HISTORICAL ATLAS

HISTORICAL ATLAS
OF THE
UNITED STATES

By CLIFFORD L. LORD
Director, New York State Historical Association
and ELIZABETH H. LORD

NEW YORK : HENRY HOLT AND COMPANY

Second printing, August, 1944

PRINTED IN THE UNITED STATES OF AMERICA

Preface

Any attempt at the serious study of historical development without a somewhat meticulous regard for geographical factors has long been discarded as an educational venture of dubious value. The map, with its own peculiar usefulness, is an established tool for the student both inside and outside the classroom.

The startlingly rapid growth and development of the United States make its history particularly susceptible to visual portrayal. The animated cartoon-map is certainly the most vivid way of showing, for instance, the tentacles of our railroad system reaching out year by year across the country, or of portraying the spread of our crop areas, the development of manufacturing regions, the westward advance of population. It may be the best way to show the spread of reform, and particularly the evolution of such pillars of our democracy as the free public school, universal suffrage, and the abolition of slavery. But movies have their limitations. They may be seen and heard, but they are difficult to study, even in classrooms. Those who lack photographic memories (and they are many) are more apt to carry away a vague impression than definite knowledge. By mapping developments in particular fields every few years, so that one can almost see them grow or shift, this atlas tries to combine the usefulness of the animated map with the advantages of being able to sit down face to face with the moving panorama of American history for study at such length as need be. That is its first excuse for being.

Its second excuse is derived from the sound increase of emphasis in the last few decades upon social and economic history. The study of geopolitics is being begun in American schools, courses in economic geography have become common, and frequent attempts have been made to study the development of many of the characteristics of our democracy from a geographical basis. Yet, just as much attention has been paid to American government but relatively little to the history of that American government, so history has been slow to adapt the techniques of the economic and political geographer to its own field, and so far has produced no serviceable handbook, sufficiently wide in scope, which so juxtaposes basic social and economic maps against those of our political history as to be useful in a general introduction to the history of the United States. The need in this field cannot be fully met for many years to come, until far more detailed research and compilation has been done in the statistics of early industry, agriculture, and transportation. But much material now exists, and its partial mapping and correlation here gives further reason for this volume.

The authors are firmly convinced of the pedagogical necessity of using such a collection of maps as these in teaching a well-rounded course in American history—are convinced that such a volume would be useful in the hands of every high school or college student of American history.

It should be clearly understood that this volume is not designed to be a reference atlas.[1] It is designed to help every student of American history along the road to that clarified, broader, integrated understanding which is the essence of intelligent education.

Every good teacher has his or her particular ideas on teaching. Therefore no attempt is made here to present any suggested class exercises. Obviously the study of the Granger movement will be enriched by attention to contemporary railroad development, to drought frequency and the major crop belts. One will find intriguing material in correlating the areas of light slaveholding in the South with the areas of Southern opposition to secession in 1860–61; the advancing frontier with the line of Indian land cessions; the routes of westward migration with the existing canals and waterways; the spread of the free public school and the liberalization of the franchise; the growth of crop and manufacturing areas and the increase of foreign trade. Liberal use has been made of the relief map of the United States in maps of exploration, communication, military campaigning, and wherever else it could be used without undue confusion of detail or loss of clarity. The direct correlation of such subjects with the topography of the region opens fur-

[1] Students wishing to consult a good reference atlas on American history should refer to C. O. Paullin (ed.), *Atlas of the Historical Geography of the United States* (Washington, 1932), or to the recent atlas accompanying the *Dictionary of American History*.

ther vistas of interest and comprehension. The imagination of both teacher and student will develop worthwhile and useful correlations along these lines far more satisfactorily than could any arbitrary set of stereotyped exercises.

The authors are indebted to many people for assistance in preparing this volume. George Robertson, of Arlington, Virginia, has contributed greatly to its usefulness by generously permitting us to reproduce the prints, so extensively used, of his revisions of the relief models of both North and South America originally prepared by E. E. Howell. The staffs of the Columbia University, the Boston and New York Public Libraries, and the American Geographical Society have been most helpful. The Carnegie Institution of Washington has graciously permitted the authors to use freely the maps of its *Atlas of the Historical Geography of the United States*, permission which has been used as noted in the section on Sources. The New Jersey Historical Records Survey, Work Projects Administration, generously granted the use, as a basis for the maps in this book, of their plottings of the development of state and territorial borders, the evolution of the federal circuit and district courts, and the maps of the votes of the House and Senate upon certain major issues, prepared for their forthcoming *Atlas of Congressional Roll Calls*. Elizabeth Smart of the Women's Christian Temperance Union, Laura Lindley of the Anti-Saloon League, Lawrence Martin of the Library of Congress, and Henrietta L. Gordon of the Child Welfare League of America have given valuable aid. Many government officials, particularly those of the Division of Statistical and Historical Research, the Bureau of Agricultural Economics, the Bureau of Plant Industry, the Soil Conservation Service, and the Forest Service in the Department of Agriculture; of the National Park Service in the Interior Department; of the Corps of Engineers, U. S. A.; of the Federal Reserve System; of the Public Roads Administration of the Federal Works Agency; of the Children's Bureau, the Women's Bureau, and the Office of the Solicitor of the Department of Labor; of the then Civil Aeronautics Commission; the Office of the Attorney-General; and officials of various states, have furnished their full and indispensable cooperation. Particularly grateful acknowledgement should be made to Amy Wadsworth Wells, whose drawing and lettering of the final copy of the maps insured the attractiveness of their ultimate form; to kind and helpful neighbors like Julie Wehr who cheerfully helped in the laborious job of applying the Ben-Day shadings; and to many academic friends for help and suggestions.

C.L.L.
E.H.L.

Cooperstown, New York,
June 12, 1943.

Sources

Government publications have been heavily drawn upon in the preparation of many of the maps of this book. Maps prepared by the Department of Agriculture have been adapted for the general maps of temperature, soil belts, regionalized types of farming, vegetation and forestation belts, drought frequency and the distribution of crops. A number of these "belt" maps are necessarily simplified. Thus the maps on regionalized types of farming (Map 12) may show Iowa in the corn belt. This, of course, does not mean that livestock, wheat, etc., are not also raised in that state. It merely indicates the predominant crop.

The map of regional watersheds was adapted from the December, 1936, *Report* of the National Resources Board, which was also consulted for the maps of rainfall, submarginal land areas, and the land retirement program. The maps of national resources were developed largely from data and maps appearing in publications of the Geological Survey. The irrigation maps were taken from the census volumes on agriculture since 1890. Pipeline routes are based on the map prepared by the *Gas and Oil Journal*.

Population maps, including those showing the distribution of residents of foreign birth, were taken, as were the maps of farm tenancy, from those published in volumes of the *Census* Reports and in some editions of the *Statistical Atlas of the United States*. The map of distribution of racial stocks in 1775 is based on the map in J. T. Adams, *The Record of America*, checked against A. B. Faust, *The German Element in the United States*.

Maps of highways eligible for federal aid were prepared from maps furnished by the Public Roads Administration of the Federal Works Agency. Maps of the development of the national parks were adapted from maps furnished by the National Park Service. National Monuments were adapted from the wall map of the Department of the Interior, 1940 edition; the dates of establishment were obtained from the Department. The Federal Reserve System furnished the map of the capitals and borders of the Reserve districts, together with data on the negligible border changes since 1914. Newspaper statistics for 1725, 1775 and 1800 were derived from Clarence Brigham's *Bibliography of American Newspapers Published Prior to 1820;* for 1860 from Kenny, *American Newspaper Directory*.

The development of the federal circuit and district courts was worked out by the Historical Records Survey of New Jersey for the forthcoming *Handbook of the Federal Circuit and District Courts*, edited by the author. Maps of votes in both Houses of Congress were compiled by the same project for the author's forthcoming *Atlas of Congressional Roll Calls*. Borders of states and territories used on all maps were also worked out by the New Jersey Historical Records Survey from the *United States Statutes At Large*, federal court decisions, and the reports of boundary commissions. It should be noted that for the period *after* 1775 these latter maps show the borders of the states as they legally were fixed at the beginning of the year indicated in the caption. Exceptions to this rule are noted in the captions. For the Colonial Period, on maps where the exact location of disputed borders is of no immediate importance to the purpose of the map, the border lines are drawn arbitrarily along the present state boundaries. Dates of treaty lines and cessions are the effective dates, i.e., the dates of ratification and acceptance respectively.

Colonial period maps were based largely on Shepherd's *Historical Atlas* (by permission of the publisher), with information added from other sources such as the *New International Encyclopaedia*. Charter lines and the colonial wars were to some degree adapted from Paullin's *Atlas of the Historical Geography of the United States* (by permission of the publishers), where an excellent textual summary of each charter appears. Data for the maps of Spanish expansion in the Southwest were taken from H. E. Bolton, *Colonization of North America*, *Spanish Borderlands*, and *Spanish Explorations in the Southwest*, and from W. E. Lowery, *Spanish Settlements Within the Present Limits of the United States*. The map of the exploration of the American West was adapted largely from Shepherd, supplemented by additional data from the *New International Encyclopaedia* and Paullin. Colonial manufacturing maps were based largely on the iron works mapped in V. S. Clark, *History of Manufactures in the United States*. Later manufacturing maps were based on textile and iron and steel statistics in *American State Papers, Finance*, vol. 2, supplemented by Clark. Still later maps are based on census figures.

Maps of abolition, free public schools, compulsory school attendance, hours of men's and women's work, and child labor were worked out from the volumes of state statutes, supplemented, in the case of the latter three, by publications of the Women's Bureau, the Children's Bureau, the Bureau of Labor Statistics, the Bureau of Labor Standards, and the Solicitor of the Department of Labor. Ratification of the Constitution is based on Orin G. Libby's famous and much-used work; ratification of the Amendments is based on the lists of ratification dates in the annotated *Constitution of the United States of America*.

The prohibition maps were worked out from Funk and Wagnalls, *Cyclopaedia of Temperance and Prohibition;* E. H. Cherrington, *Evolution of Prohibition in the United States of America;* and D. L. Colvin, *Prohibition in the United States*. Additional data were furnished by Miss Laura Lindley of the Anti-Saloon League, the officials of many states, and Miss Elizabeth Smart of the Women's Christian Temperance Union. The map of dry territory in 1919 is based on the 1919 *Handbook of the World League Against Alcoholism* (by permission). The franchise maps were compiled from K. H. Porter, *A History of Suffrage in the United States*, and the *Codes* and *Session Laws* of the several states.

The military maps have been adapted largely from Paullin, simplified to show only routes of attack, not retreat, and put on a background of the region's physical features. The maps of the Treaty of 1783, Guadalupe Hidalgo, post roads, banks and rates of travel were adapted, with permission, from the same source. The maps of the Revolutionary War were adapted from Shepherd, those of the Civil War from the atlas accompanying the *Official Records of the War of the Rebellion*, compiled by Davis, Perry and Kirkley. Maps of American participation in World War I on both the domestic and the French fronts were drawn from a number of maps in L. P. Ayres, Chief of the Statistics Branch of the General Staff, U. S. A., *The War With Germany*. M. F. Steele, *American Campaigns*, was also helpful.

The routes of westward migration, the underground railway and the slave trade were adapted from Shepherd. The map of federal land grants in aid of railroad and wagon road construction was derived from that published by the Bureau of Corporations in *The Lumber Industry*, part 1 (1913).

Canal maps were based on the list of canals and their completion dates in the Census of 1880, vol. 4. Railroad maps for the period 1840–60 were based on V. S. Clark, *History of Manufactures in the United States*, and H. V. Poor, *History of the Railroads and Canals of the United States;* those for 1870–80 on G. W. Colton, *General Atlas*. The 1854 telegraph map was adapted from Disturnell's *New Map of the United States and Canada* (1854). The map of 1922 transmission lines was derived from F. G. Baum, *Atlas of the U. S. A. Electrical Power Industry;* the 1935 lines from the wall map issued by the Federal Power Commission in that year.

The manifest destiny and expansion maps were compiled from the author's course notes, worked up over a number of years, from A. Weinberg's *Manifest Destiny*, from Harper's *Atlas of American History*, and from valuable suggestions by Basil Rauch of the Barnard faculty, whose forthcoming book on the subject will shed much new light on this interesting field.

The maps of southern opposition to secession, slaves per slaveholder, and proportion of slaves to total population were prepared from the reports of the State Secession conventions, the *Tribune Almanac and Political Reporter* and the 1860 *Census Reports*.

The college maps were prepared from statistics taken from Frasier, *American Almanac and Depository of Useful Knowledge* for the period 1830–60; from Armatraut, *An Introduction to Education* for the period before 1800; from the *Reports* of the Commissioner of Education for the years 1870–1910; and from the *Bulletins* of the Bureau of Education for the decades 1920–40. Based on such incomplete sources, these maps are not pretended to be definitive. They do, however, present a graphic and fairly complete picture of the spread of higher education.

Trade maps and the appendix of trade statistics for 1800 were derived from *American State Papers: Commerce and Navigation*, I; for 1850, from Treasury Department, *Report of the Register of the Treasury;* for 1900 from the Treasury Department, Bureau of Statistics, *Foreign Commerce and Navigation of the United States for the Year Ending June 30, 1900;* for

1938 from the volume of the same title published by the Department of Commerce, Bureau of Foreign and Domestic Commerce for the calendar year, 1938. The figures on American investments abroad are taken from R. W. Dunn, *American Foreign Investments;* and from the 1930 and 1936 surveys published by the Bureau of Foreign and Domestic Commerce; data on subsidized ship lines from P. M. Zeis, *American Shipping Policy*, and J. E. Saugstad, *Shipping and Shipbuilding Subsidies*.

Numerous sources were drawn upon for the map of the American Empire, chiefly Rand-McNally, *World Atlas*, and publications of the National Geographic Society. The latter sources were also used for the names of physical features of North and South America, the nomenclature conforming to that used by the U. S. Board of Geographic Names, while the maps of world resources and crops were adapted from those appearing in Putnam's *Commercial Atlas*.

CONTENTS

SECTION I. GENERAL MAPS

Map No. — Page

1. United States—States and Principal Cities 2-3
2. Physical Features of North America 4-5
3. Canada, Alaska, Newfoundland, and Labrador 6
4. Physical Features and Political Boundaries of South America 7
5. Regional Watersheds 8
6. Metallic Resources 8
7. Iron Ore Deposits: Hematite, Limonite, and Magnetite 9
8. Coal Deposits 9
9. Oil and Natural Gas 10
10. Vegetation and Forestation Belts 10
11. Soil Regions 11
12. Regionalized Types of Farming 11
13. Areas of Major Soil Erosion 12
14. Areas Most Suitable for a Land Retirement Program 12
15. Average Annual Precipitation 13
16. Drought Frequency (east of the Pacific Coast Mountain Ranges) 13
17. Average Temperature in January 14
18. Average Temperature in July 14
19. The American Indian: Approximate Location of Indians at the Period of Their Greatest Significance in the Westward Movement of the Frontier 15

SECTION II. COLONIAL PERIOD

20. Age of Discovery, 1486-1600 18-19
21. Spanish Exploration and Expansion in the Caribbean and Central America, 1492-1600 . . 20
22. English Colonies, Charter Grants and Frontier of Settlement, 1660 21
23. New Sweden, 1638-1655; New Netherland, 1655-1664 22
24. New Netherland, 1609-1664 22
25. English Colonies, Charter Grants, 1660-1700, and Frontier of Settlement, 1700 23
26. English Colonies, Charter Grants, 1700-1750, and Frontier of Settlement, 1750 23
27. English Expansion to 1697 24
28. French Expansion to 1697: American Campaigns of King William's War or the War of the League of Augsburg 24
29. English Expansion, 1698-1713 25
30. French Expansion, 1698-1713: American Campaigns of Queen Anne's War or the War of the Spanish Succession 25
31. English Expansion, 1714-1744 26

Map No. Page

32. French Expansion, 1714-1744: American Campaigns of King George's War or the War of the Austrian Succession . . . 26

33. English Expansion and Routes of Indian Trade with the English Colonies, 1744-1763 . . . 27

34. French Expansion, 1745-1763: American Campaigns of the French and Indian War, or the Seven Years' War . . . 27

35. Spanish Exploration and Expansion in and Near the Present Territorial Limits of the United States, 1600-1823 . . . 28

36. English Colonies, 1763-1775 . . . 28

37. Distribution of Immigrant Stock, 1775 . . . 29

38. Manufacturing Areas (Iron Works), 1775 . . . 29

39. Generalized Crop Areas, 1700 . . . 29

40. Generalized Crop Areas, 1775 . . . 29

41. Colonial Trade and Fisheries . . . 30-31

42. Male Suffrage, 1775 . . . 32

43. Colleges, 1775 . . . 32

44. Newspapers, 1725 . . . 33

45. Newspapers, 1775 . . . 33

SECTION III. 1775-1865

46. American Revolution: Campaigns of 1775-1776 . . . 37

47. American Revolution: Campaigns of 1777 . . . 37

48. American Revolution: Campaigns of 1778 . . . 38

49. American Revolution: Campaigns of 1779 . . . 38

50. American Revolution: Campaigns of 1780 . . . 39

51. American Revolution: Campaigns of 1781 . . . 39

52. American Revolution: Negotiation of the Treaty of Paris of 1783 . . . 40

53. Western Lands, 1763-1795 . . . 41

54. Creation of the National Domain: Cessions by New York of Western Land Claims and Relinquishment of the Claim to Vermont . . . 41

55. Creation of the National Domain: Cessions by Virginia and Georgia of Western Land Claims 42

56. Creation of the National Domain: Cessions by New Hampshire, Massachusetts, Connecticut, North Carolina, and South Carolina, of Western Land Claims . . . 42

57. Ratification of the Constitution . . . 43

58. Principal Posts and Routes of Westward Migration, 1775-1864 . . . 44

59. American Explorations of the West, 1803-1846 . . . 44

60. West Florida after the Treaty of Paris, 1763 . . . 45

61. West Florida Border, 1763-1787 . . . 45

62. West Florida, 1796-1821 . . . 45

63. Population Density, 1790; Line of Indian Cessions, 1783 . . . 46

64. Population Density, 1800 . . . 46

65. Population Density, Line of Indian Cessions, 1810 . . . 47

66. Population Density, 1820 . . . 48

67. Population Density; Line of Indian Cessions, 1830 . . . 49

Map No.		Page
68.	Population Density, 1840	50
69.	Population Density; Line of Indian Cessions, 1850	51
70.	Population Density, 1860	52
71.	Maine Border Dispute, 1821-1842	53
72.	Oregon Border Dispute, 1826-1872	53
73.	Lake Superior-Rainy Lake Border Dispute, 1826-1842	53
74.	Male Suffrage, 1780	54
75.	Male Suffrage, 1790	54
76.	Male Suffrage, 1800	54
77.	Male Suffrage, 1820	55
78.	Male Suffrage, 1830	55
79.	Male Suffrage, 1840	56
80.	Male Suffrage, 1850	56
81.	Male Suffrage, 1860	57
82.	States Effecting the Ratification of the First Ten Amendments to the Constitution, 1791	57
83.	States Effecting the Ratification of the Eleventh Amendment to the Constitution, 1798	57
84.	Organization of the Federal Circuit and District Courts by Act of September 24, 1789	58
85.	Federal Circuit and District Courts, 1801	58
86.	Organization of the Federal Circuit and District Courts by Act of March 8, 1802	58
87.	Federal Circuit and District Courts, 1802	58
88.	Federal Circuit and District Courts, 1807	59
89.	Federal Circuit and District Courts, 1837	59
90.	Federal Circuit and District Courts, 1861	60
91.	House Vote of January 2, 1808, on Passage of the Embargo Resolution	61
92.	House Vote of June 4, 1812, on Resolution Declaring War on Great Britain	62
93.	War of 1812: Campaigns of 1812	63
94.	War of 1812: Campaigns of 1813	63
95.	War of 1812: Campaigns of 1814; Jackson's Florida Expedition of 1818	64
96.	House Vote of May 11, 1846, Authorizing the President to Use Military and Naval Forces to Prosecute the Existing War with Mexico	65
97.	The Mexican War	66
98.	The Mexican Border, 1821-1857	67
99.	Wheat Production, 1840	68
100.	Wheat Production, 1860	68
101.	Corn Production, 1840	69
102.	Corn Production, 1860	69
103.	Cotton Production, 1840	70
104.	Cotton Production, 1860	70
105.	Cattle (excluding Dairy Cows), 1860	70
106.	Tobacco Production, 1860	71
107.	Improved Acreage, 1850	71
108.	Manufacturing Areas, 1810	72

Map No.		Page
109.	Manufacturing Areas, 1840	72
110.	Manufacturing Areas, 1860	73
111.	Banks of 1800, including All Branches of the First Bank of the United States	73
112.	Banks of 1830, including All Branches of the Second Bank of the United States	73
113.	Banks of 1850	74
114.	Main Post Roads, 1804	74
115.	Main Post Roads, 1834	75
116.	Routes of the Overland Mail and the Pony Express	75
117.	Canals to 1837	76
118.	Canals, 1837-1860	76
119.	Railroads in Operation, 1840	77
120.	Railroads in Operation, 1850	77
121.	Railroads in Operation, 1860	78
122.	First Ten Years of the Telegraph, 1844-1854	78
123.	Rates of Travel from New York, 1800	79
124.	Rates of Travel from New York, 1830	79
125.	Rates of Travel from New York, 1860	79
126.	Expansion, 1775-1830; Exports, 1800	80-81
127.	Expansion and Manifest Destiny, 1830-1860; Exports, 1850	82-83
128.	State Public School Legislation, 1790	84
129.	State Public School Legislation, 1820	84
130.	State Public School Legislation, 1830	85
131.	State Public School Legislation, 1855	85
132.	Prohibition, 1846	86
133.	Prohibition, 1856	86
134.	Colleges, 1800	87
135.	Newspapers, 1800	87
136.	Universities, Colleges, and Other Institutions of Higher Learning, 1830	87
137.	Universities, Colleges, and Other Institutions of Higher Learning, 1850	88
138.	Newspapers, 1860	88
139.	Women's Hours of Work, 1850	89
140.	Enfranchisement of Women, 1860	89
141.	Proportion of Slaves to Total Population, 1790	90
142.	Proportion of Slaves to Total Population, 1820	90
143.	Proportion of Slaves to Total Population, by County, 1840	91
144.	Proportion of Slaves to Total Population, by County, 1860	91
145.	Free Negro Population, by County, 1860	92
146.	Routes of the Underground Railway and of the Domestic Slave Trade	92
147.	Number of Slaves per Slaveholder in the South, by County, 1860	93
148.	Opposition to Secession in the South, by County, 1860-1861	93
149.	Progress of Abolition, 1800	94
150.	Progress of Abolition, 1821	94

Map No.		Page
151.	Progress of Abolition, 1840	95
152.	Progress of Abolition, 1850	95
153.	Progress of Abolition, 1854	96
154.	Progress of Abolition, 1860	96
155.	Progress of Abolition, 1863-1864	97
156.	Progress of Abolition, 1865-1868	97
157.	The War Between the States: Campaigns of 1861	98
158.	The War Between the States: Campaigns of 1862	98
159.	The War Between the States: Campaigns of 1863	99
160.	The War Between the States: Campaigns of 1864	99
161.	The War Between the States: Campaigns of 1865	100
162.	States Effecting the Ratification of the Thirteenth Amendment to the Constitution, 1865	100
163.	States Effecting the Ratification of the Fourteenth Amendment to the Constitution, 1868	101
164.	States Effecting the Ratification of the Fifteenth Amendment to the Constitution, 1870	101

SECTION IV. 1865-1941

Map No.		Page
165.	Population Density, Line of Indian Cessions, 1870	104
166.	Population Density, 1880	104
167.	Population Density, 1890	105
168.	Population Density, 1900	106
169.	Population Density, 1910	107
170.	Population Density, 1920	108
171.	Population Density, 1930	109
172.	Negro Population, 1900	110
173.	Negro Population, 1930	111
174.	Population of Foreign Birth, 1860	112
175.	Population of Foreign Birth, 1880	113
176.	Population of Foreign Birth, 1900	114
177.	Swedish- and Norwegian-born Population, 1880	115
178.	Swedish- and Norwegian-born Population, 1900	116
179.	Swedish- and Norwegian-born Population, 1930	117
180.	Irish-born Population, 1880	118
181.	Irish-born Population, 1900	119
182.	Irish-born Population, 1930	120
183.	German-born Population, 1880	121
184.	German-born Population, 1900	122
185.	German-born Population, 1930	123
186.	Male Suffrage, 1870	124
187.	Male Suffrage, 1880	124
188.	Male Suffrage, 1900	125
189.	Male Suffrage, 1910	125
190.	Suffrage, 1940	126

Map No.		Page
191.	Enfranchisement of Women, 1870	126
192.	Enfranchisement of Women, 1880	127
193.	Enfranchisement of Women, 1900	127
194.	Enfranchisement of Women, 1915	128
195.	Enfranchisement of Women, 1919	128
196.	Dates of the Establishment of Literacy Qualifications for the Franchise	129
197.	Alien Enfranchisement, 1775-1942	129
198.	States Effecting the Ratification of the Sixteenth Amendment to the Constitution, 1913	130
199.	States Effecting the Ratification of the Seventeenth Amendment to the Constitution, 1913	130
200.	States Effecting the Ratification of the Eighteenth Amendment to the Constitution, 1919	131
201.	States Effecting the Ratification of the Nineteenth Amendment to the Constitution, 1920	131
202.	States Effecting the Ratification of the Twentieth Amendment to the Constitution, 1933	132
203.	States Effecting the Ratification of the Twenty-first Amendment to the Constitution, 1933	132
204.	Federal Circuit and District Courts, 1873	133
205.	Federal Circuit and District Courts, 1911	134
206.	House Vote of April 13, 1898, on Resolution Declaring War on Spain, Taken Prior to and Lacking Unanimity of Final Action Agreeing to Conference Report	135
207.	The Spanish-American War: Caribbean Campaign	136
208.	Senate Vote of February 6, 1899, on Ratification of the Treaty of Paris	136
209.	Alaska Border Dispute, 1878-1905	137
210.	House Vote of April 5, 1917, on Resolution Declaring War on Germany	138
211.	Senate Vote of November 19, 1919, on Unconditional Ratification of the Versailles Treaty	139
212.	America in the First World War: Training Camps, Embarkation Ports, and Construction Projects	140
213.	America in the First World War: The European Front	141
214.	Wheat Production, 1890	142
215.	Wheat Production, 1920	142
216.	Wheat Production, 1940	143
217.	Corn Production, 1890	143
218.	Corn Production, 1920	144
219.	Corn Production, 1940	144
220.	Cotton Production, 1890	145
221.	Cotton Production, 1920	145
222.	Cotton Production, 1940	146
223.	Tobacco Production, 1890	146
224.	Tobacco Production, 1920	147
225.	Tobacco Production, 1940	147
226.	Cattle Trails and Cow Towns, 1880	148
227.	Cattle (excluding Dairy Cows), 1890	149
228.	Cattle (excluding Dairy Cows), 1920	149
229.	Cattle (Dairy Cows only), 1940	150
230.	Cattle (excluding Dairy Cows), 1940	150
231.	Improved Acreage, 1870	151

Map No. Page

232. Improved Acreage, 1880 151
233. Improved Acreage, 1900 152
234. Improved Acreage, 1910 152
235. Acreage in Harvested Crops, 1920 153
236. Acreage in Harvested Crops, 1930 153
237. Farm Tenancy, by Counties, 1880 154
238. Farm Tenancy, by Counties, 1910 154
239. Farm Tenancy, by Counties, 1920 155
240. Farm Tenancy, by Counties, 1930 155
241. Power Transmission Lines Carrying a Potential of 55,000 or More Volts, 1923 156
242. Power Transmission Lines Carrying a Potential of 55,000 or More Volts, 1935 156
243. Manufacturing Areas, 1900 157
244. Manufacturing Areas, 1940 157
245. Banks of 1880 158
246. Federal Reserve Districts, 1914 158
247. Railroads in Operation, 1870 159
248. Railroads in Operation, 1882 159
249. Federal Land Grants in Aid of Railroad and Wagon-Road Construction, 1828-1871 . . 160
250. Canals Constructed Since 1860 160
251. Federal Highways System, 1925 161
252. Revised Federal Highways System, 1940 161
253. Commercial Air Lines, 1920 162
254. Commercial Air Lines, 1930 162
255. Commercial Air Lines, 1940 163
256. Rates of Travel: Railroad Time from New York, 1930 163
257. Subsidized Trade Routes, under Acts of 1864 and 1891; Expansion, 1865-1904; Exports and Foreign Investments, 1900 164-165
258. Subsidized Trade Routes, under Act of 1928; Expansion, 1904-1942; Investments Abroad, 1930; Direct Investments, 1936 166-167
259. National Forests, 1900 168
260. National Forests, 1910 168
261. National Forests, 1930 169
262. National Forests, 1940 169
263. National Parks and National Monuments 170
264. Irrigated Lands, 1940 170
265. State Public School Legislation, 1870 171
266. Compulsory School Attendance, 1880 171
267. Compulsory School Attendance, 1890 172
268. Compulsory School Attendance, 1900 172
269. Compulsory School Attendance, 1920 173
270. Compulsory School Attendance: Age Limits, 1940 173
271. Universities, Colleges, and Other Institutions of Higher Learning, 1870 174

Map No.		Page
272.	Universities, Colleges, and Other Institutions of Higher Learning, 1890	174
273.	Universities, Colleges, and Other Institutions of Higher Learning, 1910	175
274.	Universities, Colleges, and Other Institutions of Higher Learning, 1930	175
275.	Prohibition, 1880	176
276.	Prohibition, 1906	176
277.	Prohibition, 1915	177
278.	Prohibition, 1919	177
279.	Dry Counties, 1919	178
280.	Dry Counties, 1942	178
281.	Child Labor: Manufacturing and/or Mercantile Employment, 1880	179
282.	Child Labor: Any Gainful Occupation, 1880	179
283.	Child Labor: Manufacturing and/or Mercantile Employment, 1890	180
284.	Child Labor: Any Gainful Occupation, 1890	180
285.	Child Labor: Manufacturing and/or Mercantile Employment, 1900	181
286.	Child Labor: Any Gainful Occupation, 1900	181
287.	Child Labor: Manufacturing and/or Mercantile Employment, 1915	182
288.	Child Labor: Any Gainful Occupation, 1915	182
289.	Child Labor: Manufacturing and/or Mercantile Employment, 1930	183
290.	Child Labor: Any Gainful Occupation, 1930	183
291.	Women's Hours of Work, 1890	184
292.	Women's Hours of Work, 1910	184
293.	Women's Hours of Work, 1920	185
294.	Women's Hours of Work, 1930	185
295.	Men's Hours of Work: Public Works and Dangerous Occupations, 1890	186
296.	Men's Hours of Work: General Occupations, 1890	186
297.	Men's Hours of Work: Public Works and Dangerous Occupations, 1900	187
298.	Men's Hours of Work: General Occupations, 1900	187
299.	Men's Hours of Work: Public Works and Dangerous Occupations, 1910	188
300.	Men's Hours of Work: General Occupations, 1910	188
301.	Men's Hours of Work: Public Works and Dangerous Occupations, 1920	189
302.	Men's Hours of Work: General Occupations, 1920	189
303.	State Action on Proposed Federal Child Labor Amendment	190
304.	Old Age Assistance: Maximum Benefit Payments, 1940	190

SECTION V. WORLD MAPS

305.	American Empire, 1942	192-193
306.	World Production of Coal	194-195
307.	World Production of Iron	196-197
308.	World Production of Petroleum and Natural Gas	198-199
309.	World Production of Aluminum and Tin	200-201
310.	World Production of Gold and Silver	202-203
311.	World Production of Copper	204-205

Map No. Page

312. World Production of Lead and Zinc 206-207
313. World Production of Wheat 208-209
314. World Production of Cotton 210-211
315. World Production of Corn 212-213
316. World Production of Tobacco 214-215
317. World Production of Cattle, Beef, Skins, and Hides 216-217

APPENDICES

I. Population, 1770-1940 220-221
II. Presidential Elections 222-227
III. Immigration by Country of Origin, 1831-1940 228
IV. Imports and Exports, 1799-1938 229-237
V. Railroad Mileage, 1840-1940 238
VI. Initiative, Referendum, and Recall 238
Index 239

Section I

GENERAL MAPS

The maps presented in this section contain generalized data on the physical features and political boundaries of our own nation and her neighbors of this hemisphere, on climate, soils, and national resources.

The student will constantly want to refer to these maps in connection with his use of the maps of the later sections. Major cities and physical features have been shown as fully as the available space will allow. Climate, soil, and vegetation belts are shown in slightly generalized form, with the elimination of unimportant local variations too small to be shown practically on maps of this scale.

The teacher may find it useful, when discussing industrial developments or the opening of new mineral strikes such as those at the Comstock Lode, or Leadville, or the Kettleman Hills field, to refer back to the maps where some of the most important deposits of natural resources are specifically labeled; or, when discussing regional planning or regional problems, to refer back to the relief model on which the watersheds are clearly outlined and labeled with the designations used by the National Resources Board. Discussion of crop belts will almost of necessity recall the student to the maps of rainfall, soil, vegetation, drought frequency, temperature belts and the particularly valuable map on regionalized types of farming. Such cross-reference will immeasurably increase one's knowledge and appreciation of the basic developments of the country.

The map of Indian locales is necessarily limited in its usefulness. Many Indian tribes, particularly the Plains Indians, migrated over vast areas before the coming of the white settlers. Others were forcibly moved to reservations and often subsequently forced to change their locale a second or third time. It is impossible on such a map as this to represent all the places where a given Indian group appeared at different times. Accordingly, this map attempts merely to show the location of an Indian group at the period when, in the authors' opinion, that group was most important or prominent in American history. An authority on Indians may quarrel with some of the selections, particularly those made in the cases of the more migratory Indians. The map is useful, however, for general study purposes.

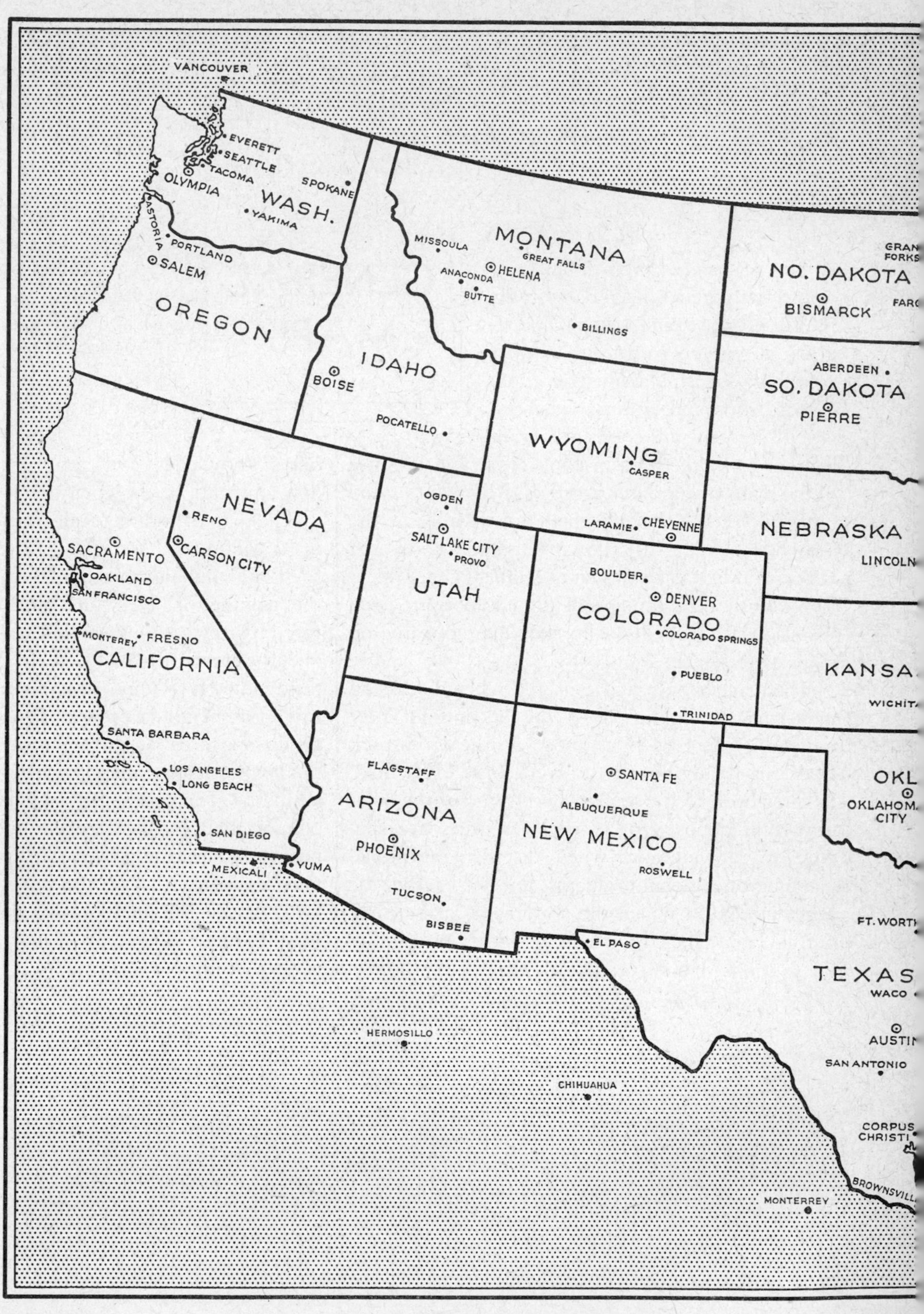

I

United States

Includes some sites of hist

ates and Principal Cities

erest not shown on other maps in this atlas

ICELAND
CAPE FAREWELL
GREENLAND
DAVIS STRAIT
LABRADOR
BAFFIN BAY
HUDSON STRAIT
BAFFINLAND
HUDSON BAY
CHESTERFIELD INLET
NELSON R.
CHURCHILL R.
REINDEER LAKE
L. WOLLASTON
LAKE WINNIPEGOSIS
ARCTIC OCEAN
GREAT BEAR LAKE
GT. SLAVE LAKE
LAKE ATHABASKA
PEACE R.
ATHABASKA R.
LITTLE SLAVE LAKE
N. SASKATCHEWAN R.
MACKENZIE R.
LIARD R.
FRASER R.
PT. BARROW
COLVILLE R.
ENDICOTT MTS.
YUKON R.
TANANA R.
COAST MTS.
BERING STRAIT
YUKON R.
ALASKA MTS.
KUSKOKWIM R.
NORTON SOUND
BERING SEA
ST. LAWRENCE IS.
ST. MATTHEW IS.
NUNIVAK IS.
BRISTOL BAY
KODIAK IS.
ALASKA PENINSULA
PRIBILOF IS.
DUTCH HARBOR
ALEUTIAN IS.
ANDREANOF IS.
AMCHITKA IS.
KISKA IS.
ATTU IS.
VANCOUVER IS.
P A
OCEAN

From the model constructed by Edwin O. Howell, revised by George Robertson

2 Physical Features of North America

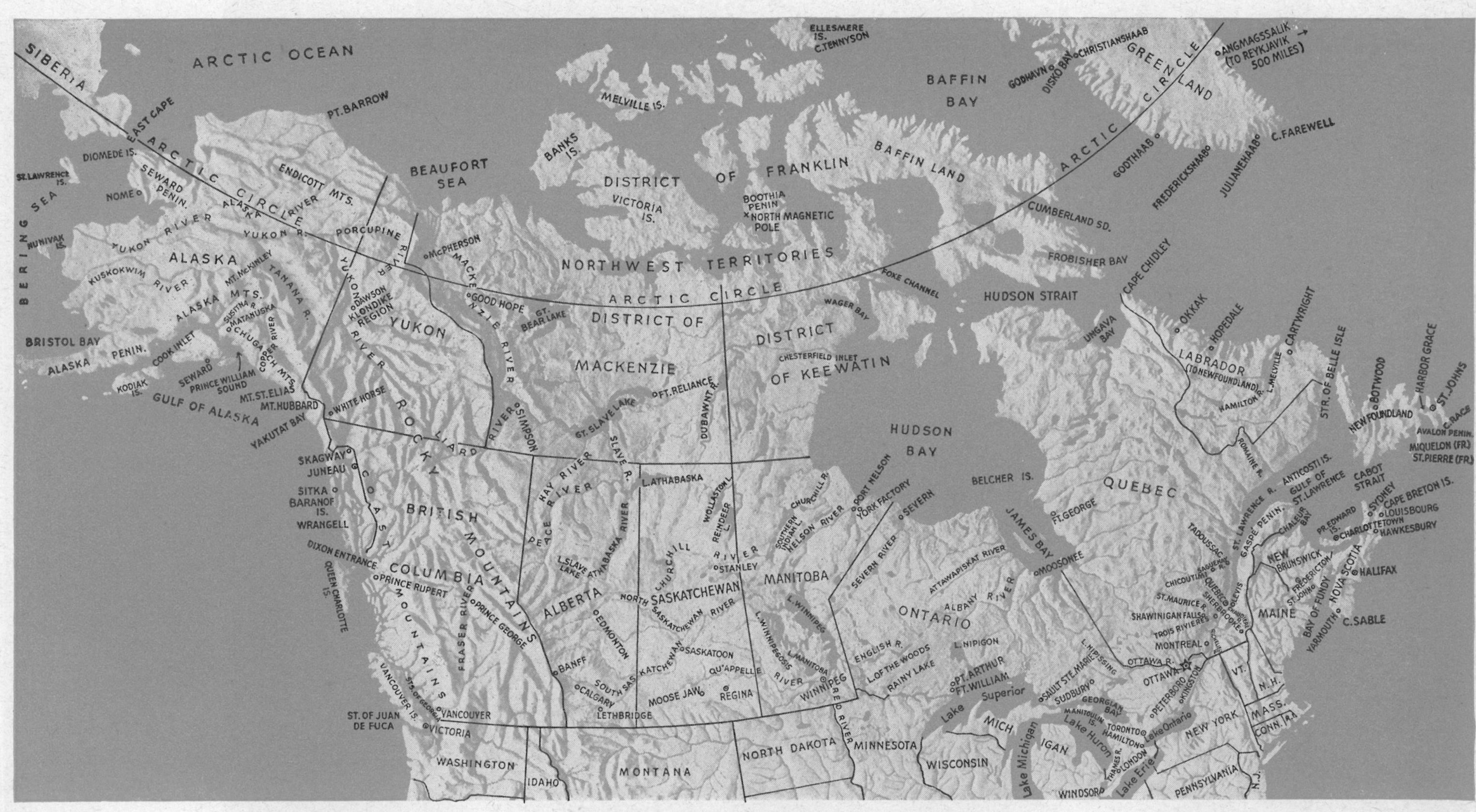

3

Canada, Alasaka, Newfoundland, and Labrador

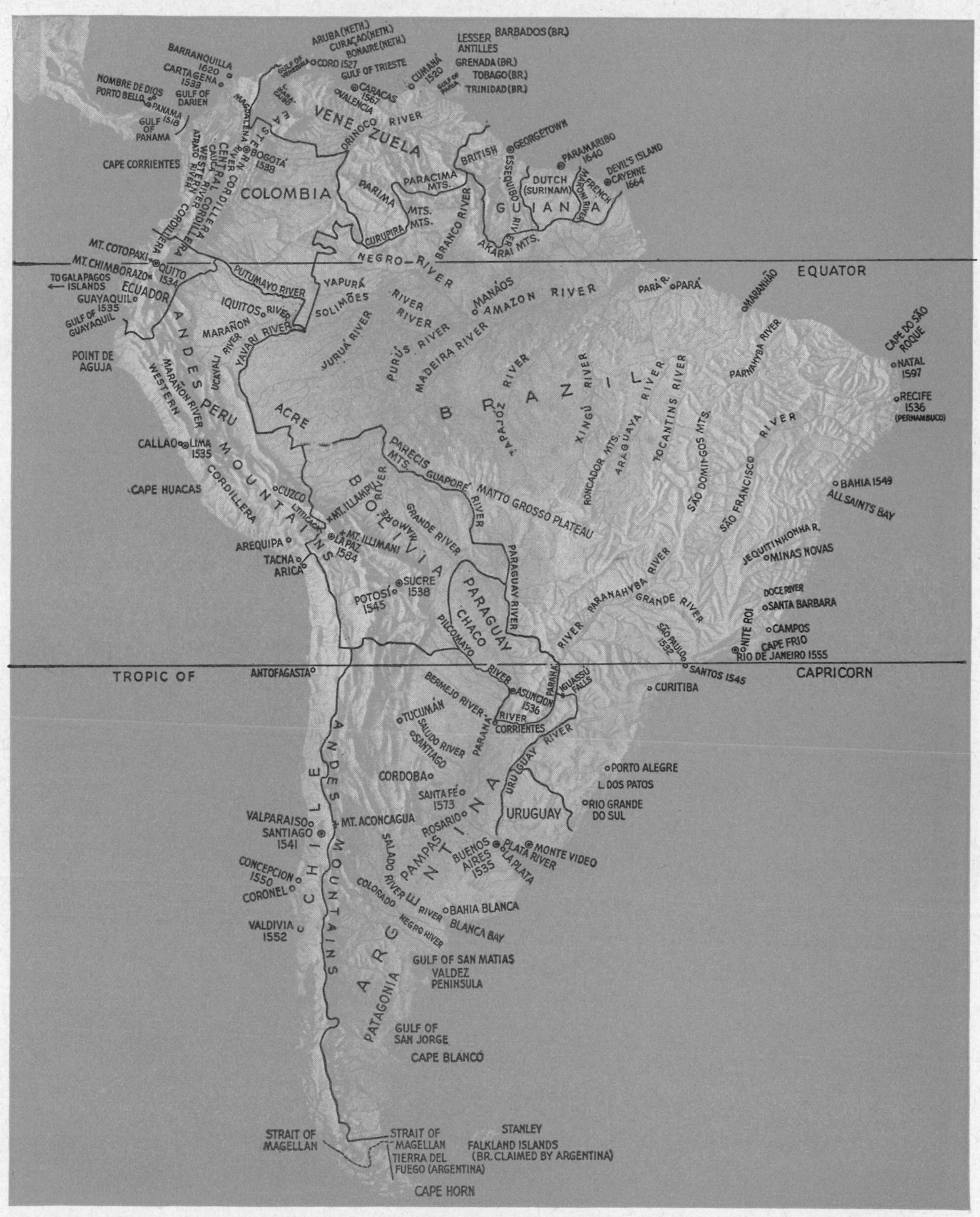

From the model constructed by Edwin O. Howell, revised by George Robertson

4

Physical Features and Political Boundaries of South America

Shows dates of colonial settlement, including those at Panama

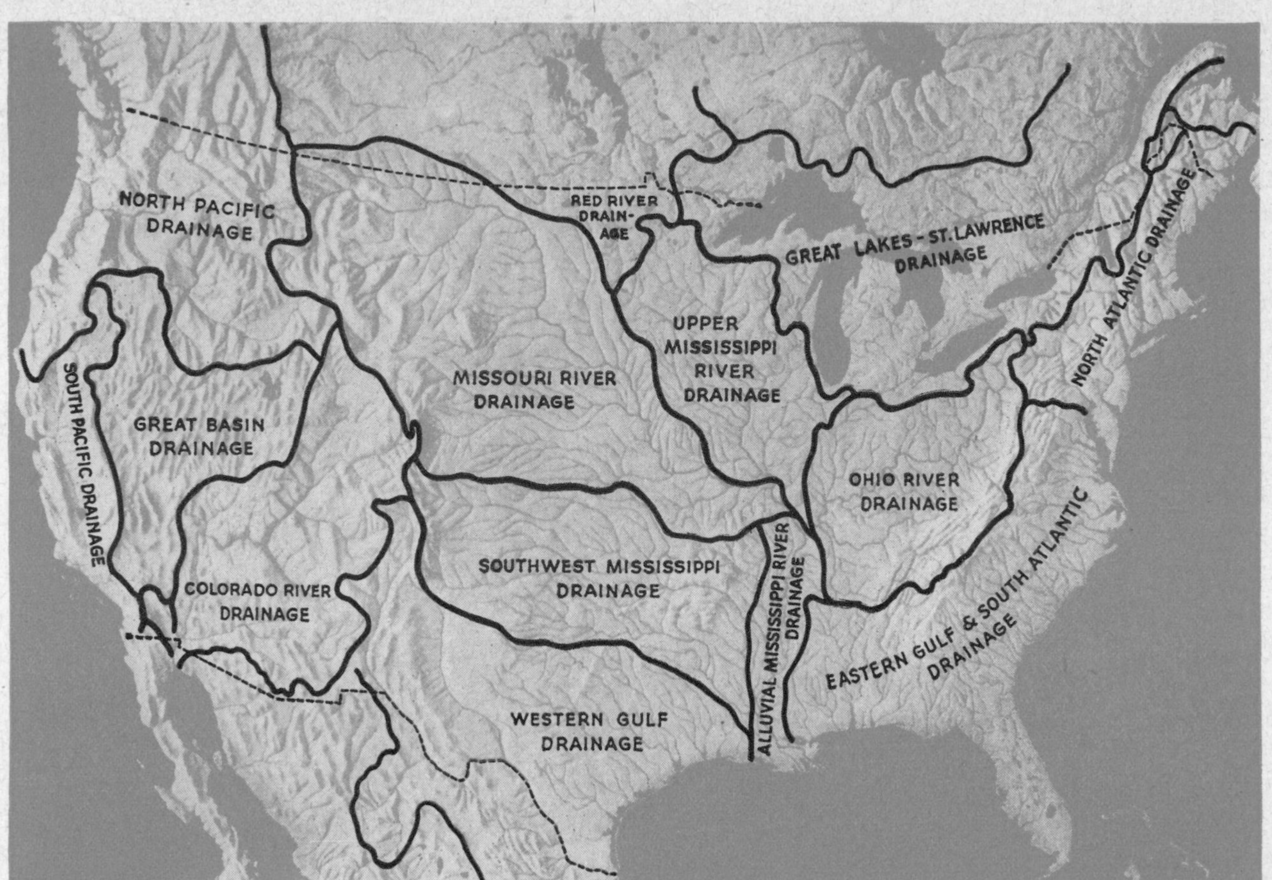

5 Regional Watersheds

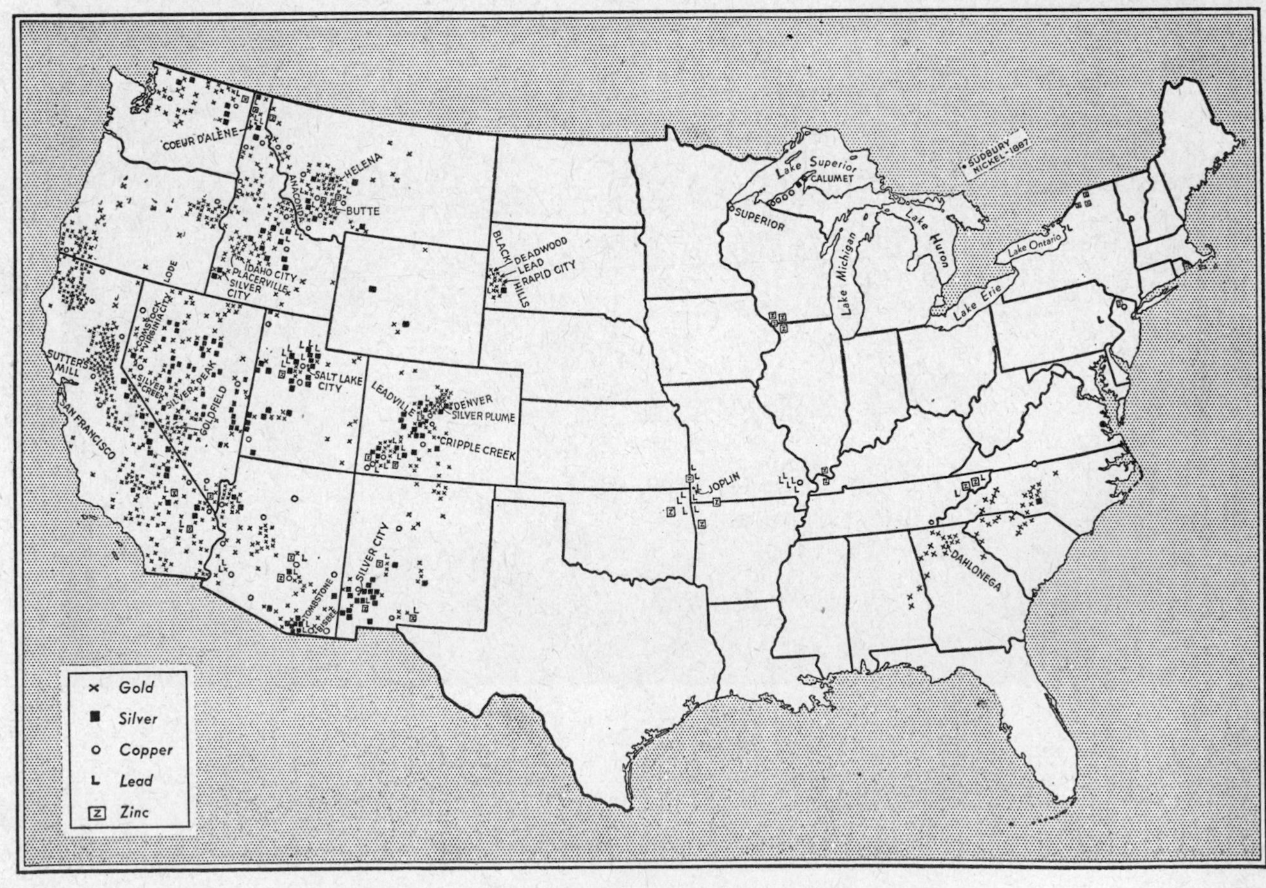

6 Metallic Resources

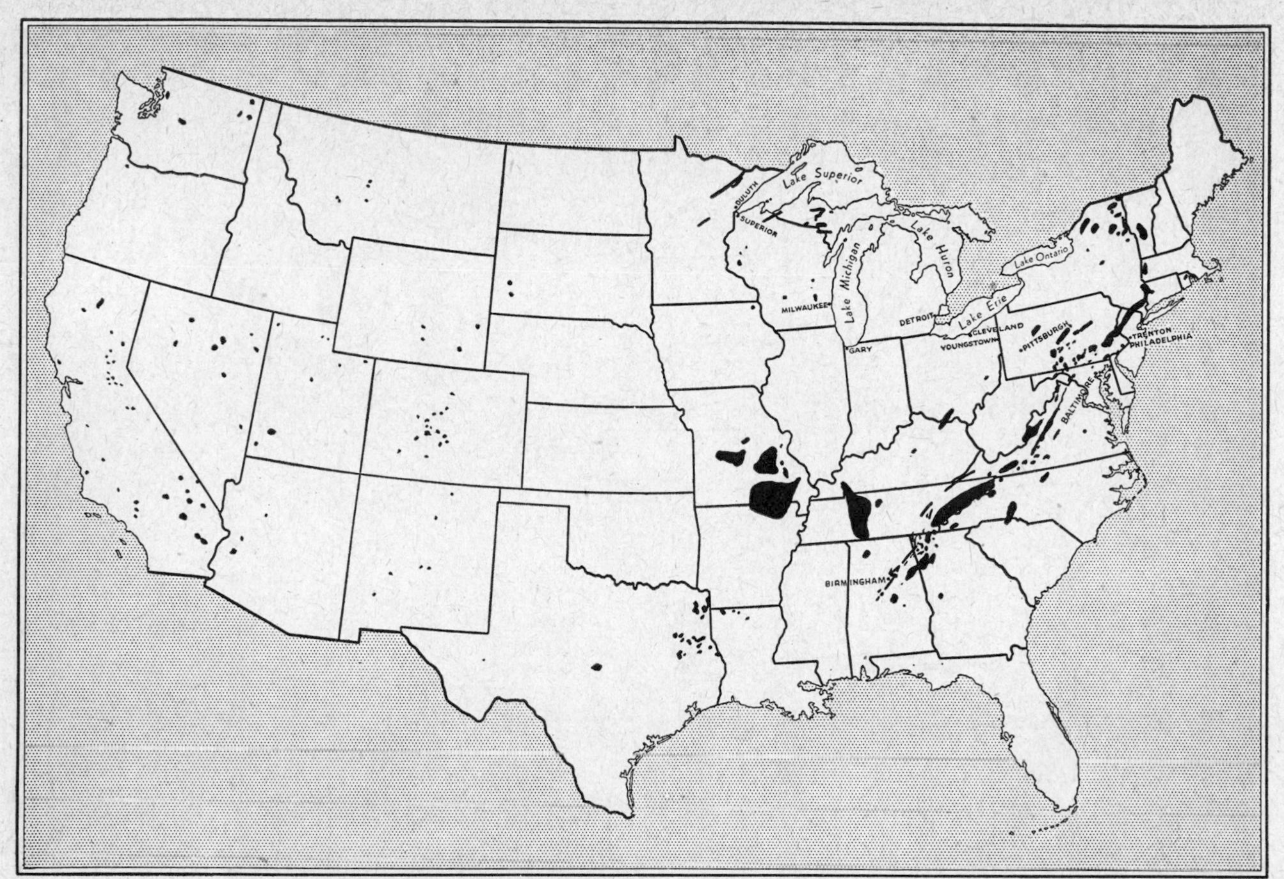

7 Iron Ore Deposits: Hematite, Limonite, and Magnetite

The principal commercial beds are located around Lake Superior, in Pennsylvania, and in Alabama

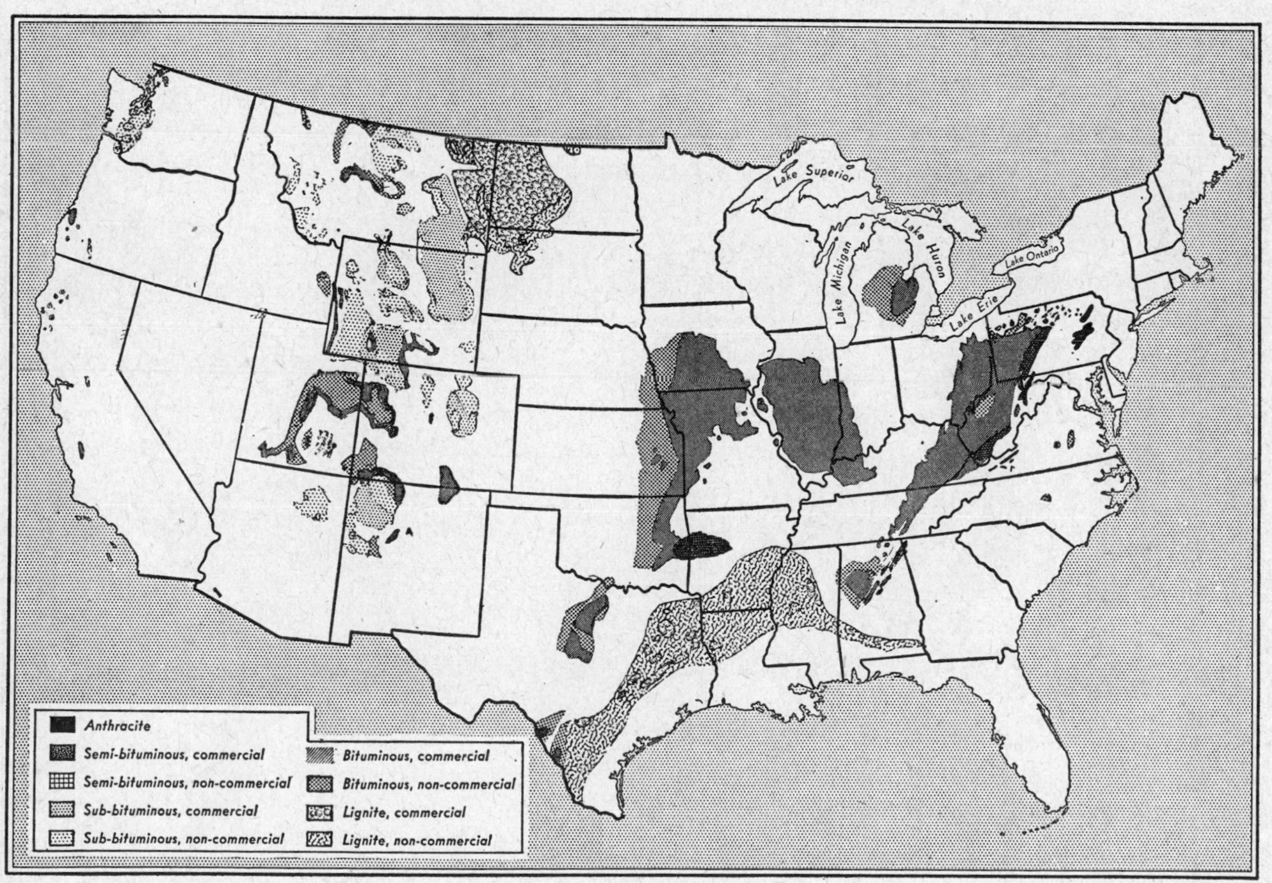

8 Coal Deposits

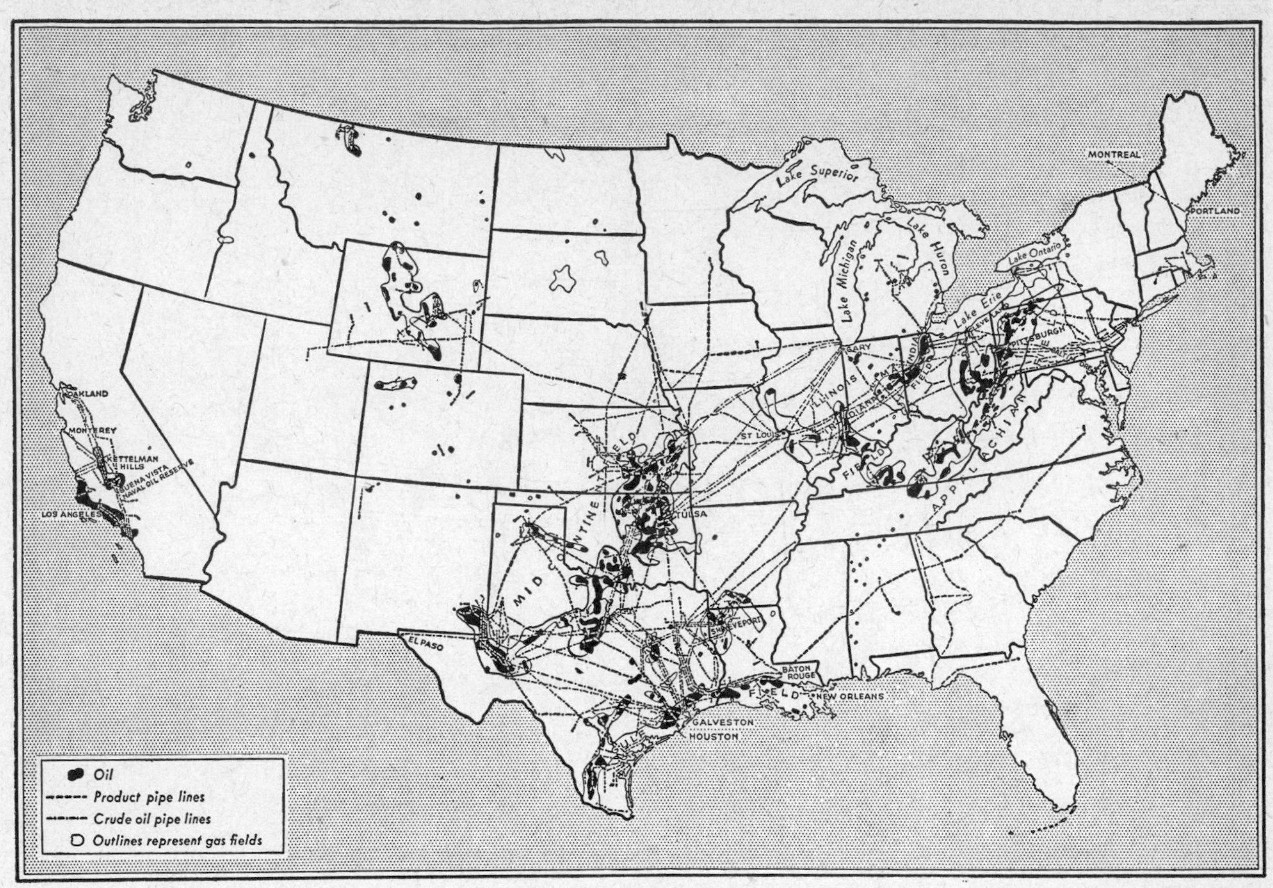

9

Oil and Natural Gas, 1942
Location and number of pipelines only approximate

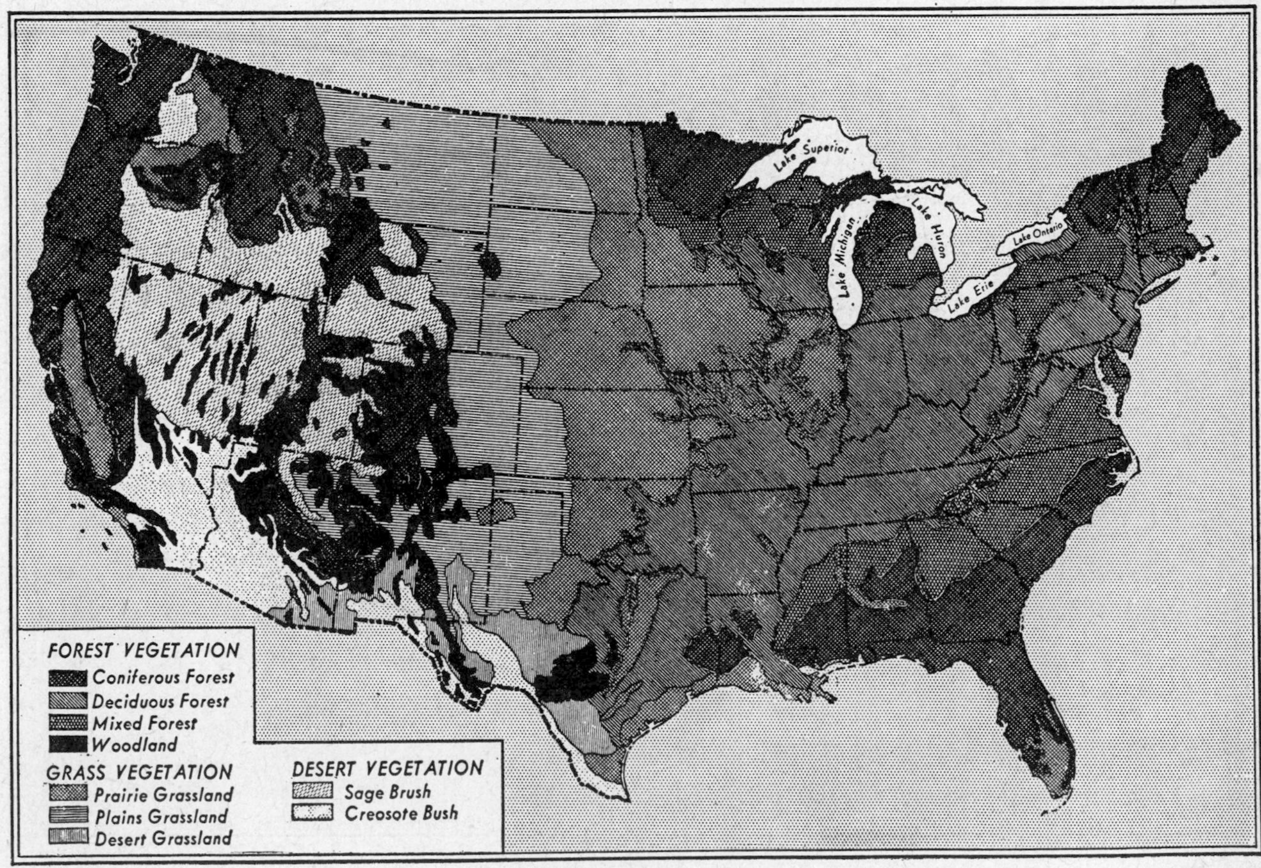

10

Vegetation and Forestation Belts

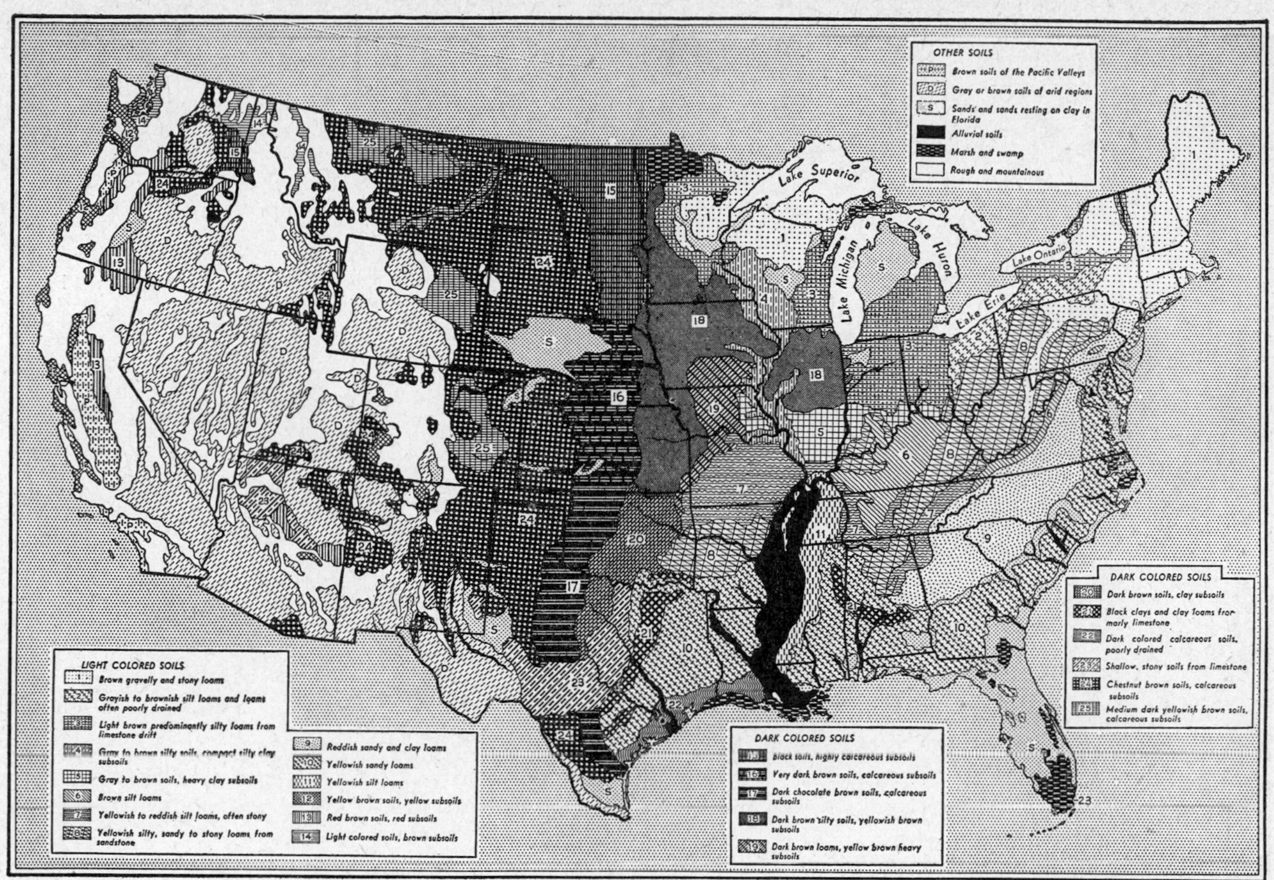

From Map Prepared by C. F. Marbut and Associates in the Soil Survey

11

Soil Regions

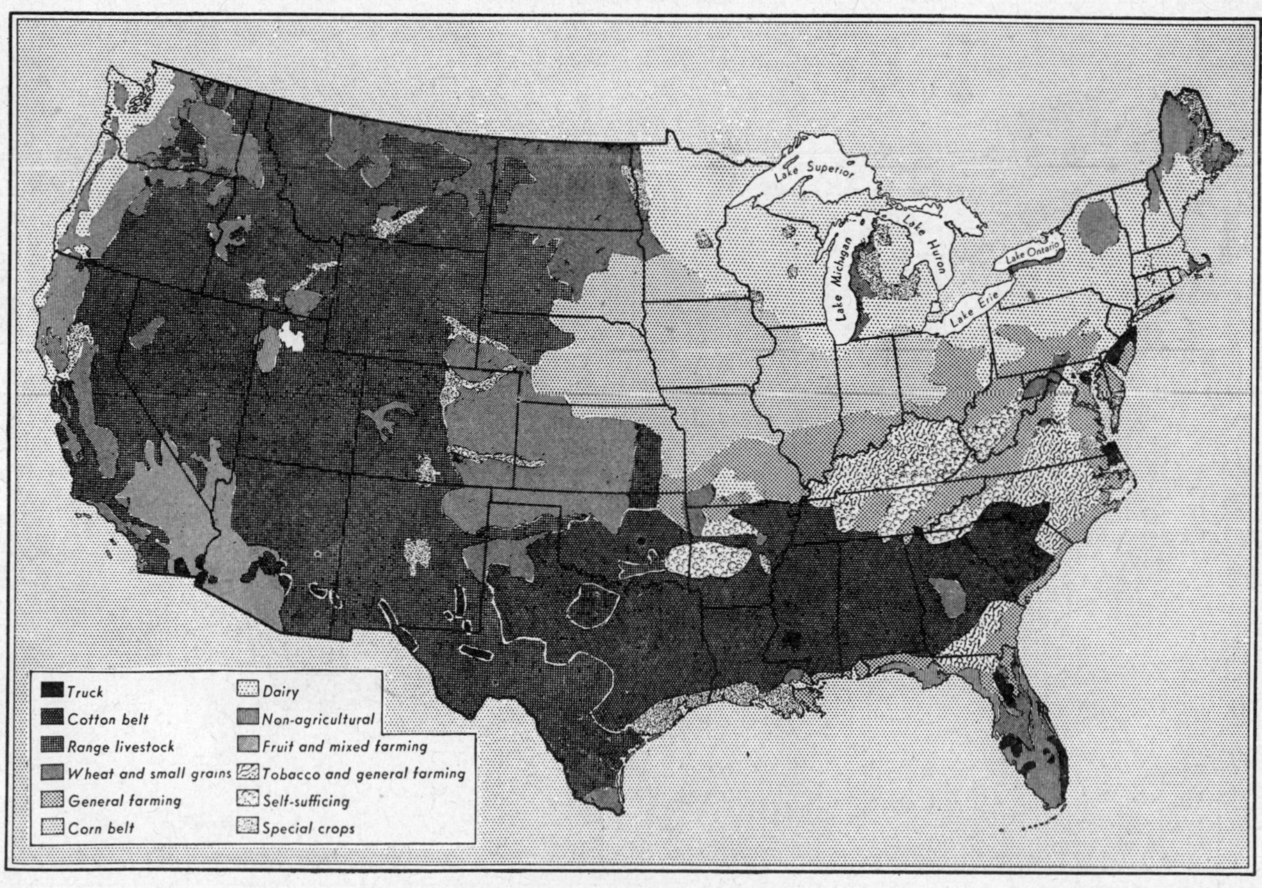

12

Regionalized Types of Farming

(For production of specific commodities see crop and cattle maps)

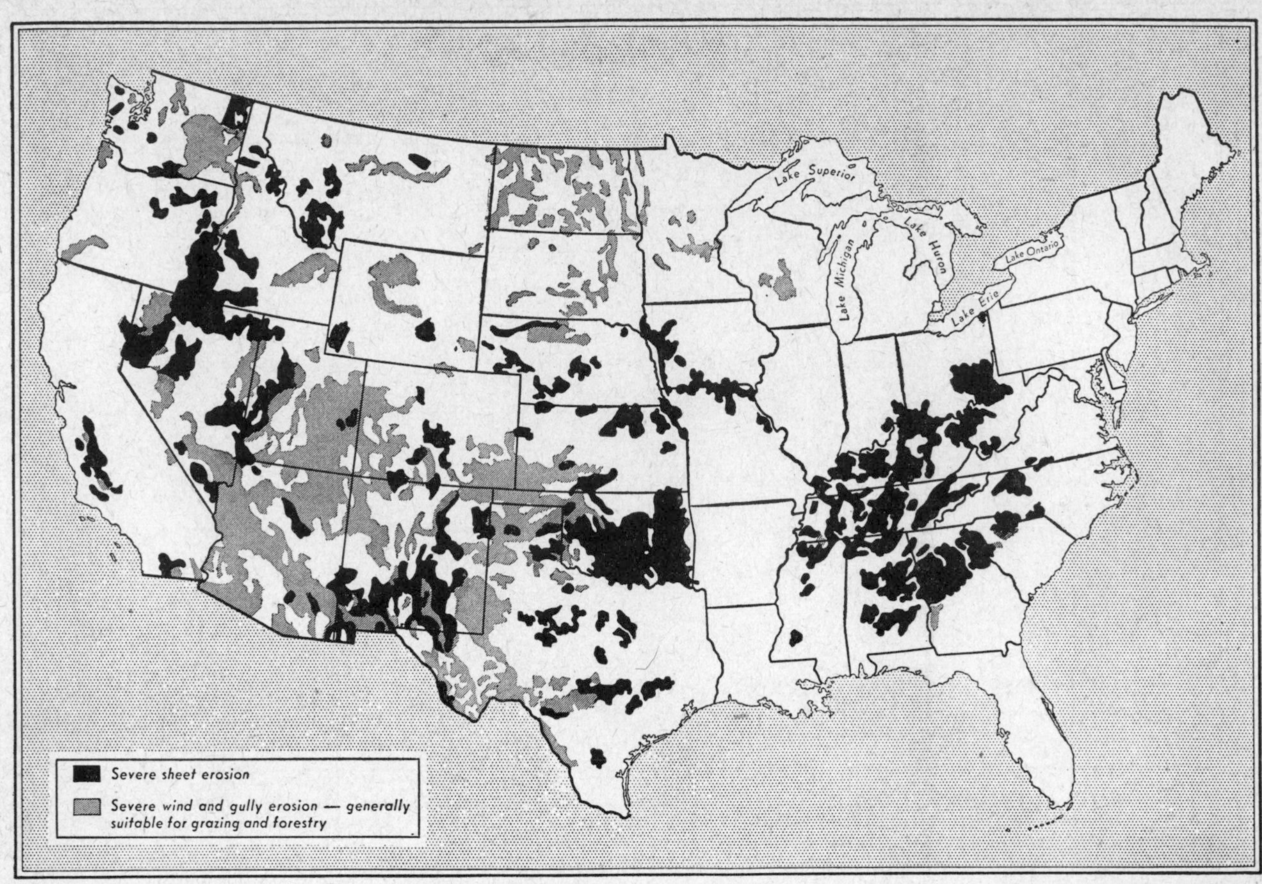

13 Areas of Major Soil Erosion

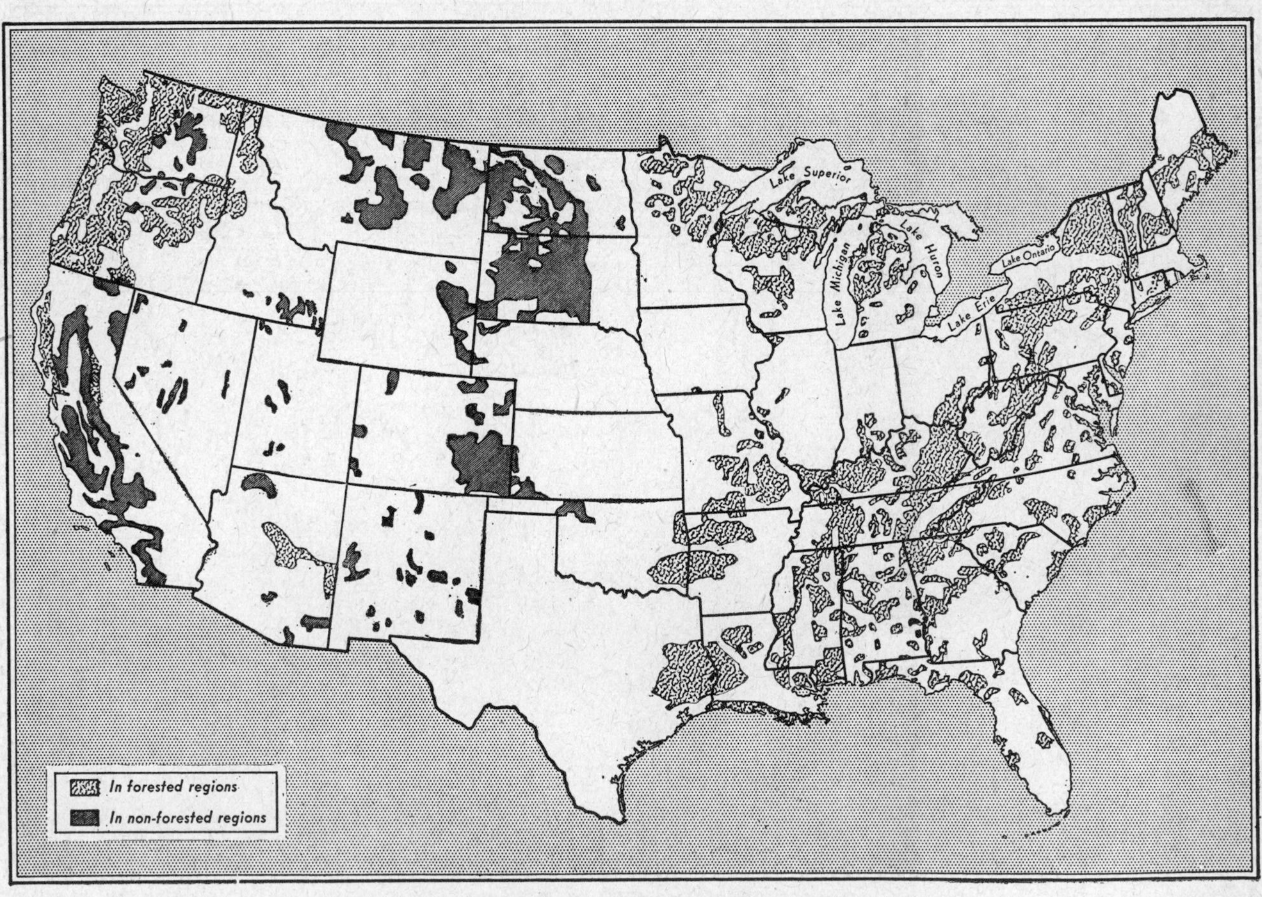

14 Areas Most Suitable for a Land Retirement Program

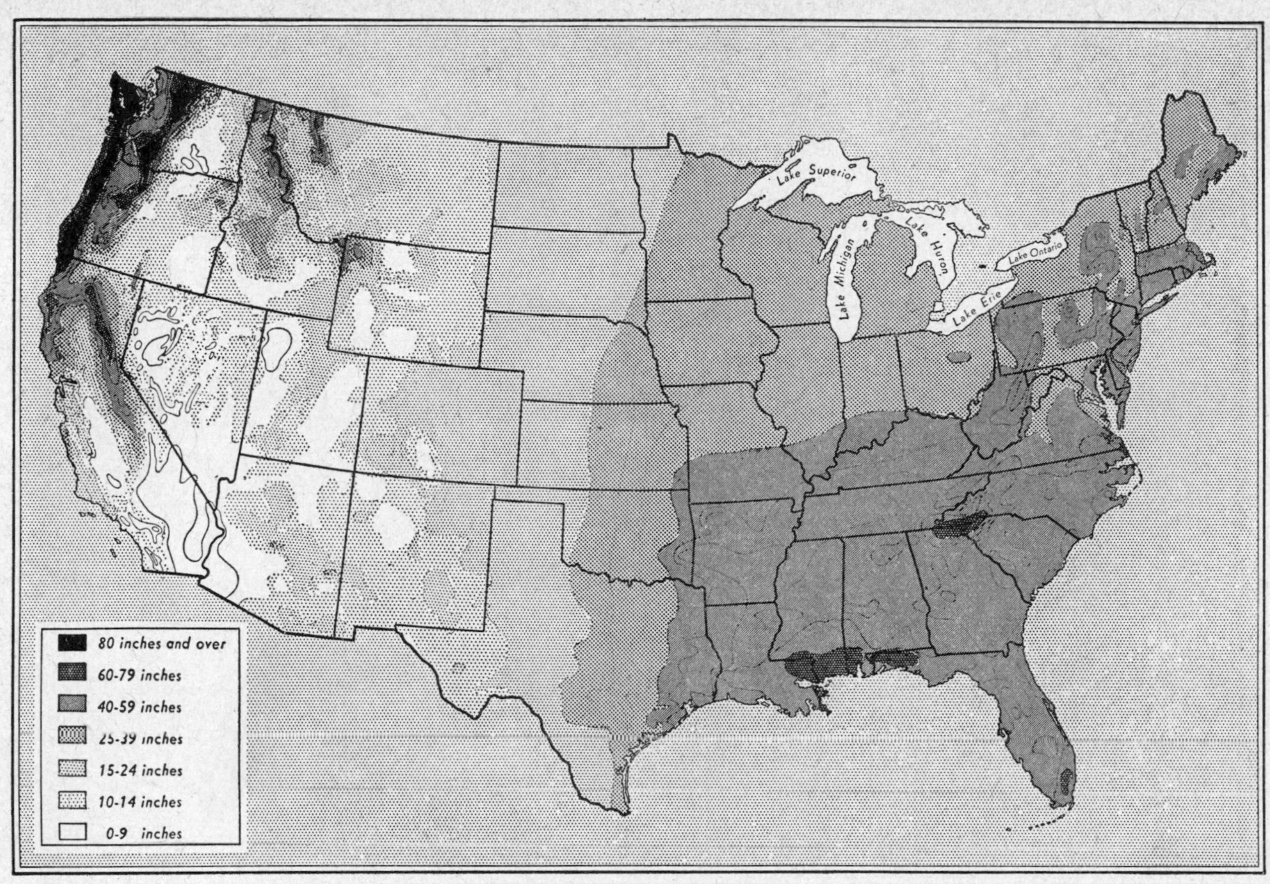

15 Average Annual Precipitation

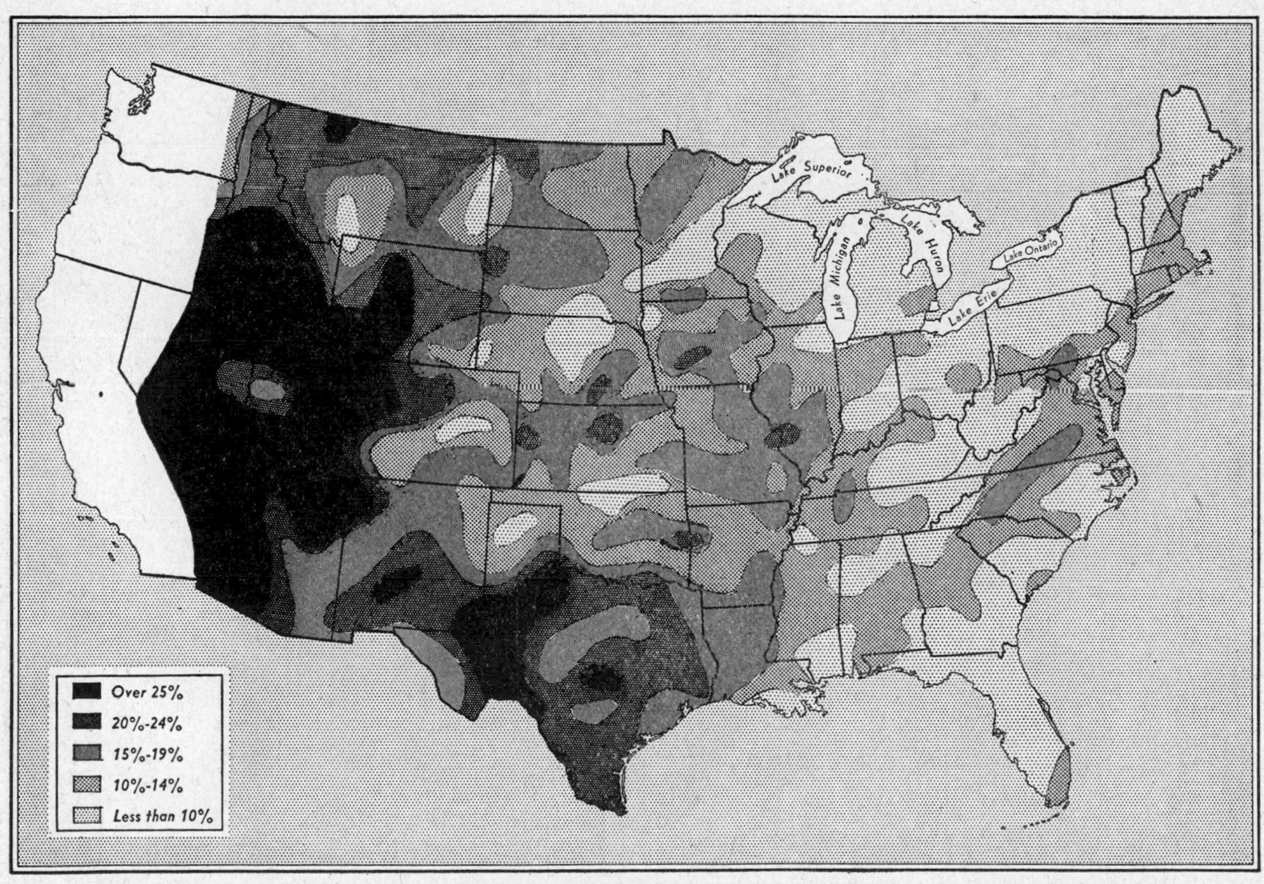

16 Drought Frequency: Percentage of Years in which Rainfall is Less than Two-thirds of Normal from May through August (East of the Pacific Coast Mountain Ranges)

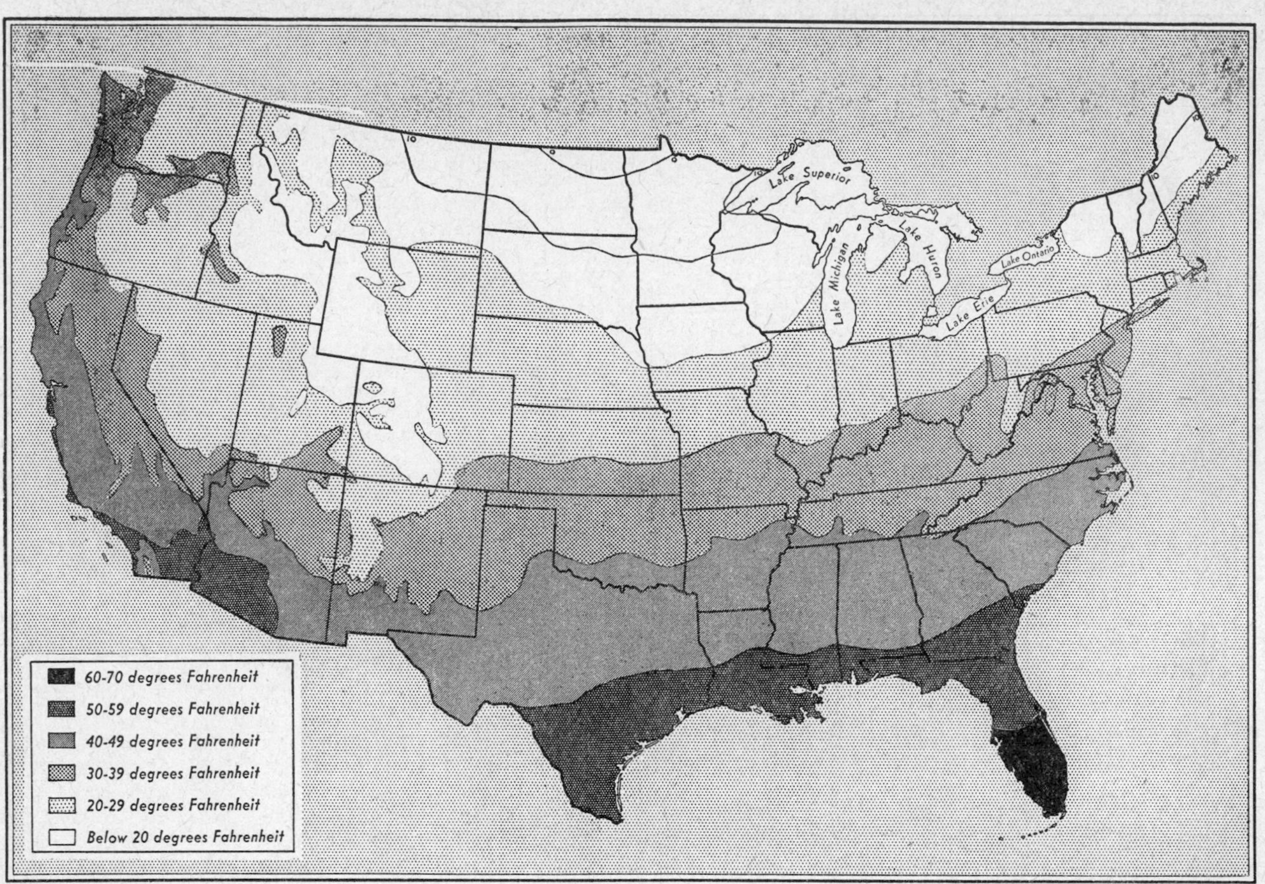

17 Average Temperature in January

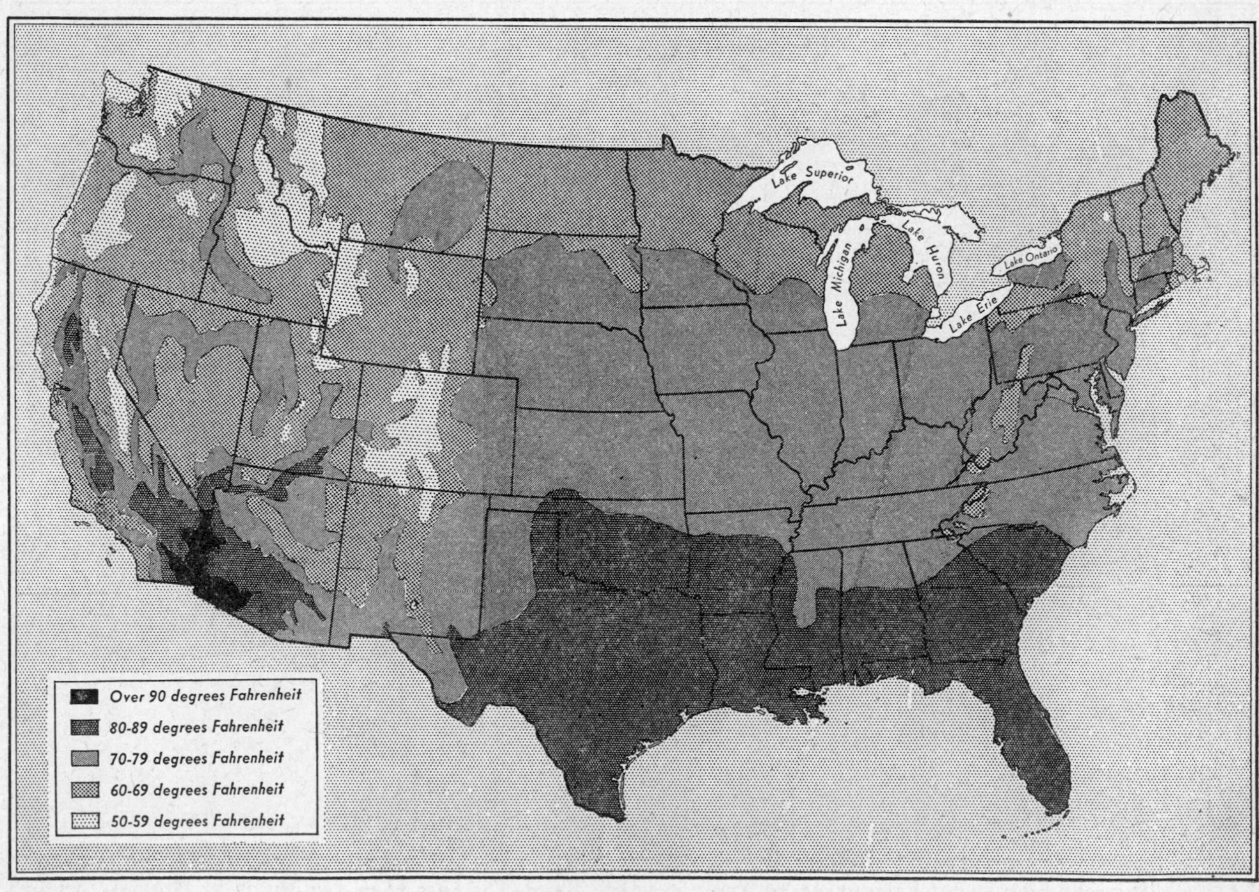

18 Average Temperature in July

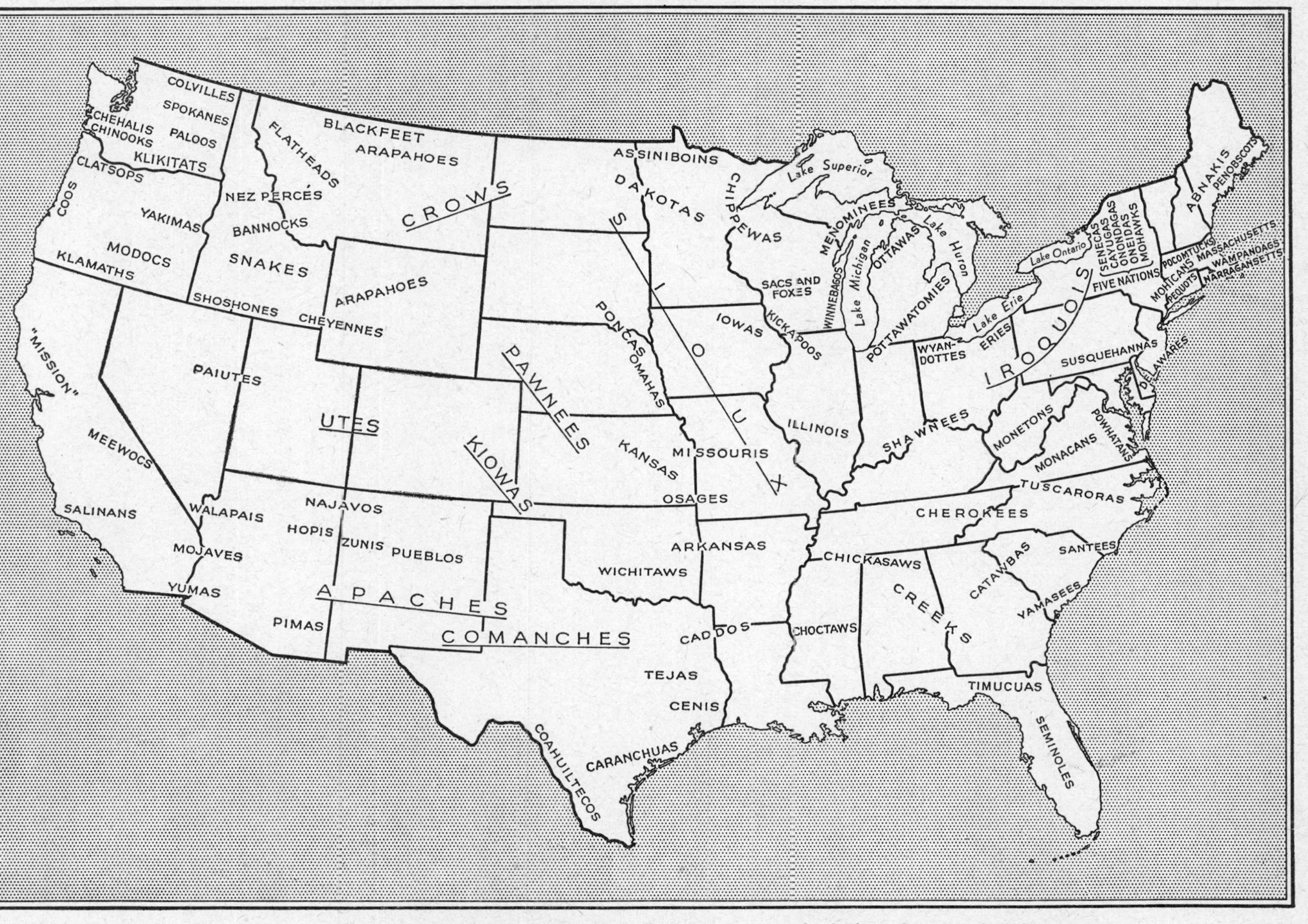

19 The American Indian: Approximate Location of Indians at the Period of Their Greatest Significance in the Westward Movement of the Frontier

The more prominent names are underlined

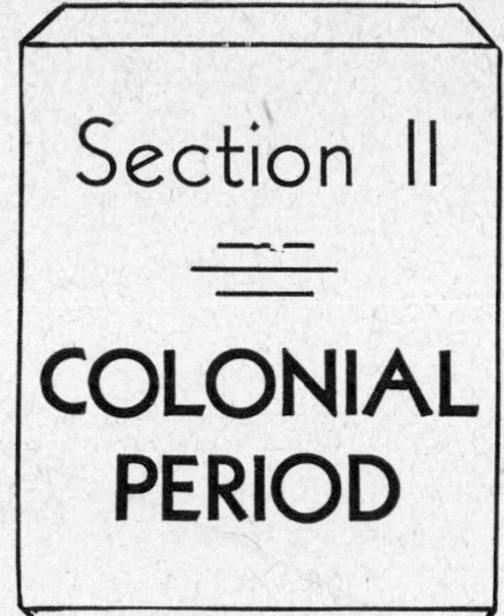

Section II

COLONIAL PERIOD

The days of exploration, early settlement, and gradual growth of the colonies and provinces prior to the Revolution constitute one of the most interesting and vital parts of our history. Yet, only too often, this important period is given the same treatment in classroom and textbook which "Early Childhood" receives in most biographies. Unfortunately, the lack of time and space which cramps its presentation in introductory courses is one factor restricting its development even here. Another is that full and reliable statistics for the period are almost unavailable, so that the economic maps are of necessity rather limited, both in number and usefulness.

After the age of exploration and after Spain had founded her enormous Colonial empire, the English began the permanent settlements along the Atlantic Coast which were to become the direct forbears of the United States.

The growth of the English colonies is shown first in the charter grants, the advancing line of population, and the expansion of frontier forts and settlements. International rivalries, determining the future course of empire, were present from the outset, though the earlier ones were destined to be somewhat dwarfed by the magnitude of the century of struggle between France and England. One can see France and Spain clash from Georgia to Texas. One can watch the fingers of settlement move out dramatically from New Netherland, absorbing New Sweden, meeting the more rapidly moving tentacles of New England in Long Island, in the Connecticut Valley and on the mouth of the Delaware. The final absorption of the Dutch settlements by the English only paved the way for the ensuing conflict for mastery of the continent between the French and the English. Few more effective methods may be found for presenting the meaning of this conflict and its course than to study the expansion of French and English posts and forts between 1688 and 1763, and to correlate the military campaigns of the four wars with this expansion and its attempt to establish hegemony of the Ohio, the Mississippi, the Great Lakes, and, of course, the fur trade. Spain meanwhile was pressing her expansion northward, but neither so far nor so fast as to come into serious conflict with the British colonials, moving westward. Trouble in that area was to wait on American independence, the Jay-Gardoqui negotiations, the Louisiana Purchase, the Texan Revolution and the Mexican War.

Franchise laws show the close restriction of the suffrage prior to the Revolution. The limits of free district school legislation mark the difficulty, despite the promise of the Massachusetts Act of 1649, which the son of the man of modest means encountered in obtaining a rudimentary education. Restricted by British legislation and far more effectively checked by transportation difficulties, manufacturing was limited largely to production for local markets. Commerce, influenced appreciably by British policies of enumeration, subsidy and empire trade, was an extremely important factor in the colonial economy in the period preceding the establishment of independence. Restrictions upon that commerce, on westward expansion, and on local self-determination, were to contribute largely to the outbreak of revolt against the government of George III. Some of the commodities, their countries of origin, and the much abused and oversimplified "triangular" routes are indicated on the map of colonial trade.

The diverse nationalities which were eventually to constitute the American nation were already in evidence prior to the Revolution, English, Dutch, Scotch-Irish and German predominating. Newspapers, always useful vehicles, as well as significant criteria, of the spread of knowledge and literacy, were already long established by the time the Revolution came to give birth to new Tory and Patriot sheets. Though many provincials relied on English institutions for higher learning, by 1775 American colleges, beginning with Harvard College in 1636, included many of our best-known universities. Many of the foundation stones of modern America were in place by April, 1775.

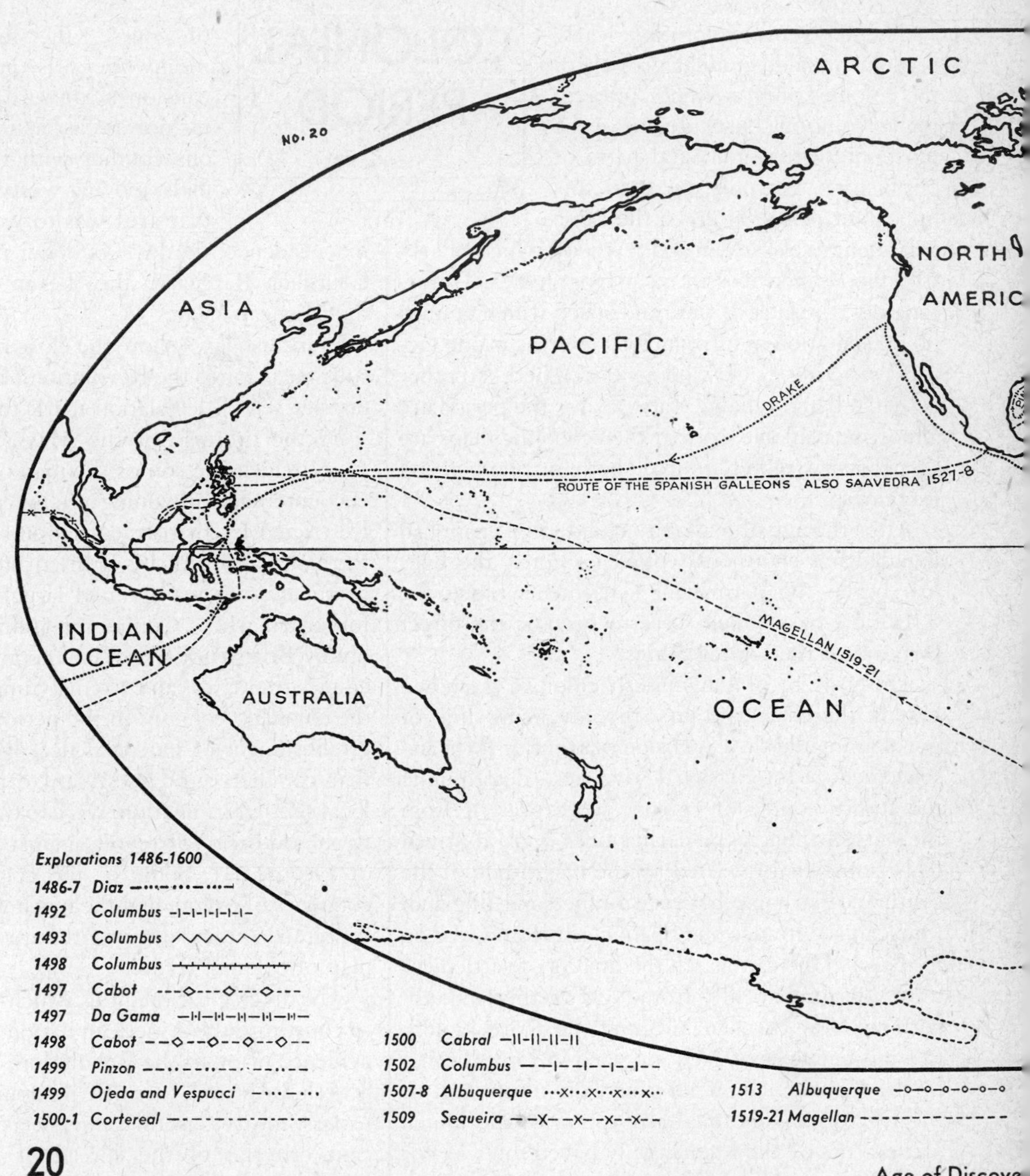

ARCTIC
No. 20
NORTH
AMERIC
ASIA
PACIFIC
DRAKE
ROUTE OF THE SPANISH GALLEONS ALSO SAAVEDRA 1527-8
INDIAN
OCEAN
MAGELLAN 1519-21
AUSTRALIA
OCEAN
Explorations 1486-1600
1486-7 Diaz
1492 Columbus
1493 Columbus
1498 Columbus
1497 Cabot
1497 Da Gama
1498 Cabot
1499 Pinzon
1499 Ojeda and Vespucci
1500-1 Cortereal
1500 Cabral
1502 Columbus
1507-8 Albuquerque
1509 Sequeira
1513 Albuquerque
1519-21 Magellan

20

Age of Discove

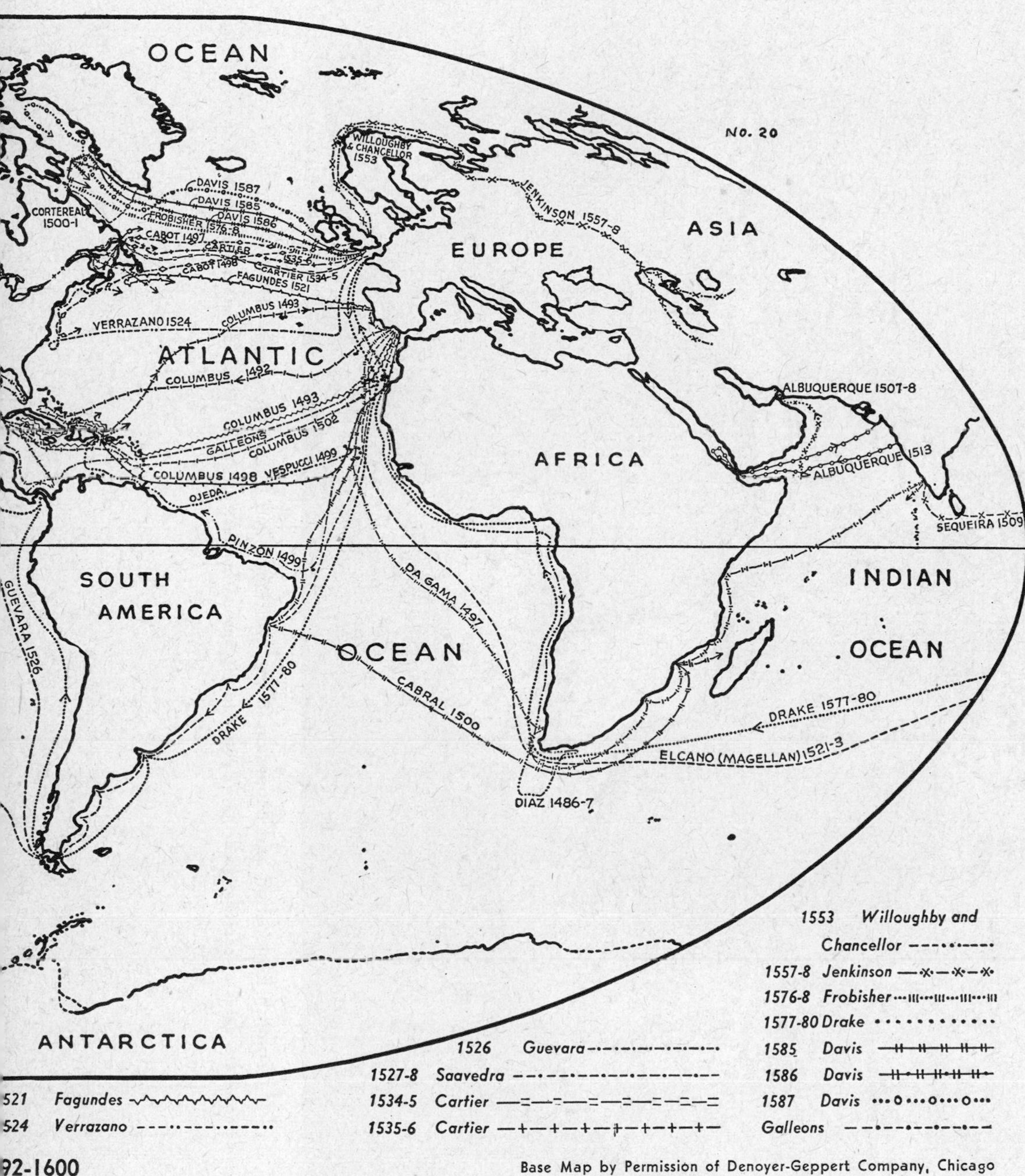
OCEAN
No. 20
WILLOUGHBY & CHANCELLOR 1553
JENKINSON 1557-8
ASIA
EUROPE
DAVIS 1587
DAVIS 1585
DAVIS 1586
CORTEREAL 1500-1
FROBISHER 1576-8
CABOT 1497
CARTIER 1534-5
FAGUNDES 1521
VERRAZANO 1524
COLUMBUS 1493
ATLANTIC
COLUMBUS 1492
ALBUQUERQUE 1507-8
COLUMBUS 1493
GALLEONS
COLUMBUS 1502
AFRICA
ALBUQUERQUE 1513
COLUMBUS 1498
VESPUCCI 1499
OJEDA
SEQUEIRA 1509
PINZON 1499
SOUTH AMERICA
DA GAMA 1497
INDIAN
OCEAN
OCEAN
GUEVARA 1526
CABRAL 1500
DRAKE 1577-80
DRAKE 1577-80
ELCANO (MAGELLAN) 1521-3
DIAZ 1486-7
ANTARCTICA
1553 Willoughby and Chancellor
1557-8 Jenkinson
1576-8 Frobisher
1577-80 Drake
1585 Davis
1586 Davis
1587 Davis
Galleons
1526 Guevara
1527-8 Saavedra
1534-5 Cartier
1535-6 Cartier
521 Fagundes
524 Verrazano
92-1600
Base Map by Permission of Denoyer-Geppert Company, Chicago

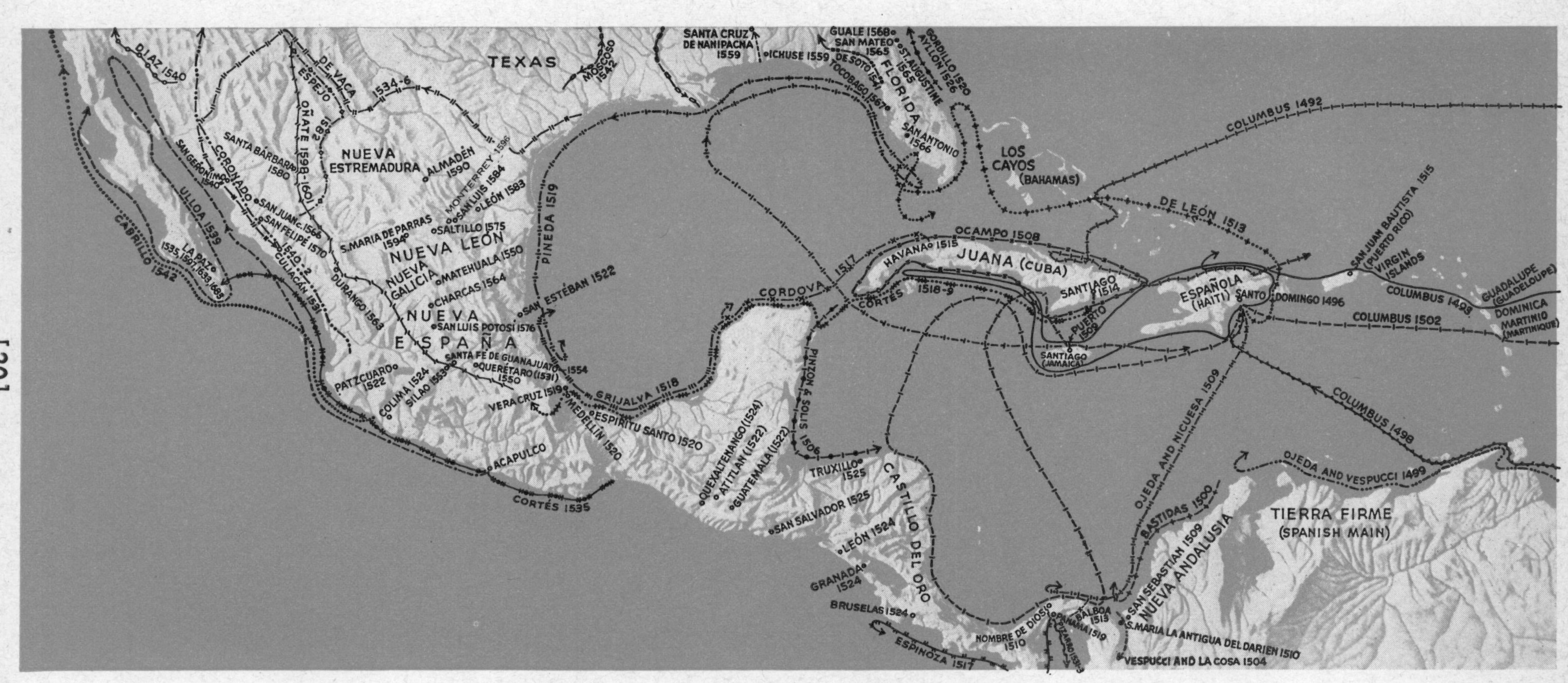

21 Spanish Exploration and Expansion in the Caribbean and Central America—1492-1600

Dates in parentheses are dates of capitulation of native towns to the Spanish conquerors. Dates without parentheses are dates of Spanish settlement

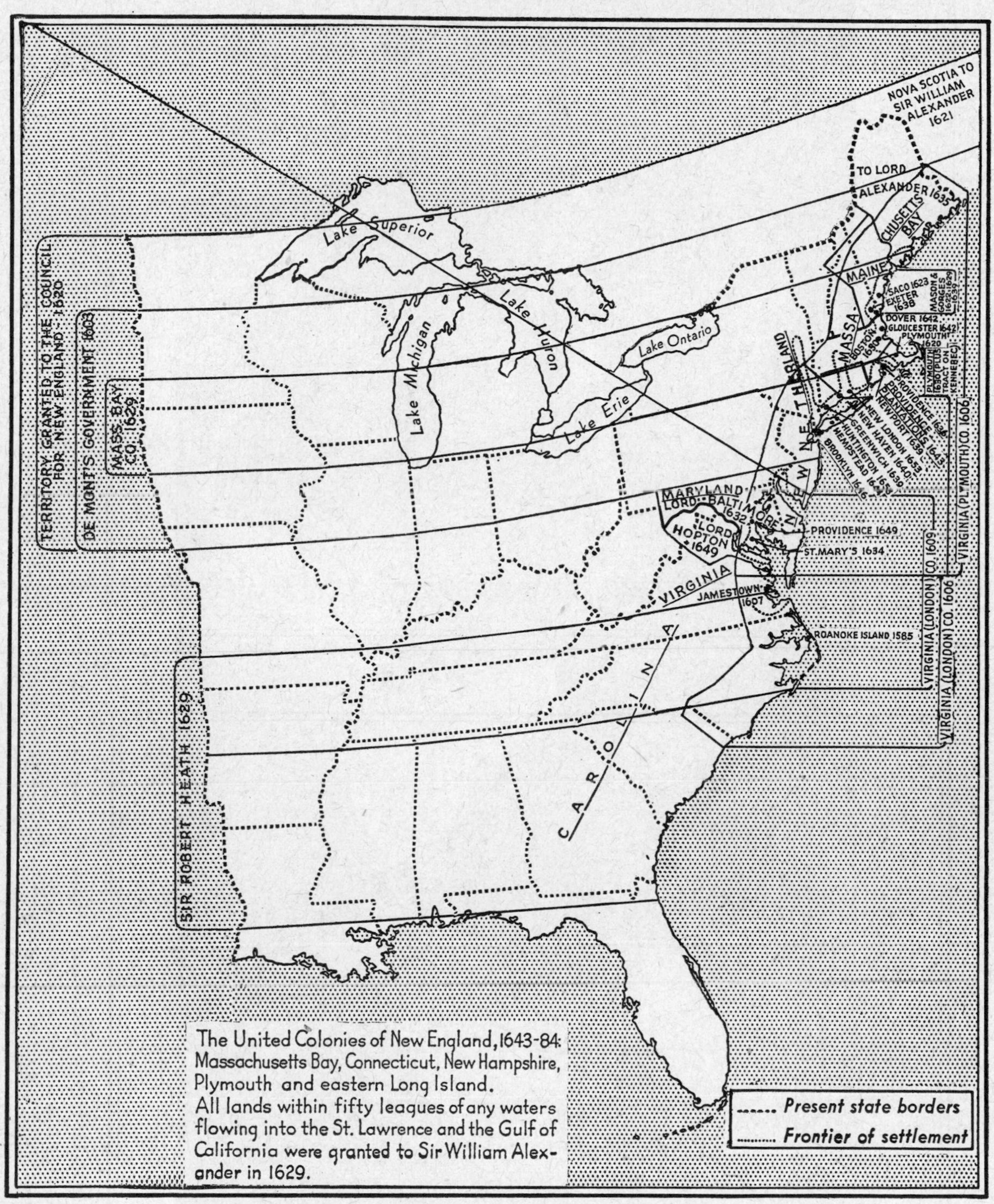
NOVA SCOTIA TO SIR WILLIAM ALEXANDER 1621
TO LORD ALEXANDER 1635
CHUSETTS BAY
MAINE
SACO 1623
EXETER 1638
MASON & GORGES
DOVER 1642
GLOUCESTER 1642
PLYMOUTH
MASSA.
BOSTON
PROVIDENCE PLANTATIONS
NEWPORT 1639
NEW LONDON 1653
NEW HAVEN 1638
GREENWICH 1640
HUNTINGTON 1653
HEMPSTEAD 1644
BROOKLYN 1646
PROVIDENCE 1636
PROVIDENCE 1643
NEW ENGLAND
NEW NETHERLAND
Lake Superior
Lake Michigan
Lake Huron
Lake Ontario
Lake Erie
TERRITORY GRANTED TO THE COUNCIL FOR NEW ENGLAND 1620
DE MONT'S GOVERNMENT 1603
MASS. BAY CO. 1629
MARYLAND
LORD BALTIMORE 1632
LORD HOPTON 1649
PROVIDENCE 1649
ST. MARY'S 1634
VIRGINIA
JAMESTOWN 1607
ROANOKE ISLAND 1585
VIRGINIA (LONDON) CO. 1609
VIRGINIA (LONDON) CO. 1606
VIRGINIA (PLYMOUTH) CO. 1606
CAROLINA
SIR ROBERT HEATH 1629
The United Colonies of New England, 1643-84:
Massachusetts Bay, Connecticut, New Hampshire,
Plymouth and eastern Long Island.
All lands within fifty leagues of any waters
flowing into the St. Lawrence and the Gulf of
California were granted to Sir William Alexander in 1629.
Present state borders
Frontier of settlement

22 English Colonies, Charter Grants, and Frontier of Settlement, 1660

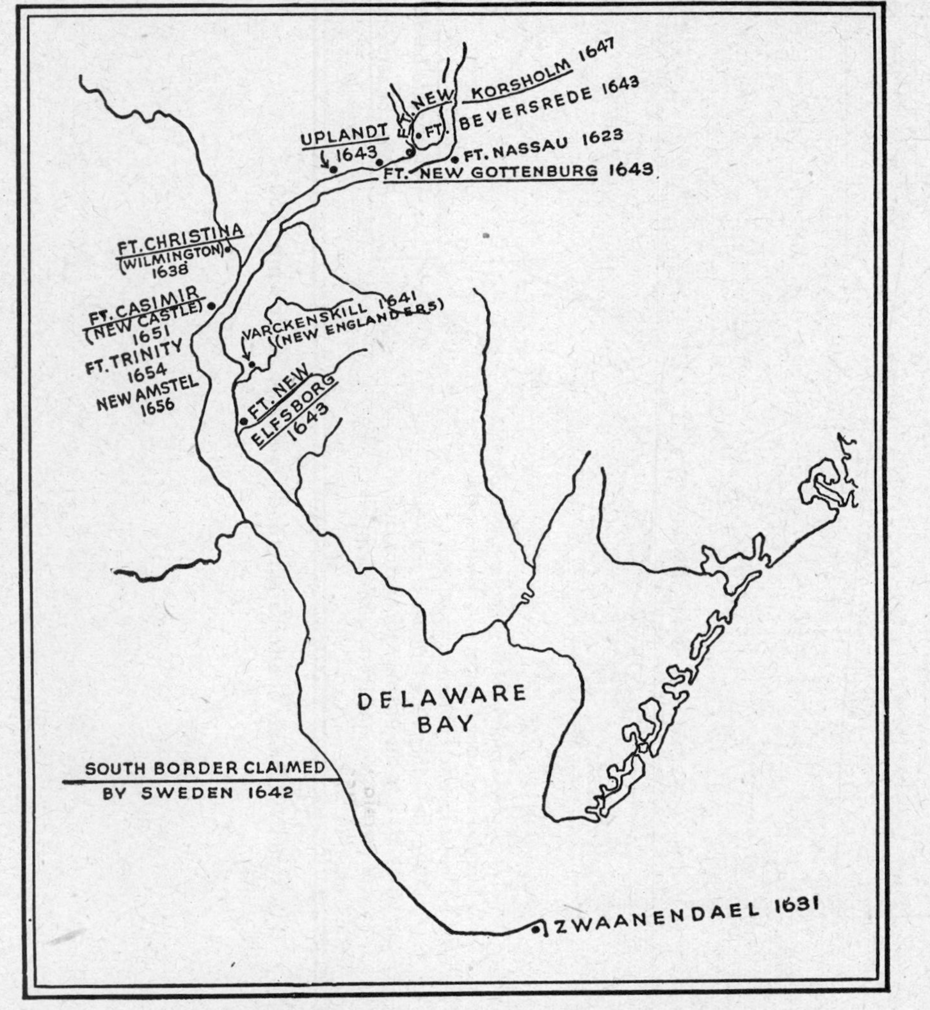

23 New Sweden, 1638-1655; New Netherland, 1655-1664
Names of Swedish settlements are underscored

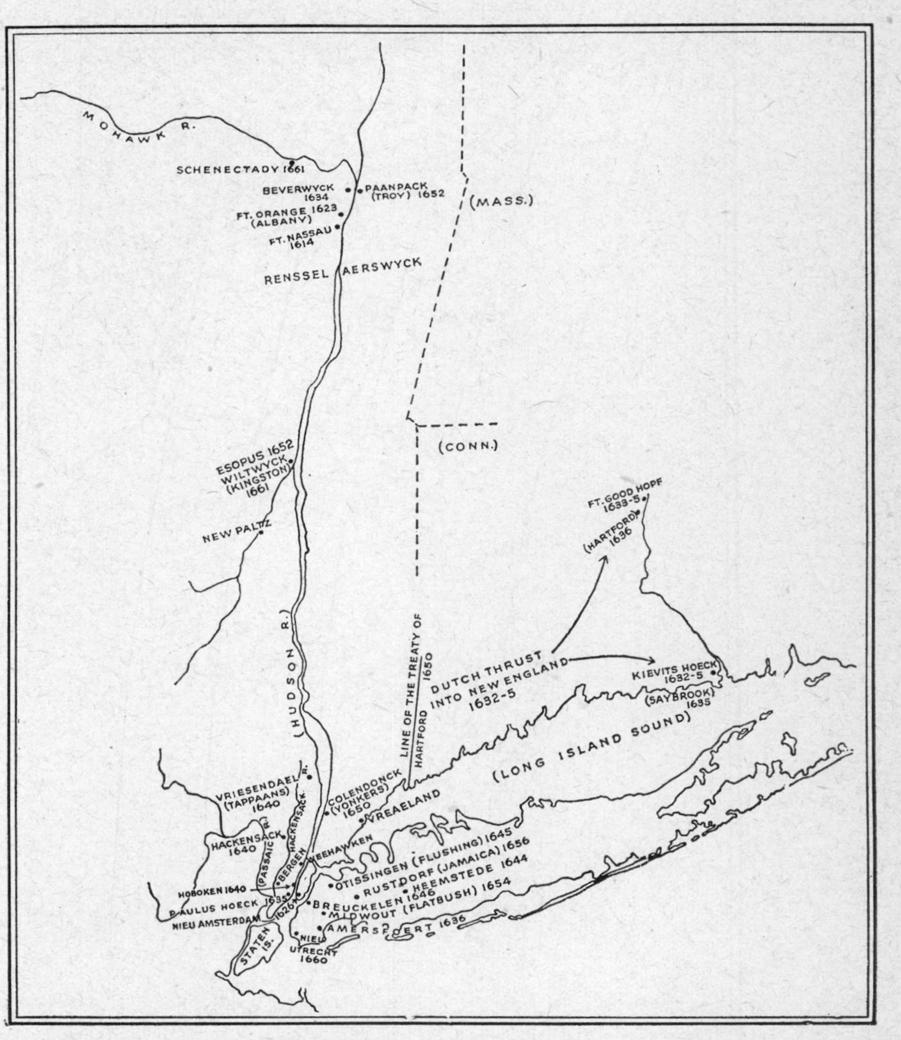

24 New Netherland, 1609-1664

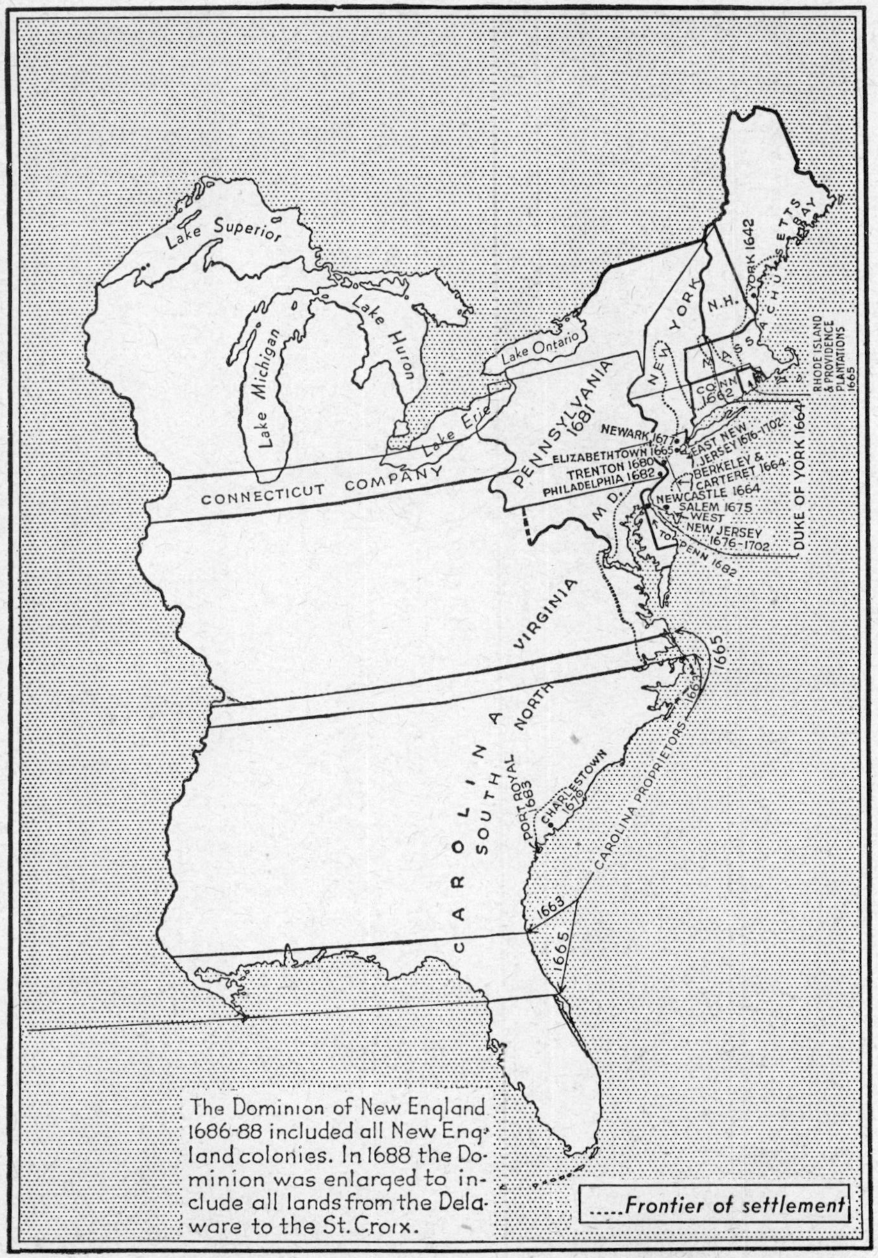

The Dominion of New England 1686-88 included all New England colonies. In 1688 the Dominion was enlarged to include all lands from the Delaware to the St. Croix.

.....Frontier of settlement

25 English Colonies, Charter Grants, 1660-1700, and Frontier of Settlement, 1700

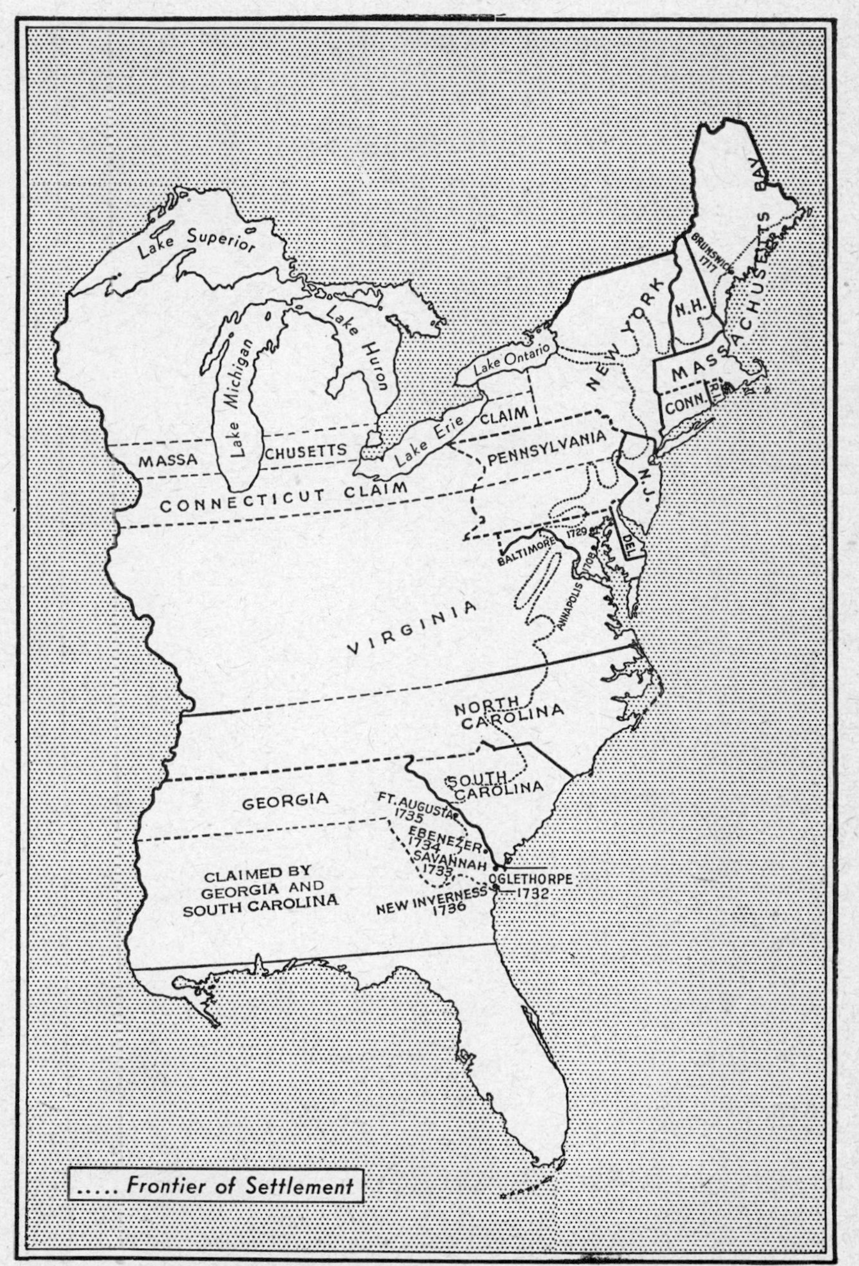

26 English Colonies, Charter Grants, 1700-1750, and Frontier of Settlement, 1750

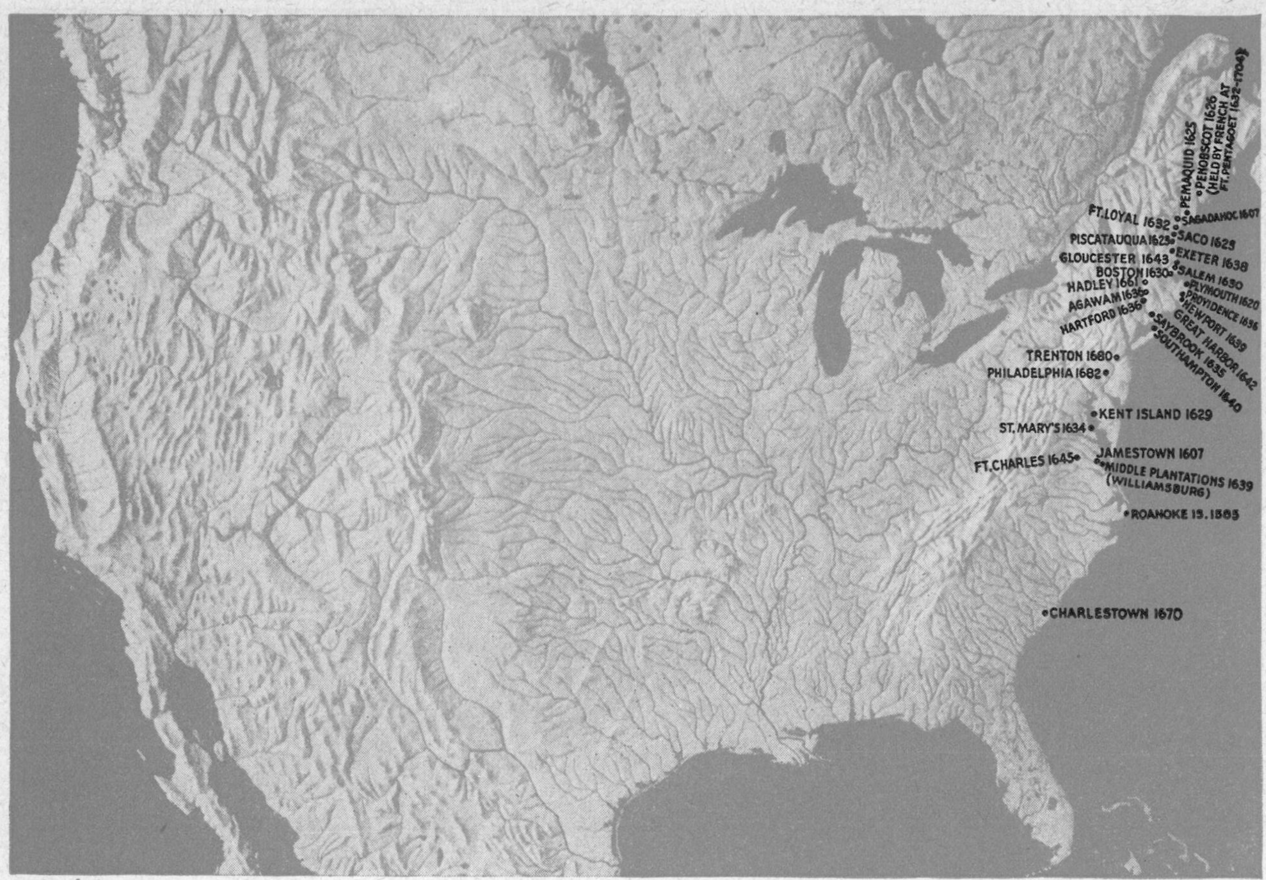

27 English Expansion to 1697

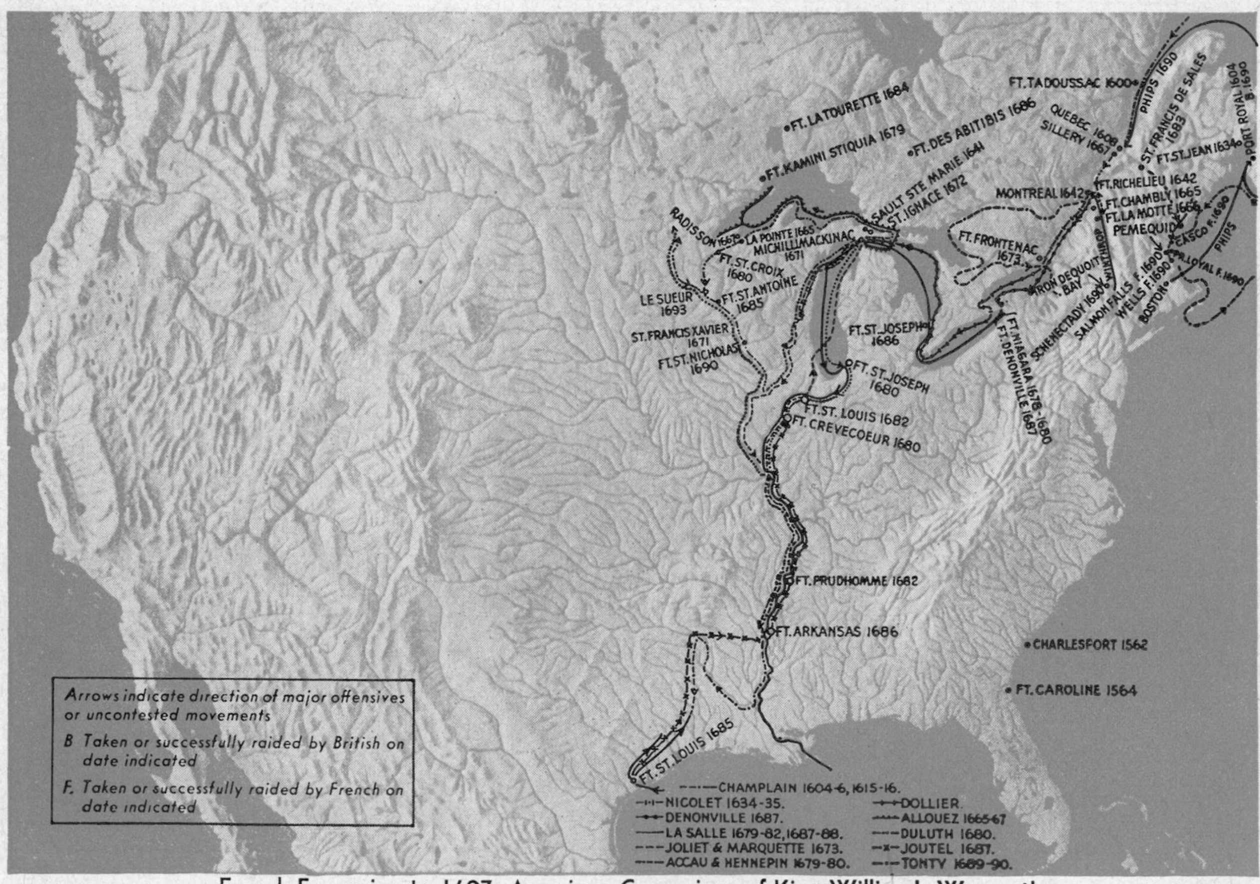

28 French Expansion to 1697: American Campaigns of King William's War or the War of the League of Augsburg

Dates approximate first settlement of sometimes ephemeral posts

For maps 27-34 the same base is used to show the relative positions of the French and the British

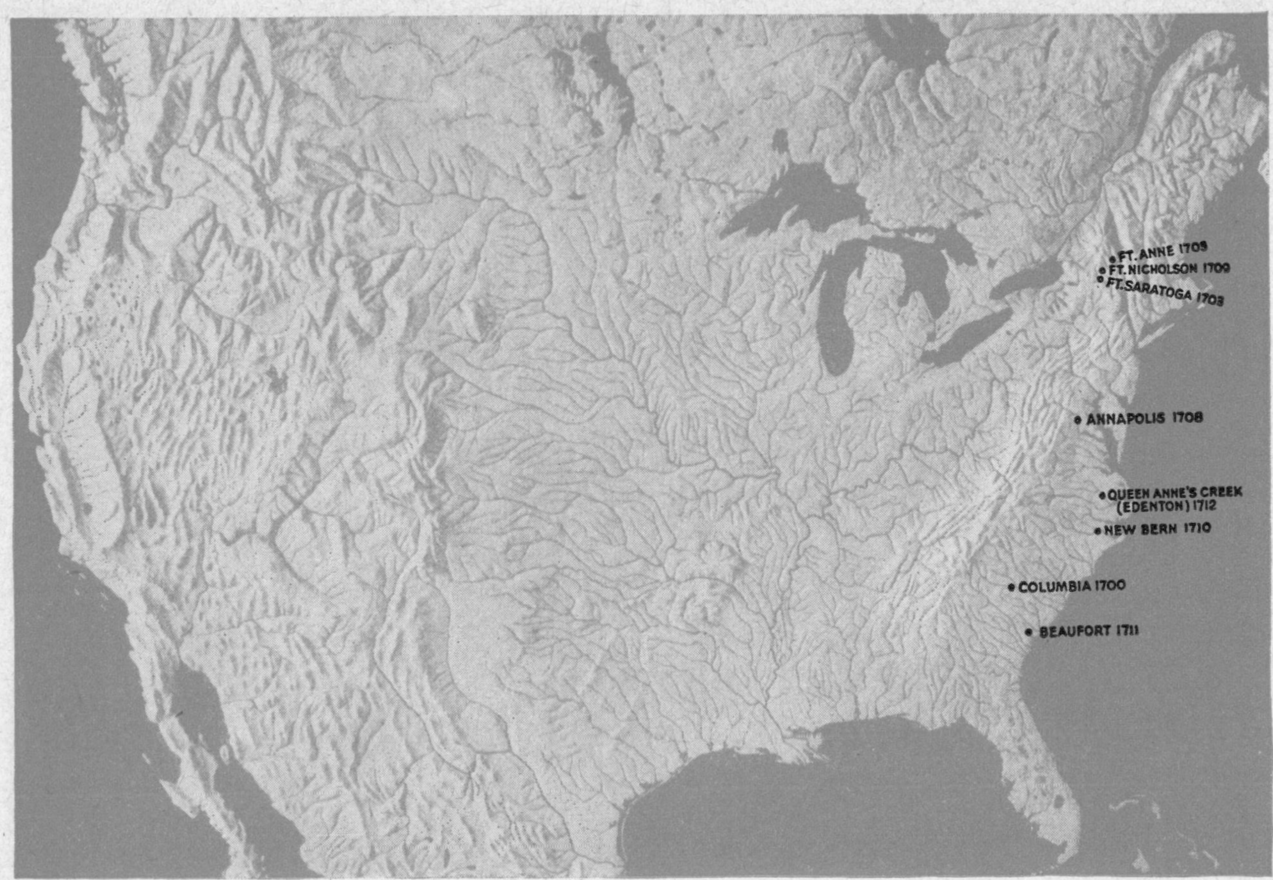

29 English Expansion, 1698-1713

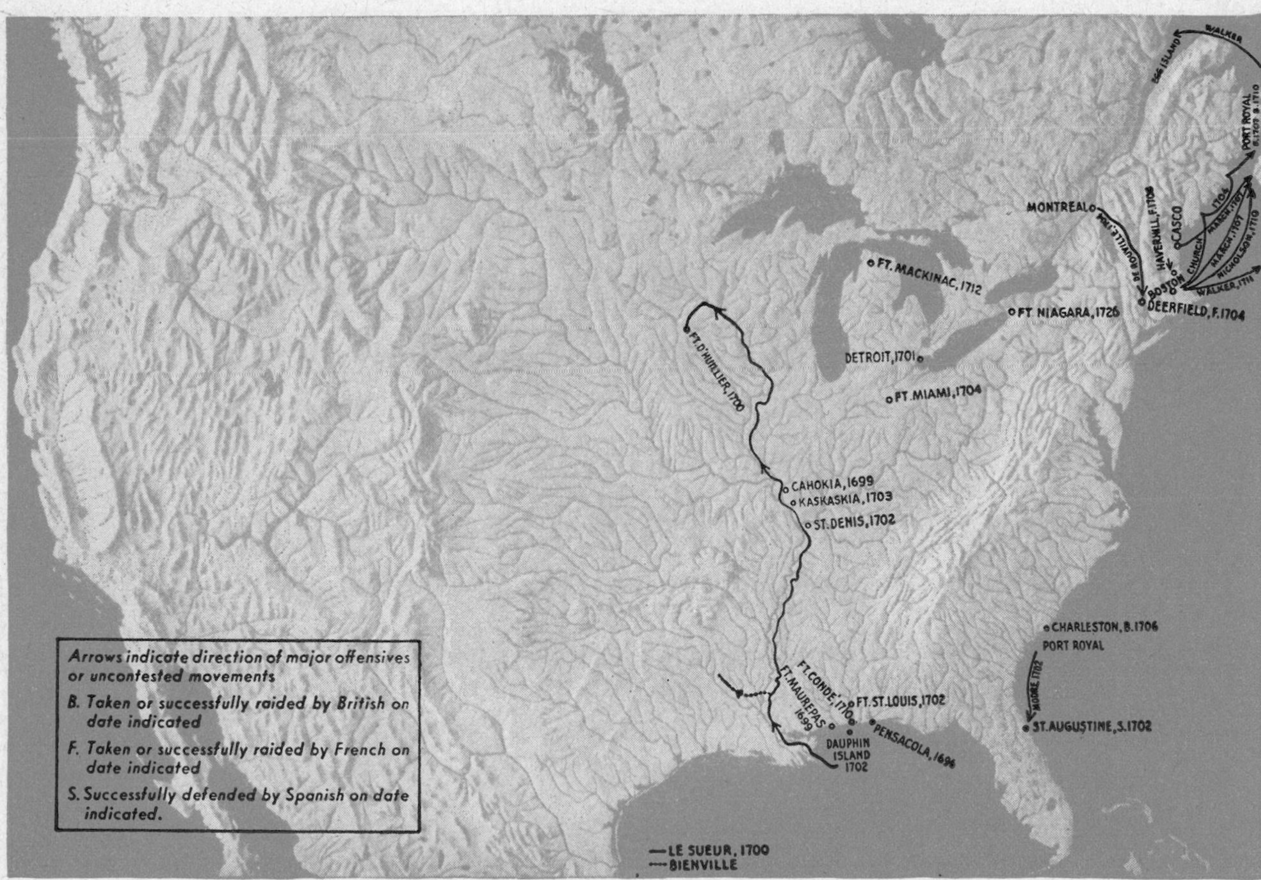

30 French Expansion, 1698-1713: American Campaigns of Queen Anne's War or the War of the Spanish Succession

Dates approximate first settlement of sometimes ephemeral posts

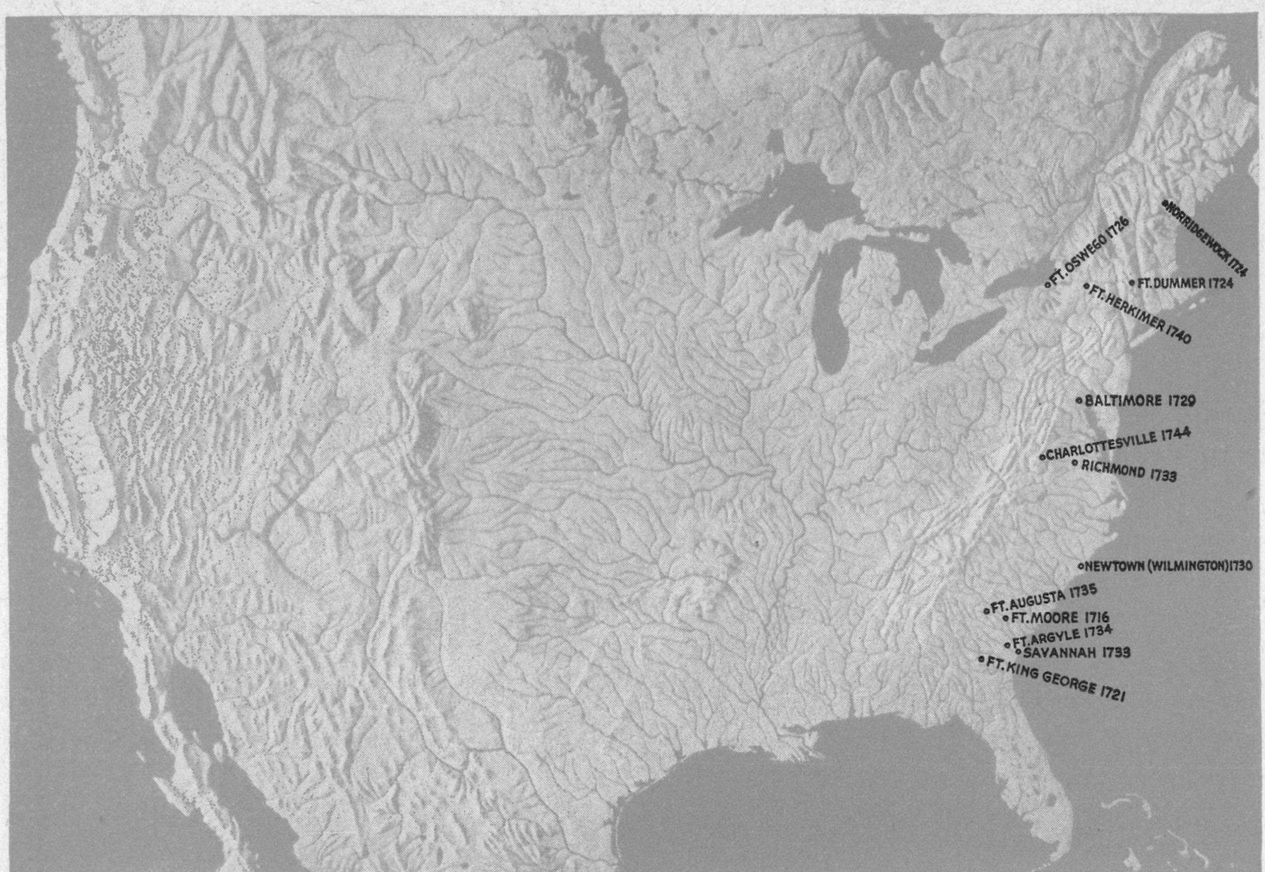

31

English Expansion, 1714-1744

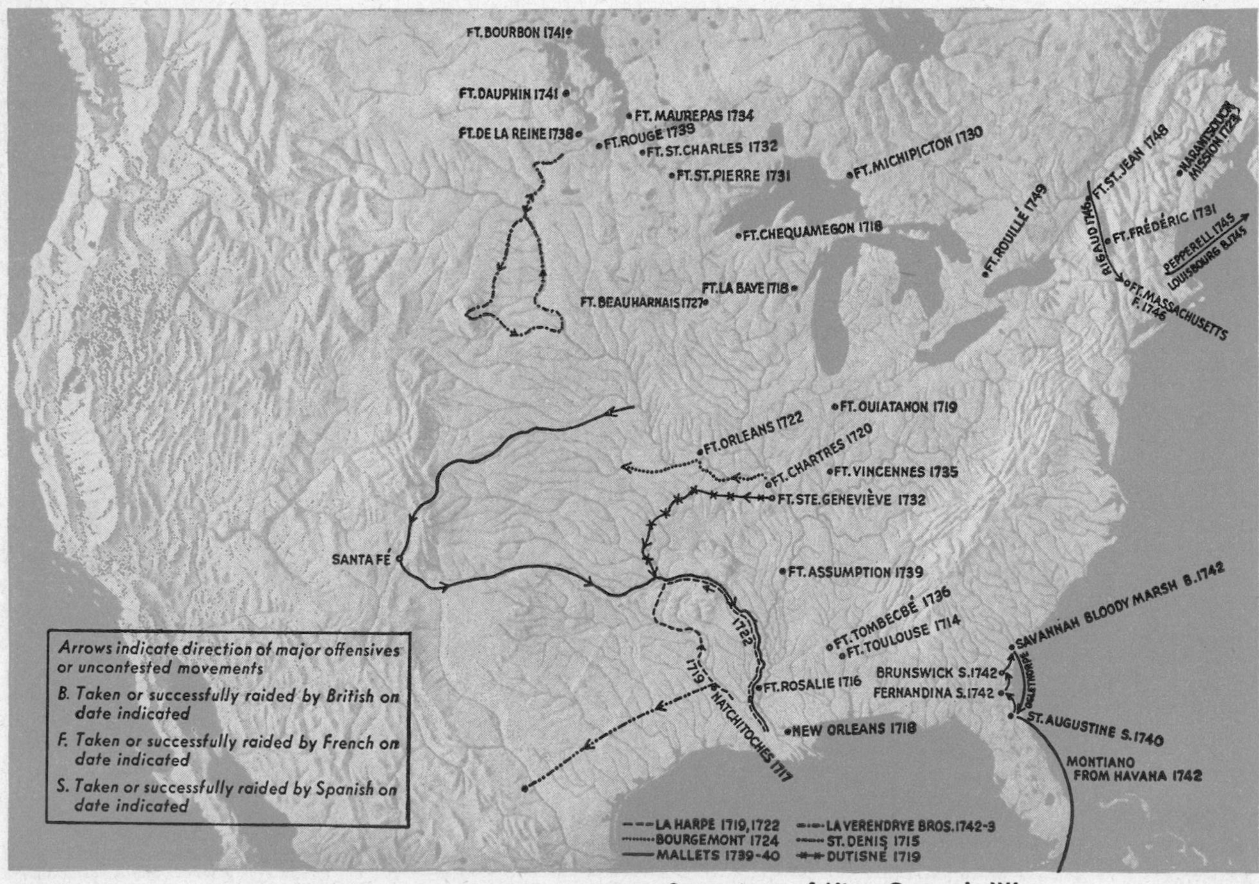

32

French Expansion, 1714-1744: American Campaigns of King George's War or the War of the Austrian Succession

Dates approximate first establishment of sometimes ephemeral posts

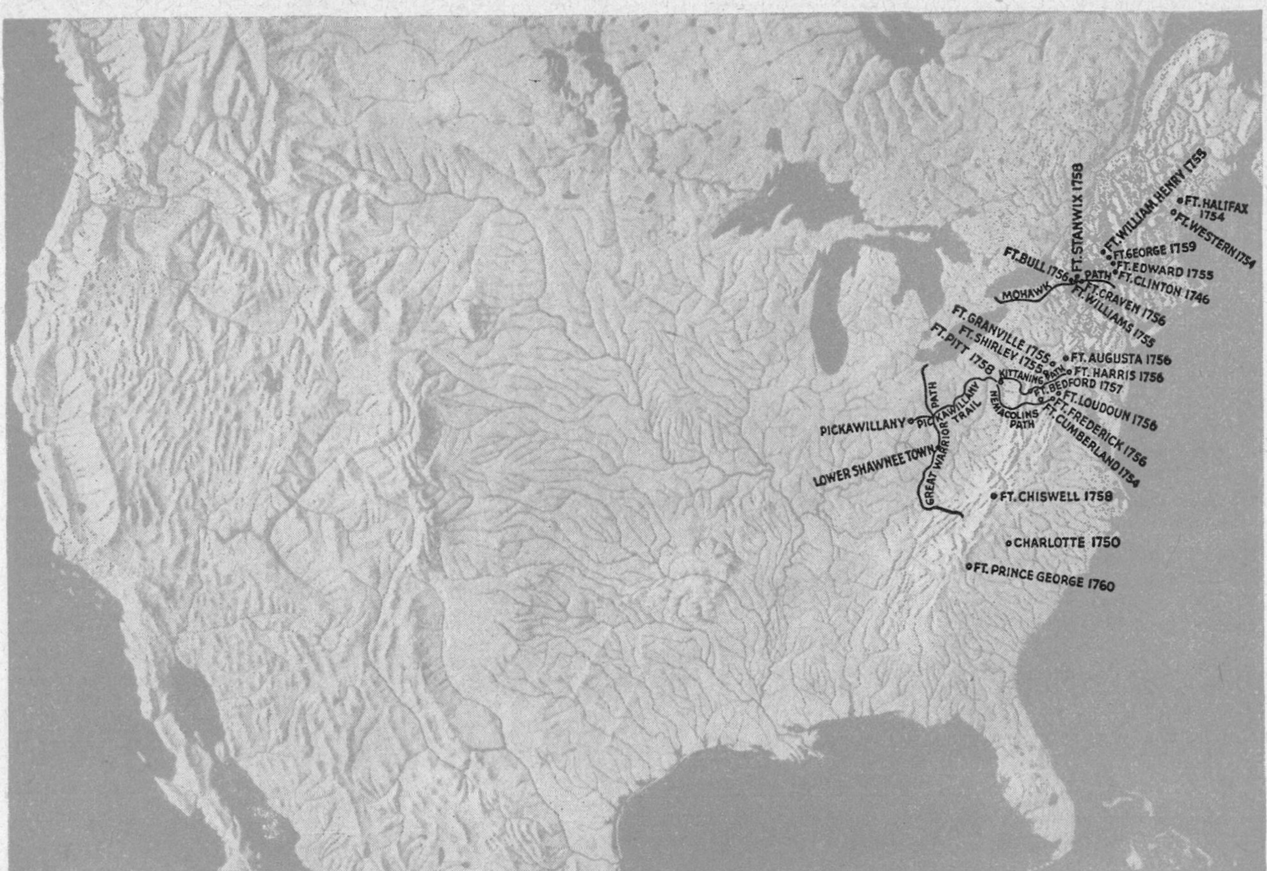

33 English Expansion and Routes of Indian Trade with the English Colonies, 1744-1763

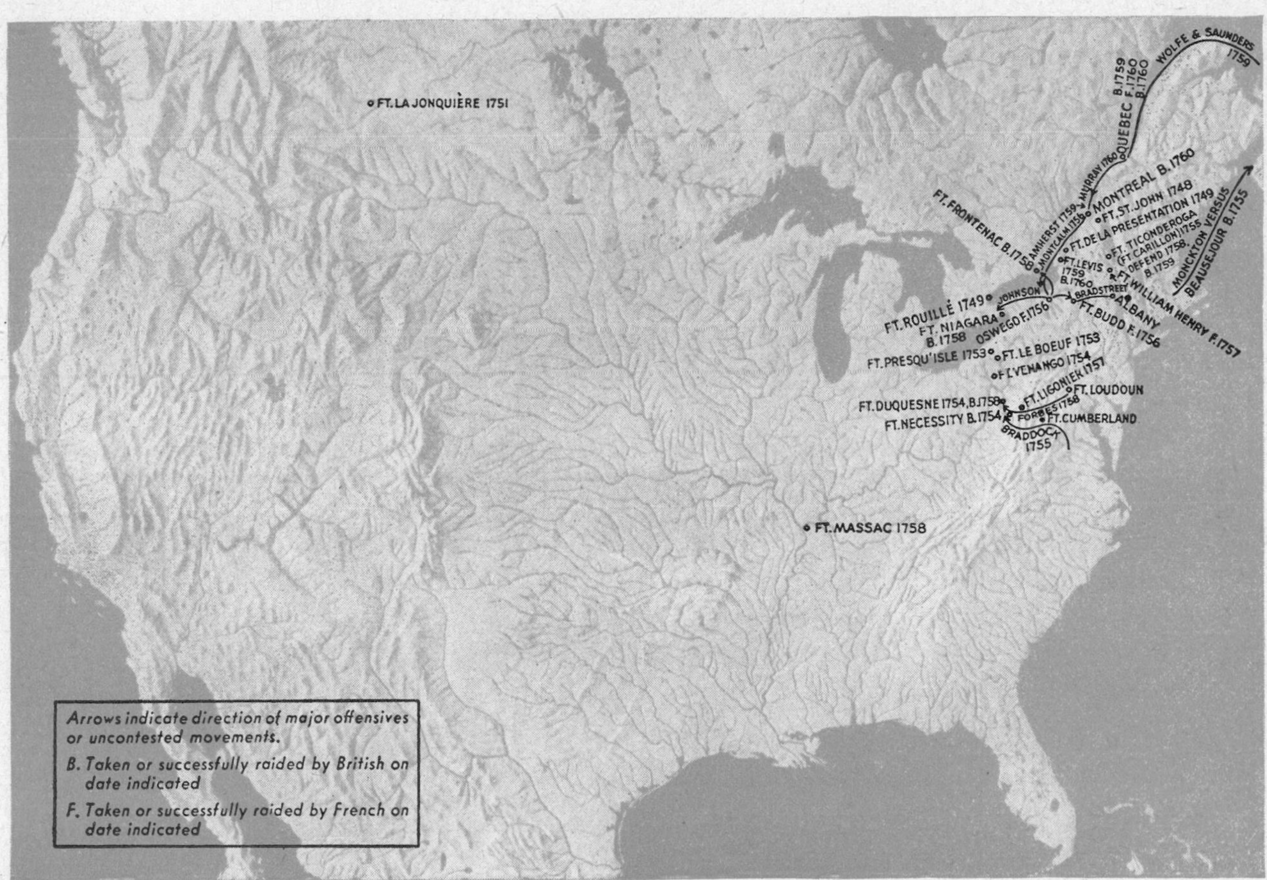

34 French Expansion, 1745-1763: American Campaigns of the French and Indian War, or the Seven Years' War

Dates approximate first establishment of sometimes ephemeral posts

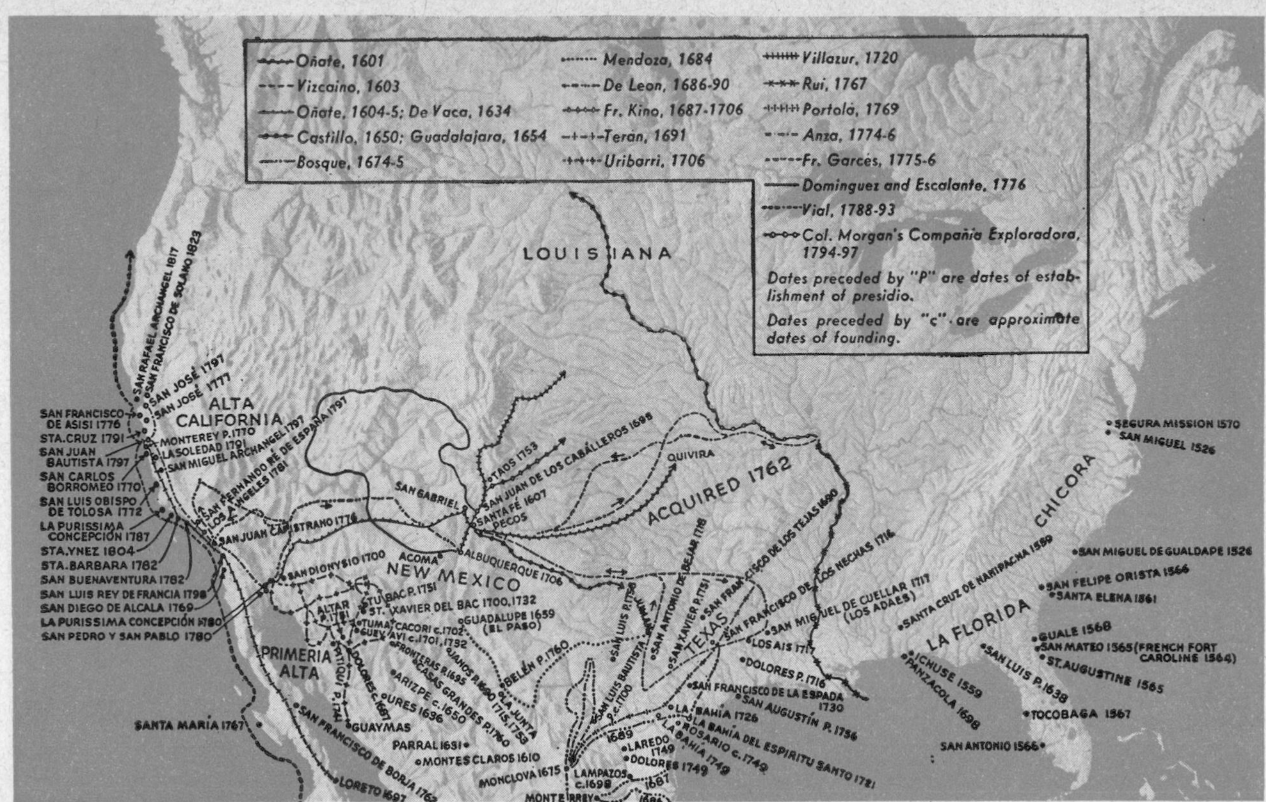

35 Spanish Exploration and Expansion in and Near the Present Territorial Limits of the United States, 1600-1823

Dates approximate first Spanish settlements

(See also Maps 49-51 for Spanish military expeditions in this area during the Revolution)

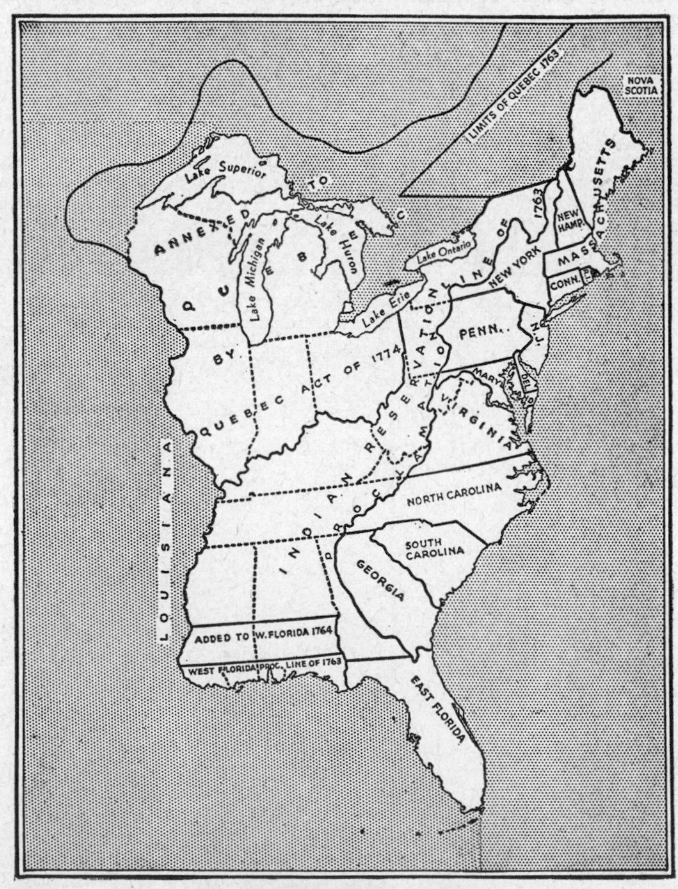

36 English Colonies, 1763-1775

The Pennsylvania-Maryland border was surveyed by Mason and Dixon in 1767

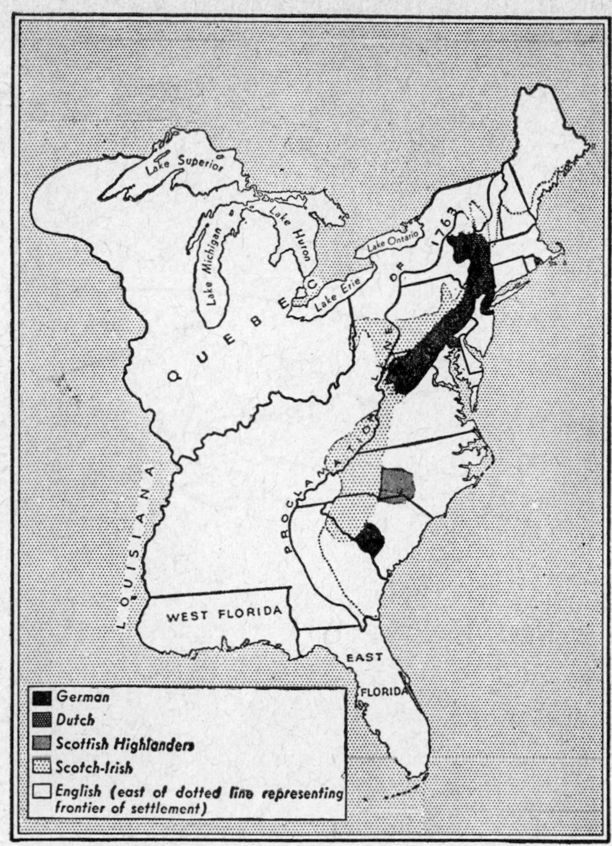

37 Distribution of Immigrant Stock, 1775

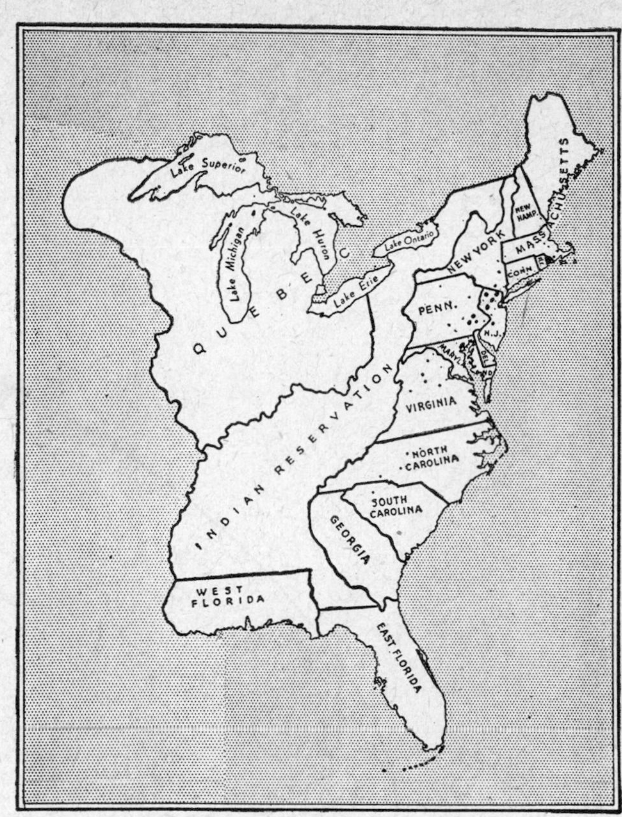

38 Manufacturing Areas (Iron Works), 1775

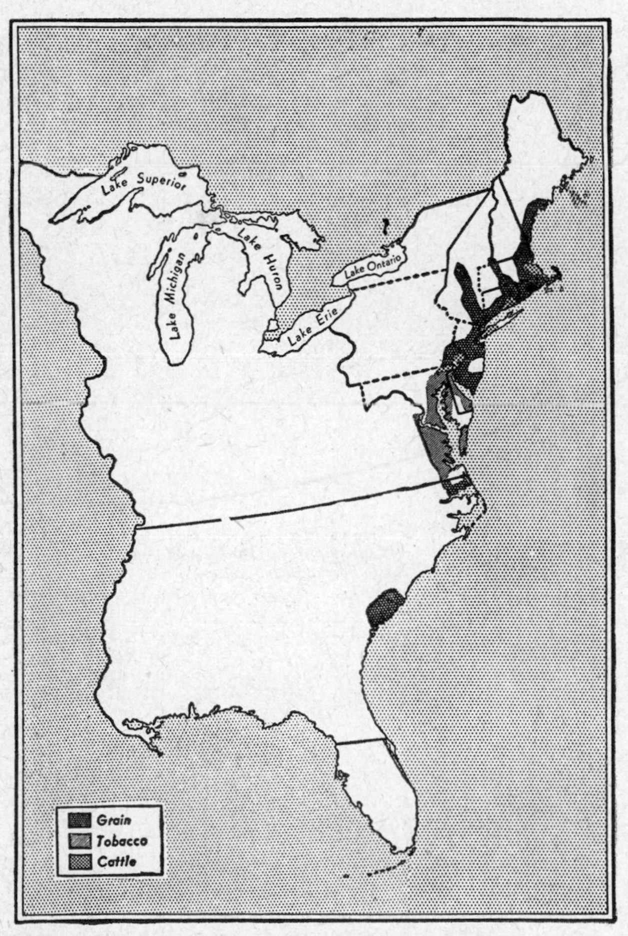

39 Generalized Crop Areas, 1700

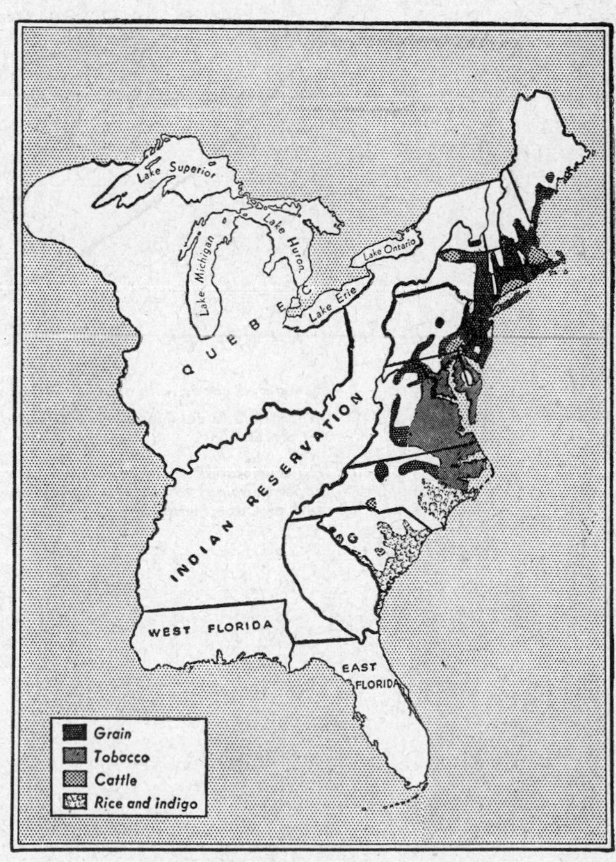

40 Generalized Crop Areas, 1775

Maps on this page give data only for the future Thirteen Original States

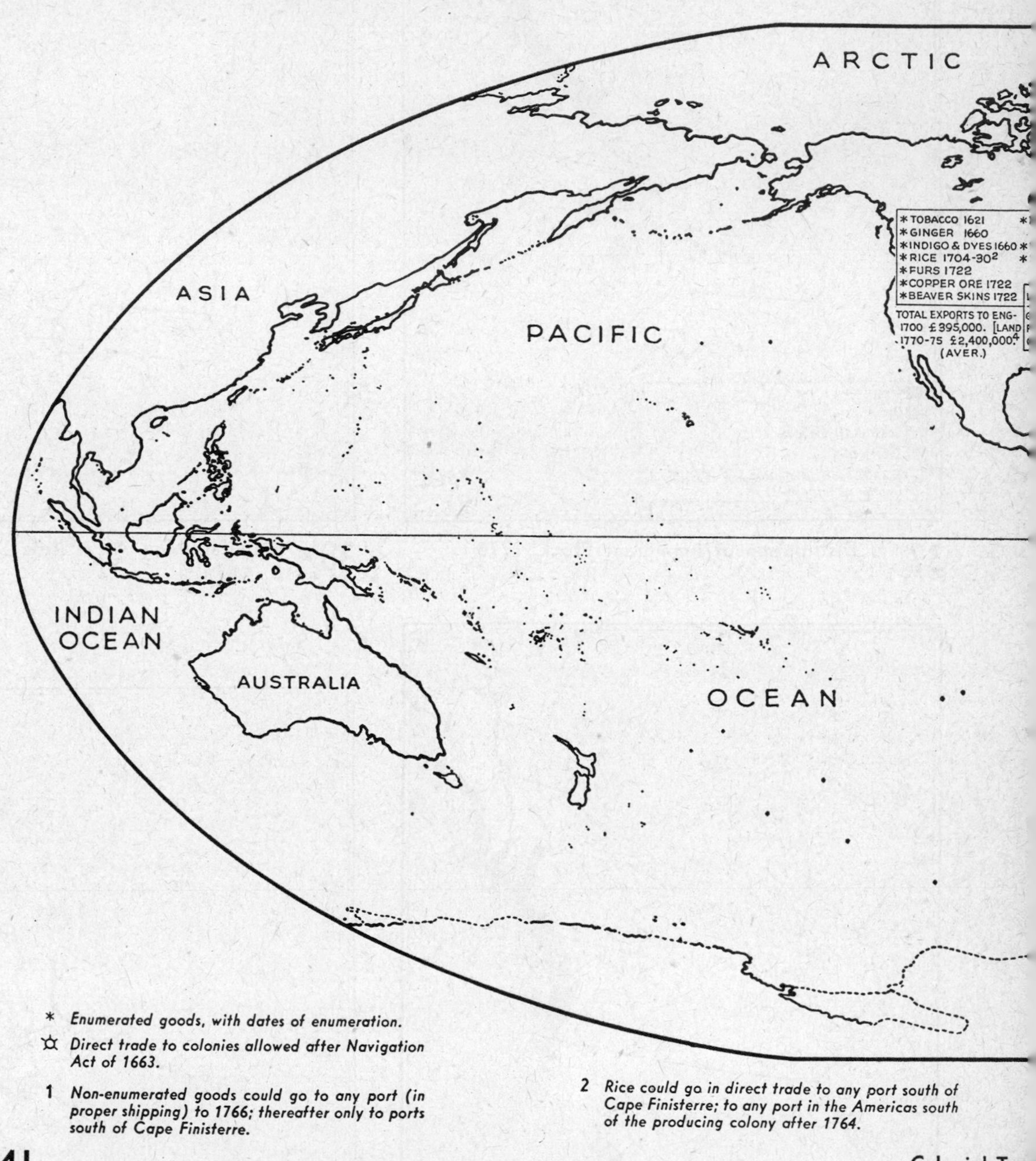

* *Enumerated goods, with dates of enumeration.*

☆ *Direct trade to colonies allowed after Navigation Act of 1663.*

1 *Non-enumerated goods could go to any port (in proper shipping) to 1766; thereafter only to ports south of Cape Finisterre.*

2 *Rice could go in direct trade to any port south of Cape Finisterre; to any port in the Americas south of the producing colony after 1764.*

41

Colonial Tra

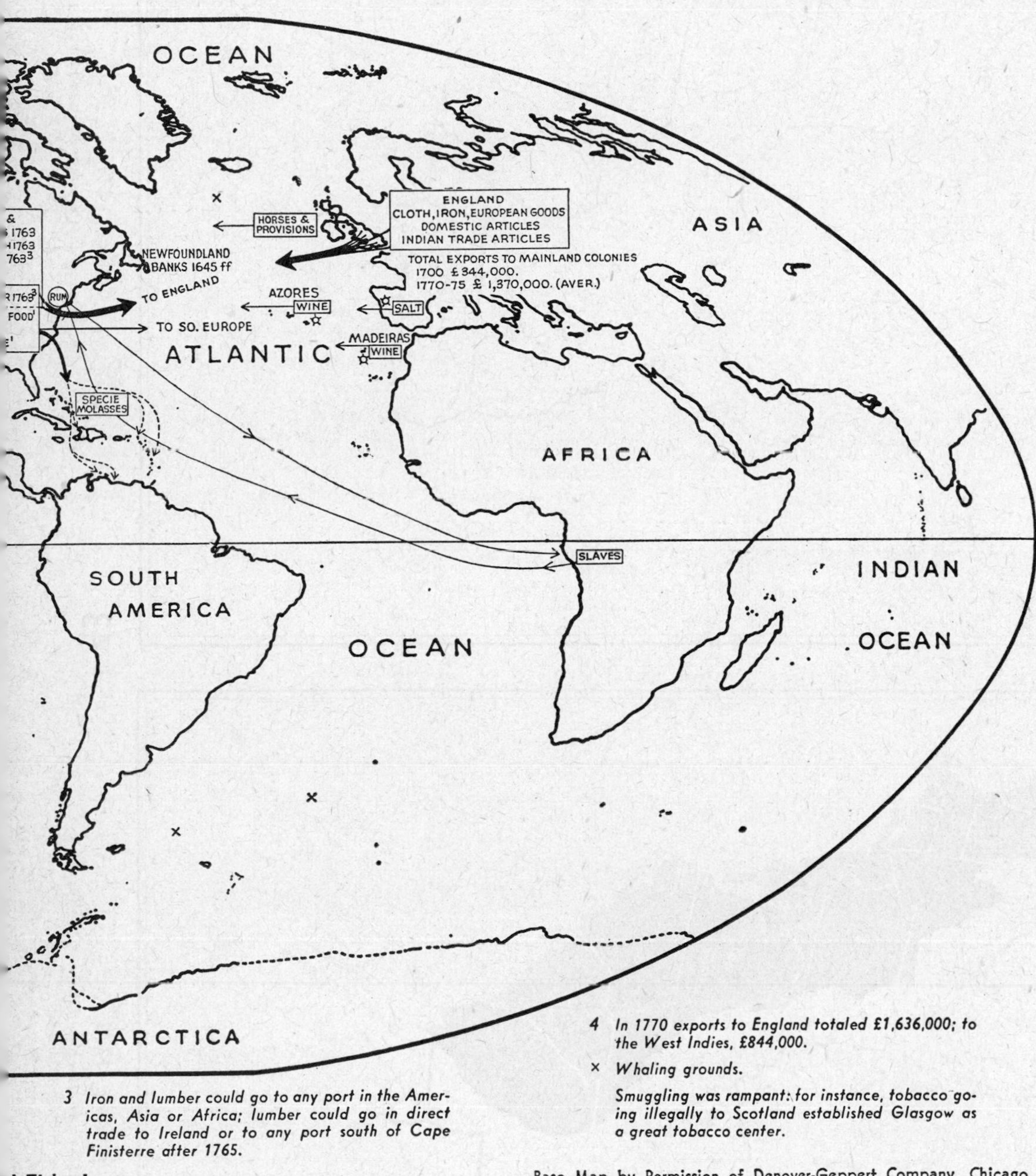

3 *Iron and lumber could go to any port in the Americas, Asia or Africa; lumber could go in direct trade to Ireland or to any port south of Cape Finisterre after 1765.*

4 *In 1770 exports to England totaled £1,636,000; to the West Indies, £844,000.*

× *Whaling grounds.*

Smuggling was rampant: for instance, tobacco going illegally to Scotland established Glasgow as a great tobacco center.

d Fisheries

Base Map by Permission of Denoyer-Geppert Company, Chicago

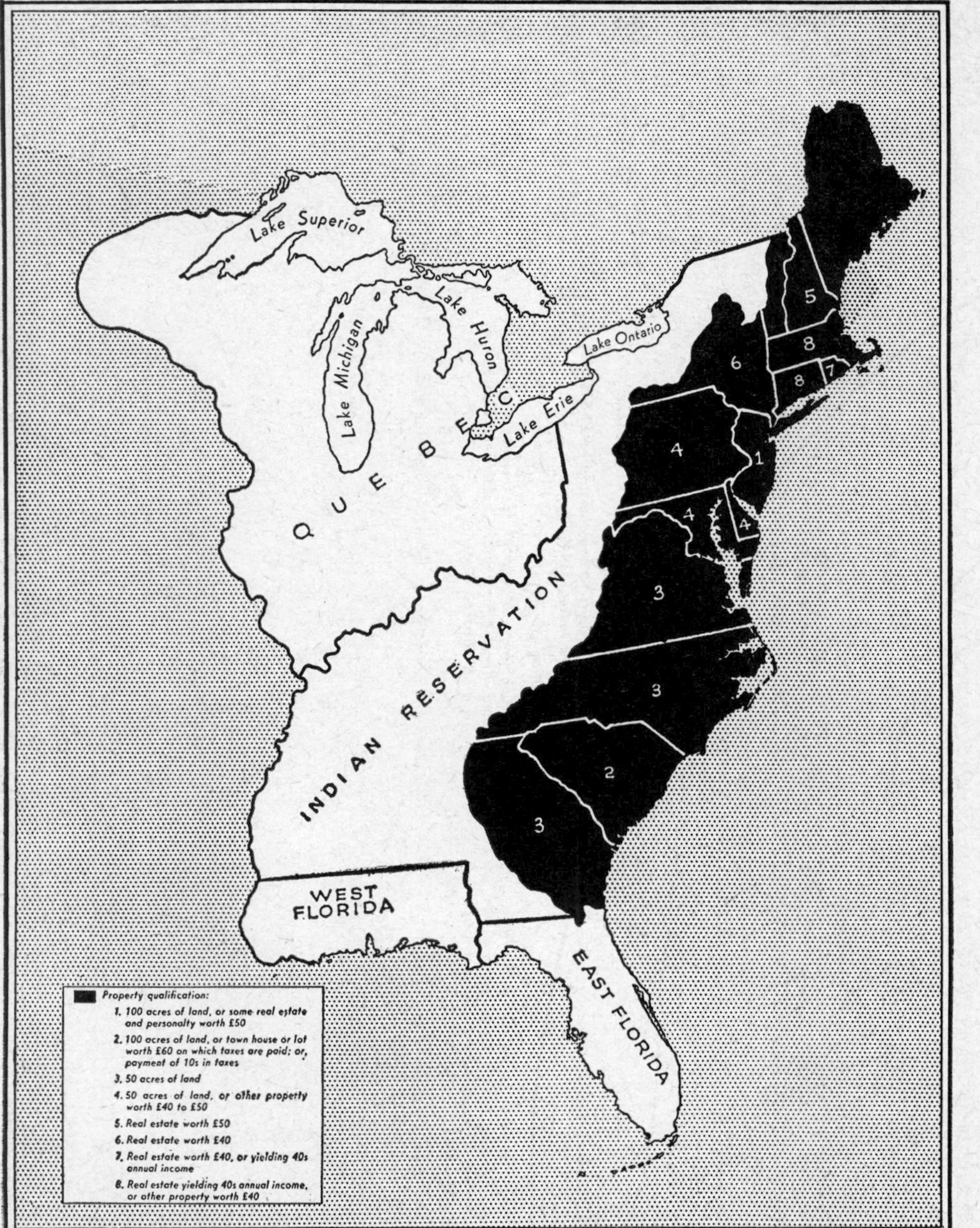

42

Male Suffrage, 1775

Maine had the same qualifications as Massachusetts; those for Vermont were not yet fully established

This map gives data only for the future thirteen original states

43

Colleges, 1775

Each dot, with date of charter, represents one college

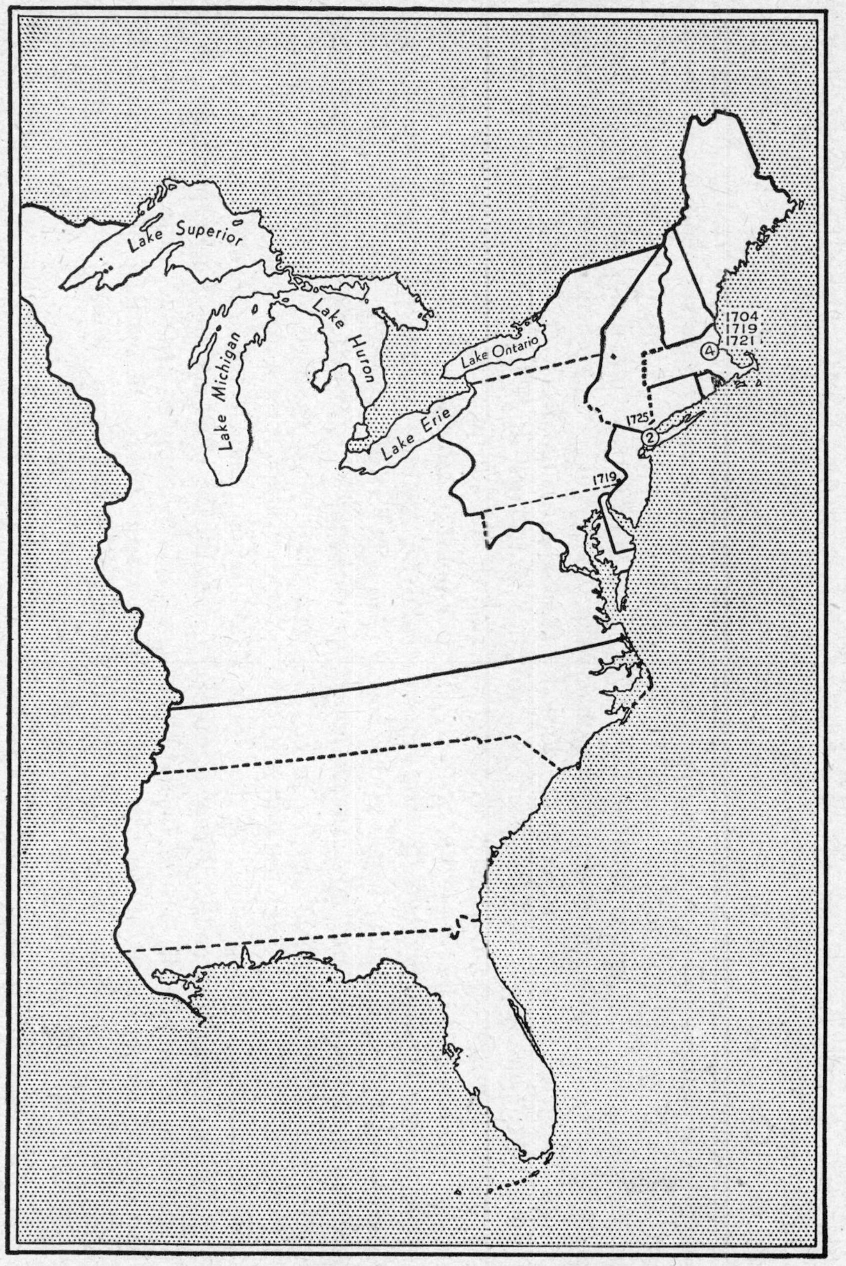

44 Newspapers, 1725

Each dot, with date of founding, represents one newspaper. Circled numerals indicate number of newspapers in a given community

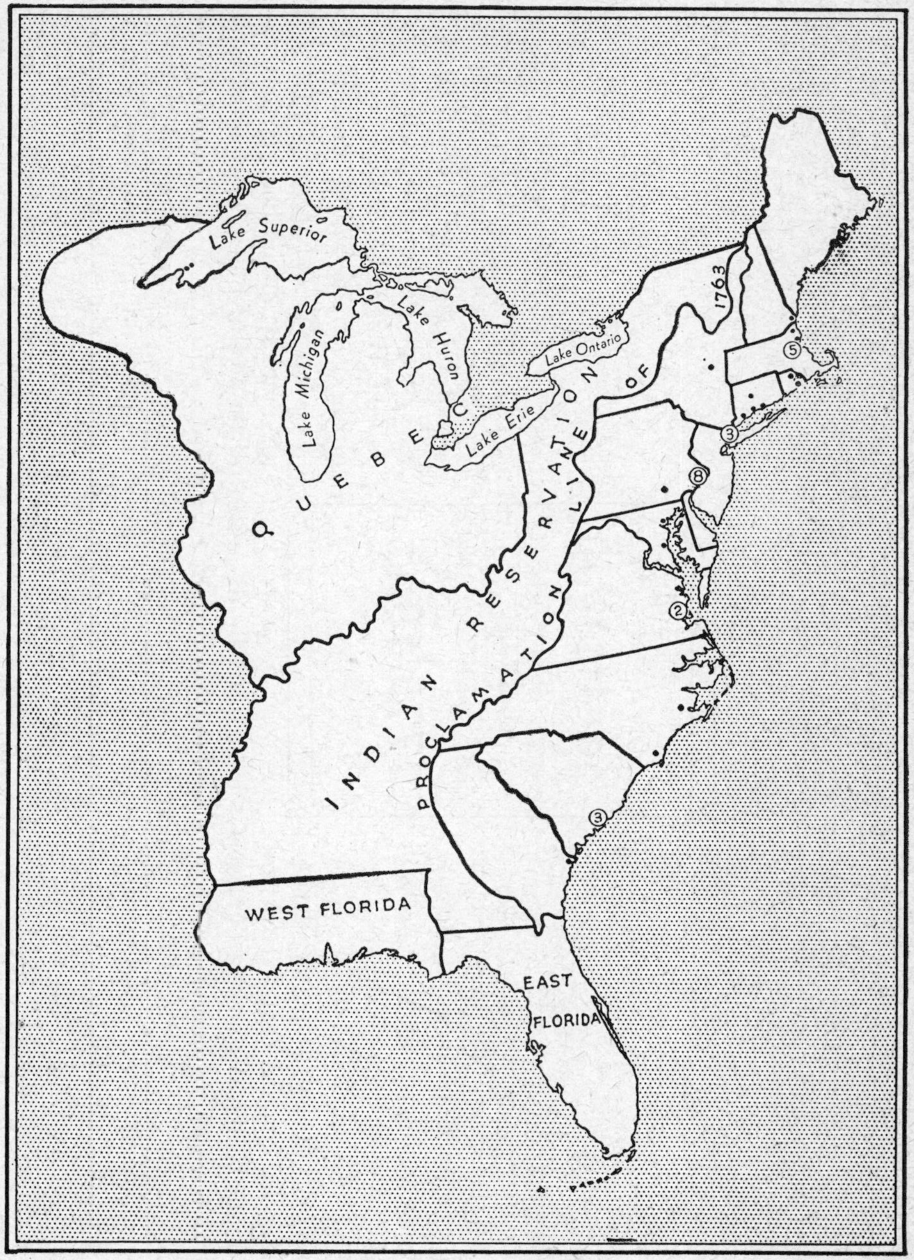

45 Newspapers, 1775

Each dot represents one paper. Circled numerals indicate number of newspapers in a given community

Section III

1775-1865

The question of the West, including the vital problem of defense against the Indians and the corollary right of settlement along the ever mobile frontier, had been in the forefront of public policy during the entire colonial era, and was to continue to absorb much of the interest and effort of the country for another hundred years after the achievement of independence. Important early developments were: (1) the removal of the legal restrictions imposed on westward migration by the Proclamation of 1763 and the "psychological" restrictions imposed by the Quebec Act of 1774; (2) the grants of huge tracts of "western" lands to the veterans of the Revolution; (3) the purchase of large areas by land companies from the Confederation Congresses; and (4) the cession by seven states of the western lands claimed under their colonial charters (limited on the maps to the territory running west to the Mississippi River, though technically the grants continued to the Pacific shores), which created the great public domain. This land, with the subsequent addition of further acquisitions on the continent, was to be split successively into territories whose government was modeled closely on that of the original Northwest Territory, created by the famous Ordinance of 1787 and widely hailed as the most successful model for colonial government, under ideal conditions, in the world.

Explorations of the West were followed by the migration of settlers, moving, on the whole, along certain well-marked and well-known routes. This movement, graphically visible on the population maps, precipitated much friction with our uneasy neighbors—with Spain over the delicate Mississippi Question; with England over sections of the Canadian border. It led to the purchase of Louisiana, the seizure of West Florida, the acquisition of East Florida, the annexation of Texas, the conflict with Mexico, the division of Oregon, and it contributed substantially to America's entrance into the War of 1812. Perforce the expansion of the whites bred conflict with the Indian, whose territory rapidly diminished, as shown by the retreat of the line of Indian cession on the population maps.

With the advancing population marched not only the political organization of states and territories, but also the courts at whose bar America received her justice, and the crops and manufactures by which the nation made its collective living.

The growth of the West was also to contribute substantially to the democratization of the American republican experiment. This development may be easily studied in the maps showing the evolution of America's franchise qualifications from high property qualifications to tax-paying requirements to universal white manhood suffrage before the Civil War: a movement which, as early as 1828, contributed decisively to, and was signalized by, the triumph of Jacksonian democracy. Extension of the suffrage brought marked changes to our political structure and system. It acted as a catalytic agent in making the "ferment" of the 1830's and 1840's effective in the drive for free public schools—to which the American workingman contributed so much impetus. It gave drive to the various reform movements of abolition, prohibition, prison management and penology, education for the blind and the handicapped, and the peace and feminist crusades—the great social counterpart of the "flowering" of New England and the extraordinary literary, cultural and religious fluxes of the day.

The American economy underwent phenomenal changes in the period between the Revolution and the Civil War. Agriculture witnessed the preliminary phases, at least, of the so-called Agricultural Revolution, spurred greatly by the rich markets for American farm products, which developed during the period, and by the county fairs of Elkanah Watson. Industry moved even farther, from the domestic handicraft era, through the early mechanization of the textile industry, to the era of big business, which, beginning in the 1850's, was rapidly advanced by the Civil War. By this time, too, the value of our manufactured products equalled that of our agricultural goods. Favorable market conditions, the enormous supply of cheap labor which successive waves of immigration furnished, adequate capital—some from abroad, some representing the plowing back of profits—and the sudden advent of a national market through the spread of the transportation network, made possible this spectacular development. Banks, many of them wildcat institutions, grew proportionately, and already individual Americans were beginning to invest their capital outside the national borders—in Canada, Mexico and Cuba. Business and the development of the country were aided by the democratization of the mail system, whose rates were rapidly lowered until the act of 1851 established a basic first-class rate of three cents for the first 3,000 miles. The rapid expansion of the facilities of the postal system reached what seemed a climax, in the 1850's, with the establishment of the Overland Mail and the Pony Express, while mail contracts gave effective government subsidy successively to stage, canal, railroad, steamship—and later airplane—companies.

With the growth of the national economy came an enormous increase in trade with Europe, the overwhelming bulk of it being carried in the rapidly growing American merchant marine. Accurate figures on the non-English trade were perforce the product of independence and the end of the British mercantilistic restrictions of our colonial commerce. But independence brought its problems for our traders as well as its advantages. Removal of Empire preference, loss of the protection of the British navy (which was to lead to unofficial naval war with France in 1797–1800, to war with the Barbary states under Jefferson, and to war with England in 1812–14), and the trade wars with England culminating in the commercial treaties of 1816 and 1830, cost many individuals dearly. On the other hand, independence put us in a position to capitalize as a neutral on the trading opportunities presented by the Napoleonic Wars, to enter the Oriental trade in 1784 in competition with the powerful East India Company, and to lay the foundations for the greatest period of our merchant marine—and for nearly a hundred years of friction with England in worldwide commercial rivalry. By the time of the Civil War, which was to deal a triple blow to American shipping, the competition of the British iron-hulled, screw-propelled steamer was already successfully driving from the seas the less efficient American packet and clipper.

The phenomenal growth of free public schools and private academies was partially reflected in the growth of the college facilities of the country, and the growth of newspapers was also symbolic of the everspreading power of an expanding press.

Our worldwide commerce, the desires of some national figures to balance the growing power of the North by southward expansion into areas where slavery would be possible and profitable, and the efforts of other leaders to escape the impending conflict by a vigorous policy of expansion, produced the era of Manifest Destiny. This concept was ideologically reinforced by a deep-rooted American belief, present throughout our history, in a national mission to "expand the areas of freedom," as Andrew Jackson phrased it—an idea which received much encouragement from the French Revolution, the achievement of Latin American independence, the liberal revolts of 1848 in Europe, the Texan Revolution and the revolts of Papineau and Mackenzie in Canada. The scenes of our commercial and physical expansion during this period constitute one of the most revealing maps of the entire period.

But throughout the thirty years between the appearance of the *Liberator* and the rebellion of Nat Turner—which automatically dried up the source springs of the anti-slavery movement in the South—and the firing on Fort Sumter, the increasingly ominous clouds of civil strife more and more obscured the less dramatic outlines of our history. The appearance of a southern cultural nationalism buttressed the rise of a southern economic nationalism, which increasingly manifested itself in debates over expansion, the tariff, slavery in the territories, land policy, railroad construction and subsidy, the roles of Yankee capital, and shipping. Through attempts to foster southern enterprise, such as southern factories, southern shipping lines to Europe and a southern transcontinental railroad, the series of trade conventions which marked the decades of the 'forties and fifties vividly emphasized the growing economic, social, and political cleavage of the sections. This conflict, of course, was to culminate in secession and four years of the costliest, bloodiest, and bitterest fighting the world had seen up to that time. Yet it is interesting to note the opposition to secession in the South itself prior to Lincoln's call for volunteers, and the relationship of that opposition to the number of slaves per slaveholder and the proportion of slaves to the total population of the South, county by county.

The issue of the war was not to be decided exclusively on the field of battle, but rather in the inner councils of the Republican party, and in the prolonged and bitter struggle between the Reconstructionists (the Radical Republicans) and the Restorationists (Democrats and Conservative Republicans, who would restore the South to its pre-war status minus its slaves). That struggle, and the predominance of Republican counsel favoring the combination of northern big business and western farming, was greatly to influence the development of the country in the succeeding sixty-five years.

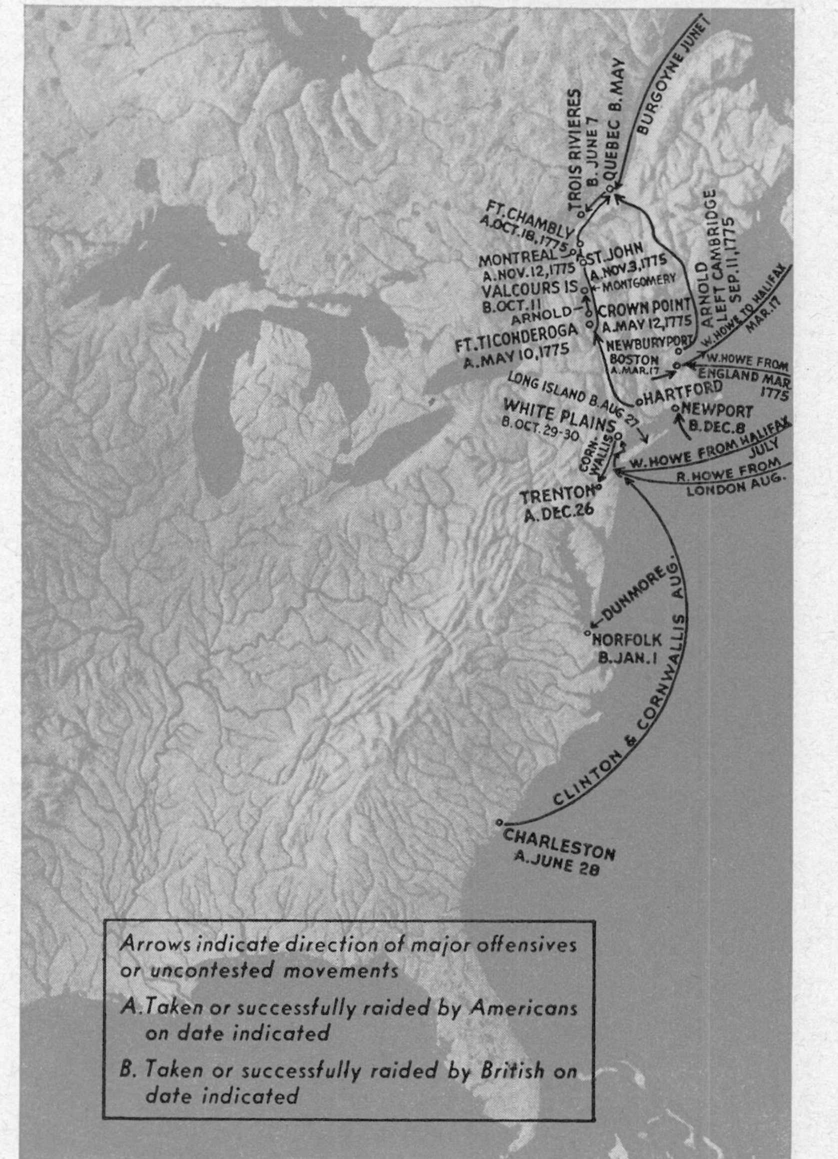

46 American Revolution: Campaigns of 1775-1776
1775 dates are so marked

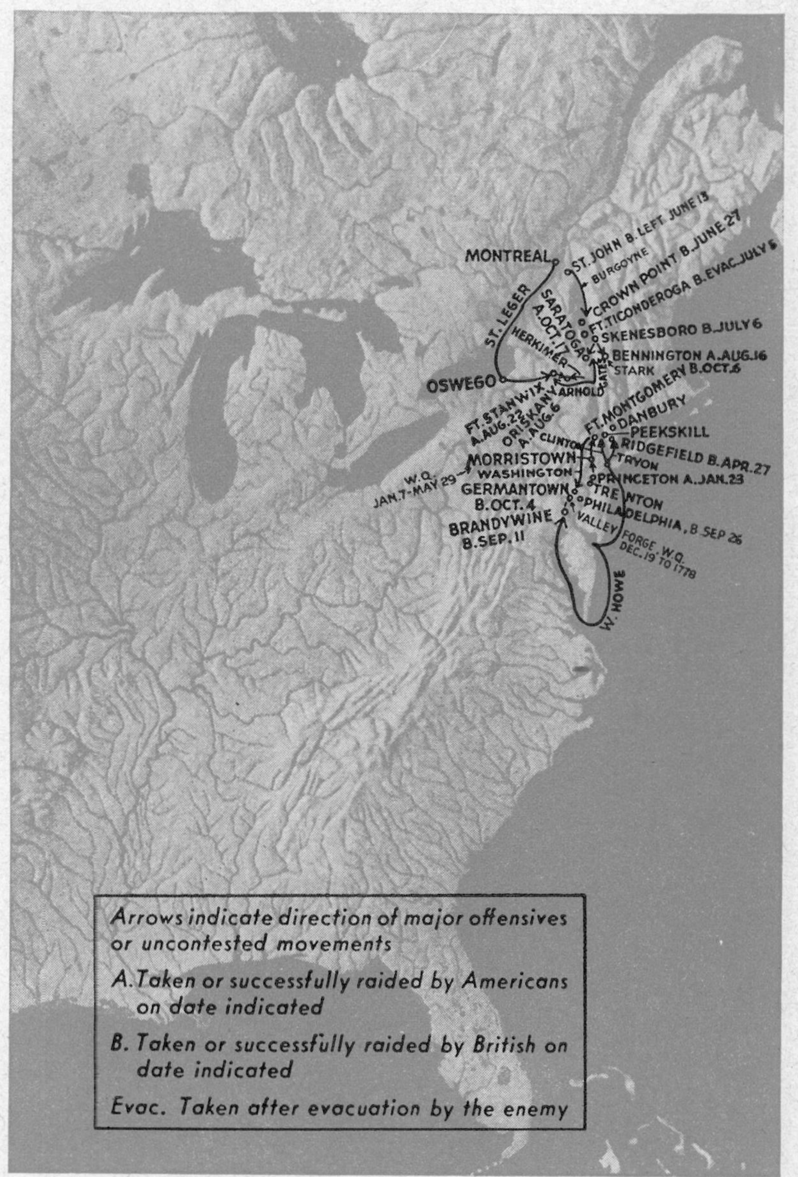

47 American Revolution: Campaigns of 1777

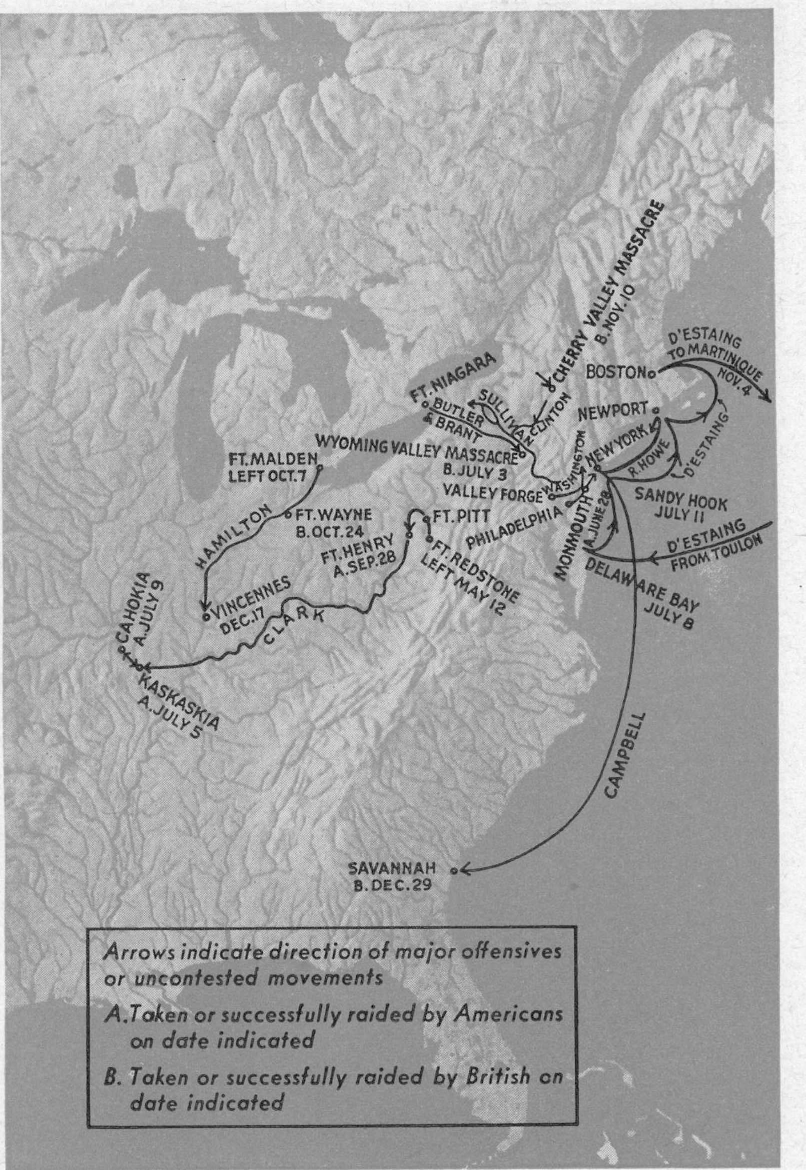

48 American Revolution: Campaigns of 1778

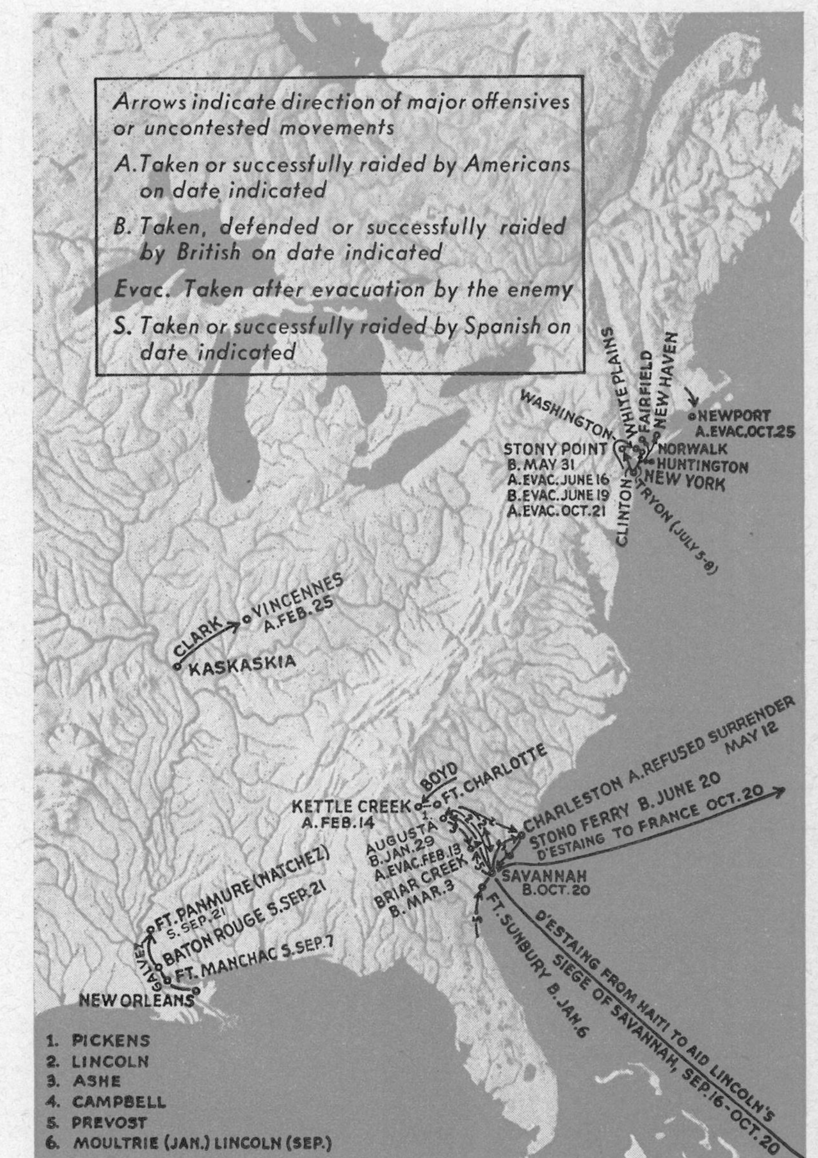

49 American Revolution: Campaigns of 1779

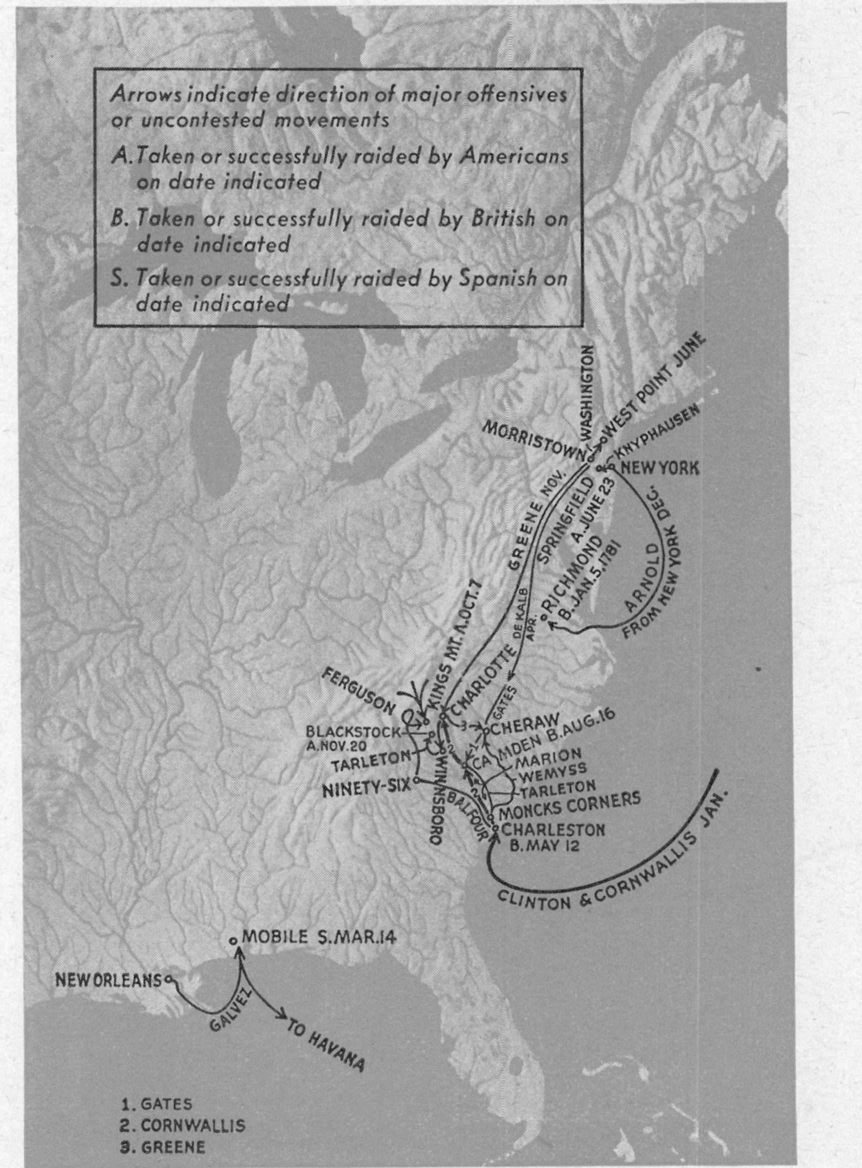

50 American Revolution: Campaigns of 1780

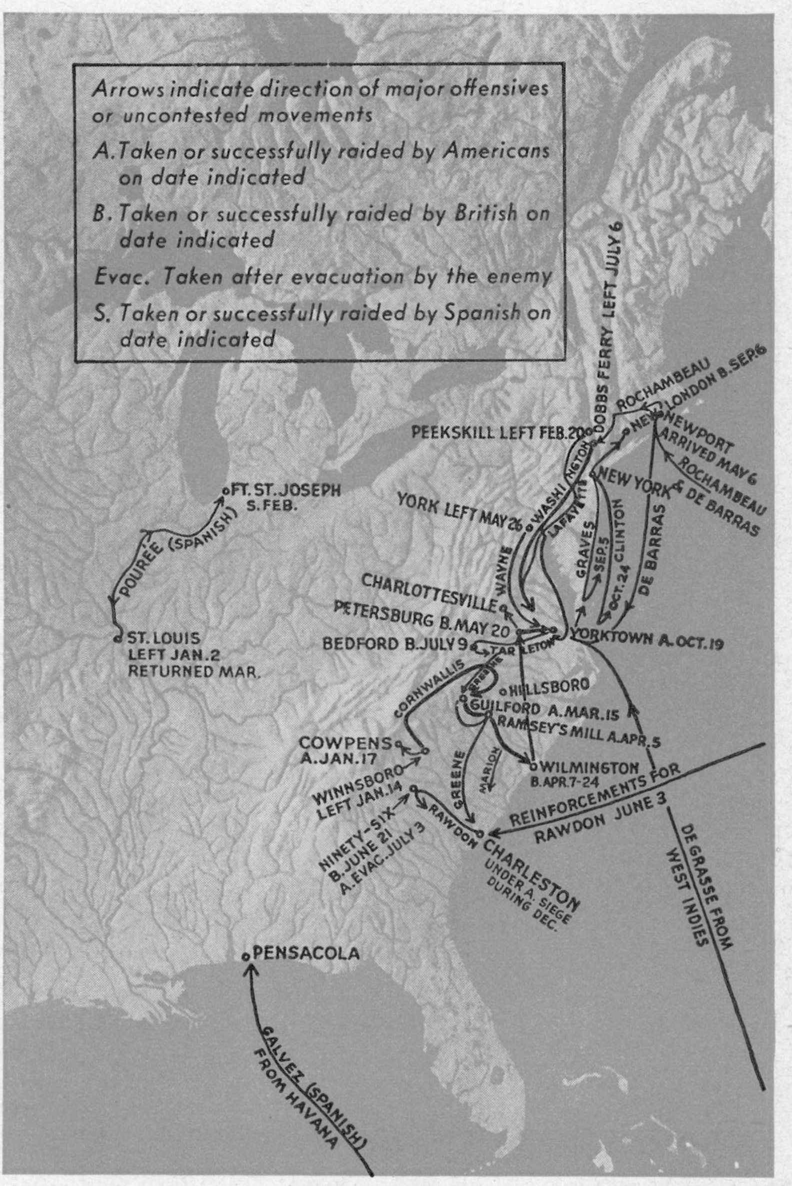

51 American Revolution: Campaigns of 1781

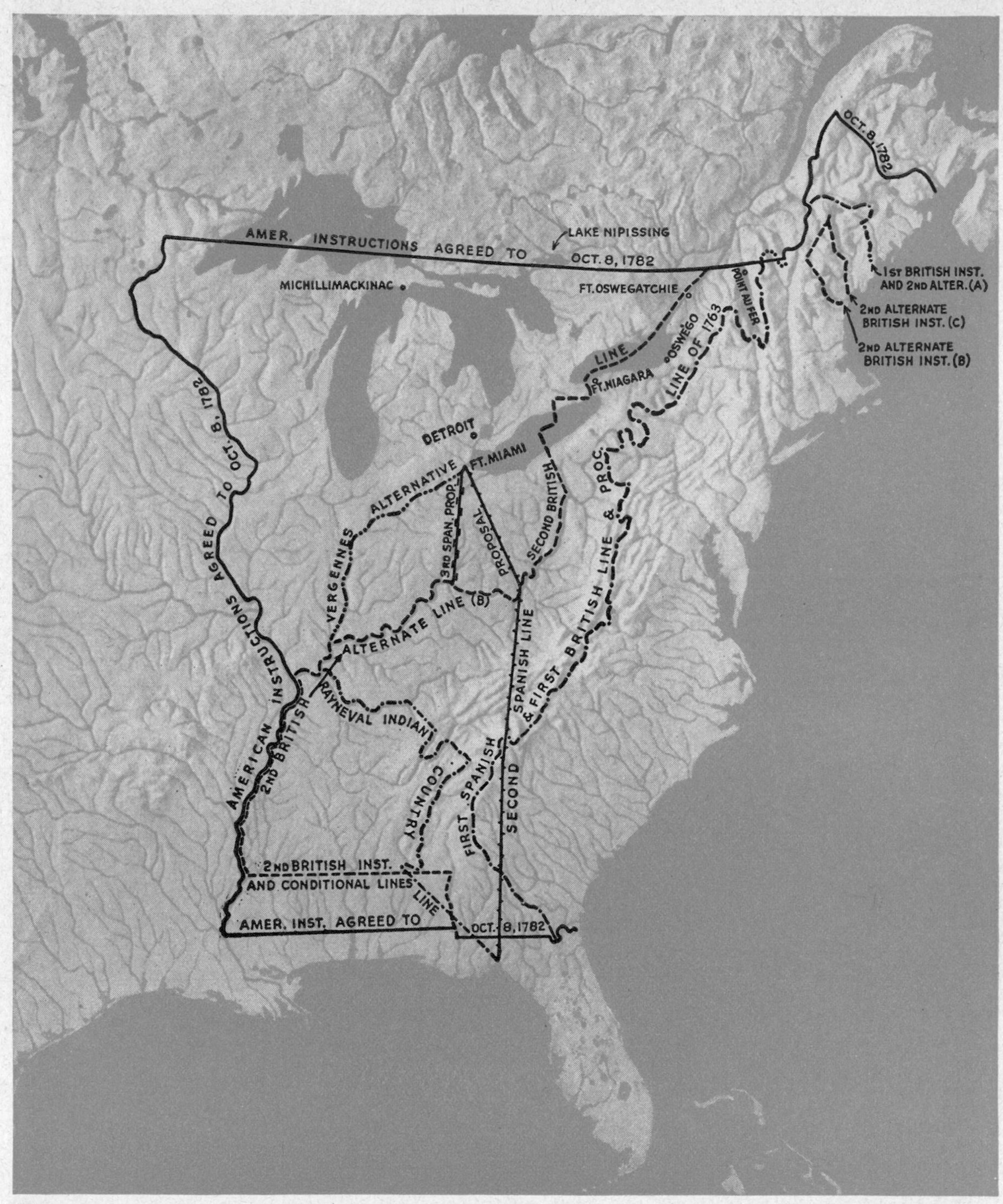

52 American Revolution: Negotiation of the Treaty of Paris of 1783

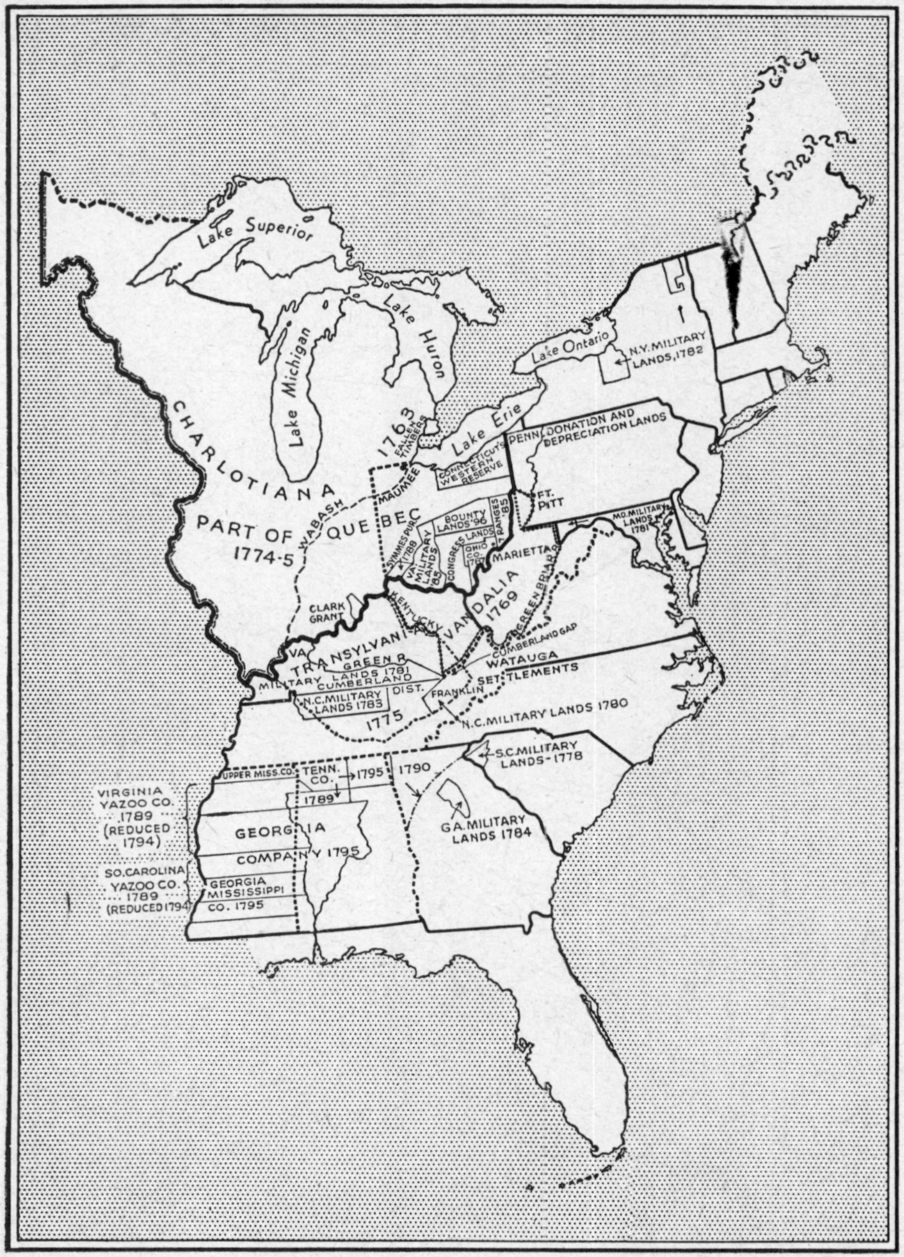

53 Western Lands, 1763-1795

(See Maps 25-26)

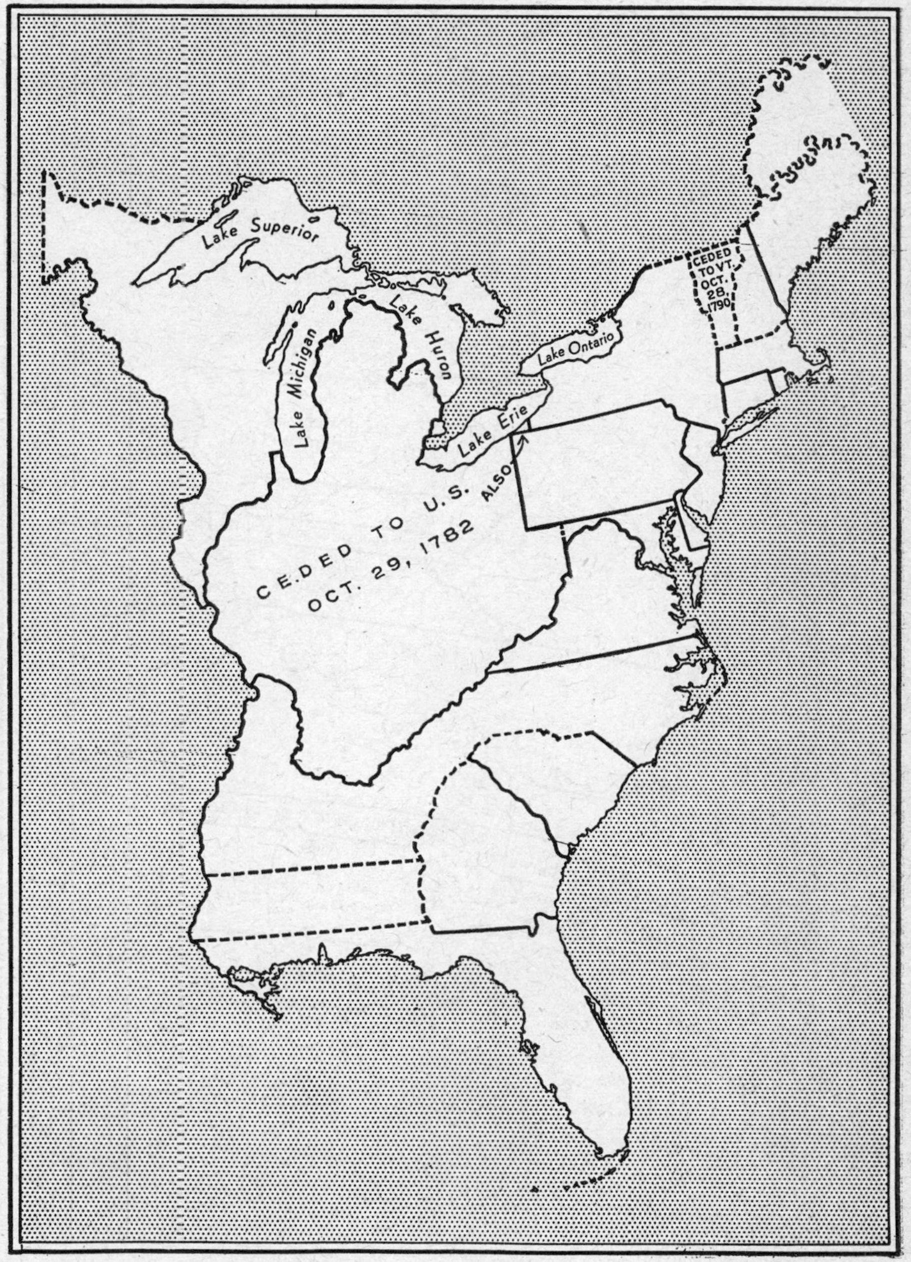

54 Creation of the National Domain: Cessions by New York of Western Land Claims and Relinquishment of the Claim to Vermont

(See Maps 25-26)

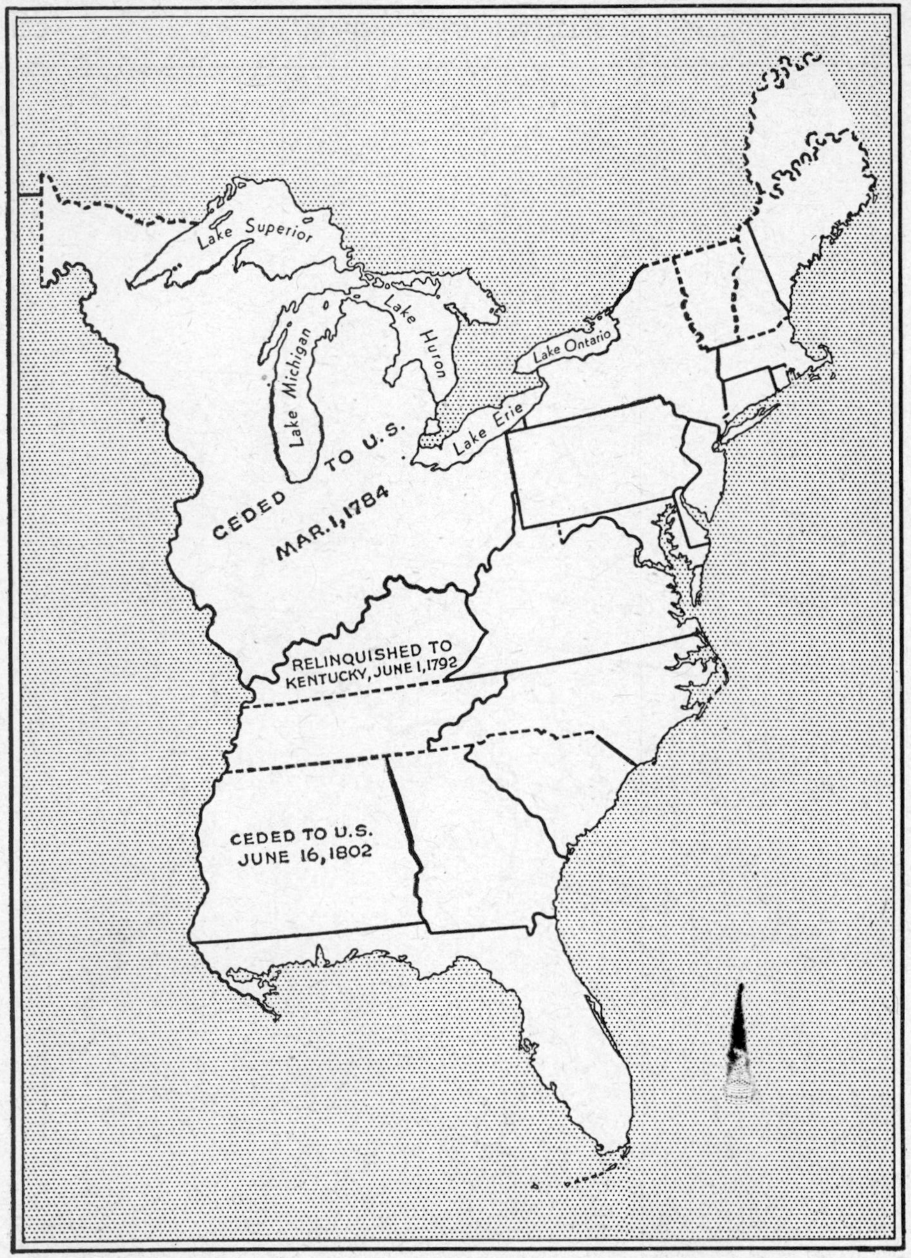

55 Creation of the National Domain: Cessions by Virginia and Georgia of Western Land Claims

(See Maps 25-26)

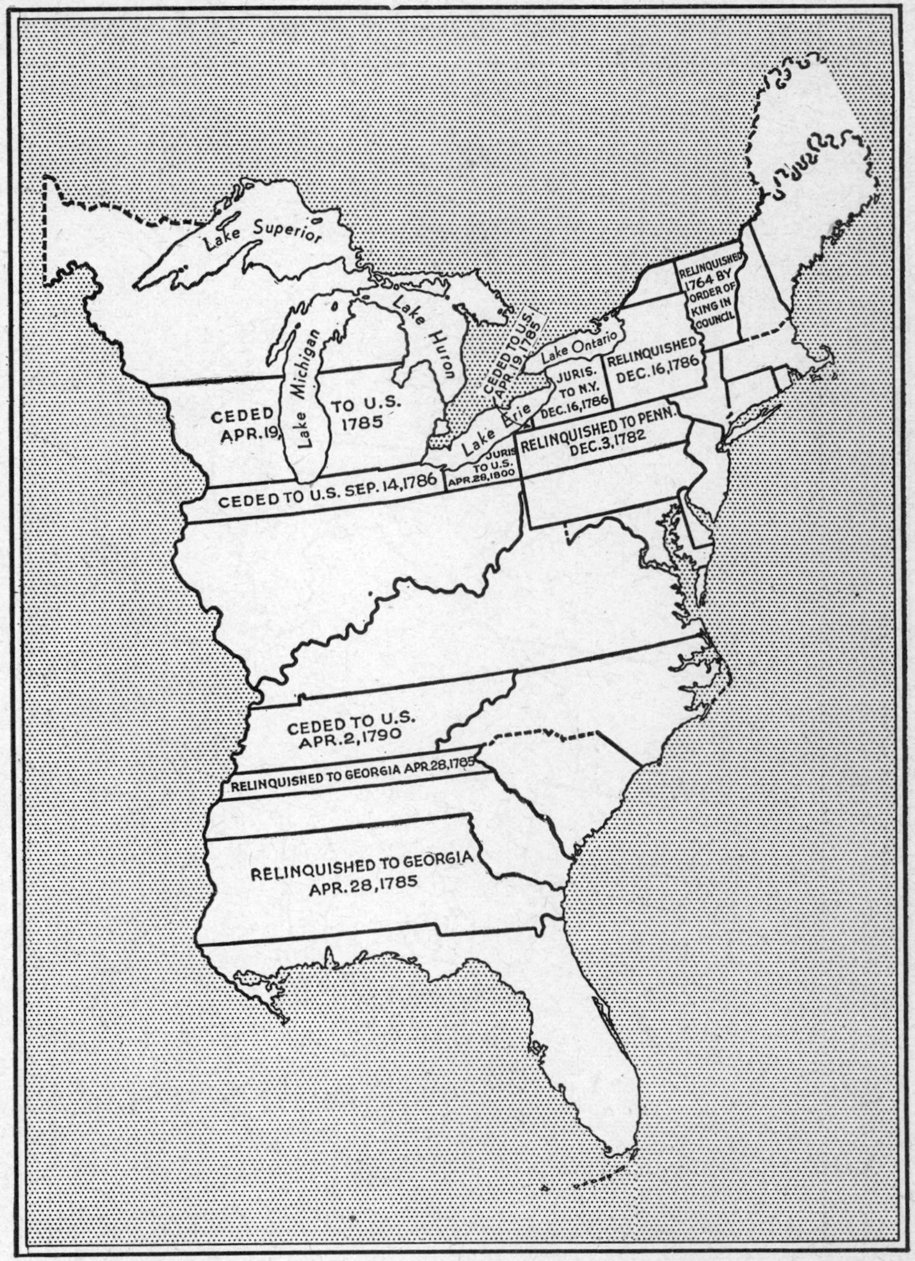

56 Creation of the National Domain: Cessions by New Hampshire, Massachusetts, Connecticut, North Carolina, and South Carolina of Western Land Claims

(See Maps 25-26)

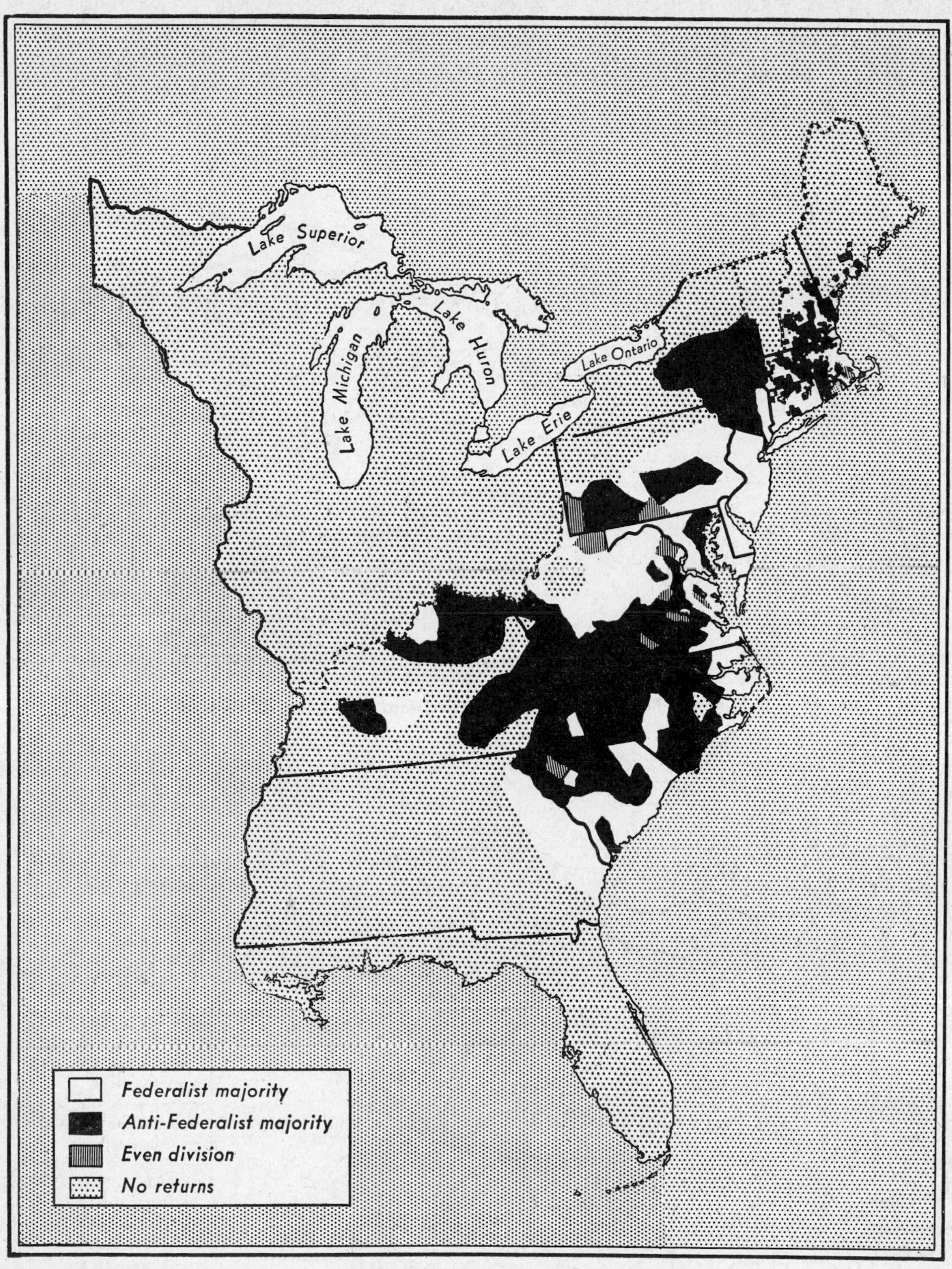

57 Ratification of the Constitution

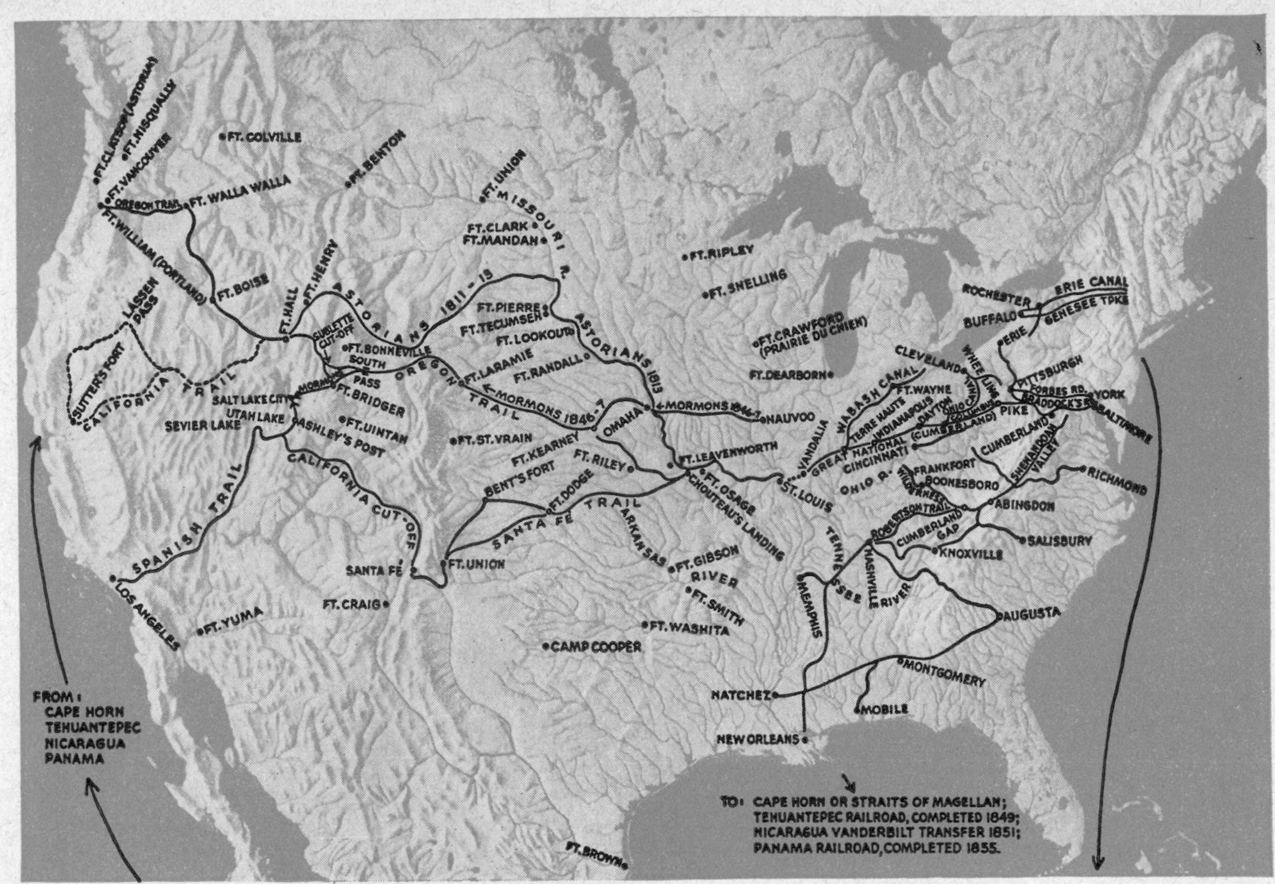

58 Principal Posts and Routes of Westward Migration, 1775-1864

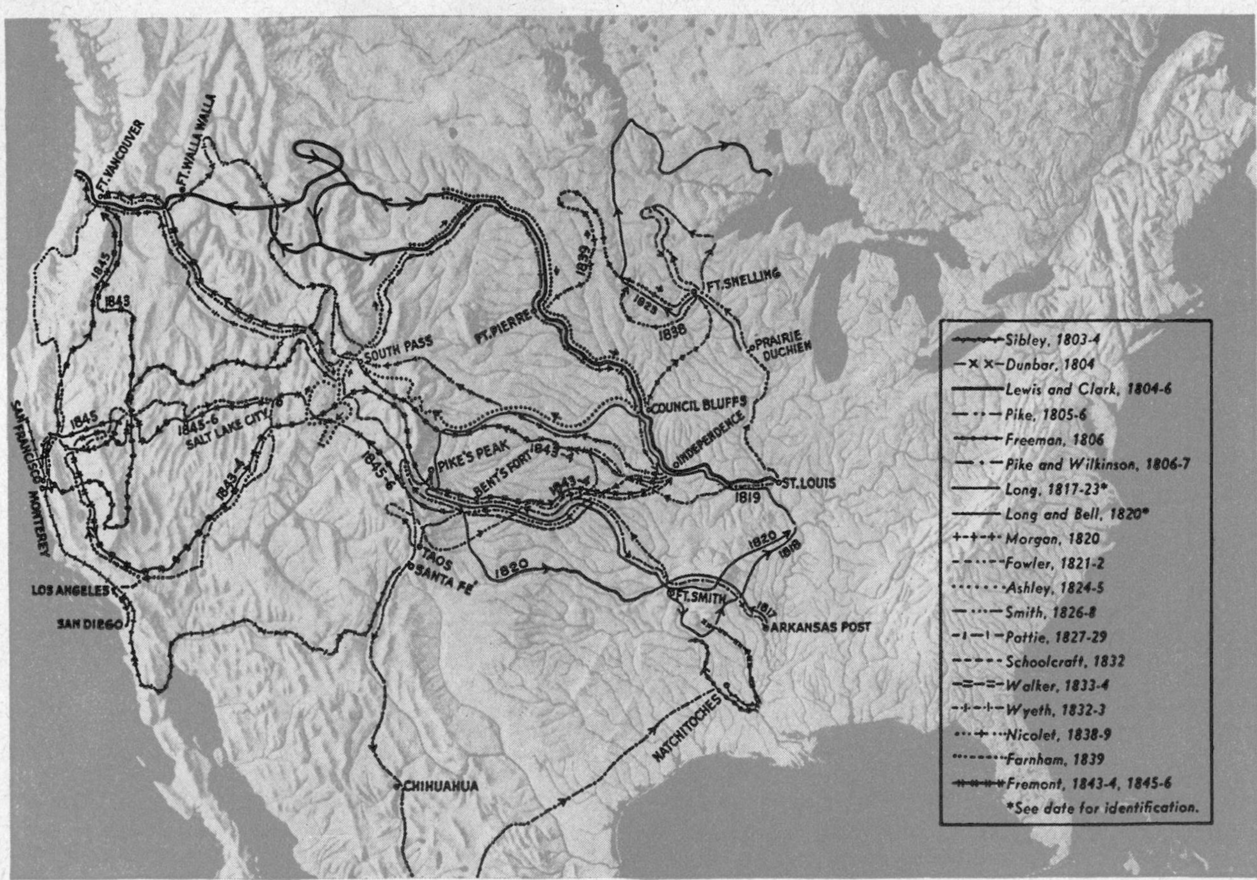

59 American Explorations of the West, 1803-1846

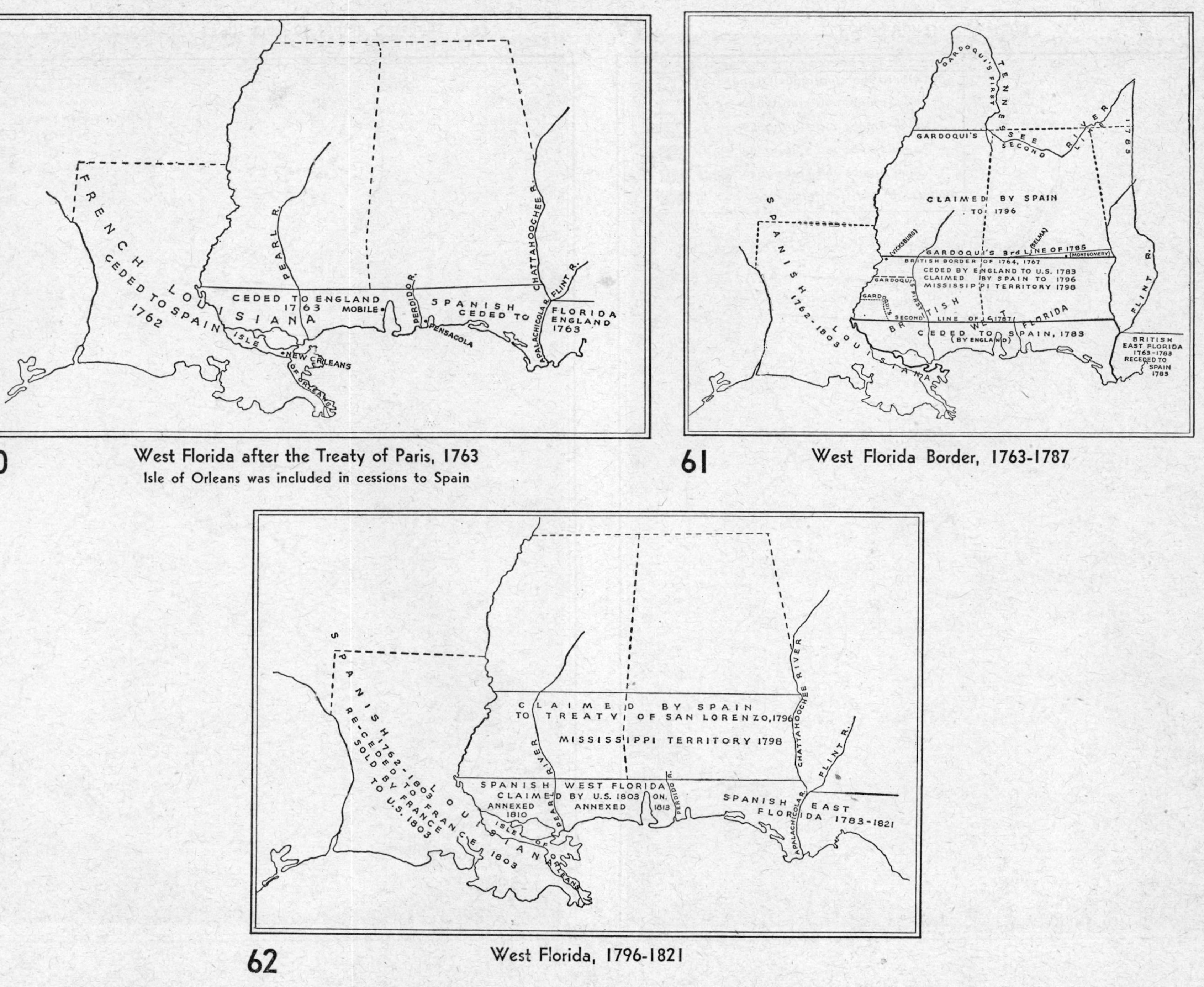

60 West Florida after the Treaty of Paris, 1763
Isle of Orleans was included in cessions to Spain

61 West Florida Border, 1763-1787

62 West Florida, 1796-1821

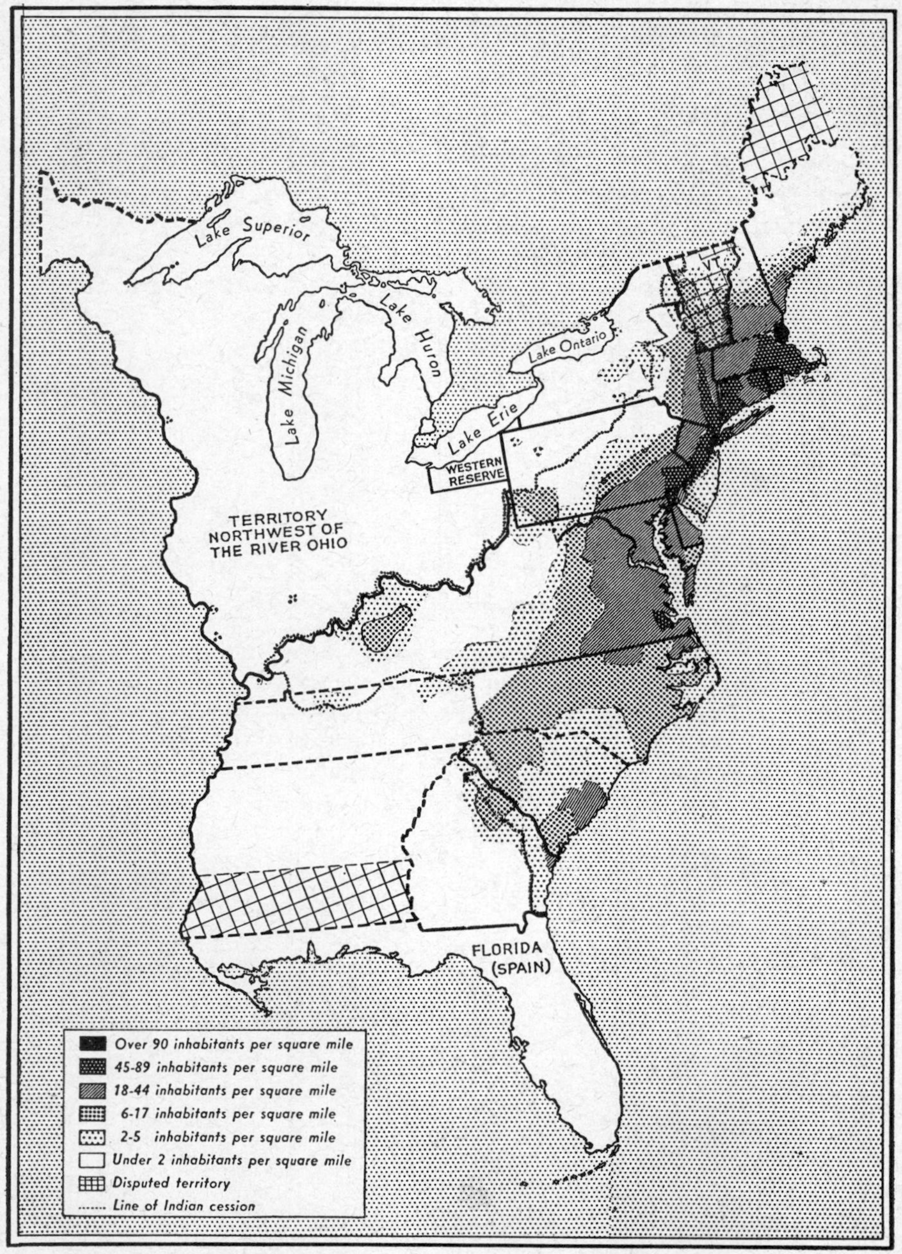

63 Population Density, 1790; Line of Indian Cessions, 1783

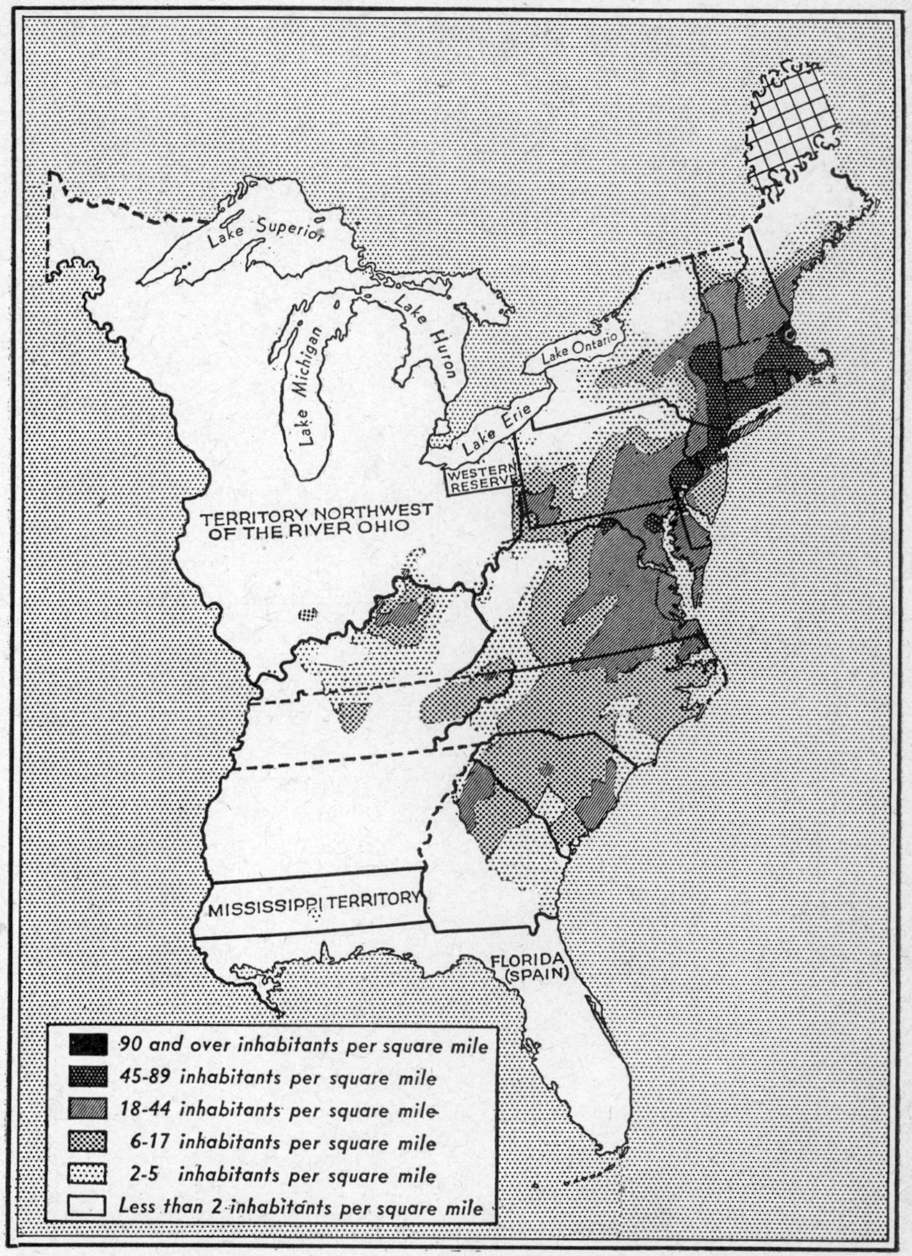

64 Population Density, 1800

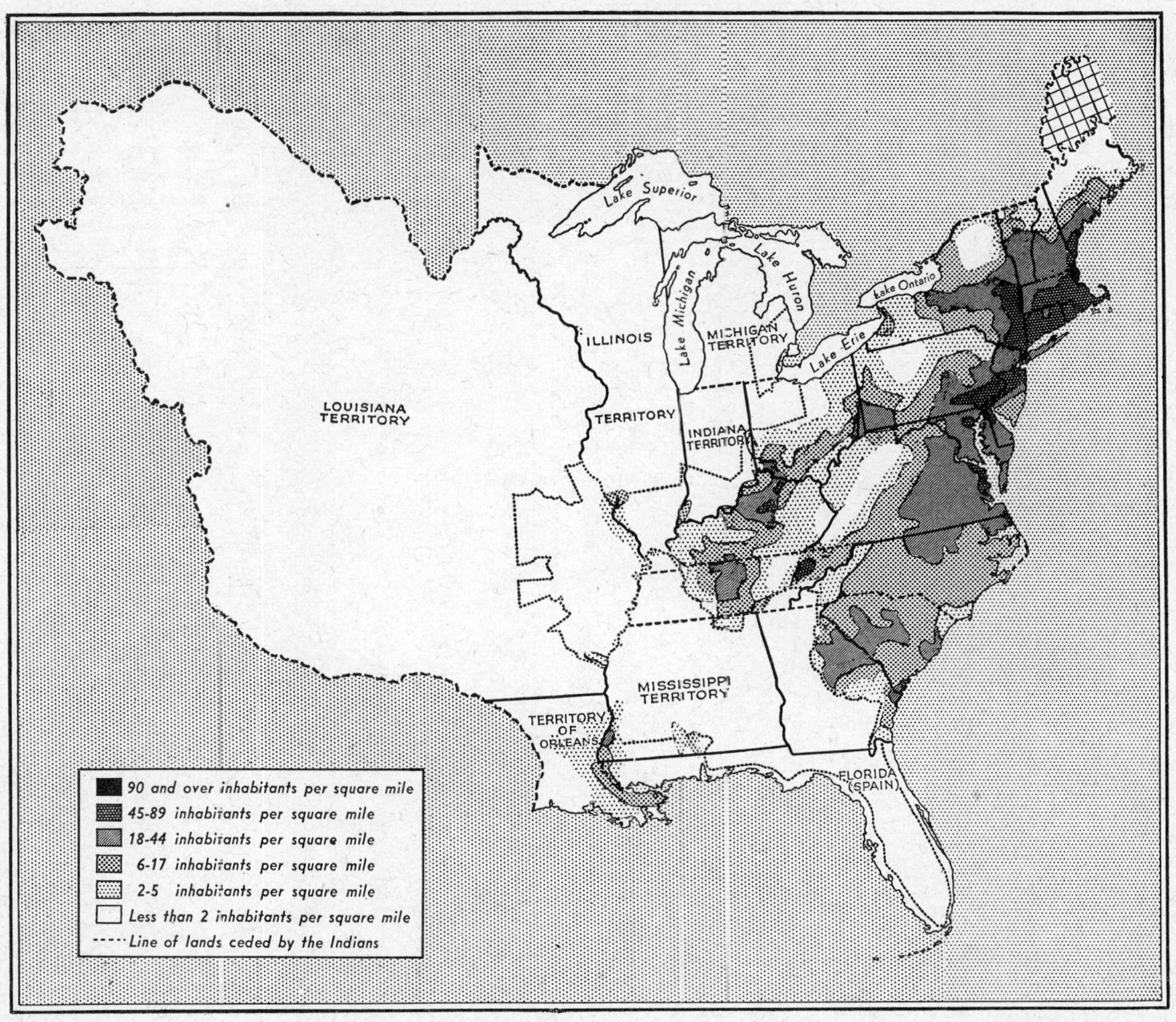

65 Population Density, Line of Indian Cessions, 1810

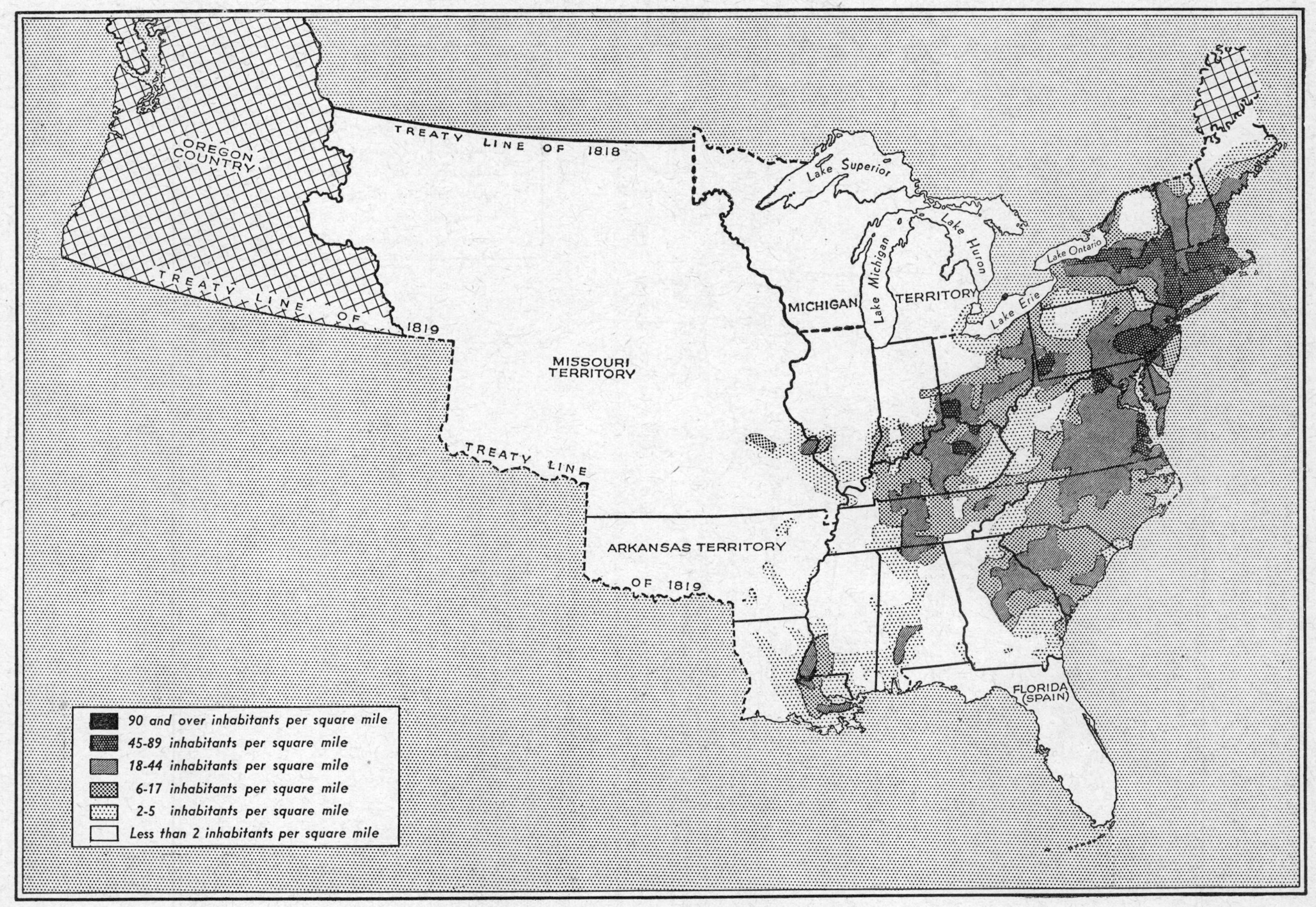
OREGON COUNTRY
TREATY LINE OF 1818
TREATY LINE OF 1819
MISSOURI TERRITORY
TREATY LINE
ARKANSAS TERRITORY
OF 1819
Lake Superior
Lake Michigan
Lake Huron
MICHIGAN TERRITORY
Lake Ontario
Lake Erie
FLORIDA (SPAIN)
90 and over inhabitants per square mile
45-89 inhabitants per square mile
18-44 inhabitants per square mile
6-17 inhabitants per square mile
2-5 inhabitants per square mile
Less than 2 inhabitants per square mile

66

Population Density, 1820

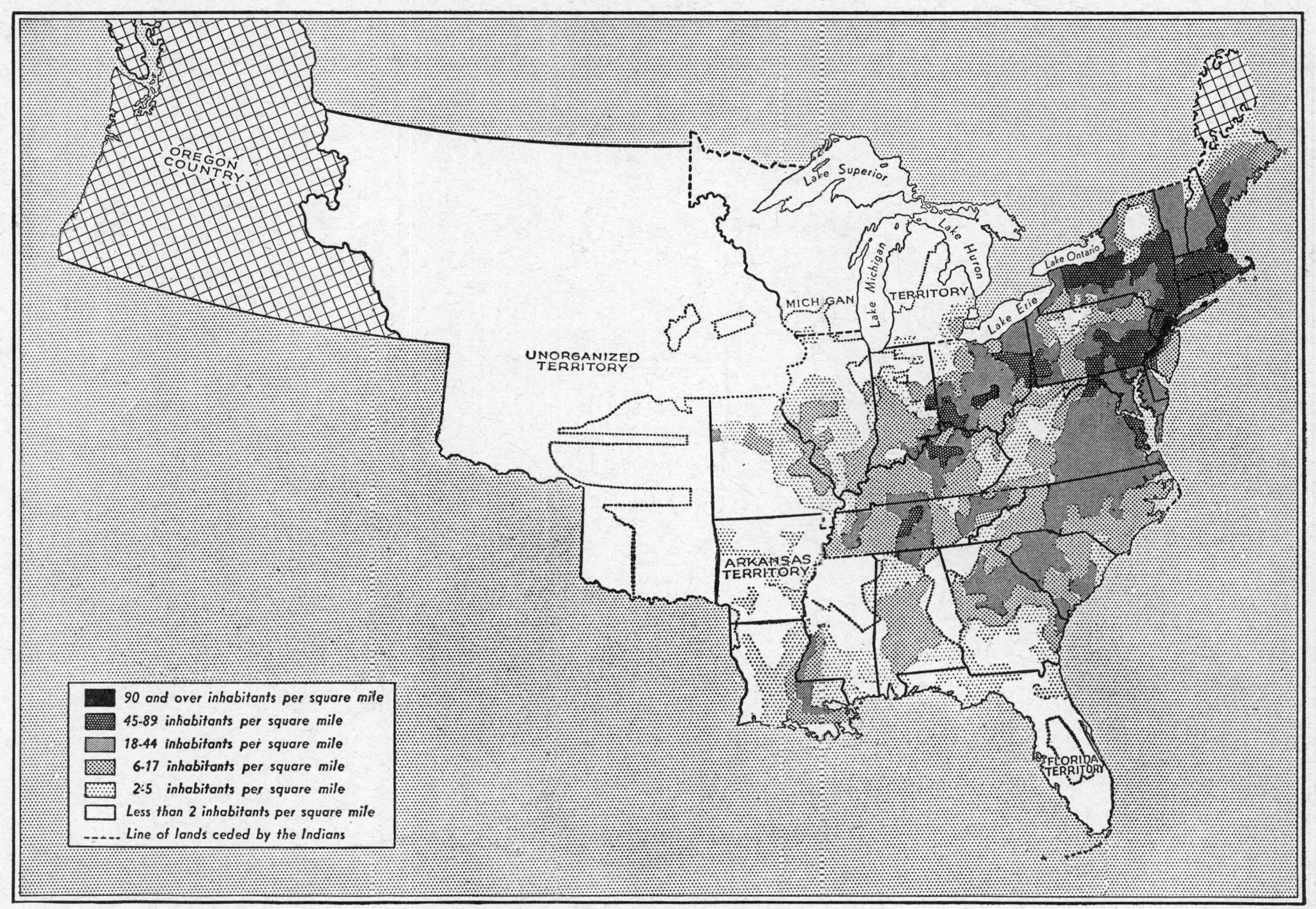

67

Population Density, Line of Indian Cessions, 1830

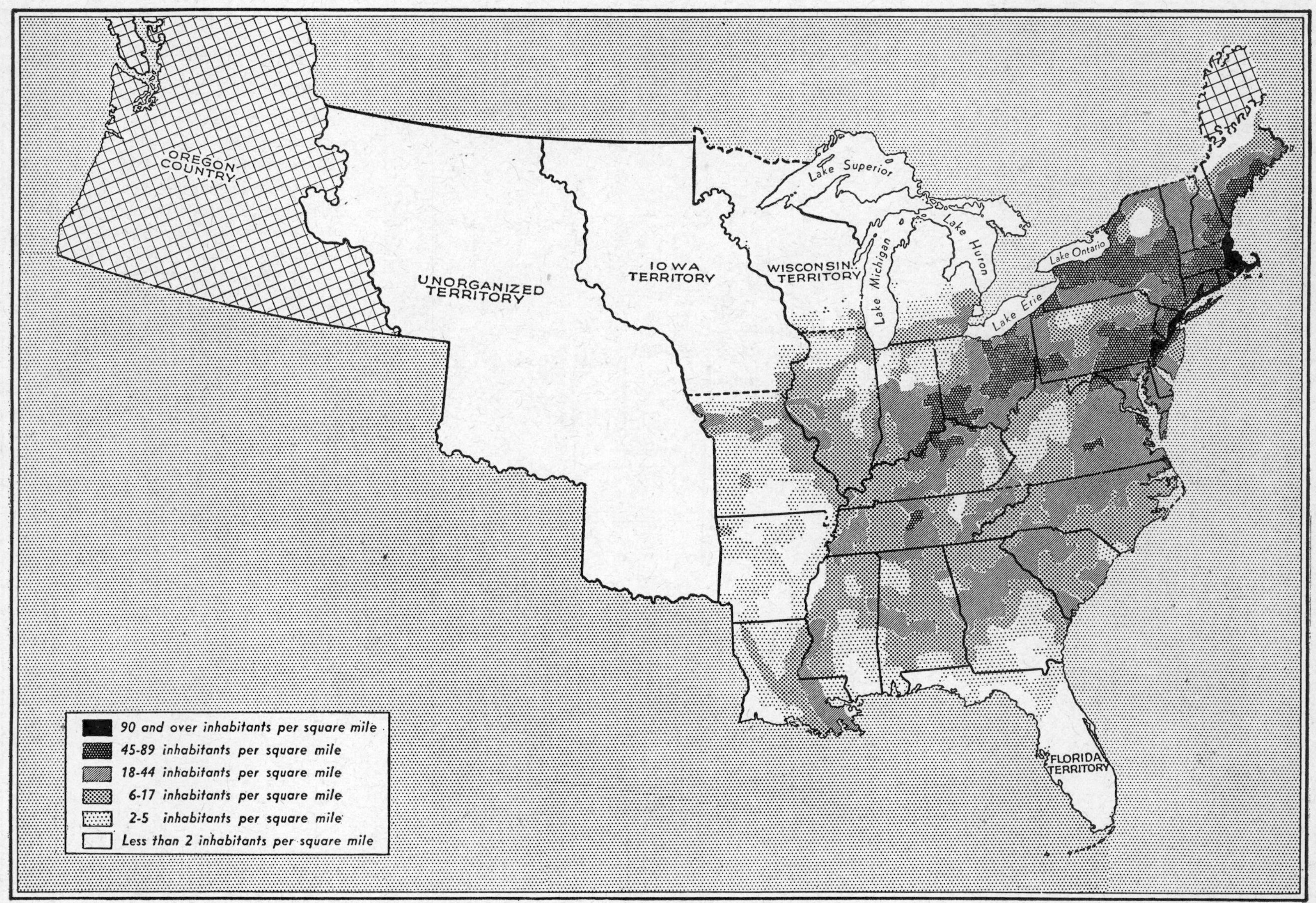
OREGON COUNTRY
UNORGANIZED TERRITORY
IOWA TERRITORY
WISCONSIN TERRITORY
Lake Superior
Lake Michigan
Lake Huron
Lake Erie
Lake Ontario
FLORIDA TERRITORY
90 and over inhabitants per square mile
45-89 inhabitants per square mile
18-44 inhabitants per square mile
6-17 inhabitants per square mile
2-5 inhabitants per square mile
Less than 2 inhabitants per square mile

68 Population Density, 1840

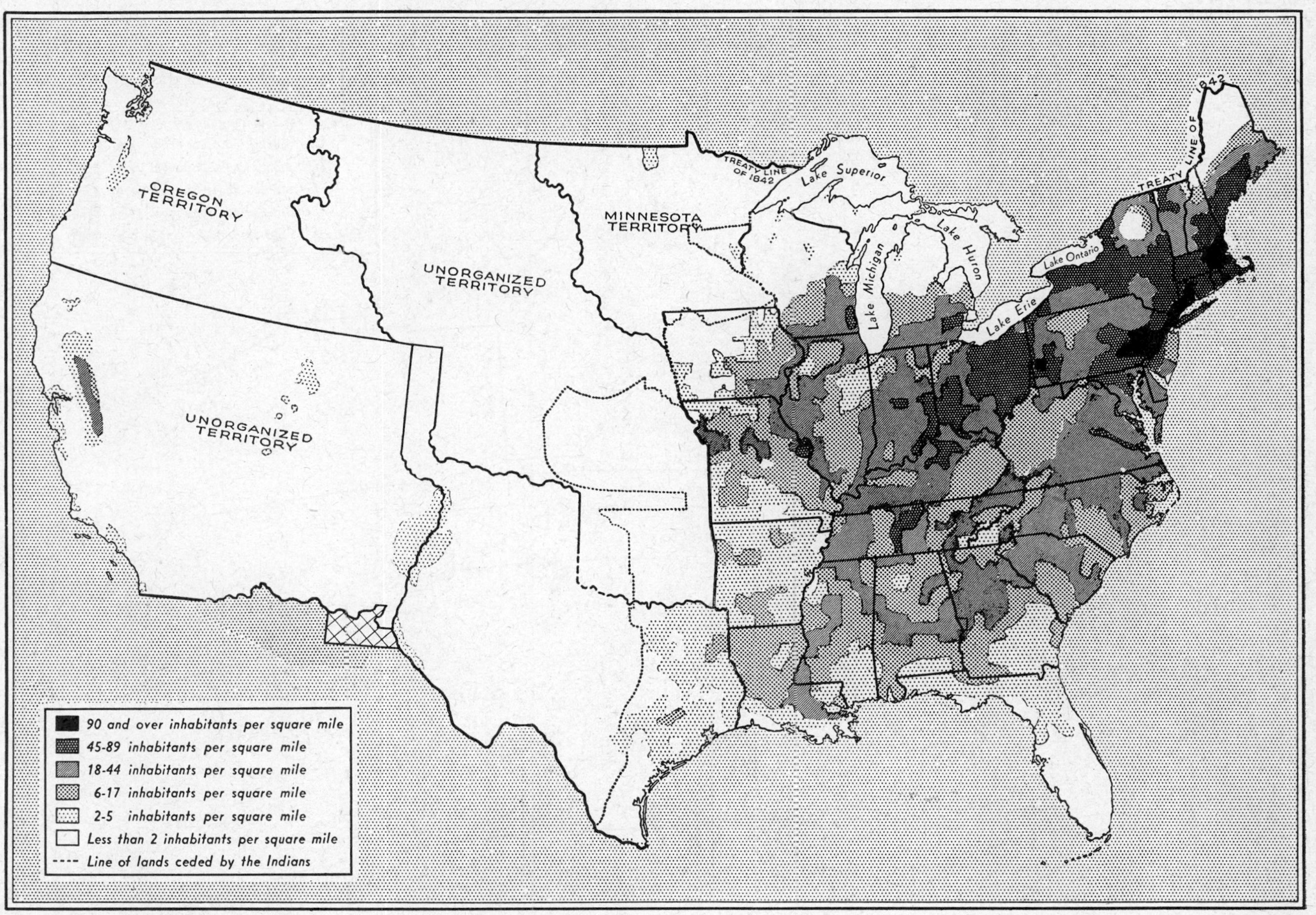

69 Population Density, Line of Indian Cessions, 1850

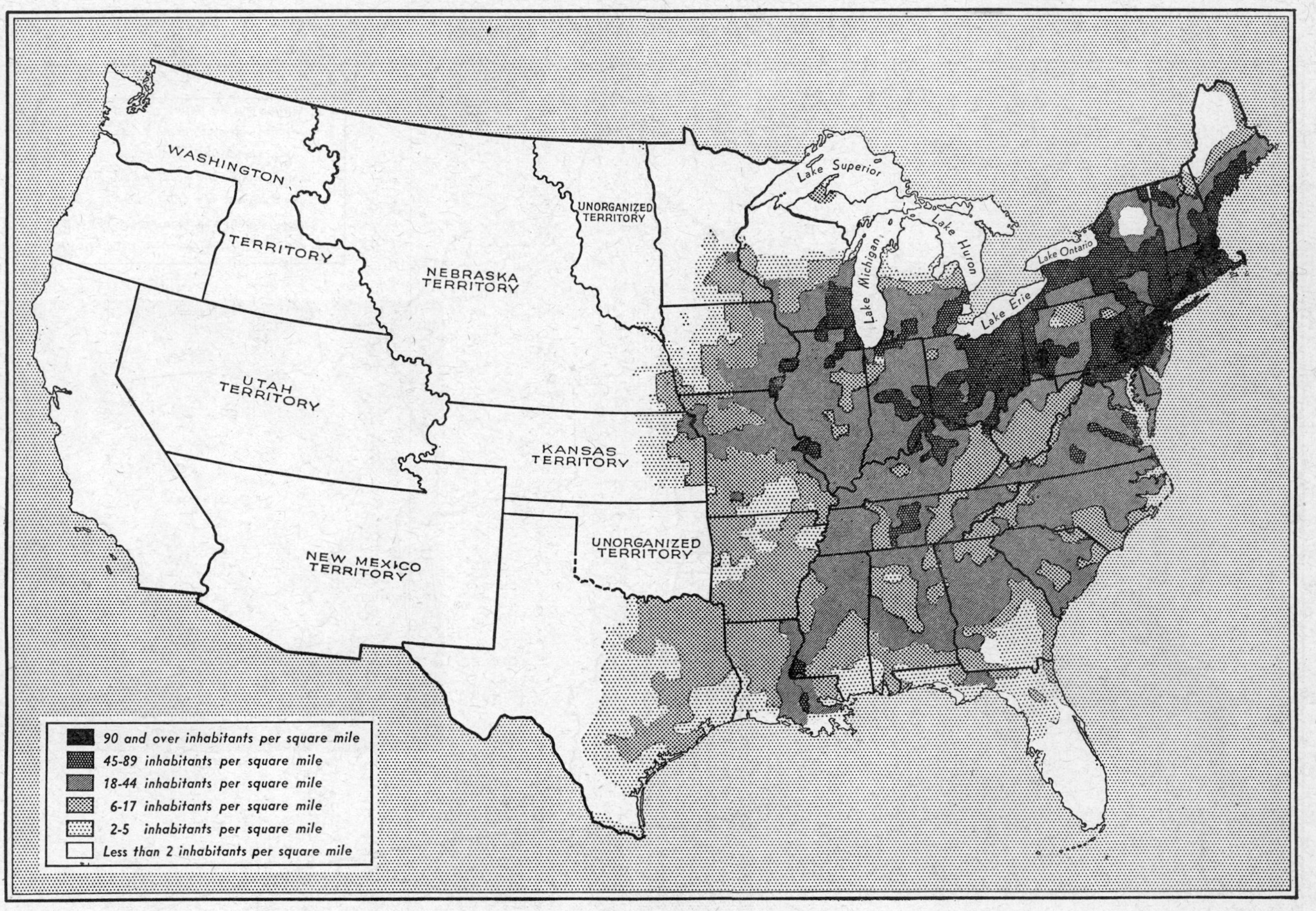
WASHINGTON
TERRITORY
NEBRASKA TERRITORY
UNORGANIZED TERRITORY
UTAH TERRITORY
KANSAS TERRITORY
UNORGANIZED TERRITORY
NEW MEXICO TERRITORY
Lake Superior
Lake Michigan
Lake Huron
Lake Erie
Lake Ontario
90 and over inhabitants per square mile
45-89 inhabitants per square mile
18-44 inhabitants per square mile
6-17 inhabitants per square mile
2-5 inhabitants per square mile
Less than 2 inhabitants per square mile

70

Population Density, 1860

—— MAXIMUM U.S. CLAIM 1821-42
- - - - MAXIMUM BRITISH CLAIM 1821-42
········ LINE AWARDED BY THE KING OF THE NETHERLANDS, 1831
-·-·-·- LINE PROPOSED BY GT. BRITAIN 1835, 1842
+++++ LINE PROPOSED BY UNITED STATES 1836
-·-·-·- LINE PROPOSED BY UNITED STATES 1842
—— FINAL BORDER FIXED 1842

71 Maine Border Dispute, 1821-1842

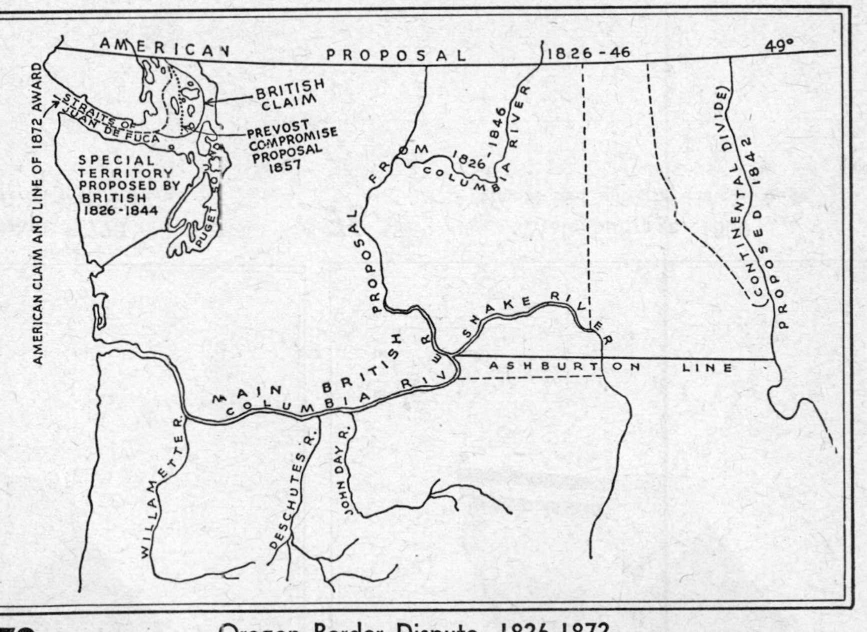

72 Oregon Border Dispute, 1826-1872

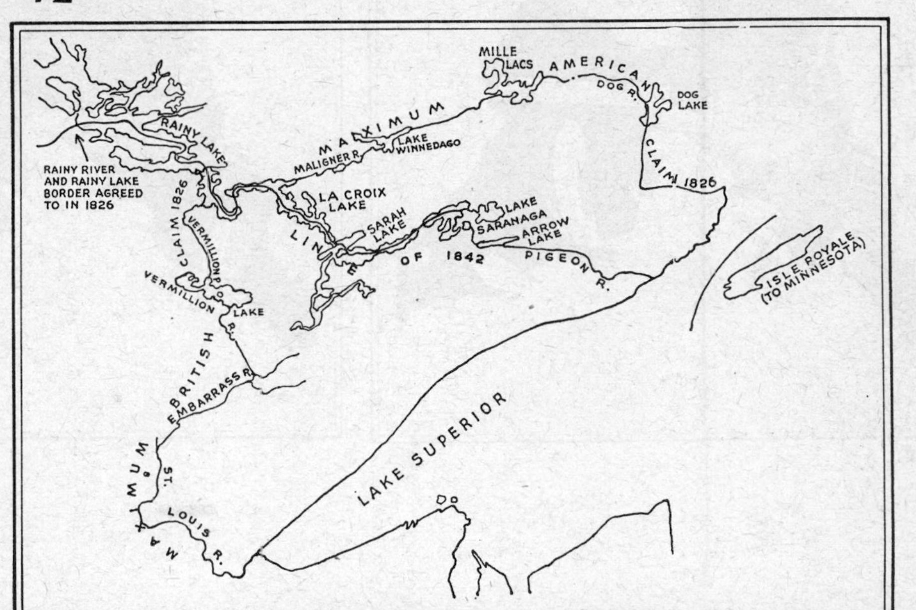

73 Lake Superior-Rainy Lake Border Dispute, 1826-1842

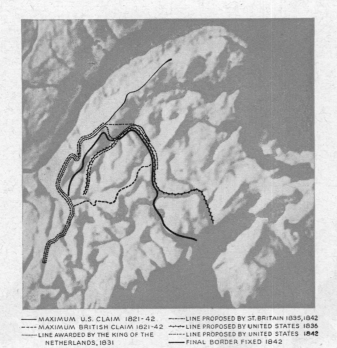

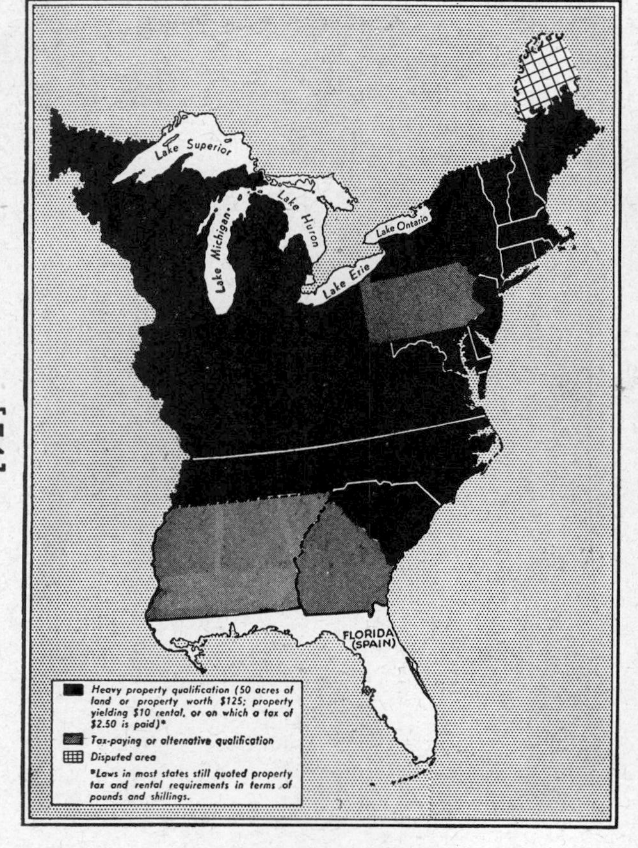

74 Male Suffrage, 1780

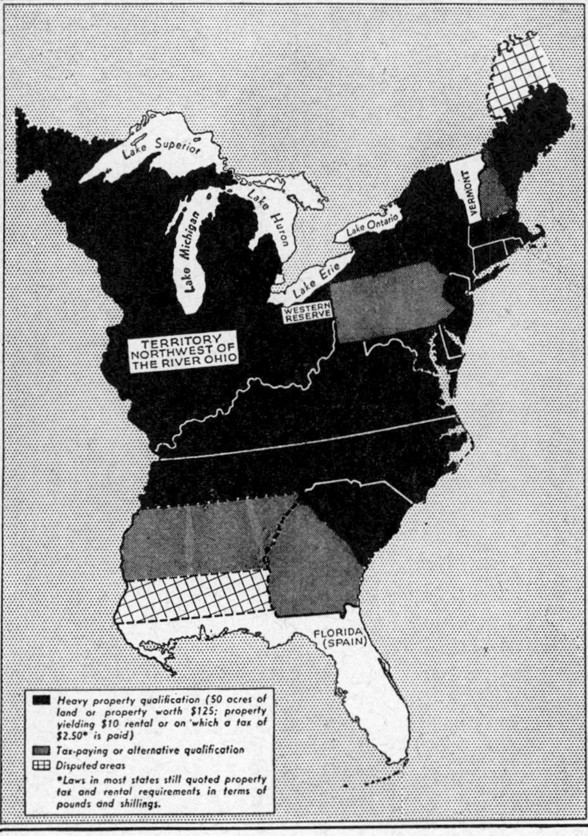

75 Male Suffrage, 1790

Vermont had universal male suffrage

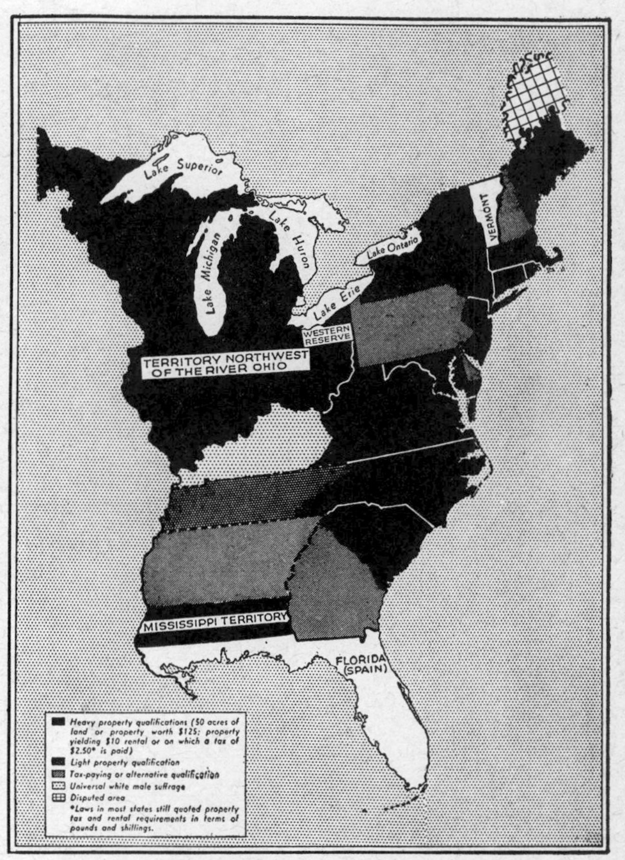

76 Male Suffrage, 1800

Vermont had universal male suffrage

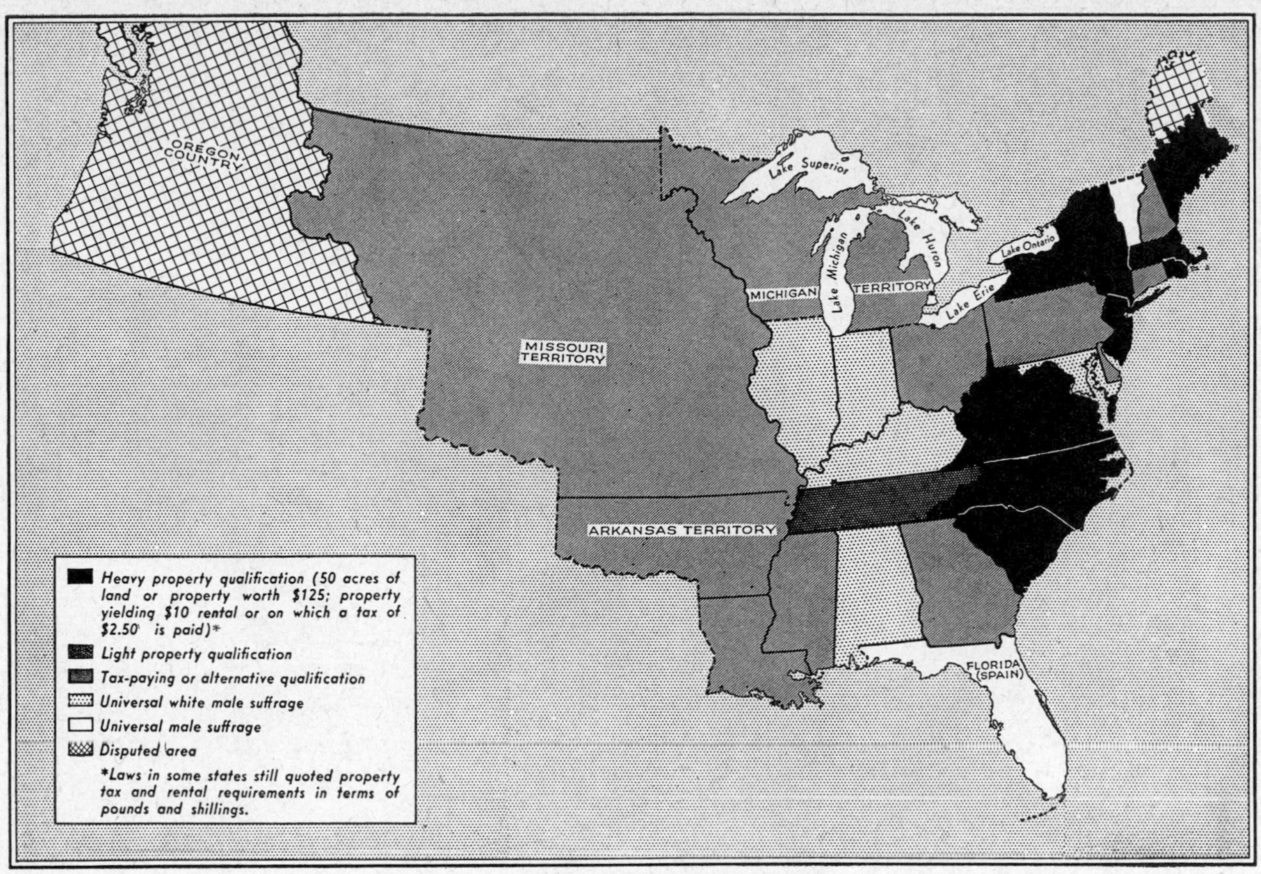

77 Male Suffrage, 1820

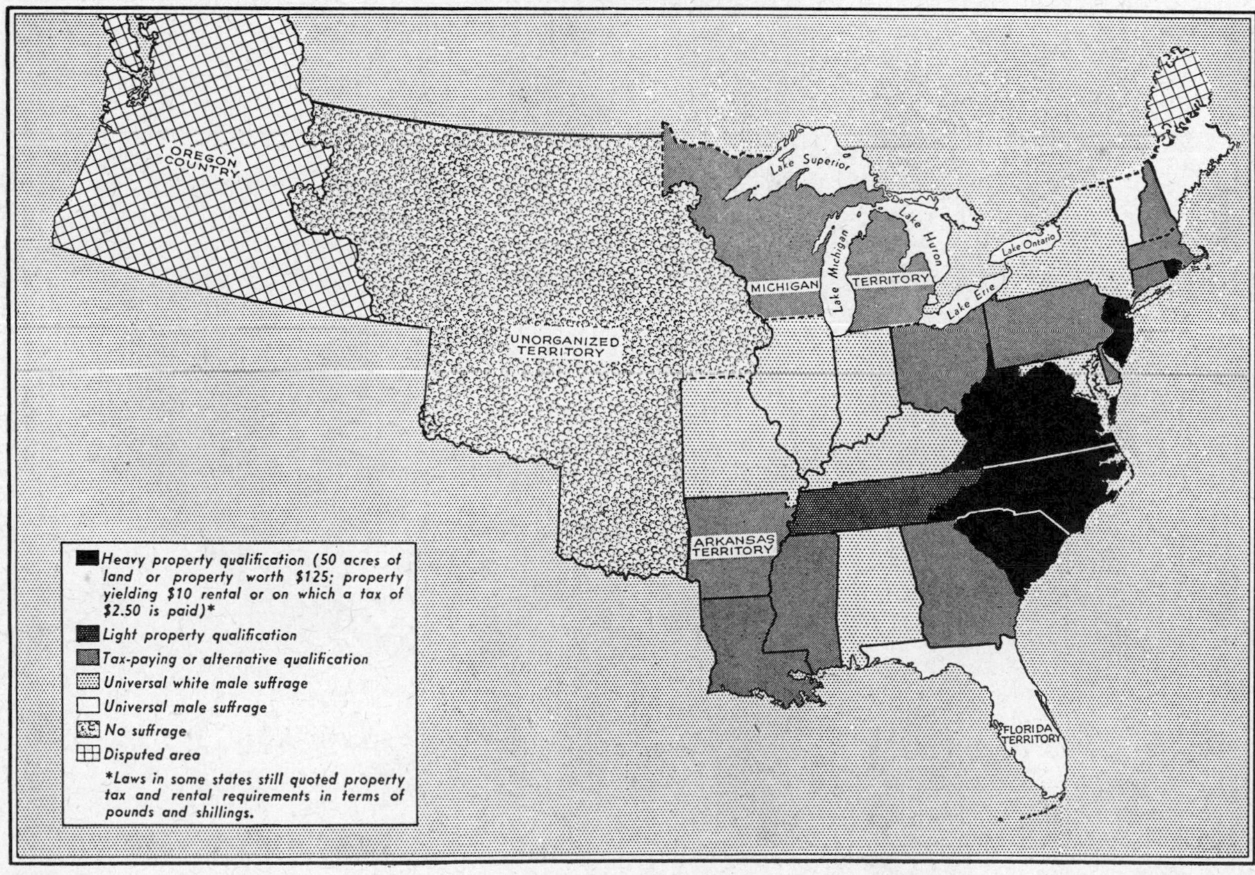

78 Male Suffrage, 1830

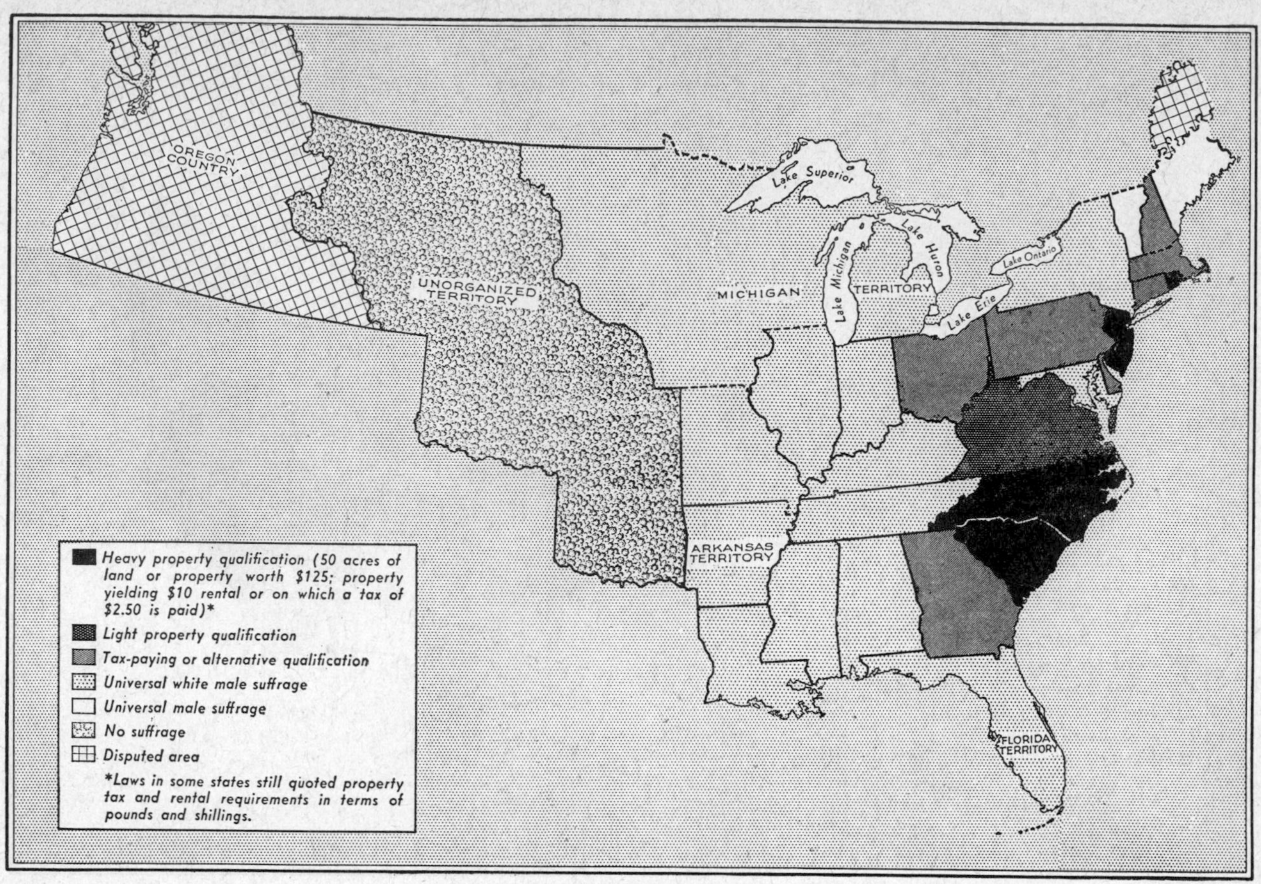

79 Male Suffrage, 1840

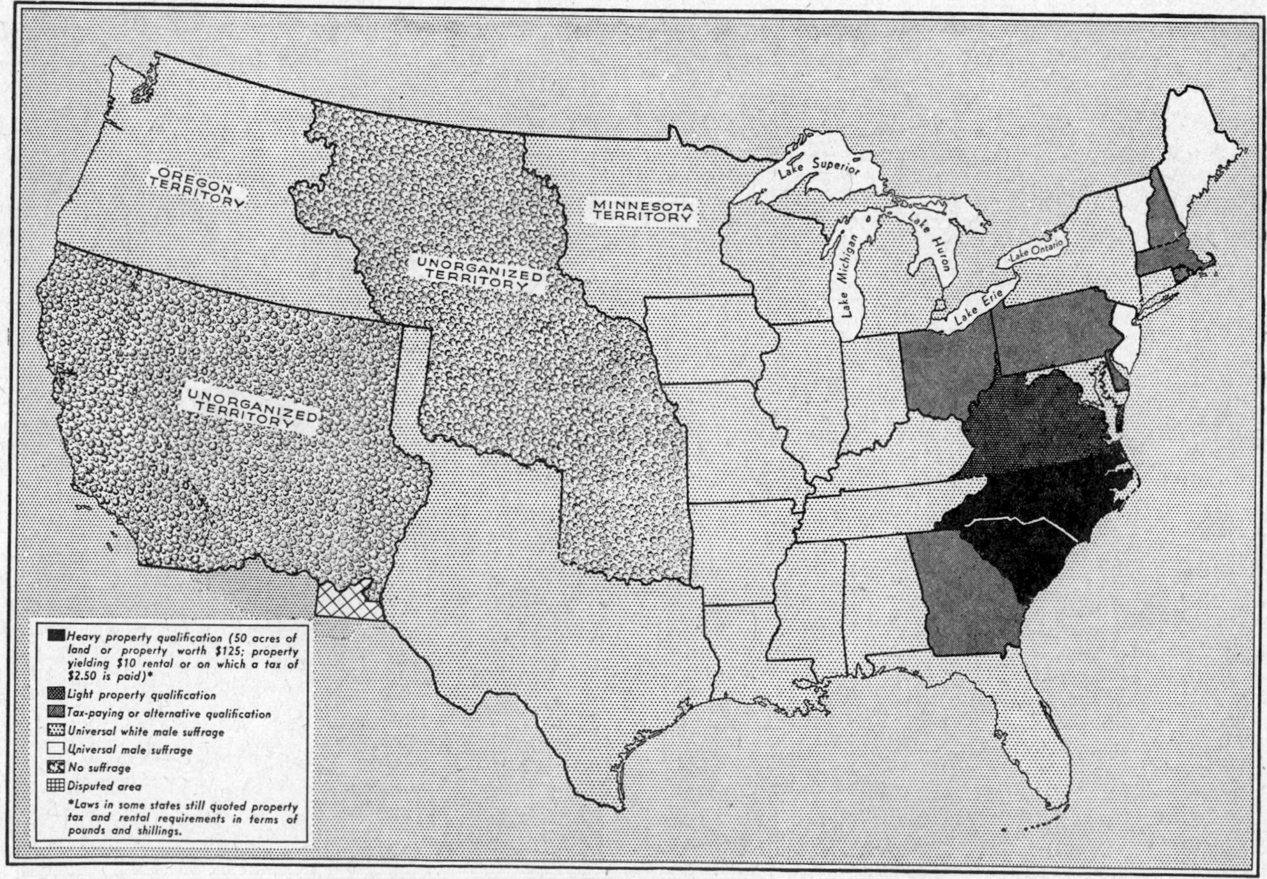

80 Male Suffrage, 1850

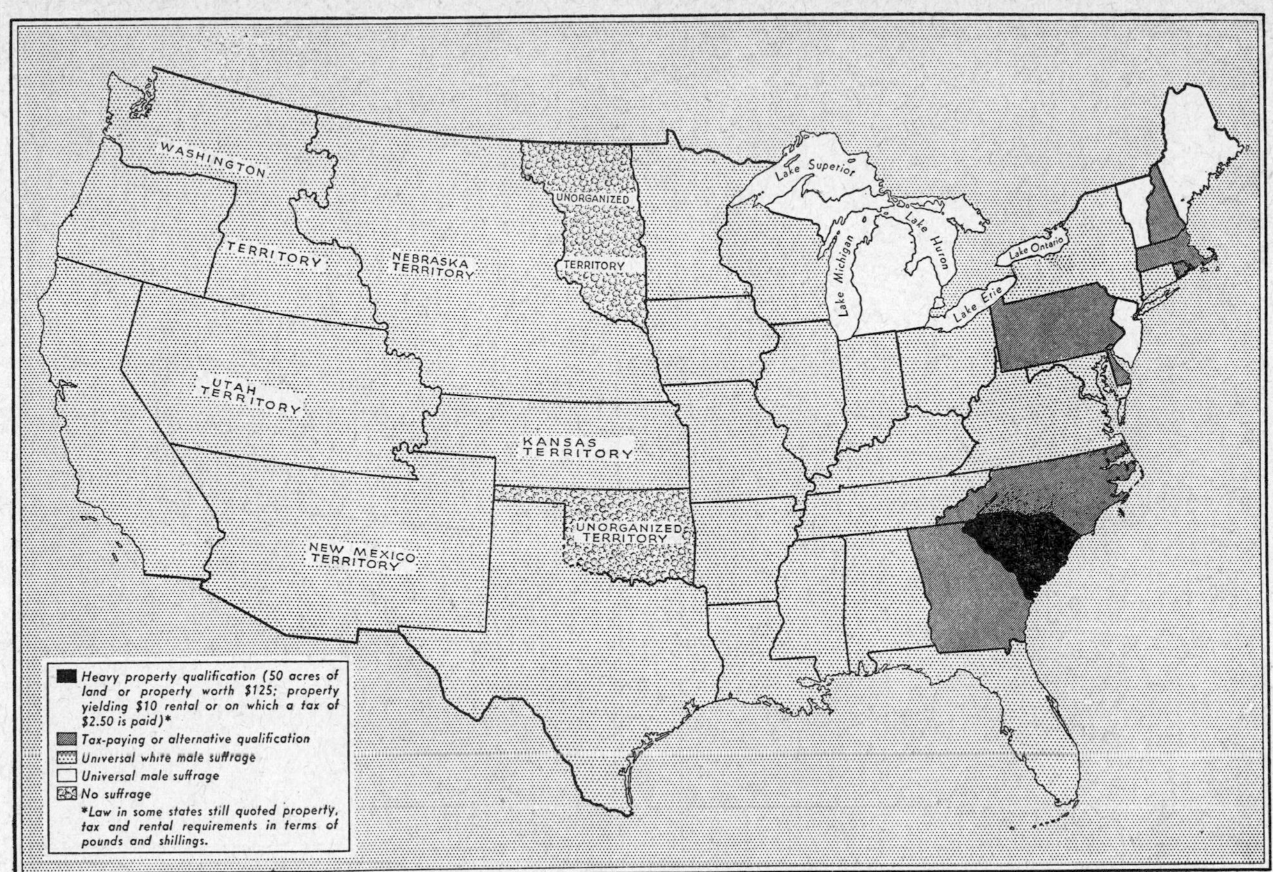

81 Male Suffrage, 1860

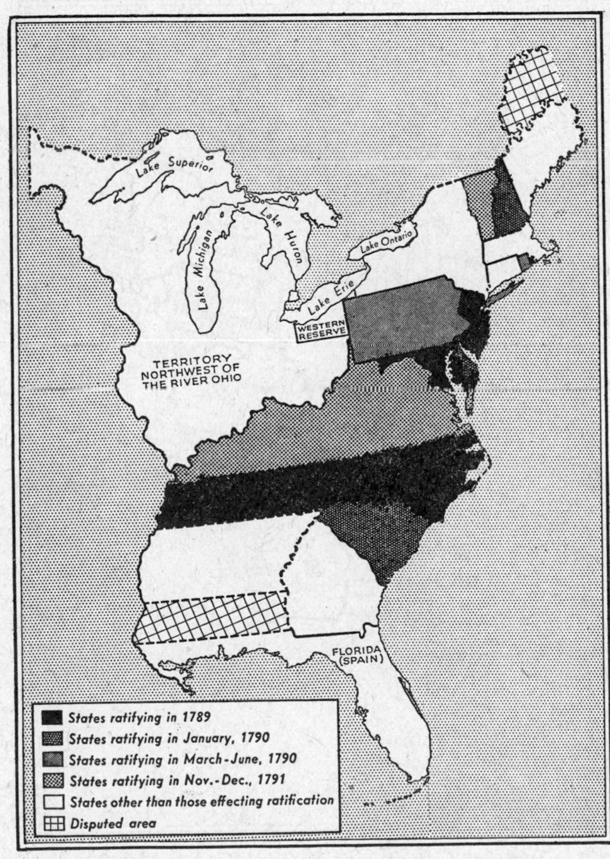

82 States Effecting the Ratification of the First Ten Amendments to the Constitution, 1791

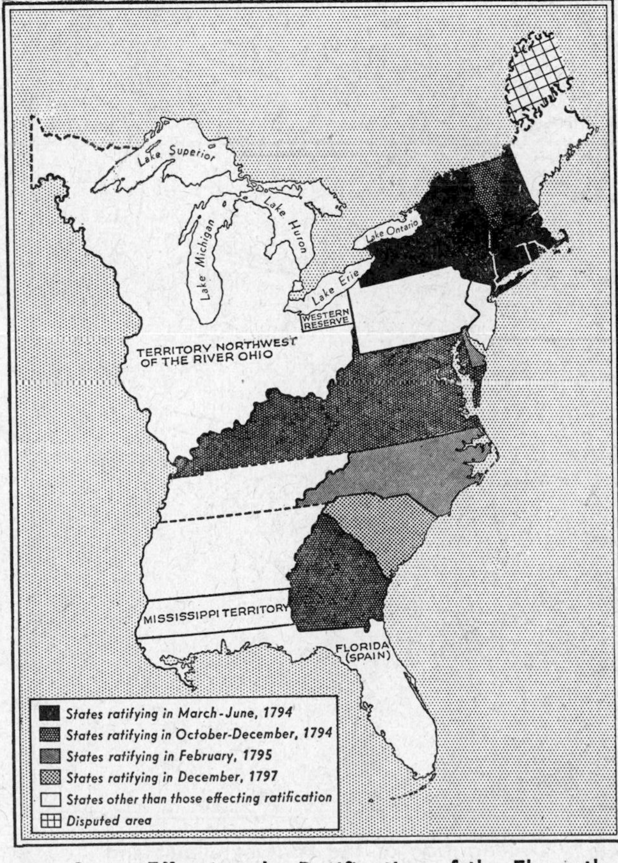

83 States Effecting the Ratification of the Eleventh Amendment to the Constitution, 1798

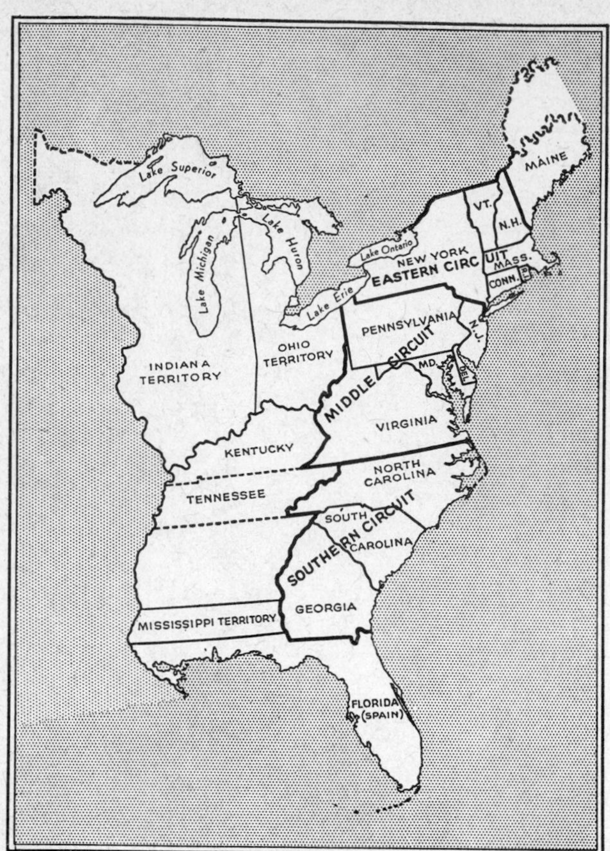

84 Organization of the Federal Circuit and District Courts by Act of September 24, 1789

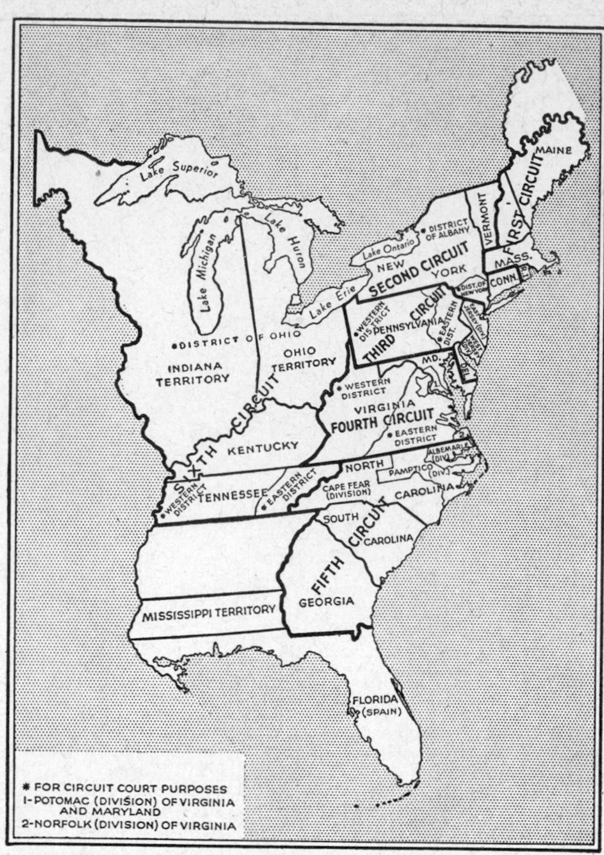

85 Federal Circuit and District Courts, 1801

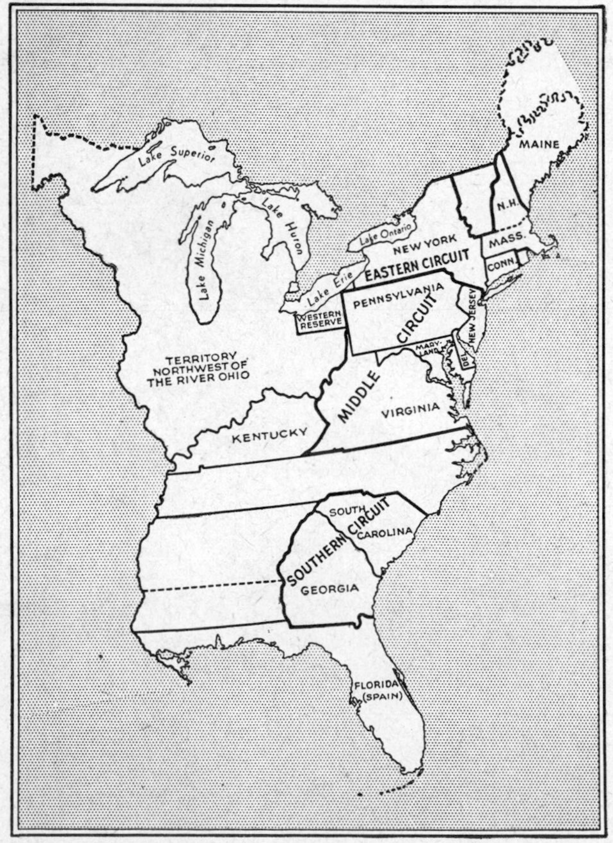

86 Organization of the Federal Circuit and District Courts by Act of March 8, 1802

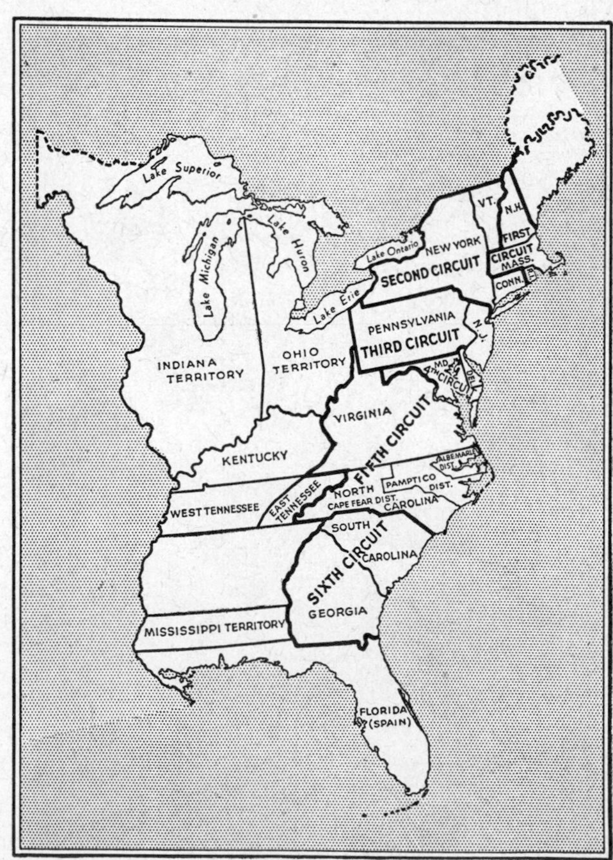

87 Federal Circuit and District Courts, 1802

In maps on this page circuit court borders are marked by heavy lines; district court borders by medium lines; division borders by light lines

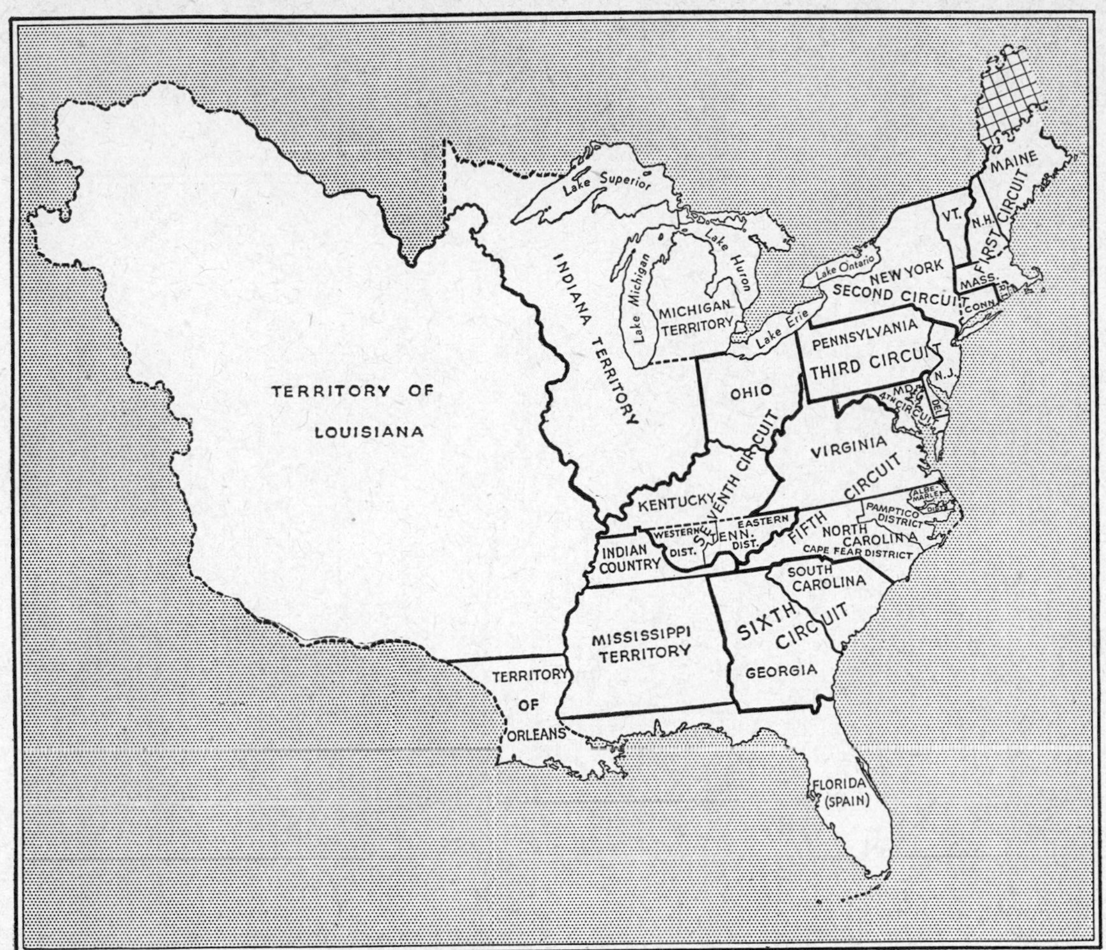

88 Federal Circuit and District Courts, 1807

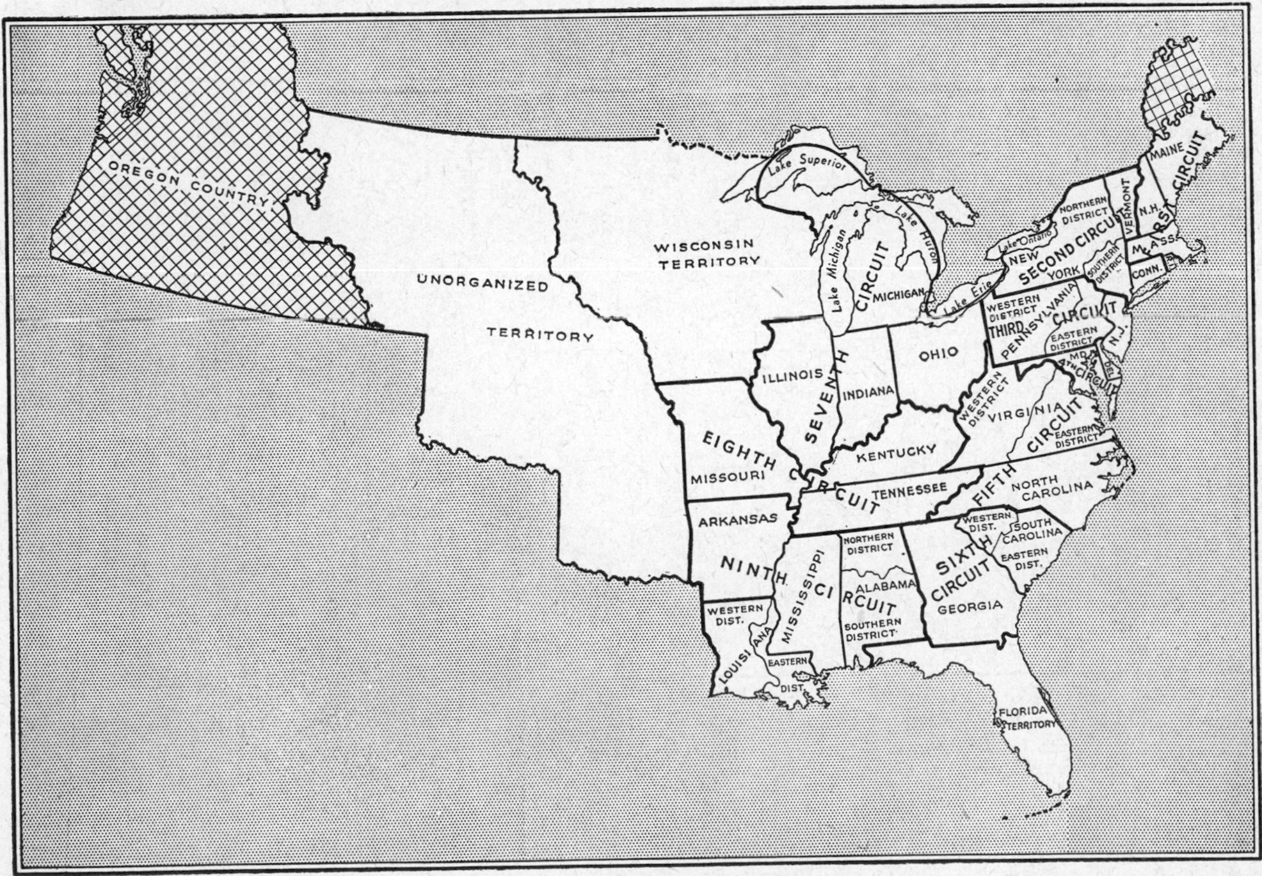

89 Federal Circuit and District Courts, 1837

In maps on this page circuit court borders are marked by heavy lines; district court borders by medium lines

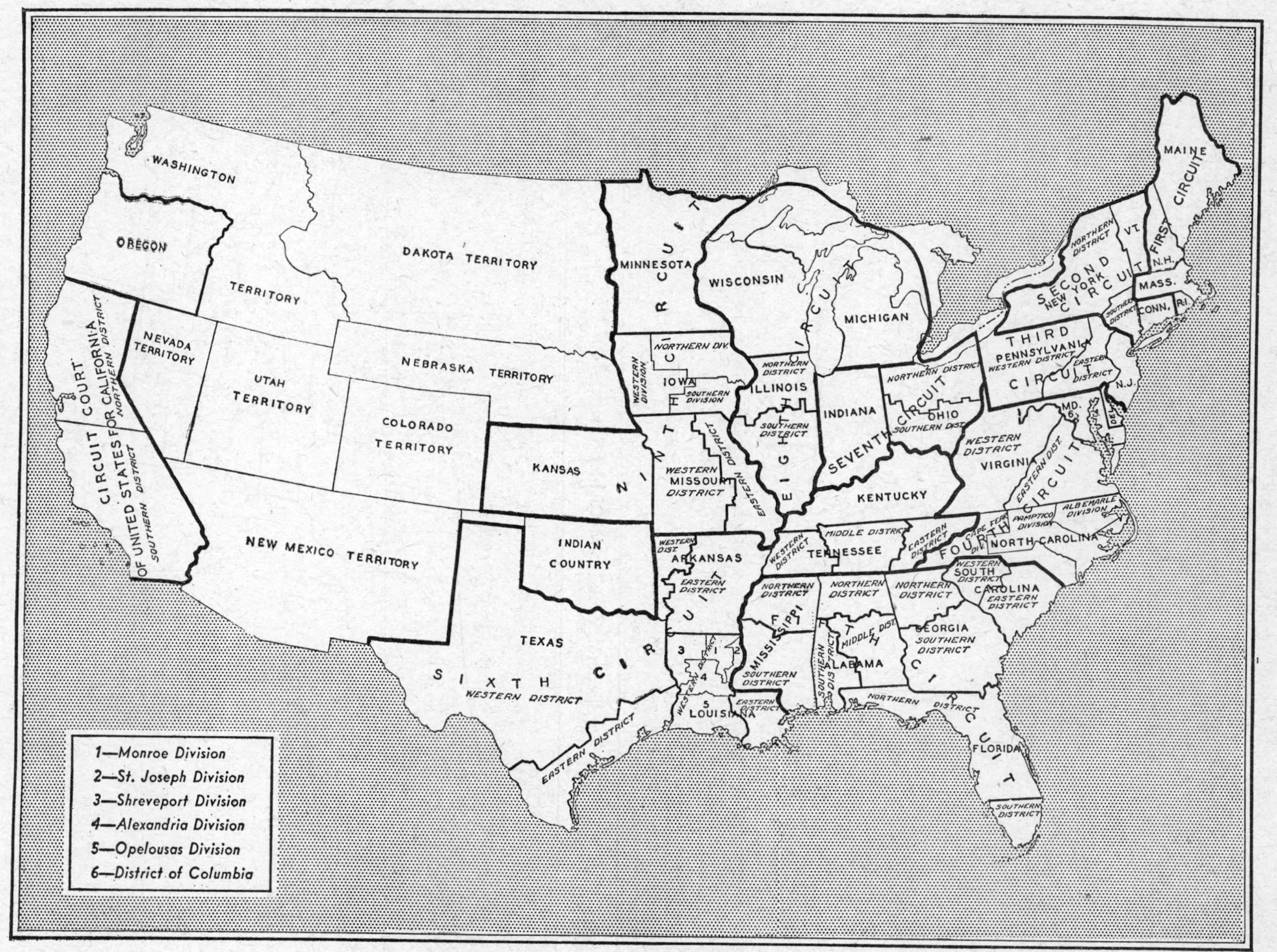

90 Federal Circuit and District Courts, 1861

Circuit court borders are marked by heavy lines; district court borders by medium lines; division borders by light lines.

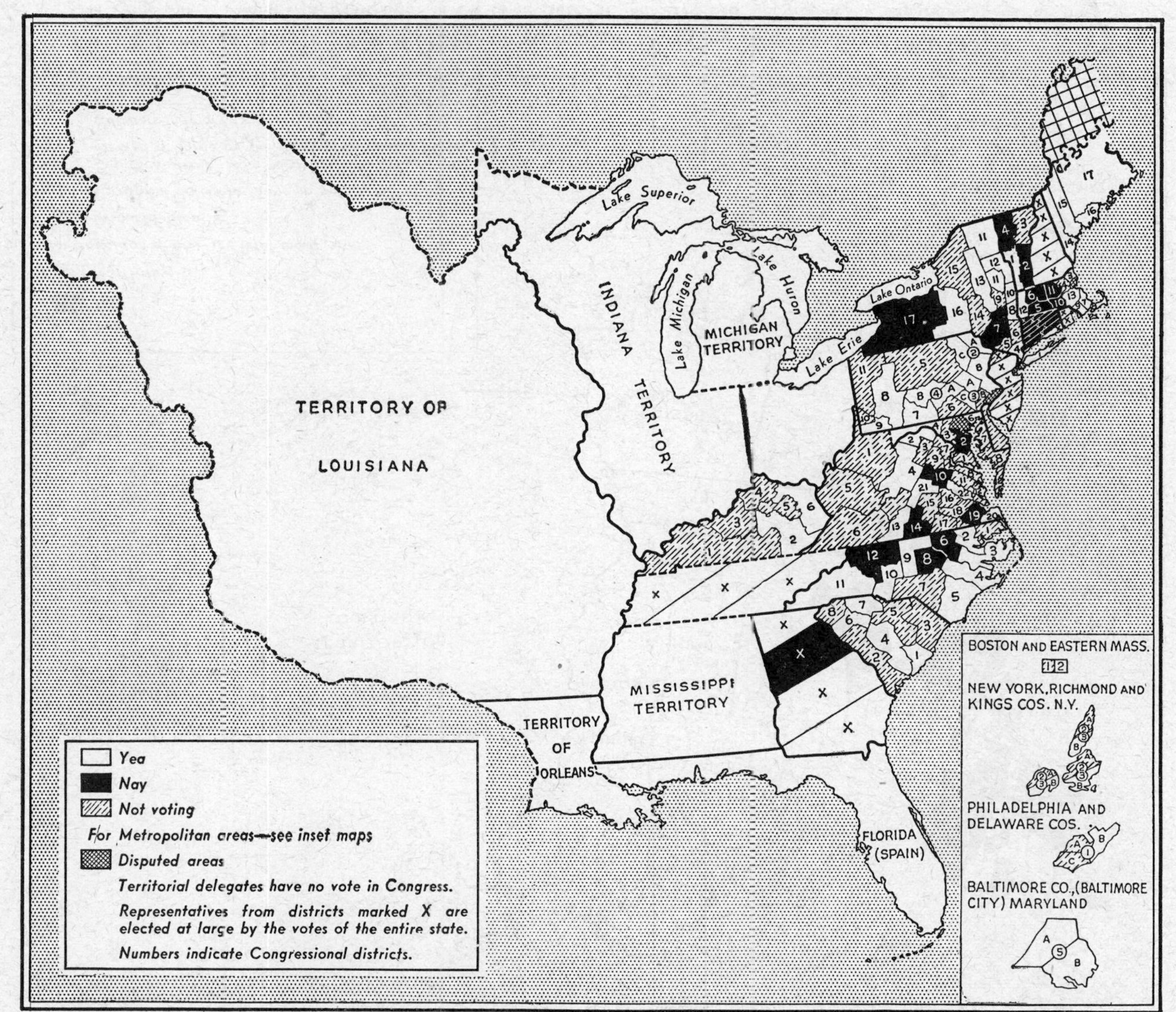

91 House Vote of January 2, 1808, on Passage of the Embargo Resolution

In cases where a number is repeated in the same state, it indicates two parts of the same district

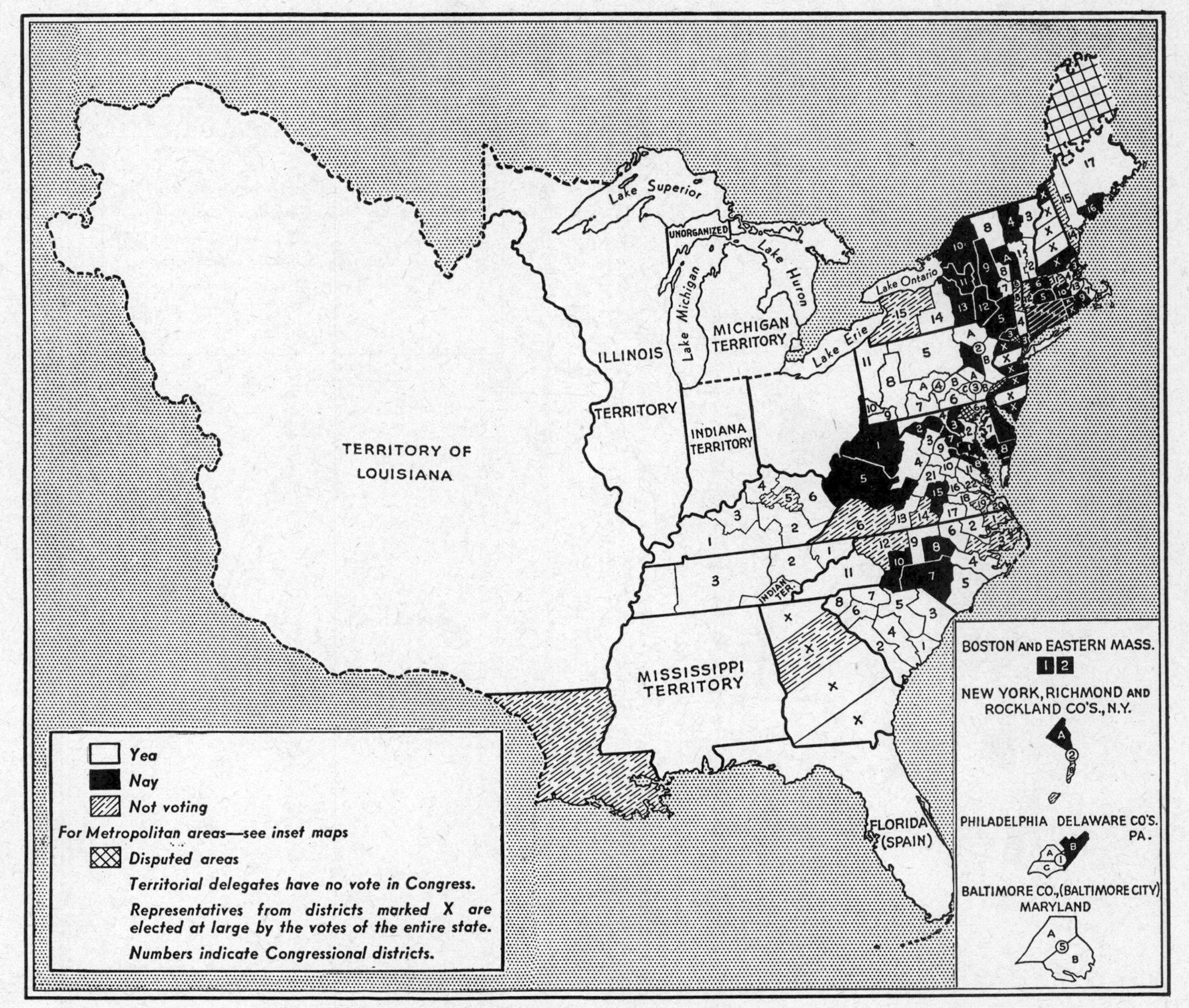

92 House Vote of June 4, 1812, on Resolution Declaring War on Great Britain

In cases where a number appears twice in the same state, it indicates two geographically separated parts of the same congressional district

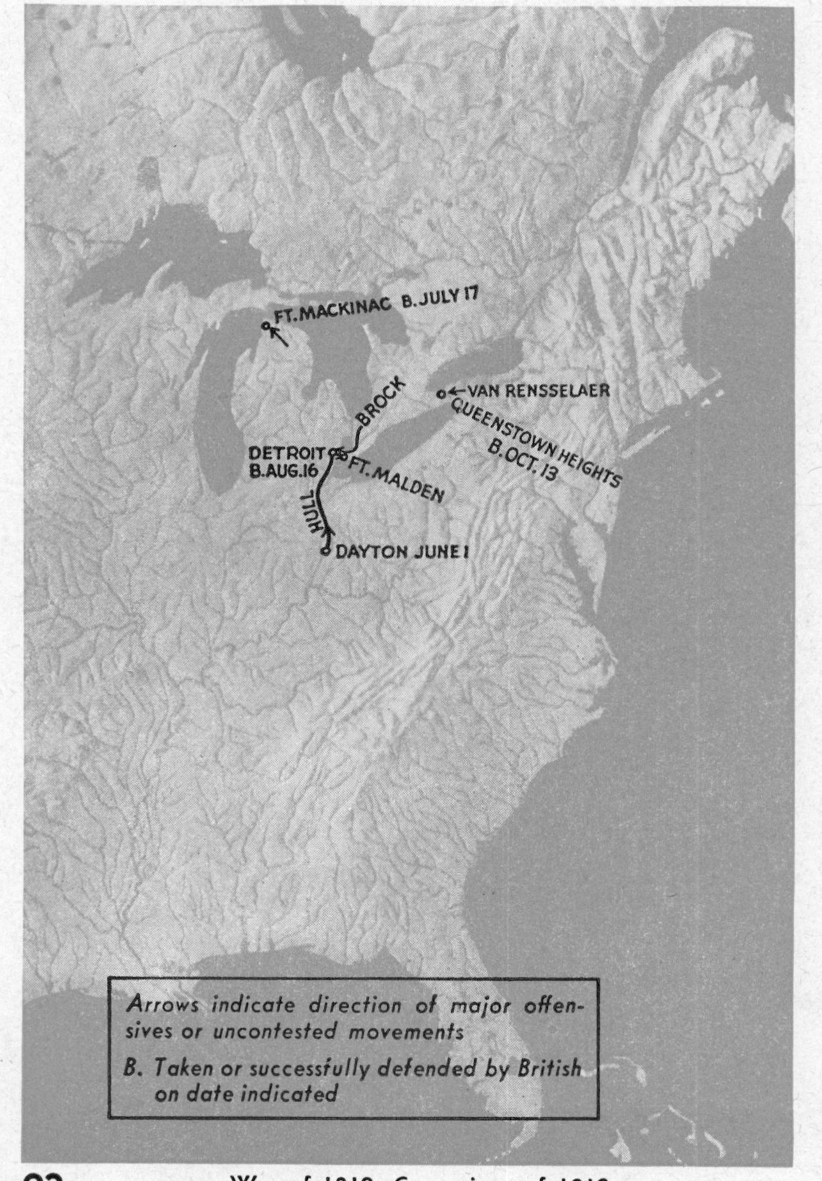

93 War of 1812: Campaigns of 1812

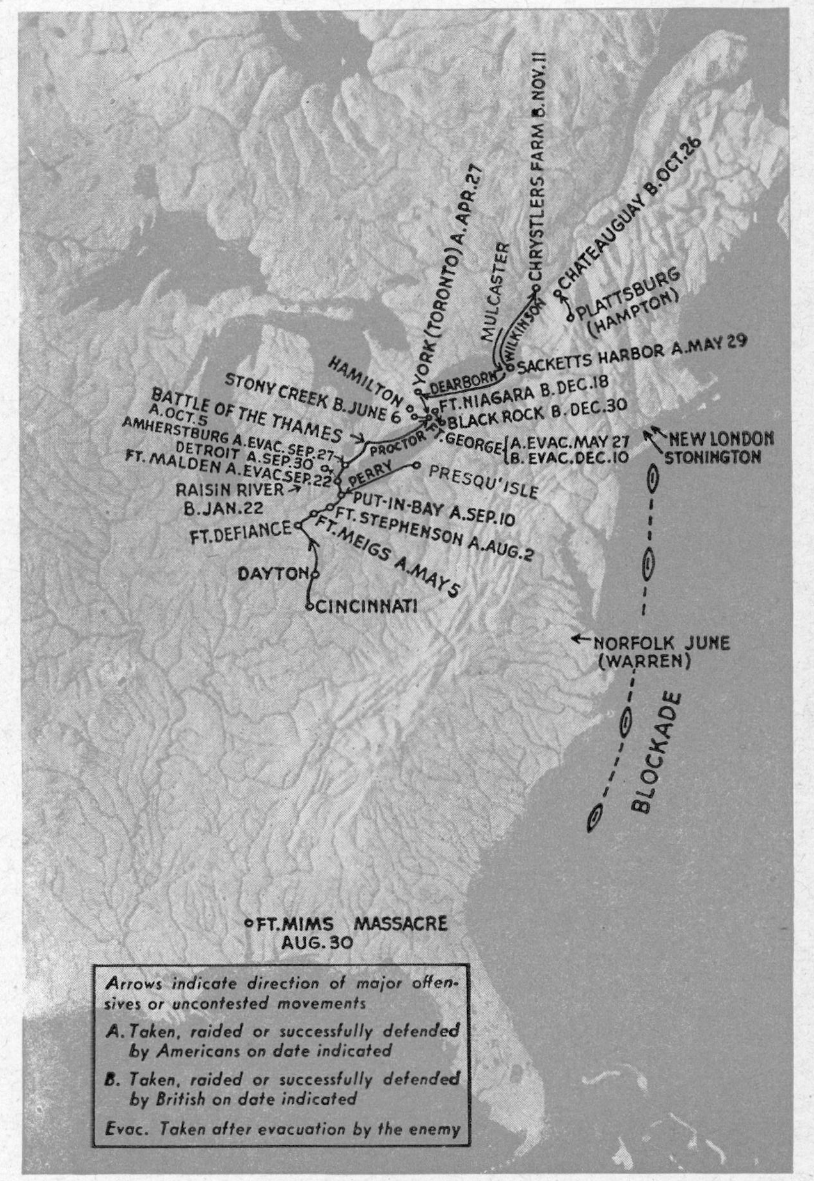

94 War of 1812: Campaigns of 1813

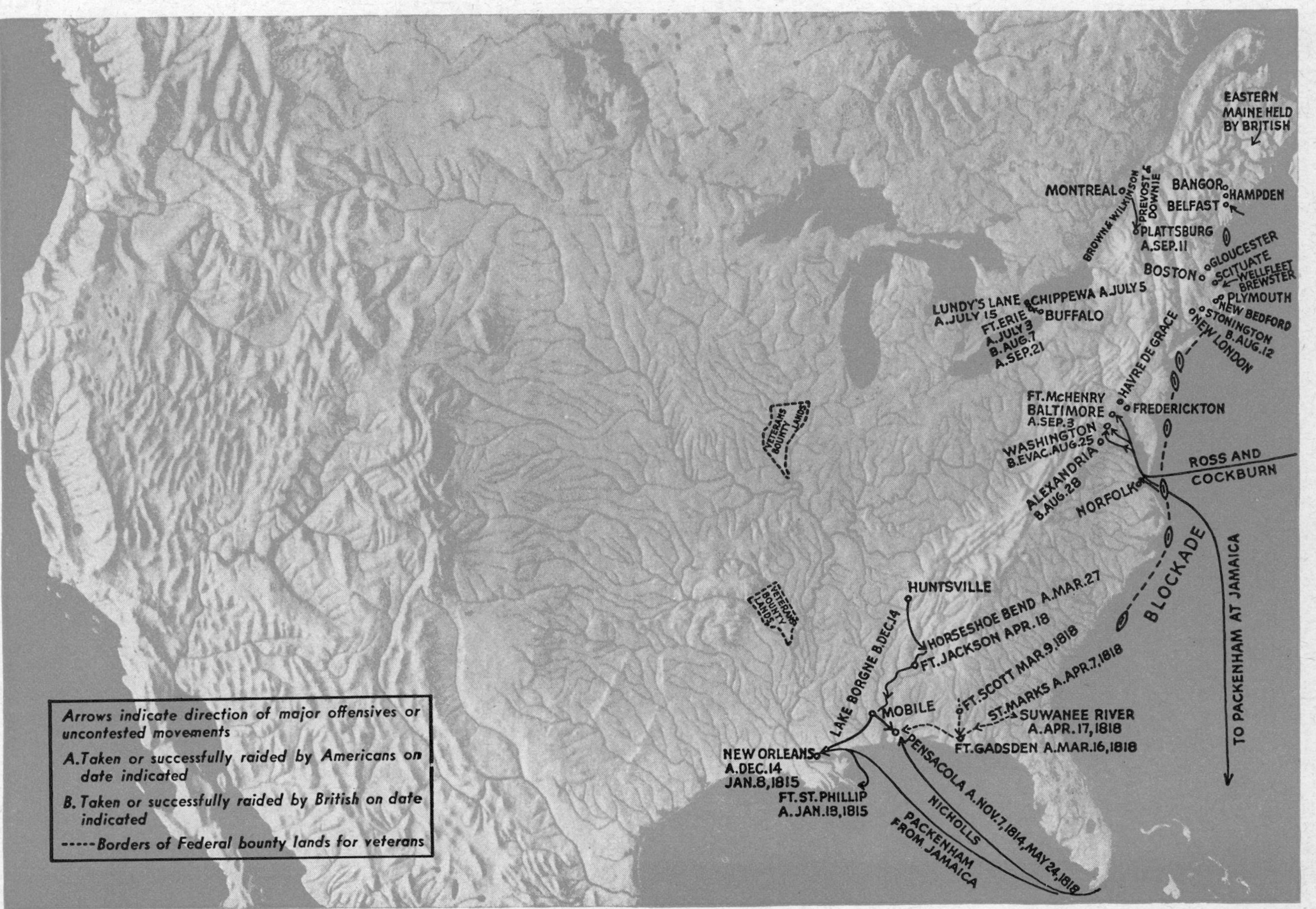
EASTERN MAINE HELD BY BRITISH
MONTREAL
BROWN & WILKINSON
PREVOST & DOWNIE
BANGOR
HAMPDEN
BELFAST
PLATTSBURG A.SEP.11
GLOUCESTER
BOSTON
SCITUATE
WELLFLEET
BREWSTER
PLYMOUTH
NEW BEDFORD
STONINGTON B.AUG.12
NEW LONDON
CHIPPEWA A.JULY 5
LUNDY'S LANE A.JULY 15
FT.ERIE A.JULY 3 B.AUG.7 A.SEP.21
BUFFALO
HAVRE DE GRACE
FT. McHENRY BALTIMORE A.SEP.3
FREDERICKTON
WASHINGTON B.EVAC.AUG.25
ALEXANDRIA B.AUG.28
NORFOLK
ROSS AND COCKBURN
BLOCKADE
TO PACKENHAM AT JAMAICA
VETERANS BOUNTY LANDS
VETERANS BOUNTY LANDS
HUNTSVILLE
HORSESHOE BEND A.MAR.27
FT.JACKSON APR.18
FT.SCOTT MAR.9,1818
ST.MARKS A.APR.7,1818
SUWANEE RIVER A.APR.17,1818
FT.GADSDEN A.MAR.16,1818
LAKE BORGNE B.DEC.14
MOBILE
PENSACOLA A.NOV.7,1814,MAY 24,1818
NICHOLLS
PACKENHAM FROM JAMAICA
NEW ORLEANS A.DEC.14 JAN.8,1815
FT.ST.PHILLIP A.JAN.18,1815
Arrows indicate direction of major offensives or uncontested movements
A. Taken or successfully raided by Americans on date indicated
B. Taken or successfully raided by British on date indicated
-----Borders of Federal bounty lands for veterans

95 War of 1812: Campaigns of 1814; Jackson's Florida Expedition of 1818

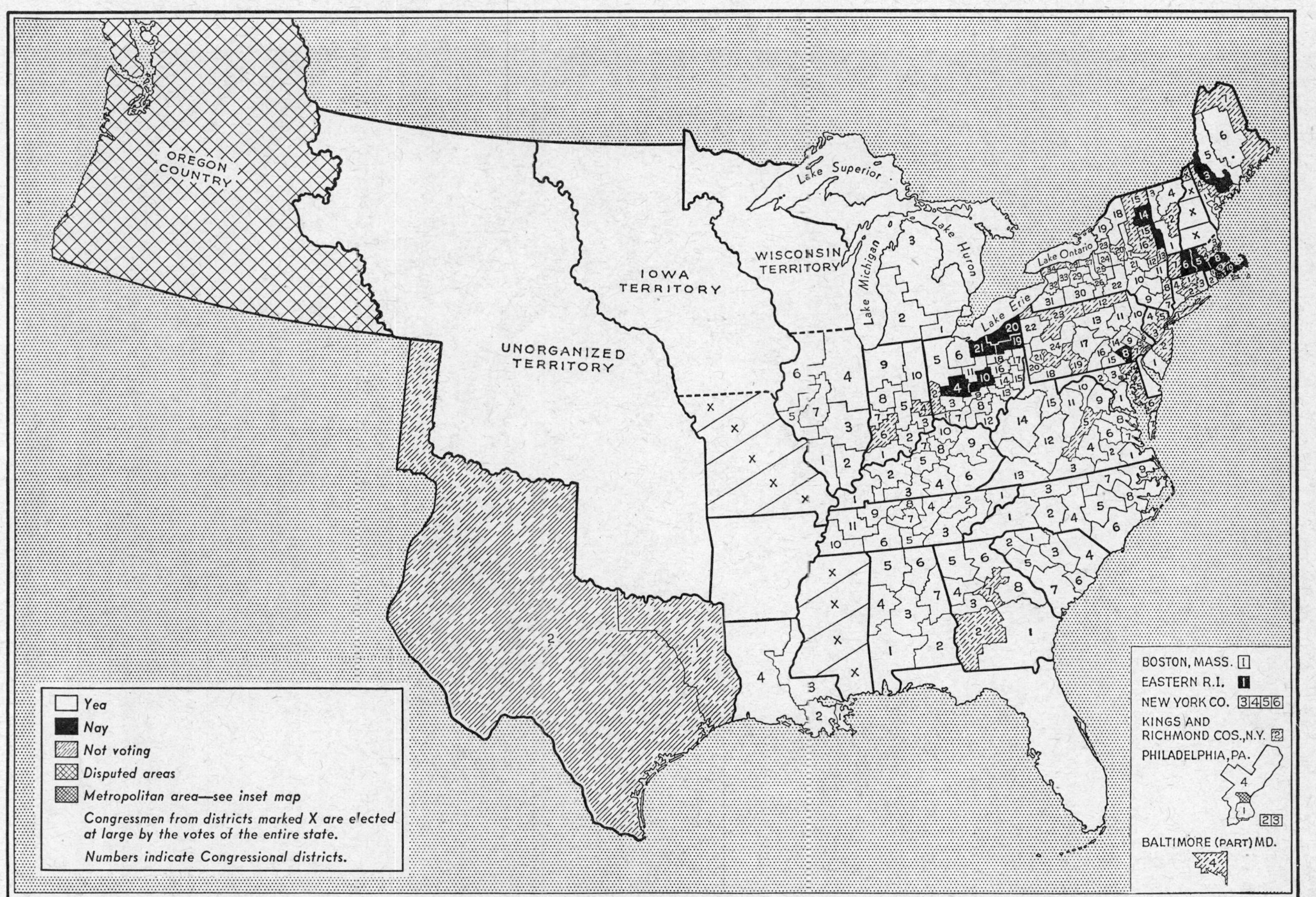

96 House Vote of May 11, 1846, Authorizing the President to Use Military and Naval Forces to Prosecute the Existing War with Mexico

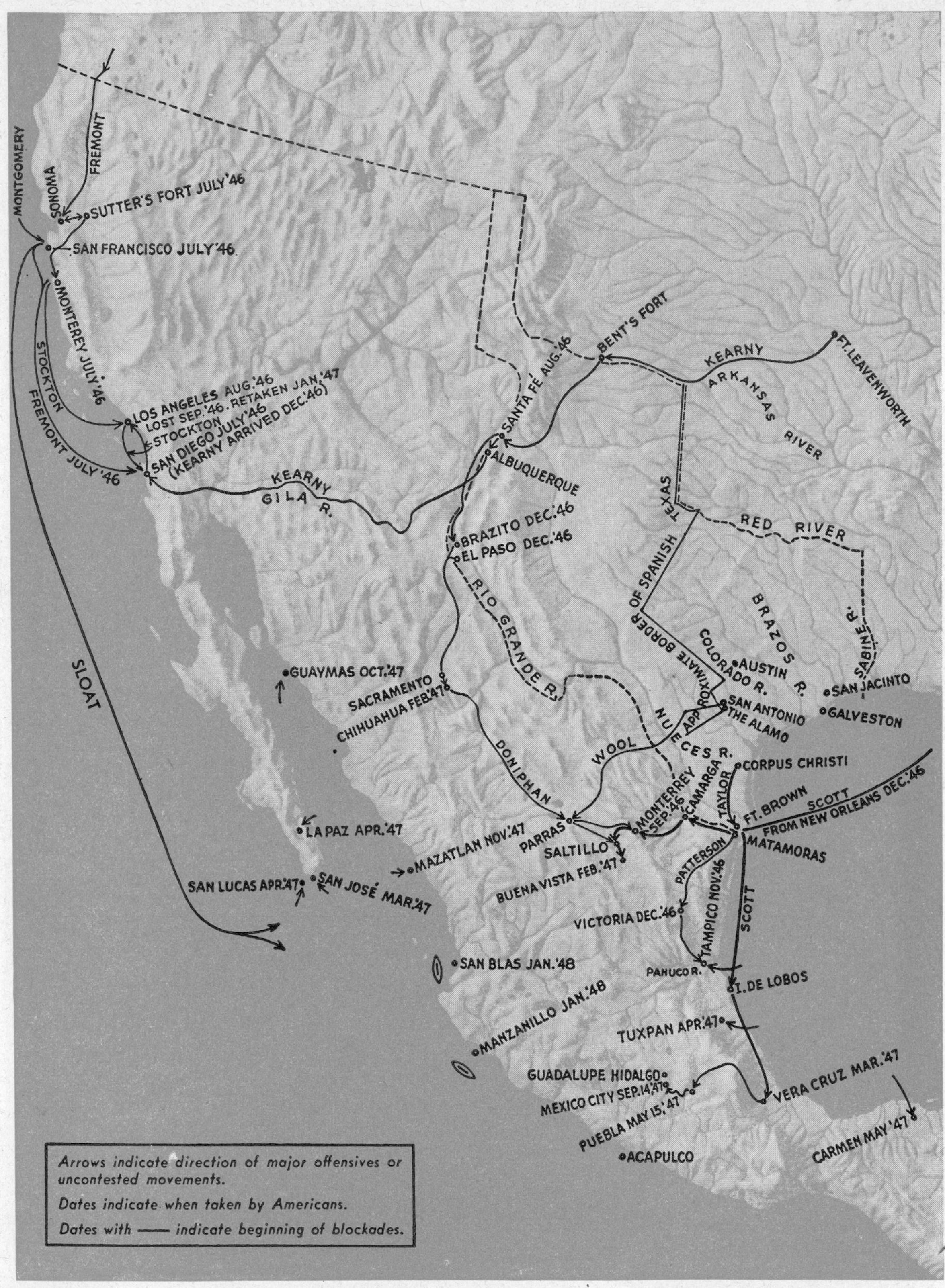

97 The Mexican War

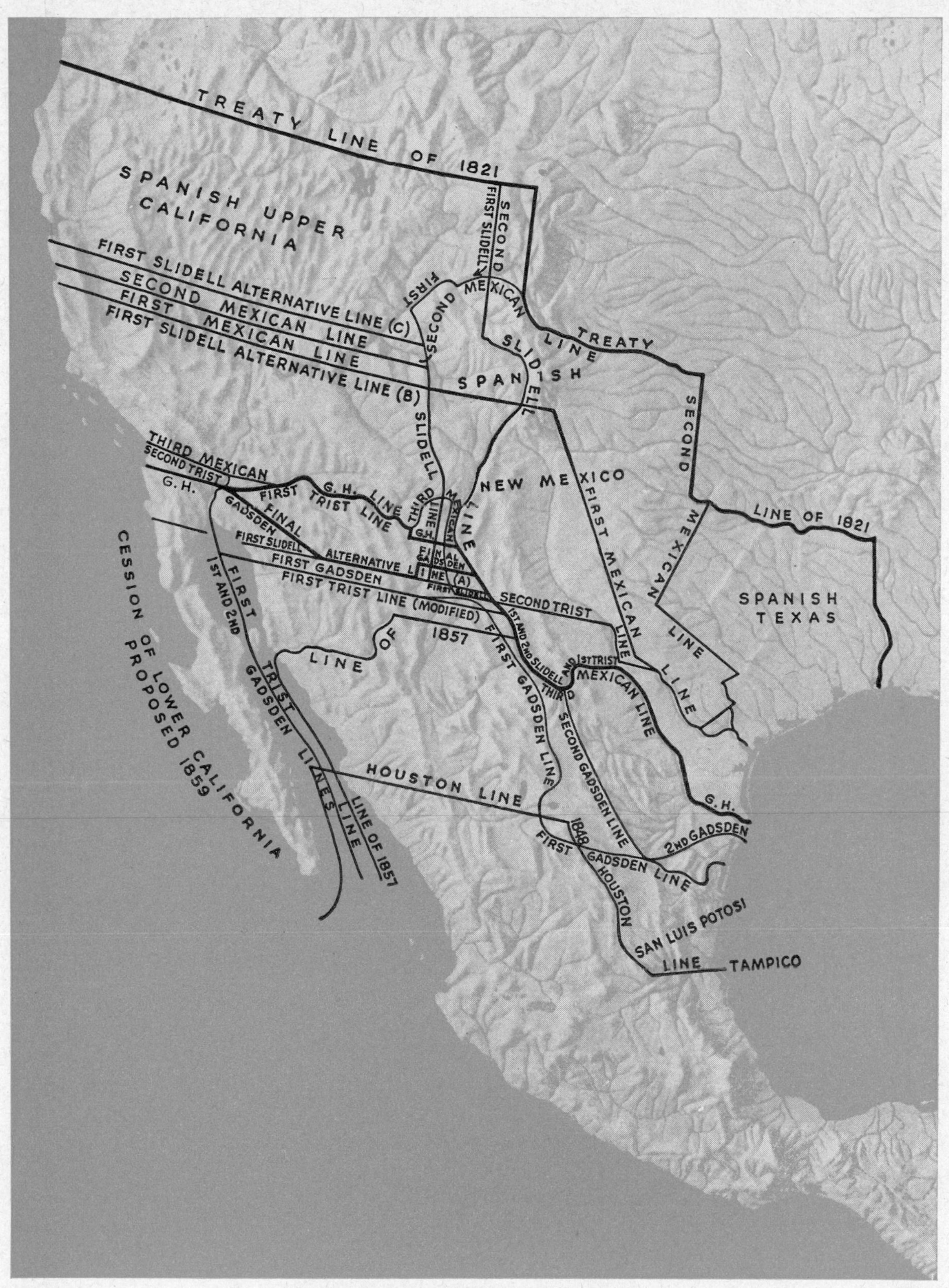

98

The Mexican Border, 1821-1857

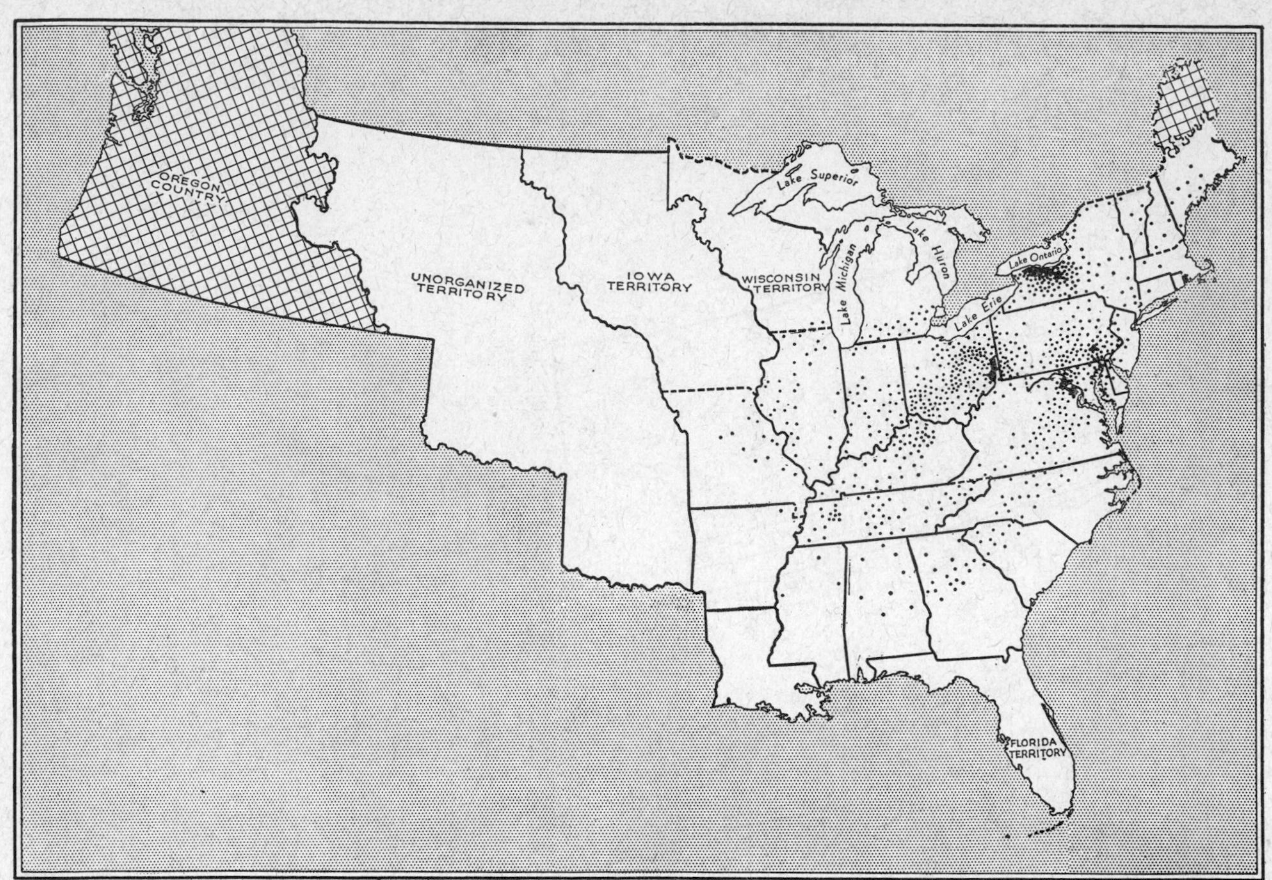

99

Wheat Production, 1840

Each dot represents 100,000 bushels; total crop, 84,823,272 bushels

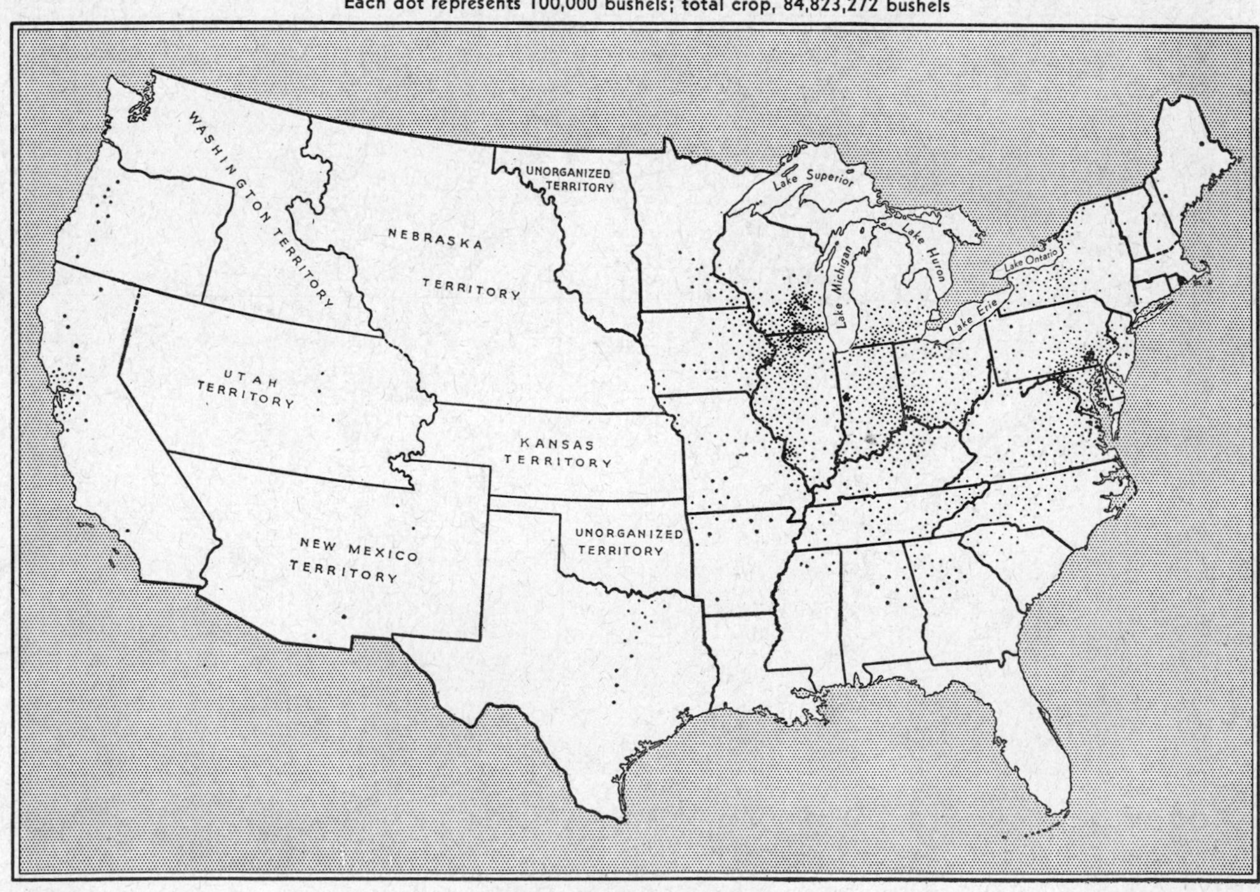

100

Wheat Production, 1860

Each dot represents 100,000 bushels; total crop, 173,104,924 bushels

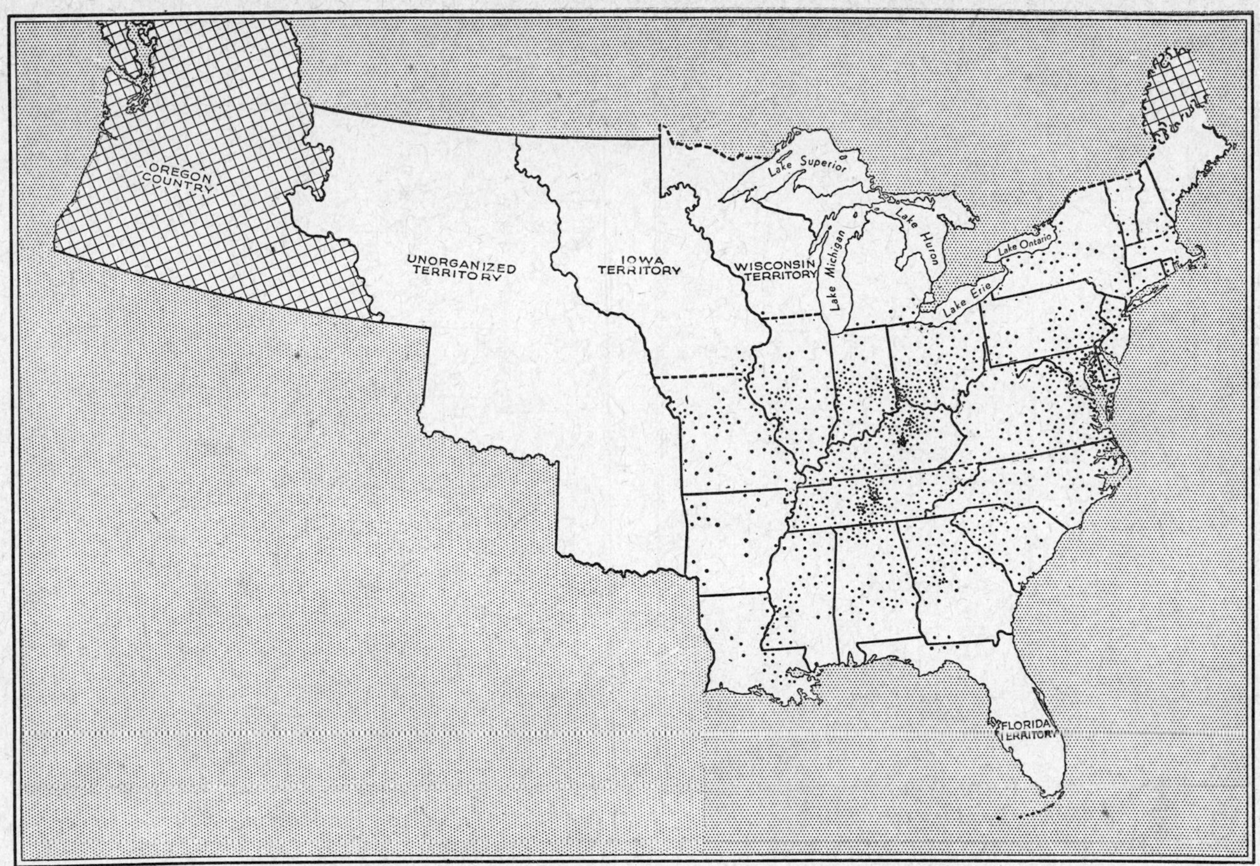

101 Corn Production, 1840

Each dot represents 300,000 bushels; total crop, 377,531,875 bushels

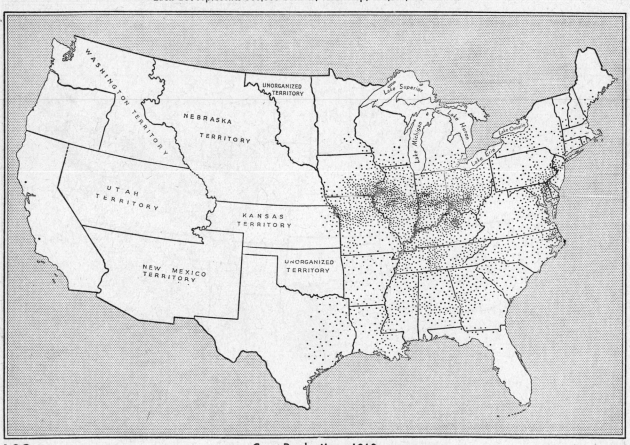

102 Corn Production, 1860

Each dot represents 300,000 bushels; total crop, 838,792,740 bushels

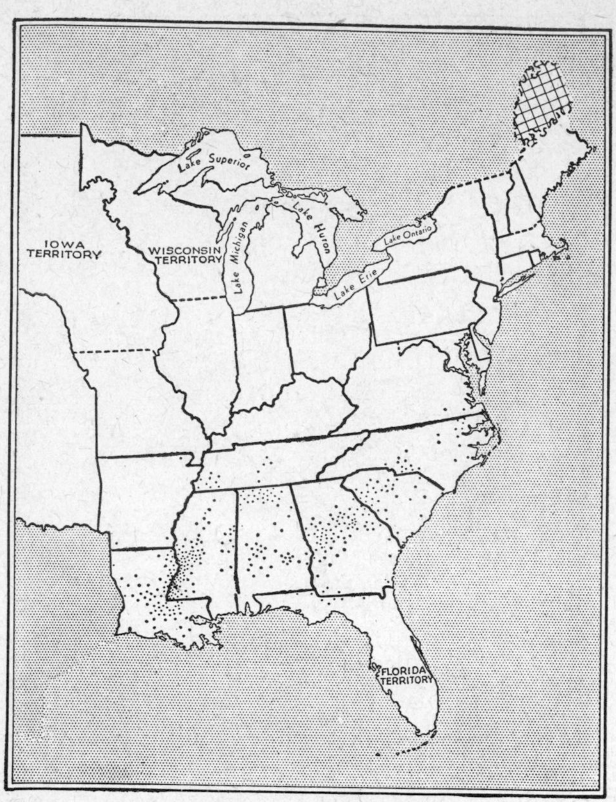

103 Cotton Production, 1840
Each dot represents 4,000 500-lb. bales; total crop, 1,976,198 500-lb. bales

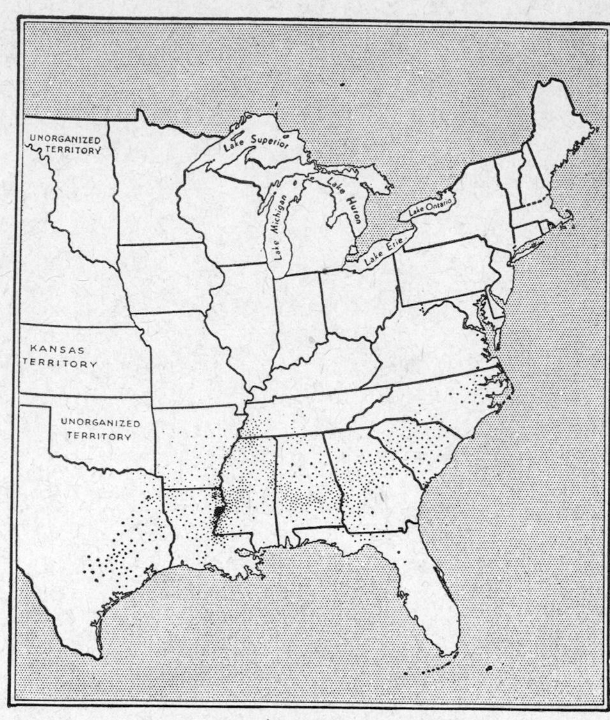

104 Cotton Production, 1860
Each dot represents 4,000 500-lb. bales; total crop, 4,309,641 500-lb. bales

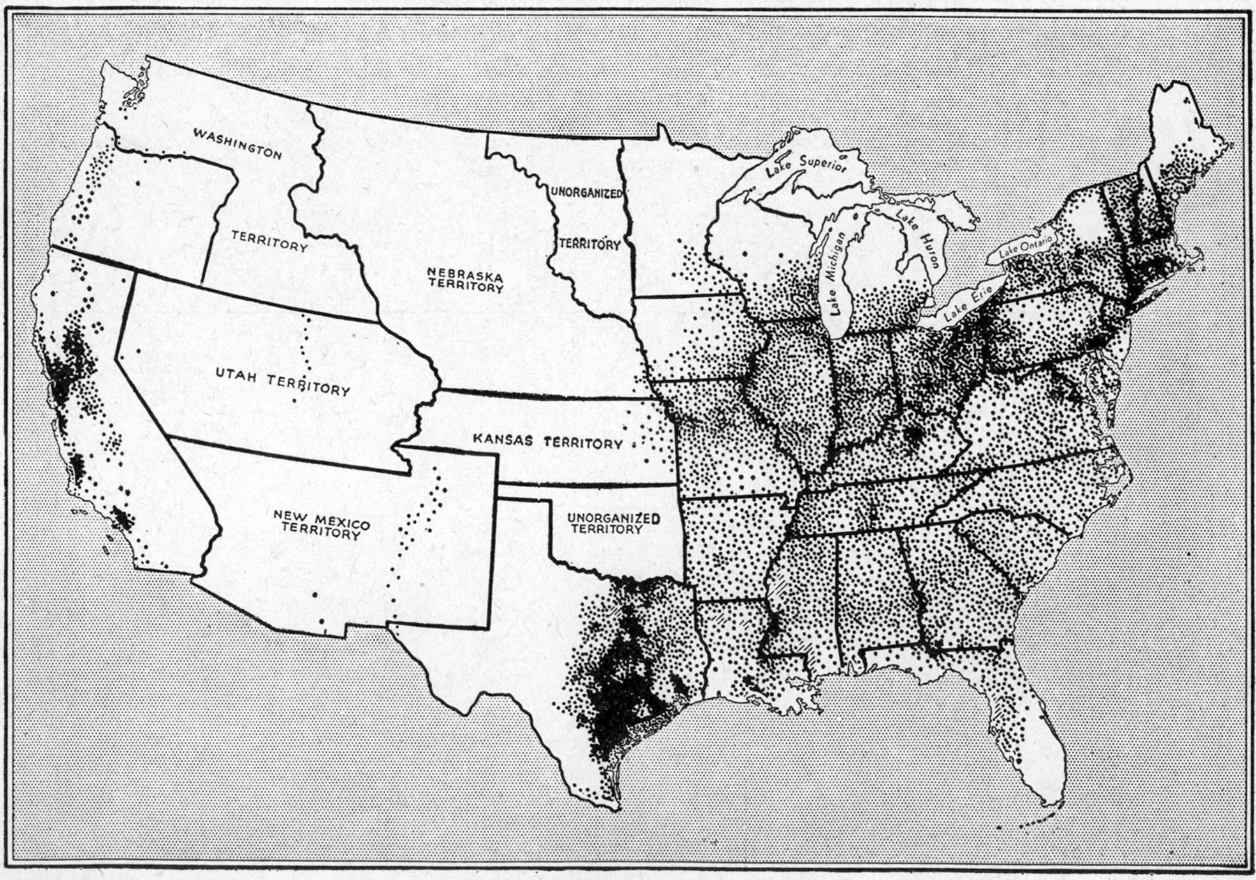

105 Cattle (Excluding Dairy Cows), 1860
Each dot represents 2,000 head; total, 8,585,735 head

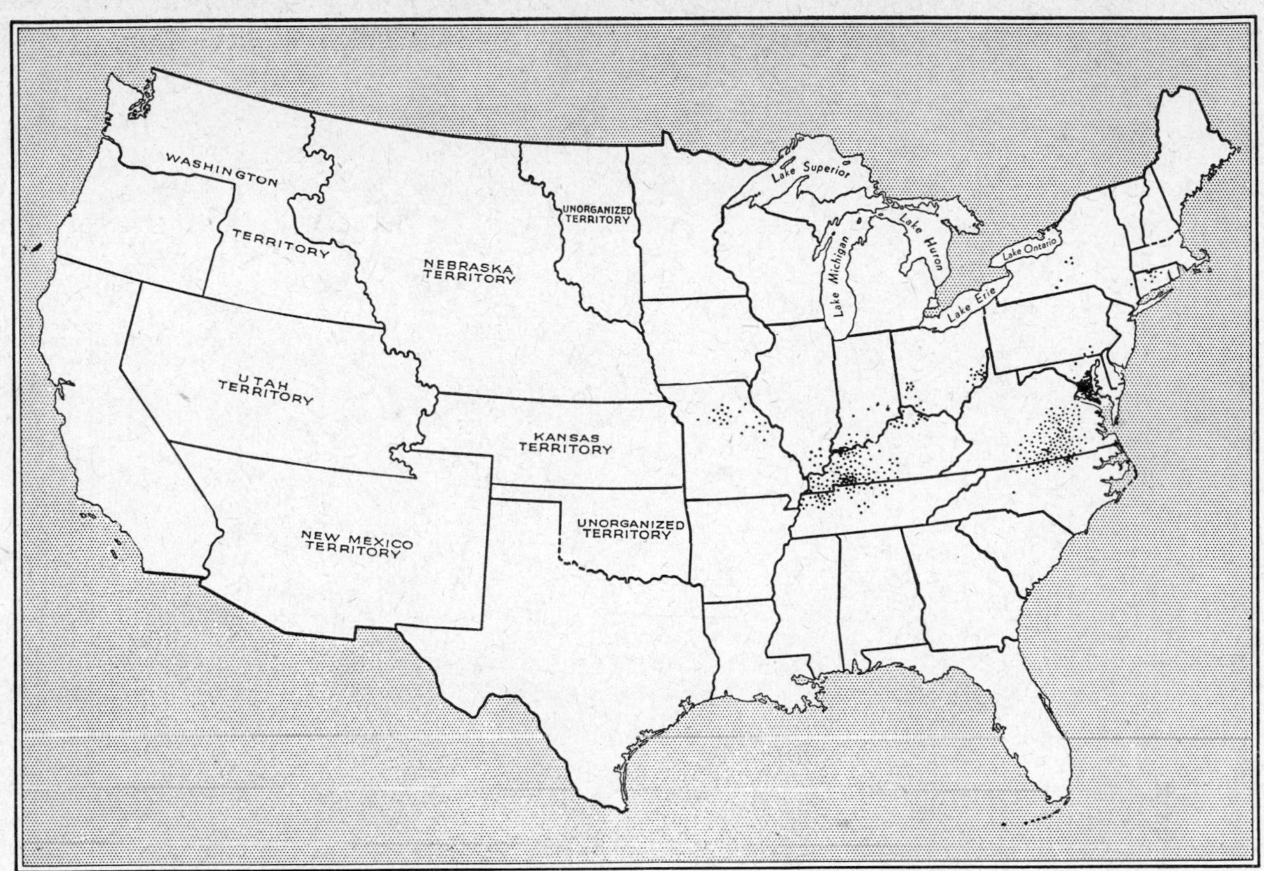

106

Tobacco Production, 1860

Each dot represents 1,000,000 lbs.; total crop, 434,209,461 lbs.

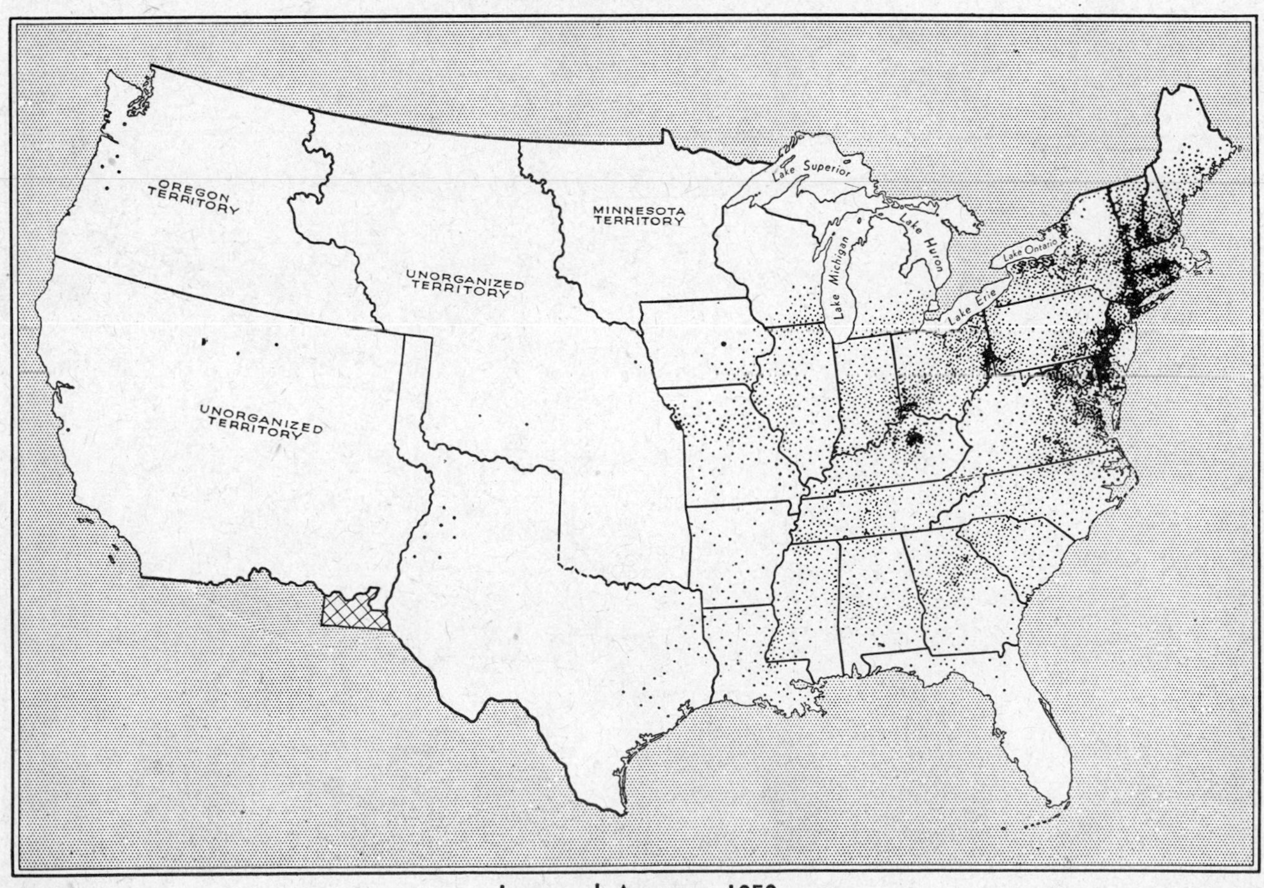

107

Improved Acreage, 1850

Each dot represents 25,000 acres; total, 113,632,614 acres

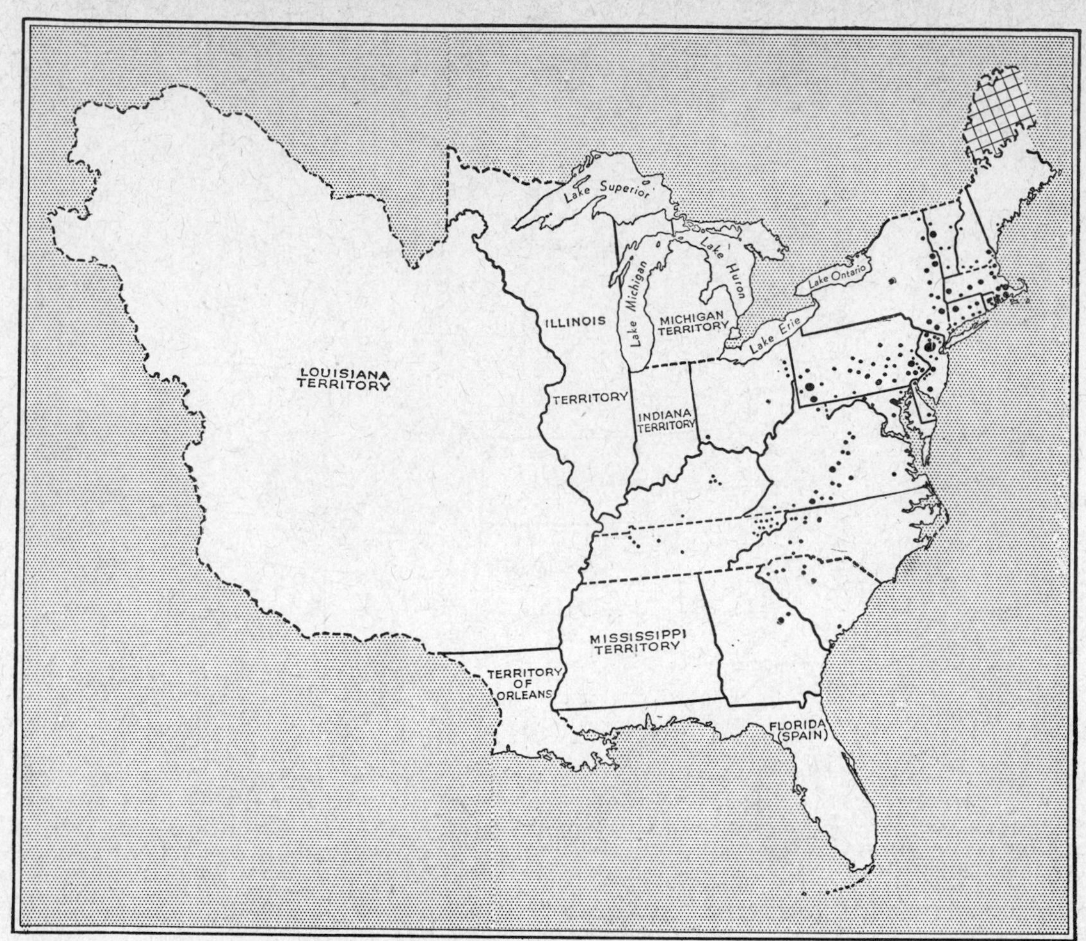

108 **Manufacturing Areas, 1810**

Based on iron, steel, and textiles, together with cities having more than 5,000 industrial employees

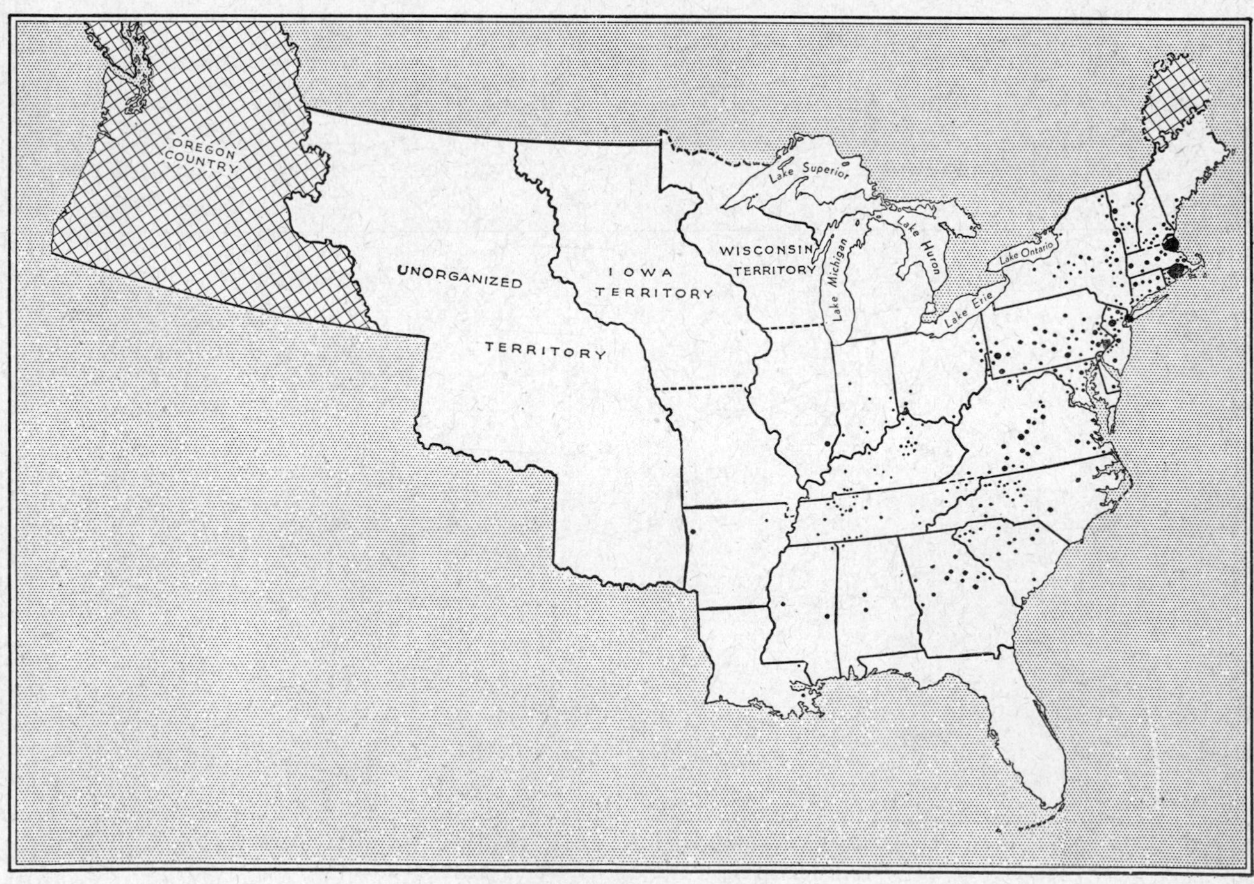

109 **Manufacturing Areas, 1840**

Based on iron, steel, and textiles, together with cities having more than 5,000 industrial employees

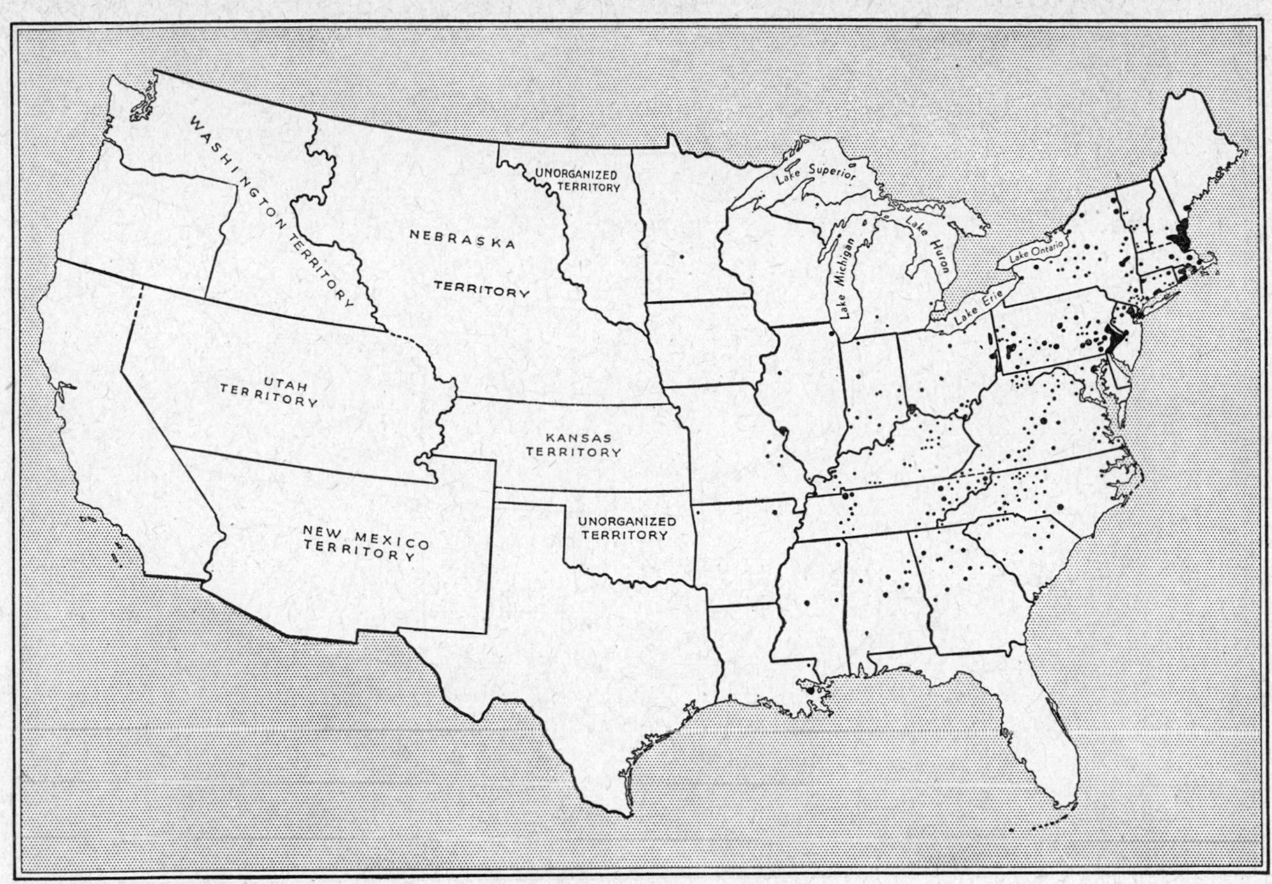

110 **Manufacturing Areas, 1860**

Based on iron, steel, and textiles, together with cities having more than 5,000 industrial employees

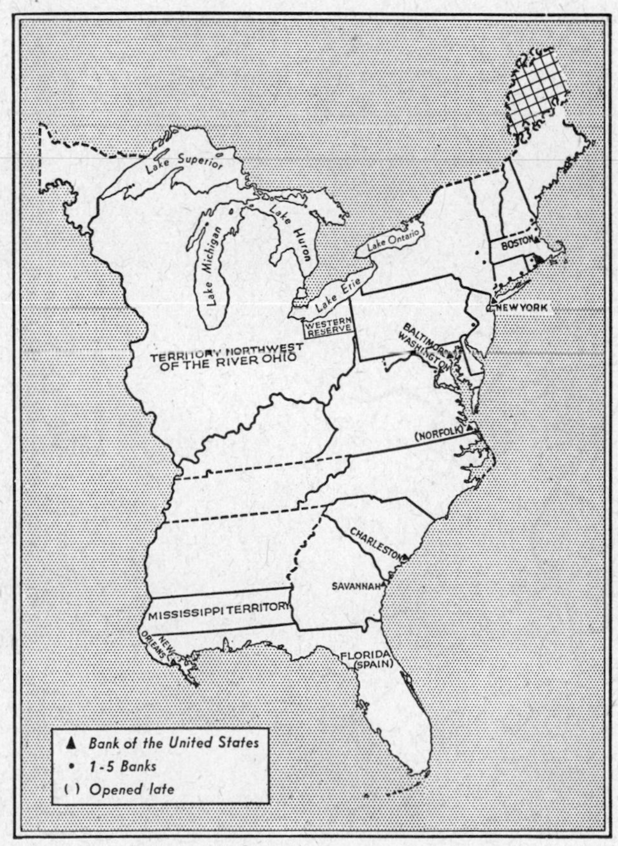

111 Banks of 1800, Including All Branches of the First Bank of the United States

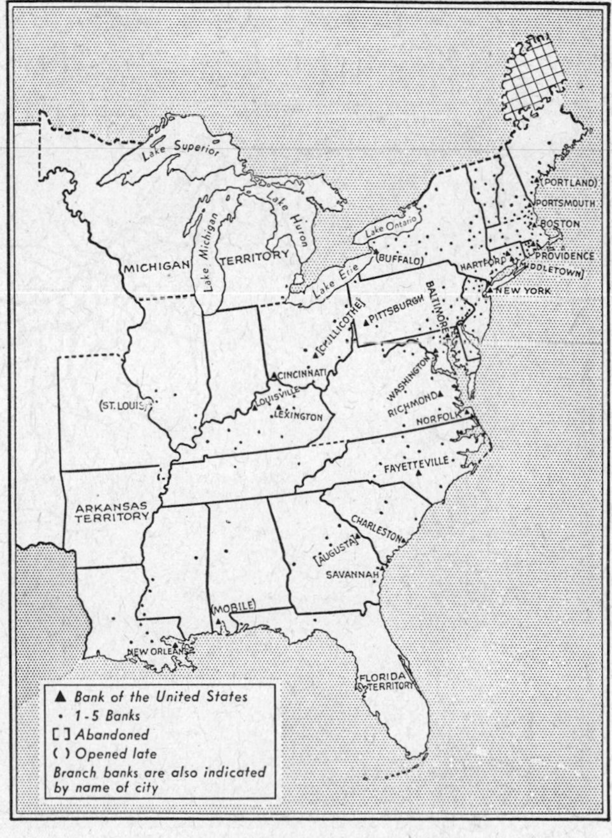

112 Banks of 1830, Including All Branches of the Second Bank of the United States

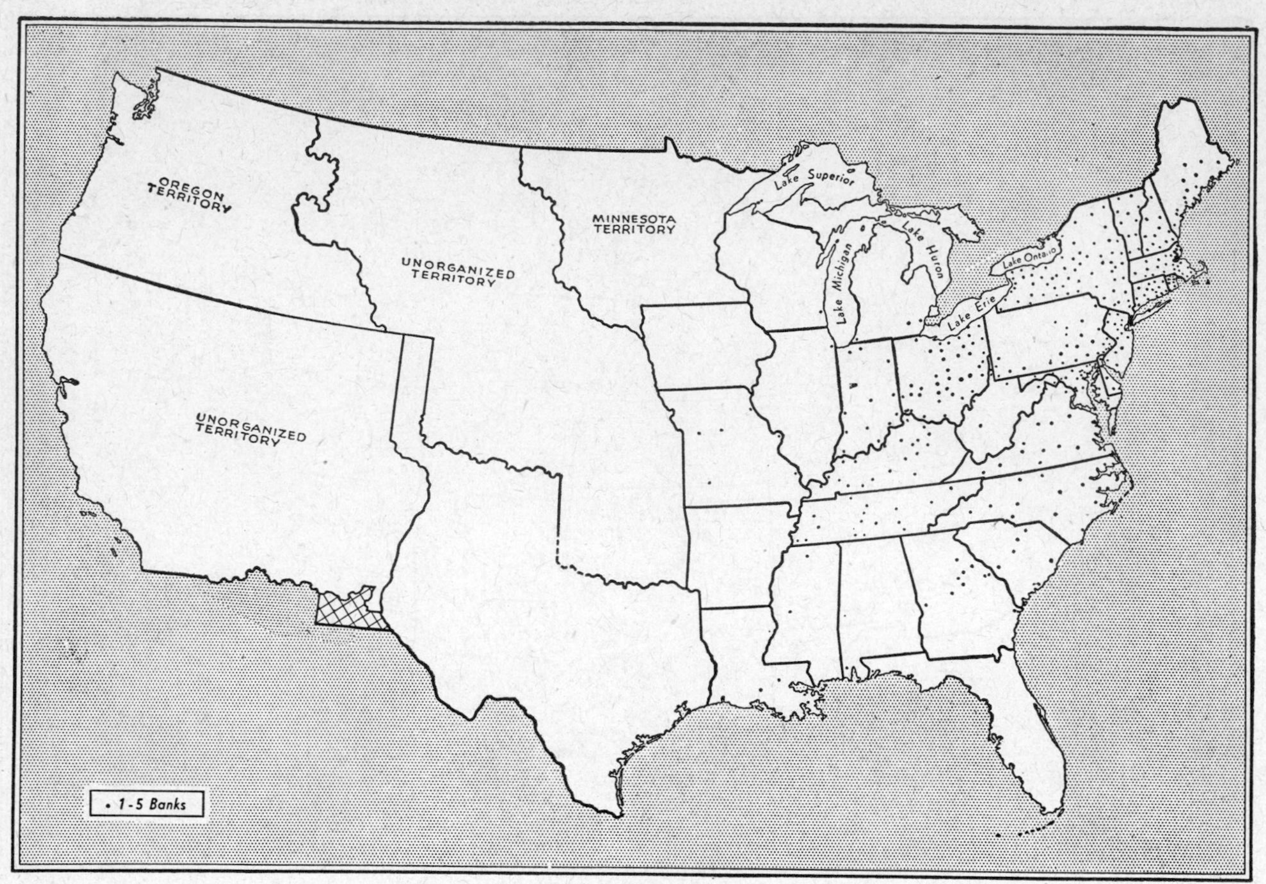

113 Banks of 1850

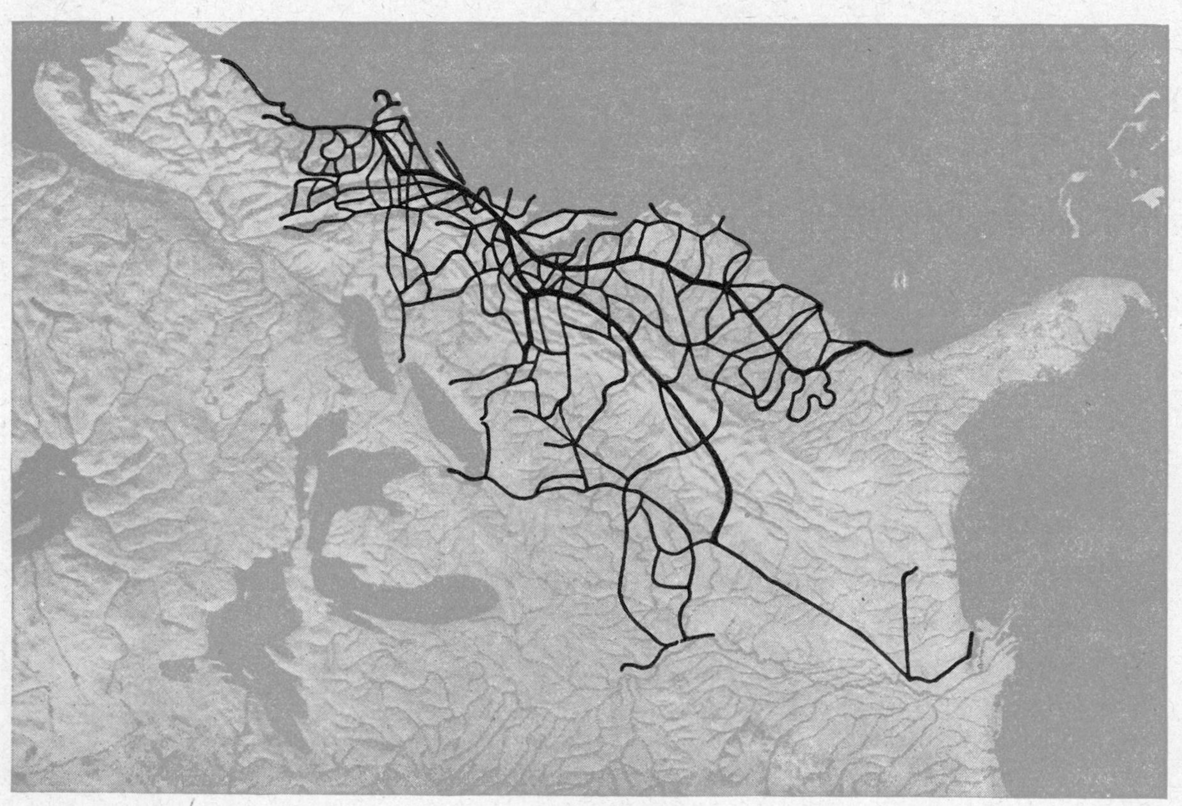

114 Main Post Roads, 1804
Heavier lines indicate routes most used

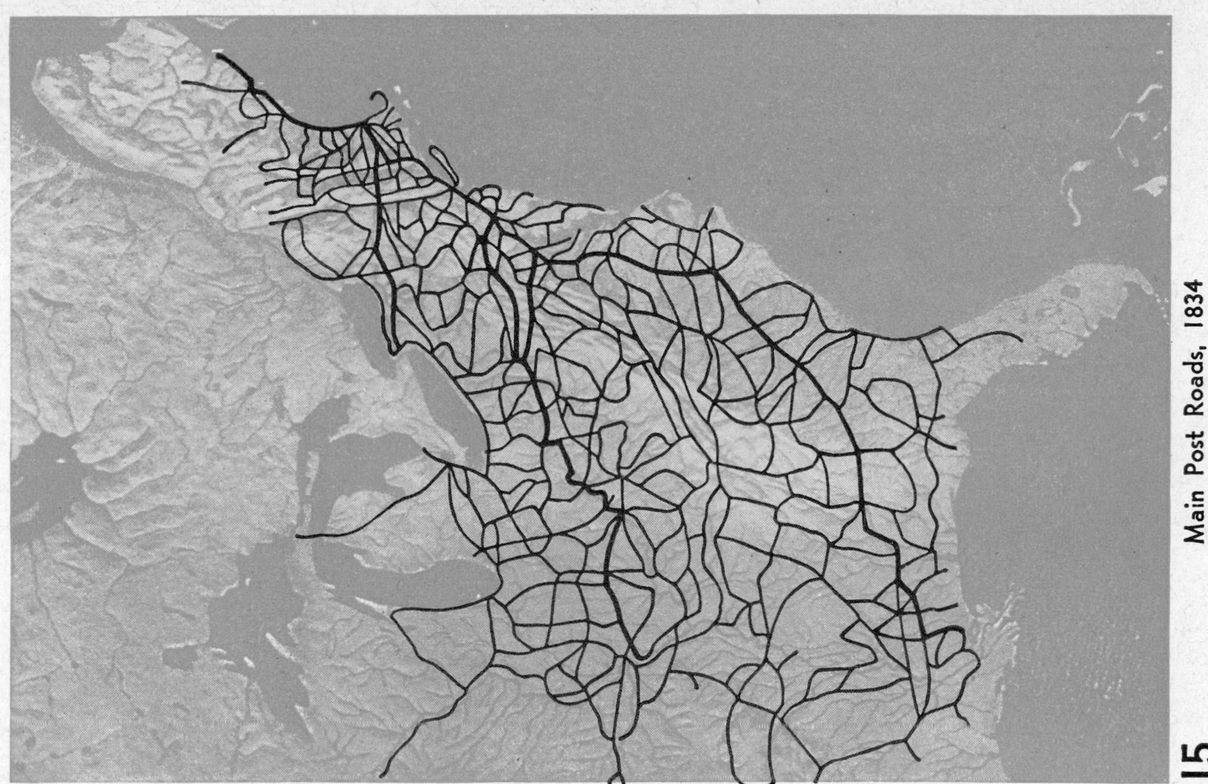

115 Main Post Roads, 1834
Heavier lines indicate routes most used

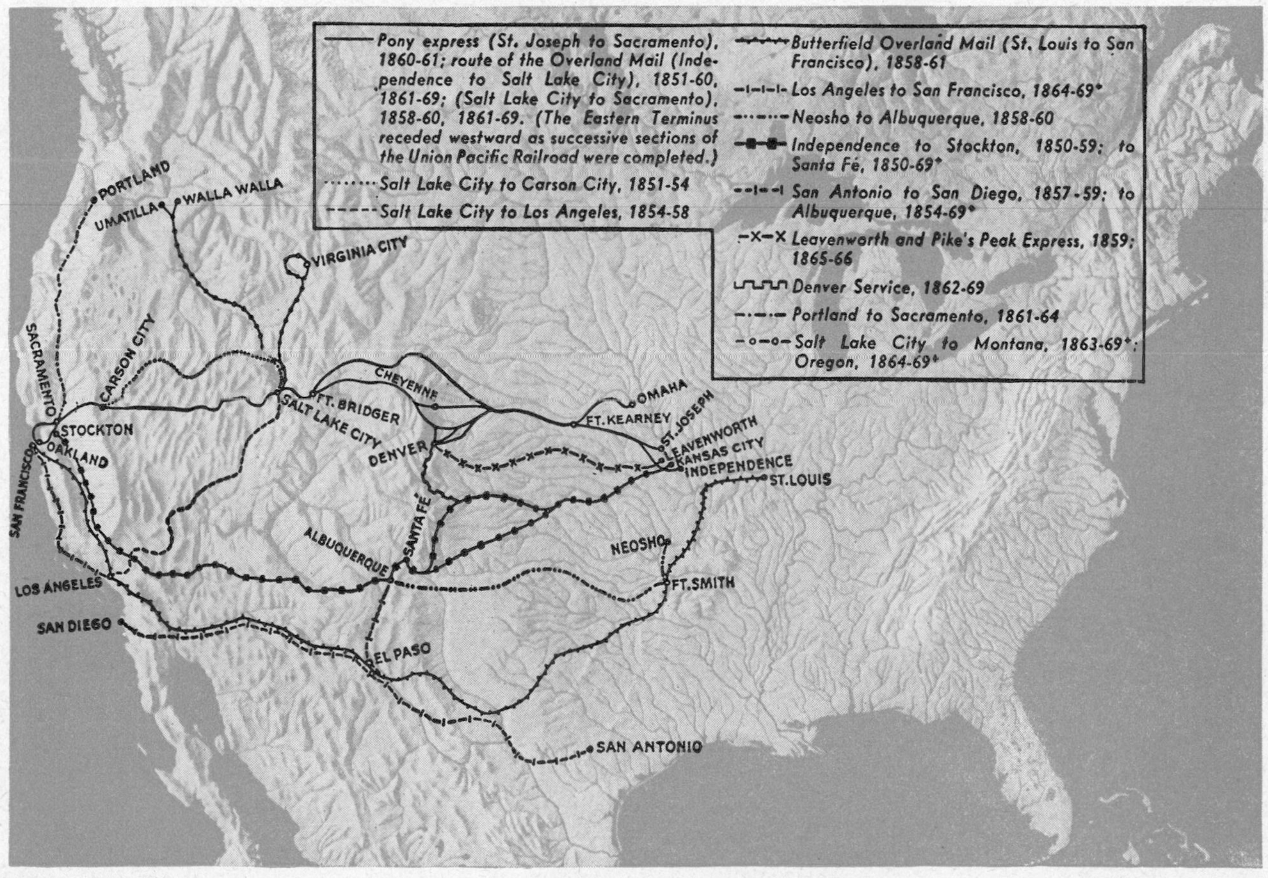

116 Routes of the Overland Mail and the Pony Express

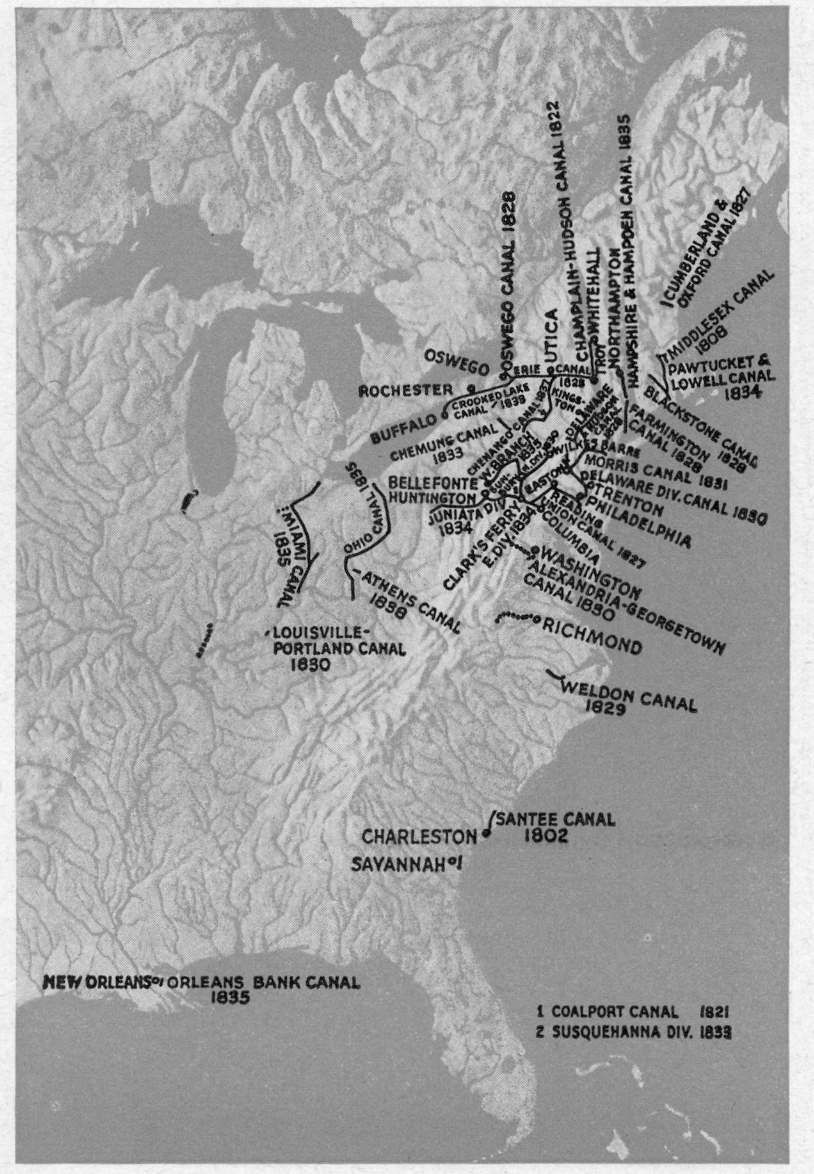

117 Canals to 1837

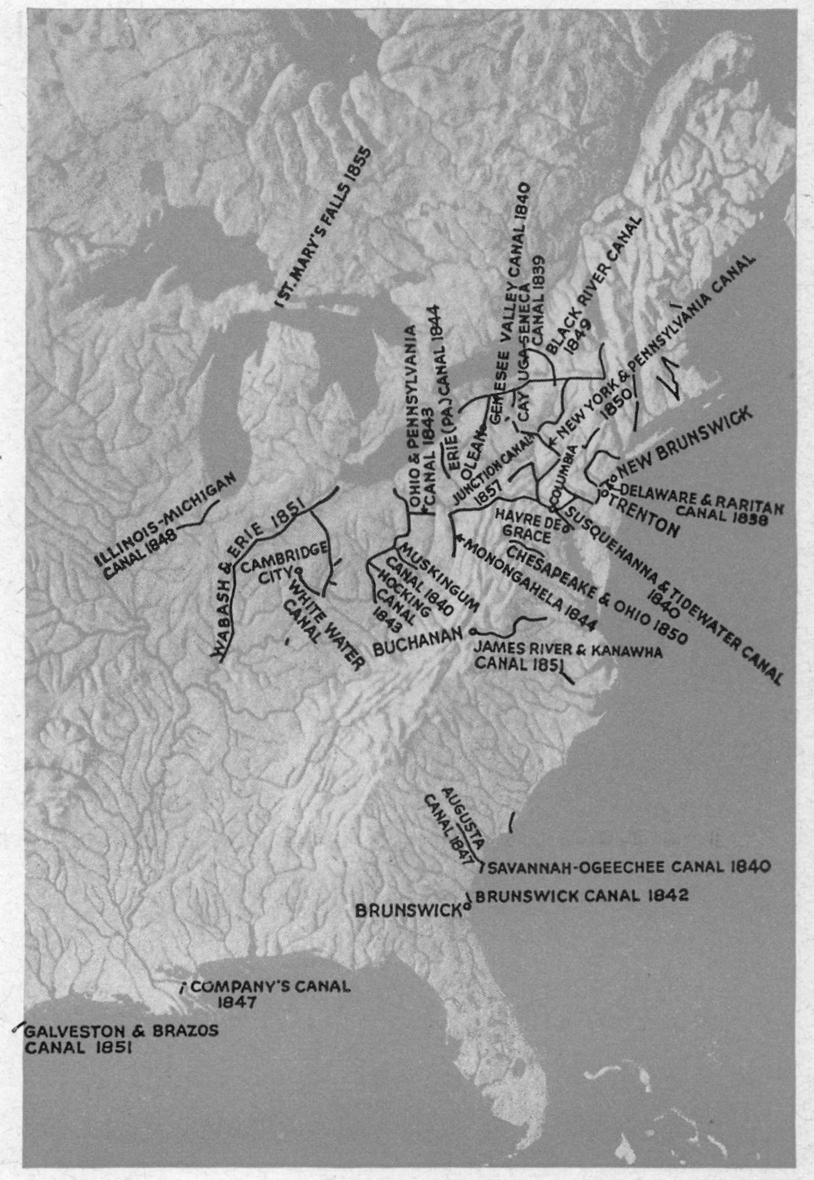

118 Canals, 1837-1860

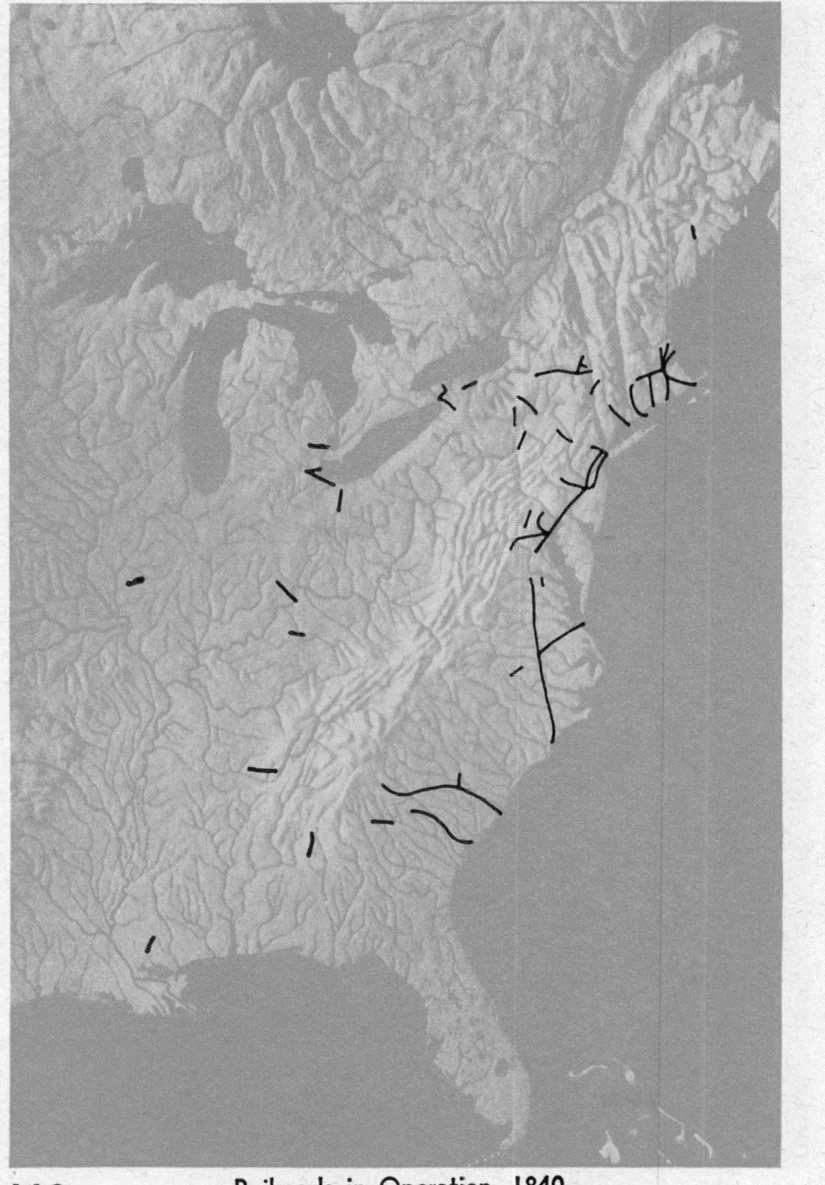

119 Railroads in Operation, 1840

For railroad mileage statistics, see Appendix V

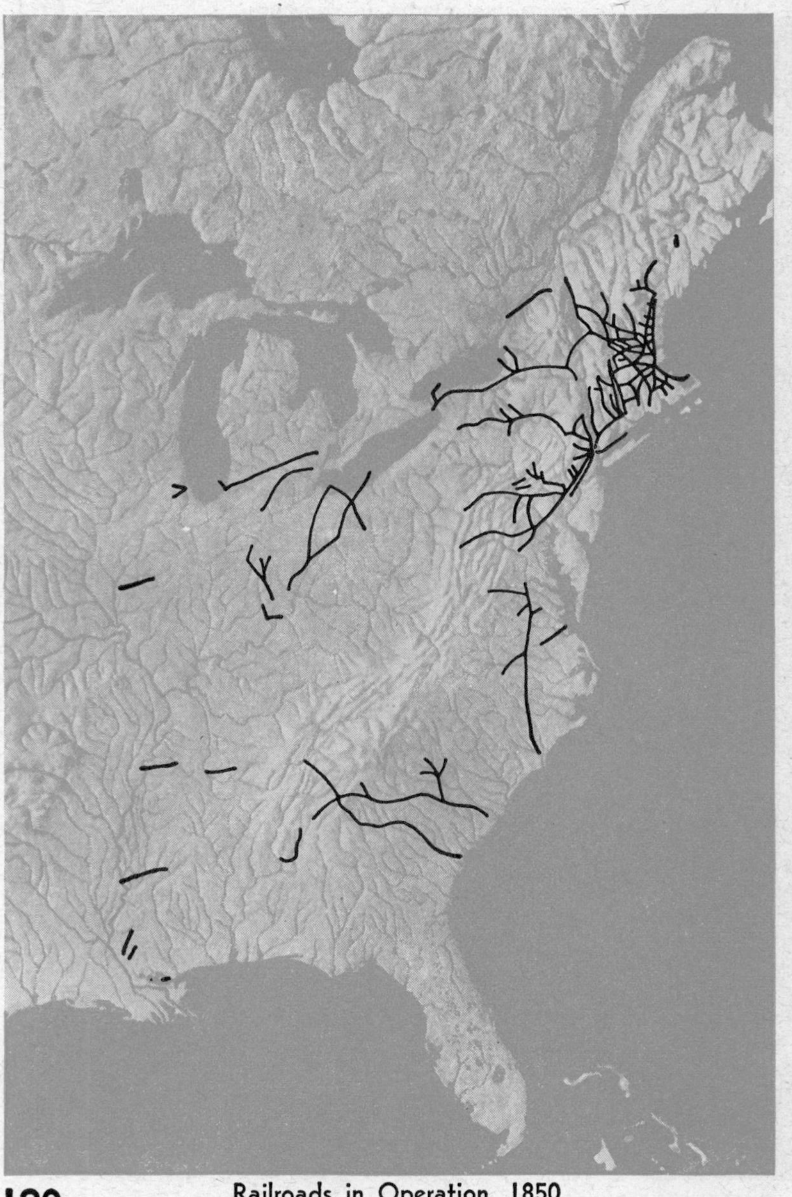

120 Railroads in Operation, 1850

For railroad mileage statistics, see Appendix V

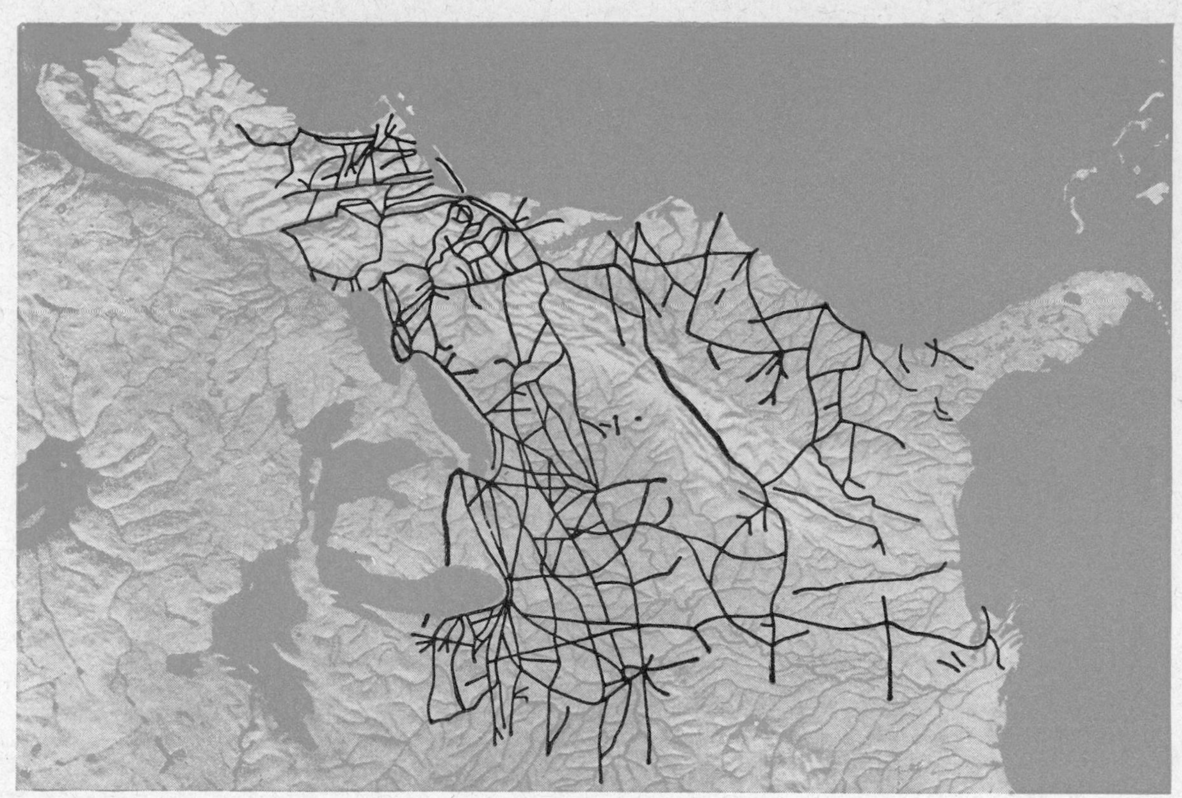

121 **Railroads in Operation, 1860**

For railroad mileage statistics, see Appendix V

122 **First Ten Years of the Telegraph, 1844-1854**

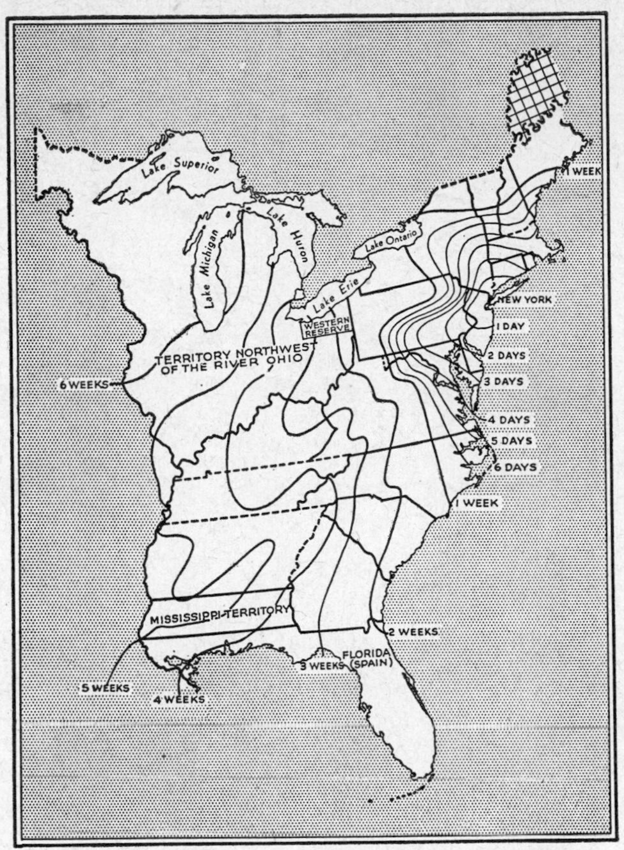

123 Rates of Travel from New York, 1800

124 Rates of Travel from New York, 1830

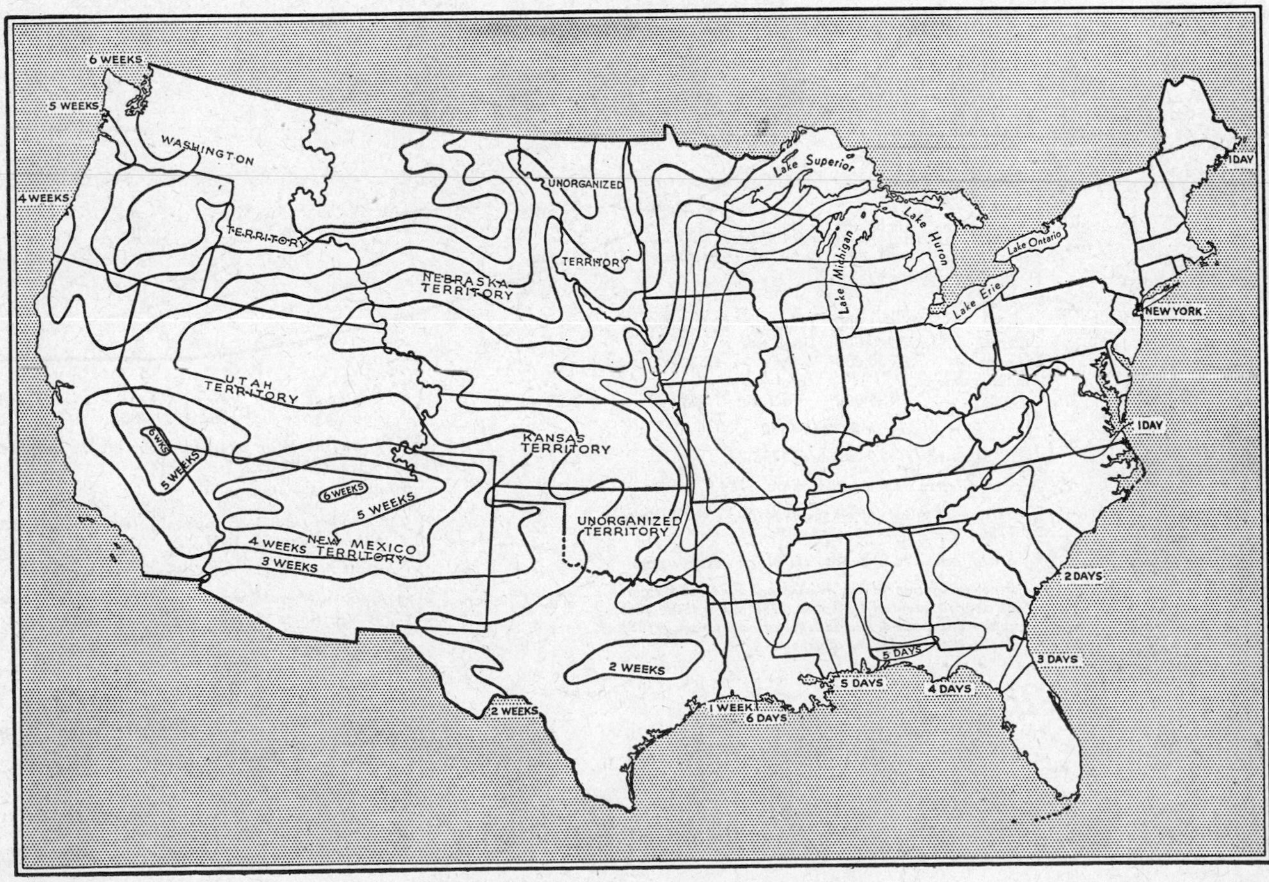

125 Rates of Travel from New York, 1860

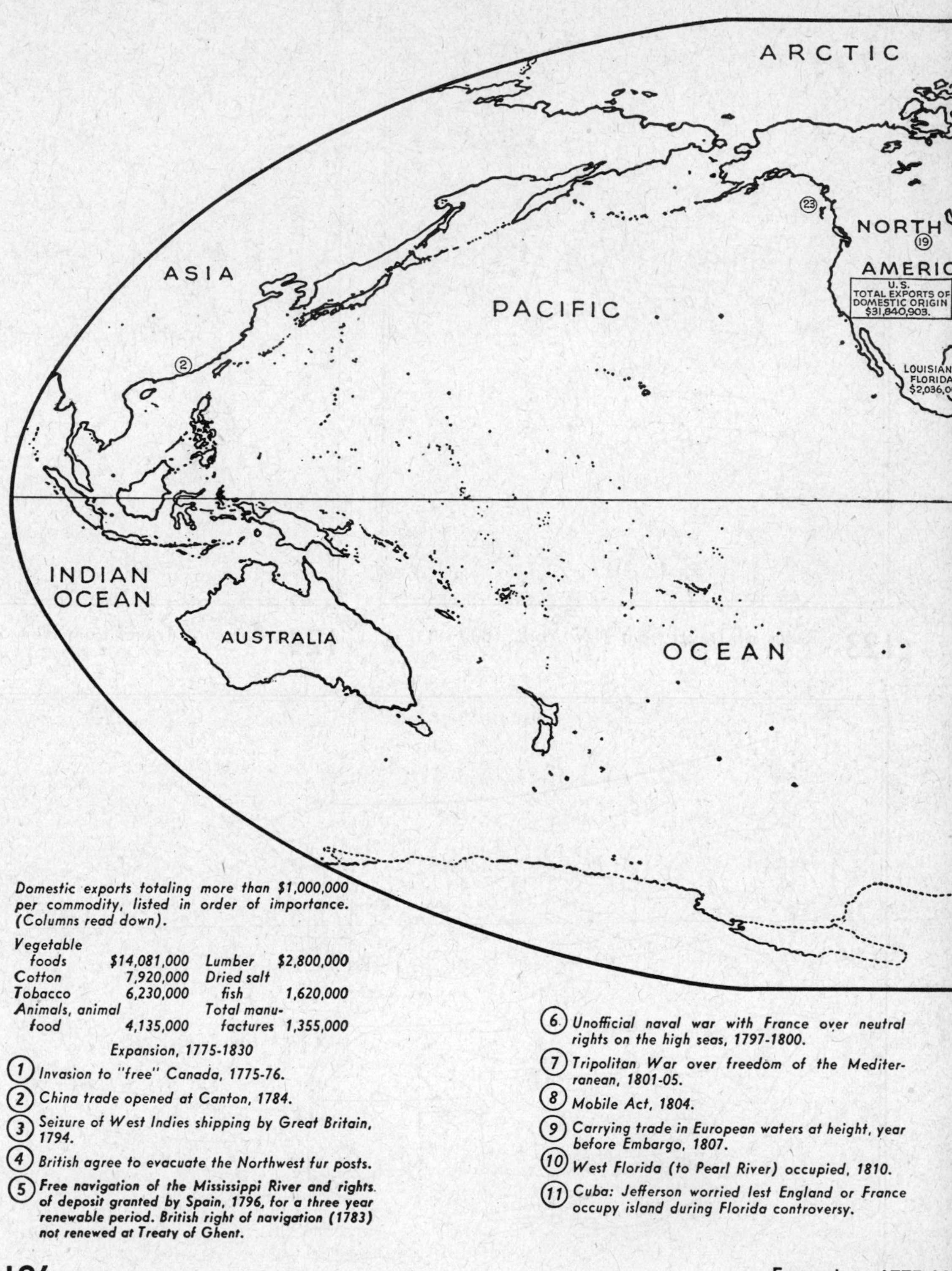

Domestic exports totaling more than $1,000,000 per commodity, listed in order of importance. (Columns read down).

Vegetable foods	*$14,081,000*	*Lumber*	*$2,800,000*
Cotton	*7,920,000*	*Dried salt fish*	*1,620,000*
Tobacco	*6,230,000*	*Total manufactures*	*1,355,000*
Animals, animal food	*4,135,000*		

Expansion, 1775-1830

1. *Invasion to "free" Canada, 1775-76.*
2. *China trade opened at Canton, 1784.*
3. *Seizure of West Indies shipping by Great Britain, 1794.*
4. *British agree to evacuate the Northwest fur posts.*
5. *Free navigation of the Mississippi River and rights of deposit granted by Spain, 1796, for a three year renewable period. British right of navigation (1783) not renewed at Treaty of Ghent.*
6. *Unofficial naval war with France over neutral rights on the high seas, 1797-1800.*
7. *Tripolitan War over freedom of the Mediterranean, 1801-05.*
8. *Mobile Act, 1804.*
9. *Carrying trade in European waters at height, year before Embargo, 1807.*
10. *West Florida (to Pearl River) occupied, 1810.*
11. *Cuba: Jefferson worried lest England or France occupy island during Florida controversy.*

126

Expansion, 1775-18
For further trade statist

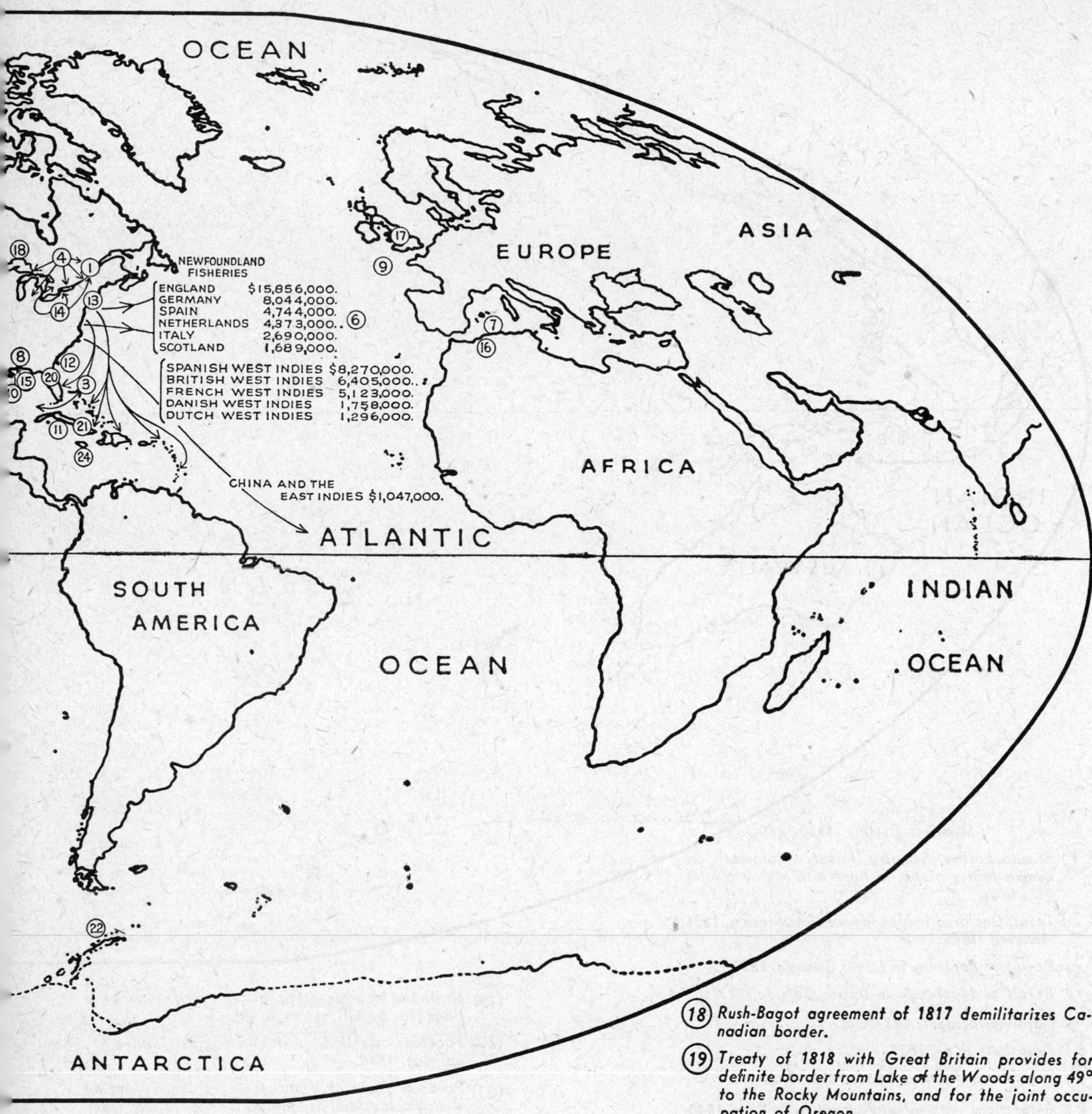

(12) *Amelia Island: seized from Spain, 1811.*

(13) *Tariff walls raised to semi-protectionist levels for first time, 1812.*

(14) *Canadian invasions, 1812-13.*

(15) *West Florida (Pearl River to Perdido River), occupied 1813.*

(16) *Decatur Expedition and Barbary pirates, 1815.*

(17) *Reciprocal trade relations established with England by commercial convention of 1815, replacing annual grant of restricted trade privileges extended to American bottoms since 1783.*

(18) *Rush-Bagot agreement of 1817 demilitarizes Canadian border.*

(19) *Treaty of 1818 with Great Britain provides for definite border from Lake of the Woods along 49° to the Rocky Mountains, and for the joint occupation of Oregon.*

(20) *East Florida purchased from Spain, 1821: U. S. claims to Texas surrendered.*

(21) *Secretary Adams rejects Canning proposal for joint British-American renunciation of territorial interests in Latin-America (Cuba).*

(22) *Nathaniel Palmer, American whaler, discovers Antarctica, 1821.*

(23) *Russian extension of Alaskan claims in Ukase of 1821 helps produce Monroe Doctrine.*

(24) *Commercial Treaty of 1830 opens West Indies and Canadian trade to U. S. ships without major restrictions.*

Base Map by Permission of Denoyer-Geppert Company, Chicago

ports, 1800

e Appendix IV

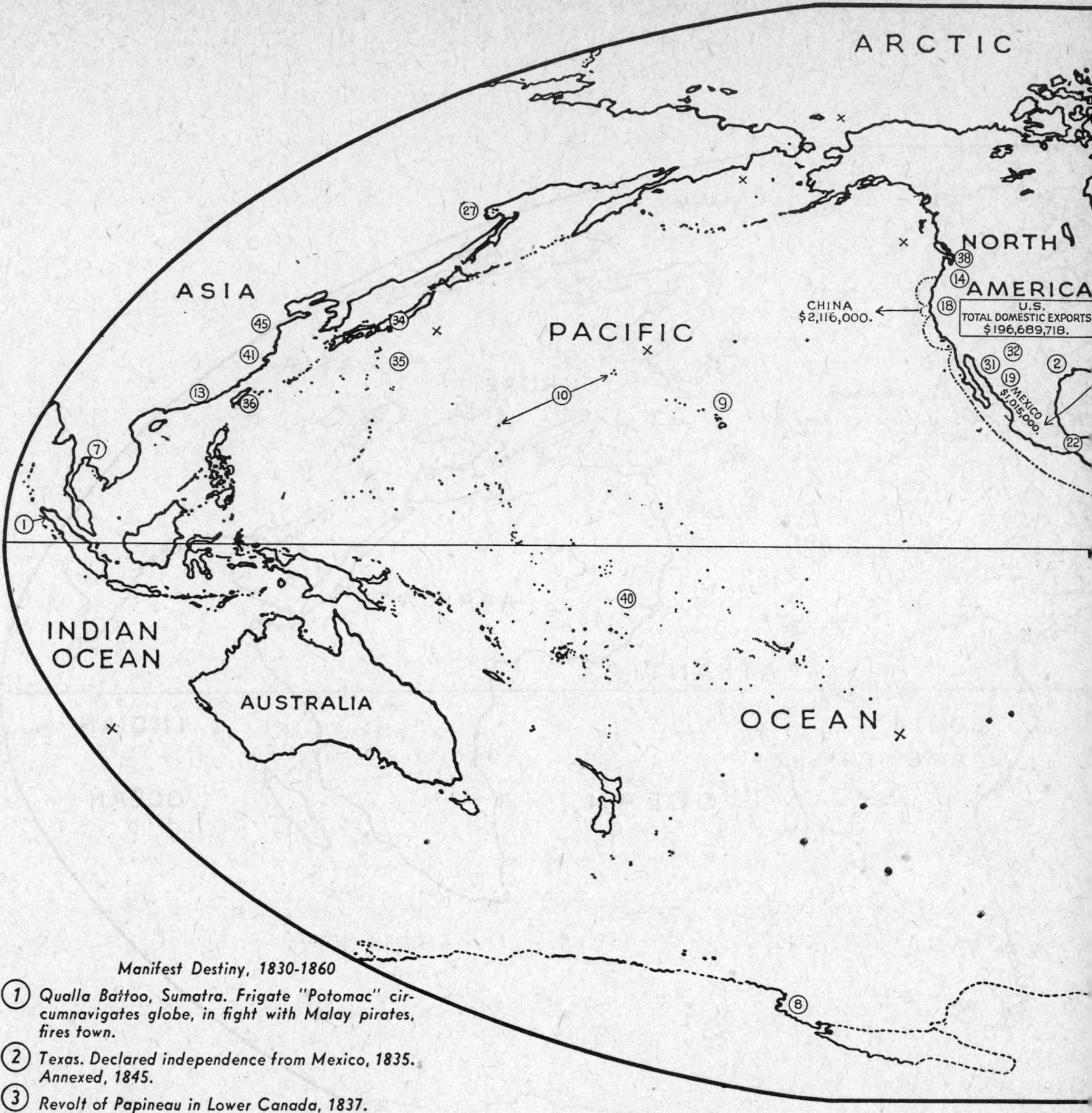

Manifest Destiny, 1830-1860

(1) Qualla Battoo, Sumatra. Frigate "Potomac" circumnavigates globe, in fight with Malay pirates, fires town.

(2) Texas. Declared independence from Mexico, 1835. Annexed, 1845.

(3) Revolt of Papineau in Lower Canada, 1837.

(4) Revolt of Mackenzie in Upper Canada, 1837.

(5) Caroline Incident, 1837.

(6) Aroostook War, 1837.

(7) Siam: trade treaties, 1836, 1856.

(8) Antarctica: segment discovered by Wilkes, 1840.

(9) Hawaii. Practical protectorate announced, 1843. Kamehameha offers formal protectorate, 1849; 1852 treaty of annexation not ratified. Important base for Oriental trade and North Pacific whaling fleets.

(10) Wake Island: claimed by Lt. Wilkes, 1841; Midway Island discovered by Capt. N. C. Brooks, 1859.

(11) Santo Domingo offers self as protectorate, 1844. American speculators active in the 1850's.

(12) Greytown, Nicaragua: British seizure produces Polk Corollary to the Monroe Doctrine, 1848.

(13) Wanghia: treaty with China opens additional ports to U. S. trade, 1844.

(14) Oregon: border controversy with Great Britain settled, 1846.

(15) Repeal of British Corn Laws ends Empire preference for Canadian grains, leads to unrest and to Reciprocity Treaty of 1854-64.

(16) New Granada: 1846 treaty provides for transit rights in Panama.

(17) **Hise treaties with Nicaragua and Honduras, 1848.**

(18) **War with Mexico: annexation of New Mexico, Utah and Upper California, 1848.**

(19) Northern Mexico: proposals for further annexations (for details, see map 98).

(20) Yucatan: asks U. S. protection against native uprising, 1848.

(21) Panama: scene of ventures of William F. Aspinwall; Pacific Mail Steamship Co. opens line from Panama City to California, 1848; Panama Railroad completed, 1855.

(22) Isthmus of Tehuantepec: negotiations for transit rights, 1849, 1851; secured by Gadsden Treaty, 1854; used by U. S. mails, 1859.

(23) Cuba: Polk offers $100,000,000, 1848; Lopez filibustering expeditions, 1850, 1851; renunciation of territorial ambitions in Cuba rejected by U. S., 1852; "Black Warrior" incident, Ostend Manifesto, Quitman expedition, 1854; Buchanan proposes purchase, 1858; Ridley expedition, 1858.

(24) Tigre Island, Gulf of Fonseca: U. S. flag raised abortively, 1849, to thwart British plans.

(25) Hungary: liberal revolts there and elsewhere, 1848-49; U. S. sentiment expressed in Hulsemann note to Austria and in receptions here to Kossuth.

(26) Chincha Islands: negotiations with Peru, 1850, over guano deposits.

(27) Amur River: P. D. Collins plans American steamship line and trading posts.

(28) Capital export begins to Canadian banks and mines, Mexican railroads and banks.

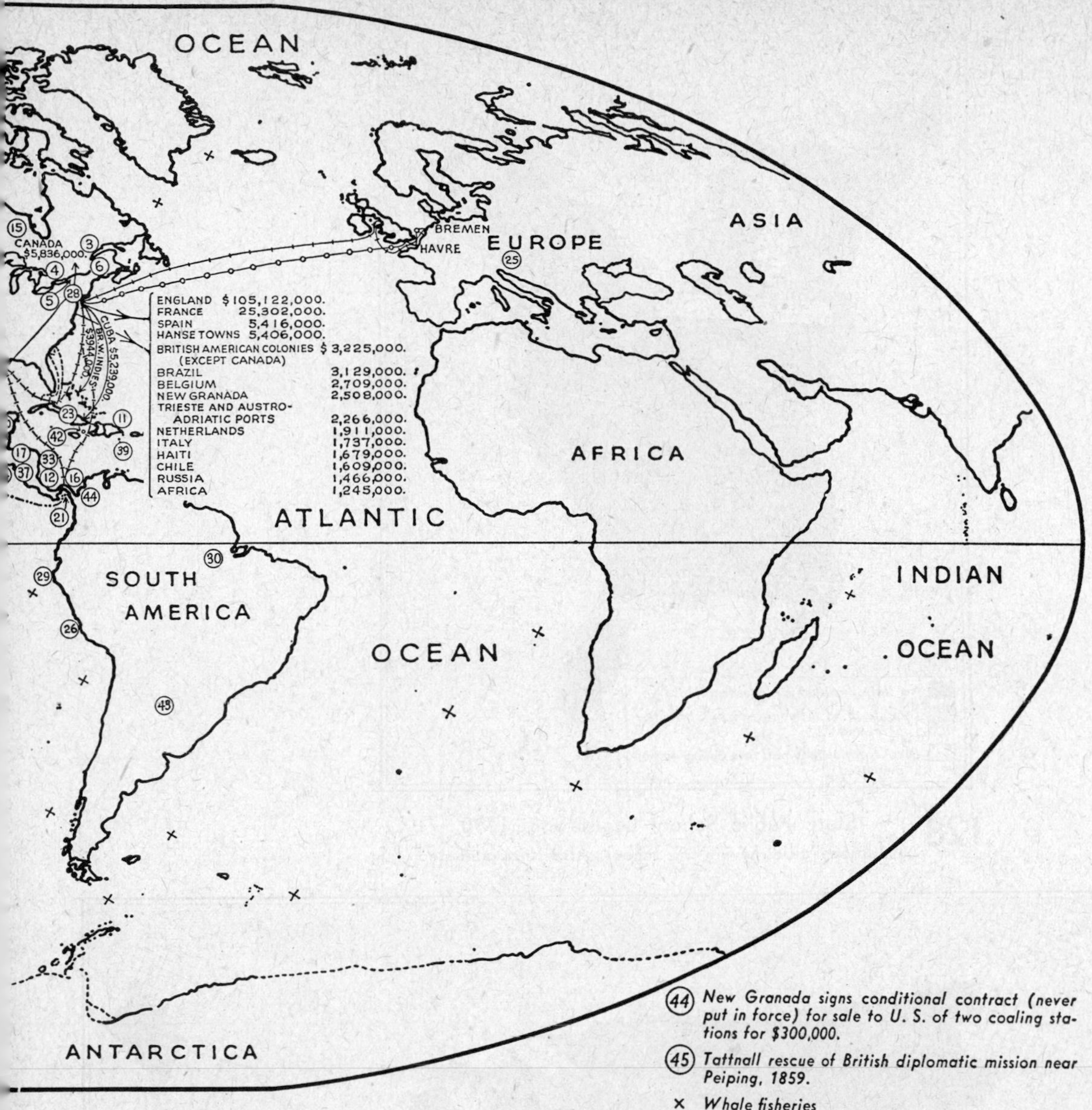

(29) *Lobos Islands: diplomatic exchange with Peru over guano rights, 1852.*

(30) *Maury explorations of the Amazon, 1852-53; regarded as prelude to control.*

(31) *William Walker invades Sonora; established rebel government, 1853.*

(32) *Two more filibustering expeditions into Mexico, Gadsden Purchase, 1854.*

(33) *Greytown: bombarded by American warship in support of Transit Company, 1854.*

(34) *Kanagawa: treaty negotiated by Perry, opening Japanese trade to U. S., 1853-54.*

(35) *Bonin Islands: claimed by Perry, 1853; claimed by Japan, 1861.*

(36) *Formosa: seizure recommended by Perry, 1854; flag abortively raised.*

(37) *William Walker filibusters in Nicaragua, 1855, 1857.*

(38) *Juan de Fuca: U. S. seizes island disputed with England, 1855.*

(39) *Alta Vela, giving rise to the Guano Act of 1856: basis of claims to guano islands thereafter.*

(40) ***Swains Island occupied by Jennings family.***

(41) ***Tsinan forts, Shanghai, bombarded, 1857.***

(42) ***Navassa: guano island claimed, 1858.***

(43) ***Paraguay: punitive naval expedition avenges 1856 attack on "Water Witch," 1859.***

(44) *New Granada signs conditional contract (never put in force) for sale to U. S. of two coaling stations for $300,000.*

(45) *Tattnall rescue of British diplomatic mission near Peiping, 1859.*

× *Whale fisheries*

Subsidized Steamship Lines

—o—o—o— ***Ocean Steam Navigation Company***

—+—+—+— ***Collins Line***

—I—I—I— ***New York to Chagres***

—··—··— ***Pacific Mail Line***

— — — -·- ***Charleston-Havana***

Foreign Trade — 1851

Domestic Exports Totaling More than $1,000,000 per Commodity, Listed in Order of Importance (Columns Read Down):

Cotton	*$112,315,000*	*Iron manufactures*	*$1,876,000*
Gold and silver coin	*18,070,000*	*Indian corn*	*1,763,000*
Flour	*10,524,000*	*Beef, tallow, hides*	*1,690,000*
Tobacco	*9,219,000*	*Wearing apparel*	*1,212,000*
Cotton piece goods	*7,241,000*	*Snuff and tobacco manufactures*	*1,144,000*
Pork, bacon, lard	*4,368,000*	*Butter and cheese*	*1,125,000*
Staves, shingles, boards	*2,349,000*	*Naval stores*	*1,064,000*
Rice	*2,171,000*	*Spermaceti oil*	*1,045,000*
Wood manufactures	*2,076,000*	*Wheat*	*1,026,000*

Base Map by Permission of Denoyer-Geppert Company, Chicago

stiny, 1830-1860; Exports, 1850

Appendix IV

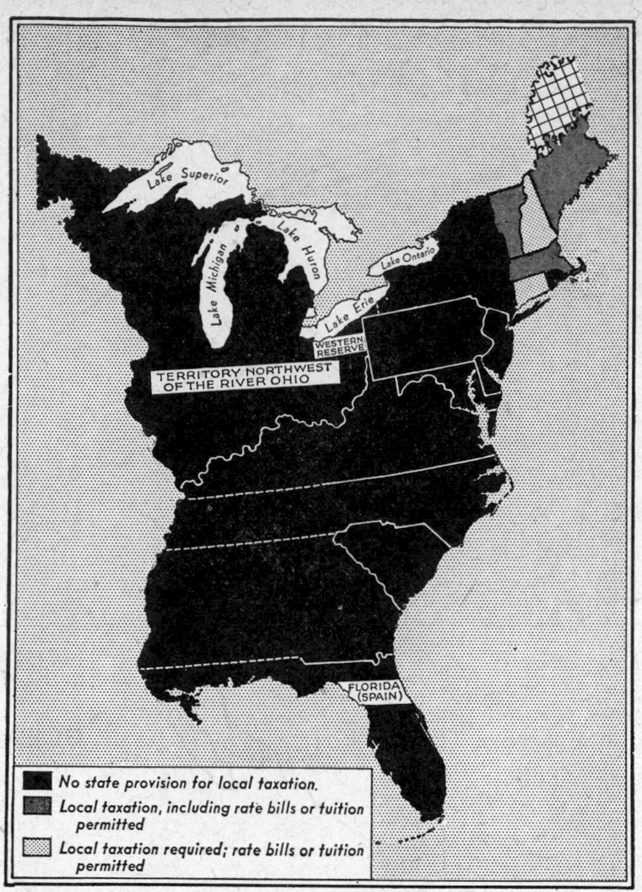

128 State Public School Legislation, 1790

Additional cities having free school systems not indicated

OREGON COUNTRY

Lake Superior

Lake Michigan

Lake Huron

Lake Ontario

Lake Erie

MICHIGAN TERRITORY

MISSOURI TERRITORY

ARKANSAS TERRITORY

FLORIDA (SPAIN)

No state provision for local taxation.

No state provision for local taxation, but state aid for education of the poor

Local taxation, including rate bills or tuition permitted

Local taxation required; rate bills or tuition permitted

1. State aid to free schools but preference given poor children

2. To be used for the education of the poor

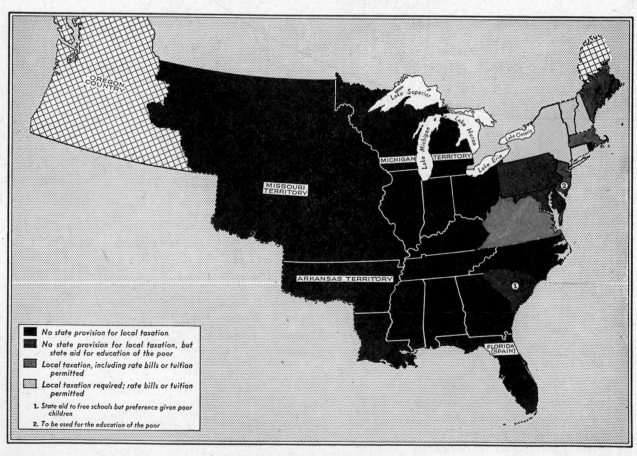

129 State Public School Legislation, 1820

Additional cities having free school systems not indicated

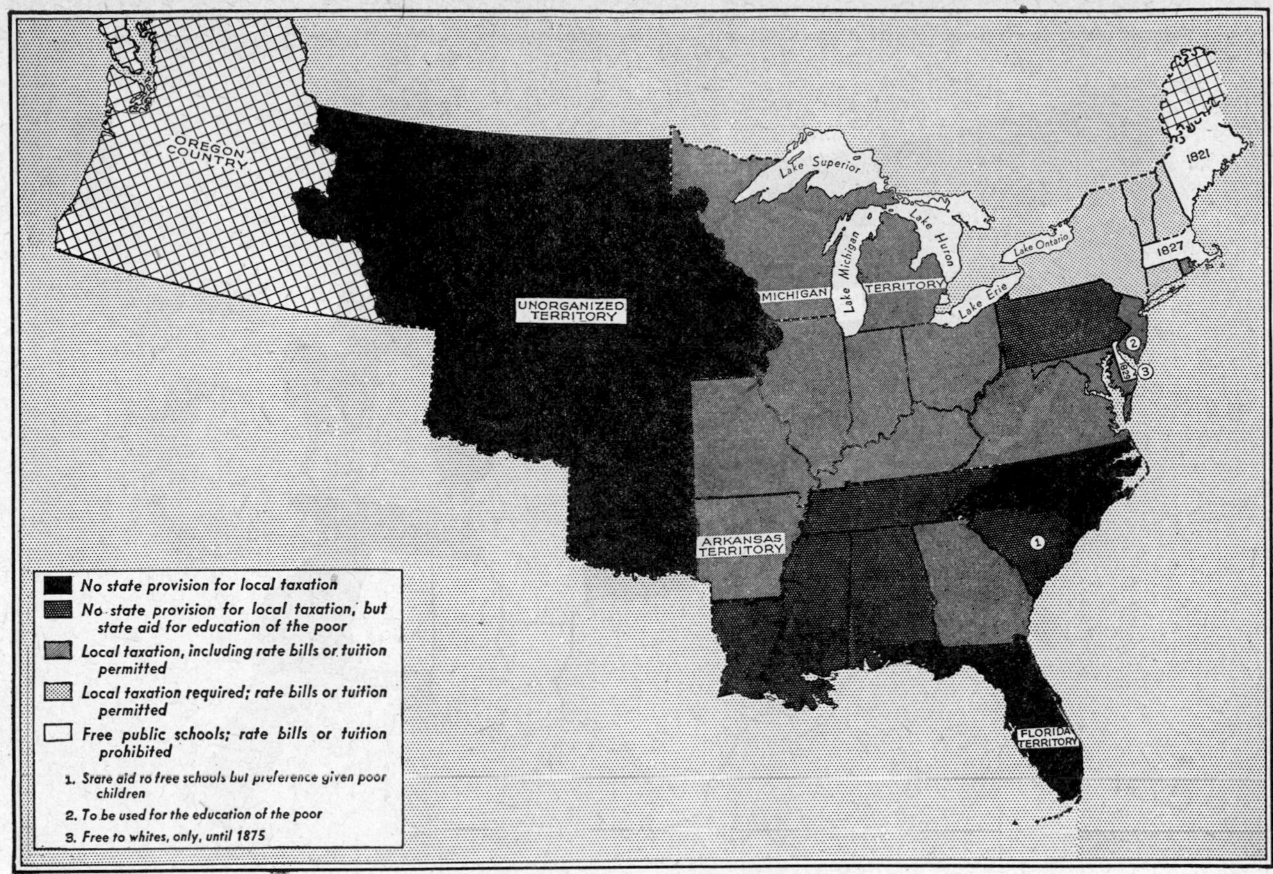

130

State Public School Legislation, 1830

Additional cities having free school systems not indicated

WASHINGTON TERRITORY 1854
OREGON TERRITORY 4
NEBRASKA TERRITORY
MINNESOTA TERRITORY 1851
UTAH TERRITORY
KANSAS TERRITORY
NEW MEXICO TERRITORY
UNORGANIZED TERRITORY
Lake Superior
Lake Michigan
Lake Huron
Lake Ontario
Lake Erie
1852
1851
1854
1853
1851
1852 3
1
2

No state provision for local taxation
No state provision for local taxation, but state aid for education of the poor
Local taxation, including rate bills or tuition permitted
Local taxation required; rate bills or tuition permitted
Free public schools; rate bills or tuition prohibited
1. State aid to free schools but preference given poor children
2. Free to whites, only, until 1875
3. Free to whites, only, until 1872
4. Had territorial school tax which yielded insufficient funds; no-permission law for local taxation

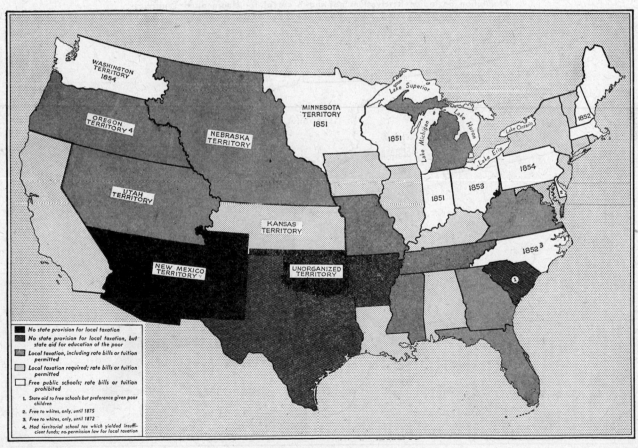

131

State Public School Legislation, 1855

Additional cities having free school systems not indicated

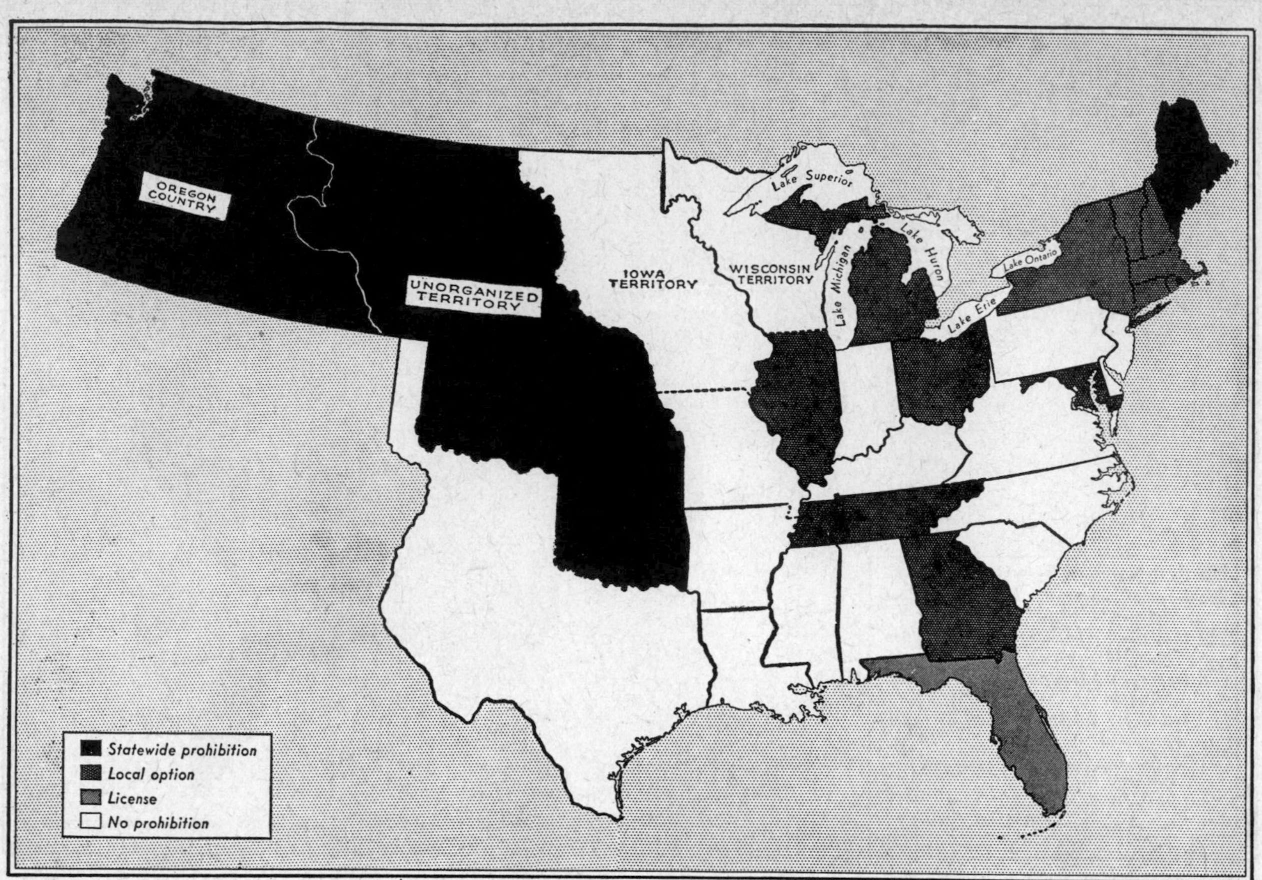

132 **Prohibition, 1846**

Prohibition on Indian Reservations not shown except for Unorganized Territories

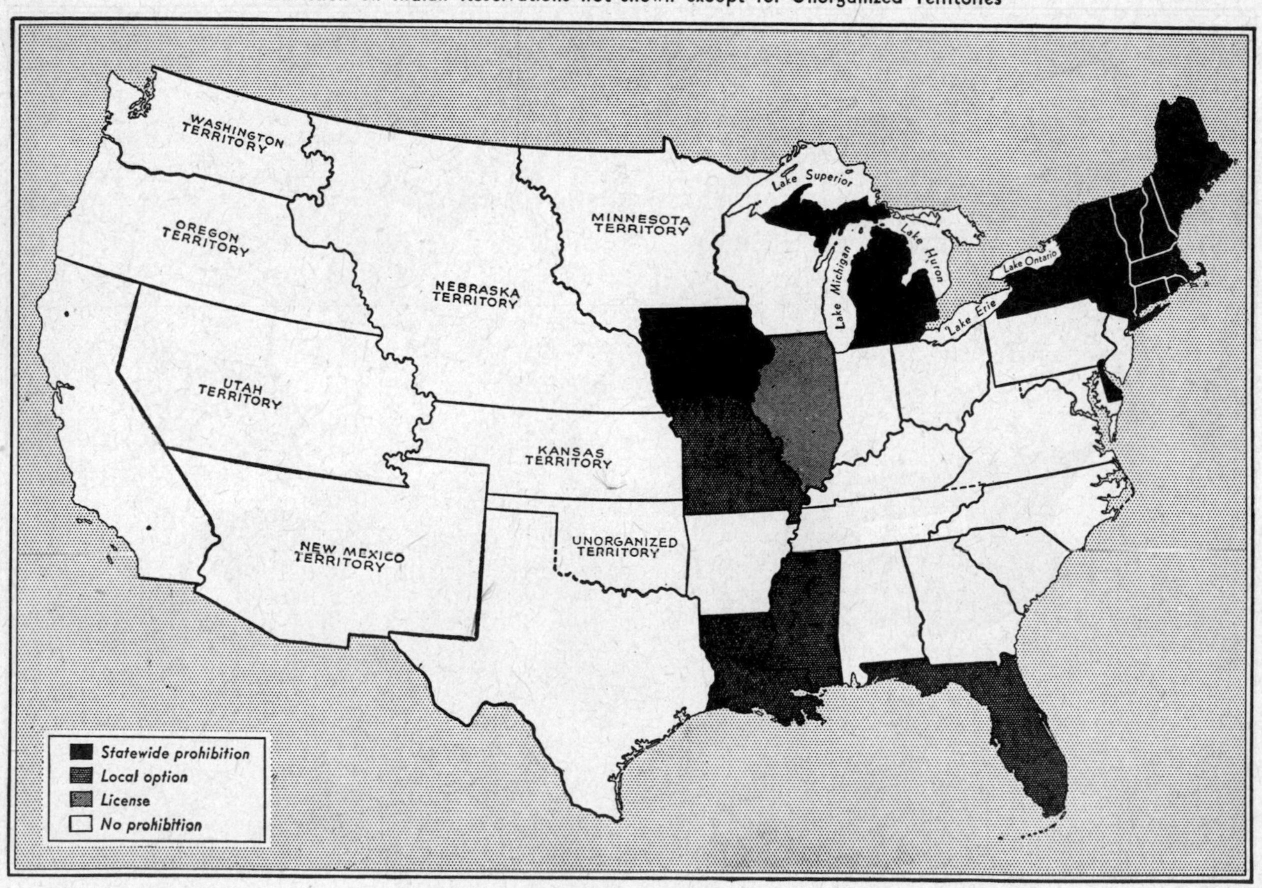

133 **Prohibition, 1856**

Prohibition on Indian Reservations not shown

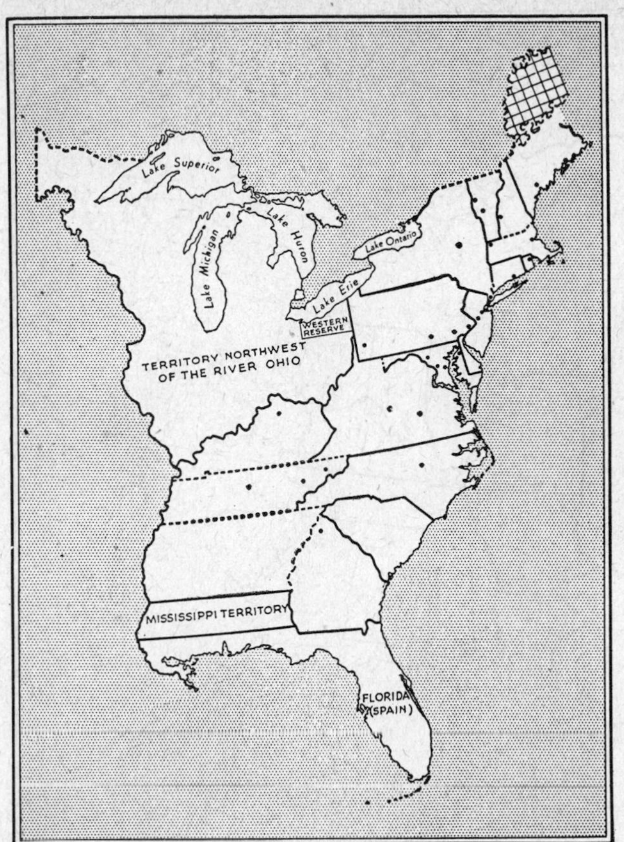

134 Colleges, 1800
Each dot represents one men's college

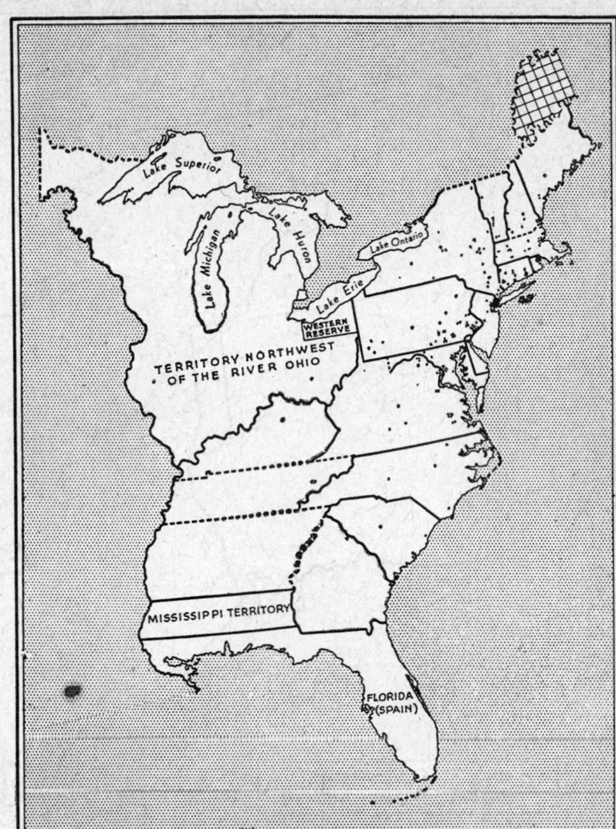

135 Newspapers, 1800
Each dot represents one paper

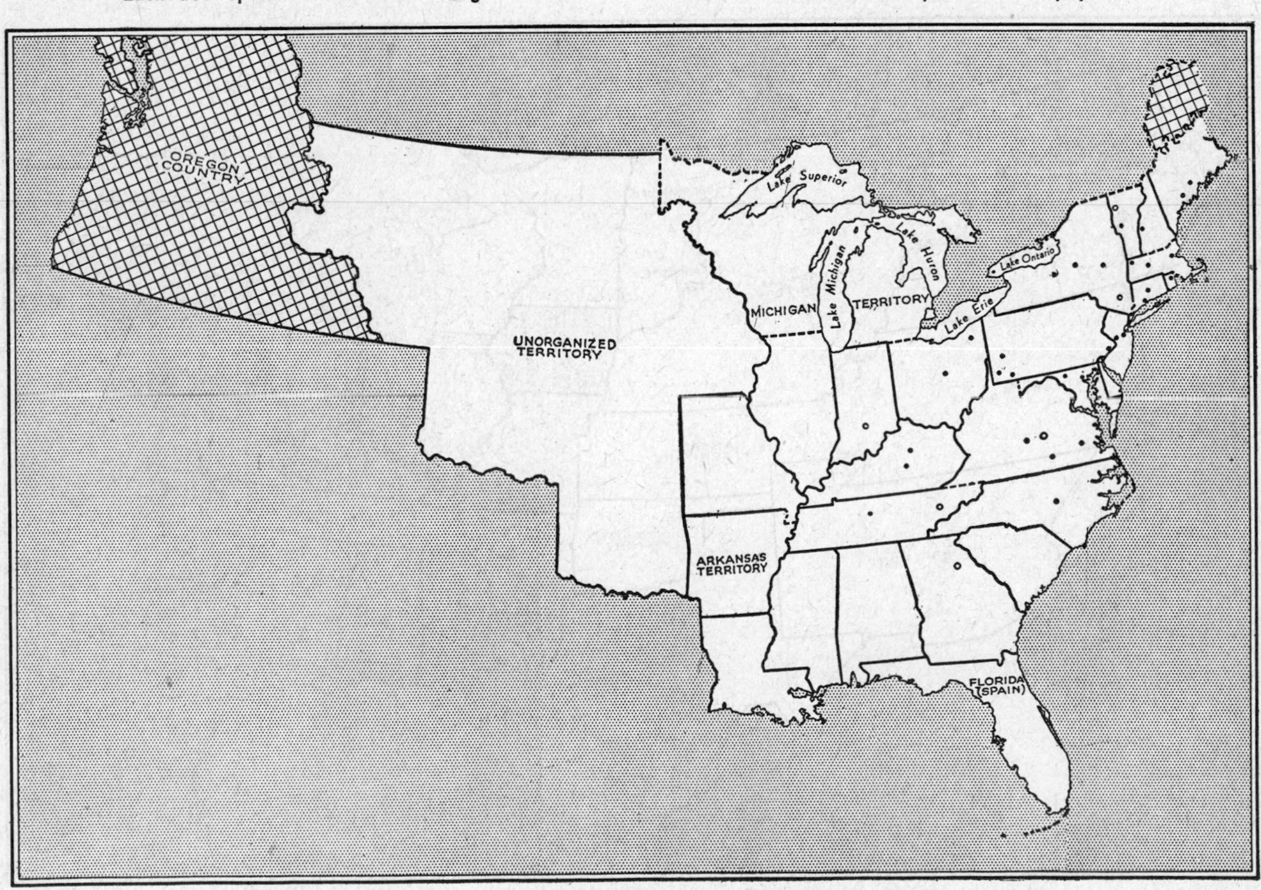

136 Universities, Colleges, and Other Institutions of Higher Learning, 1830
Each dot represents one men's college; each circle represents one public institution

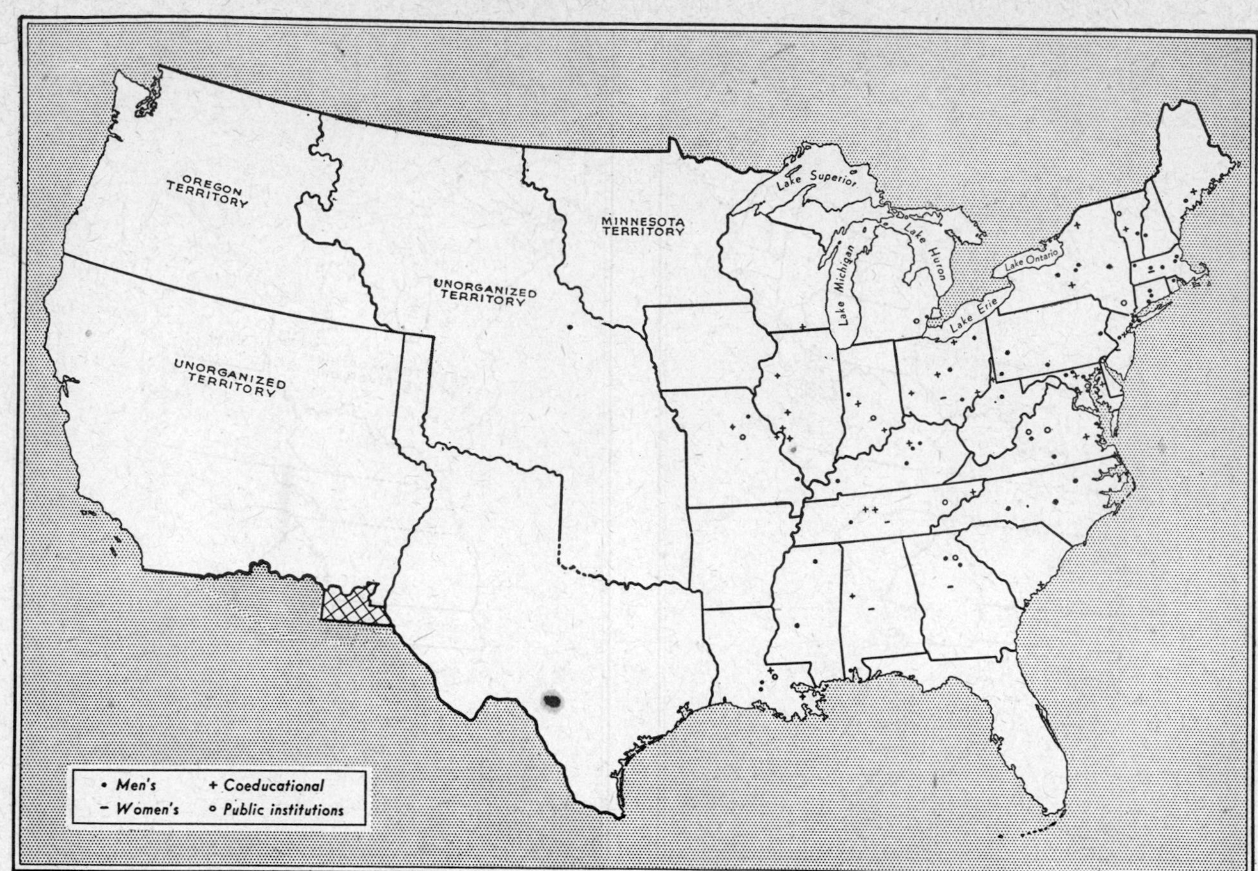

137 Colleges, 1850

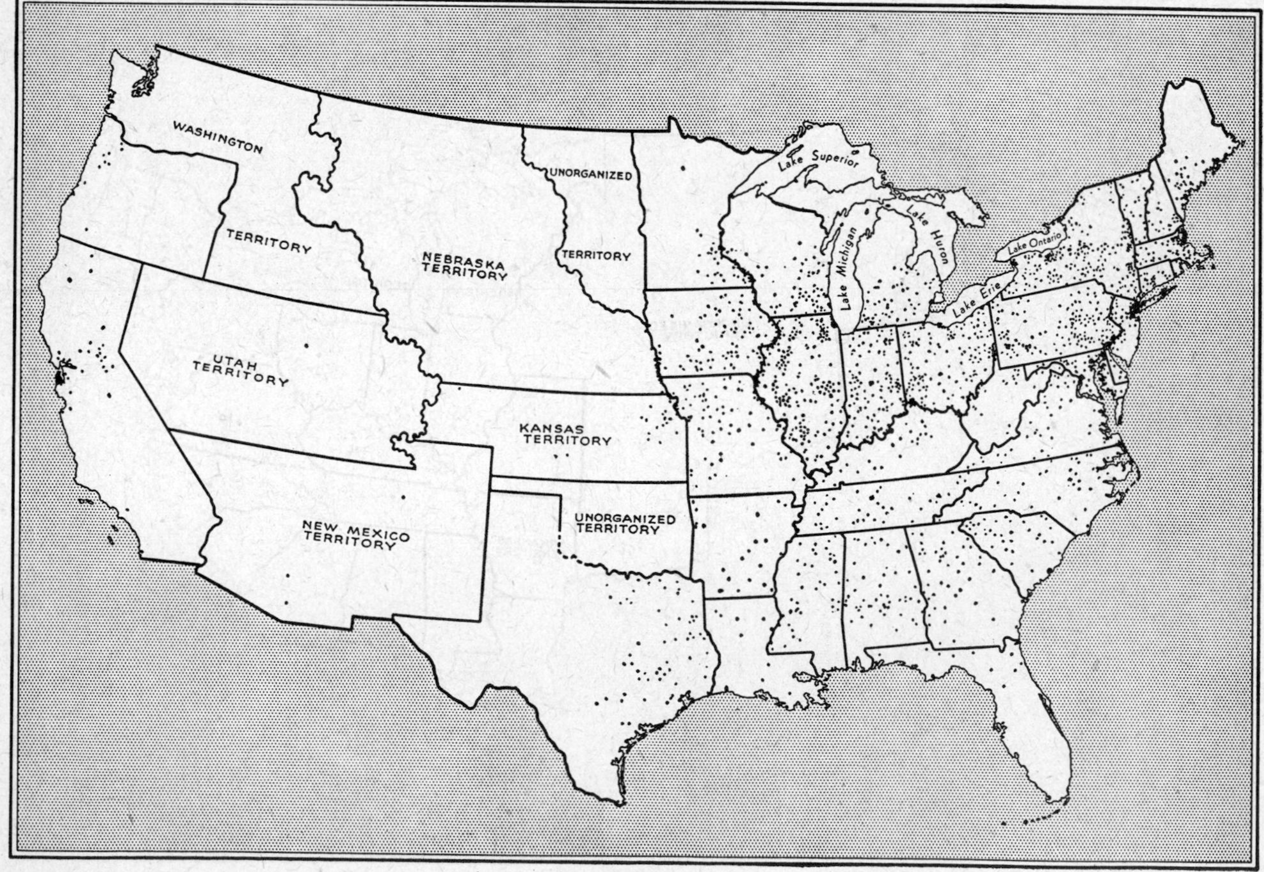

138 Newspapers, 1860
Each dot represents 1-5 papers

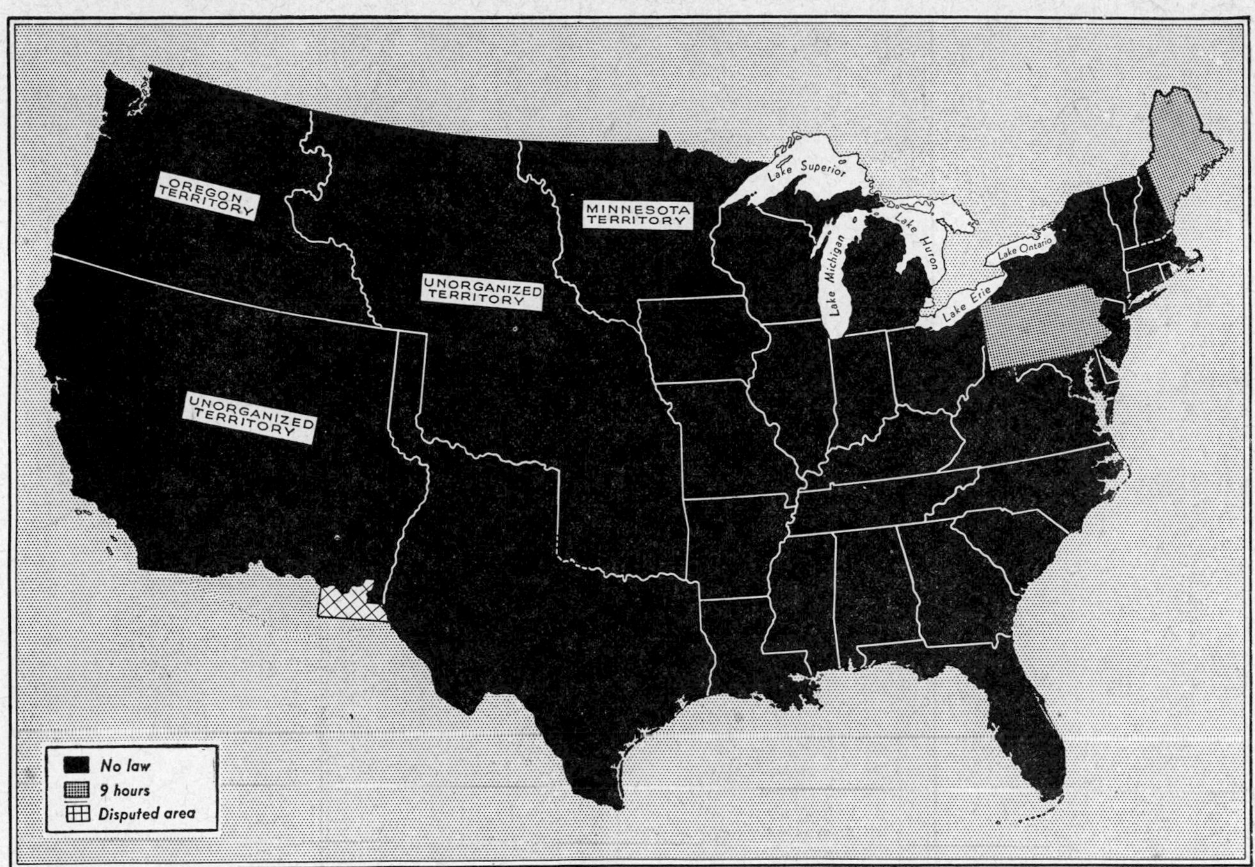

139 Women's Hours of Work, 1850

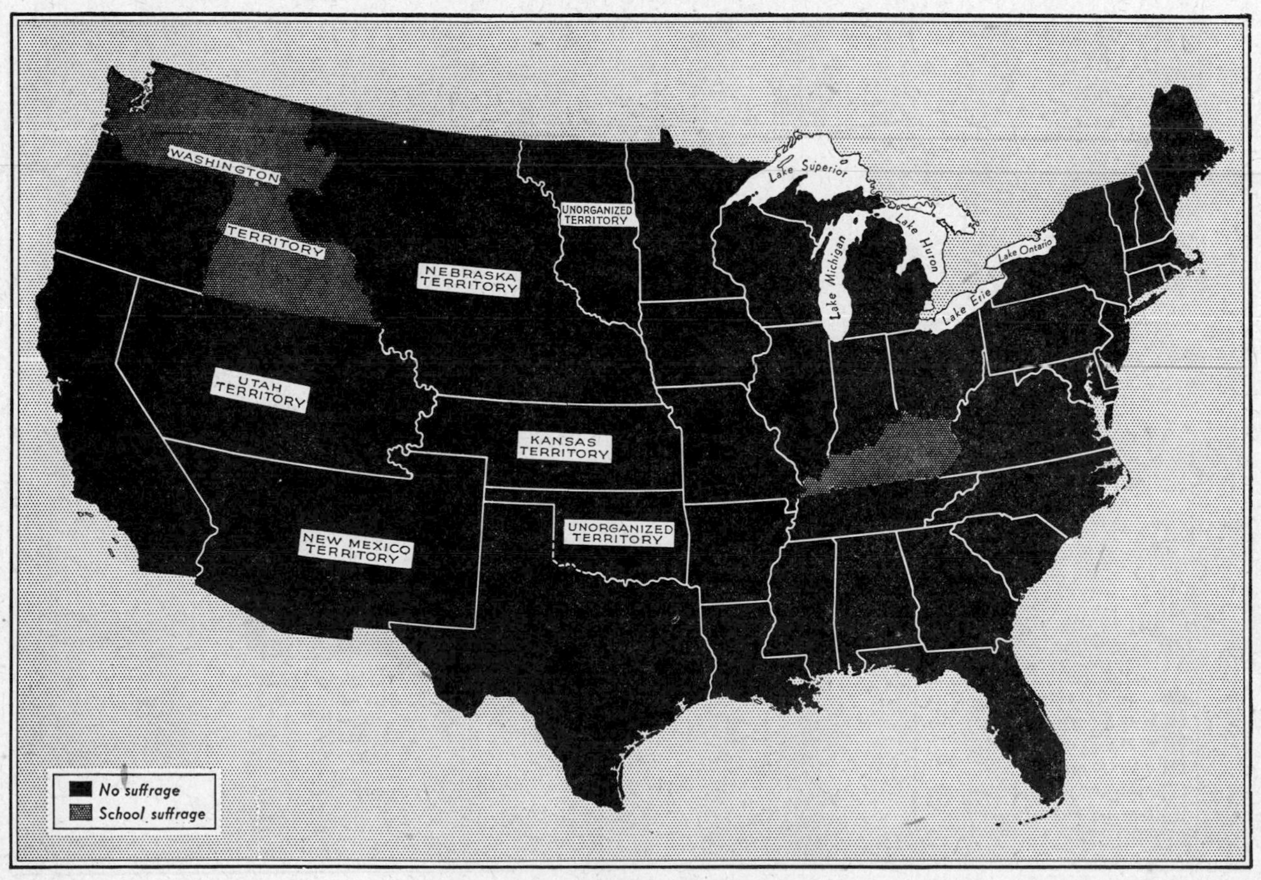

140 Enfranchisement of Women, 1860

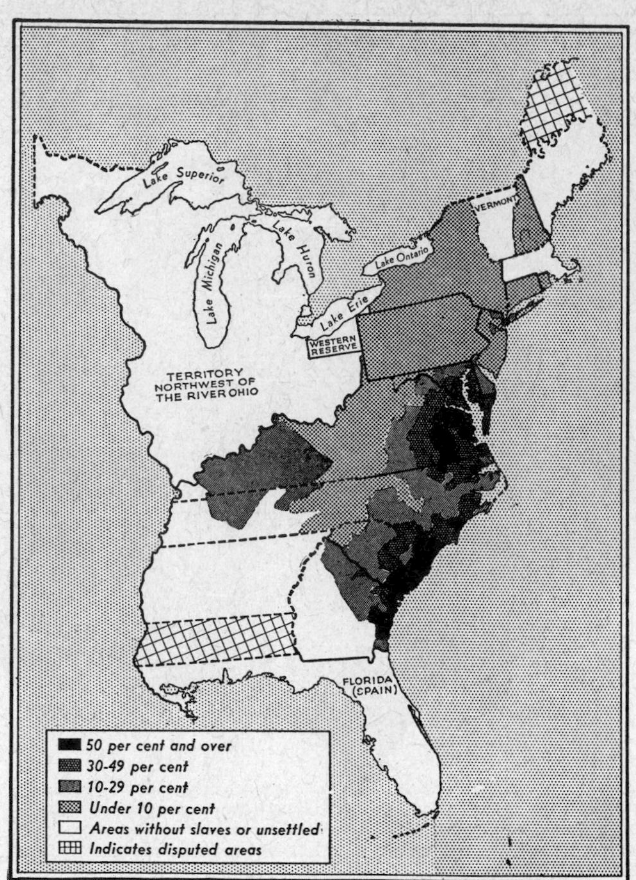

141 Proportion of Slaves to Total Population, 1790

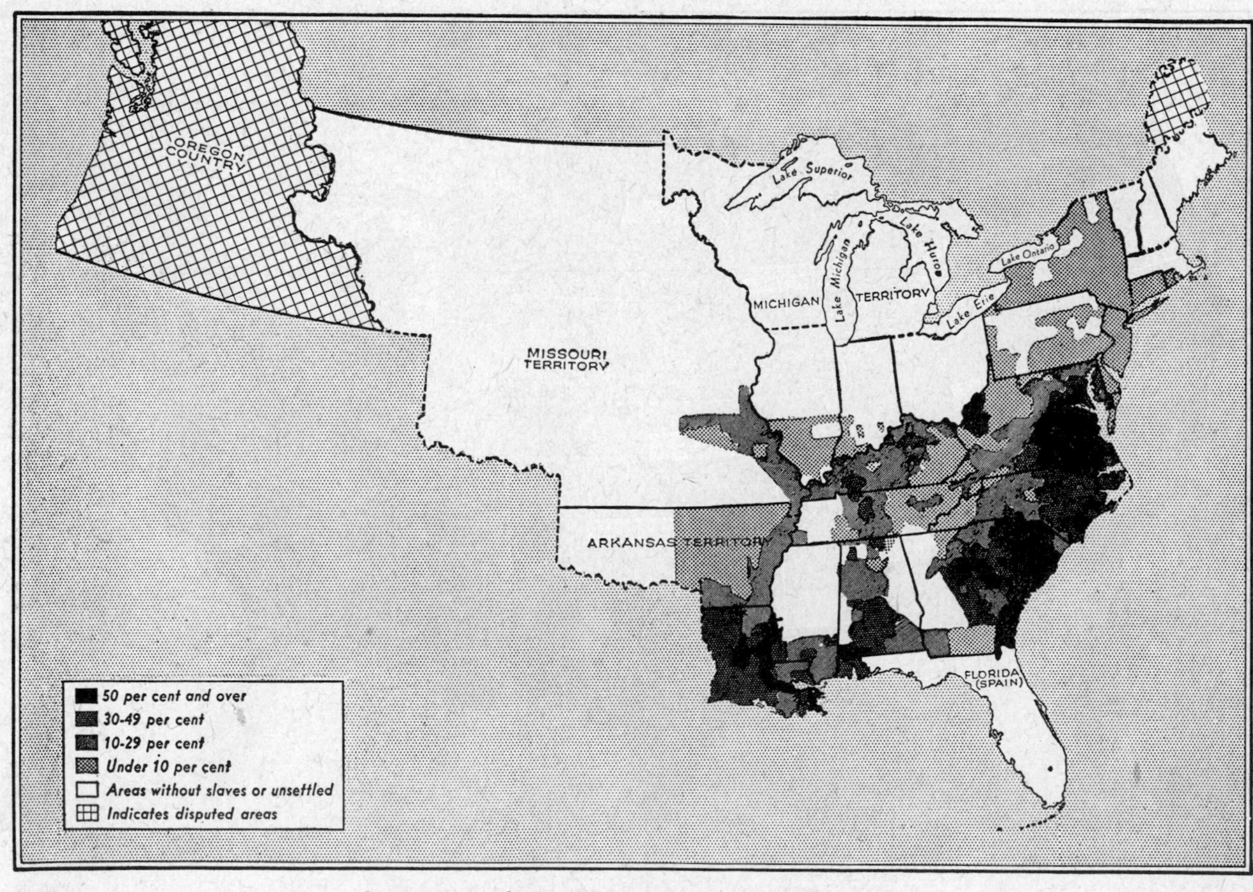

142 Proportion of Slaves to Total Population, 1820

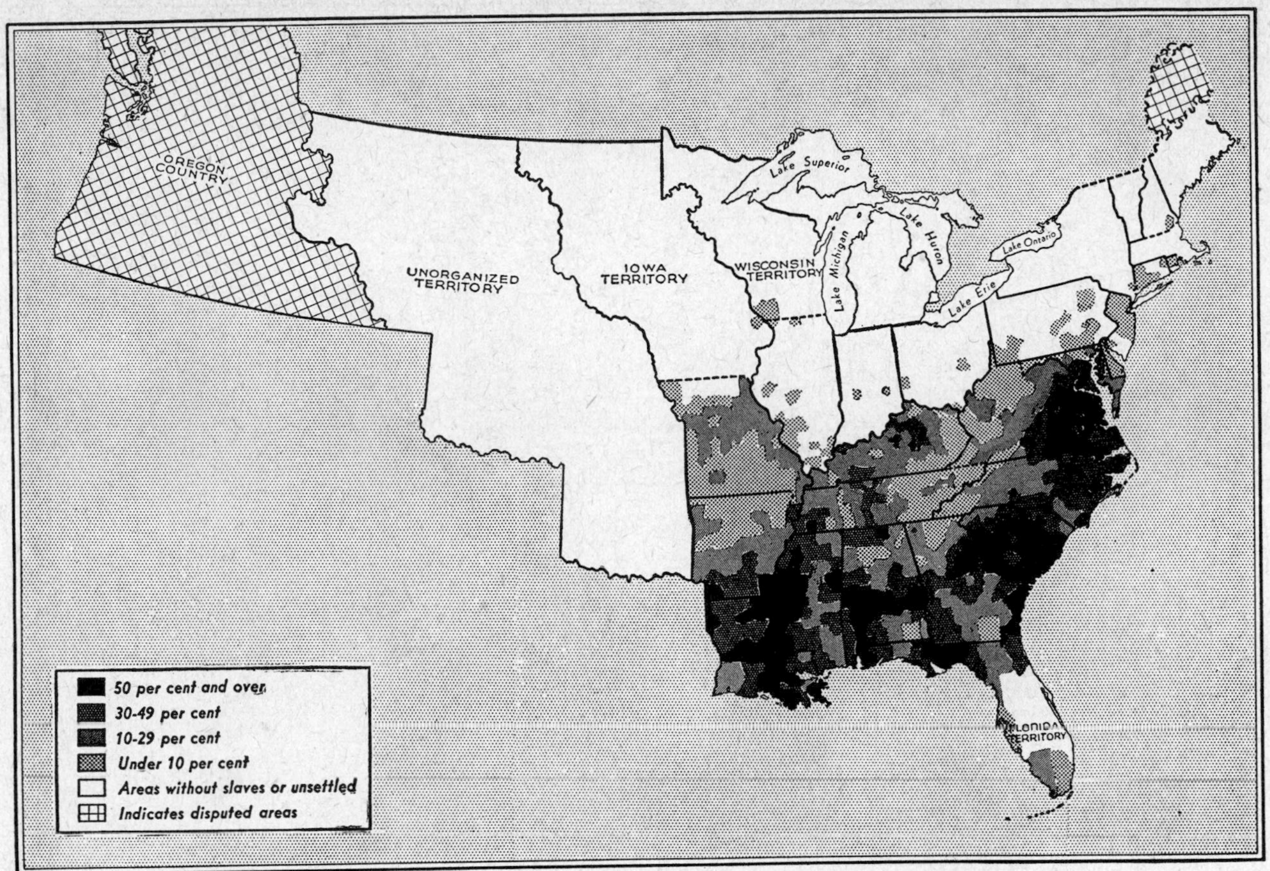

143 Proportion of Slaves to Total Population, by County, 1840

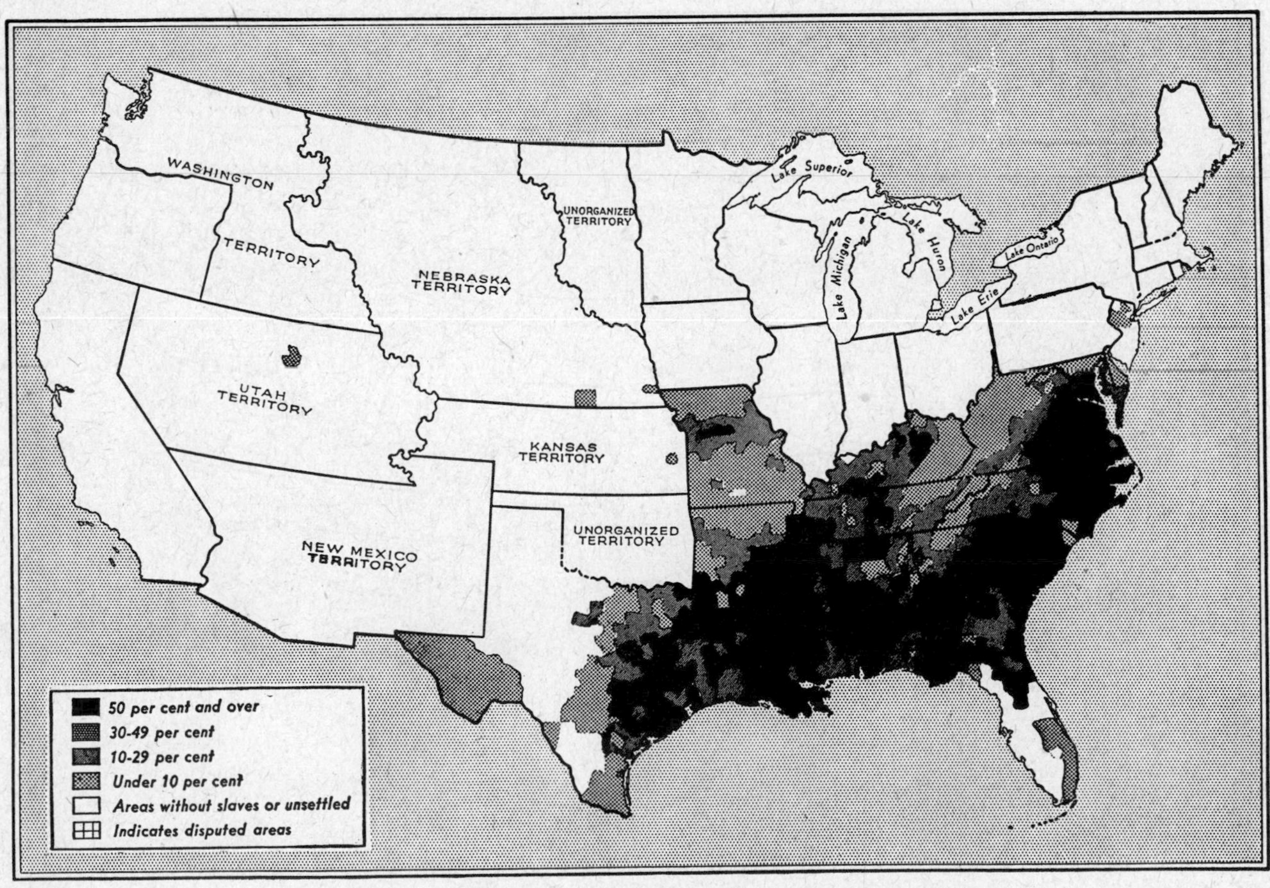

144 Proportion of Slaves to Total Population, by County, 1860

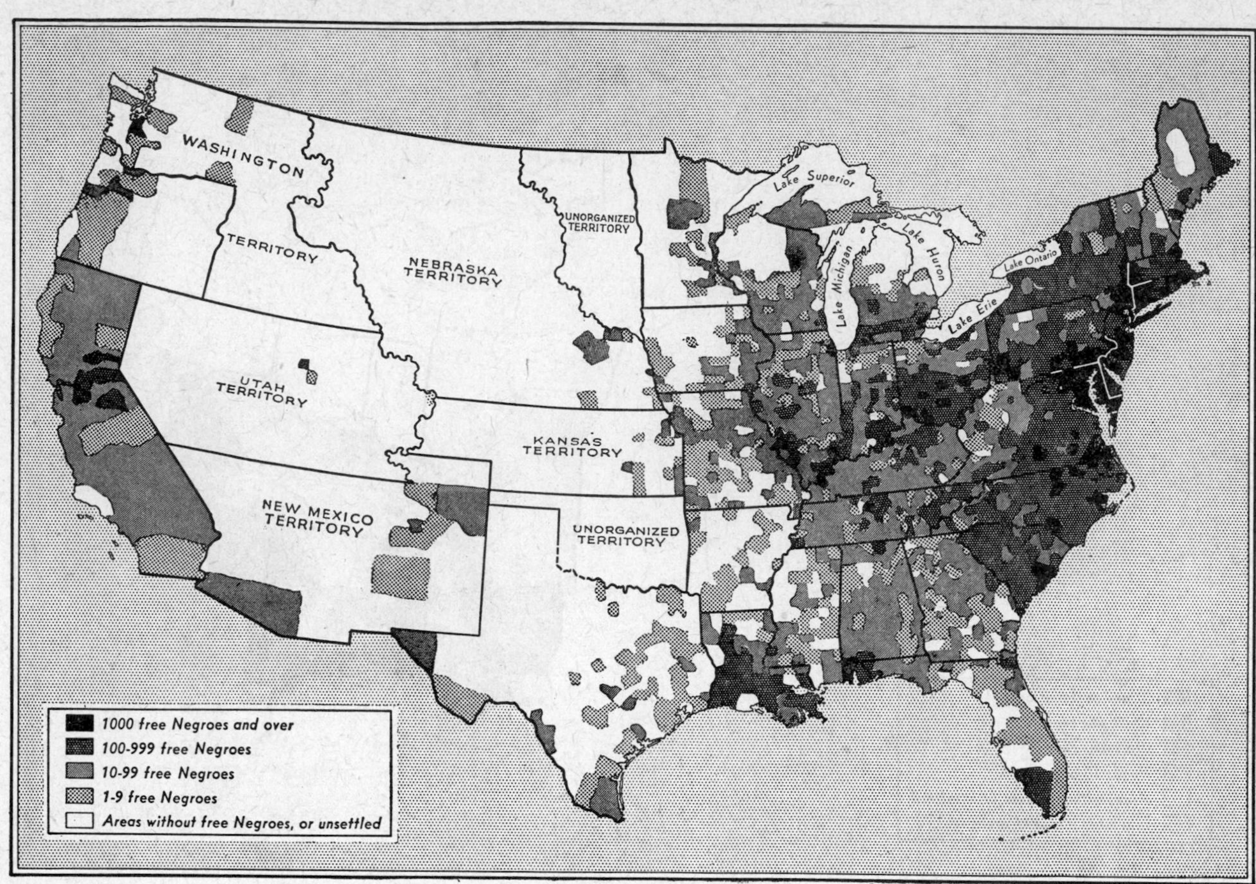

145 Free Negro Population, by County, 1860

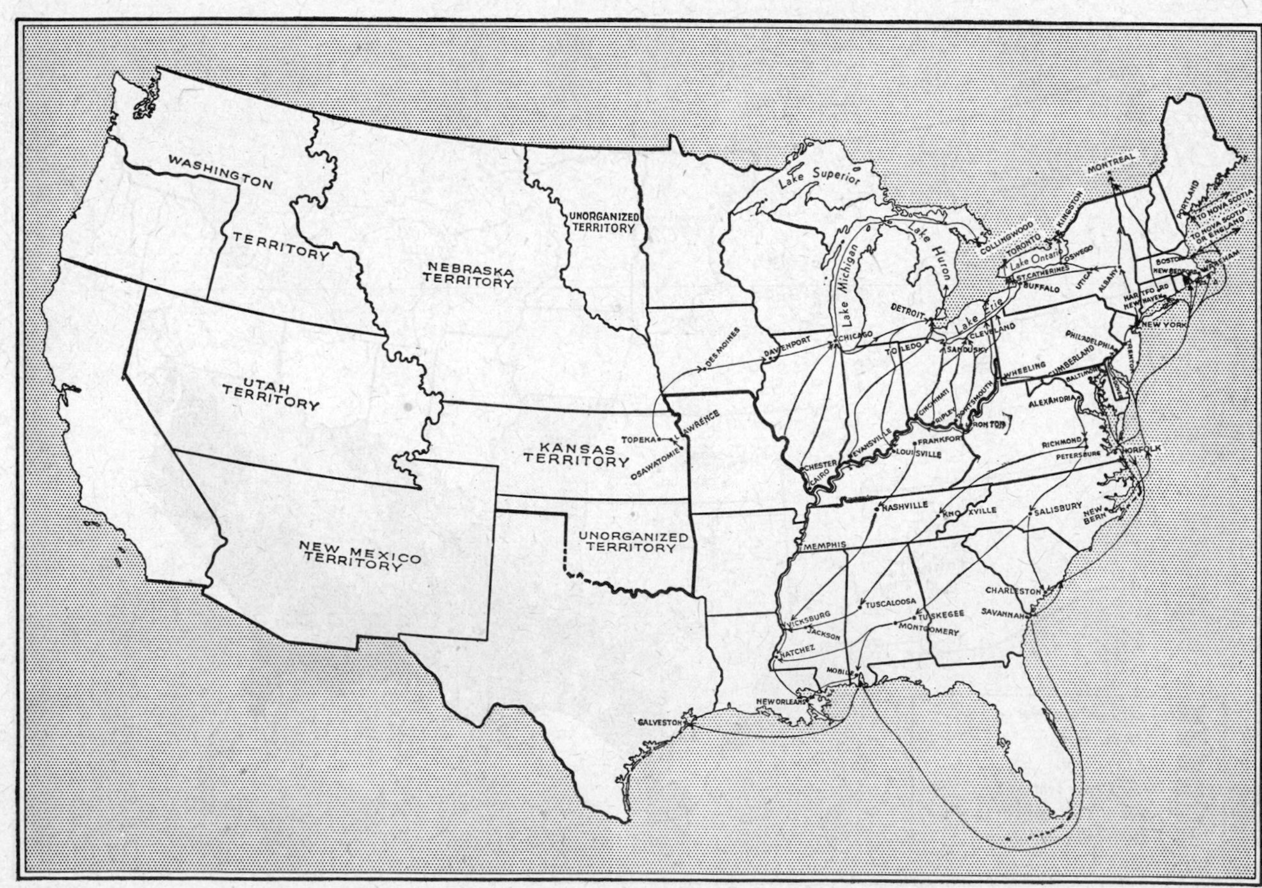

146 Routes of the Underground Railway and of the Domestic Slave Trade

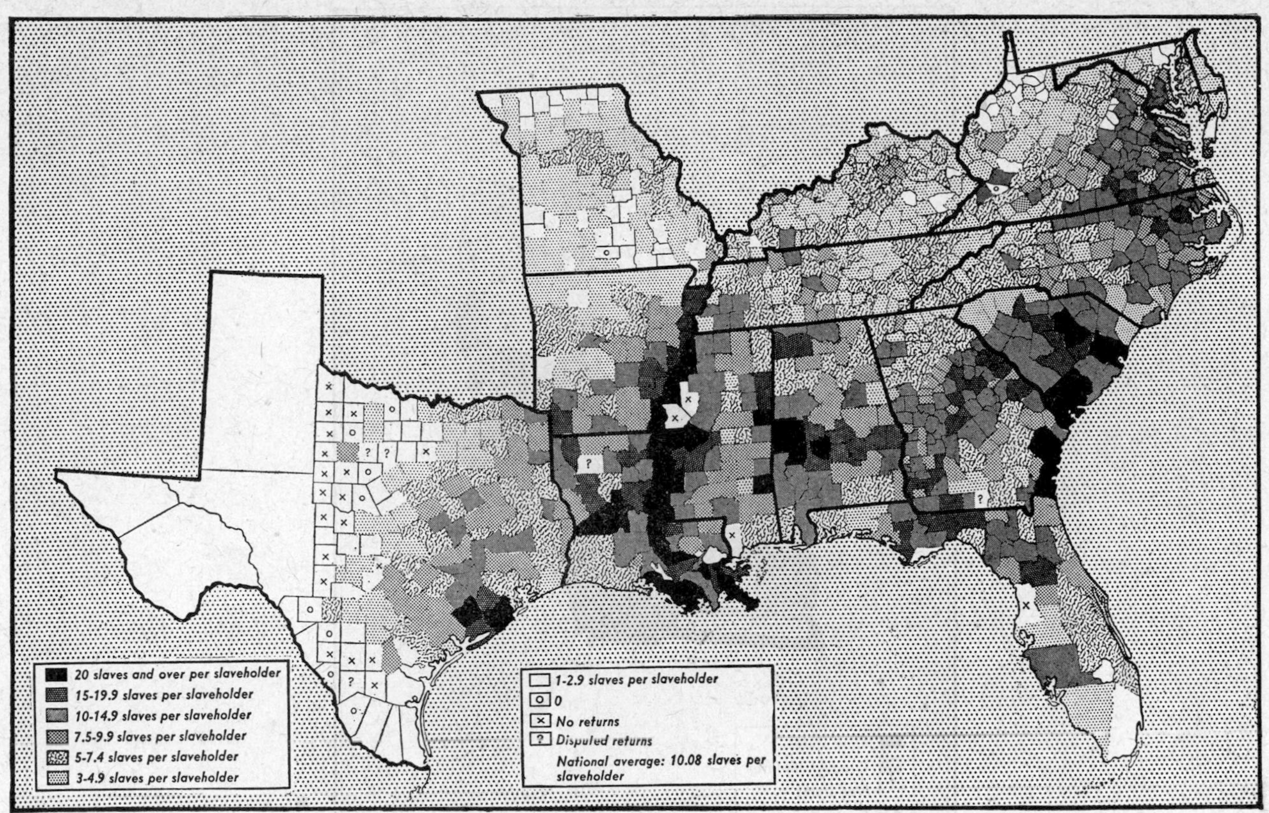

147 Number of Slaves per Slaveholder in the South, by County, 1860

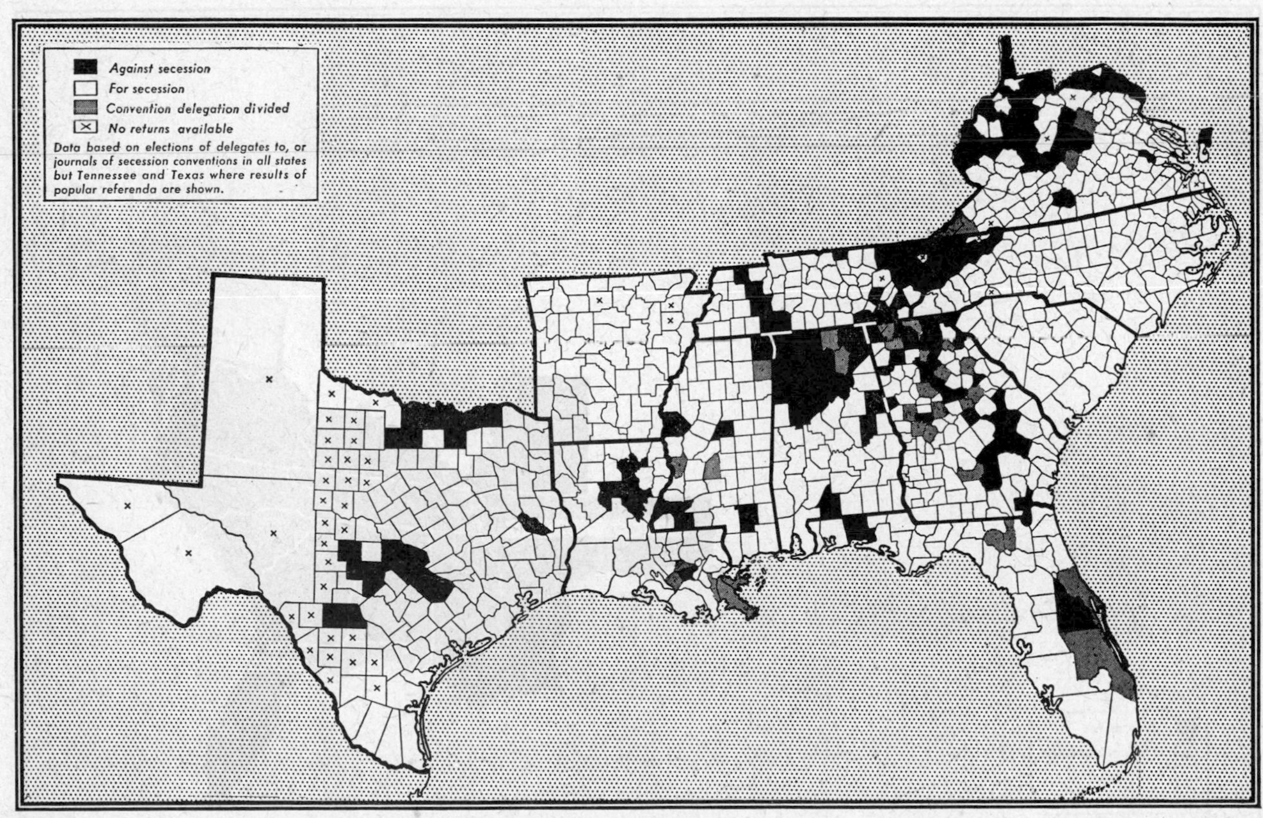

148 Opposition to Secession in the South, by County, 1860-1861

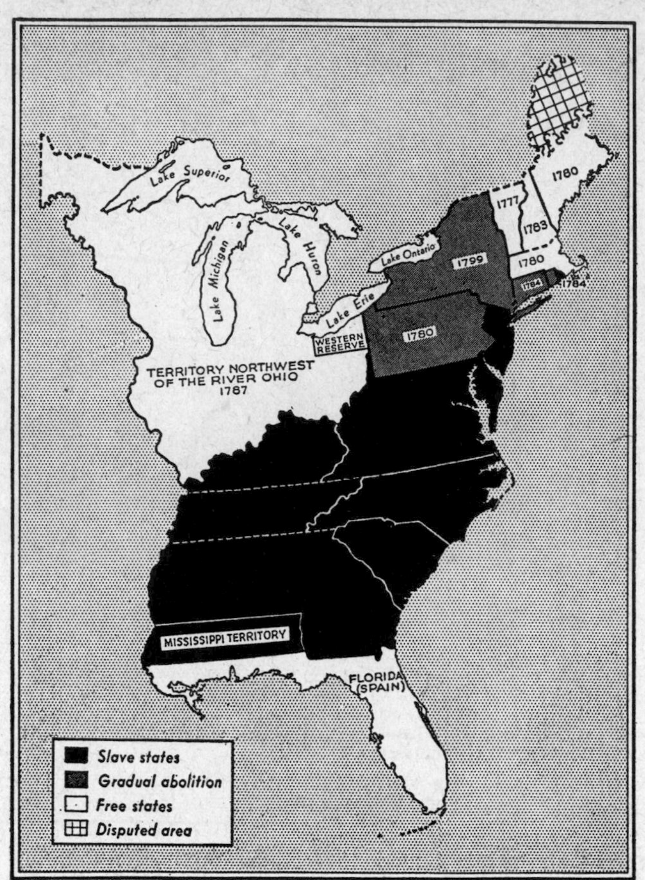

149

Progress of Abolition, 1800

Dates are those of adoption of gradual or complete abolition

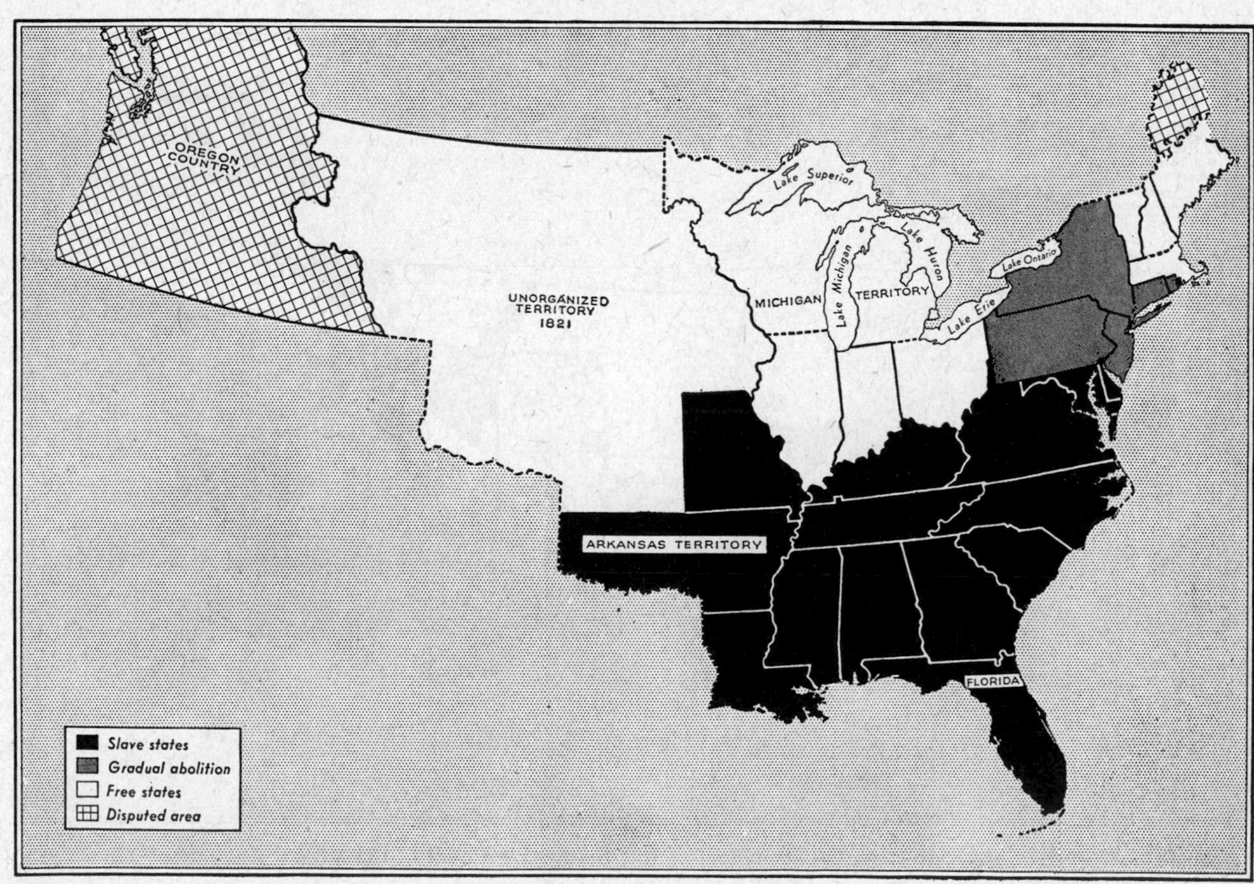

150

Progress of Abolition, 1821

Dates are those of adoption of gradual or complete abolition

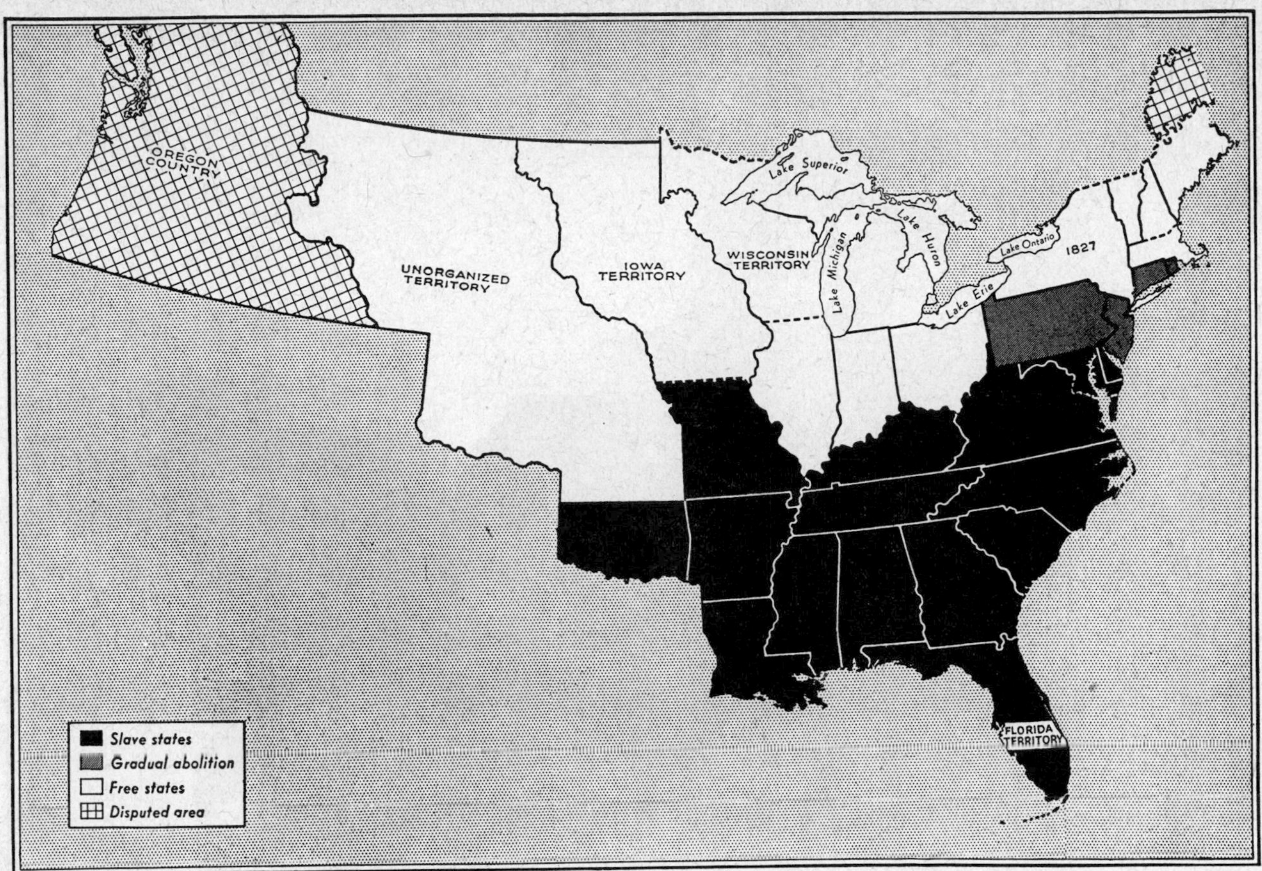

151

Progress of Abolition, 1840

Dates are those of adoption of gradual or complete abolition

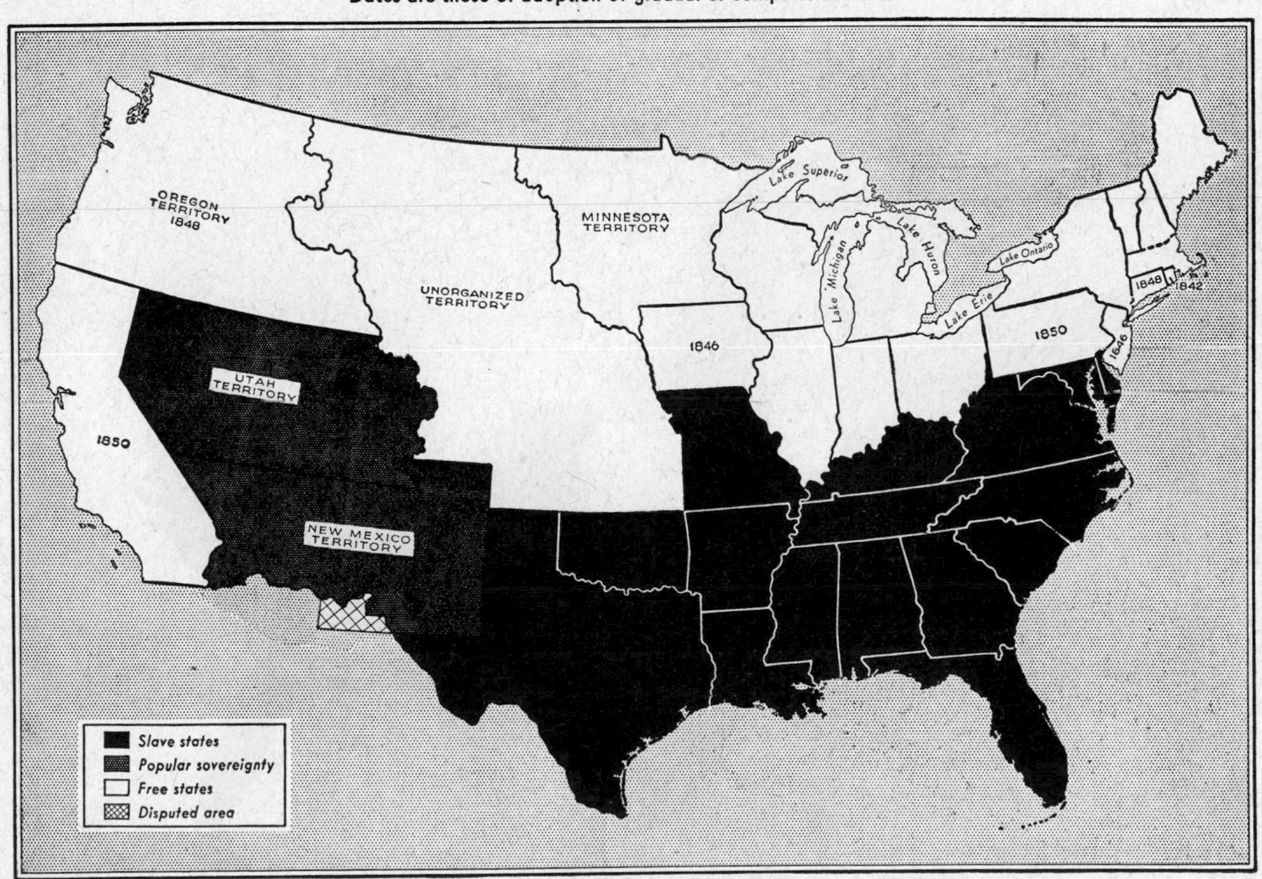

152

Progress of Abolition, 1850

Dates are those of adoption of gradual or complete abolition

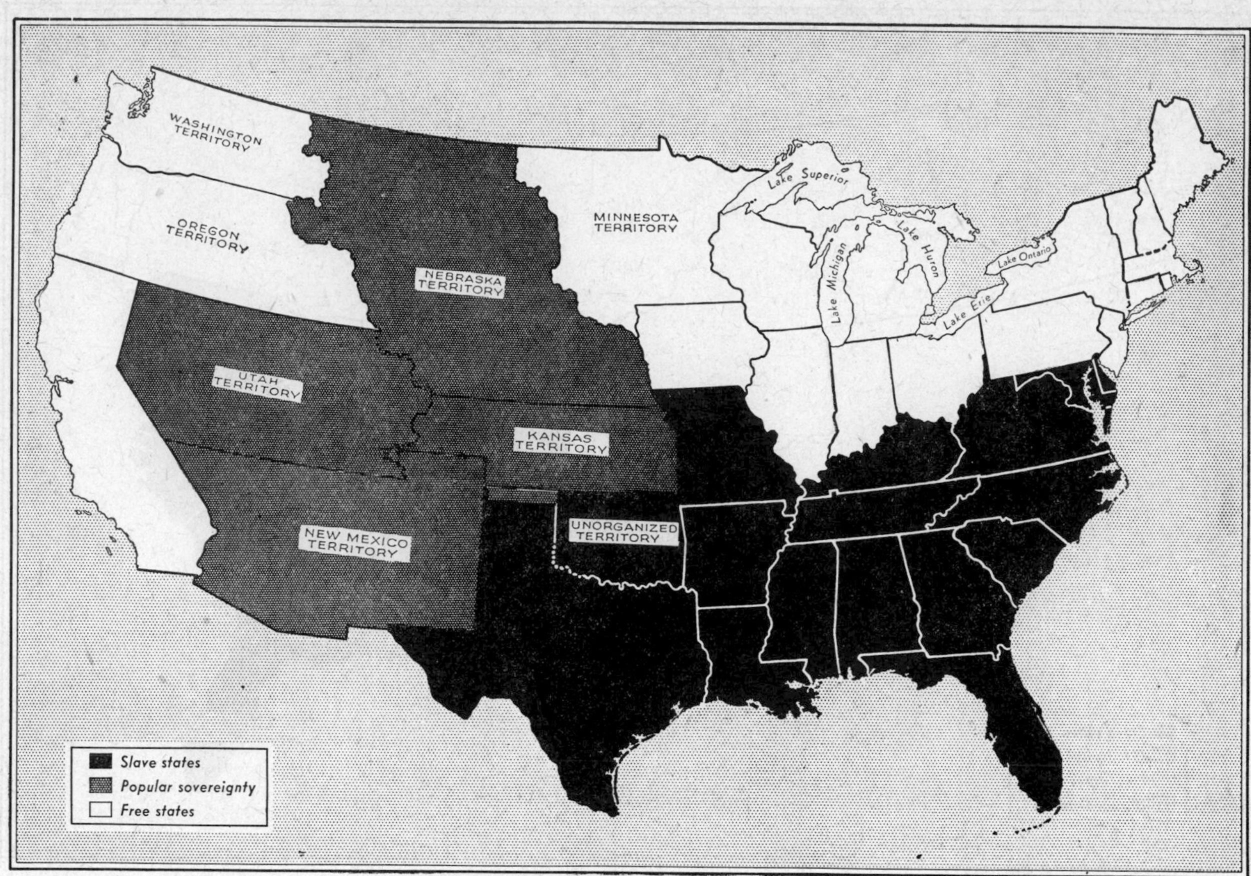

153 Progress of Abolition, 1854

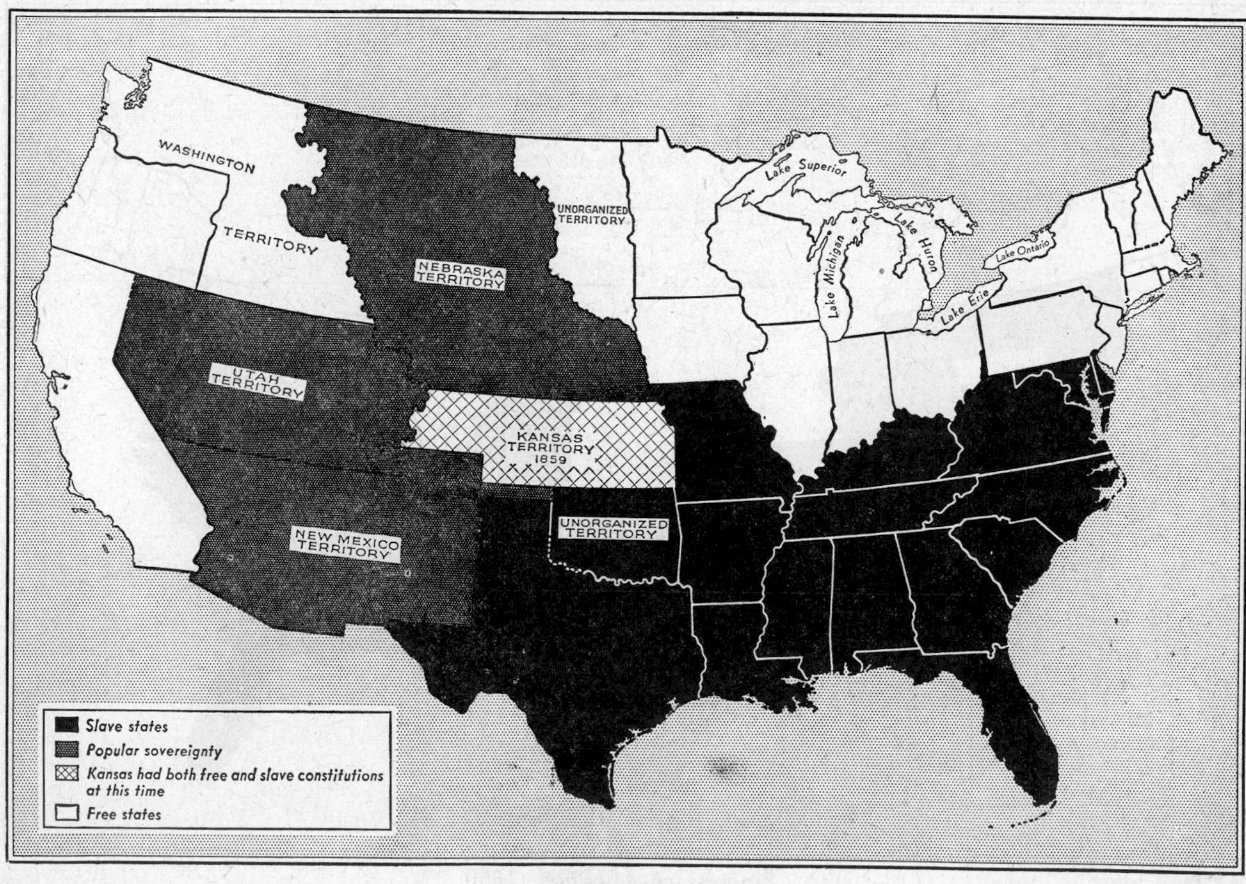

154 Progress of Abolition, 1860

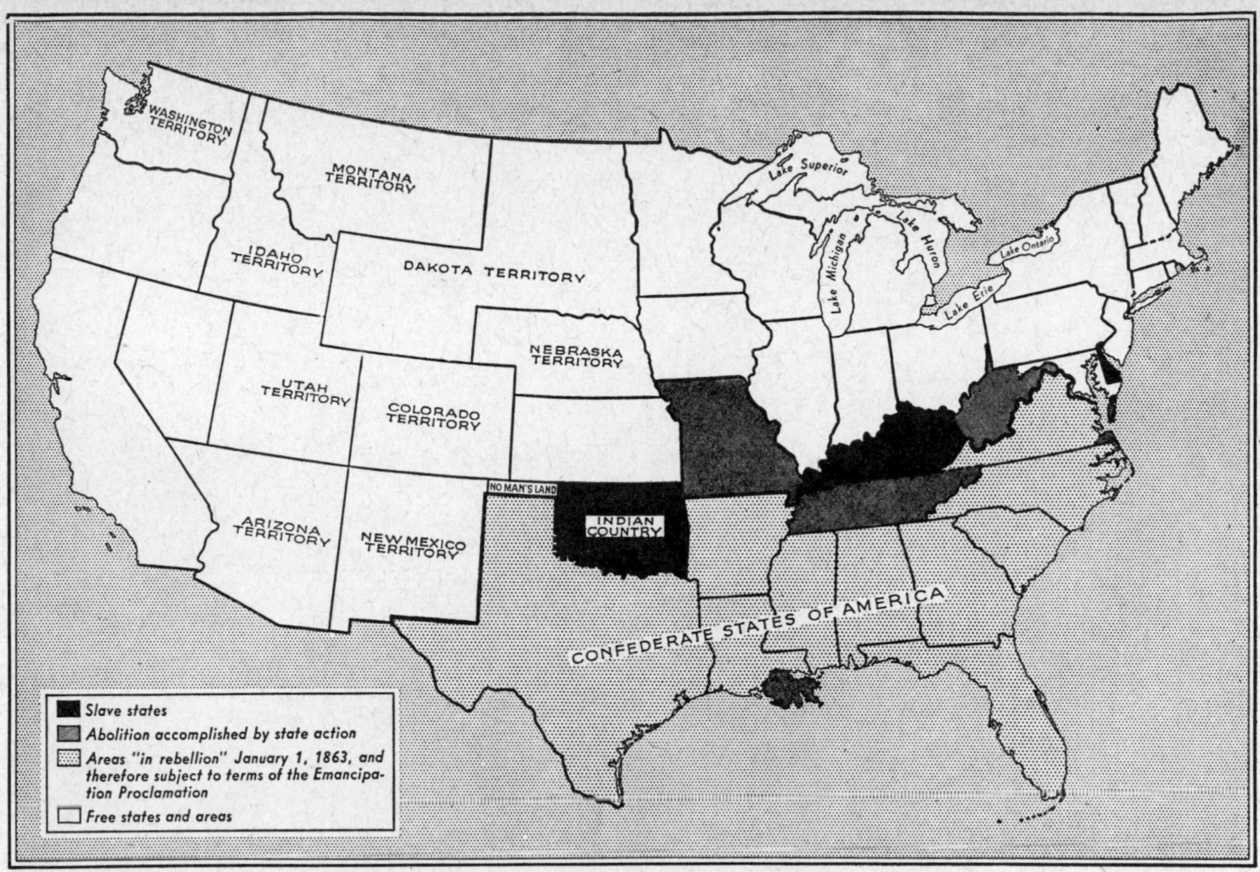

155

Progress of Abolition, 1863-1864

State and territorial borders shown are those of late 1864. In areas of Union military occupation in Louisiana, Virginia, etc., Emancipation Proclamation had no legal applicability and state action in 1864 effected abolition therein.

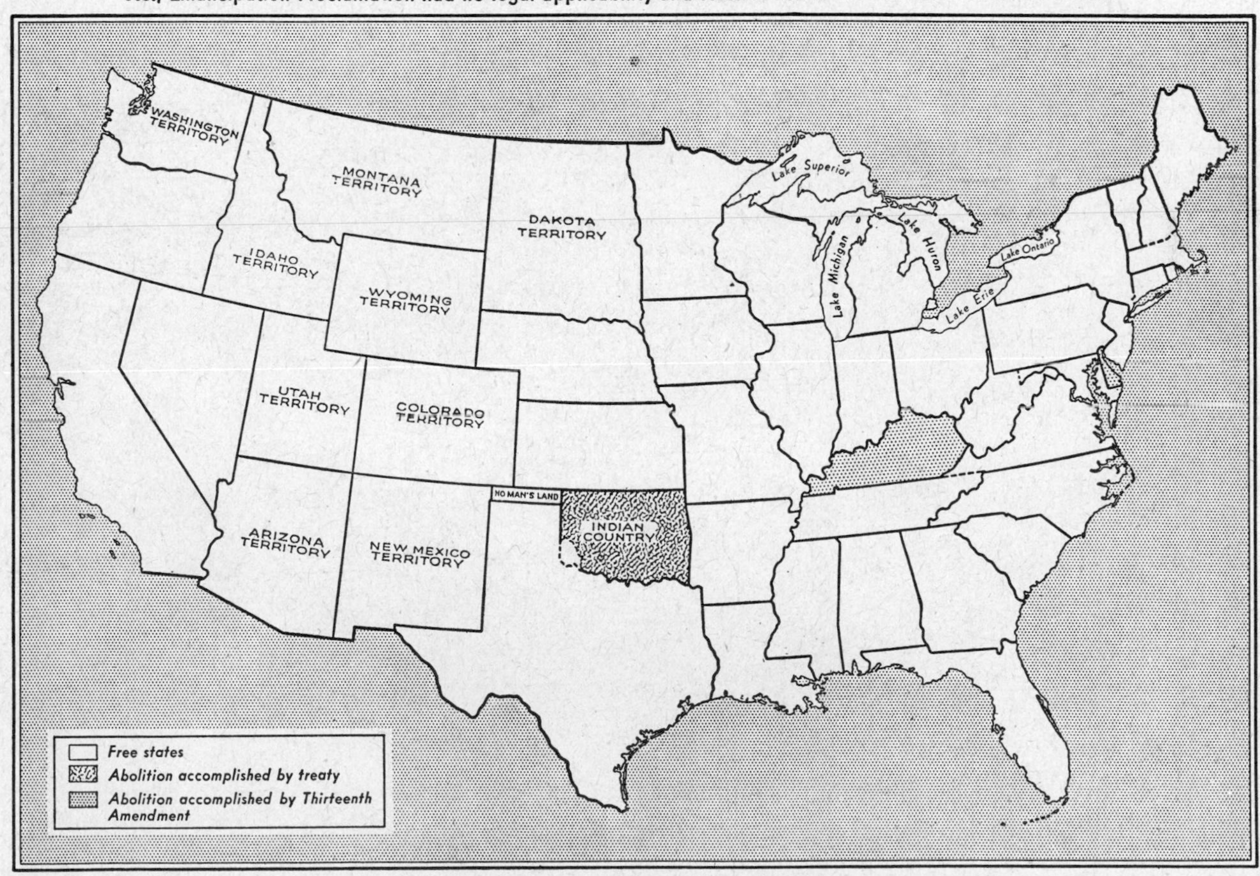

156

Progress of Abolition, 1865-1868

State and territorial borders shown are those of late 1868

(For disputed border between Texas and Indian Country, see map 204)

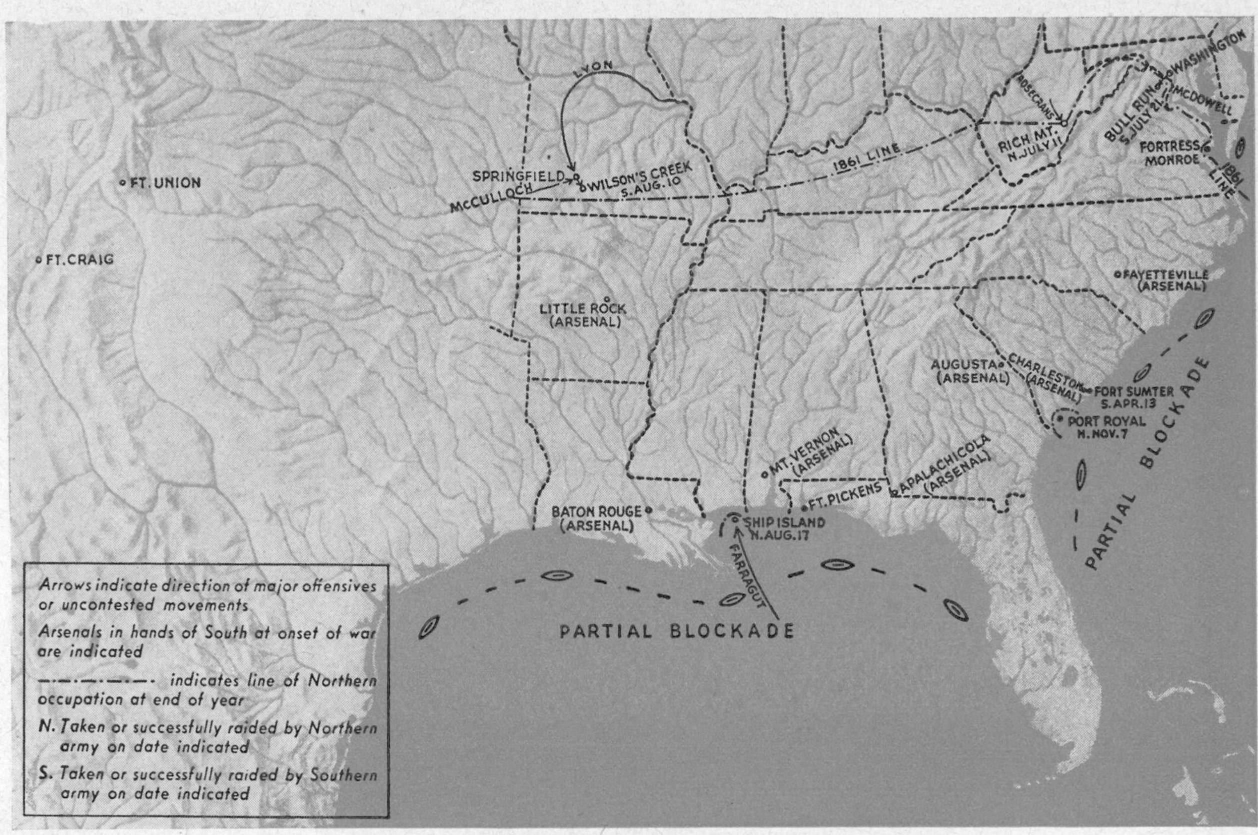

157 The War Between the States: Campaigns of 1861

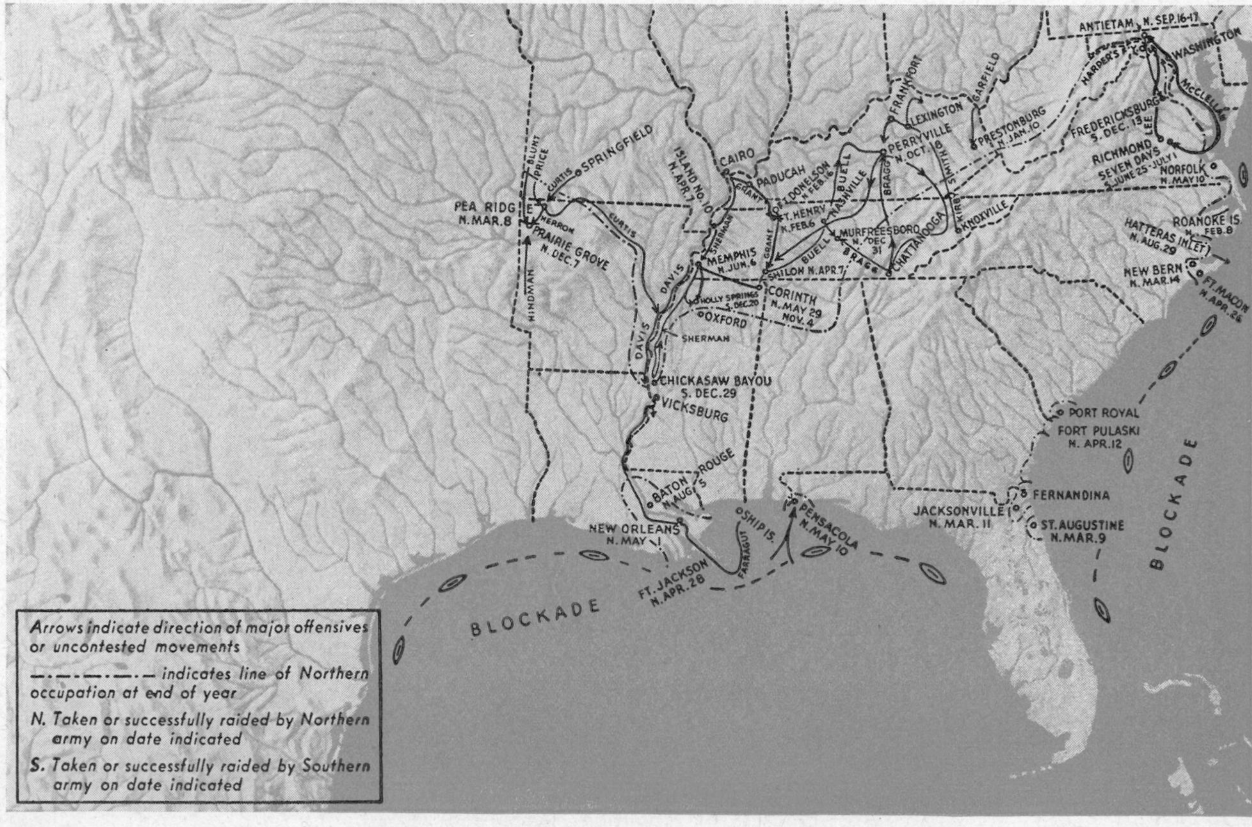

158 The War Between the States: Campaigns of 1862

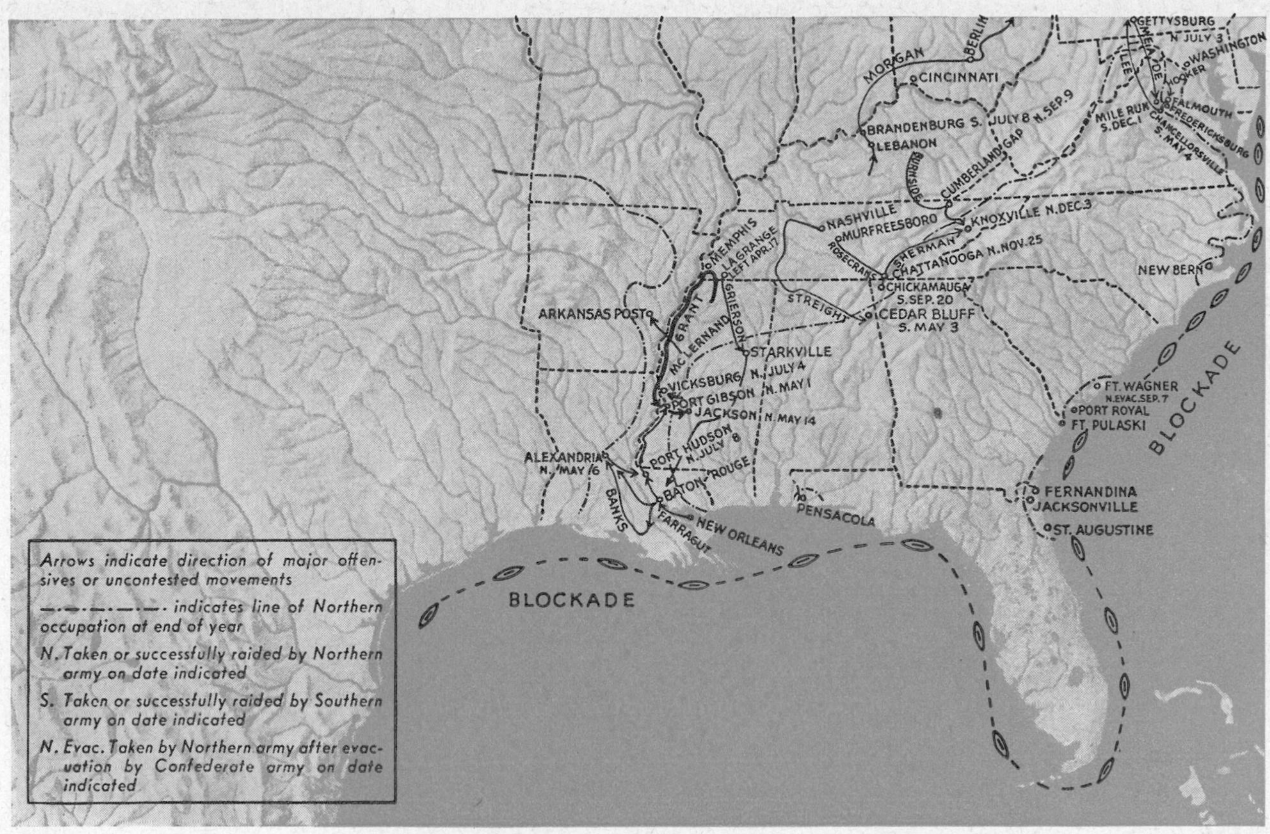

159 The War Between the States: Campaigns of 1863

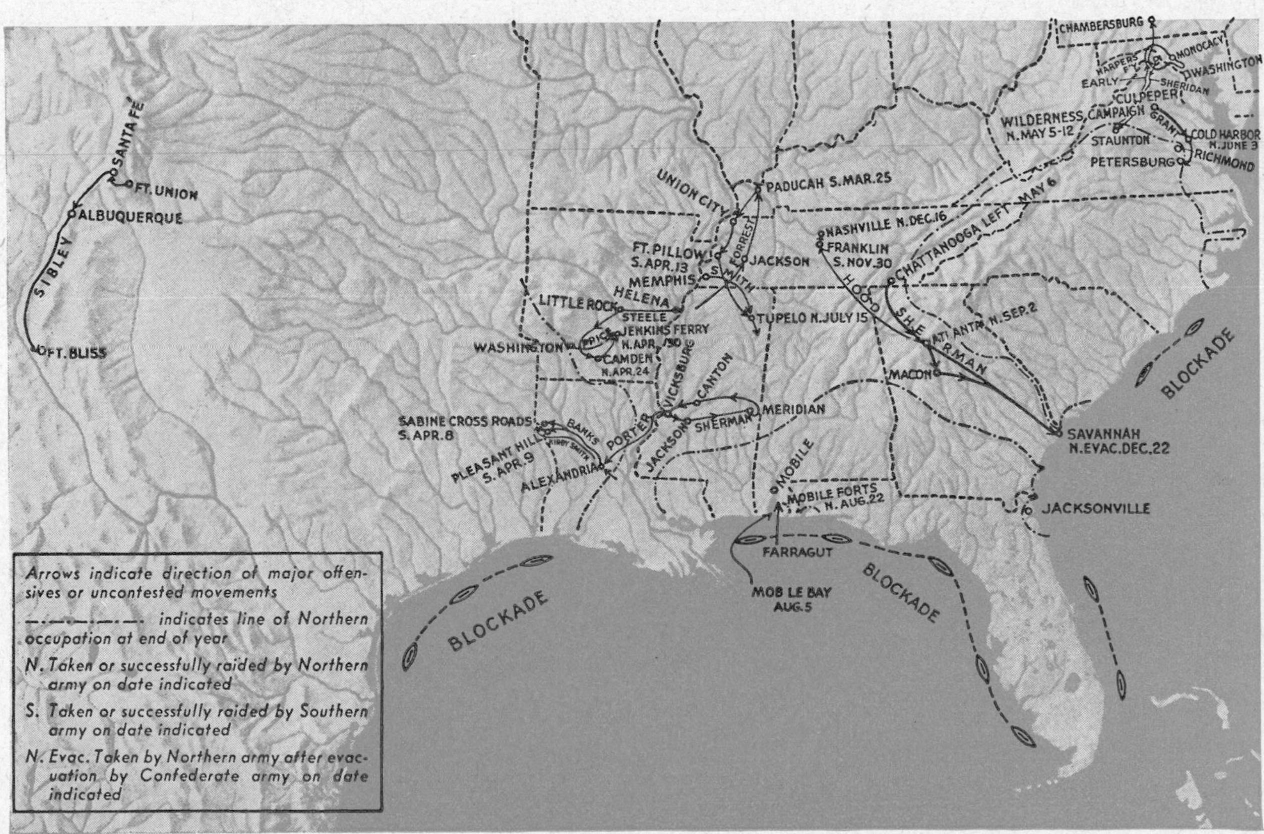

160 The War Between the States: Campaigns of 1864

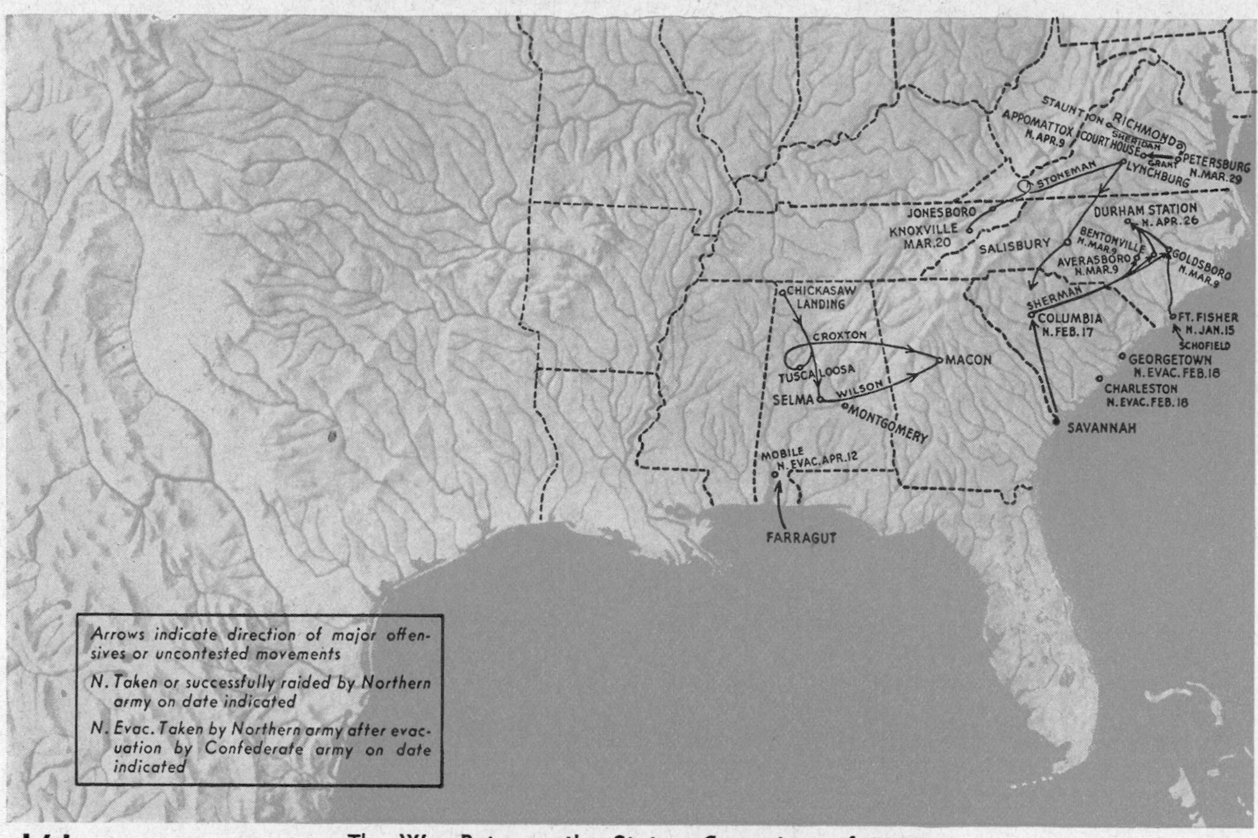

161 The War Between the States: Campaigns of 1865

Kirby Smith, commander in the Trans-Mississippi West, and last Confederate general in the field, after a fruitless trip to Houston to see about continuing the fight, surrendered his forces, including Buckner's men at Shreveport and Price's Missourians, to General Canby at New Orleans, May 26, 1865.

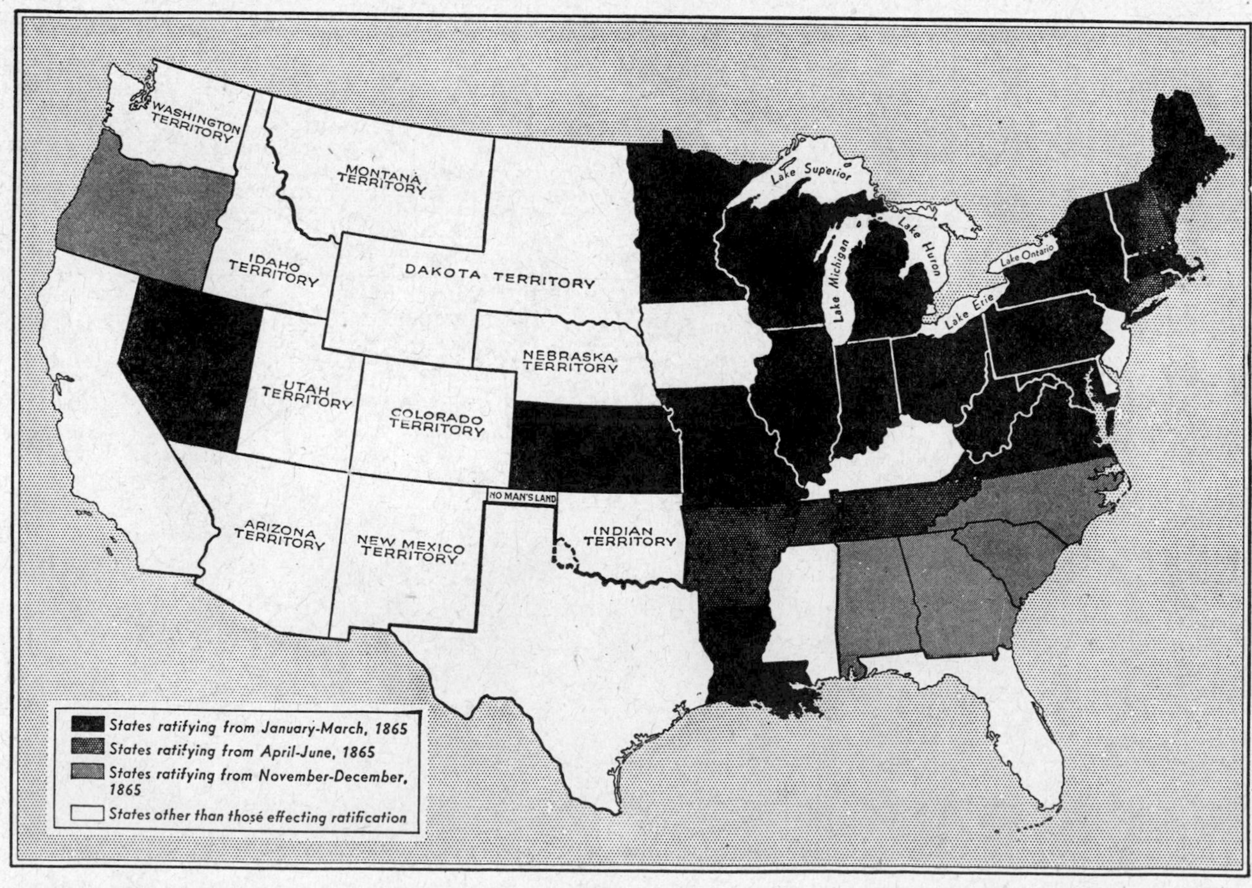

162 States Effecting the Ratification of the Thirteenth Amendment to the Constitution, 1865

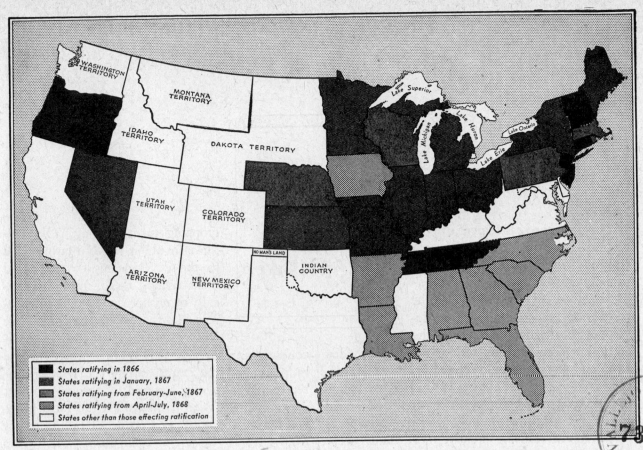

163 States Effecting the Ratification of the Fourteenth Amendment to the Constitution, 1868

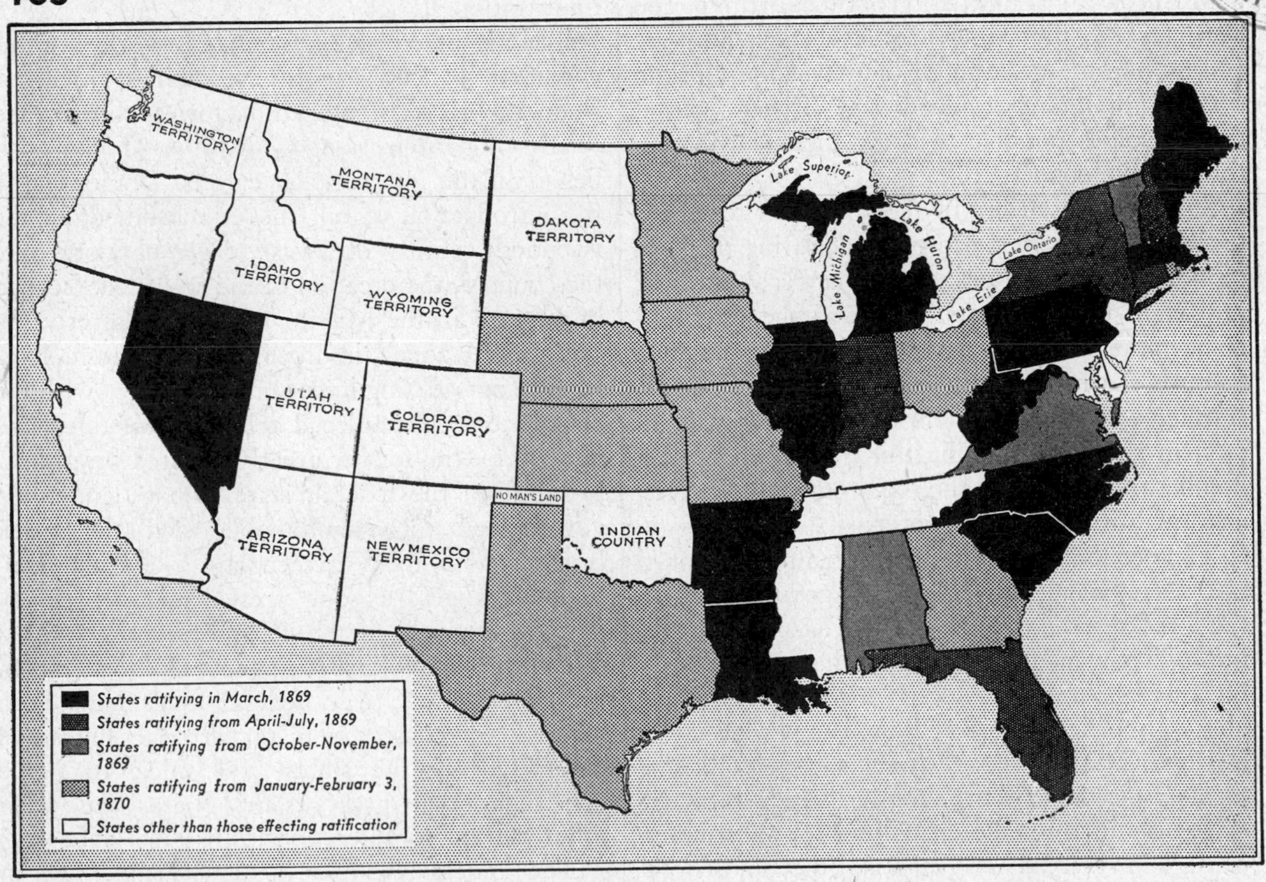

164 States Effecting the Ratification of the Fifteenth Amendment to the Constitution, 1870

Section IV

1865-1941

The continued movement of population westward after the war resulted in the so-called (and misleadingly called) "disappearance" of the frontier, as shown on the population map of 1890. This development meant the end of the cattle kingdom (already seriously crippled by disease and particularistic state-restrictive legislation) and also the evolution of the age-old Indian problem from a military to a civil and social status, far more than it signalized the end of free public homesteads. Actually more lands were patented in the decade of the 1890's than ever before in a comparable period of time. In this period also, for the first time in our history, accurate census figures were taken of the national origin of our immigrant residents and citizens, and it thus becomes possible to show their distribution through the country.

Suffrage, extended by some states to aliens taking out their first papers or declaring their intention of seeking citizenship, underwent three important developments: one was the establishment in the South of various legal devices designed to curb the newly won franchise of the Negro; another was the extension, slowly but surely, of woman suffrage; and the third, in an increasing number of states, was the requirement of literacy as a qualification of the voter.

The economic growth of the country continued at a phenomenal rate. It brought great benefits in the form of an enormously improved and generally improving, standard of living, with a tremendously increased national income. It also brought grave abuses, which Grangers, Populists, Progressives and New Dealers were to attack successively. The farming picture saw the slow but steady recovery of the South from the chaos of 1865. Disruption of the old slave labor system and the almost total lack of fluid capital speeded the evolution of share-cropping farm tenancy. Over-enthusiasm about western farming led to the development of share and cash tenancy there, most dramatically on unsuccessful irrigation projects like that in the Uncompahgre Valley. Such overexpansion, encouraged in the early part of this period by the railroads and the states and territories, and directly and indirectly fostered by the government during World War I, intensified the farm problem during the prolonged period of falling prices from 1871 to 1897, and again from 1920 to the establishment of the Agricultural Adjustment Administration.

The manufacturing and business world saw the evolution of pools, trusts, combines, mergers, trade associations, branch factories abroad, and finally of participation by many American businesses in the international cartels. Domestically, the introduction of oil, the establishment in the twentieth century of a vast power network over the country, the creation of the so-called "second mill zone" in the Middle West, and latterly the "third mill zone" in the industrial South, have been of outstanding importance, together with the completion of the railroad, telegraph and telephone networks—the former greatly assisted by grants-in-aid from the federal, state, county and town governments. The automobile and the truck brought with them tremendous social and economic changes, as our present great highway systems evolved, first haphazardly and then, beginning in New Jersey, under state supervision. Still later, since 1921, federal funds have been allotted to construction on arterial highways designated by the states, and since 1941 the construction of great traffic routes has been influenced by considerations of national defense.

The Federal Reserve System, inaugurated in 1914, brought a much needed elasticity and uniformity to the currency of the country. It gave added stability to member banks through the pooling of reserves, and constituted a marked improvement over the system established by the National Banking Acts of 1863 and 1864, which, in their turn, had brought an appreciable improvement over the chaotic conditions of earlier days.

Integration of the country, well begun by the roads, canals and particularly the railroads of the previous period, continued, and indeed was accelerated. The length of time required to move from one place to another rapidly decreased, until, with the advent of the modern airplane, the entire country lay within the compass of a single day's trip, and the continent could be crossed in approximately half a day. This development not only made drastic changes in business and social habits, but obviously introduced fundamental innovations in the strategy of national defense.

Just before the turn of the century, our aggressively expanding business economy turned enthusiastically to a search for increased foreign markets. Simultaneously, America began for the first time to export capital in really significant quantities and to shift gradually from the position of a debtor nation to that of creditor—an evolution which reached its climax with dramatic swiftness during World War I. This export of capital came after a long series of post-Civil War leaders, like Seward and Grant, had urged further acquisitions of trade and defense bases, and after others, such as Blaine, had tried unsuccessfully to build up our economic relations with Latin America. Through capital export, America achieved true status as a world power. This development, flanked by the revival of ship subsidies for the languishing American merchant marine, the tardy rebuilding of American naval power, and the doctrines of the influential A. T. Mahan, coincided neatly and logically with the acquisition of empire through the Spanish-American War. It led to the establishment of the Republic of Panama and the building of the Panama Canal. It was essential background for the Portsmouth Conference, and for the participation of the United States in the Algeciras Conference. It took the interesting form of dollar diplomacy both in the Caribbean, with resulting strain on our relations with the rest of Latin America, and in the Orient, where, reinforcing the slightly earlier but closely related Open Door policy, it laid for thirty-seven years the bases for an inevitable conflict with Japan. It also brought increasing collisions with the recently industrialized new naval power, Germany, and had obvious connections with our entrance into World Wars I and II.

After the prodigal waste of resources which more or less inevitably characterized much of the early expansion of American enterprise, a marked conservation drive began about the turn of the century, when for the first time the conservation movement entered the field of national rather than state action. This departure resulted in the creation of the national parks, national monuments, and national forests, the beginnings of the reclamation movement under the Newlands Act of 1902, and the very important report of the Inland Waterways Commission which foreshadowed in 1907 the general line of watershed development and land-use policy to be followed years later by the Franklin Roosevelt administrations.

The development of the public school system was also forwarded by the beginning of effective compulsory school attendance laws, which were in part an oblique attack on the problem of child labor. Colleges, particularly coeducational institutions, spread rapidly with the enormous increase of free public high school education and with the increasing emancipation of women. The states have increasingly attacked the child labor question, with mixed results. The federal government stepped into the picture in the latter days of the New Freedom, more successfully in the days of NRA and again briefly in 1940. The failure of the attempt to add an amendment to the Constitution banning child labor furnishes the subject for an interesting map when compared with the maps of population and manufacturing. Other social legislation included limitations on the hours of labor of both men and women, a reform which was based on the long crusade of organized labor dating back to the 1820's and including Ira Steward's campaign for the eight-hour day, the Knights of Labor, the ill-fated general strike of 1886, and the early opposition of the American Federation of Labor. This legislation progressed first in dangerous occupations and public works, then in mercantile and manufacturing occupations, and finally in blanket regulations governing work of all types in the states. Federal action, beginning with regulations on the hours of labor of federal employees, workers on government contracts, and interstate carriers, became general only with the passage of the Wages and Hours Act in 1937.

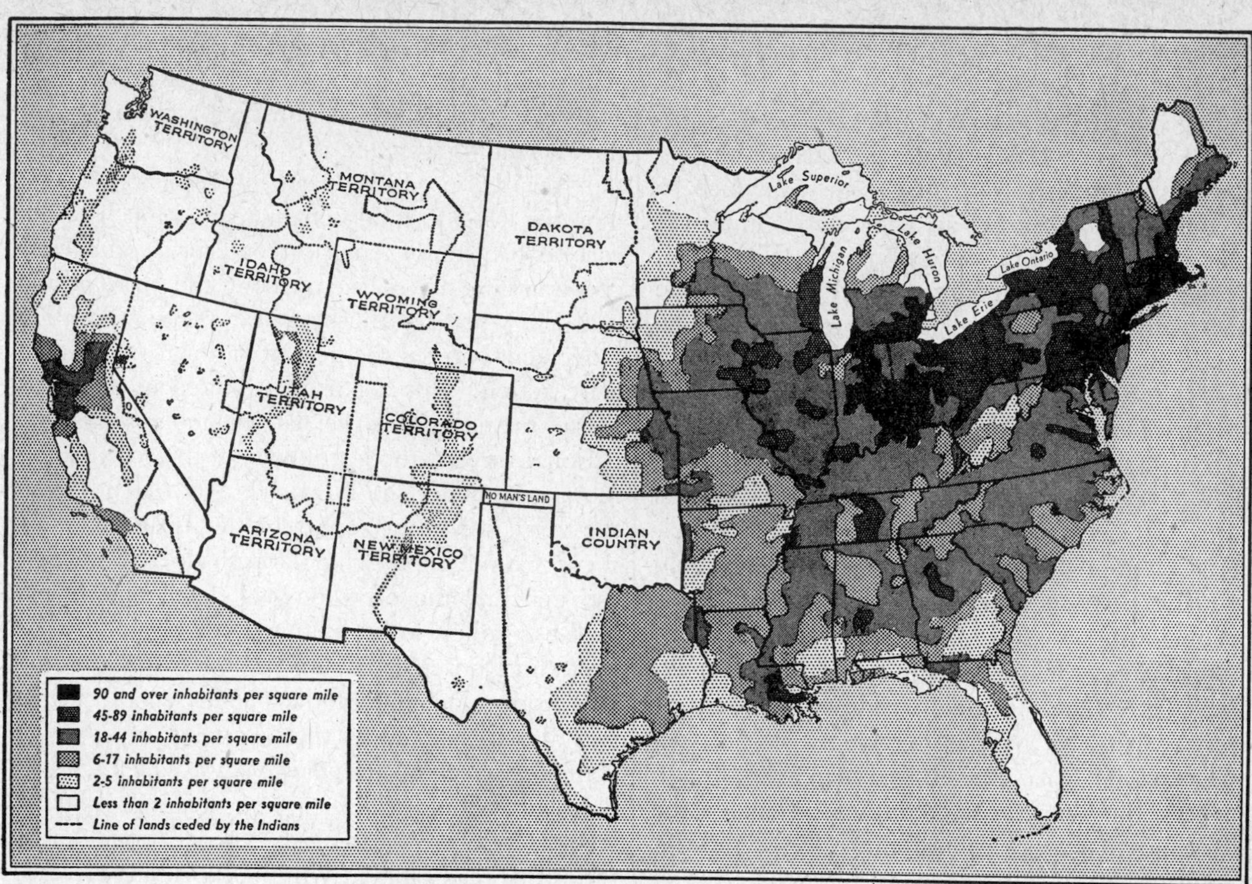

165 Population Density, Line of Indian Cessions, 1870

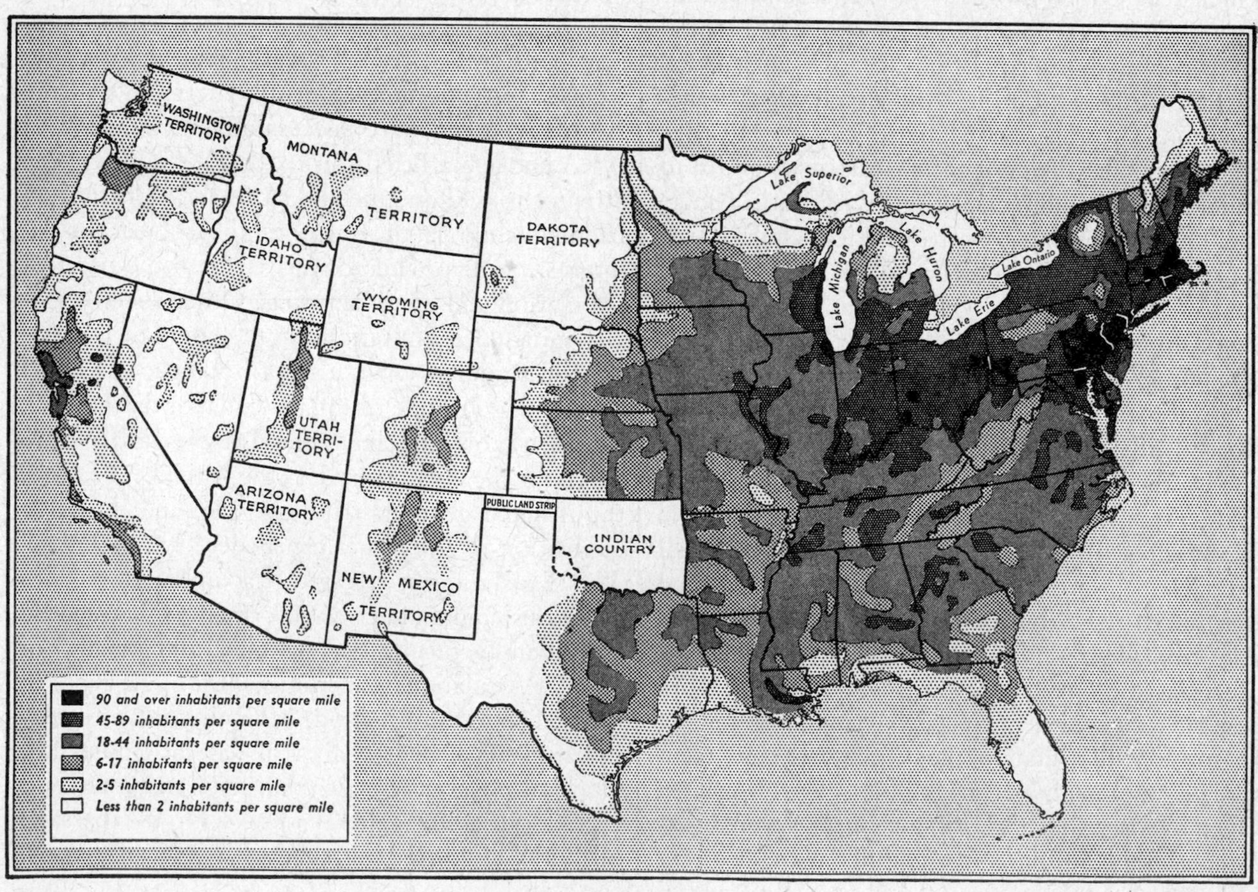

166 Population Density, 1880

90 and over inhabitants per square mile
45-89 inhabitants per square mile
18-44 inhabitants per square mile
6-17 inhabitants per square mile
2-5 inhabitants per square mile
Less than 2 inhabitants per square mile

167

Population Density, 1890

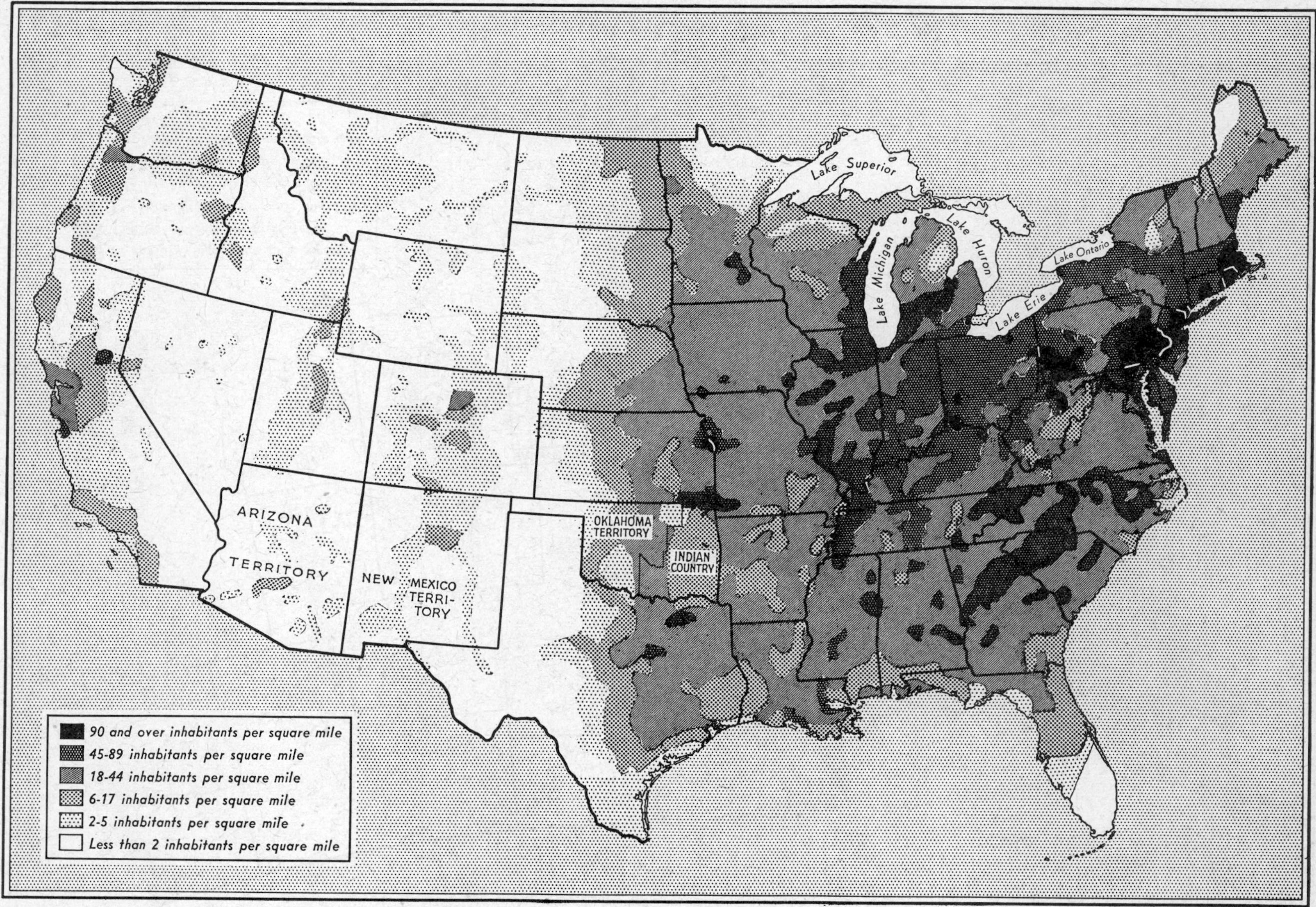

Lake Superior
Lake Michigan
Lake Huron
Lake Ontario
Lake Erie
ARIZONA TERRITORY
NEW MEXICO TERRITORY
OKLAHOMA TERRITORY
INDIAN COUNTRY
90 and over inhabitants per square mile
45-89 inhabitants per square mile
18-44 inhabitants per square mile
6-17 inhabitants per square mile
2-5 inhabitants per square mile
Less than 2 inhabitants per square mile

168

Population Density, 1900

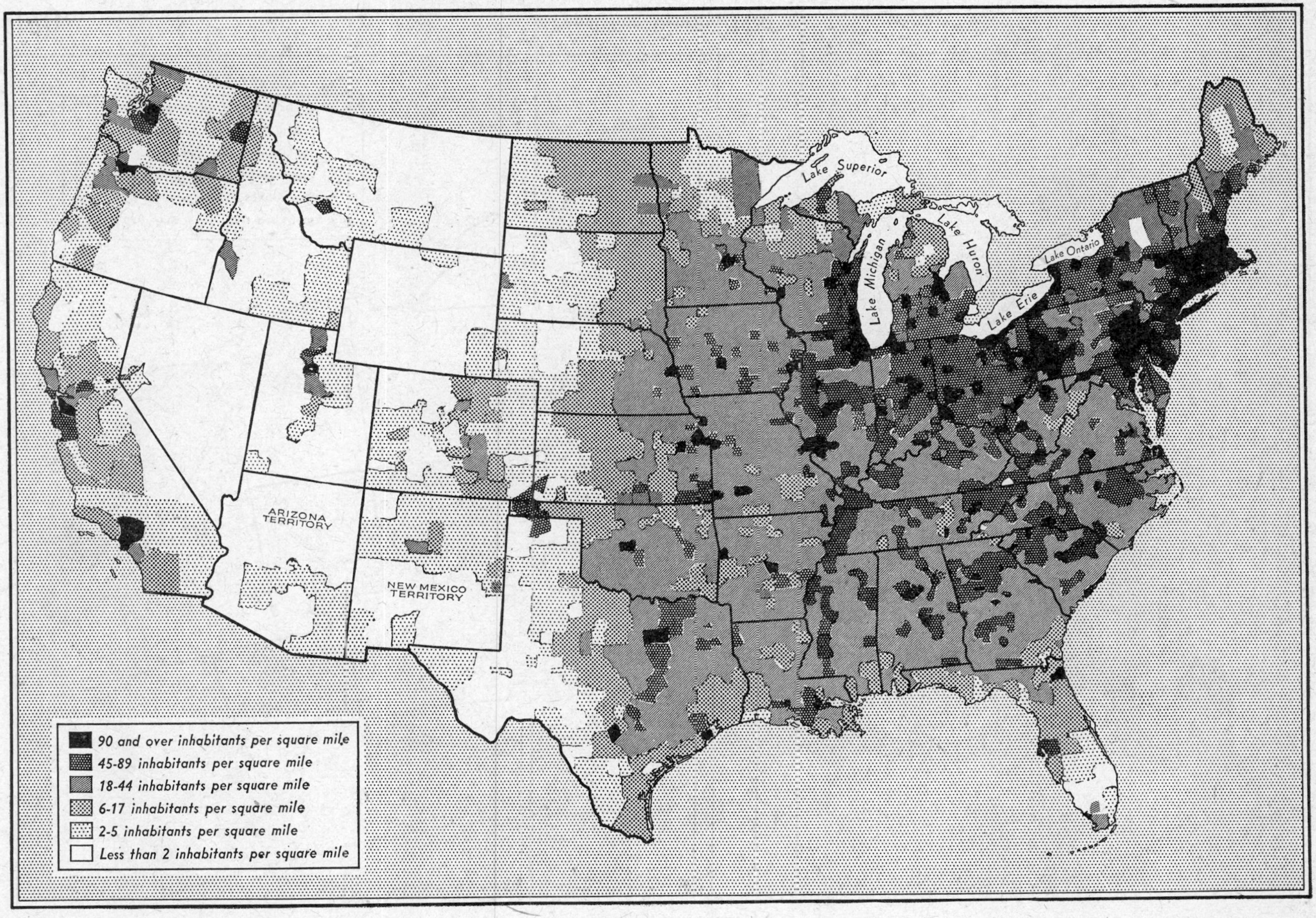

Lake Superior
Lake Michigan
Lake Huron
Lake Ontario
Lake Erie
ARIZONA TERRITORY
NEW MEXICO TERRITORY

90 and over inhabitants per square mile
45-89 inhabitants per square mile
18-44 inhabitants per square mile
6-17 inhabitants per square mile
2-5 inhabitants per square mile
Less than 2 inhabitants per square mile

169

Population Density, 1910

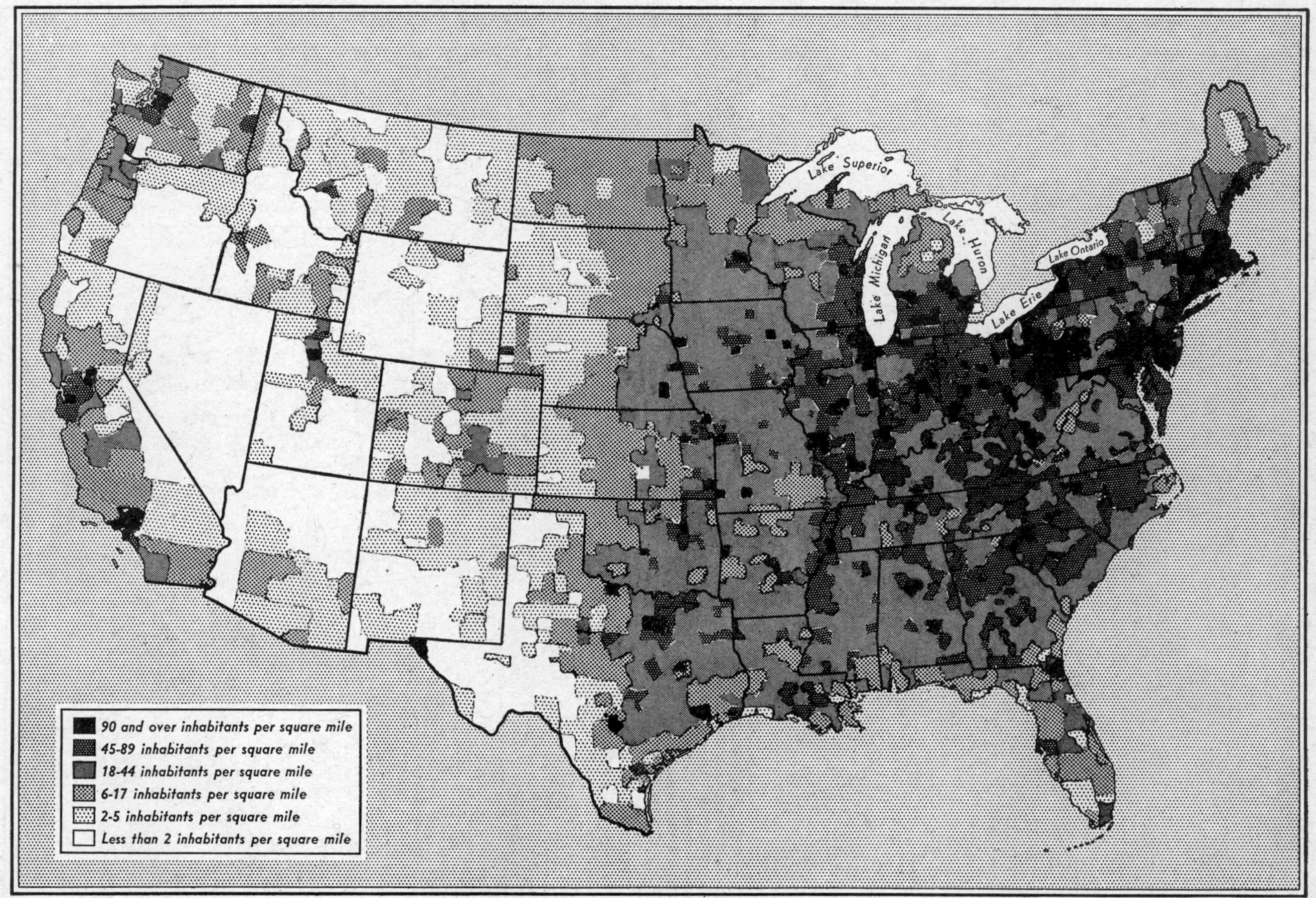

Lake Superior
Lake Michigan
Lake Huron
Lake Ontario
Lake Erie
90 and over inhabitants per square mile
45-89 inhabitants per square mile
18-44 inhabitants per square mile
6-17 inhabitants per square mile
2-5 inhabitants per square mile
Less than 2 inhabitants per square mile

170 Population Density, 1920

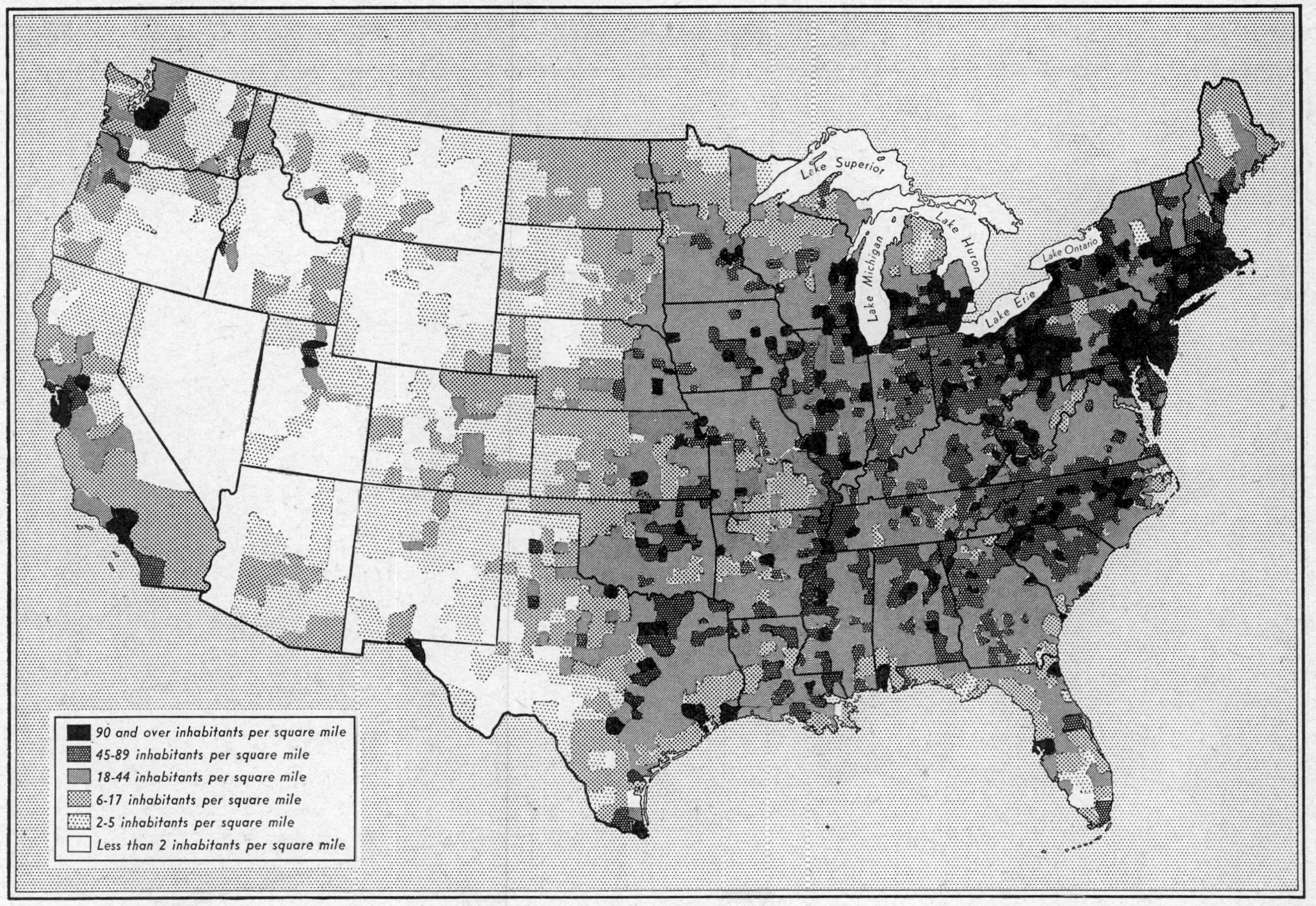
Lake Superior
Lake Michigan
Lake Huron
Lake Ontario
Lake Erie
90 and over inhabitants per square mile
45-89 inhabitants per square mile
18-44 inhabitants per square mile
6-17 inhabitants per square mile
2-5 inhabitants per square mile
Less than 2 inhabitants per square mile

171

Population Density, 1930

Lake Superior
Lake Michigan
Lake Huron
Lake Ontario
Lake Erie
OKLAHOMA TERRITORY
INDIAN COUNTRY
ARIZONA TERRITORY
NEW MEXICO TERRITORY
50 per cent and over
30-49 per cent
10-29 per cent
Under 10 per cent
Areas without colored population, or unsettled

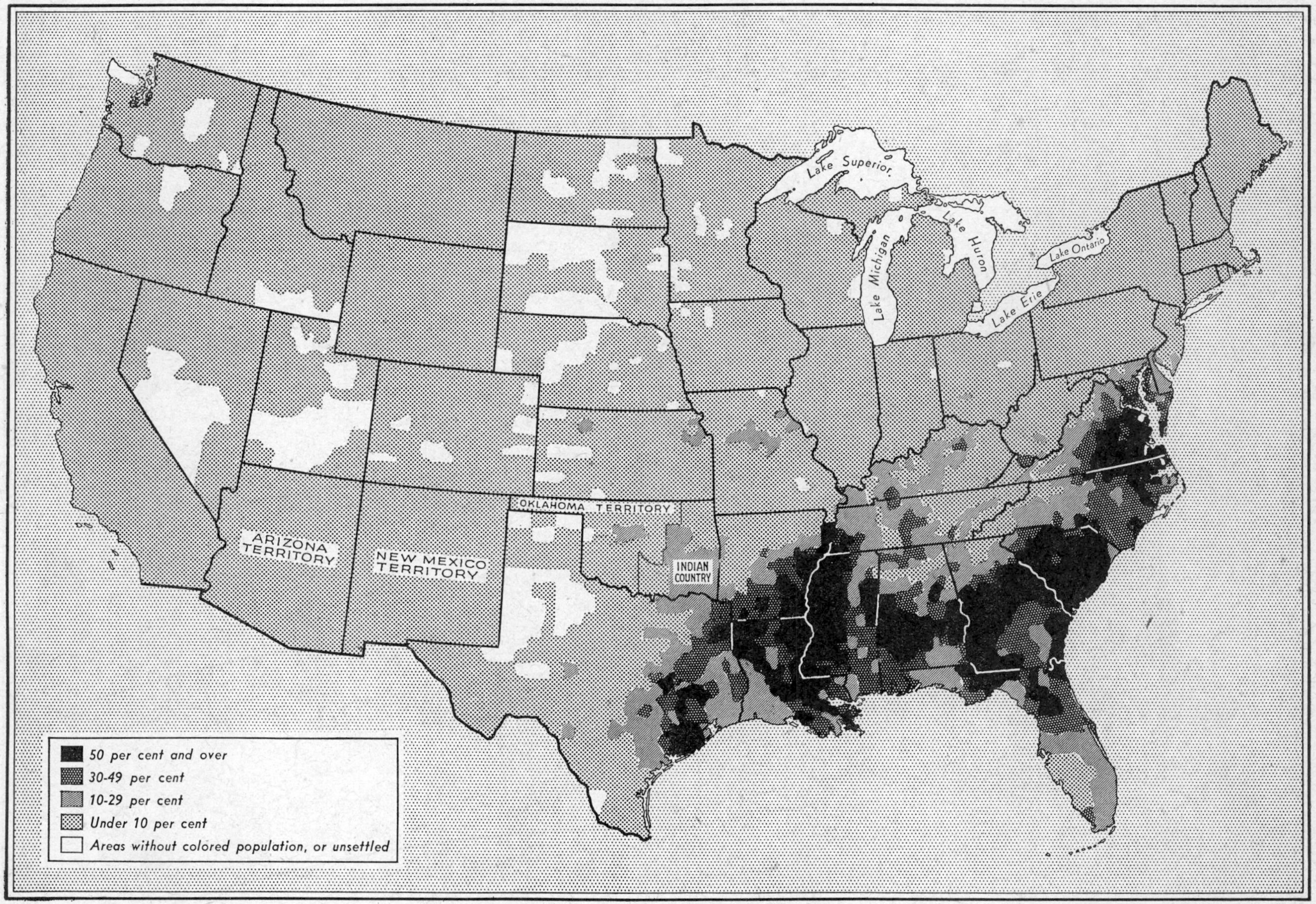

172

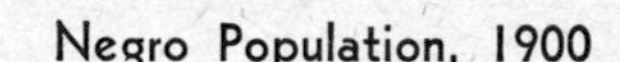

Negro Population, 1900

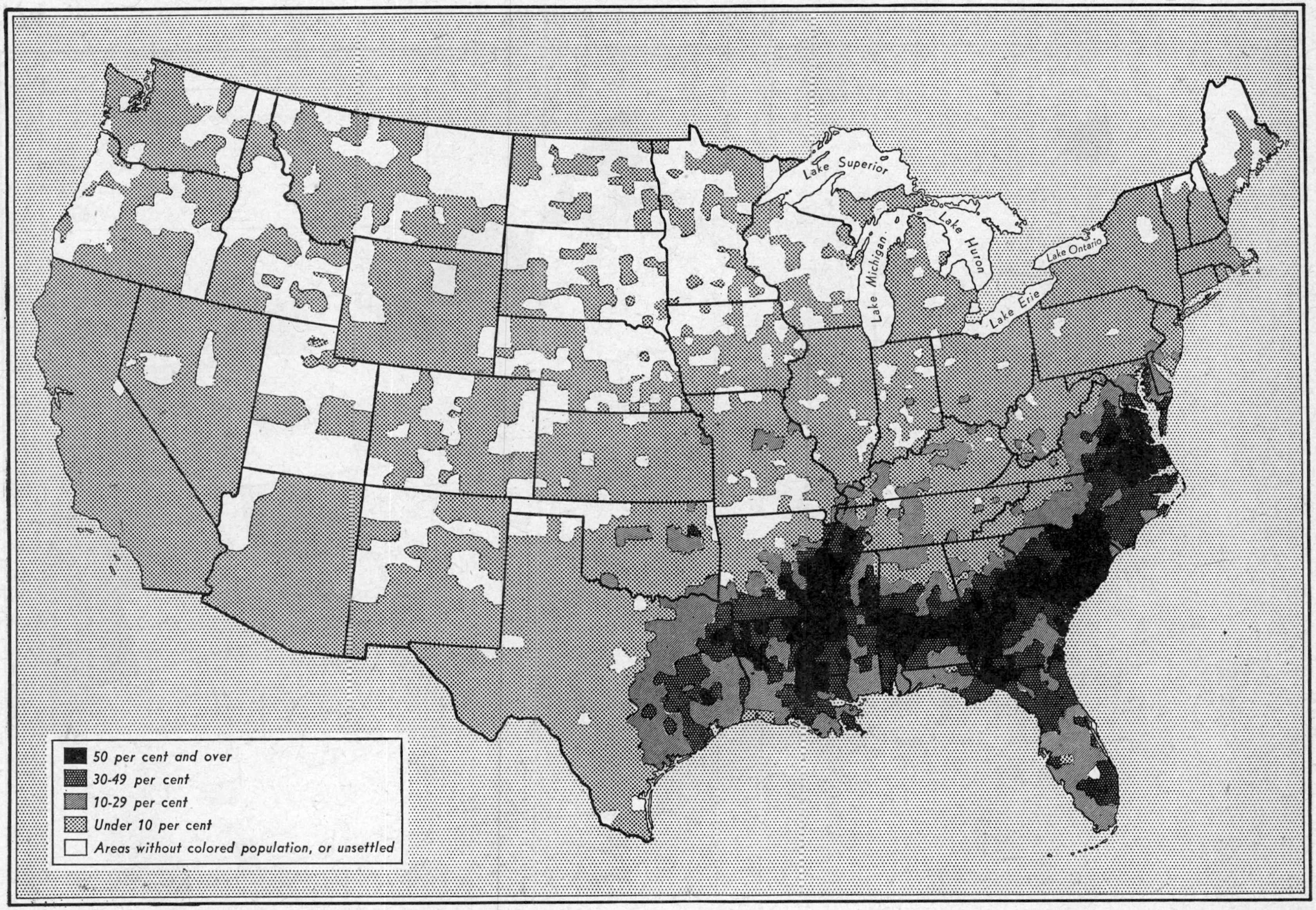

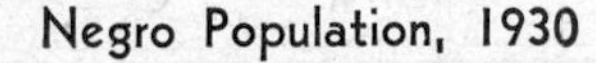

173

Negro Population, 1930

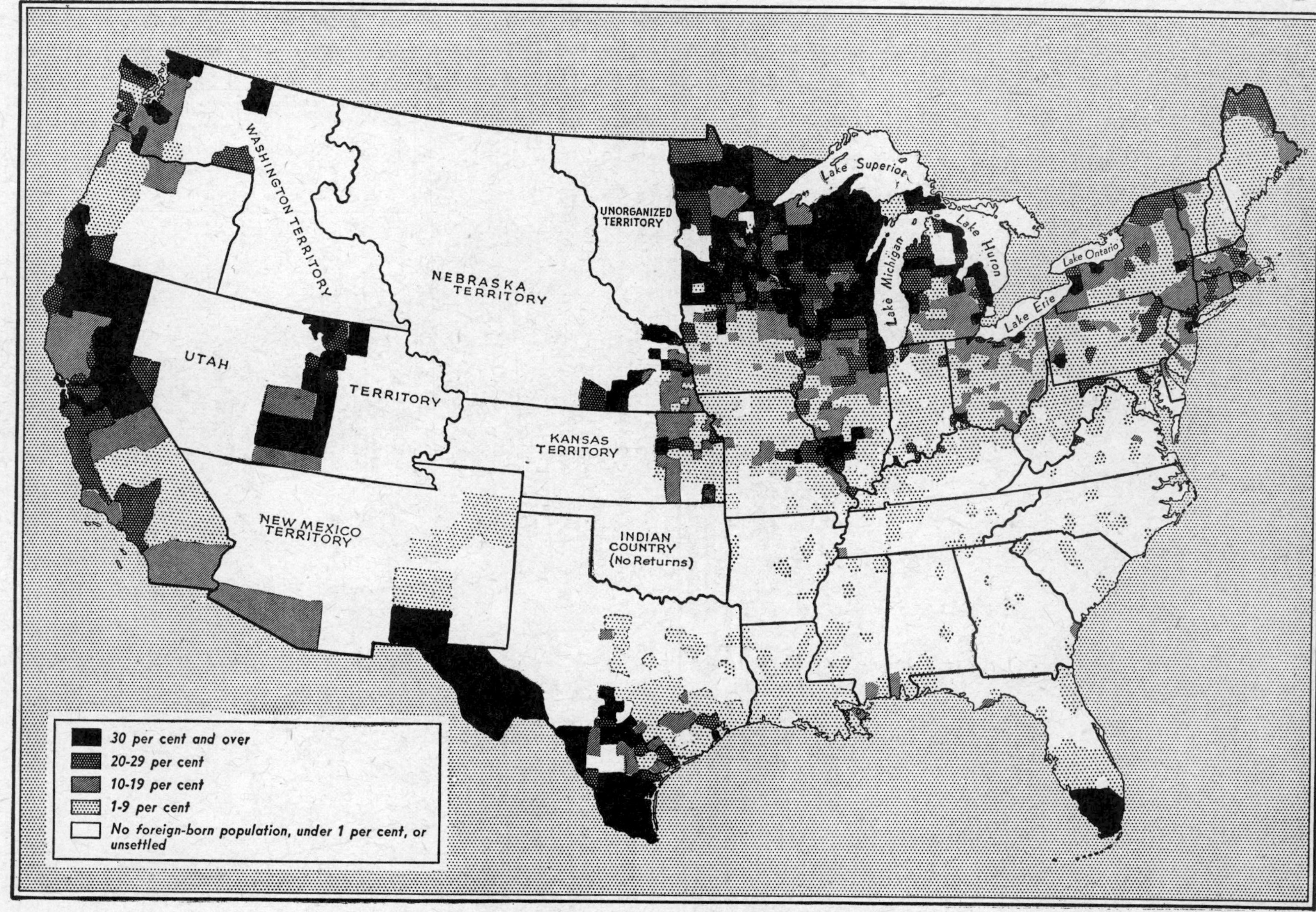

174

Population of Foreign Birth, 1860

175

Population of Foreign Birth, 1880

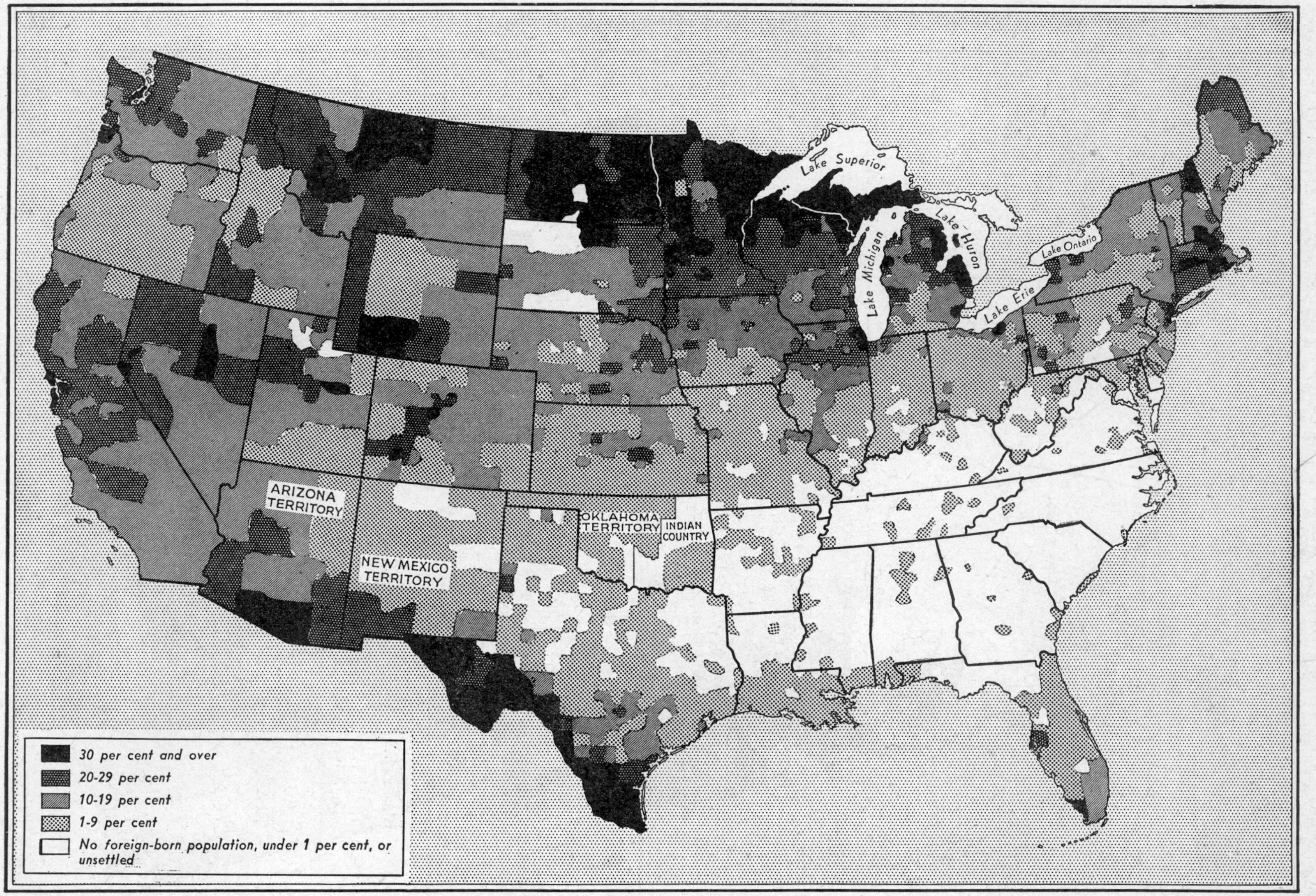

Lake Superior
Lake Michigan
Lake Huron
Lake Erie
Lake Ontario
ARIZONA TERRITORY
NEW MEXICO TERRITORY
OKLAHOMA TERRITORY
INDIAN COUNTRY

30 per cent and over
20-29 per cent
10-19 per cent
1-9 per cent
No foreign-born population, under 1 per cent, or unsettled

176

Population of Foreign Birth, 1900

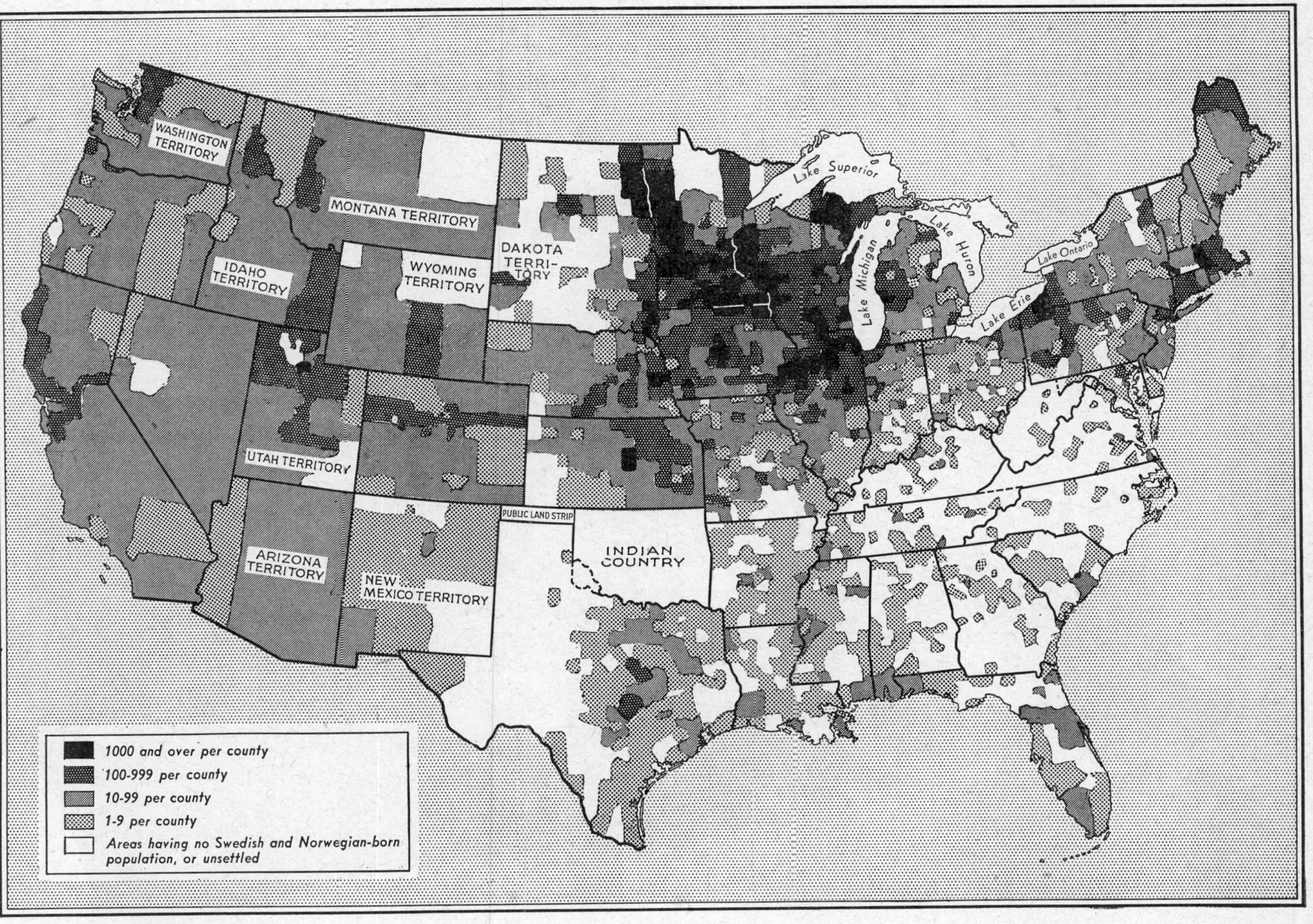

177

Swedish- and Norwegian-born Population, 1880

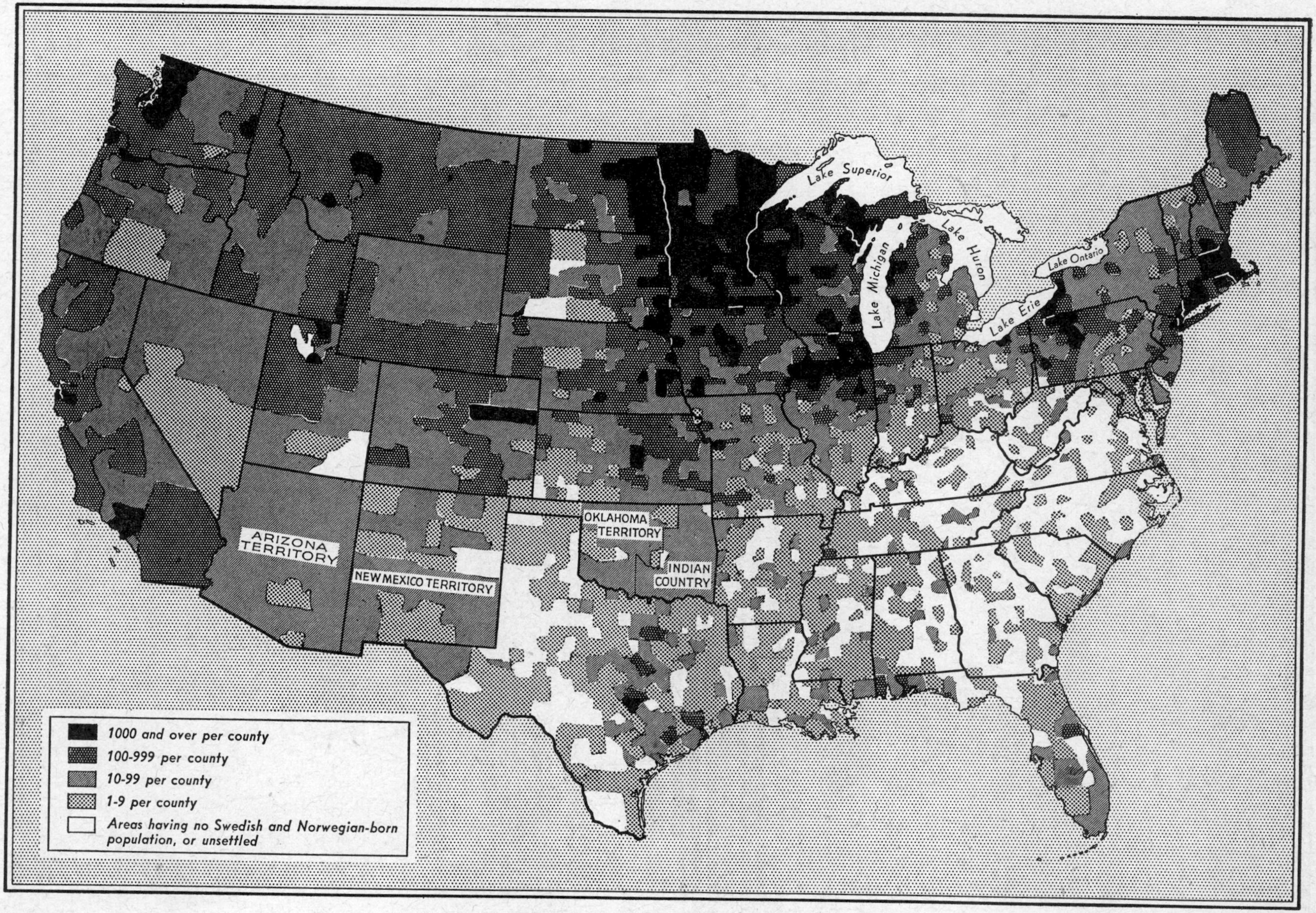

Lake Superior
Lake Michigan
Lake Huron
Lake Ontario
Lake Erie
ARIZONA TERRITORY
NEW MEXICO TERRITORY
OKLAHOMA TERRITORY
INDIAN COUNTRY

1000 and over per county
100-999 per county
10-99 per county
1-9 per county
Areas having no Swedish and Norwegian-born population, or unsettled

178 Swedish- and Norwegian-born Population, 1900

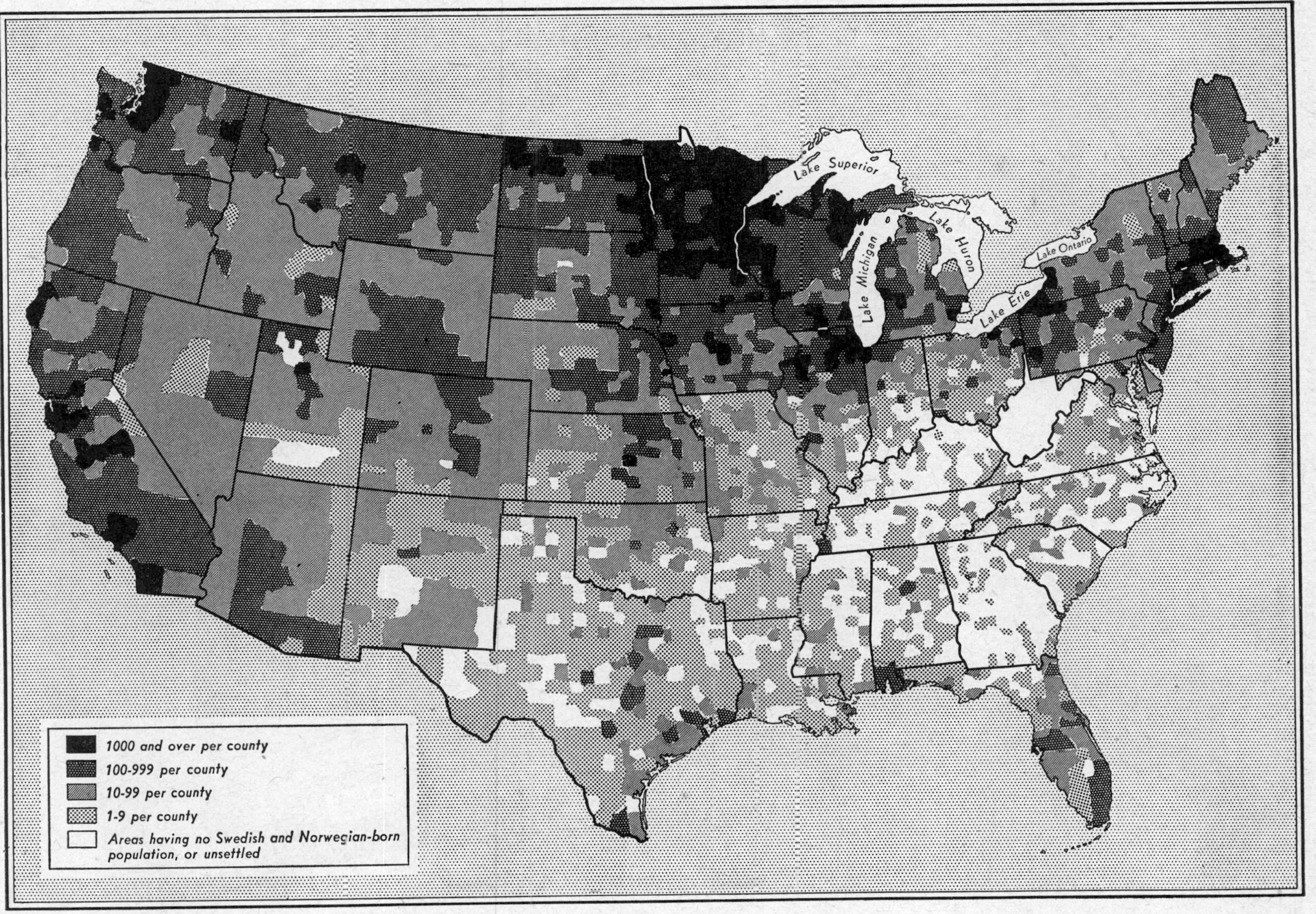

179

Swedish- and Norwegian-born Population, 1930

WASHINGTON TERRITORY
MONTANA TERRITORY
DAKOTA TERRI- TORY
IDAHO TERRITORY
WYOMING TERRITORY
UTAH TERRITORY
ARIZONA TERRI- TORY
NEW MEXICO TERRITORY
PUBLIC LAND STRIP
INDIAN COUNTRY
Lake Superior
Lake Michigan
Lake Huron
Lake Erie
Lake Ontario
1000 and over per county
100-999 per county
10-99 per county
1-9 per county
Areas having no Irish-born population, or unsettled

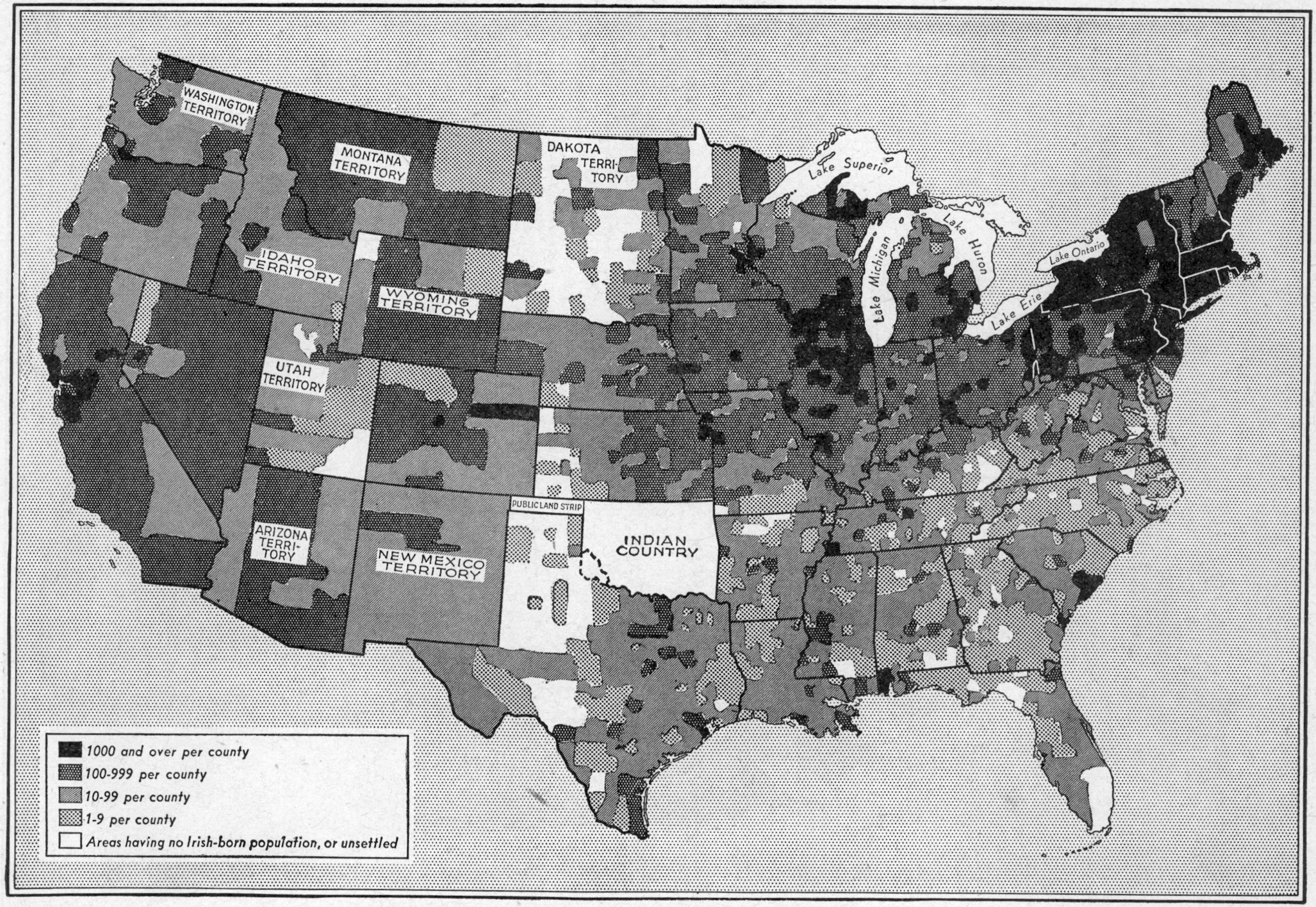

180 Irish-born Population, 1880

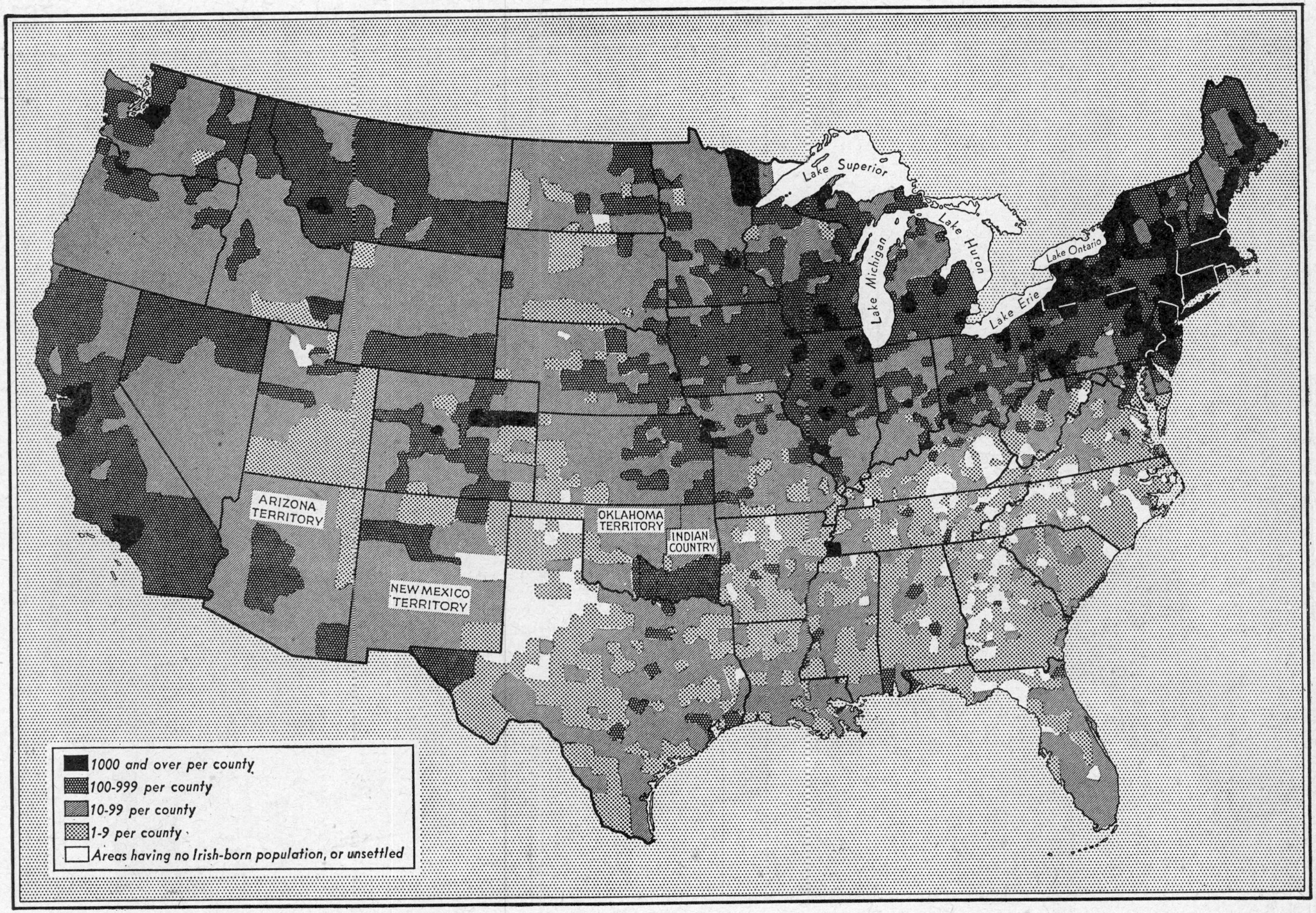

Lake Superior
Lake Michigan
Lake Huron
Lake Ontario
Lake Erie
ARIZONA TERRITORY
NEW MEXICO TERRITORY
OKLAHOMA TERRITORY
INDIAN COUNTRY

1000 and over per county
100-999 per county
10-99 per county
1-9 per county
Areas having no Irish-born population, or unsettled

181

Irish-born Population, 1900

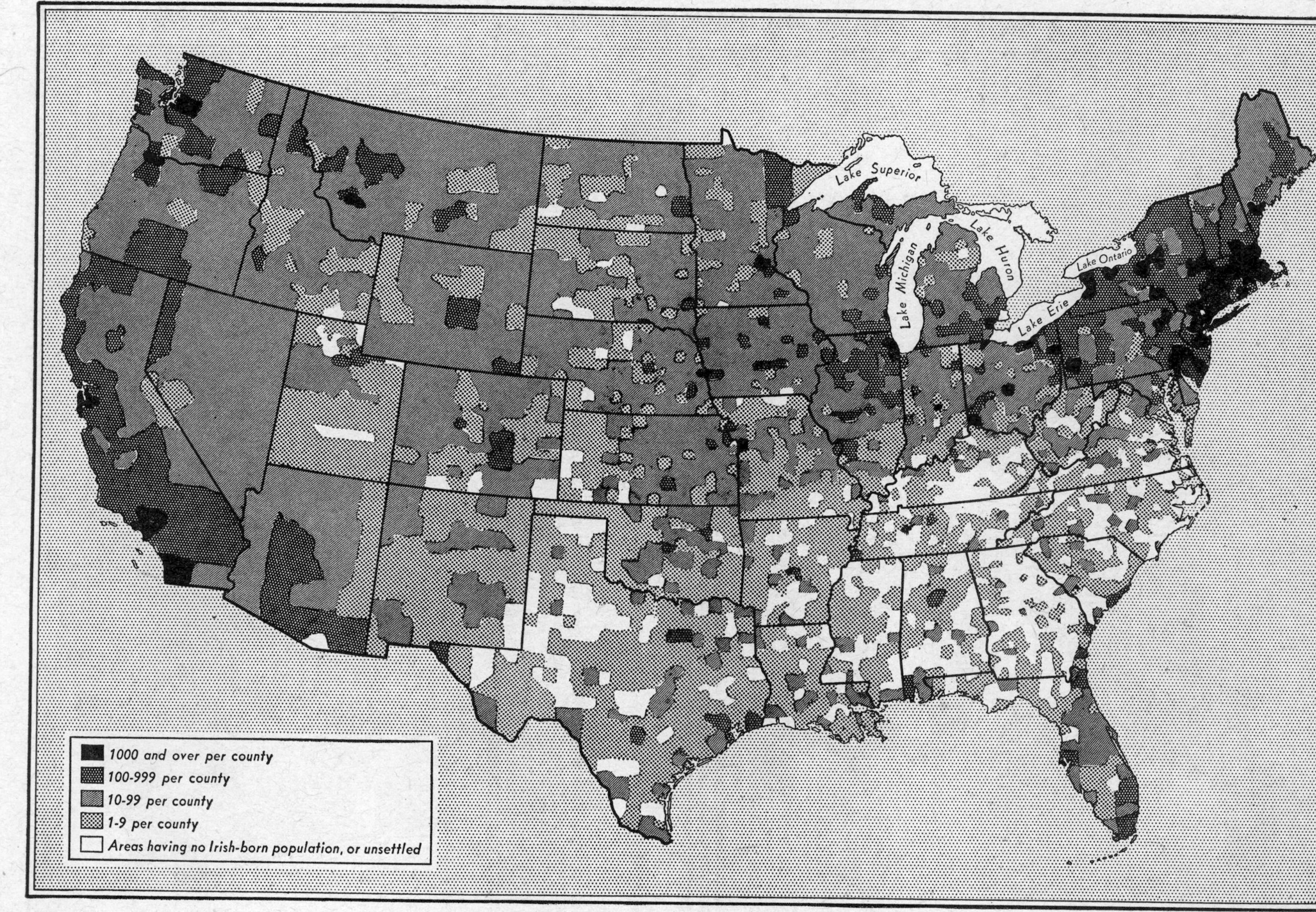

182 Irish-born Population, 1930

WASHINGTON TERRITORY
MONTANA TERRITORY
IDAHO TERRITORY
WYOMING TERRITORY
DAKOTA TERRI-TORY
UTAH TER-RITORY
ARIZONA TERRITORY
NEW MEXICO TERRITORY
PUBLIC LAND STRIP
INDIAN COUNTRY
Lake Superior
Lake Michigan
Lake Huron
Lake Erie
Lake Ontario
1000 and over per county
100-999 per county
10-99 per county
1-9 per county
Areas having no German-born population, or unsettled

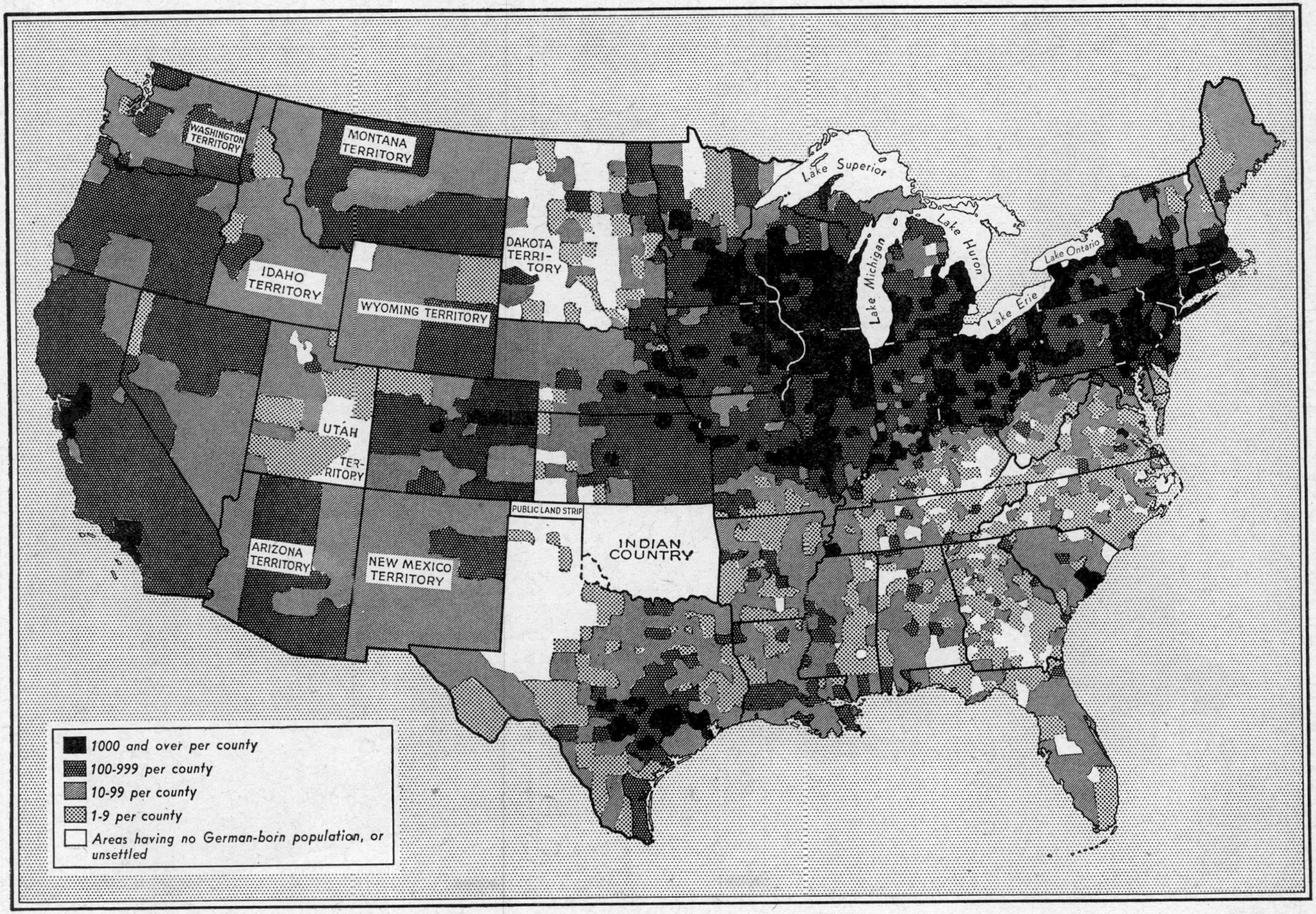

183

German-born Population, 1880

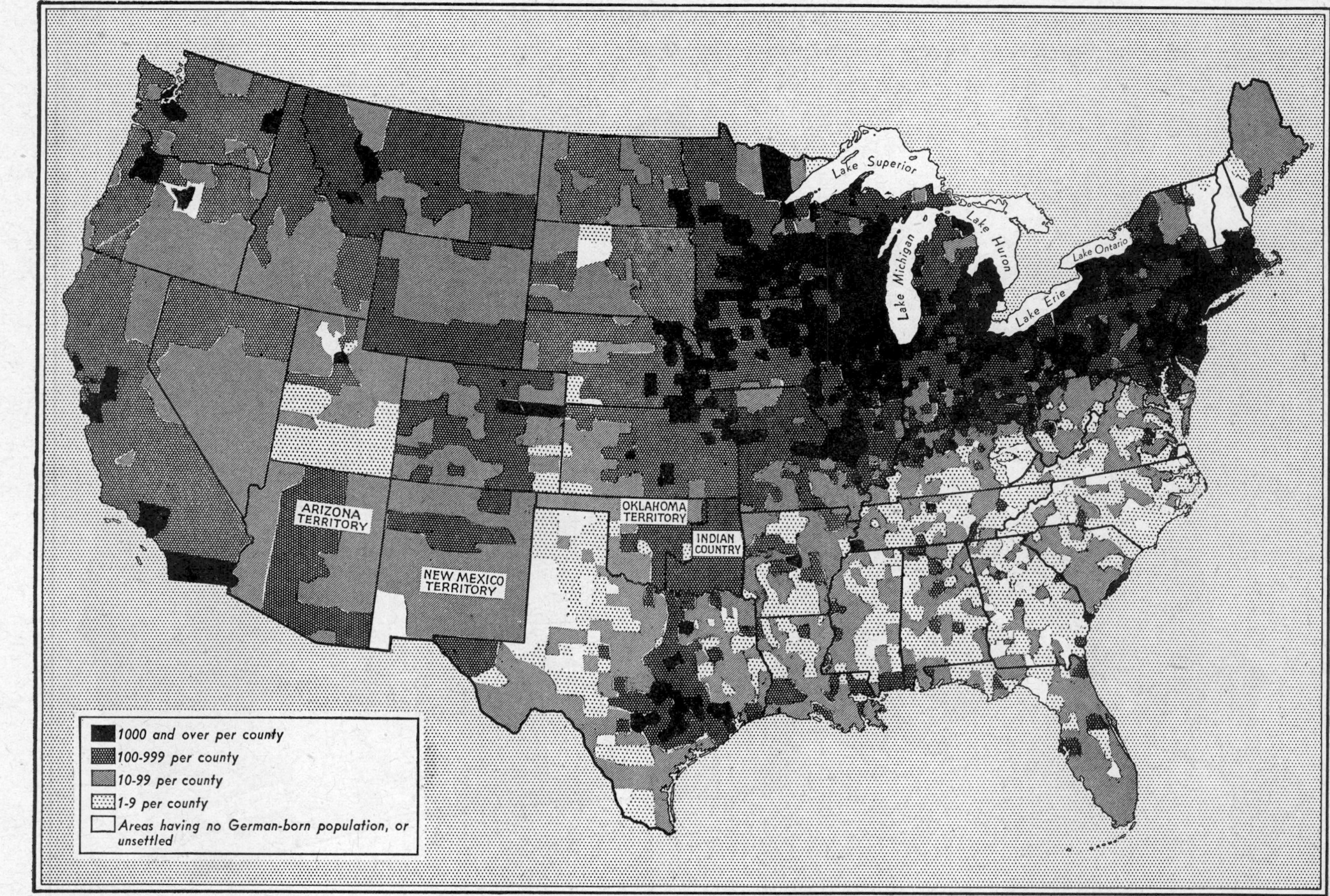

184 German-born Population, 1900

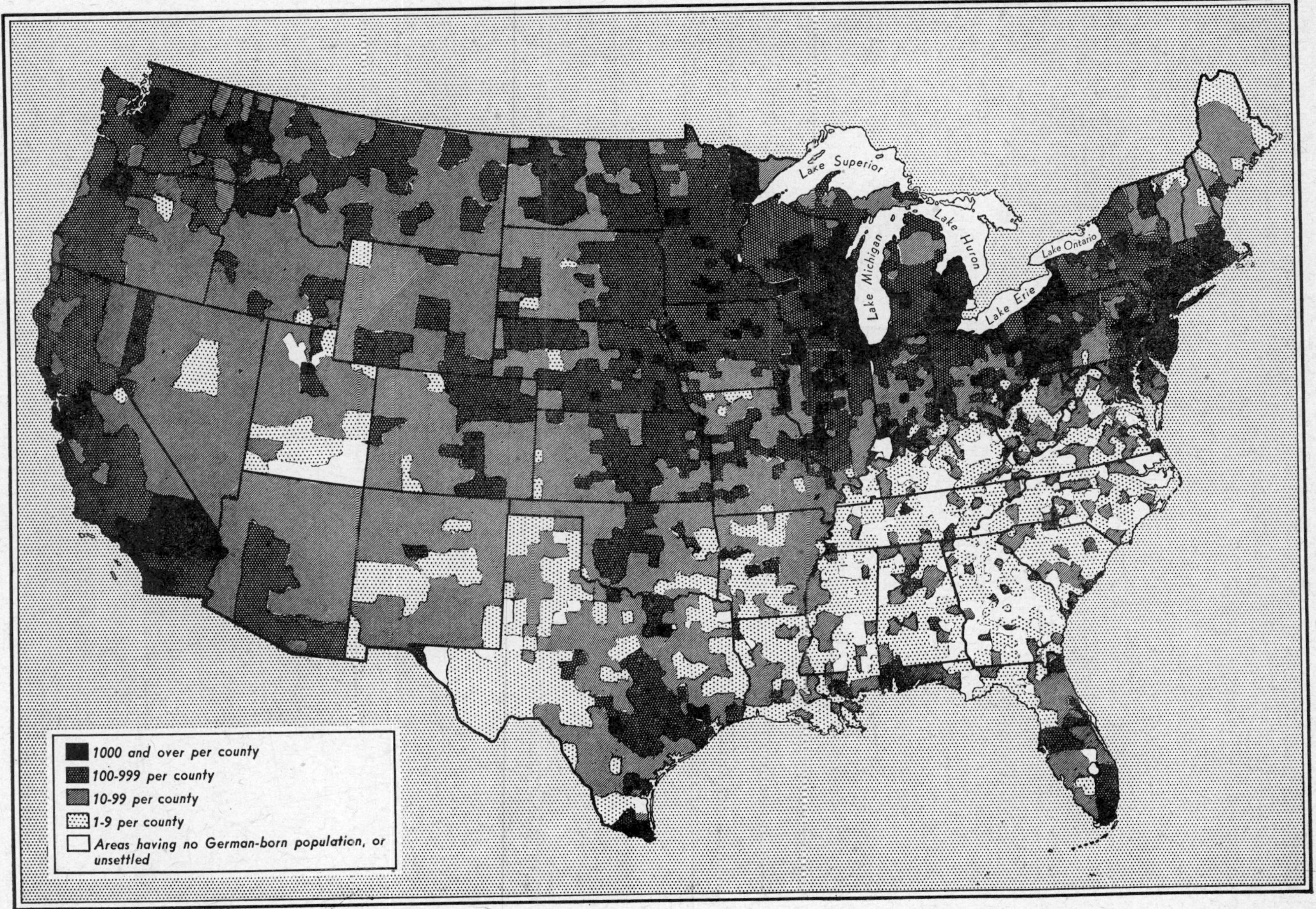

185

German-born Population, 1930

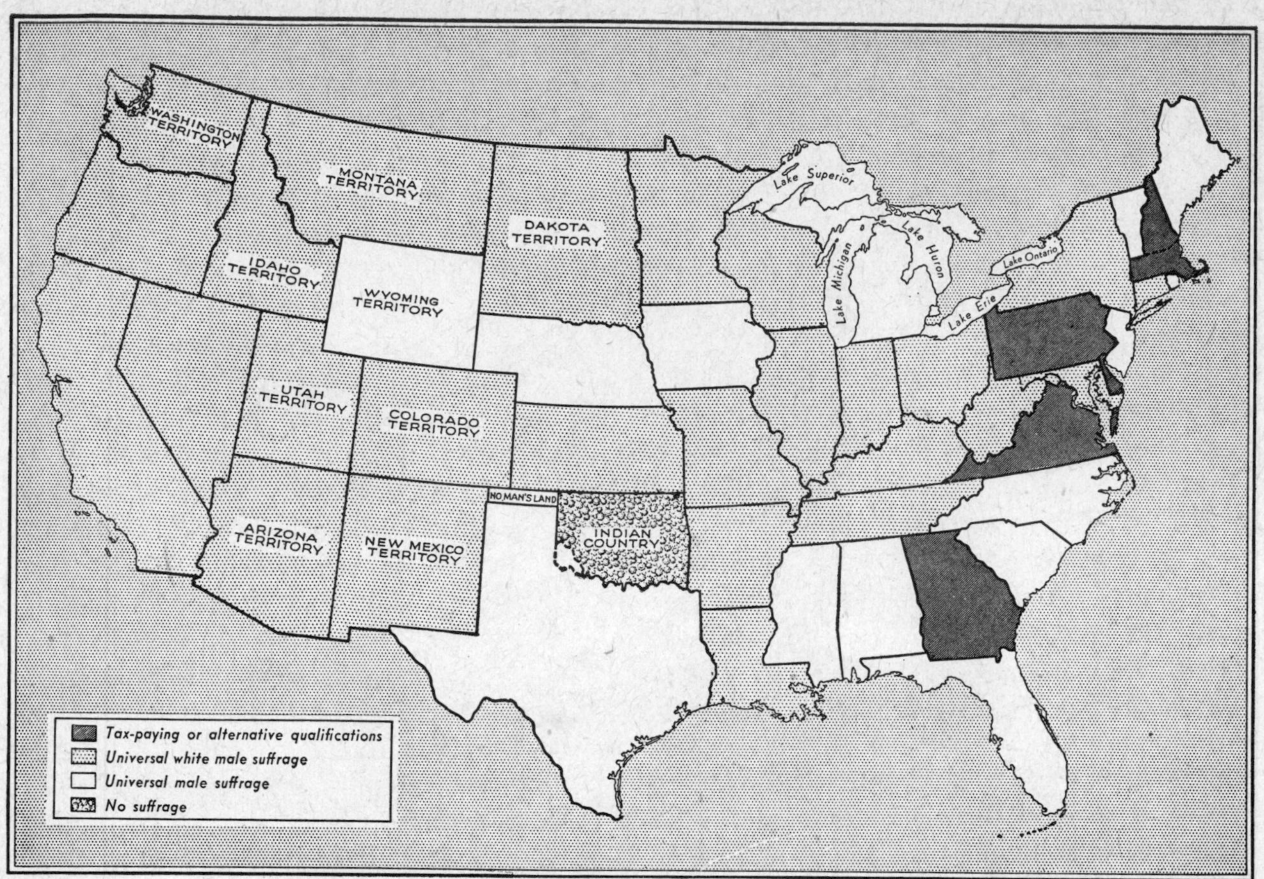

186 Male Suffrage, 1870

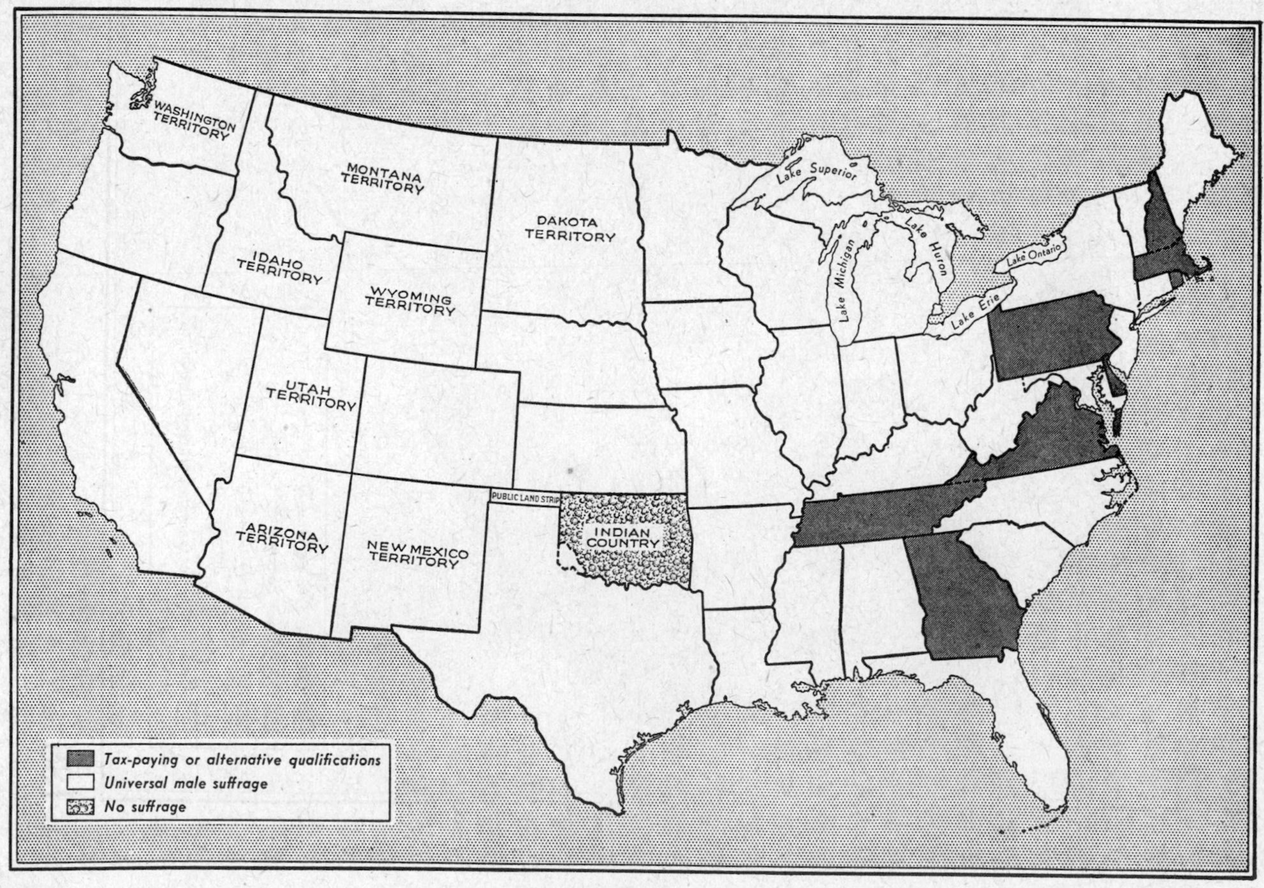

187 Male Suffrage, 1880

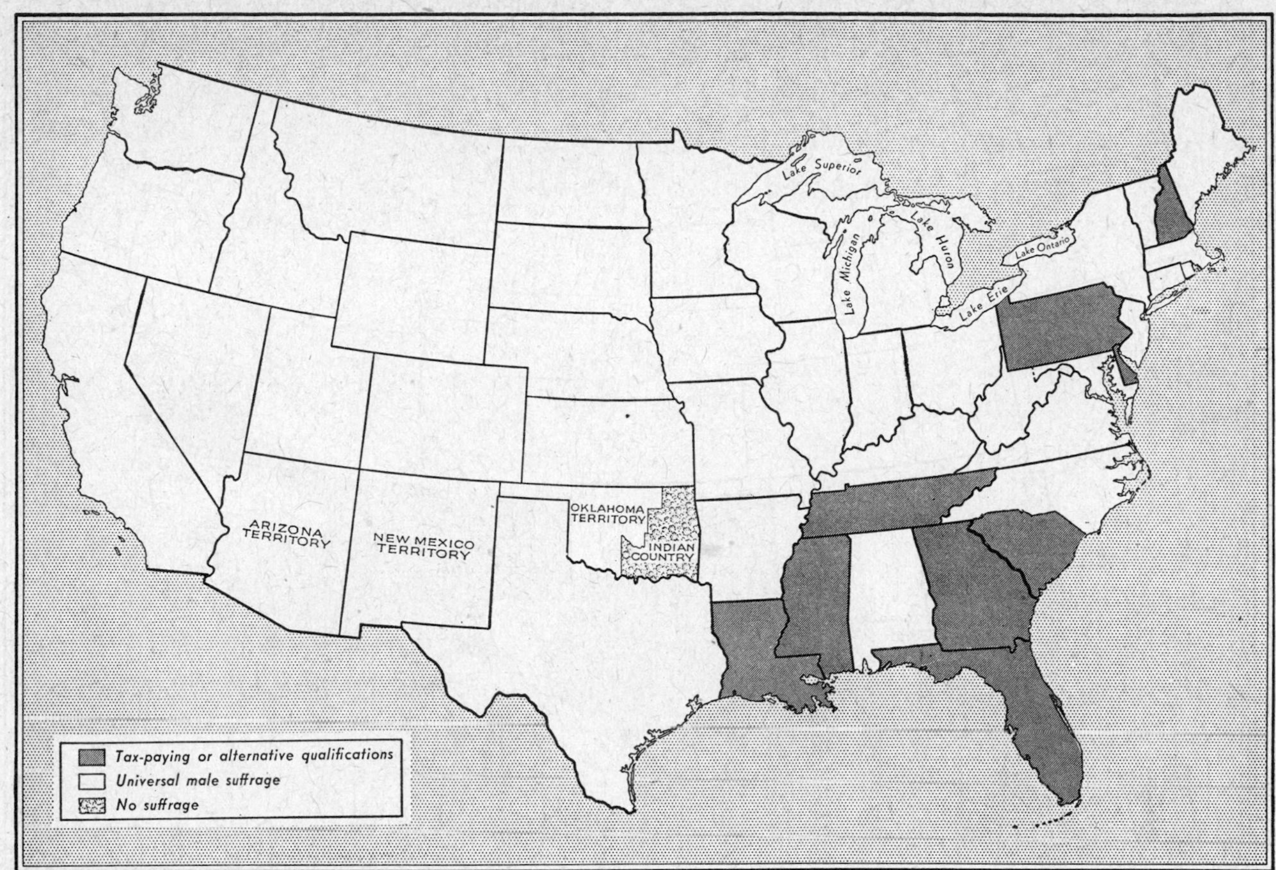

188 Male Suffrage, 1900

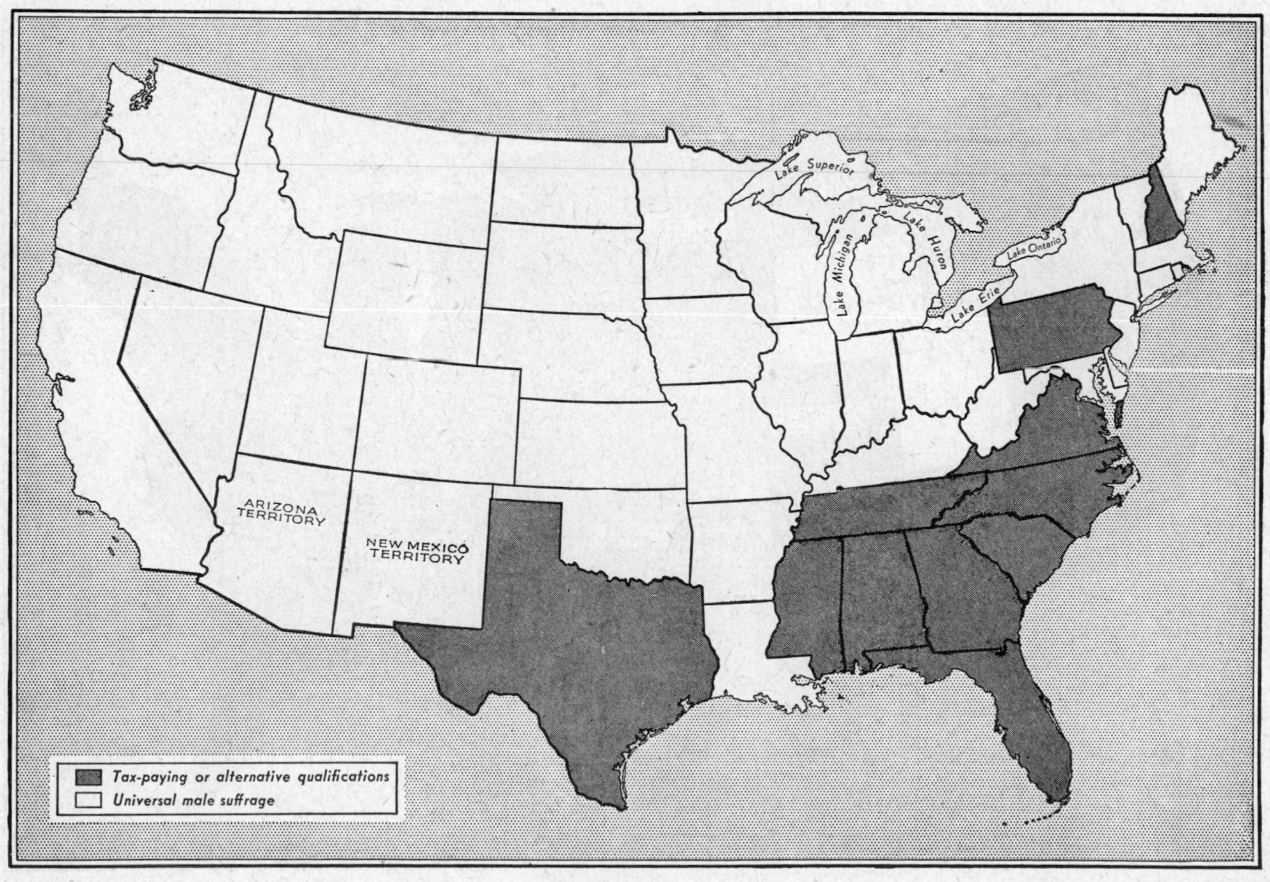

189 Male Suffrage, 1910

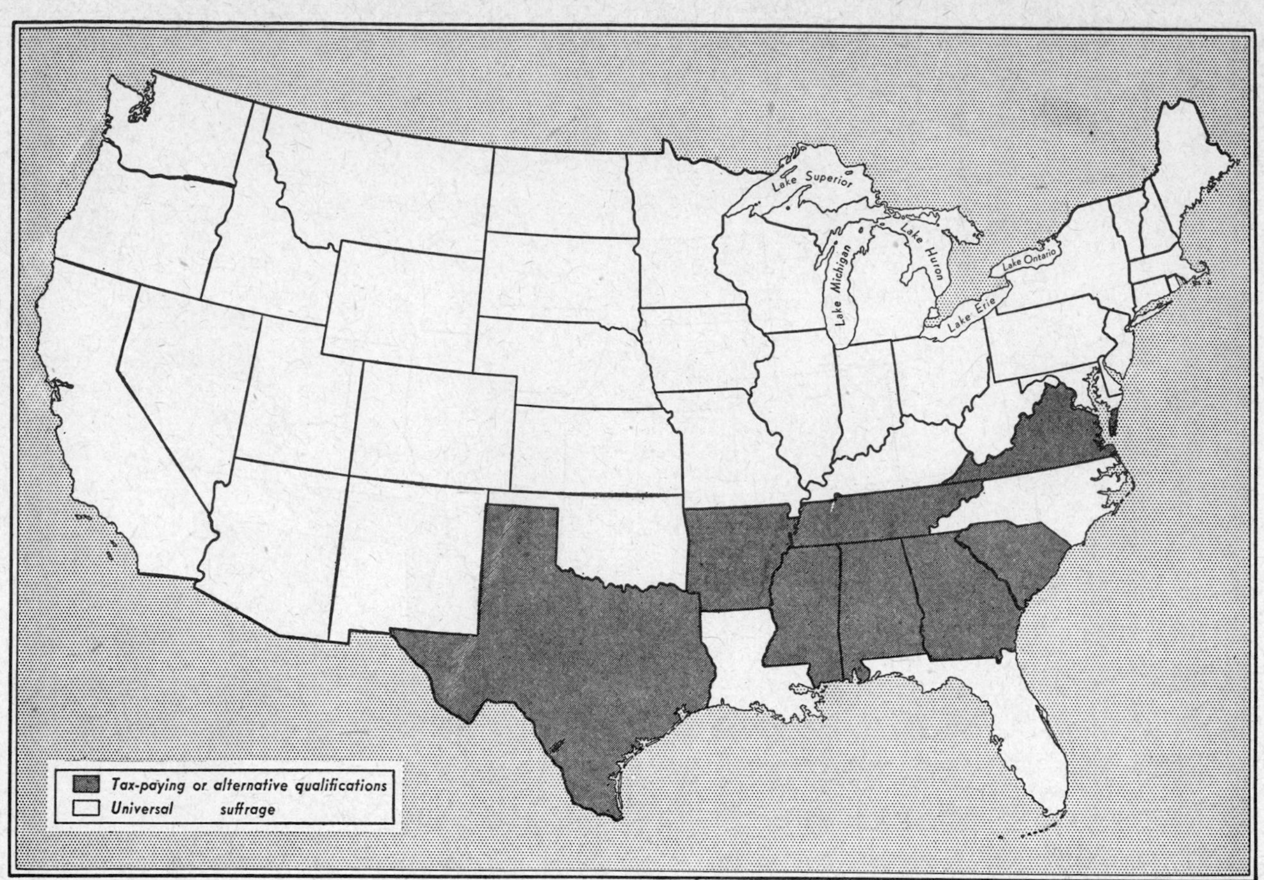

190 Suffrage, 1940

(See also literary requirements on map 196)

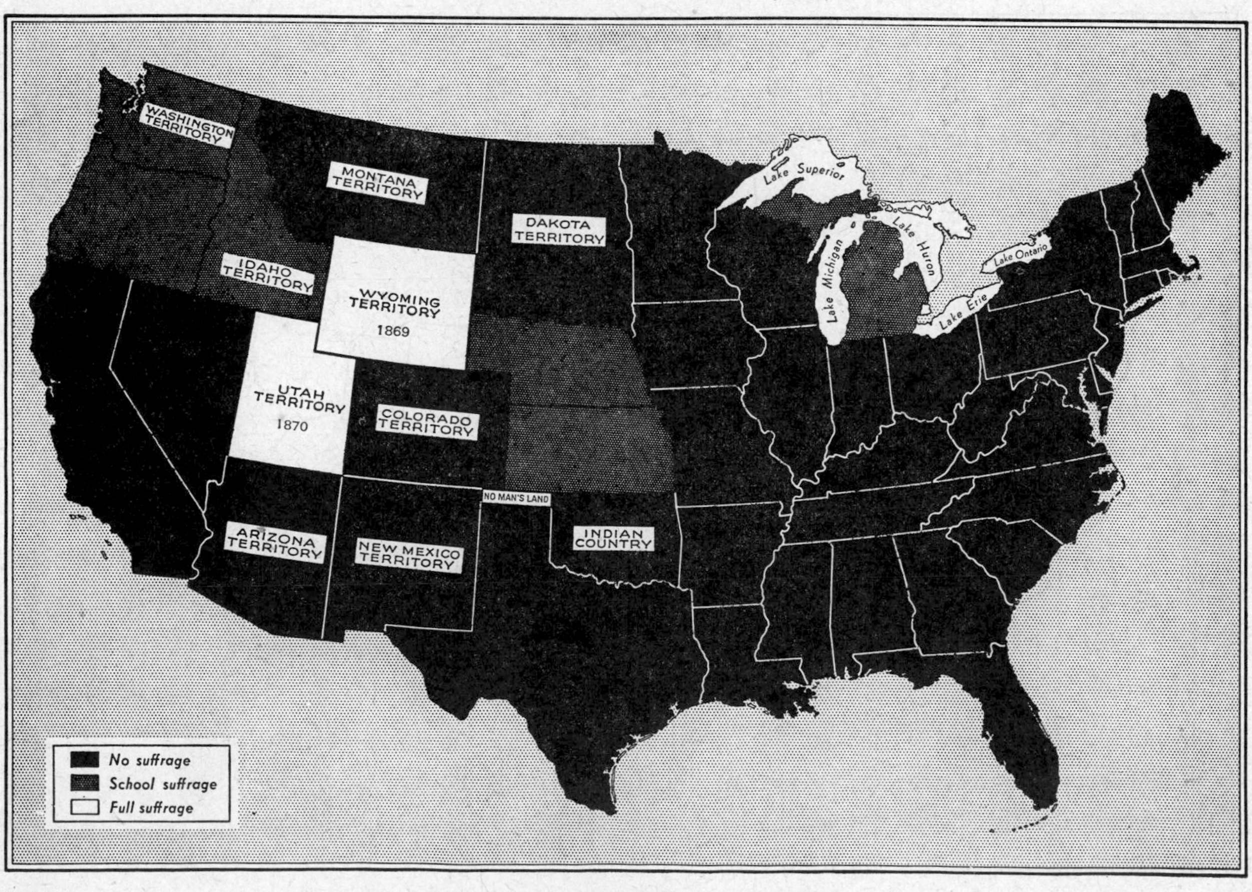

191 Enfranchisement of Women, 1870

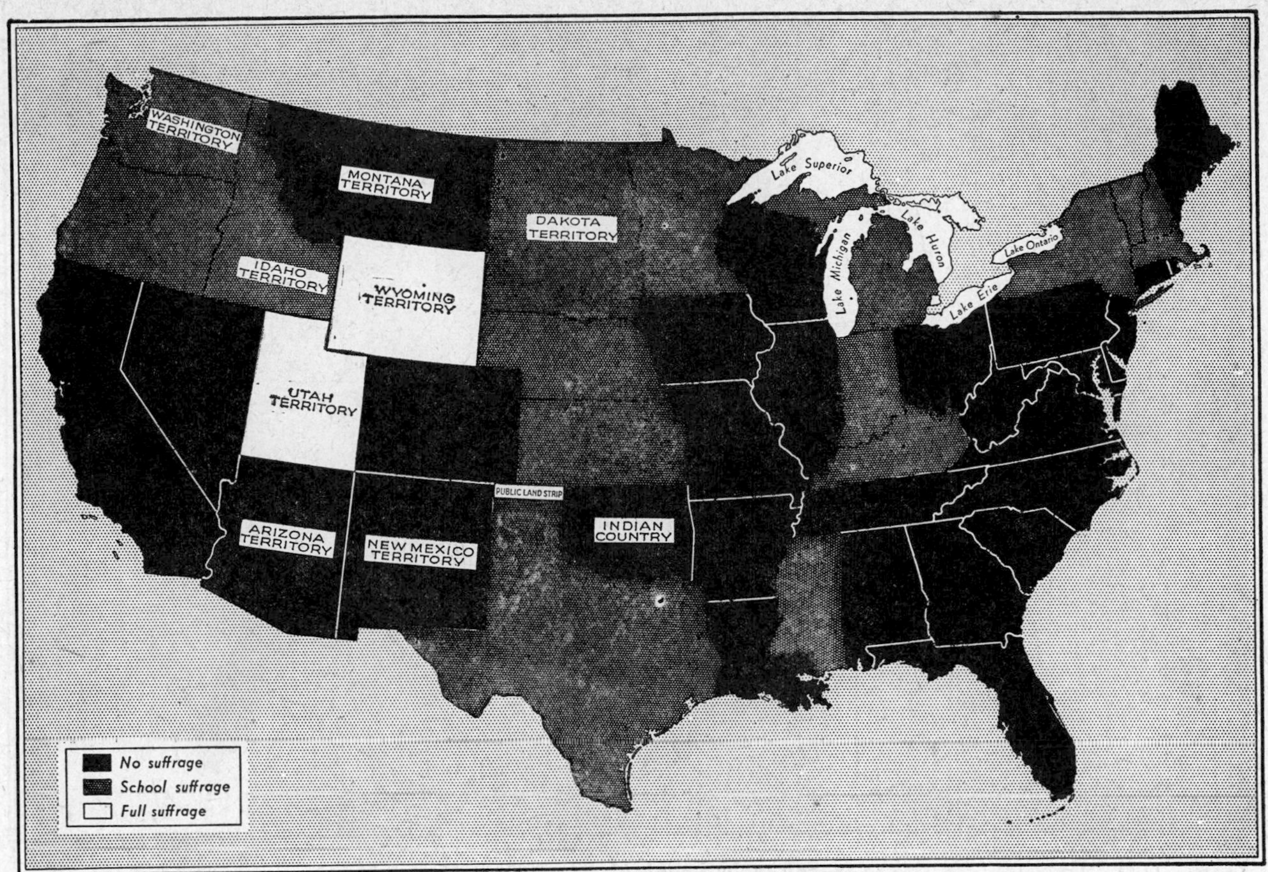

192 Enfranchisement of Women, 1880

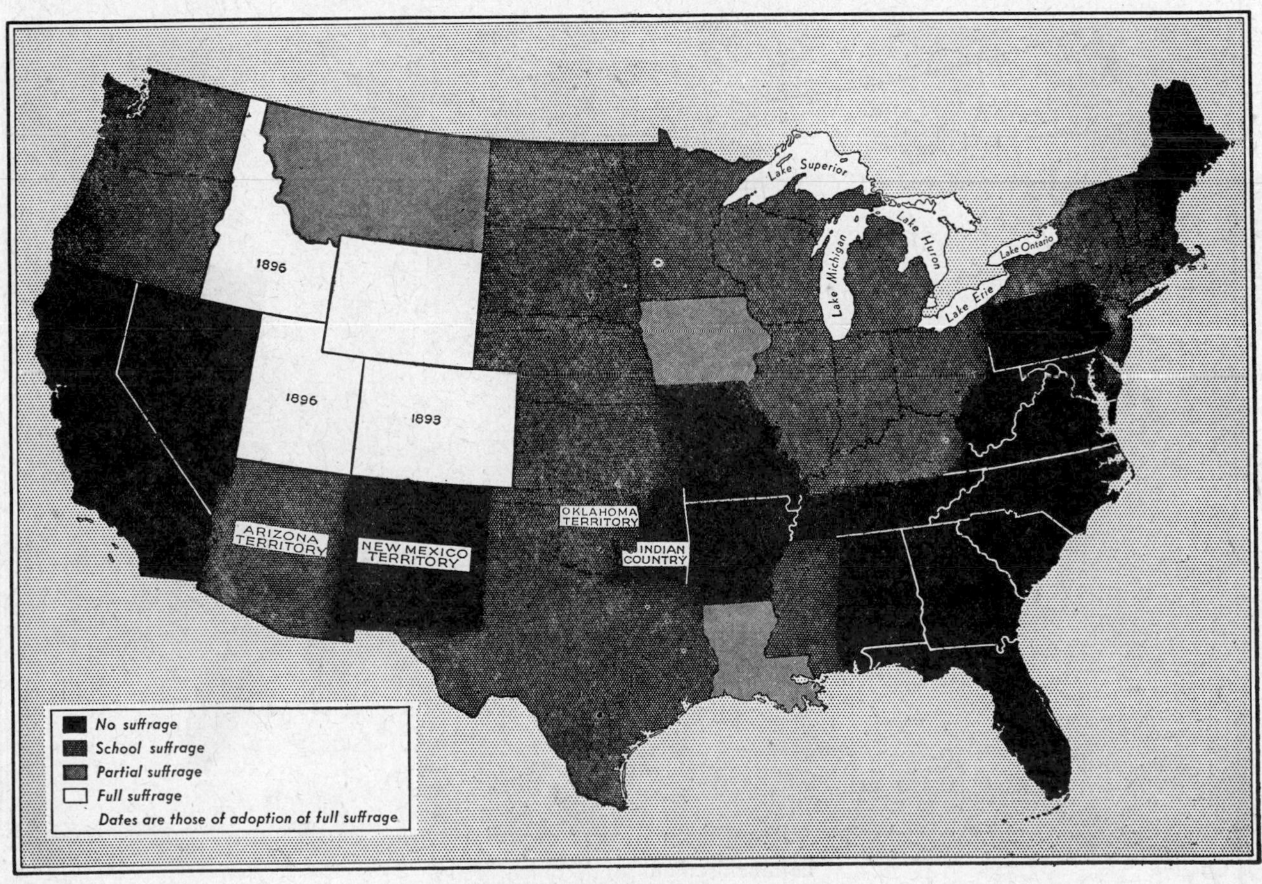

193 Enfranchisement of Women, 1900

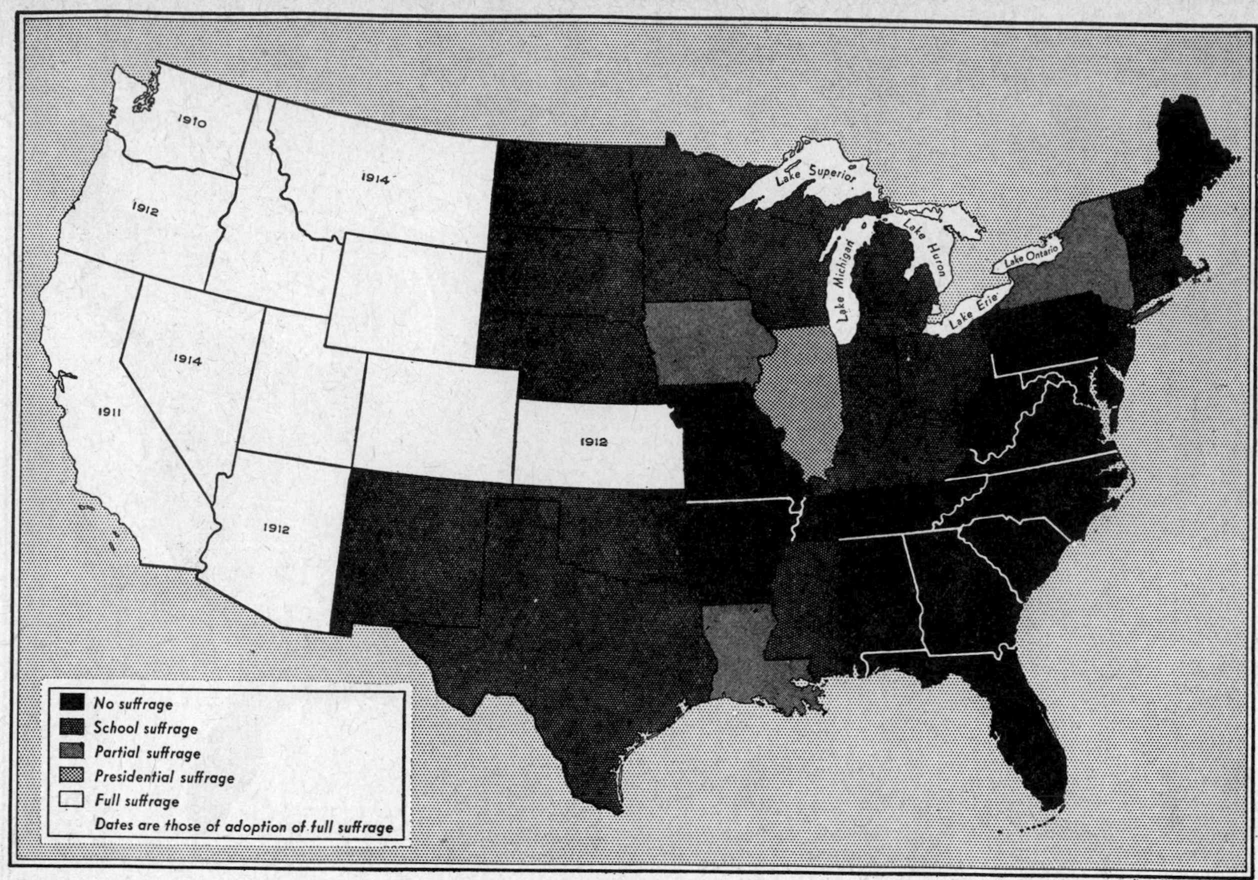

194 Enfranchisement of Women, 1915

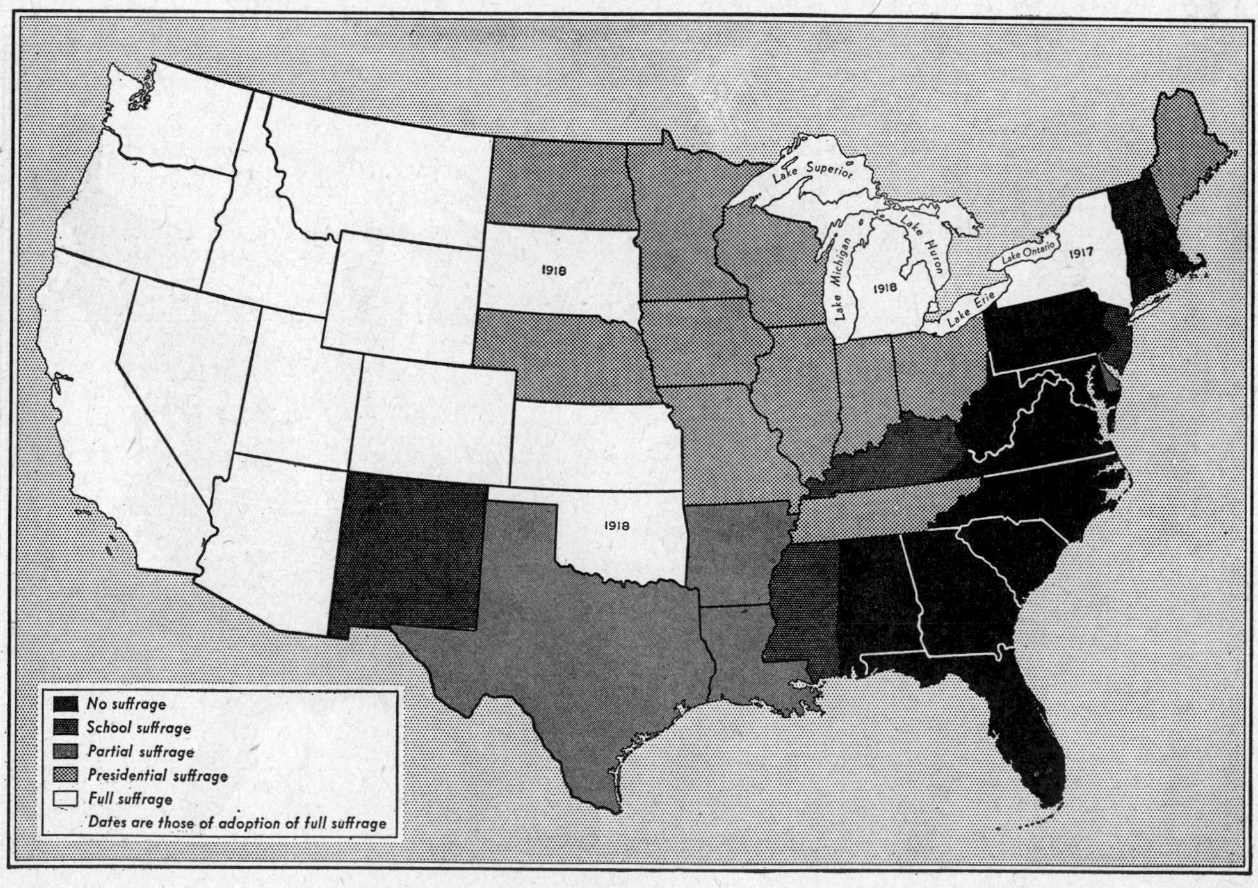

195 Enfranchisement of Women, 1919

The Nineteenth Amendment in 1920 extended suffrage to women in all states

(See maps 190 and 196 for suffrage qualifications)

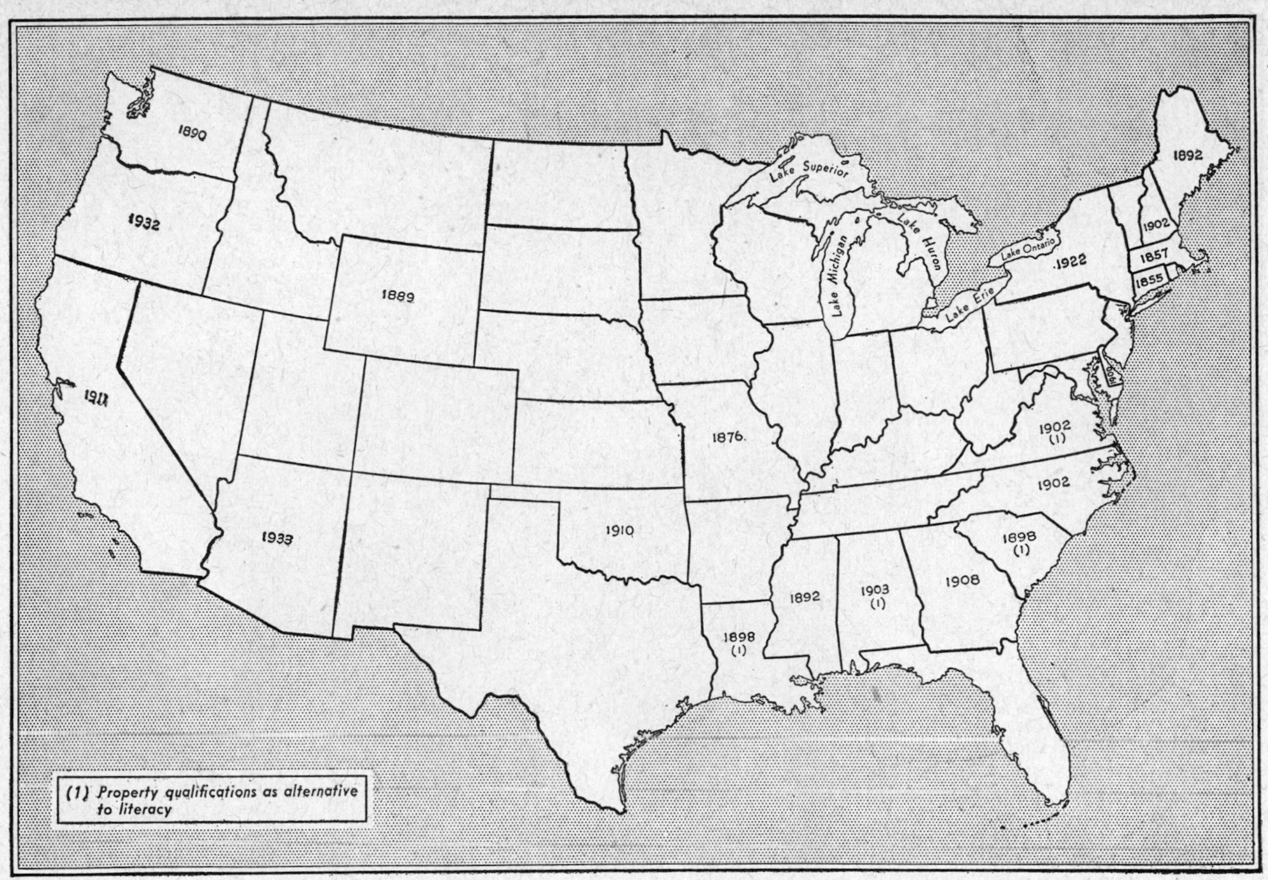

196 Dates of the Establishment of Literacy Qualifications for the Franchise

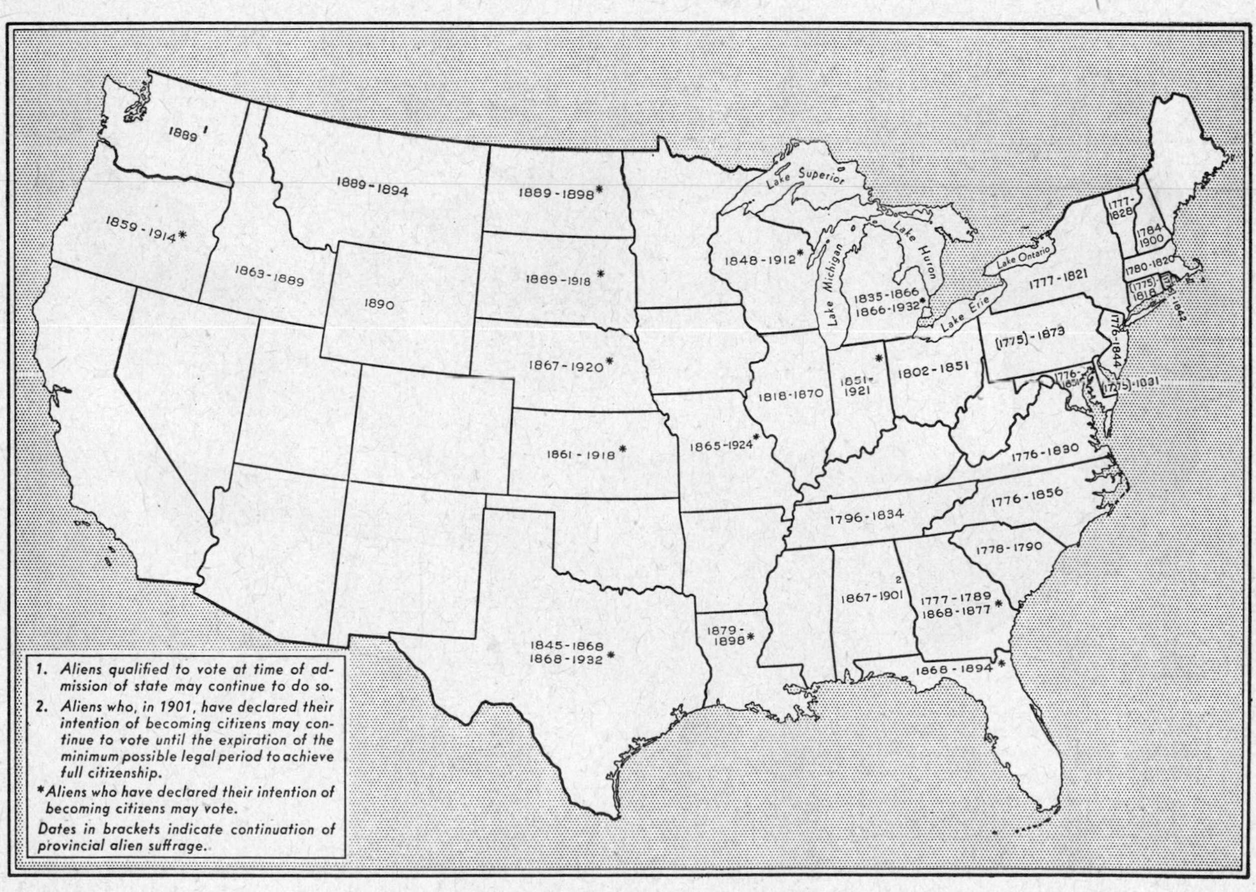

197 Alien Enfranchisement, 1775-1942

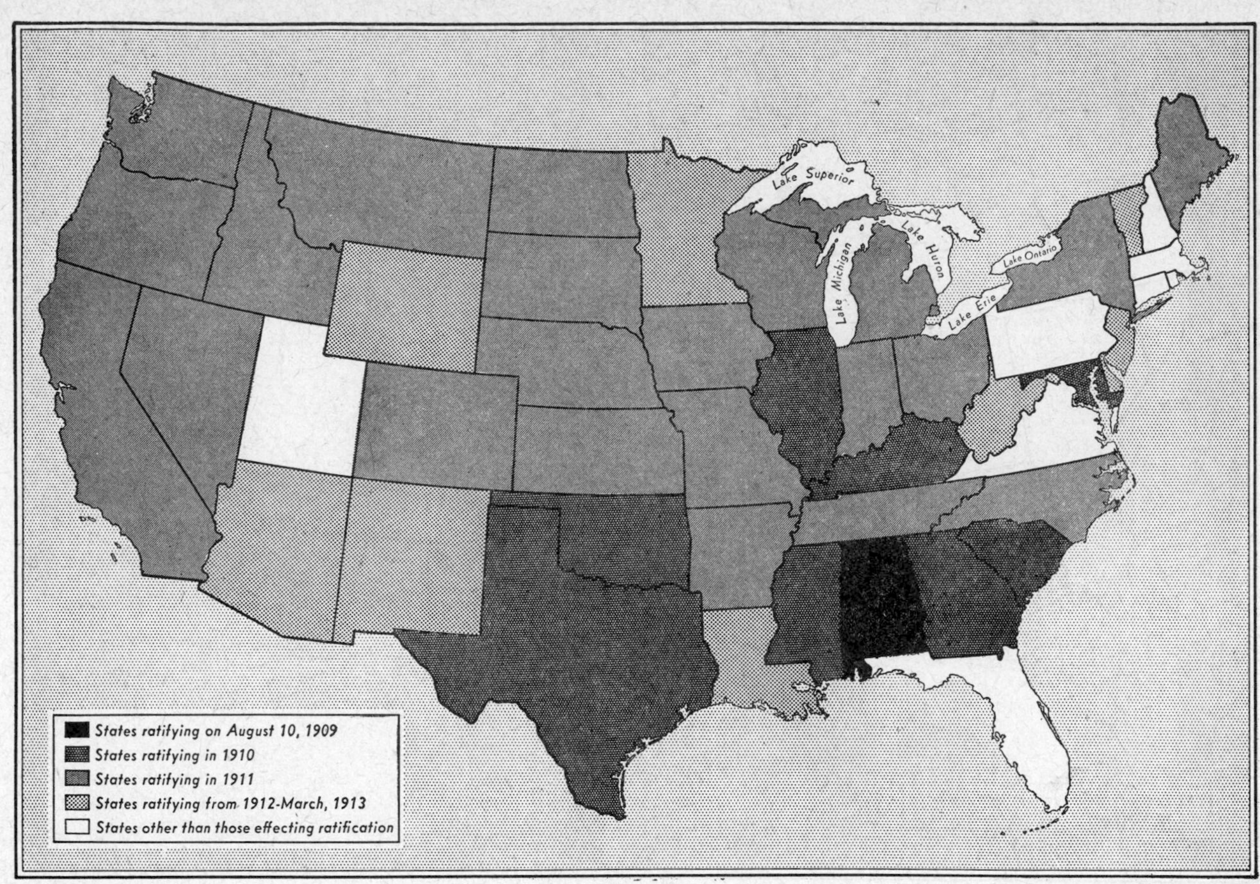

198 States Effecting the Ratification of the Sixteenth Amendment to the Constitution, 1913

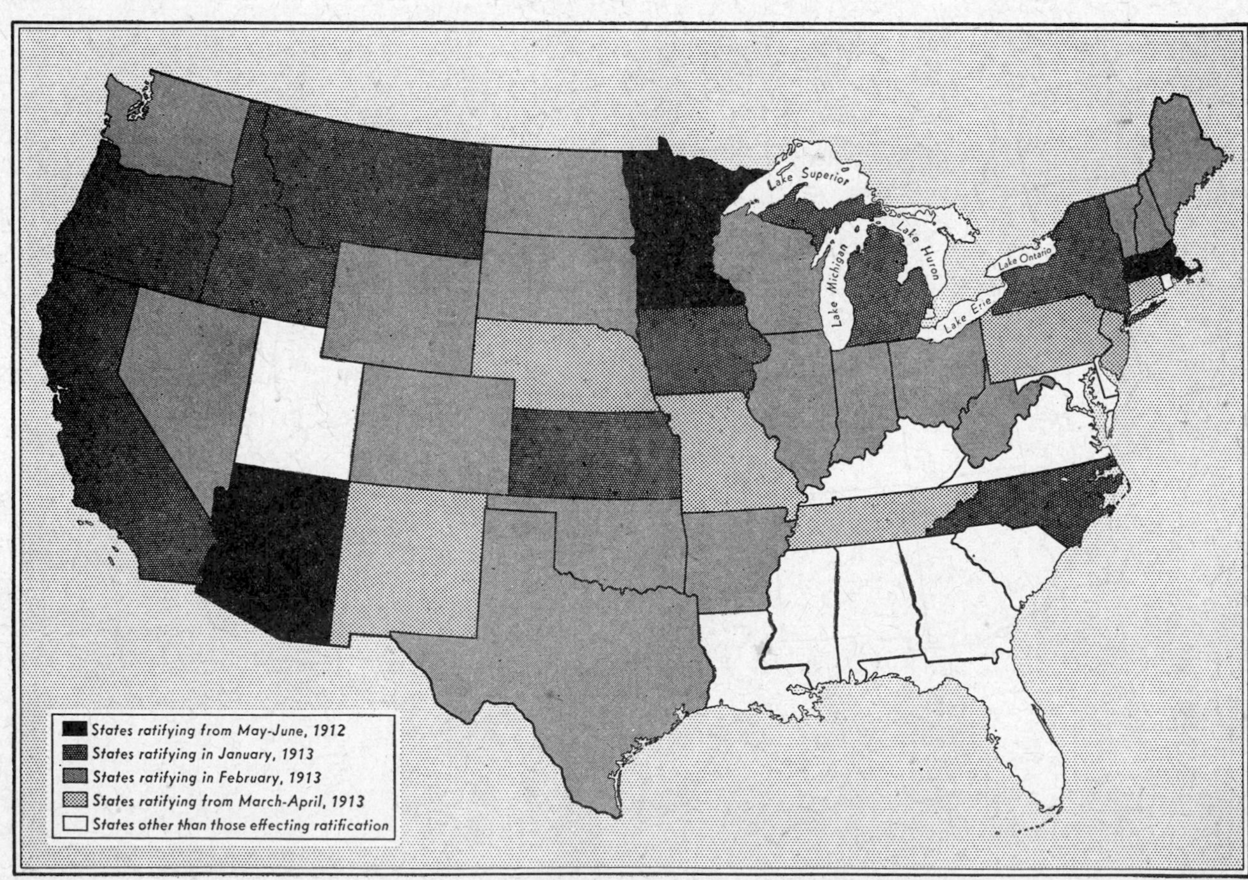

199 States Effecting the Ratification of the Seventeenth Amendment to the Constitution, 1913

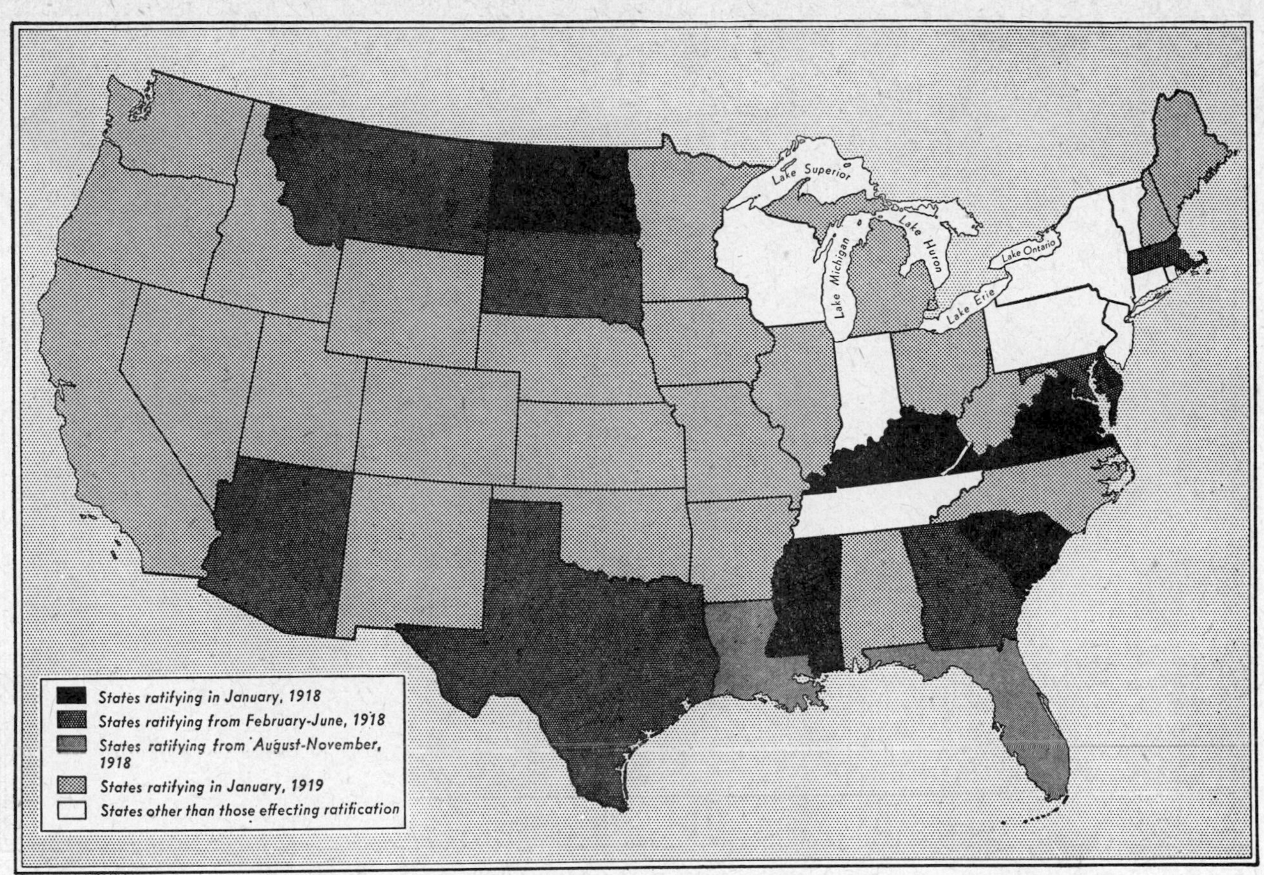

200 States Effecting the Ratification of the Eighteenth Amendment to the Constitution, 1919

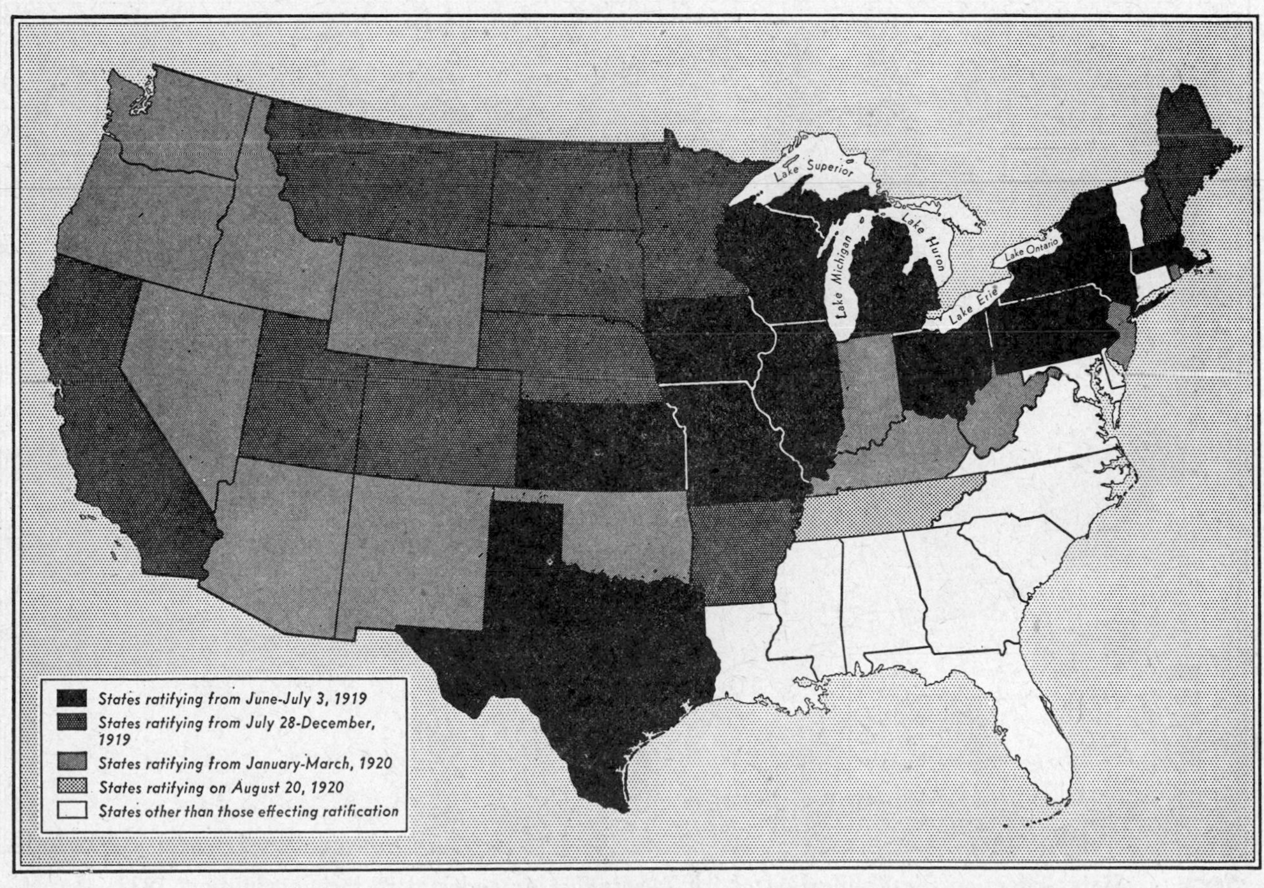

201 States Effecting the Ratification of the Nineteenth Amendment to the Constitution, 1920

Lake Superior
Lake Michigan
Lake Huron
Lake Ontario
Lake Erie

- States ratifying from March-April, 1932
- States ratifying from June-September, 1932
- States ratifying from January-February 6, 1933
- States other than those effecting ratification

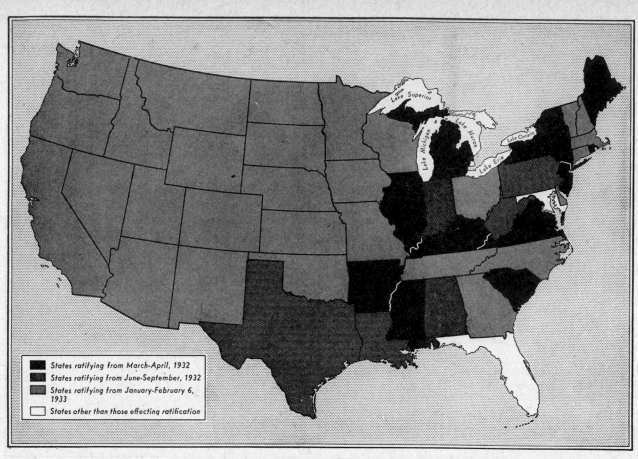

202 States Effecting the Ratification of the Twentieth Amendment to the Constitution, 1933

Lake Superior
Lake Michigan
Lake Huron
Lake Ontario
Lake Erie

- States ratifying from April-May, 1933
- States ratifying from June-August, 1933
- States ratifying from September-October, 1933
- States ratifying from November-December 5, 1933
- States other than those effecting ratification

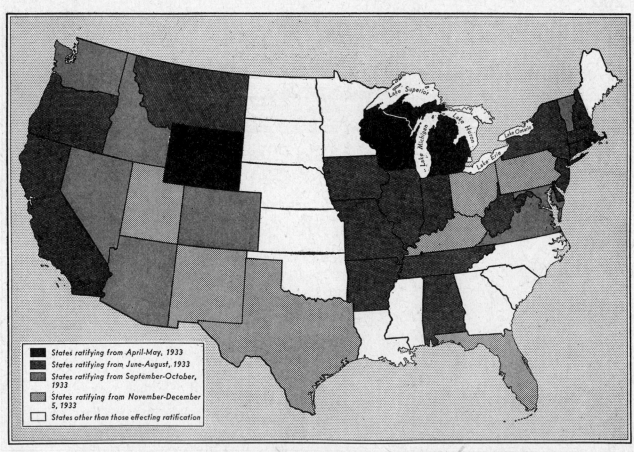

203 States Effecting the Ratification of the Twenty-first Amendment to the Constitution, 1933

(For proposed child labor amendment, see map 303)

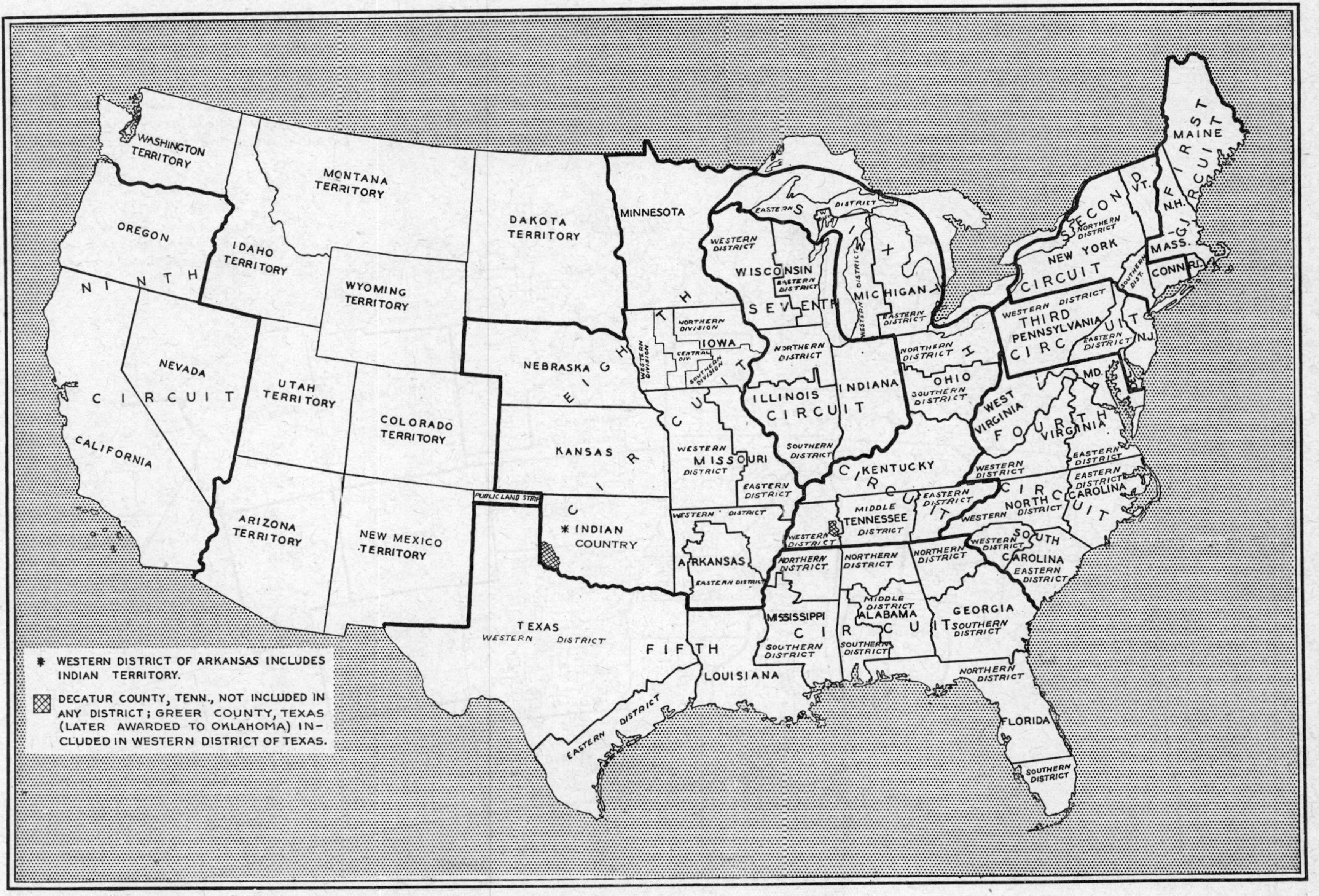

204 **Federal Circuit and District Courts, 1873**

Circuit court borders are marked by heavy lines; district court borders by medium lines; division borders by light lines

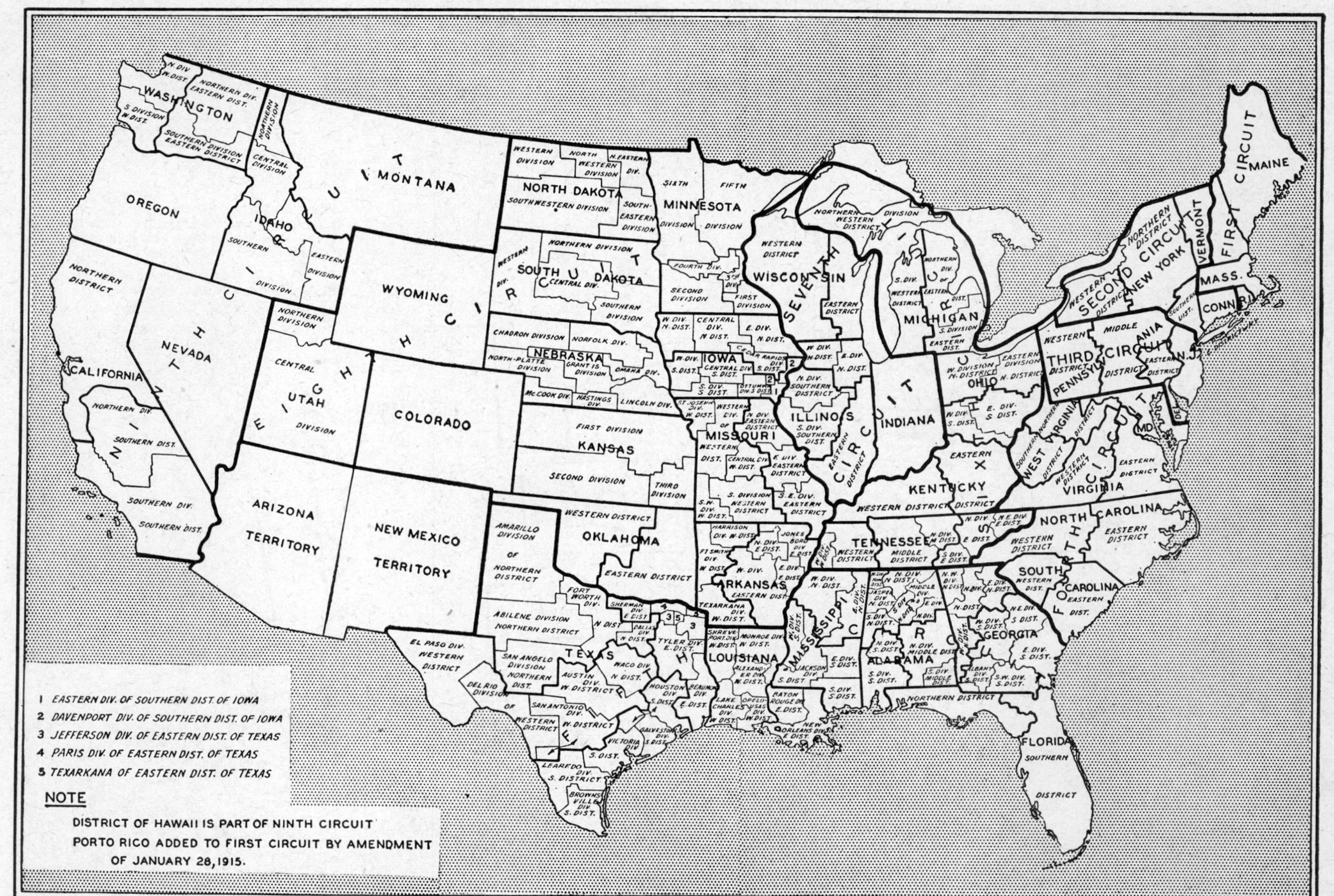

205

Federal Circuit and District Courts, 1911

Circuit court borders are marked by heavy lines; district court borders by medium lines; division borders by light lines

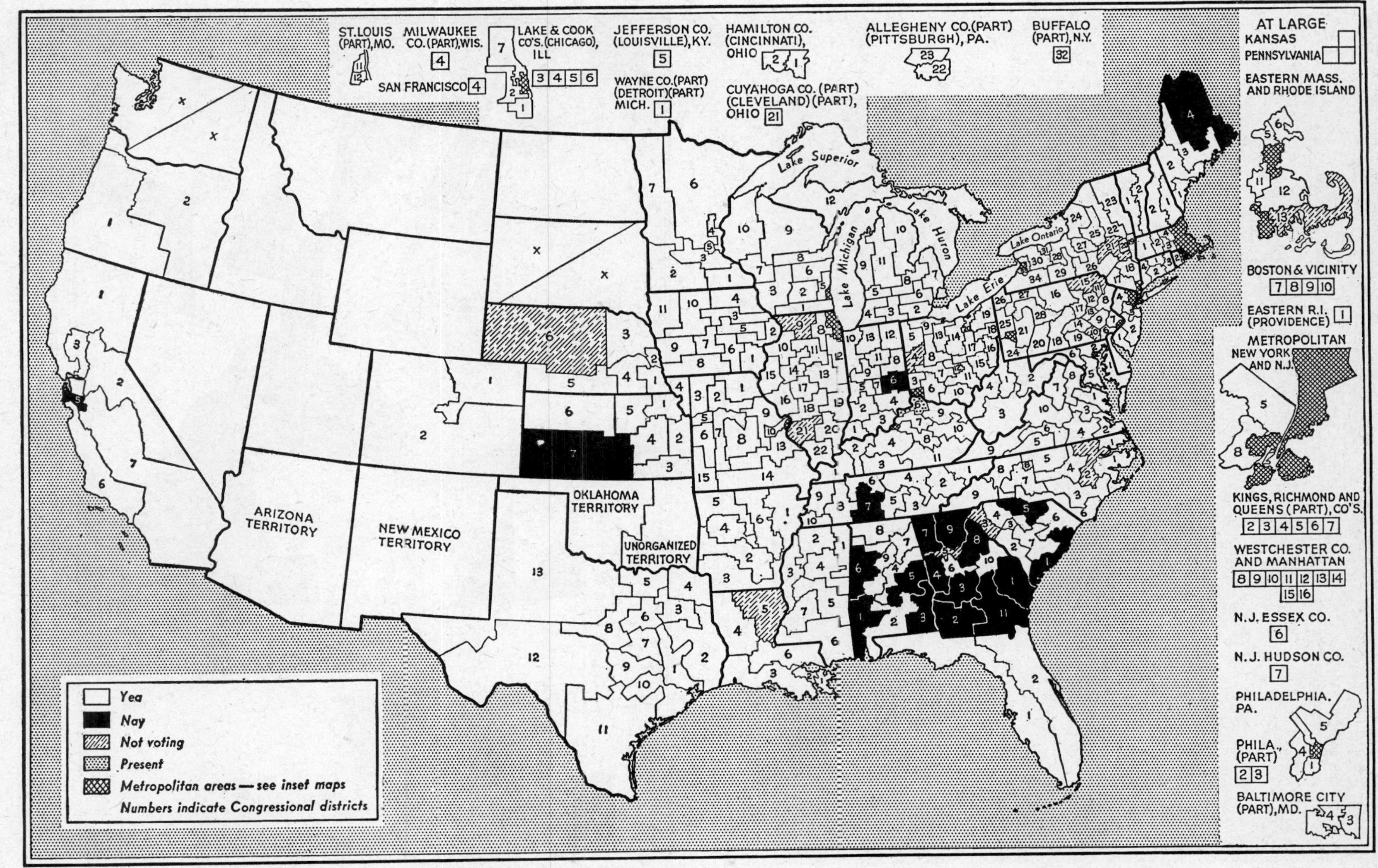

206 House Vote of April 13, 1898, on Resolution Declaring War on Spain, Taken Prior to and Lacking Unanimity of Final Action Agreeing to Conference Report

In cases where a number is repeated in the same state, it indicates two geographically separated parts of the same district.

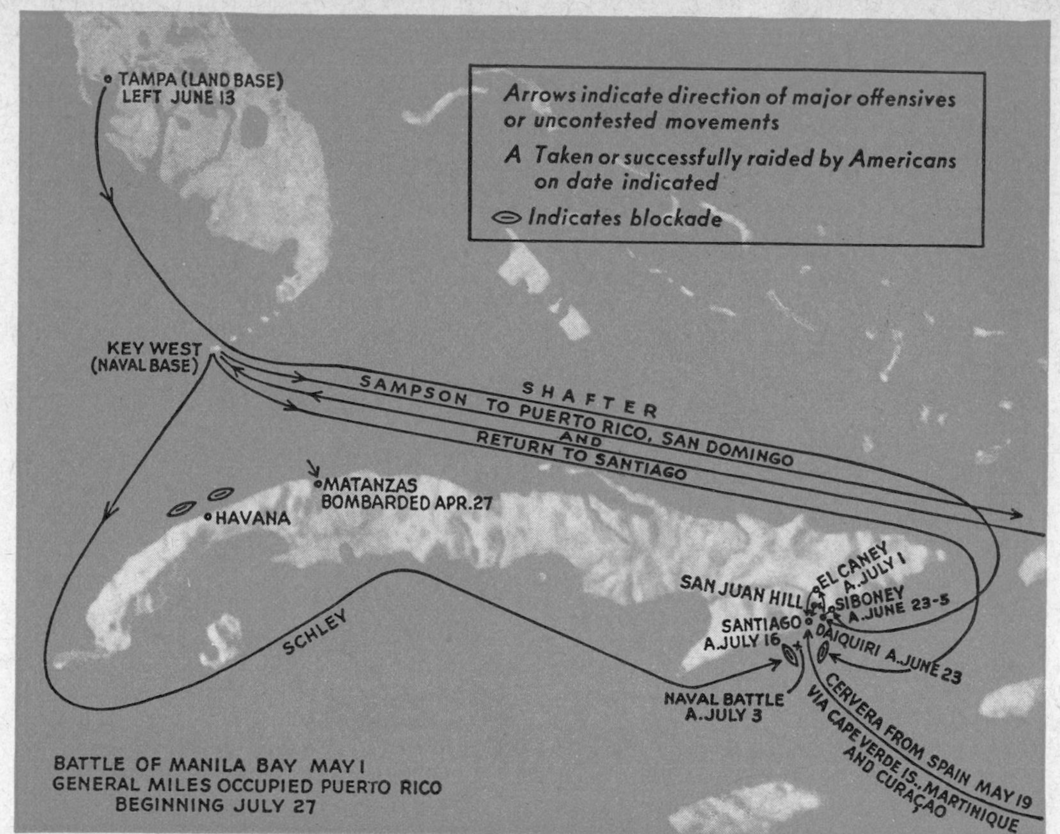

207 The Spanish-American War: Caribbean Campaign

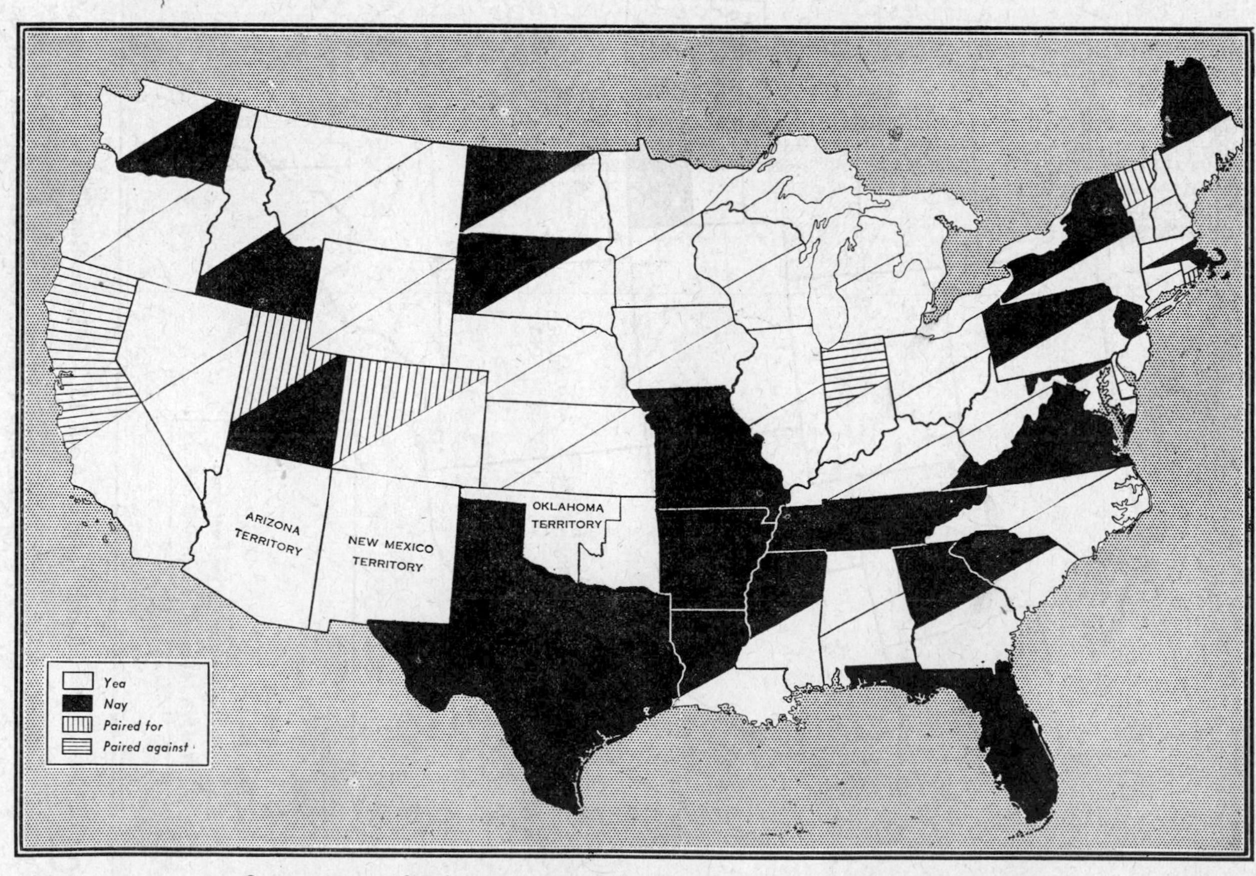

208 Senate Vote of February 6, 1899, on Ratification of the Treaty of Paris

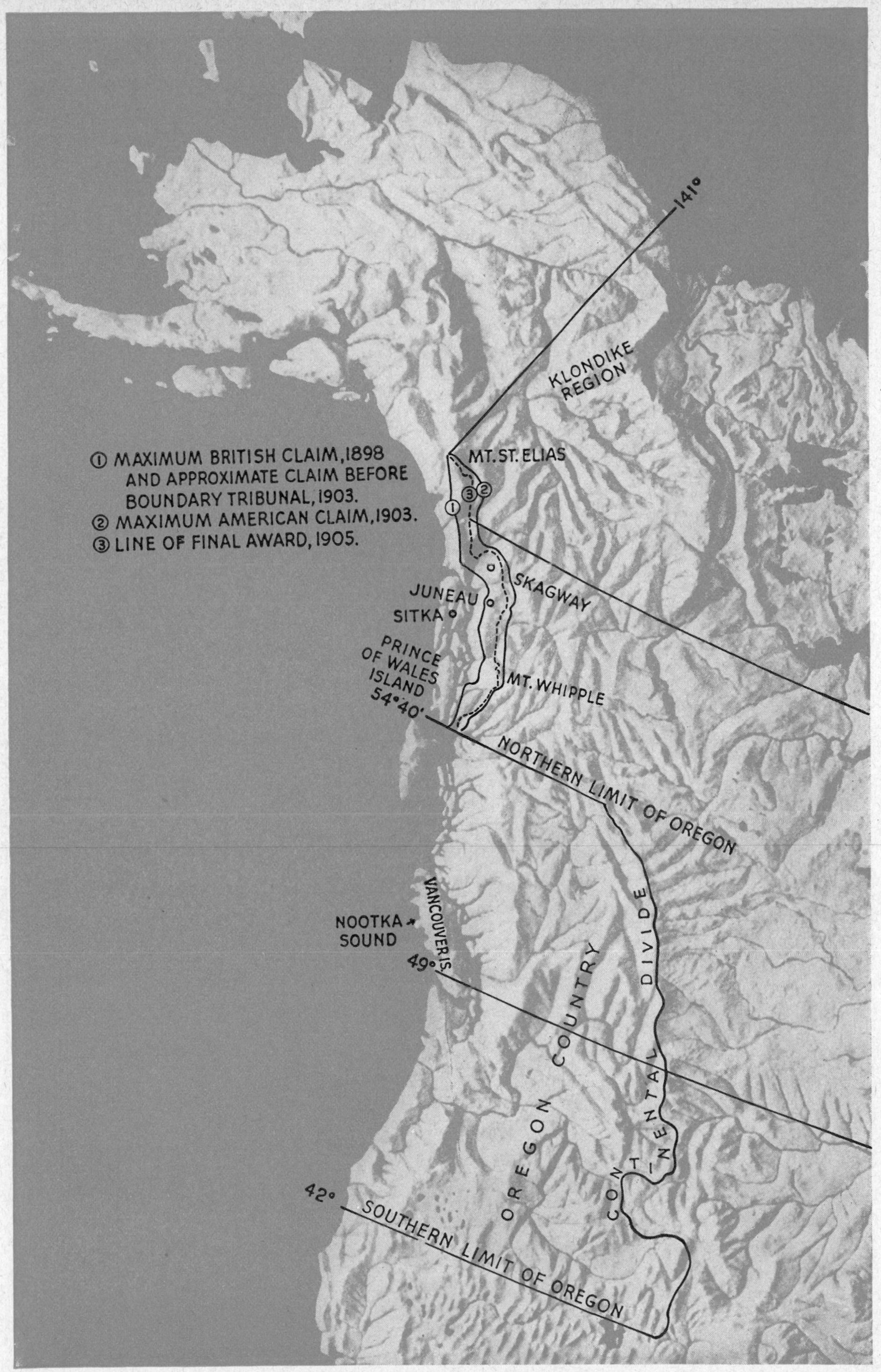
141°
KLONDIKE REGION
① MAXIMUM BRITISH CLAIM, 1898 AND APPROXIMATE CLAIM BEFORE BOUNDARY TRIBUNAL, 1903.
② MAXIMUM AMERICAN CLAIM, 1903.
③ LINE OF FINAL AWARD, 1905.
MT. ST. ELIAS
SKAGWAY
JUNEAU
SITKA
PRINCE OF WALES ISLAND
MT. WHIPPLE
54°40'
NORTHERN LIMIT OF OREGON
VANCOUVER IS.
NOOTKA SOUND
49°
OREGON COUNTRY
CONTINENTAL DIVIDE
42°
SOUTHERN LIMIT OF OREGON

209 Alaska Border Dispute, 1878-1905

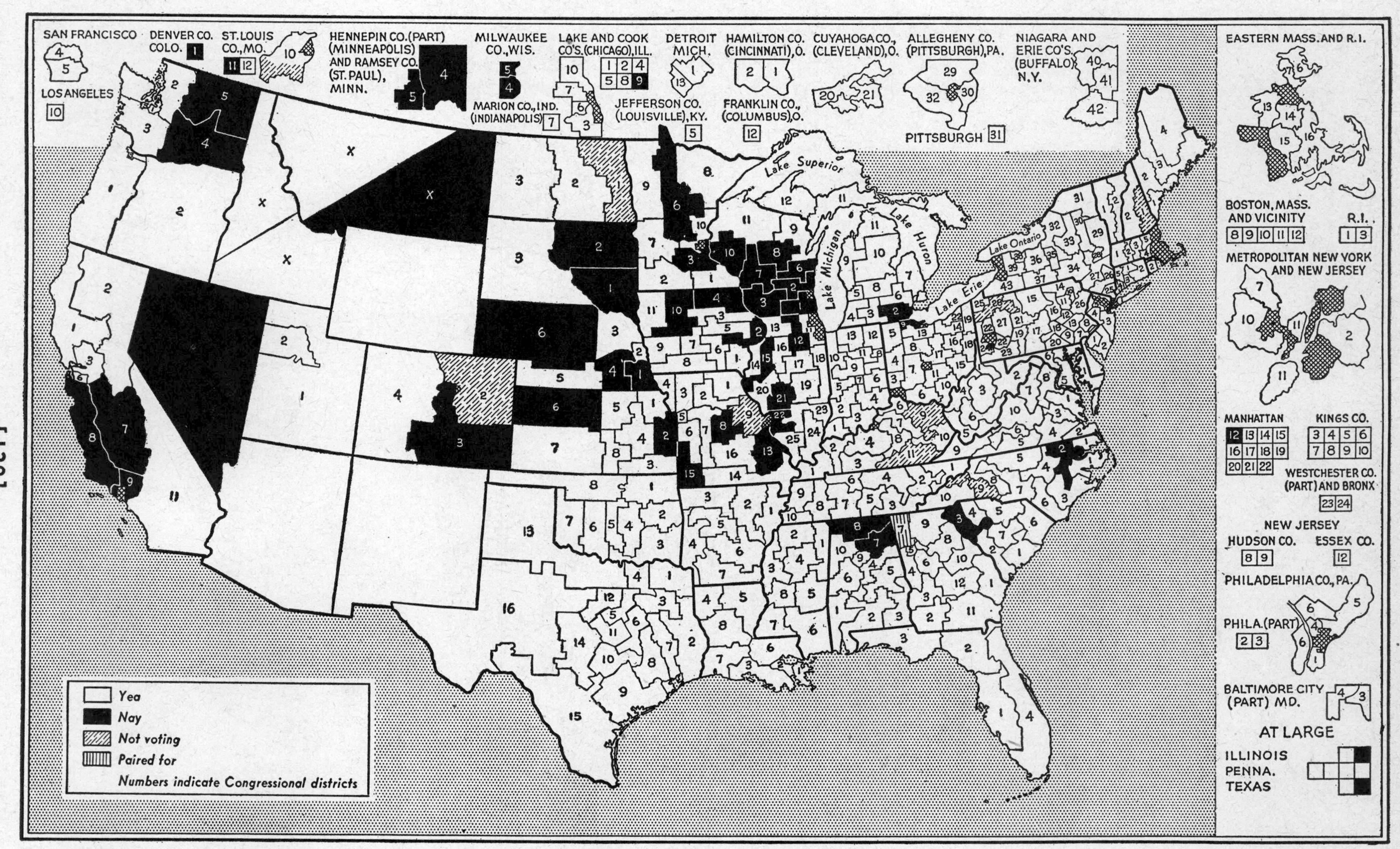

House Vote of April 5, 1917, on Resolution Declaring War on Germany

In cases where a number is repeated in the same state, it indicates two parts of the same district

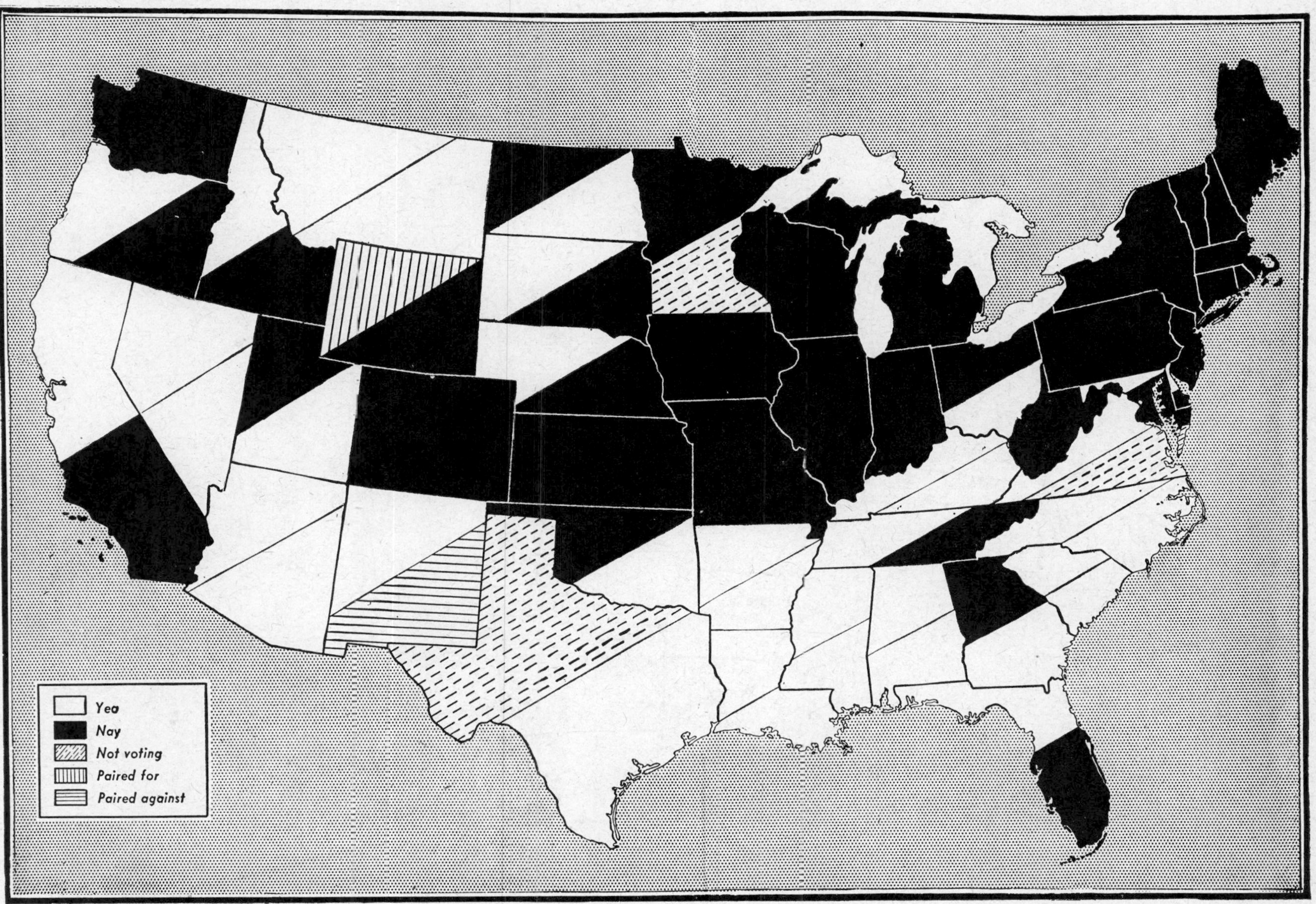

211 Senate Vote of November 19, 1919, on Unconditional Ratification of the Versailles Treaty

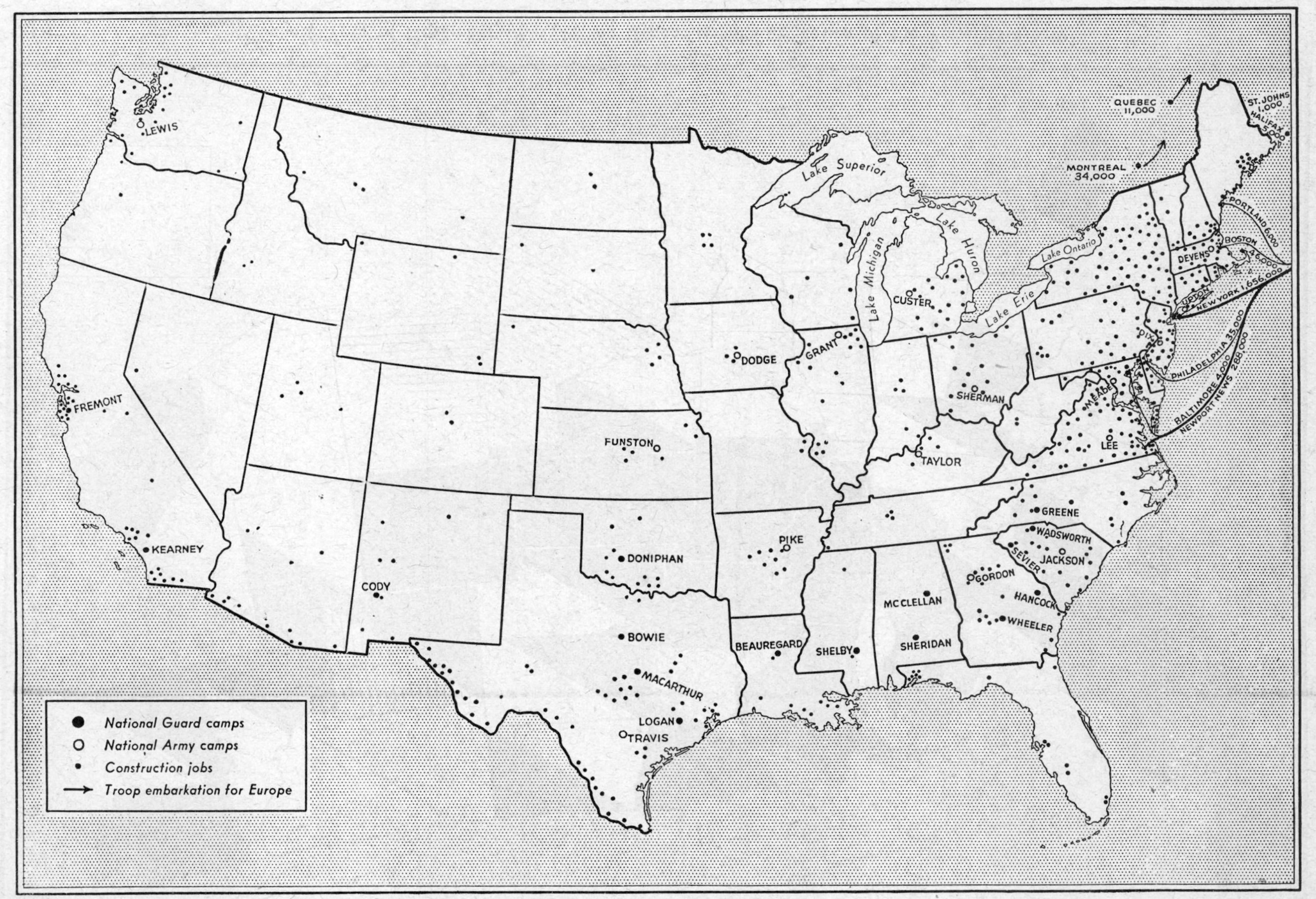

212 America in the First World War: Training Camps, Embarkation Ports, and Construction Projects

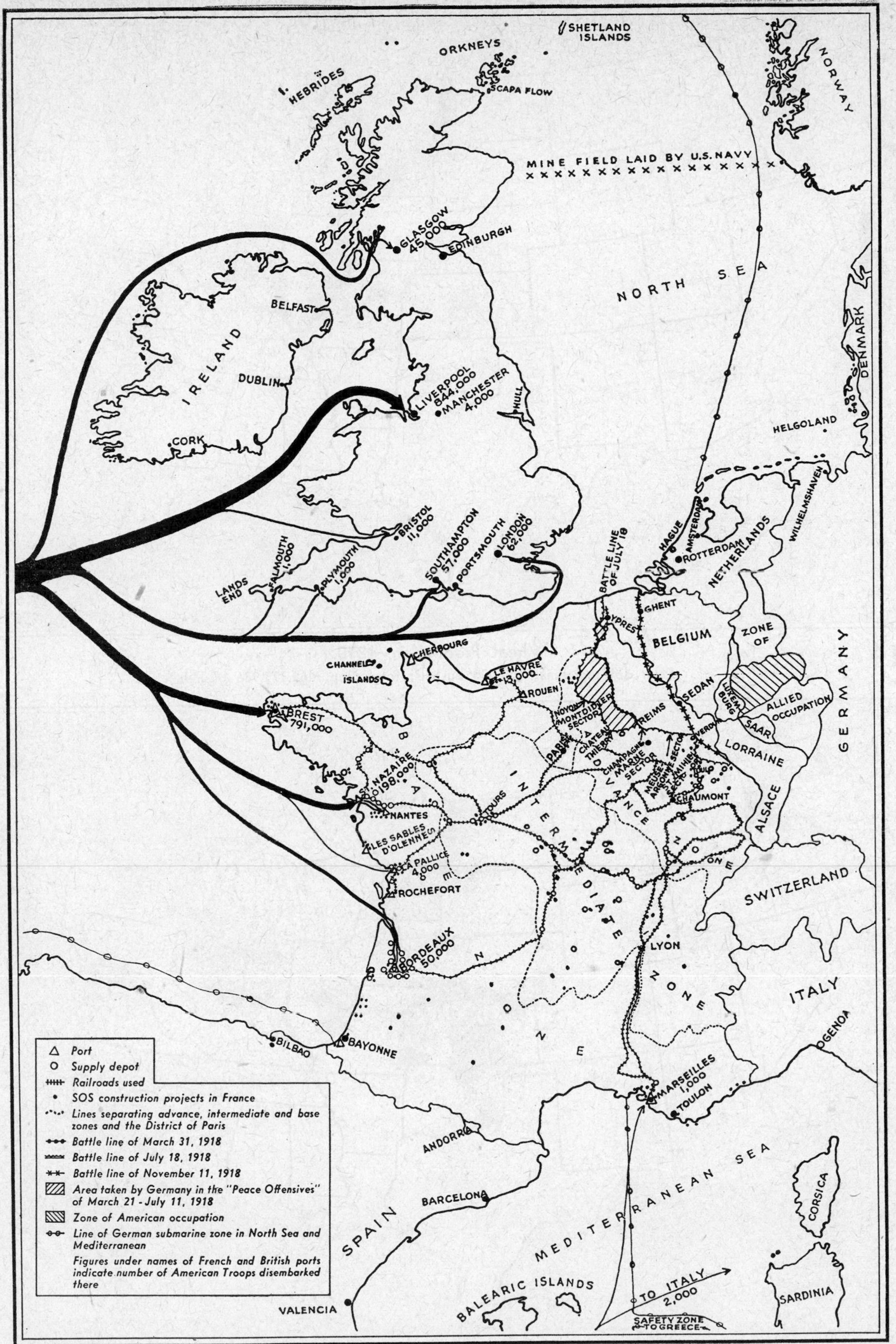

213

America in the First World War: The European Front

Sea routes indicated are those of American troop transports

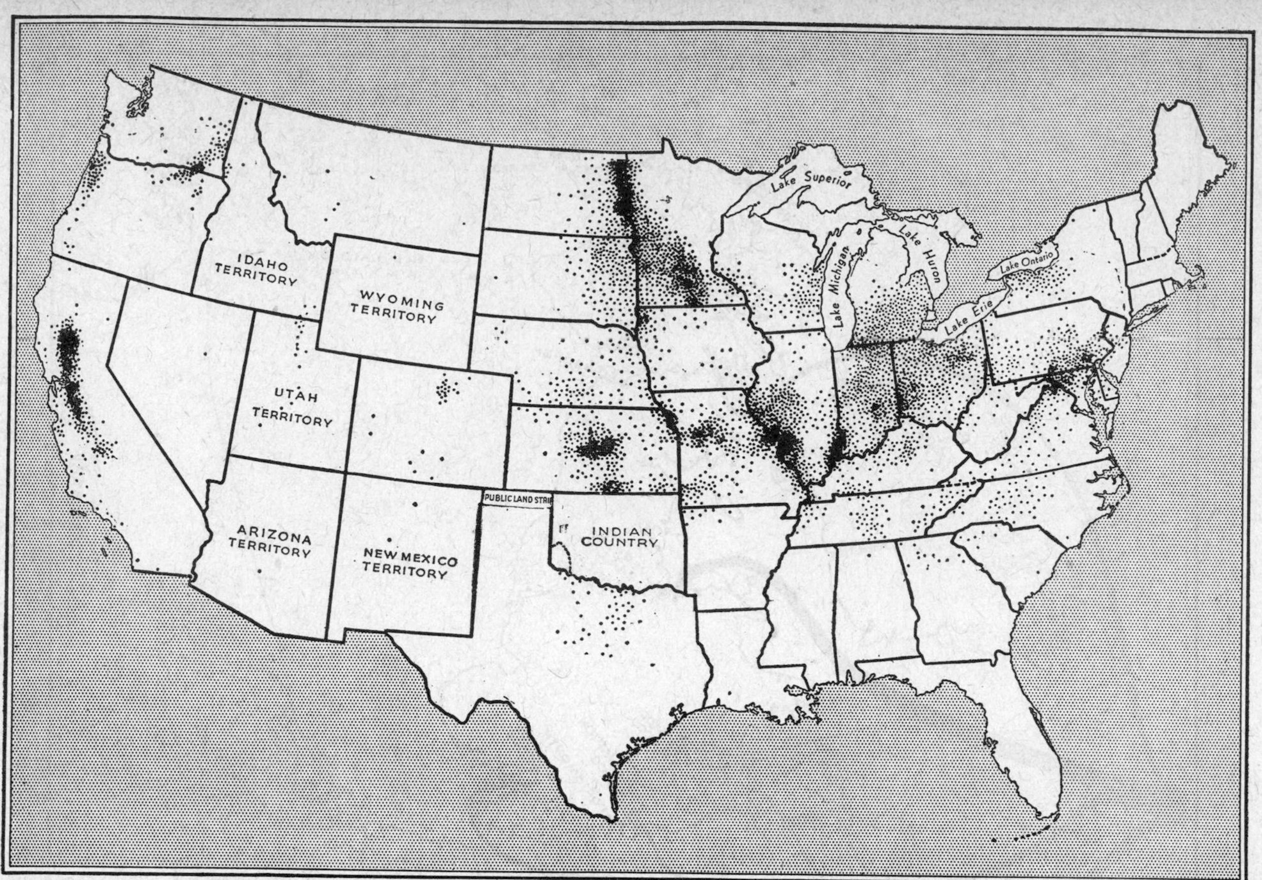

214 Wheat Production, 1890

Each dot represents 100,000 bushels; total crop, 468,373,986 bushels

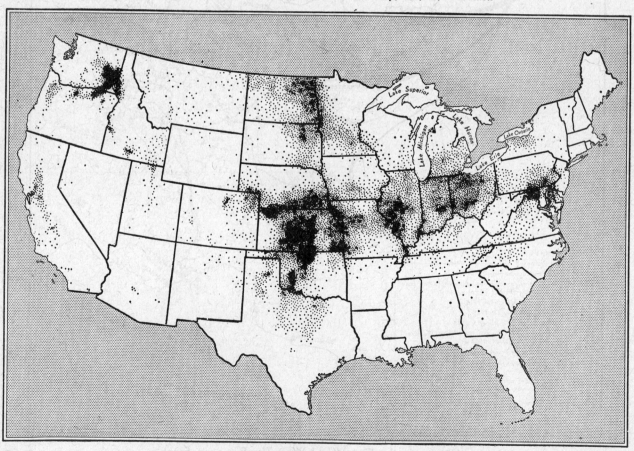

215 Wheat Production, 1920

Each dot represents 100,000 bushels; total crop, 945,403,215 bushels

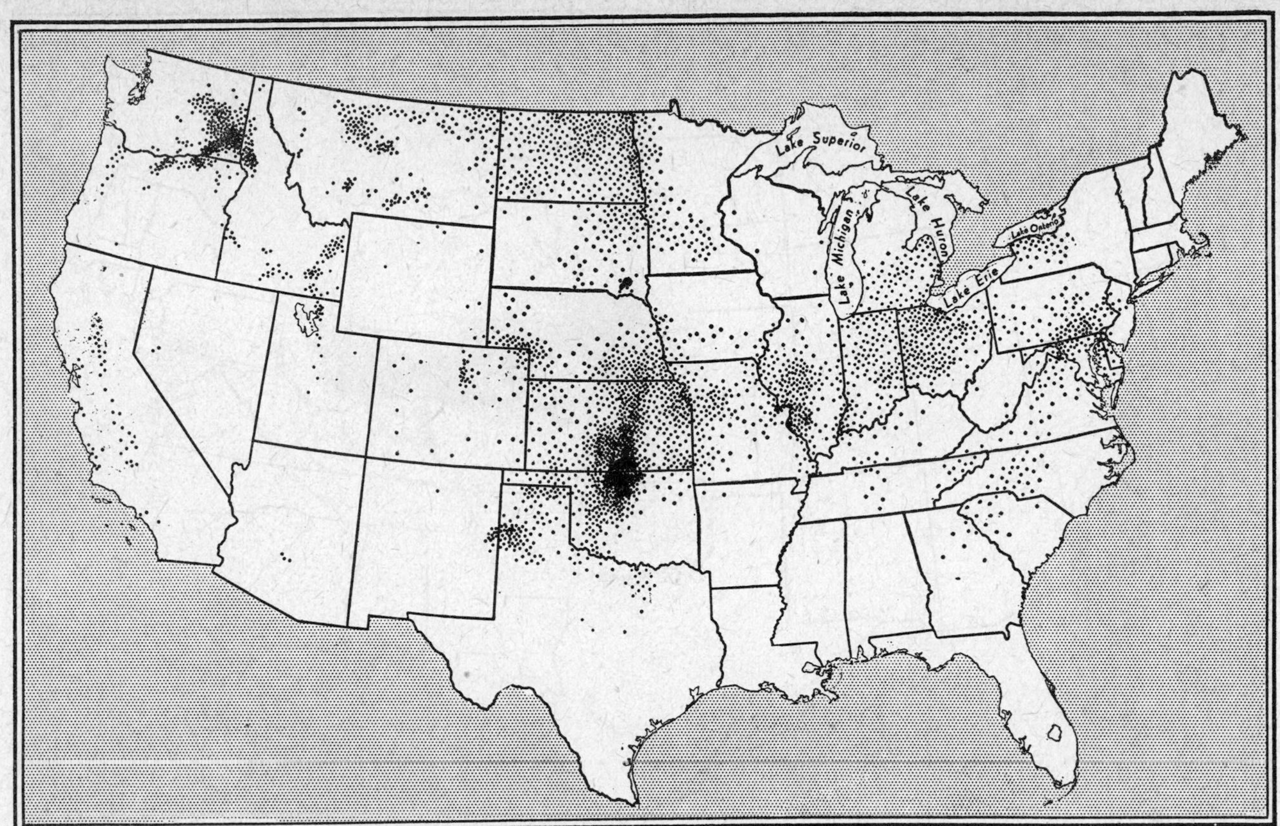

216

Wheat Production, 1940

Each dot represents 10,000 acres; total crop, 708,851,958 bushels

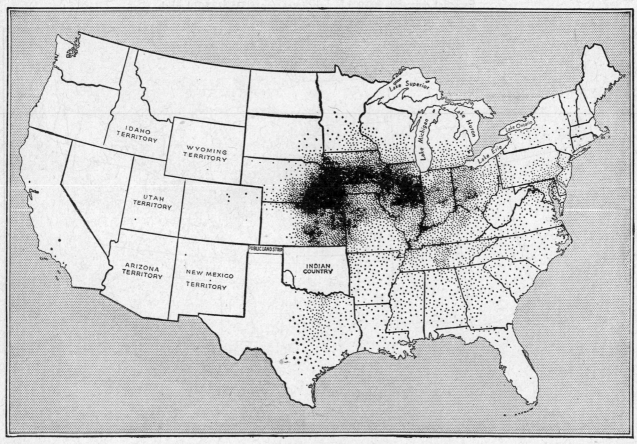

Lake Superior
Lake Michigan
Lake Huron
Lake Ontario
Lake Erie
IDAHO TERRITORY
WYOMING TERRITORY
UTAH TERRITORY
ARIZONA TERRITORY
NEW MEXICO TERRITORY
PUBLIC LAND STRIP
INDIAN COUNTRY

217

Corn Production, 1890

Each dot represents 300,000 bushels; total crop, 2,122,327,547 bushels

218

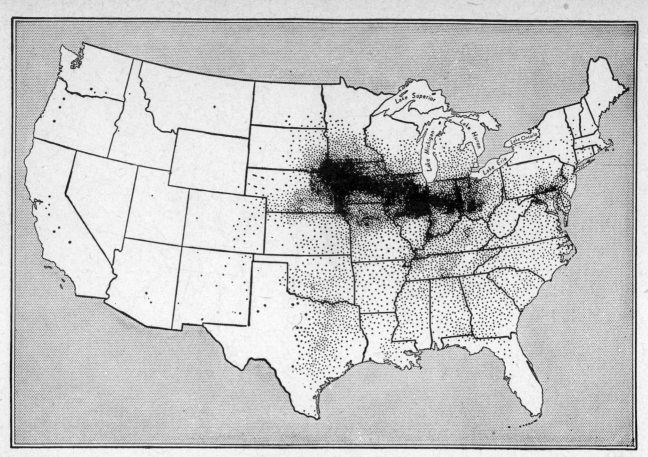

Corn Production, 1920

Each dot represents 300,000 bushels; total crop, 2,345,832,507 bushels

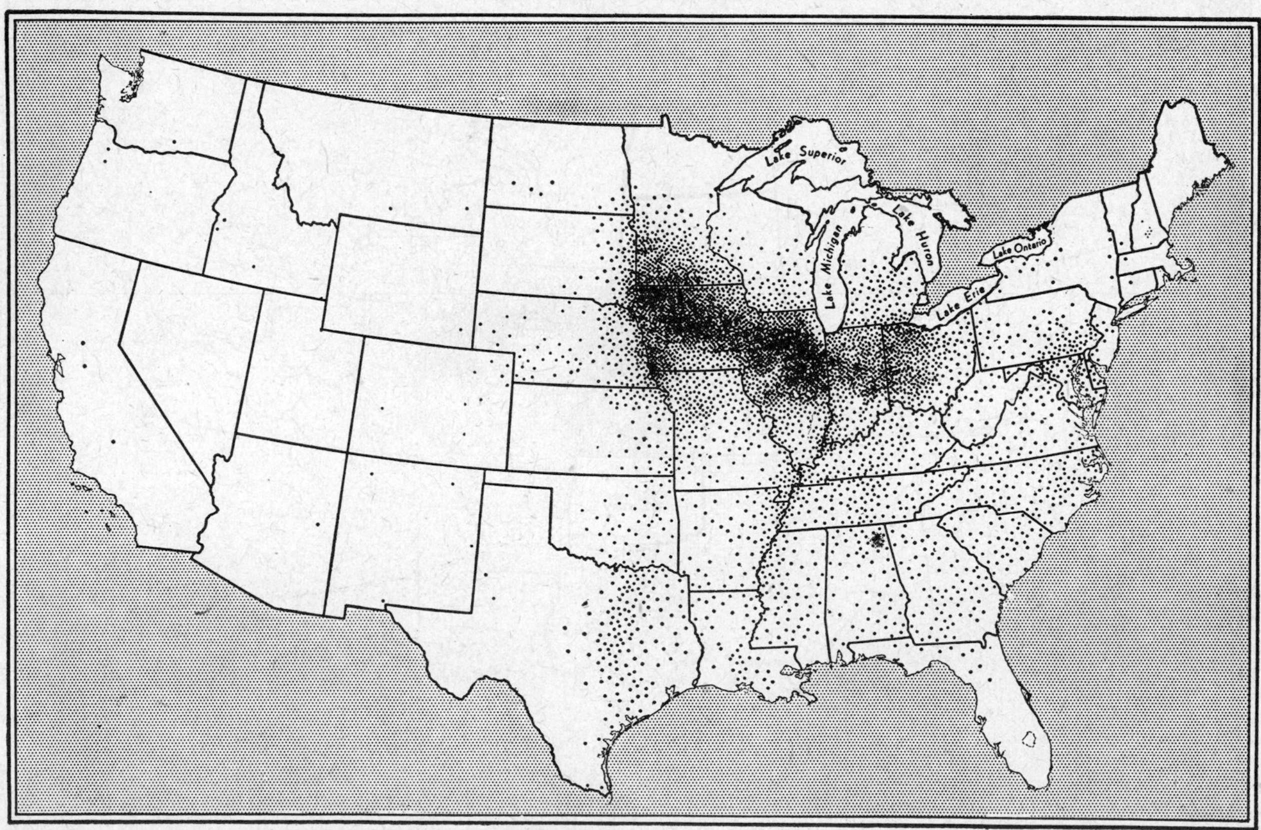

219

Corn Production, 1940

Each dot represents 500,000 bushels; total crop, 2,311,399,935 bushels

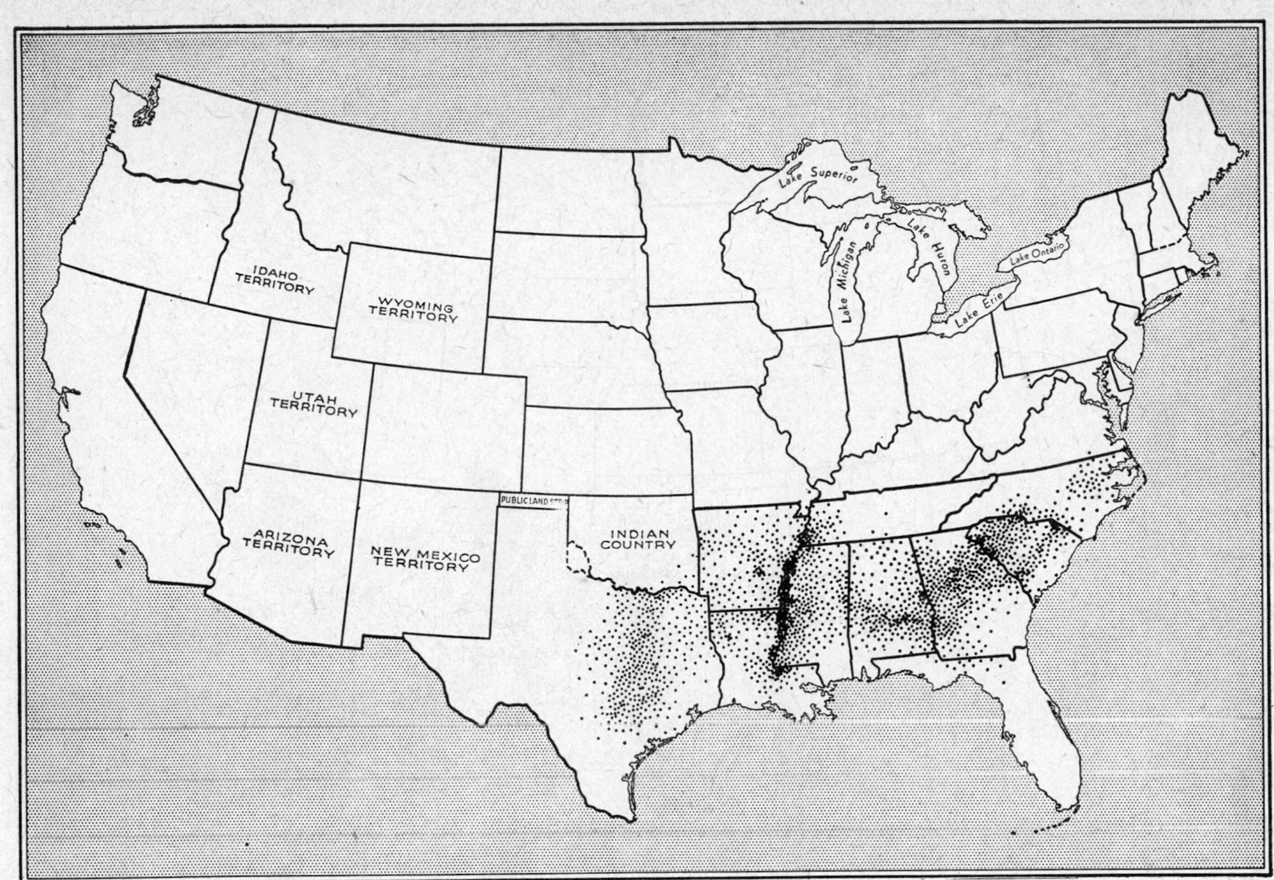

220 **Cotton Production, 1890**

Each dot represents 4,000 500-lb. bales; total crop, 7,472,511 500-lb. bales

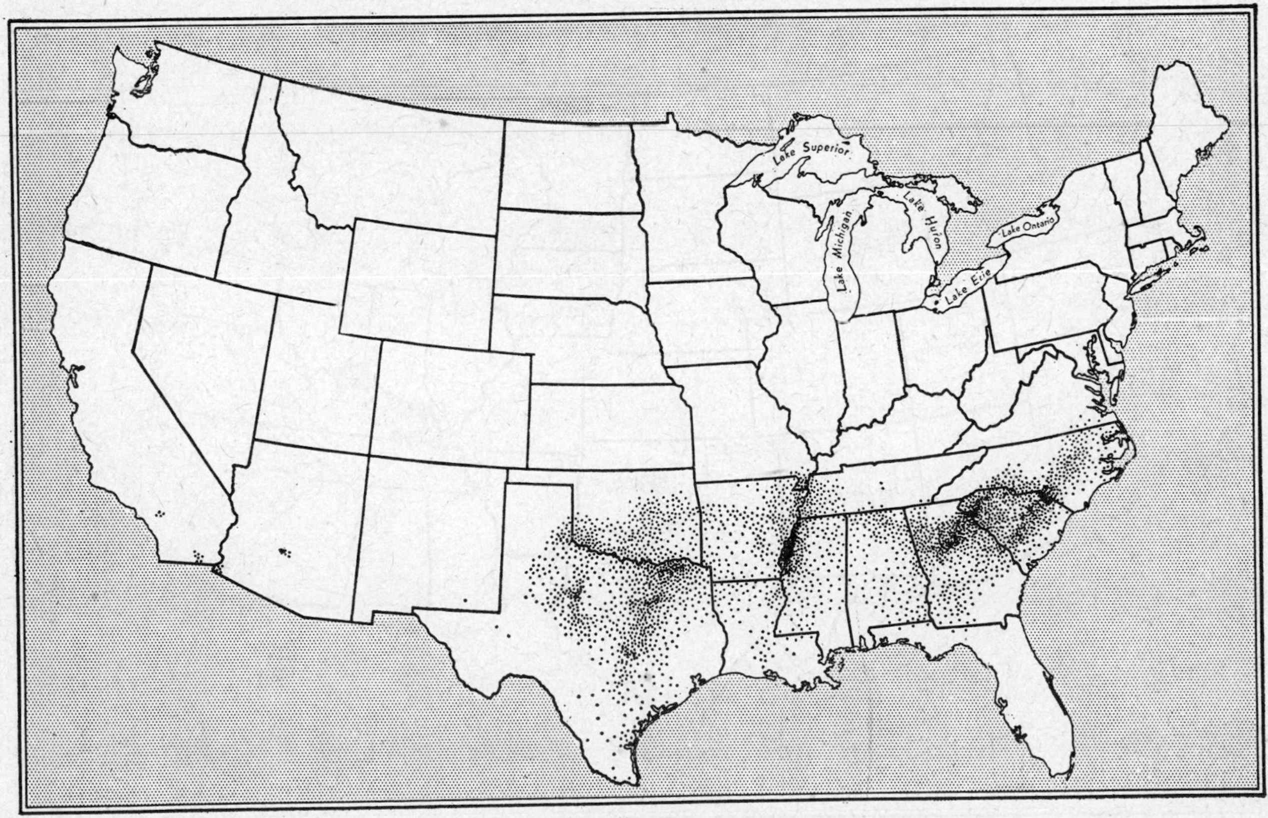

221 **Cotton Production, 1920**

Each dot represents 4,000 500-lb. bales; total crop, 11,376,130 500-lb. bales

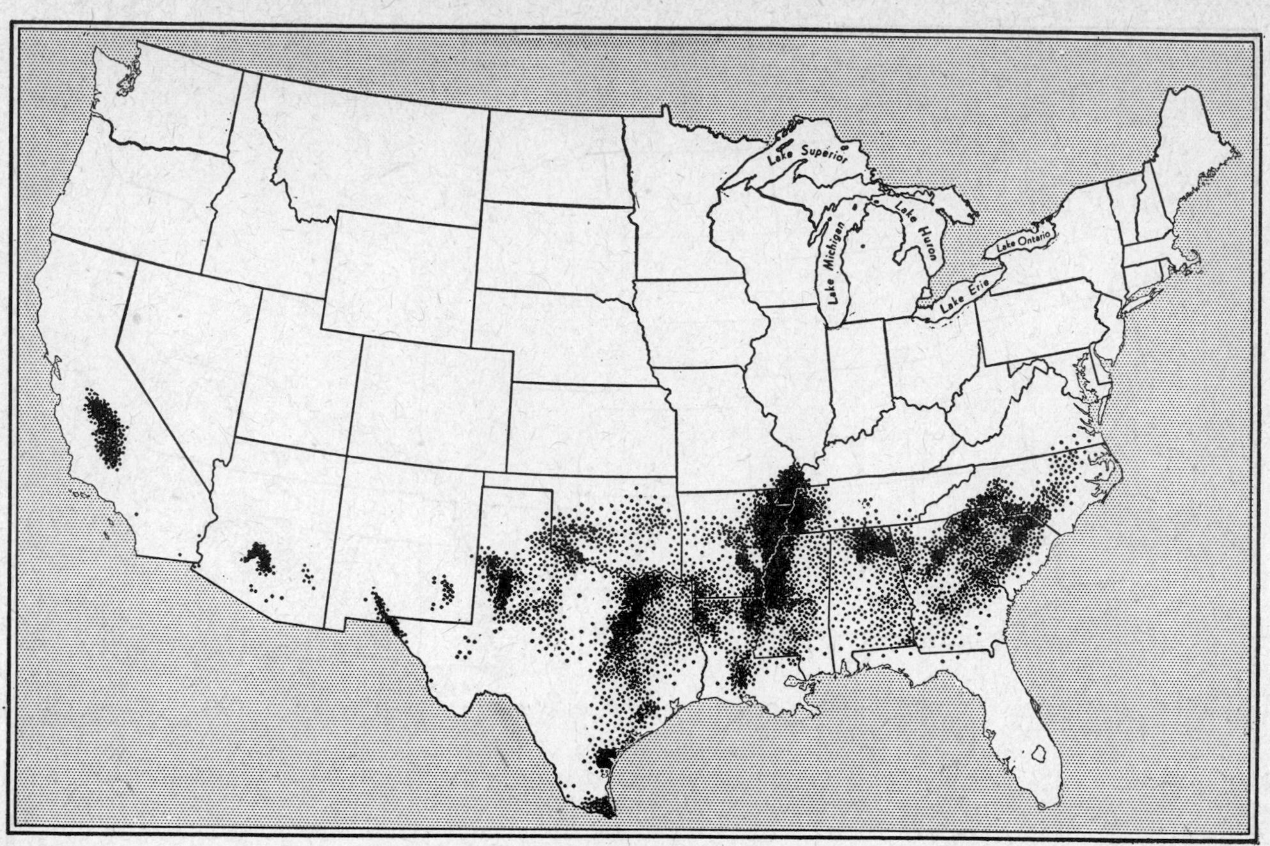

222 Cotton Production, 1940

Each dot represents 2,000 500-lb. bales; total crop, 11,481,300 500-lb. bales

Lake Superior
Lake Michigan
Lake Huron
Lake Ontario
Lake Erie
IDAHO TERRITORY
WYOMING TERRITORY
UTAH TERRITORY
PUBLIC LAND STRIP
ARIZONA TERRITORY
NEW MEXICO TERRITORY
INDIAN COUNTRY

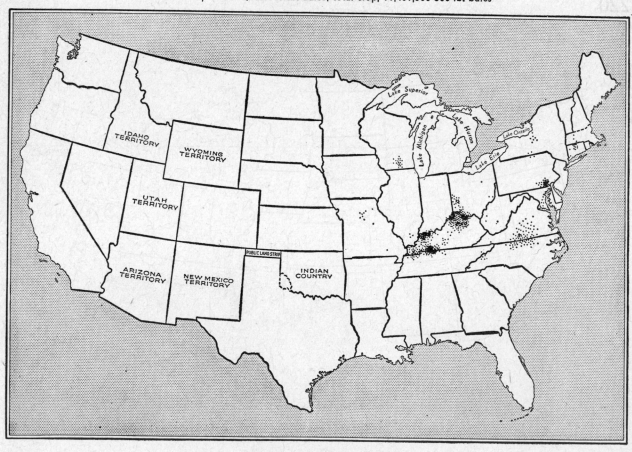

223 Tobacco Production, 1890

Each dot represents 1,000,000 lbs.; total crop, 488,256,646 lbs.

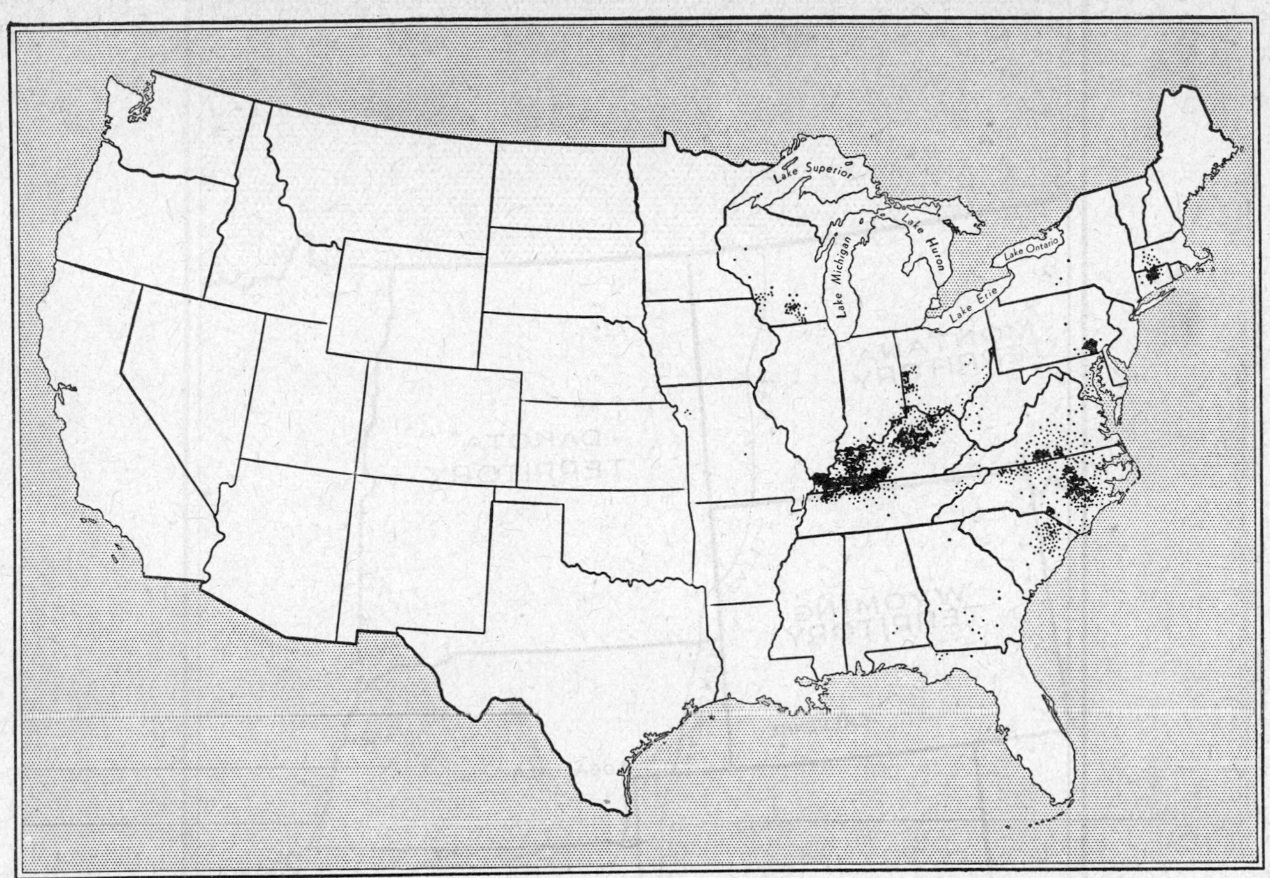

224

Tobacco Production, 1920

Each dot represents 1,000,000 lbs.; total crop, 1,371,504,261 lbs.

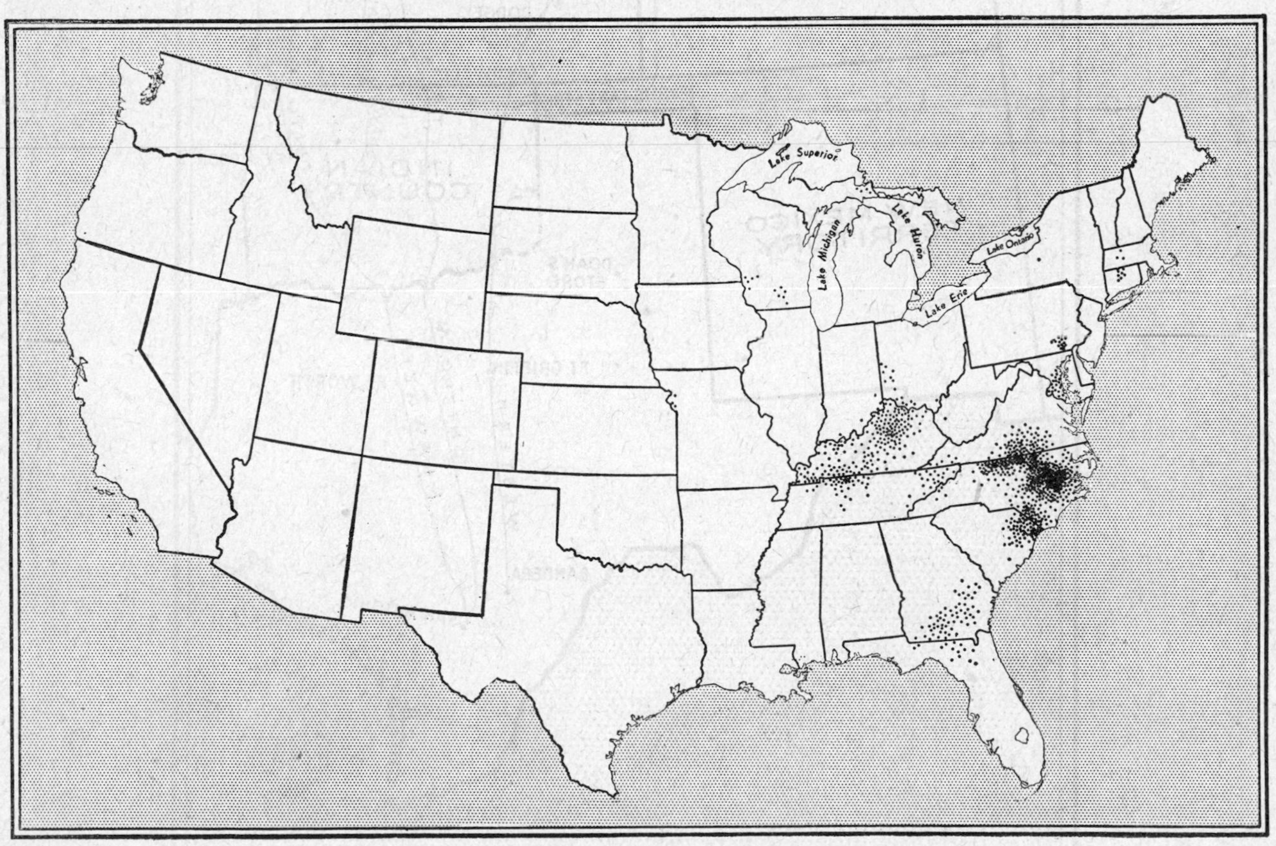

225

Tobacco Production, 1940

Each dot represents 2,000 acres; total crop, 1,699,727,914 lbs.

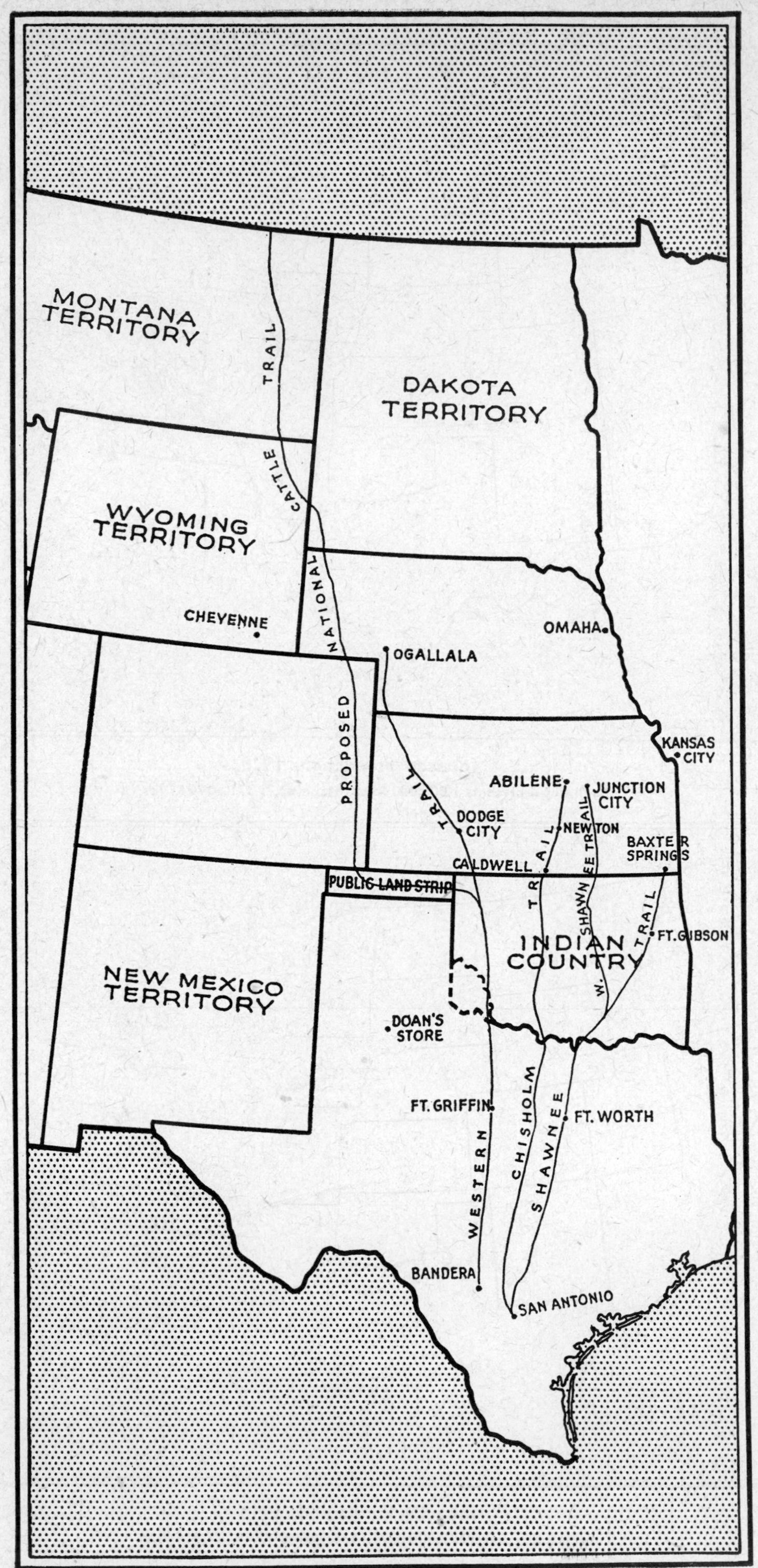

MONTANA TERRITORY
DAKOTA TERRITORY
WYOMING TERRITORY
CHEYENNE
OMAHA
OGALLALA
KANSAS CITY
ABILENE
JUNCTION CITY
DODGE CITY
NEWTON
BAXTER SPRINGS
CALDWELL
PUBLIC LAND STRIP
INDIAN COUNTRY
FT. GIBSON
NEW MEXICO TERRITORY
DOAN'S STORE
FT. GRIFFIN
FT. WORTH
BANDERA
SAN ANTONIO
PROPOSED NATIONAL CATTLE TRAIL
WESTERN TRAIL
CHISHOLM TRAIL
SHAWNEE TRAIL
W. SHAWNEE TRAIL

Cattle Trails and Cow Towns, 1880

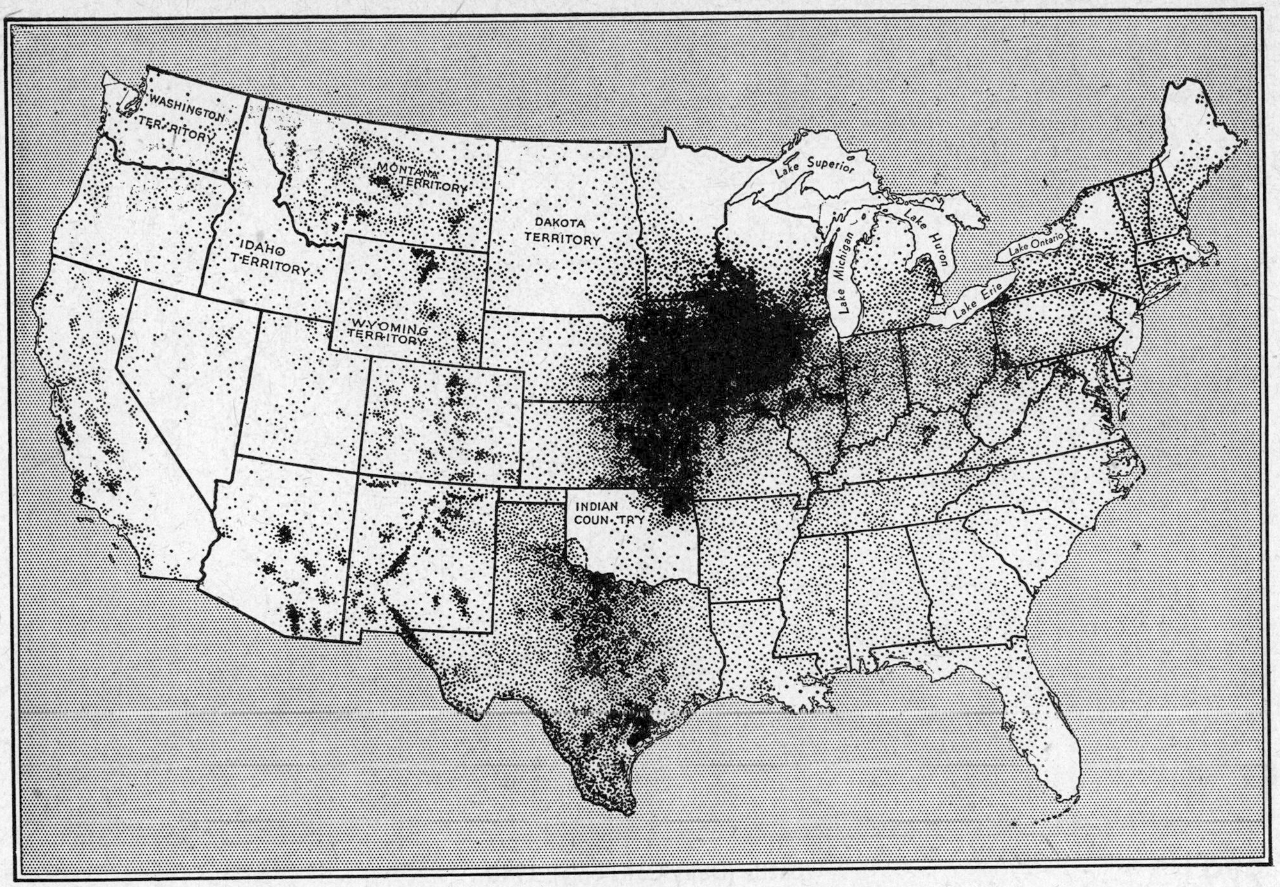

WASHINGTON TERRITORY
MONTANA TERRITORY
DAKOTA TERRITORY
IDAHO TERRITORY
WYOMING TERRITORY
INDIAN COUNTRY
Lake Superior
Lake Michigan
Lake Huron
Lake Ontario
Lake Erie

227

Cattle (Excluding Dairy Cows), 1890

Each dot represents 2,000 head; total, 34,851,622 head

Lake Superior
Lake Michigan
Lake Huron
Lake Ontario
Lake Erie

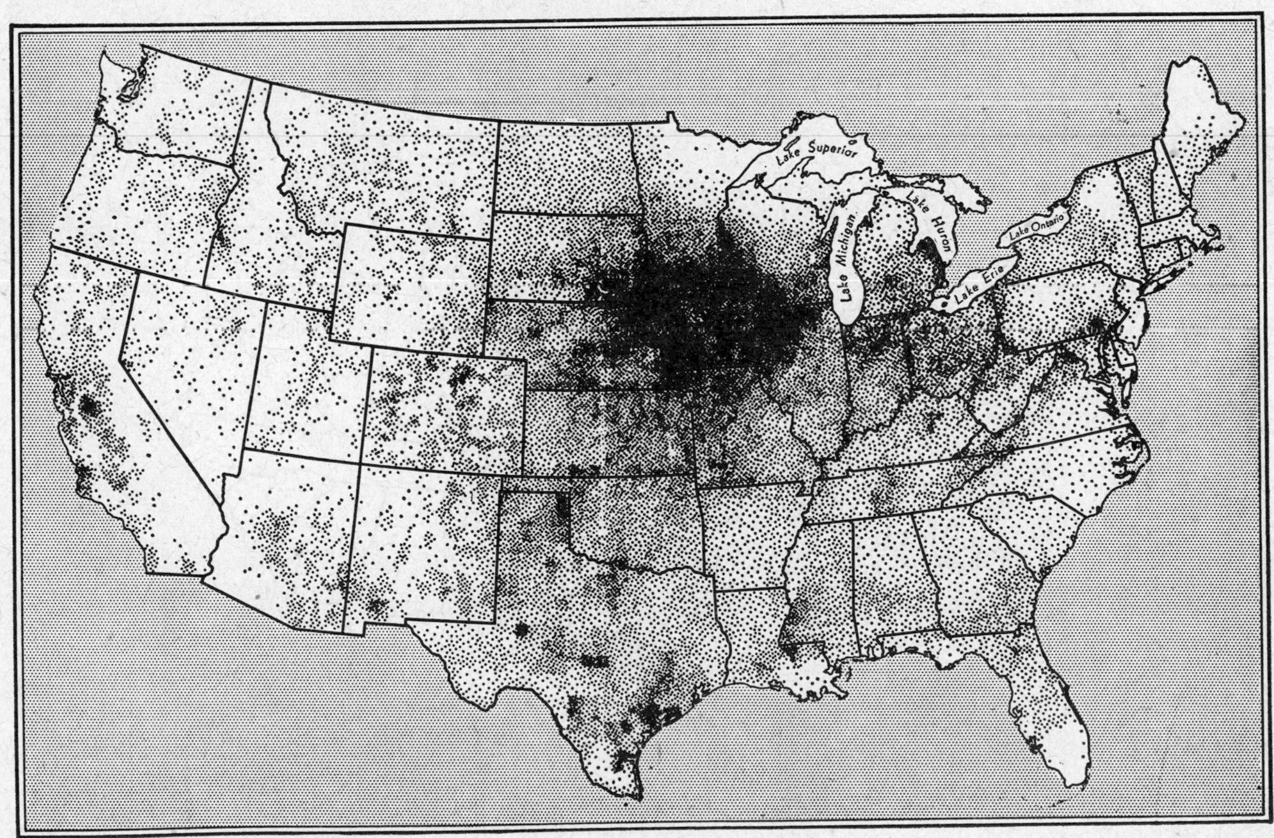

228

Cattle (Excluding Dairy Cows), 1920

Each dot represents 2,000 head; total, 46,977,000 head

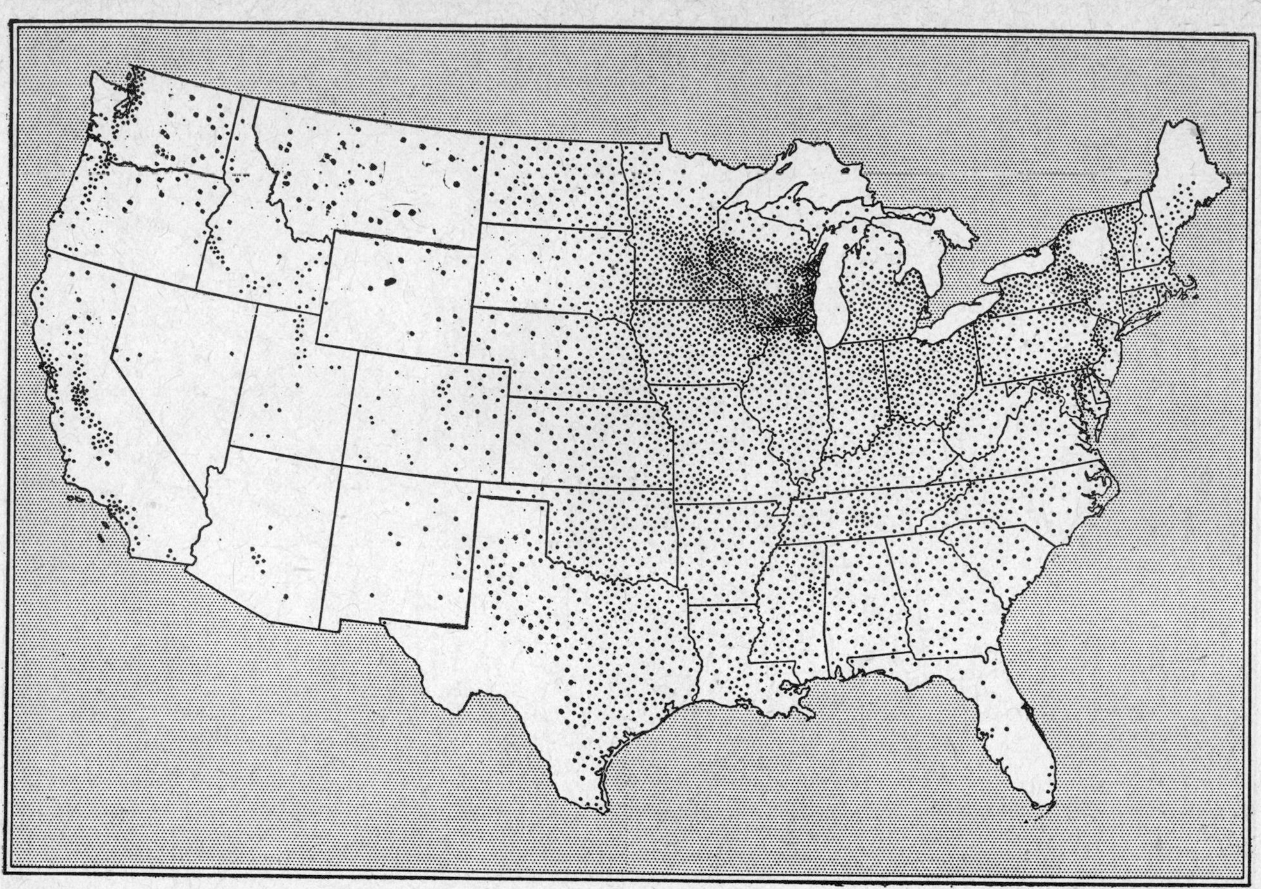

229 Cattle (Dairy Cows only), 1940

Each dot represents 5,000 head; total, 24,074,424 head

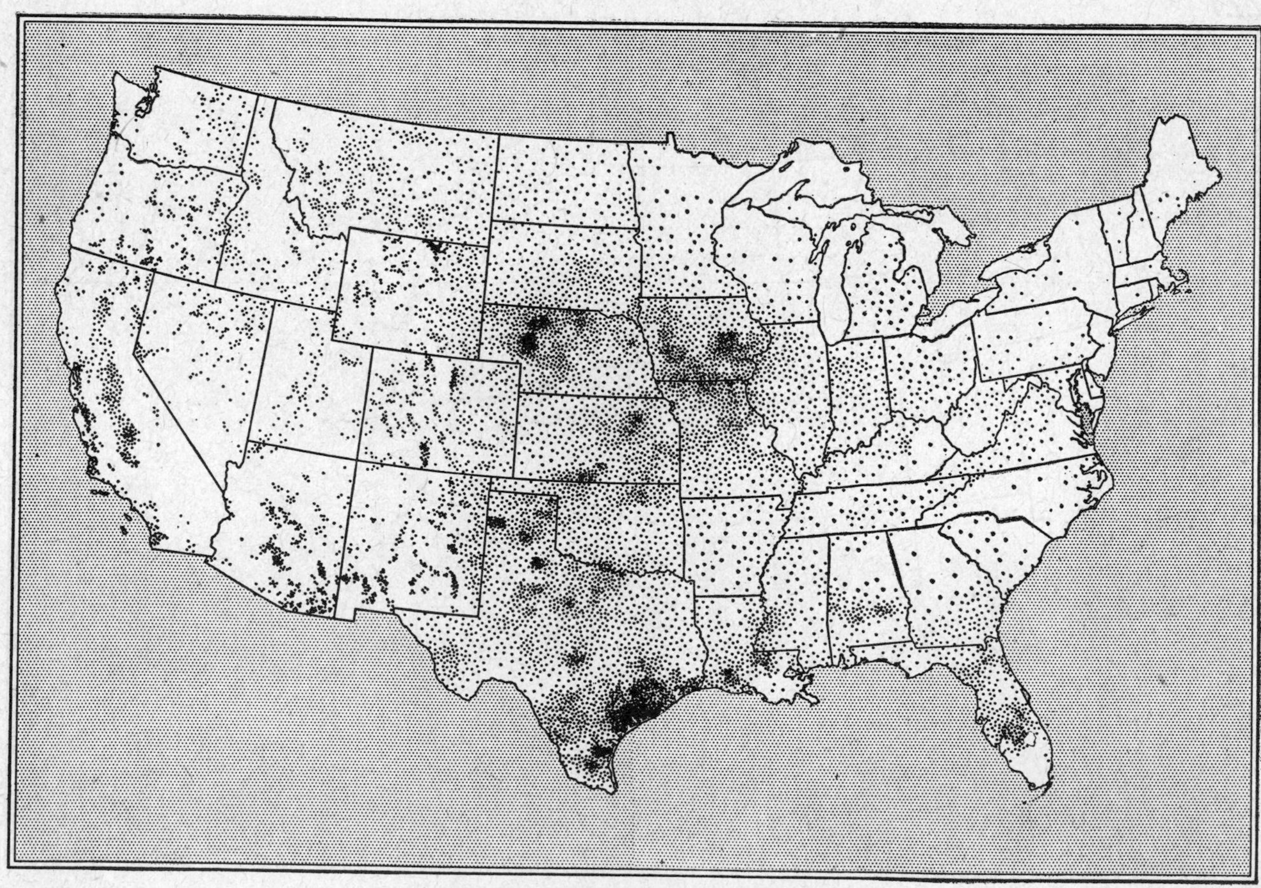

230 Cattle (Excluding Dairy Cows), 1940

Each dot represents 1,000 head; total, 9,448,671 head

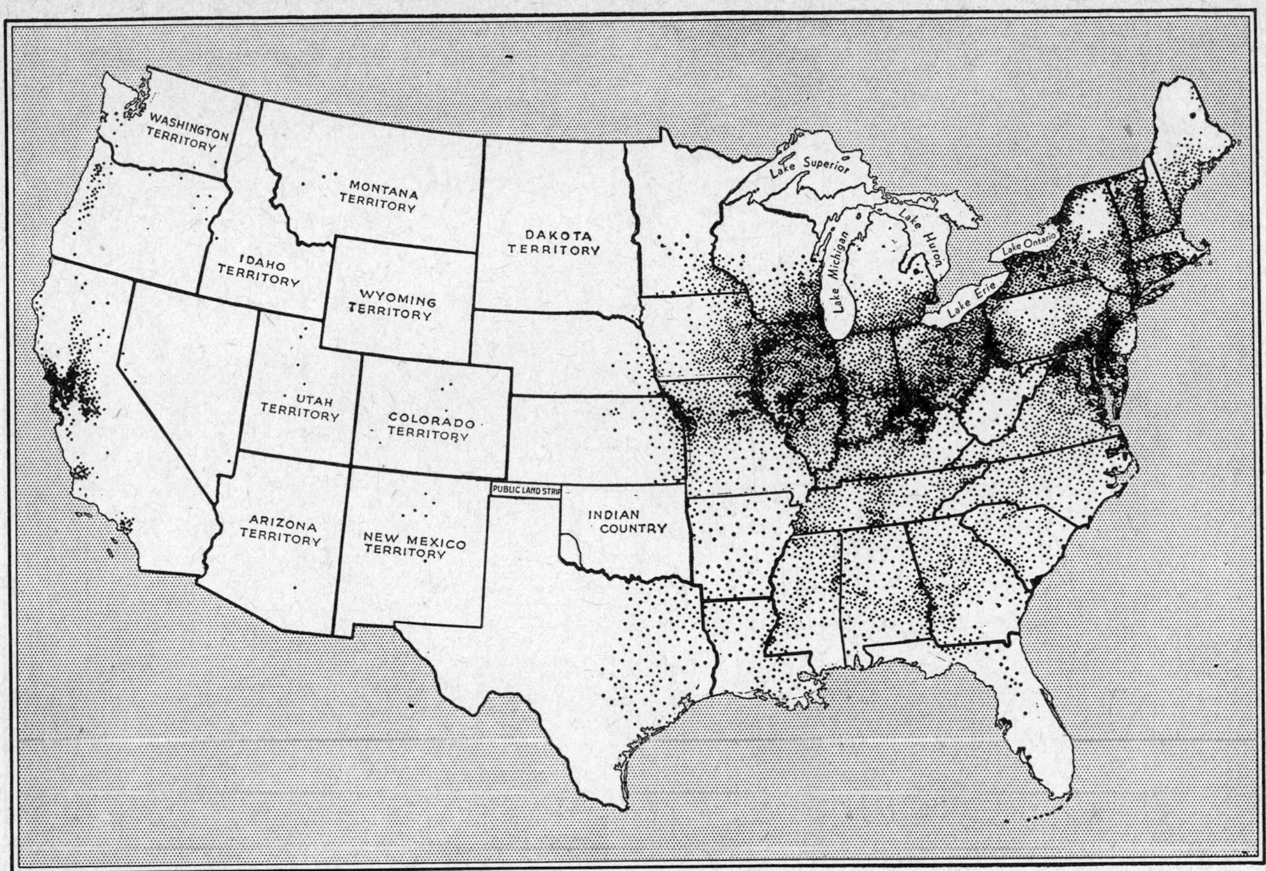

231 Improved Acreage, 1870

Each dot represents 25,000 acres; total, 188,921,099 acres

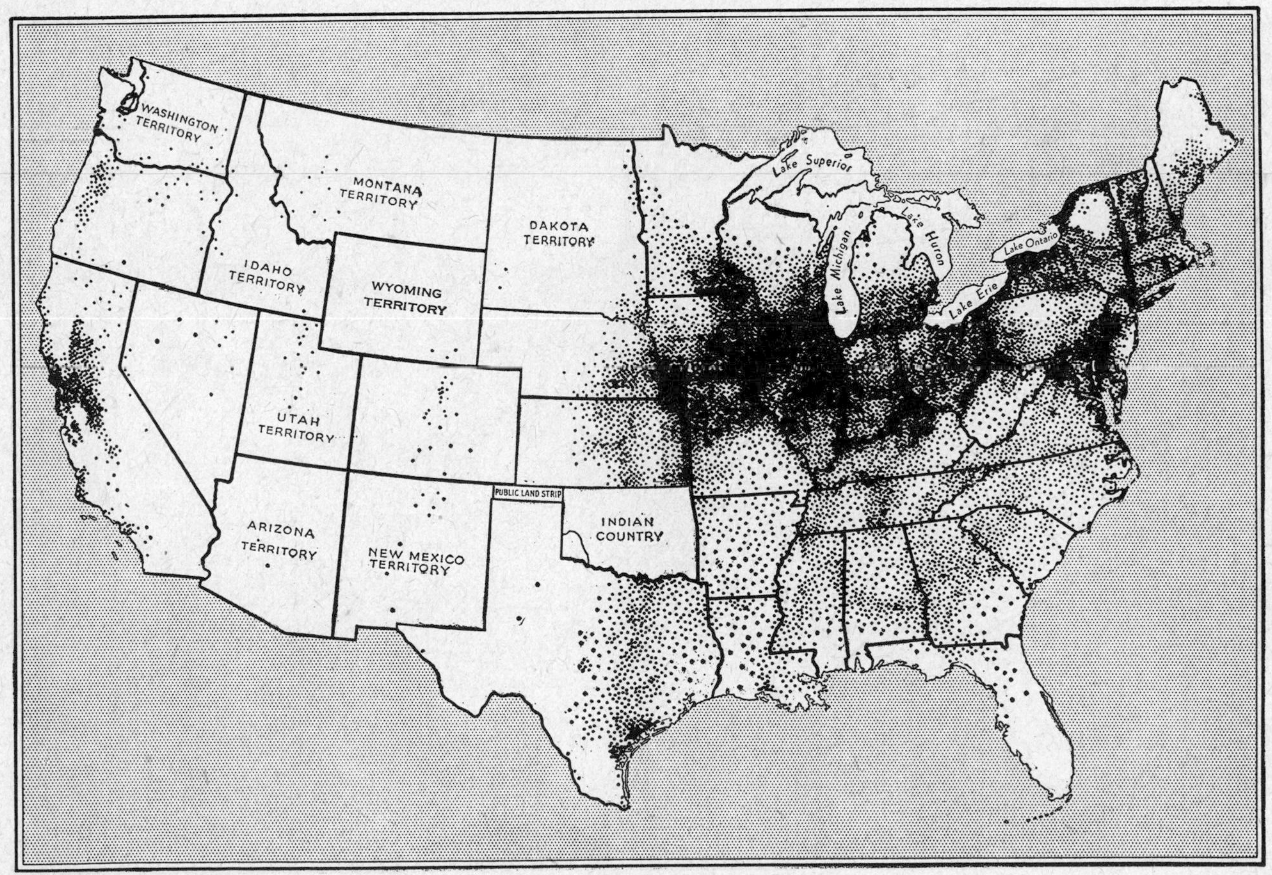

232 Improved Acreage, 1880

Each dot represents 25,000 acres; total, 284,771,042 acres

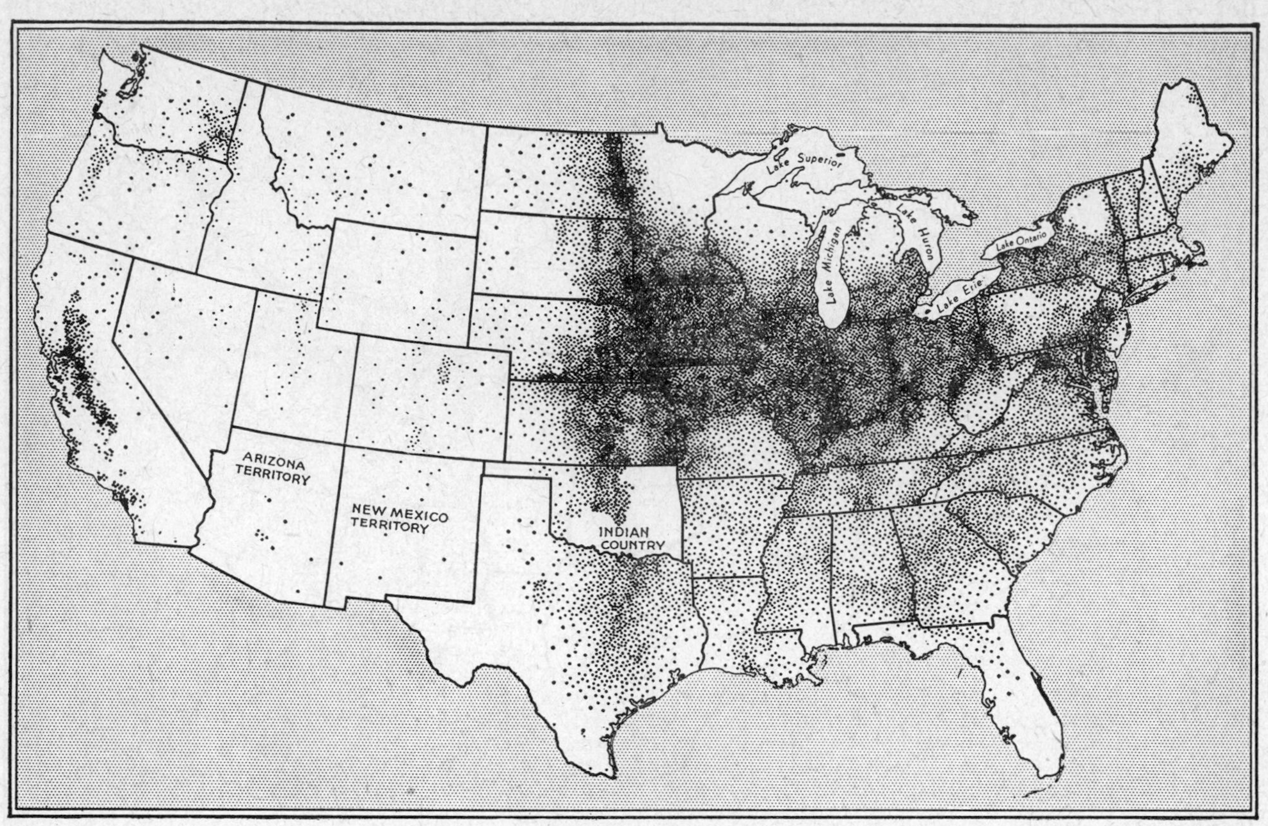

233 Improved Acreage, 1900

Each dot represents 25,000 acres; total, 414,498,487 acres

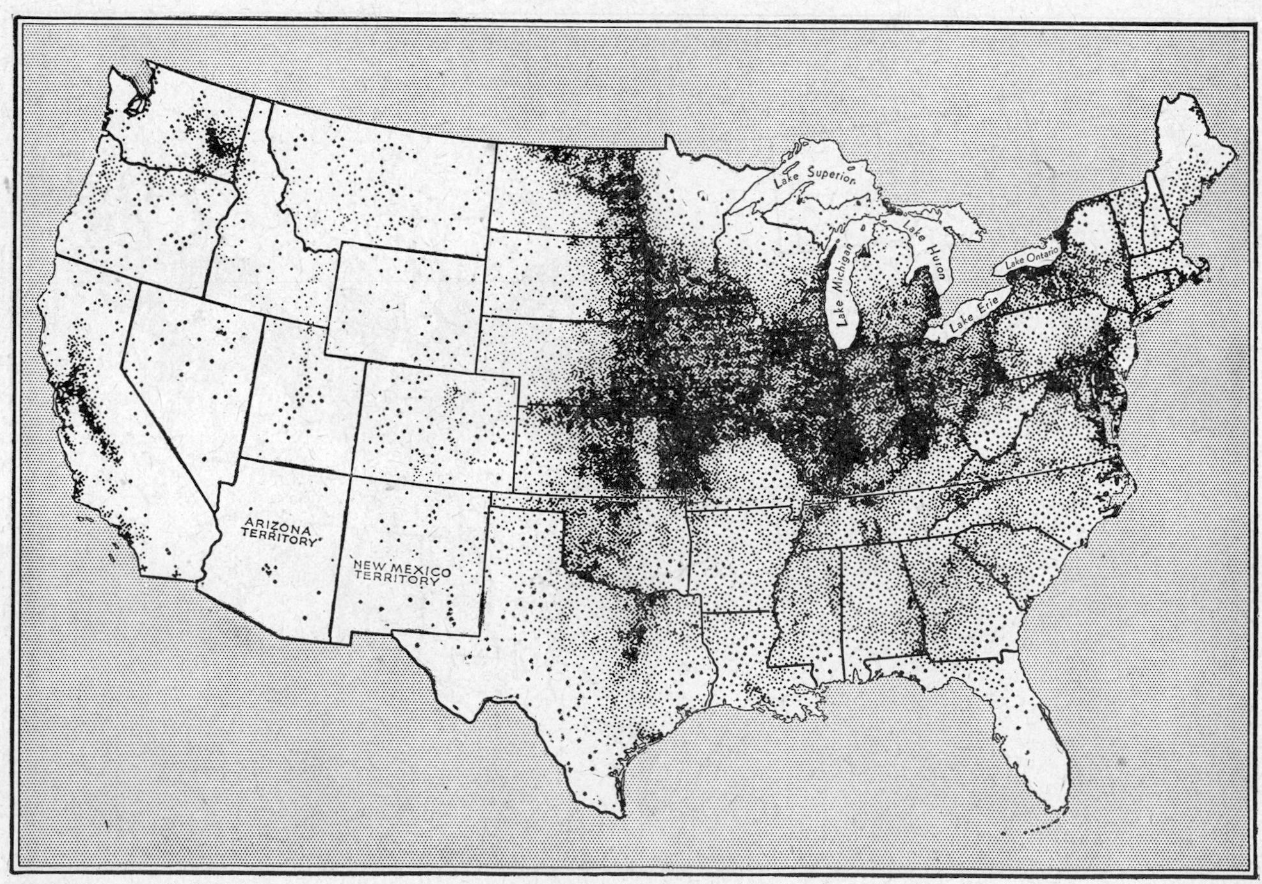

234 Improved Acreage, 1910

Each dot represents 25,000 acres; total, 478,451,756 acres

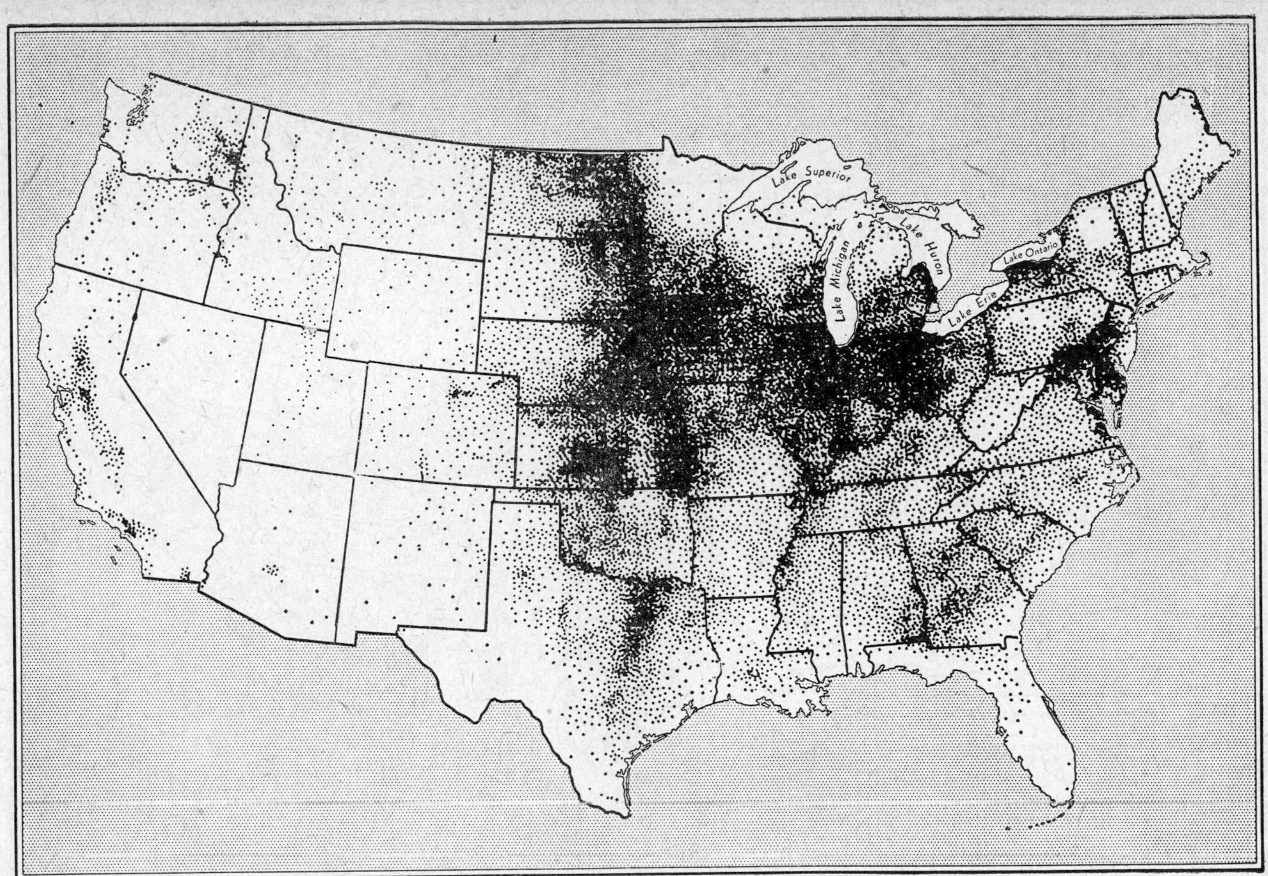

235

Acreage in Harvested Crops, 1920

Each dot represents 25,000 acres; total, 503,073,007 acres

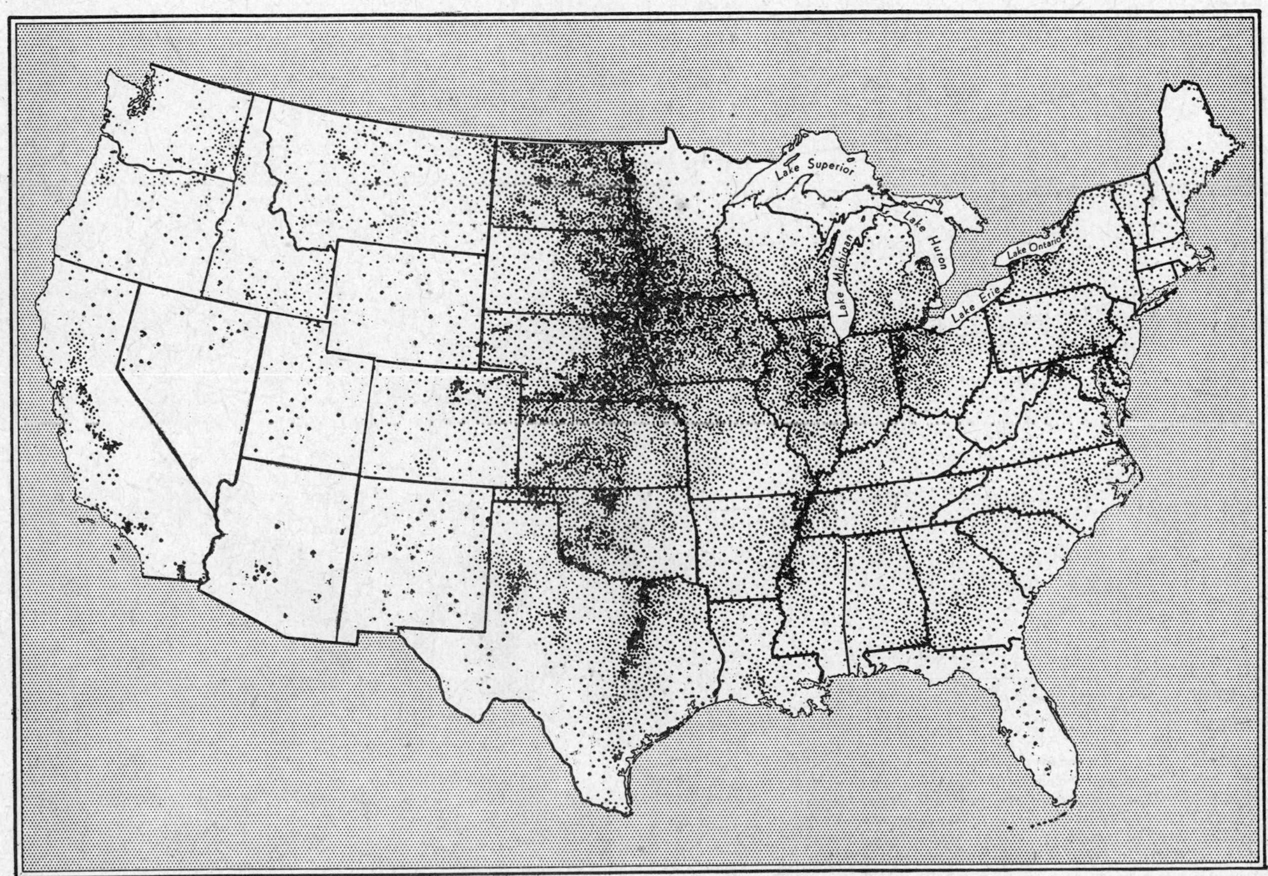

236

Acreage in Harvested Crops, 1930

Each dot represents 25,000 acres; total, 522,395,804 acres

WASHINGTON TERRITORY
MONTANA TERRITORY
DAKOTA TERRITORY
IDAHO TERRITORY
WYOMING TERRITORY
UTAH TERRITORY
PUBLIC LAND STRIP
INDIAN COUNTRY
ARIZONA TERRITORY
NEW MEXICO TERRITORY
Lake Superior
Lake Michigan
Lake Huron
Lake Ontario
Lake Erie

70 per cent and over of all farms operated by tenants
60-69 per cent and over of all farms operated by tenants
50-59 per cent and over of all farms operated by tenants
40-49 per cent and over of all farms operated by tenants
30-39 per cent and over of all farms operated by tenants
20-29 per cent and over of all farms operated by tenants
10-19 per cent and over of all farms operated by tenants
Under 10 per cent of all farms operated by tenants

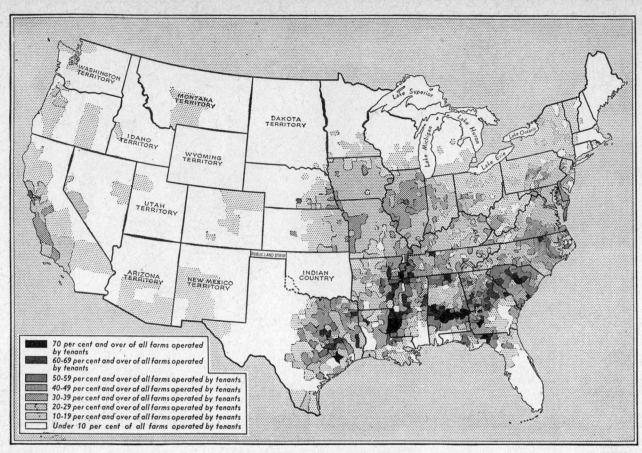

237 Farm Tenancy, by Counties, 1880

ARIZONA TERRITORY
NEW MEXICO TERRITORY
Lake Superior
Lake Michigan
Lake Huron
Lake Ontario
Lake Erie

75 per cent and over of all farms operated by tenants
60-74 per cent and over of all farms operated by tenants
50-59 per cent and over of all farms operated by tenants
40-49 per cent and over of all farms operated by tenants
30-39 per cent and over of all farms operated by tenants
20-29 per cent and over of all farms operated by tenants
10-19 per cent and over of all farms operated by tenants
Under 10 per cent of all farms operated by tenants

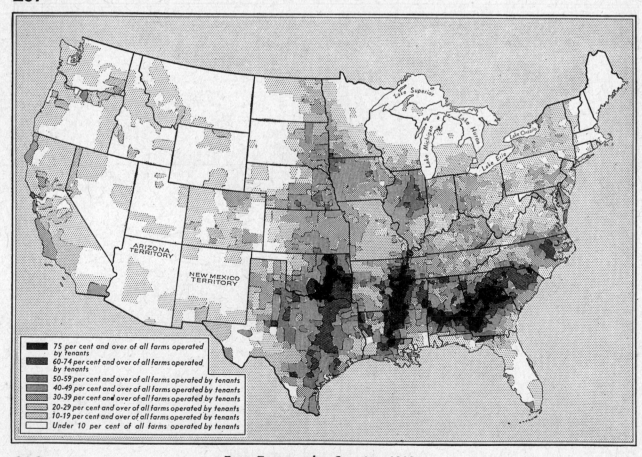

238 Farm Tenancy, by Counties, 1910

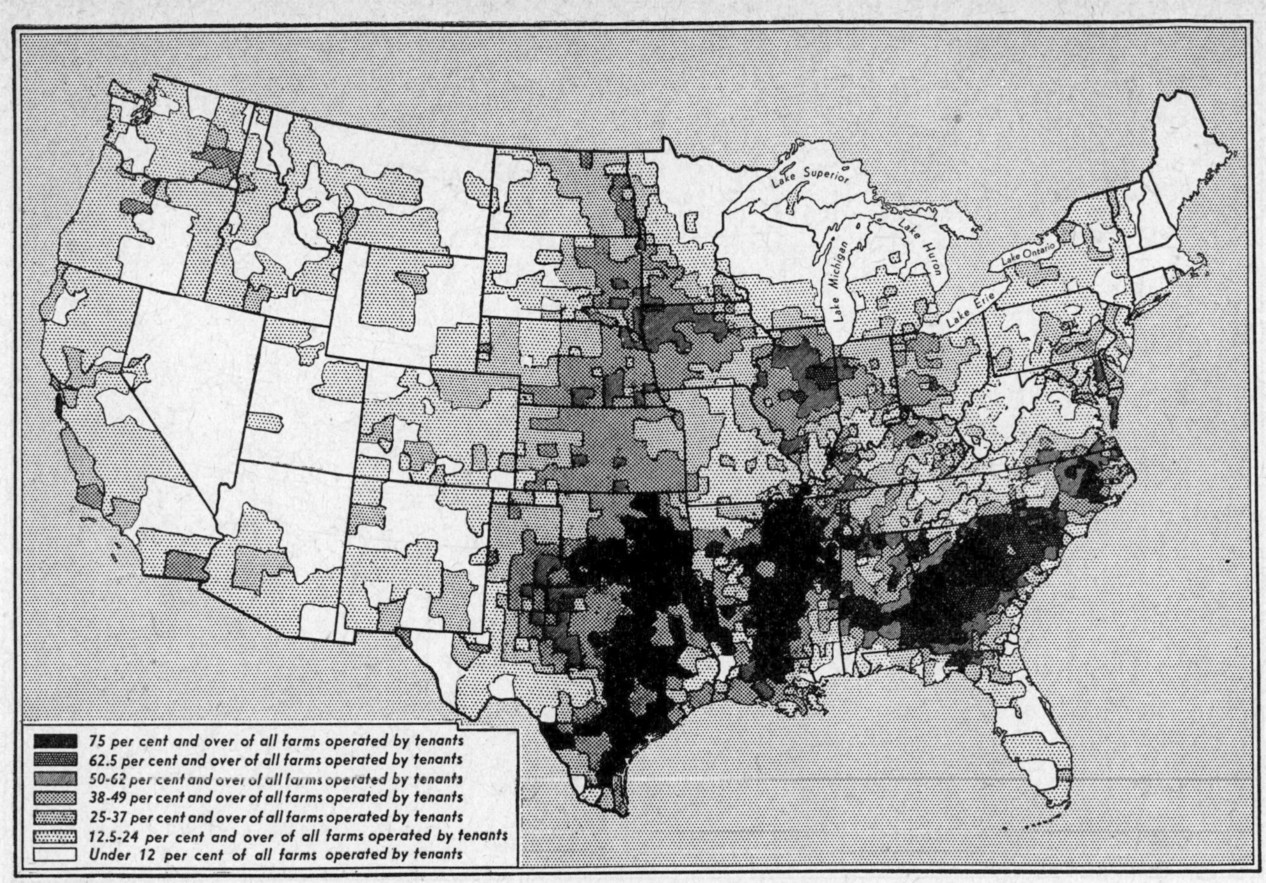

239 Farm Tenancy, by Counties, 1920

Lake Superior
Lake Michigan
Lake Huron
Lake Ontario
Lake Erie

80 per cent and over of all farms operated by tenants
60-79 per cent and over of all farms operated by tenants
40-59 per cent and over of all farms operated by tenants
20-39 per cent and over of all farms operated by tenants
Under 20 per cent of all farms operated by tenants

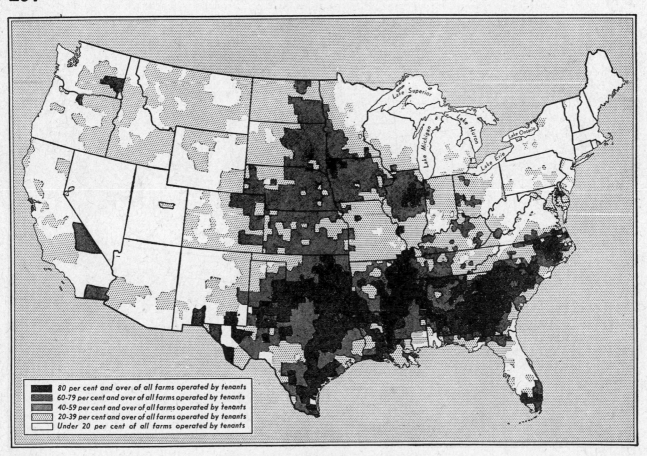

240 Farm Tenancy, by Counties, 1930

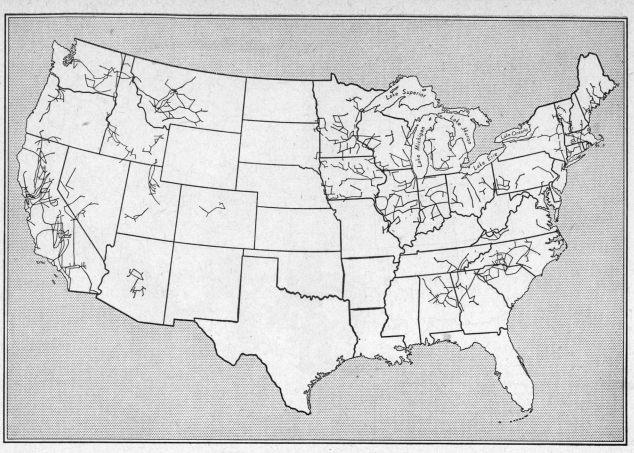

241 Power Transmission Lines Carrying a Potential of 55,000 or More Volts, 1923

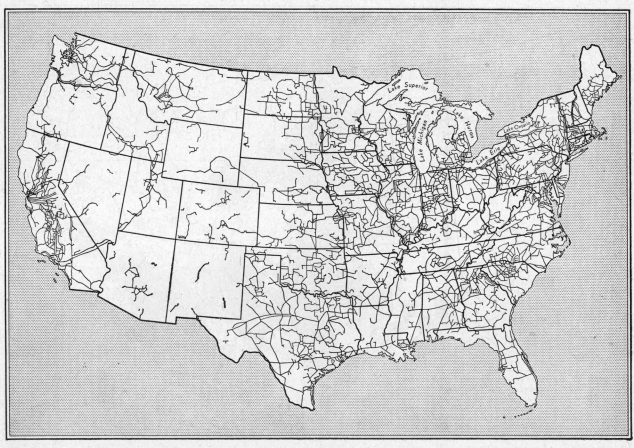

242 Power Transmission Lines Carrying a Potential of 55,000 or More Volts, 1935

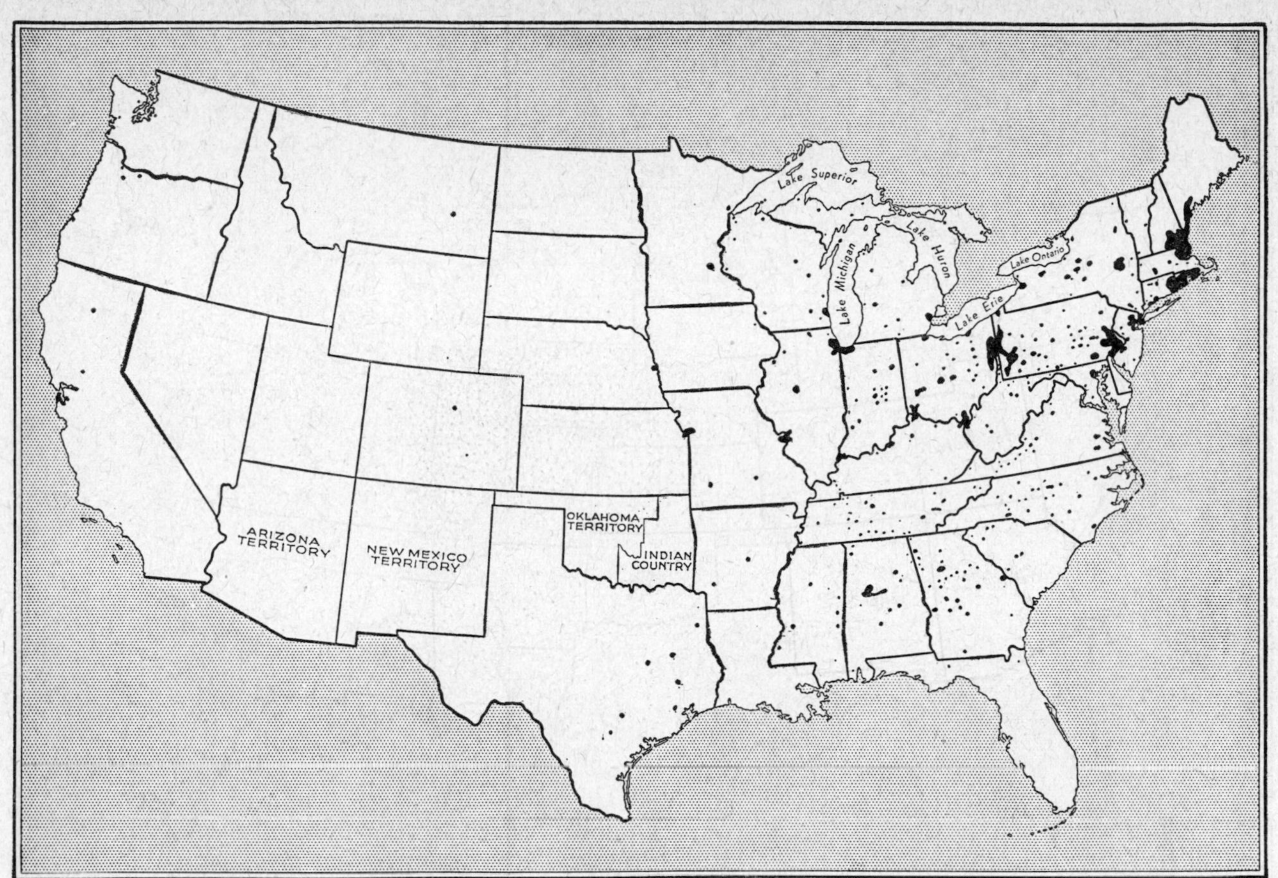

243

Manufacturing Areas, 1900

Based on iron, steel, and textiles, together with cities having more than 5,000 industrial employees

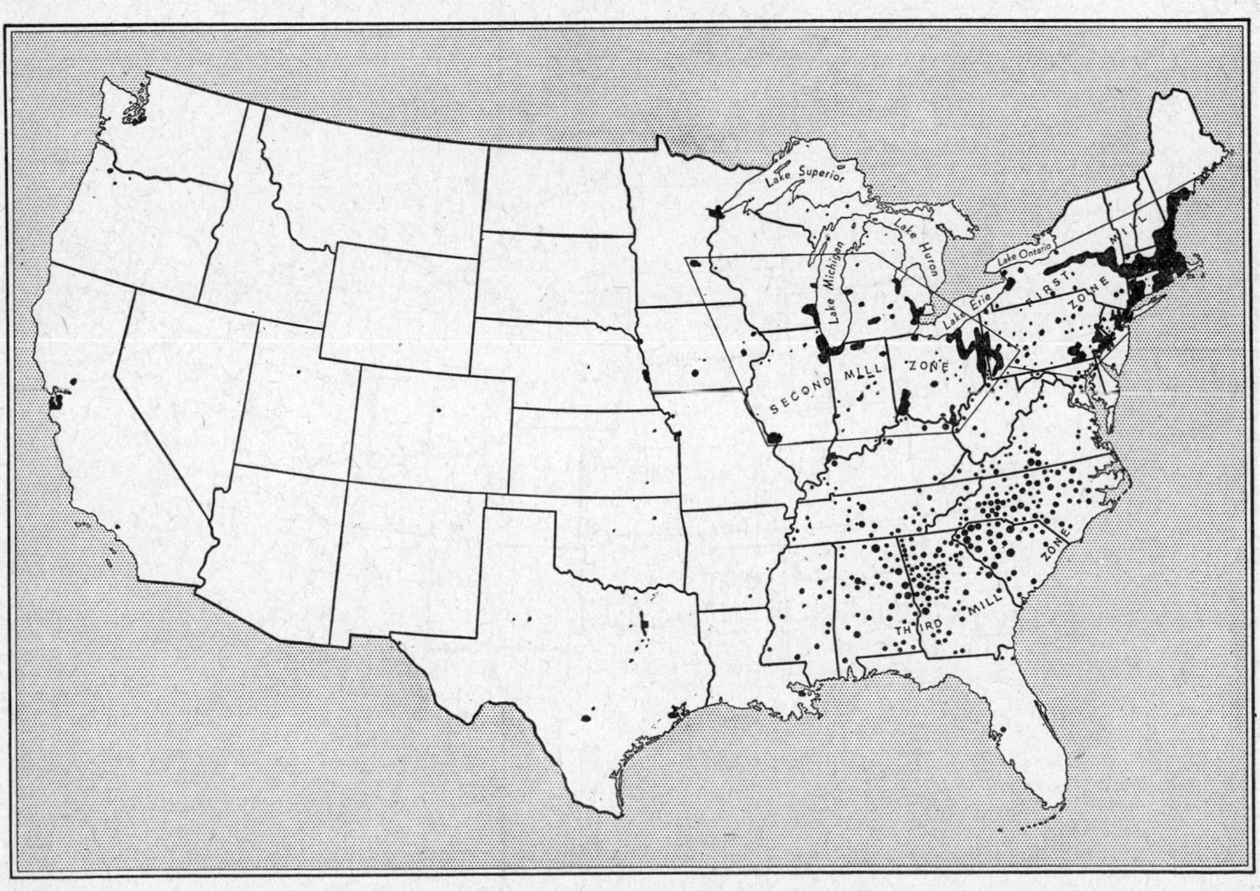

244

Manufacturing Areas, 1940

Based on iron, steel, and textiles, together with cities having more than 5,000 industrial employees

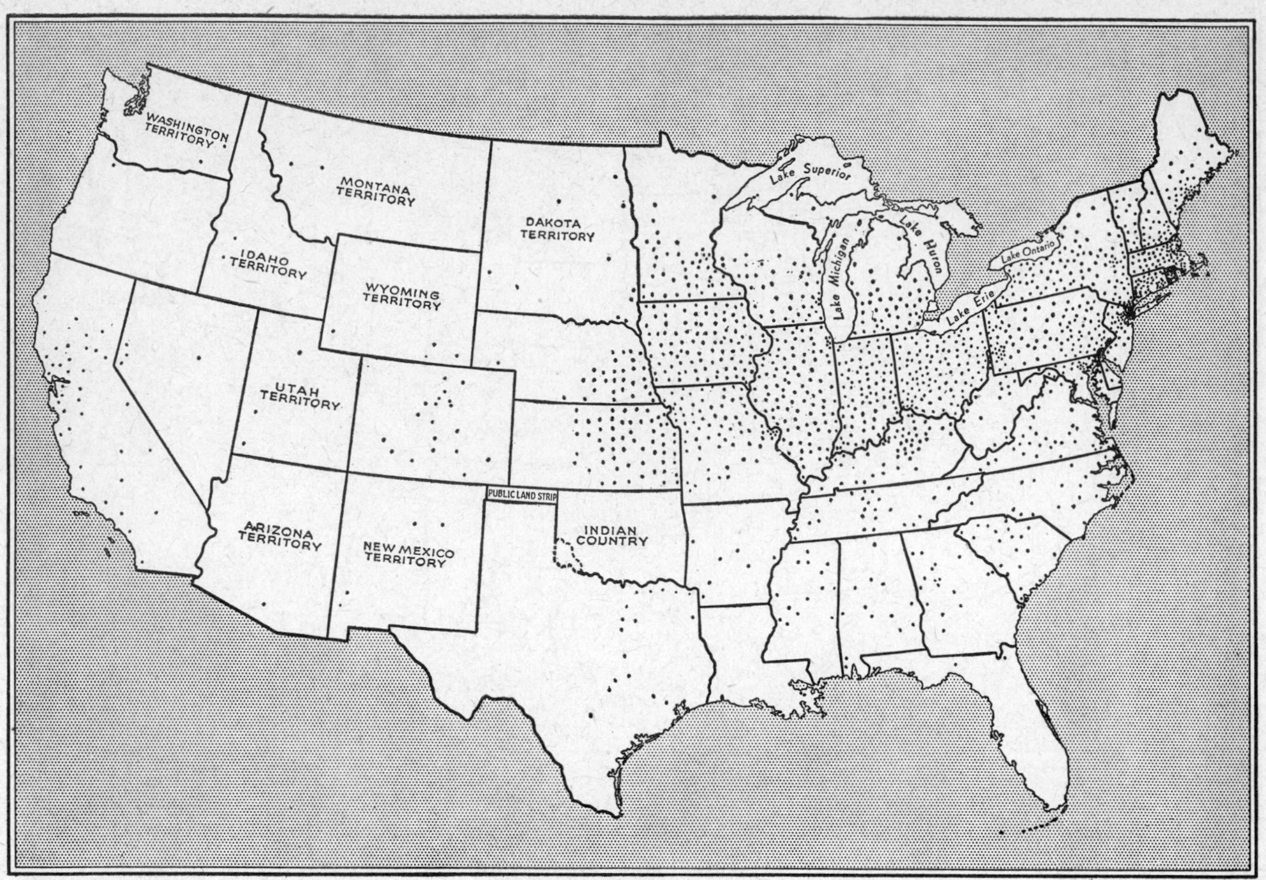

245

Banks of 1880
Each dot represents 1-5 banks

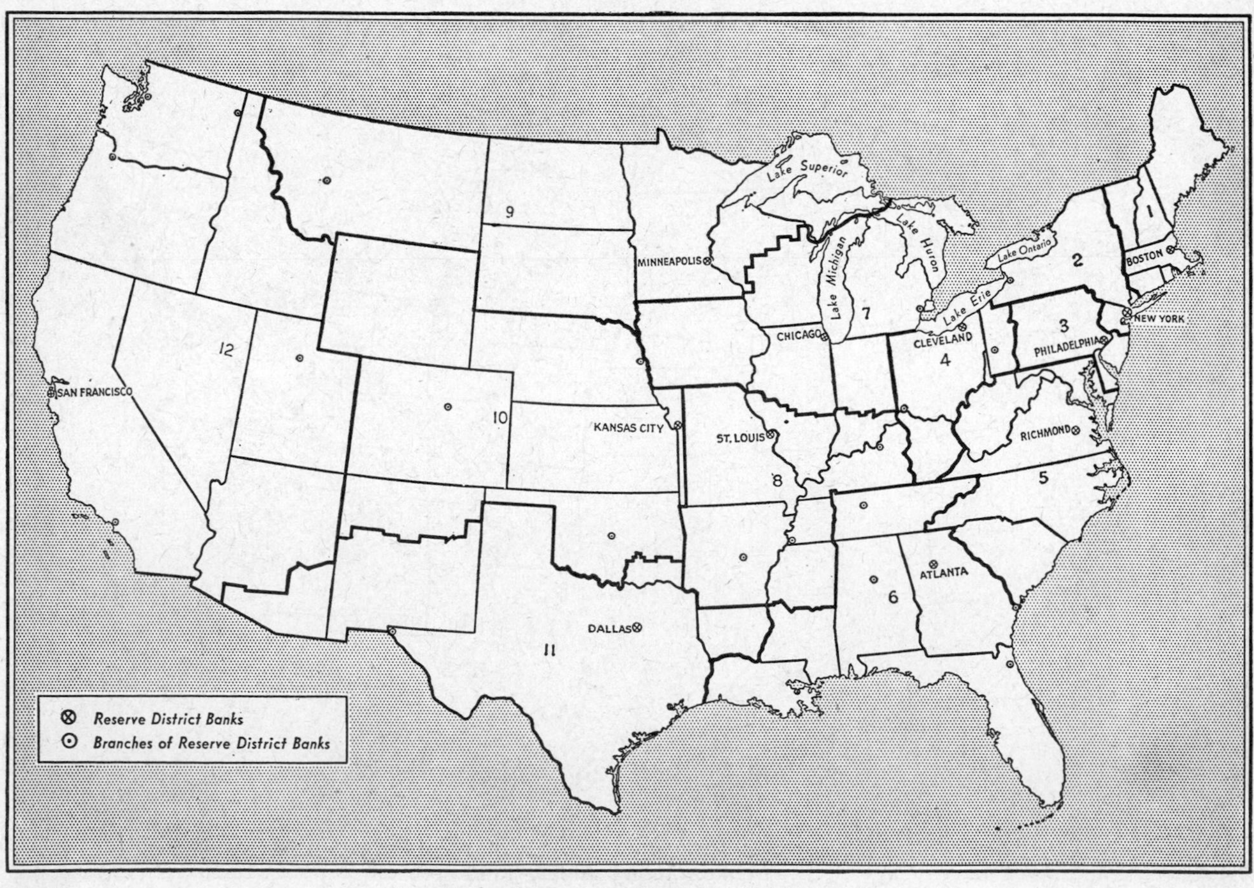

246

Federal Reserve Districts, 1914

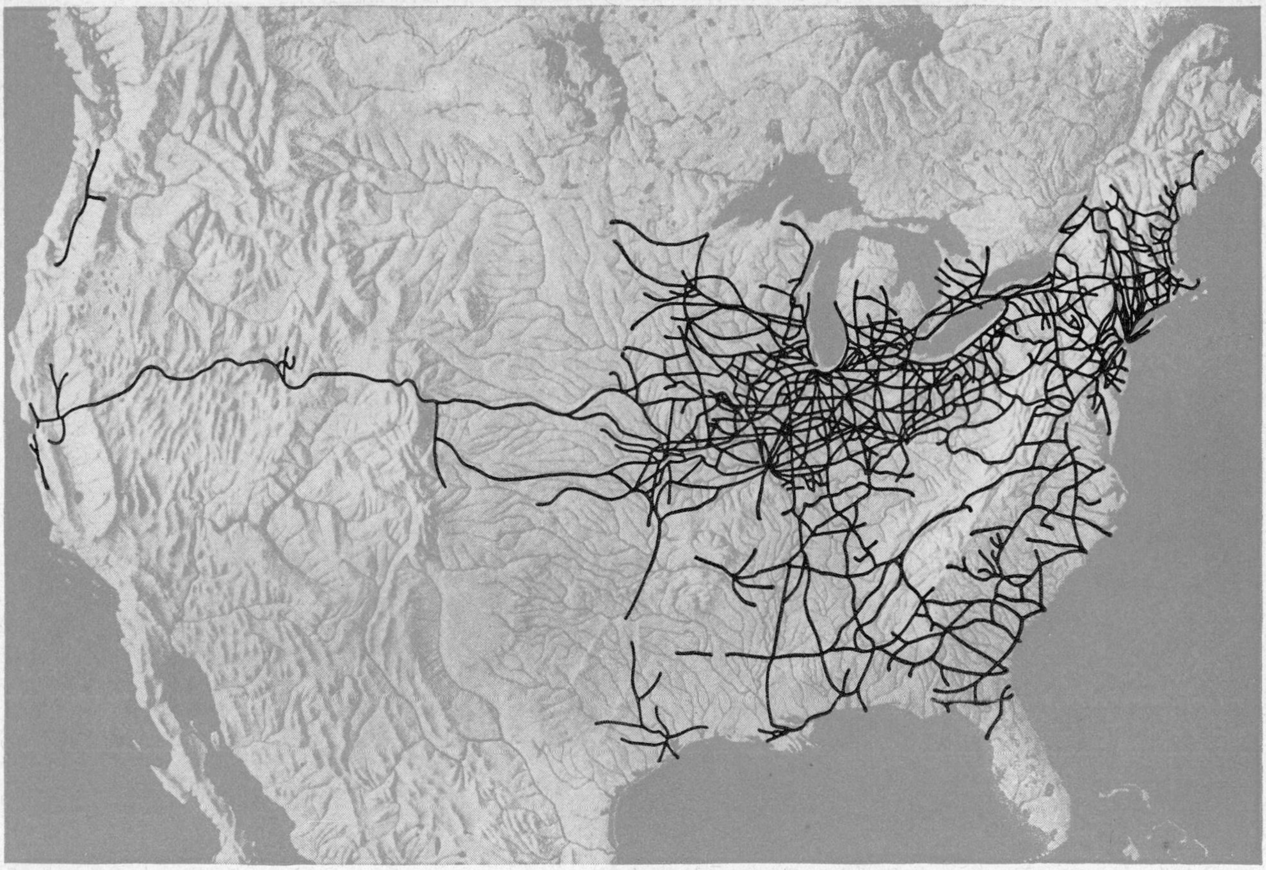

247 **Railroads in Operation, 1870**

For railroad mileage statistics, see Appendix V

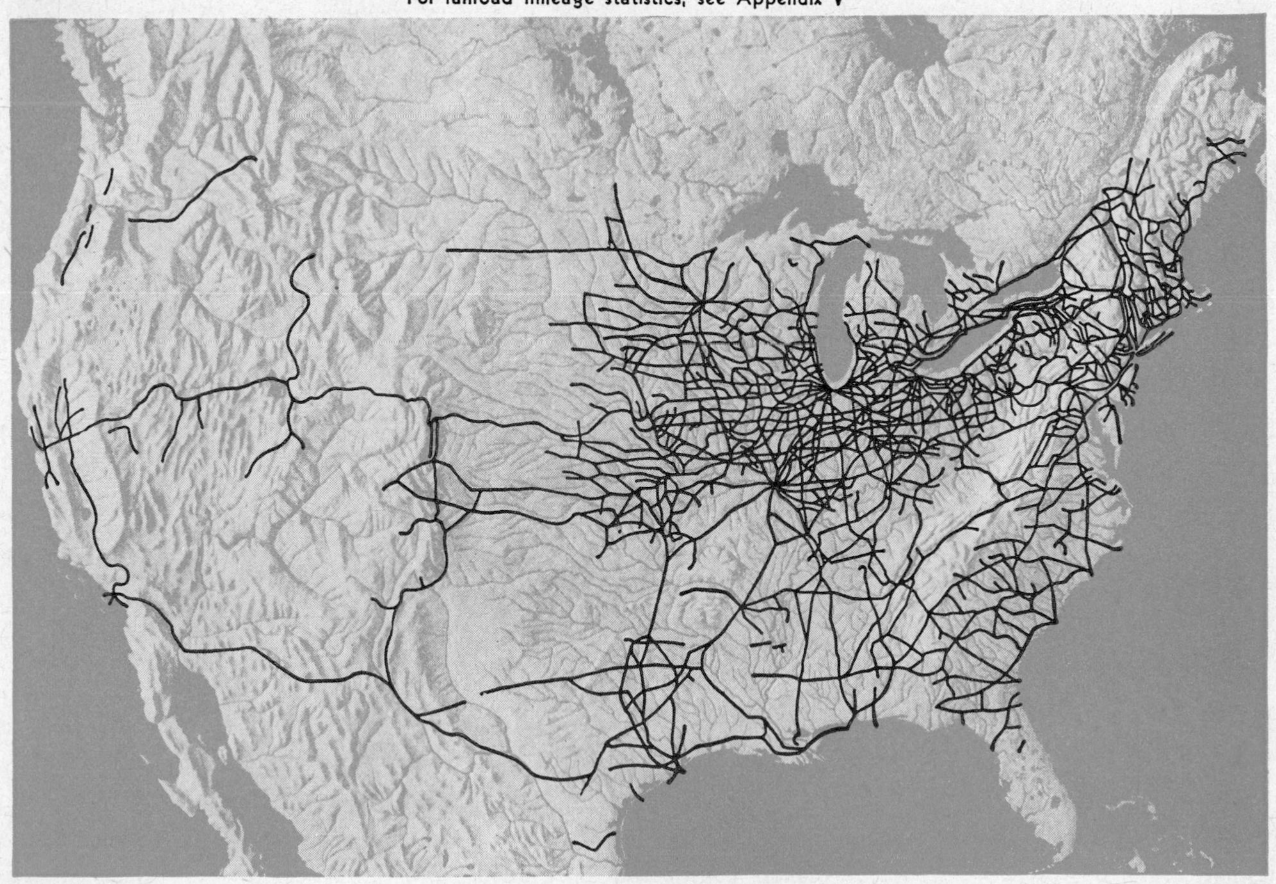

248 **Railroads in Operation, 1882**

For railroad mileage statistics, see Appendix V

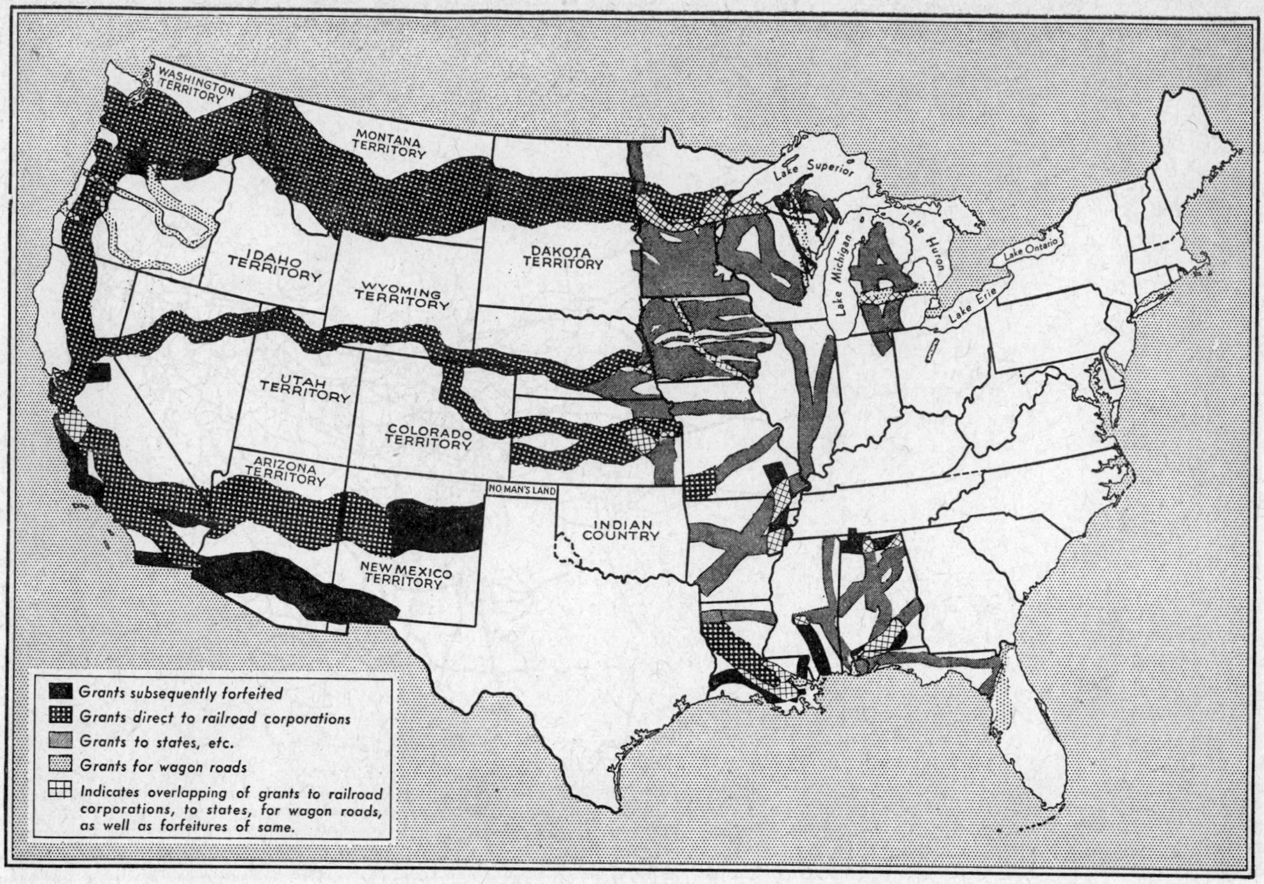

249 Federal Land Grants in Aid of Railroad and Wagon-Road Construction, 1828-1871

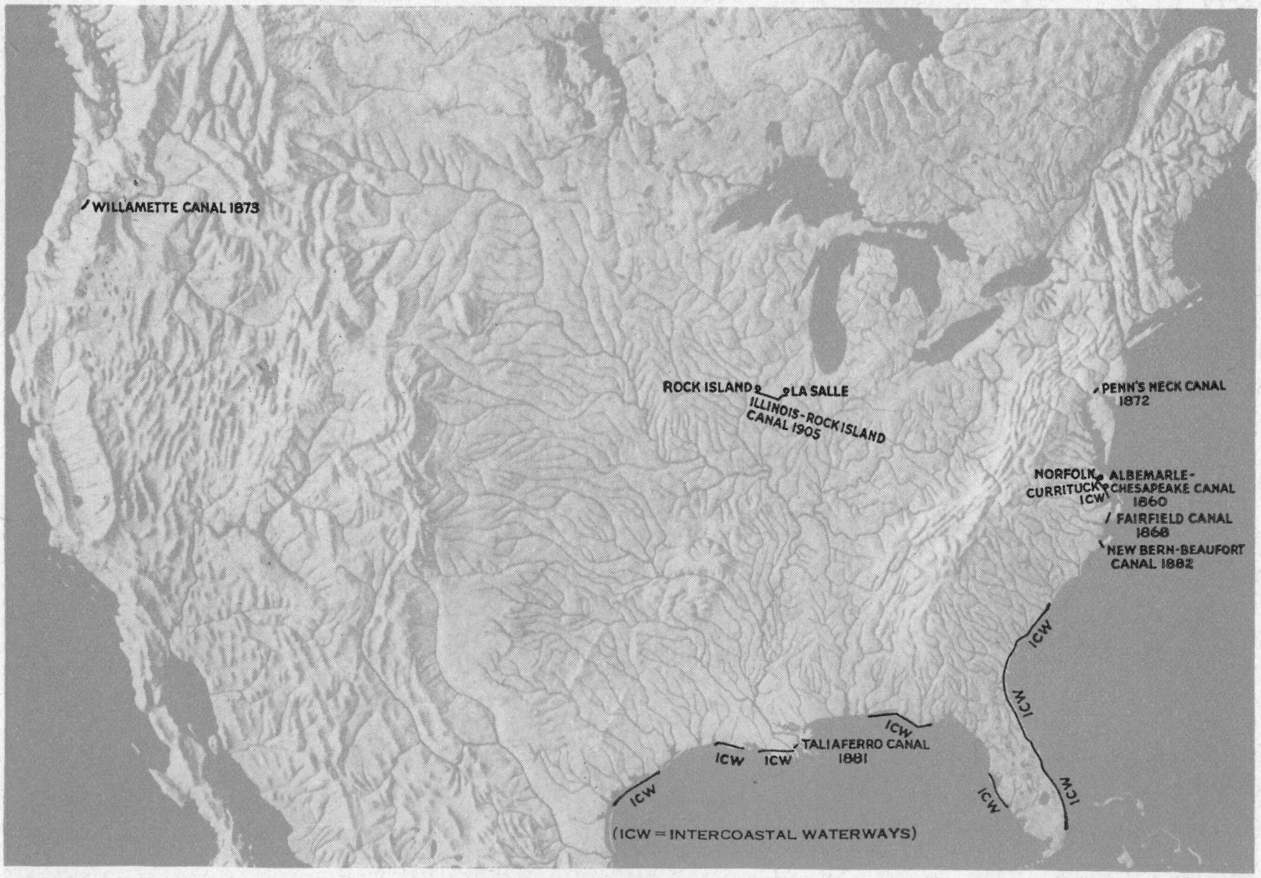

250 Canals Constructed Since 1860

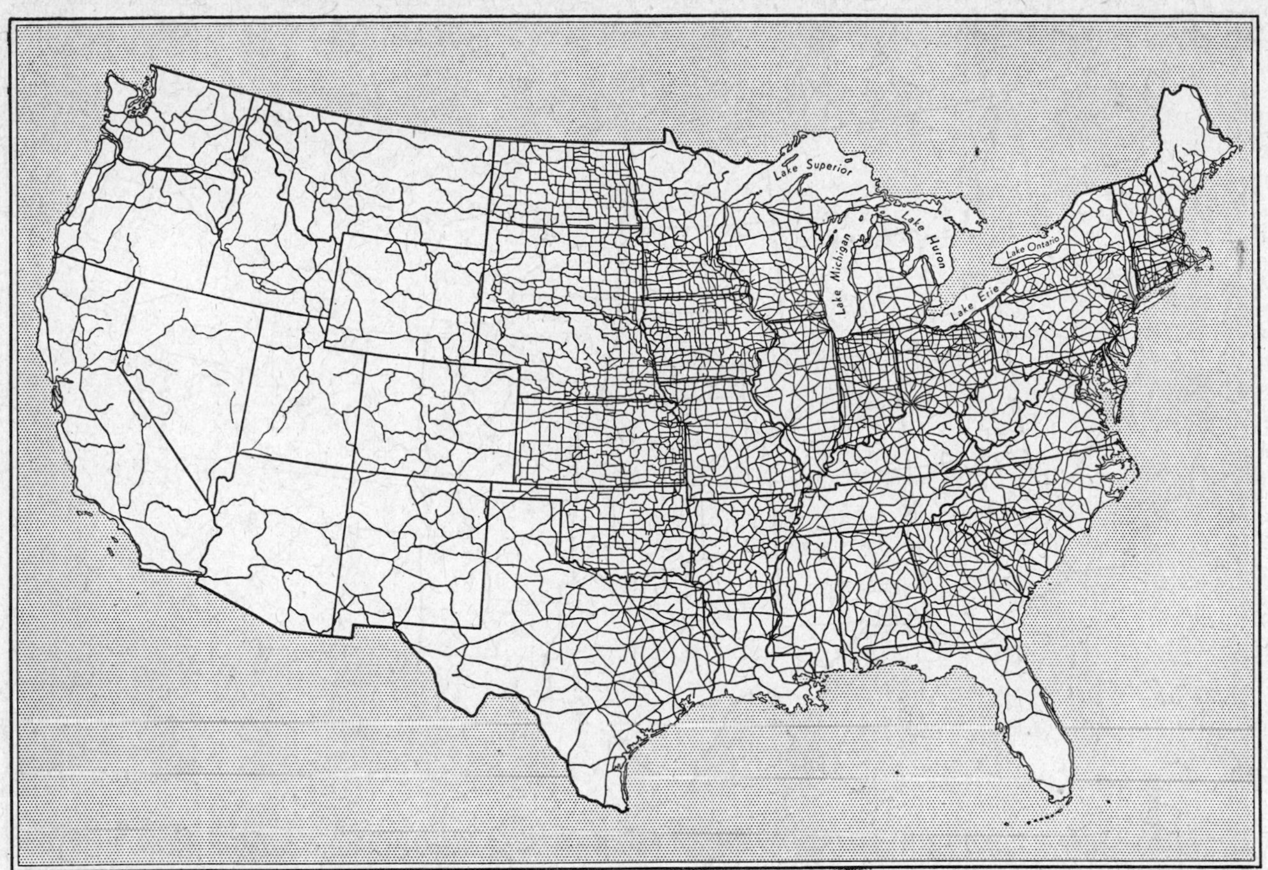

251 Federal Highways System, 1925

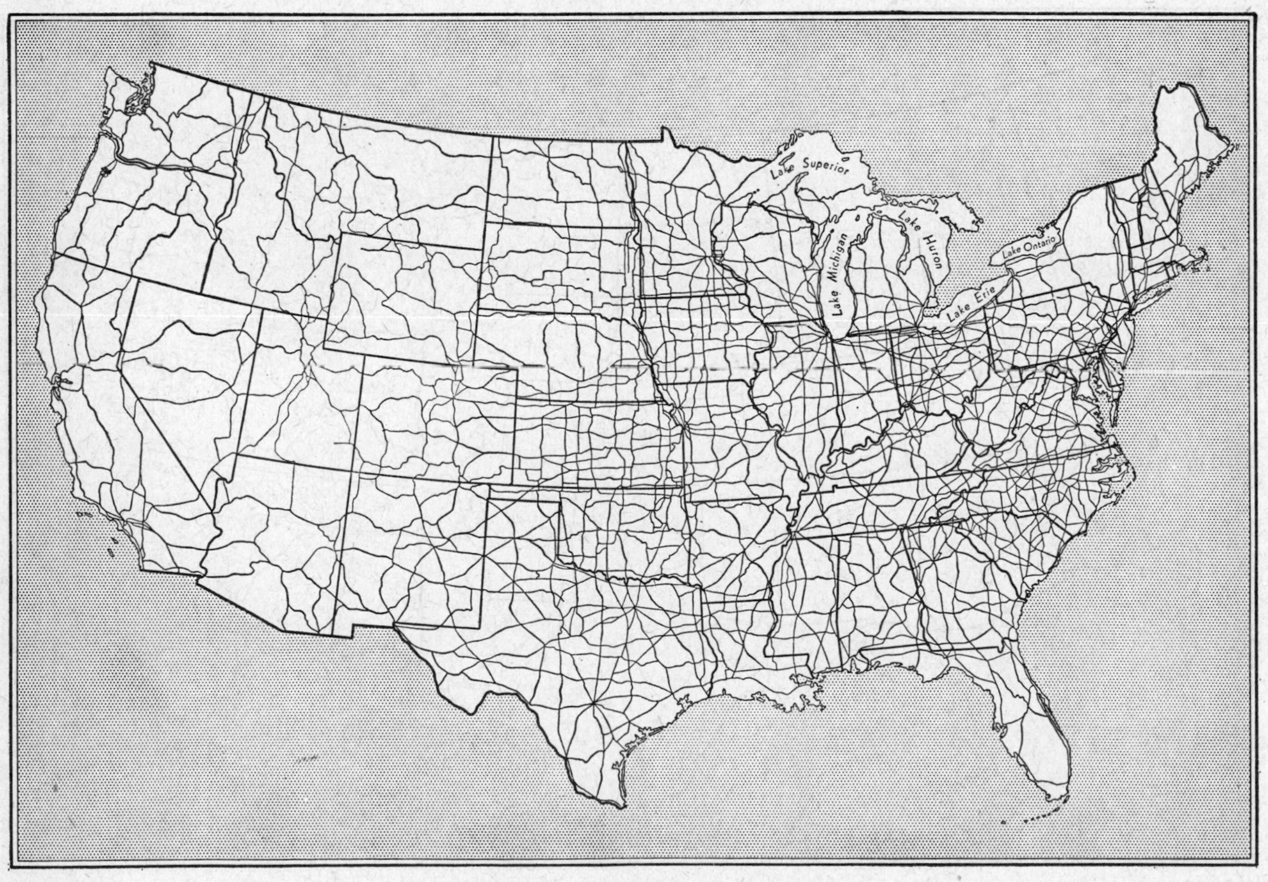

252 Revised Federal Highways System, 1940

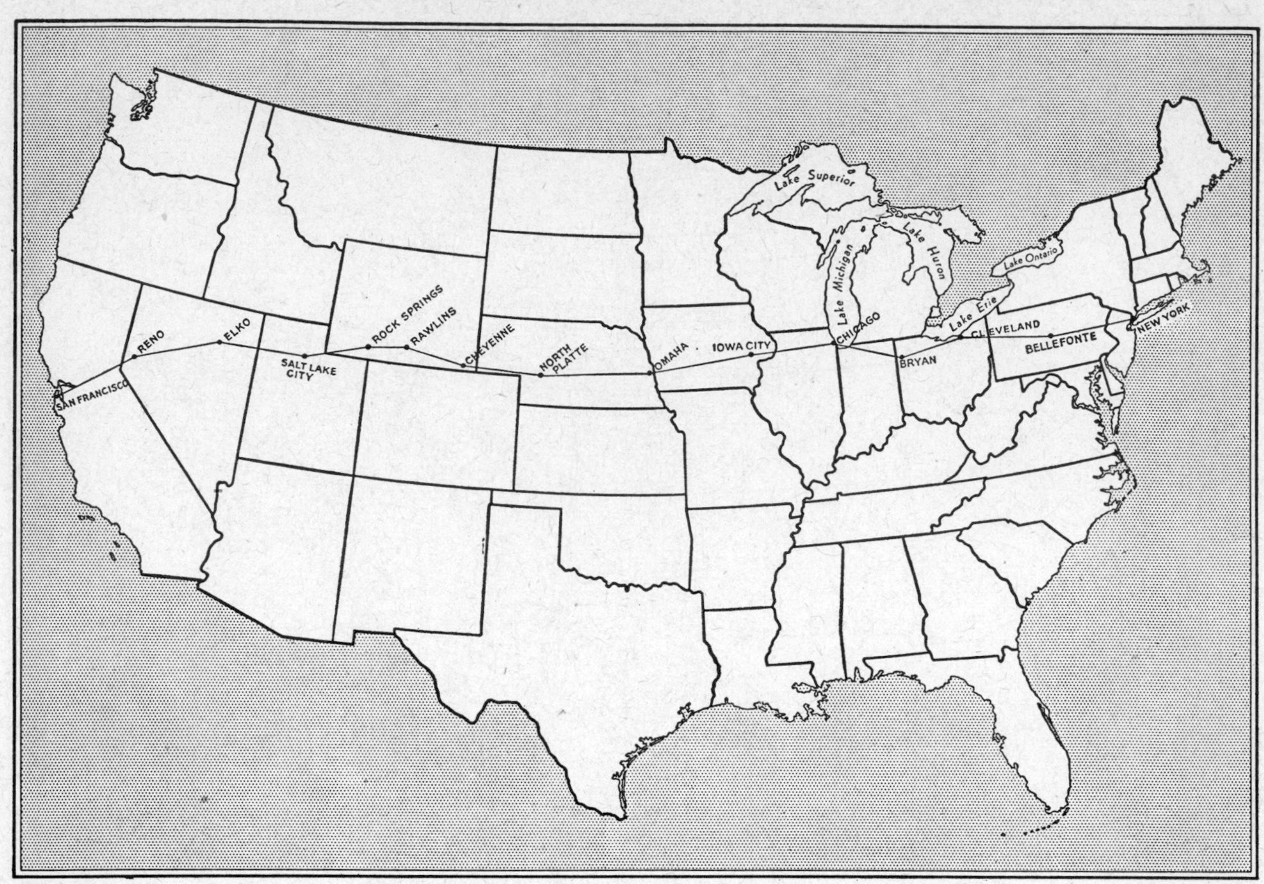

253 Commercial Air Lines, 1920

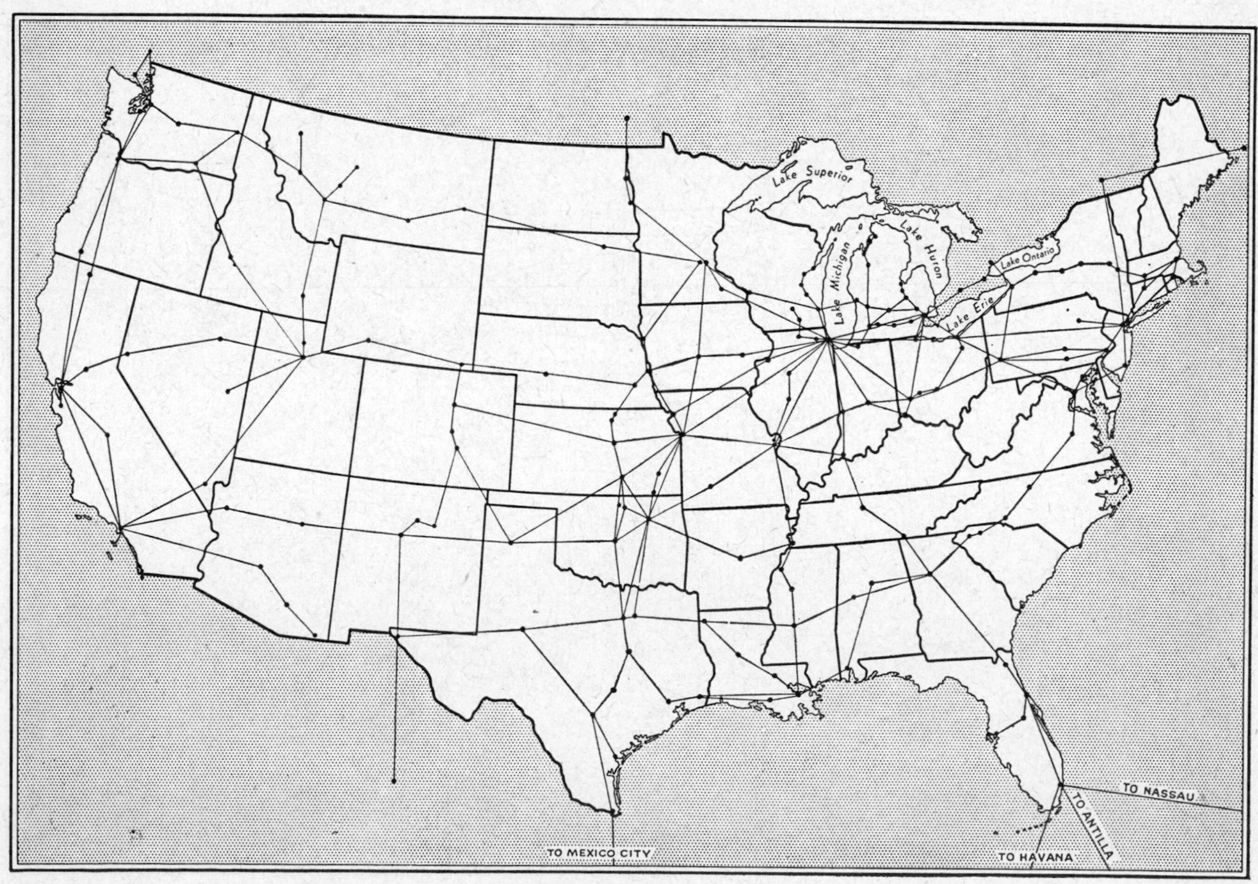

254 Commercial Air Lines, 1930

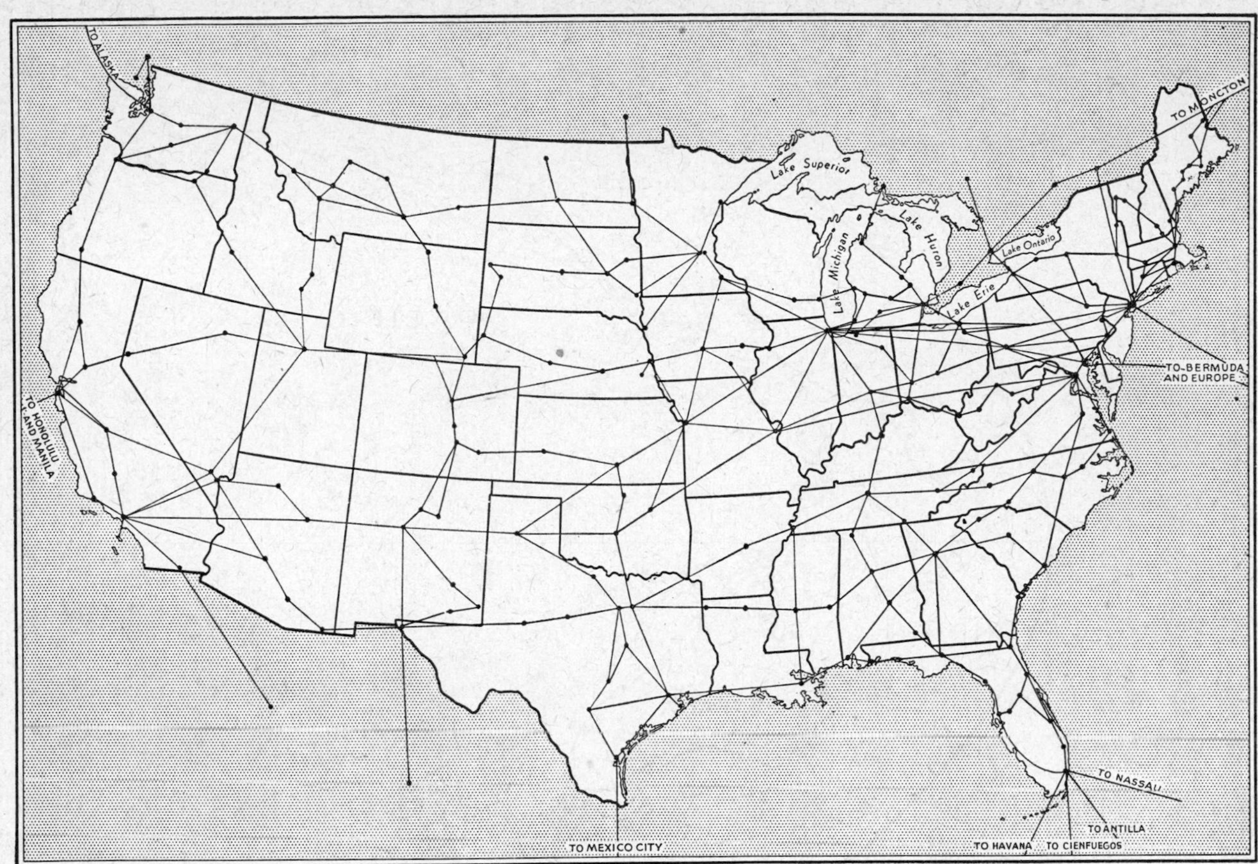

255

Commercial Air Lines, 1940

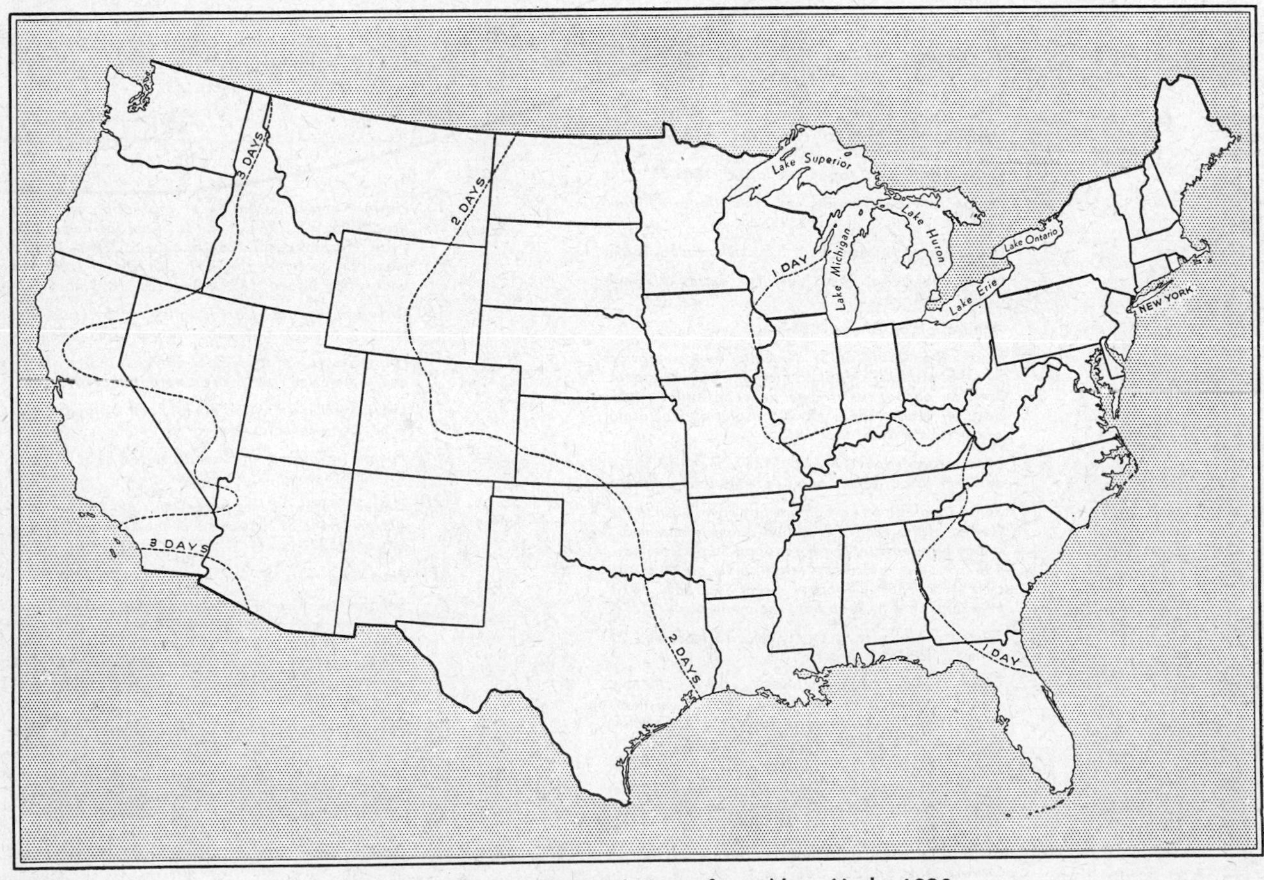

256

Rates of Travel: Railroad Time from New York, 1930

Commercial flying time Coast to Coast, 1930, 36 hours; 1940, 16 hours

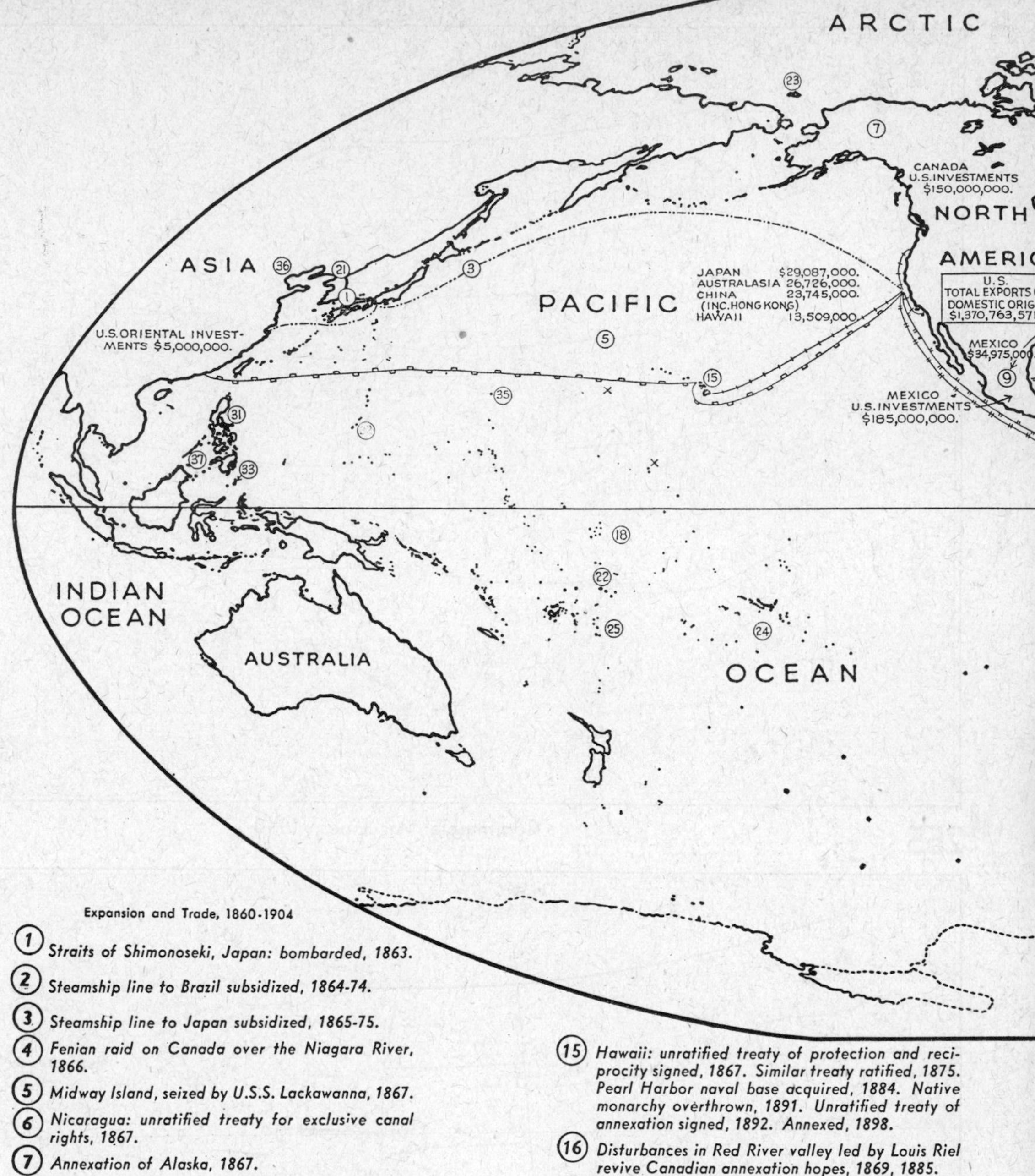

Expansion and Trade, 1860-1904

(1) *Straits of Shimonoseki, Japan: bombarded, 1863.*

(2) *Steamship line to Brazil subsidized, 1864-74.*

(3) *Steamship line to Japan subsidized, 1865-75.*

(4) *Fenian raid on Canada over the Niagara River, 1866.*

(5) *Midway Island, seized by U.S.S. Lackawanna, 1867.*

(6) *Nicaragua: unratified treaty for exclusive canal rights, 1867.*

(7) *Annexation of Alaska, 1867.*

(8) *Haiti offers Mole of St. Nicholas for assumption by U. S. of Haiti's debt to France, 1867. President Johnson announces it may be necessary to take over all Haiti, 1867. House resolution declaring protectorate defeated, 1869.*

(9) *French forces leave Mexico, 1867. General Sheridan sent to border to point up American protests.*

(10) *Santo Domingo offers Samaná Bay naval base to the United States, 1867. President Johnson announces it may be necessary to take over all Santo Domingo, 1867. House resolution establishing protectorate defeated, 1869. Babcock Treaties, 1869, 1870. Warships sent to keep Baez régime in power, 1870.*

(11) *Purchase of Culebra and Culebrita discussed by Seward, 1867.*

(12) *Cuba: President Johnson announces it may be necessary to take over the island, 1867. Ten Years War, 1868-78. Virginius incident, 1873. Spanish-American War, 1898. Platt Amendment, 1901-34.*

(13) *Danish West Indies: unratified treaty of cession to the United States for $7,500,000, signed, 1867; unratified treaty of cession for $5,000,000, signed, 1902; ceded for $25,000,000, 1917.*

(14) *St. Bartholomew: purchase contemplated by Seward from Sweden, 1867.*

(15) *Hawaii: unratified treaty of protection and reciprocity signed, 1867. Similar treaty ratified, 1875. Pearl Harbor naval base acquired, 1884. Native monarchy overthrown, 1891. Unratified treaty of annexation signed, 1892. Annexed, 1898.*

(16) *Disturbances in Red River valley led by Louis Riel revive Canadian annexation hopes, 1869, 1885.*

(17) *House resolution to declare all West Indies islands under American protection defeated, 1869.*

(18) *House resolution to declare all Pacific islands under American protection defeated, 1869.*

(19) *Fenian "invasions" of Canada halted at St. Albans, Vt., and Malone, N. Y., 1870.*

(20) *United States secures perpetual right of free navigation of the St. Lawrence in the Treaty of Washington, 1871.*

(21) *Ping-Yang forts, Korea, bombarded, 1871.*

(22) *Samoa: unratified treaty giving the United States exclusive rights at Pago Pago signed, 1872. Similar treaty ratified, 1878. Crisis with England and Germany, 1889. Tripartite condominion, 1889-99. Annexation arranged, 1899; formally accepted by Congress, 1929.*

(23) *Possession claimed to Wrangell, Bennett, Henrietta and Jeanette Islands, 1881.*

(24) *Approximately 70 guano islands, mostly in the South Pacific, bonded and claimed under the Guano Act of 1867 by 1884, including Swain's, Johnston's , Palmyra*, Baker, Howland, Kingman Reef, Navassa (1858), Swan (1863), Quito Sueño, Serrana and Seranilla Banks, Roncador Cay.*

257 Subsidized Trade Routes, Under Acts of 1864 and I

For further

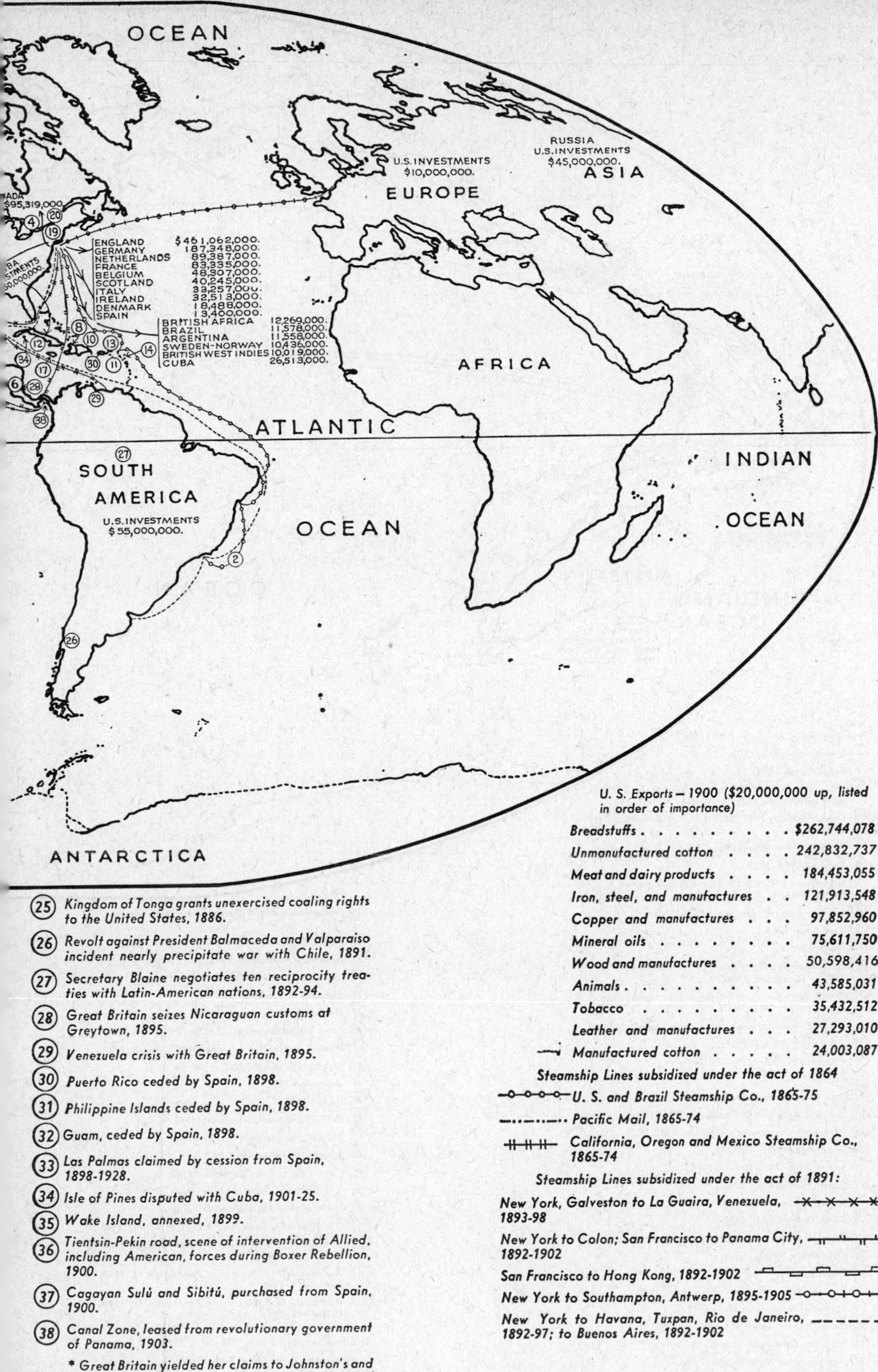

(25) Kingdom of Tonga grants unexercised coaling rights to the United States, 1886.

(26) Revolt against President Balmaceda and Valparaiso incident nearly precipitate war with Chile, 1891.

(27) Secretary Blaine negotiates ten reciprocity treaties with Latin-American nations, 1892-94.

(28) Great Britain seizes Nicaraguan customs at Greytown, 1895.

(29) Venezuela crisis with Great Britain, 1895.

(30) Puerto Rico ceded by Spain, 1898.

(31) Philippine Islands ceded by Spain, 1898.

(32) Guam, ceded by Spain, 1898.

(33) Las Palmas claimed by cession from Spain, 1898-1928.

(34) Isle of Pines disputed with Cuba, 1901-25.

(35) Wake Island, annexed, 1899.

(36) Tientsin-Pekin road, scene of intervention of Allied, including American, forces during Boxer Rebellion, 1900.

(37) Cagayan Sulú and Sibitú, purchased from Spain, 1900.

(38) Canal Zone, leased from revolutionary government of Panama, 1903.

* Great Britain yielded her claims to Johnston's and Palmyra Islands in view of Hawaiian claim of annexation in 1862.

x Whale fisheries.

U. S. Exports — 1900 ($20,000,000 up, listed in order of importance)

Breadstuffs	$262,744,078
Unmanufactured cotton	242,832,737
Meat and dairy products	184,453,055
Iron, steel, and manufactures	121,913,548
Copper and manufactures	97,852,960
Mineral oils	75,611,750
Wood and manufactures	50,598,416
Animals	43,585,031
Tobacco	35,432,512
Leather and manufactures	27,293,010
Manufactured cotton	24,003,087

Steamship Lines subsidized under the act of 1864

-o-o-o-o- U. S. and Brazil Steamship Co., 1865-75

-.-.-.-.- Pacific Mail, 1865-74

-+-+-+- California, Oregon and Mexico Steamship Co., 1865-74

Steamship Lines subsidized under the act of 1891:

New York, Galveston to La Guaira, Venezuela, 1893-98 —x—x—x—x—

New York to Colon; San Francisco to Panama City, 1892-1902

San Francisco to Hong Kong, 1892-1902

New York to Southampton, Antwerp, 1895-1905 -o-+-o-+-o-+-o

New York to Havana, Tuxpan, Rio de Janeiro, 1892-97; to Buenos Aires, 1892-1902 — — — — —

Base Map by Permission of Denoyer-Geppert Company, Chicago

pansion, 1865-1904; Exports and Foreign Investments, 1900

atistics, see Appendix IV

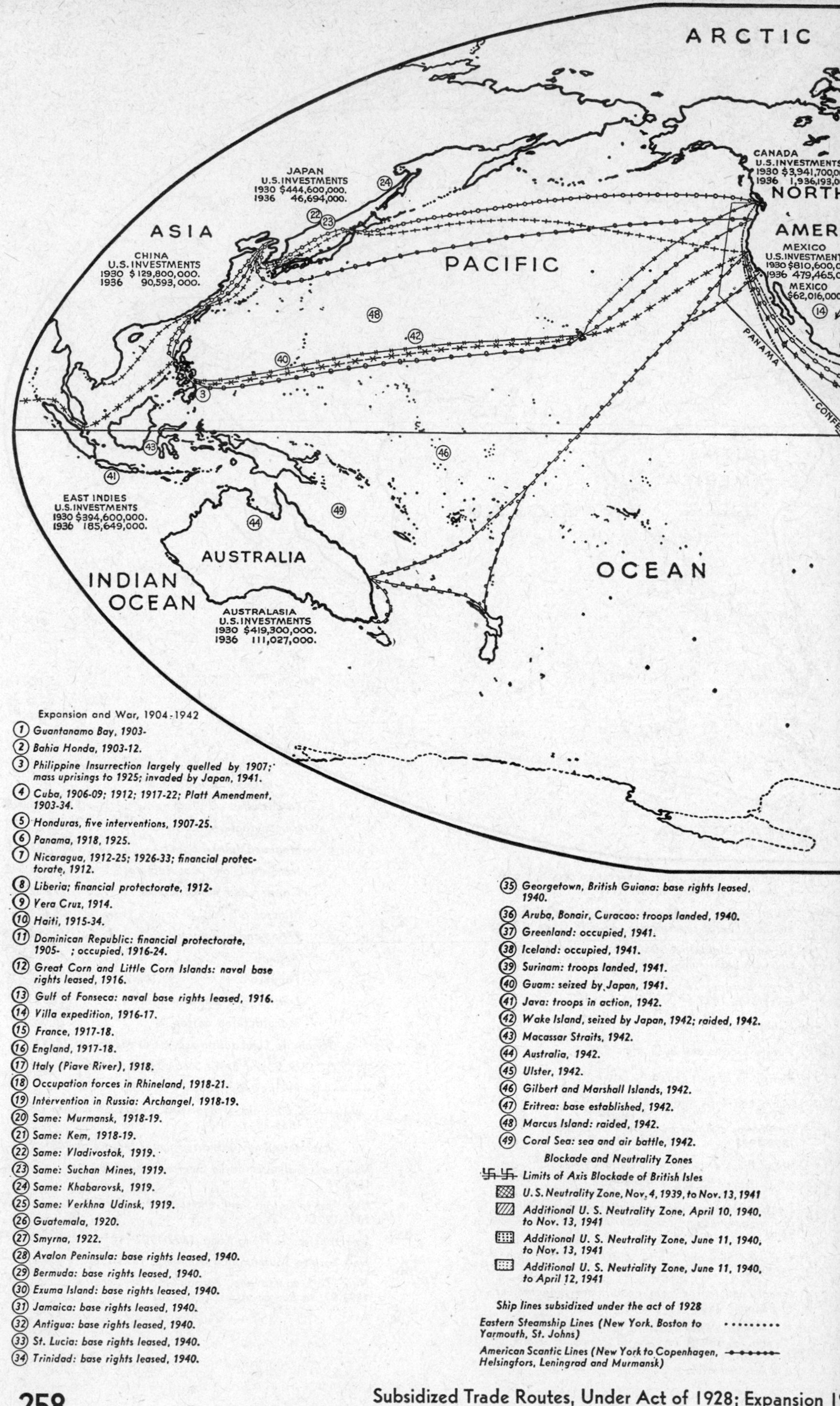
ARCTIC
CANADA
U.S. INVESTMENTS
1930 $3,941,700,000.
1936 1,936,193,000.
NORTH
AMERIC
MEXICO
U.S. INVESTMENTS
1930 $810,600,000
1936 479,465,000
MEXICO
$62,016,000.
JAPAN
U.S. INVESTMENTS
1930 $444,600,000.
1936 46,694,000.
ASIA
CHINA
U.S. INVESTMENTS
1930 $129,800,000.
1936 90,593,000.
PACIFIC
PANAMA
CONFER
EAST INDIES
U.S. INVESTMENTS
1930 $394,600,000.
1936 185,649,000.
AUSTRALIA
INDIAN
OCEAN
OCEAN
AUSTRALASIA
U.S. INVESTMENTS
1930 $419,300,000.
1936 111,027,000.
Expansion and War, 1904-1942
1 Guantanamo Bay, 1903-
2 Bahia Honda, 1903-12.
3 Philippine Insurrection largely quelled by 1907; mass uprisings to 1925; invaded by Japan, 1941.
4 Cuba, 1906-09; 1912; 1917-22; Platt Amendment, 1903-34.
5 Honduras, five interventions, 1907-25.
6 Panama, 1918, 1925.
7 Nicaragua, 1912-25; 1926-33; financial protectorate, 1912.
8 Liberia; financial protectorate, 1912-
9 Vera Cruz, 1914.
10 Haiti, 1915-34.
11 Dominican Republic: financial protectorate, 1905- ; occupied, 1916-24.
12 Great Corn and Little Corn Islands: naval base rights leased, 1916.
13 Gulf of Fonseca: naval base rights leased, 1916.
14 Villa expedition, 1916-17.
15 France, 1917-18.
16 England, 1917-18.
17 Italy (Piave River), 1918.
18 Occupation forces in Rhineland, 1918-21.
19 Intervention in Russia: Archangel, 1918-19.
20 Same: Murmansk, 1918-19.
21 Same: Kem, 1918-19.
22 Same: Vladivostok, 1919.
23 Same: Suchan Mines, 1919.
24 Same: Khabarovsk, 1919.
25 Same: Verkhna Udinsk, 1919.
26 Guatemala, 1920.
27 Smyrna, 1922.
28 Avalon Peninsula: base rights leased, 1940.
29 Bermuda: base rights leased, 1940.
30 Exuma Island: base rights leased, 1940.
31 Jamaica: base rights leased, 1940.
32 Antigua: base rights leased, 1940.
33 St. Lucia: base rights leased, 1940.
34 Trinidad: base rights leased, 1940.
35 Georgetown, British Guiana: base rights leased, 1940.
36 Aruba, Bonair, Curacao: troops landed, 1940.
37 Greenland: occupied, 1941.
38 Iceland: occupied, 1941.
39 Surinam: troops landed, 1941.
40 Guam: seized by Japan, 1941.
41 Java: troops in action, 1942.
42 Wake Island, seized by Japan, 1942; raided, 1942.
43 Macassar Straits, 1942.
44 Australia, 1942.
45 Ulster, 1942.
46 Gilbert and Marshall Islands, 1942.
47 Eritrea: base established, 1942.
48 Marcus Island: raided, 1942.
49 Coral Sea: sea and air battle, 1942.
Blockade and Neutrality Zones
Limits of Axis Blockade of British Isles
U. S. Neutrality Zone, Nov. 4, 1939, to Nov. 13, 1941
Additional U. S. Neutrality Zone, April 10, 1940, to Nov. 13, 1941
Additional U. S. Neutrality Zone, June 11, 1940, to Nov. 13, 1941
Additional U. S. Neutrality Zone, June 11, 1940, to April 12, 1941
Ship lines subsidized under the act of 1928
Eastern Steamship Lines (New York, Boston to Yarmouth, St. Johns)
American Scantic Lines (New York to Copenhagen, Helsingfors, Leningrad and Murmansk)

Subsidized Trade Routes, Under Act of 1928; Expansion 19

For further t

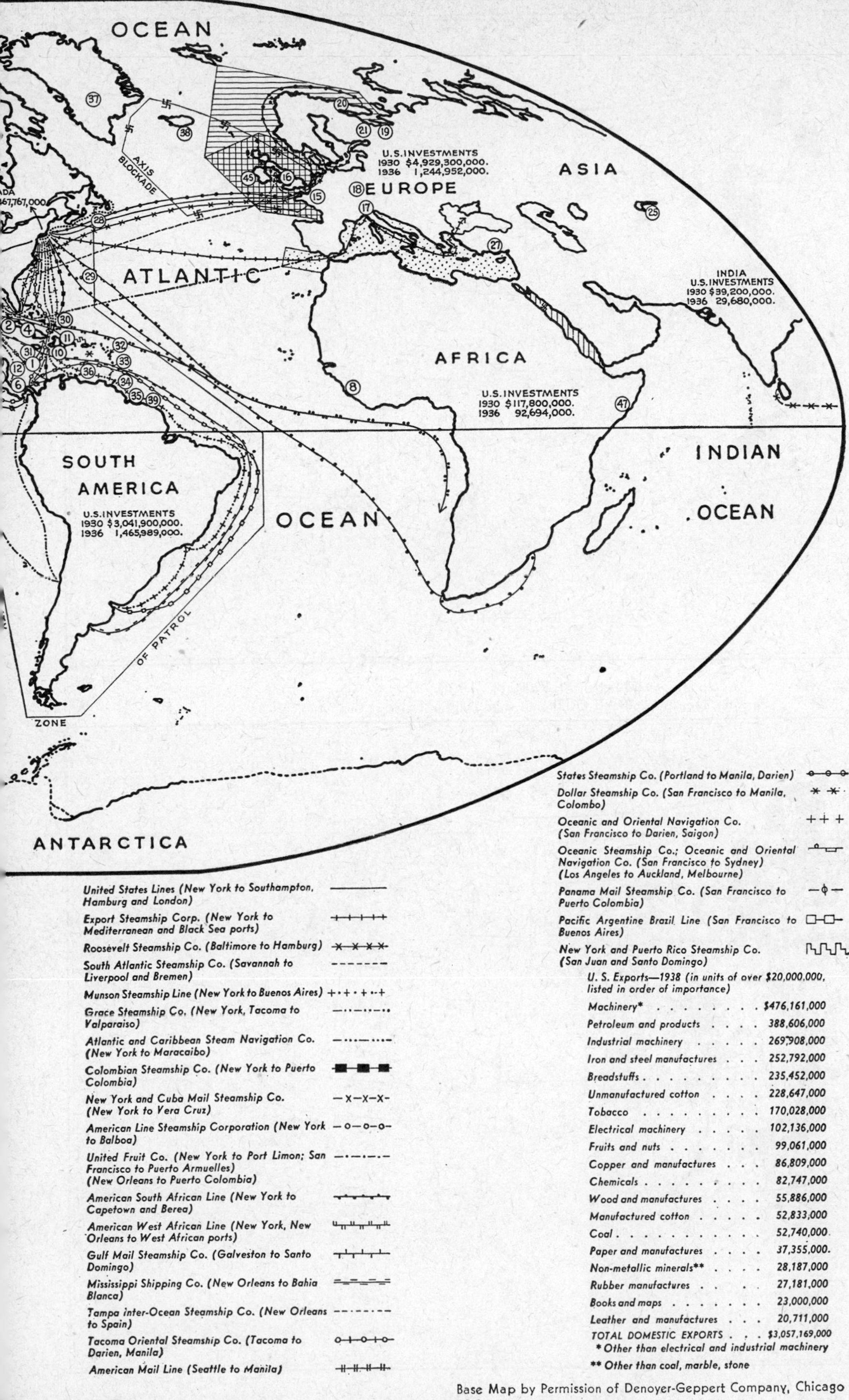

U. S. Exports—1938 (in units of over $20,000,000, listed in order of importance)

*Machinery**	$476,161,000
Petroleum and products	388,606,000
Industrial machinery	269,908,000
Iron and steel manufactures	252,792,000
Breadstuffs	235,452,000
Unmanufactured cotton	228,647,000
Tobacco	170,028,000
Electrical machinery	102,136,000
Fruits and nuts	99,061,000
Copper and manufactures	86,809,000
Chemicals	82,747,000
Wood and manufactures	55,886,000
Manufactured cotton	52,833,000
Coal	52,740,000
Paper and manufactures	37,355,000
*Non-metallic minerals***	28,187,000
Rubber manufactures	27,181,000
Books and maps	23,000,000
Leather and manufactures	20,711,000
TOTAL DOMESTIC EXPORTS	$3,057,169,000

** Other than electrical and industrial machinery*

*** Other than coal, marble, stone*

Base Map by Permission of Denoyer-Geppert Company, Chicago

2; Investments Abroad 1930; Direct Investments, 1936

istics, see Appendix IV

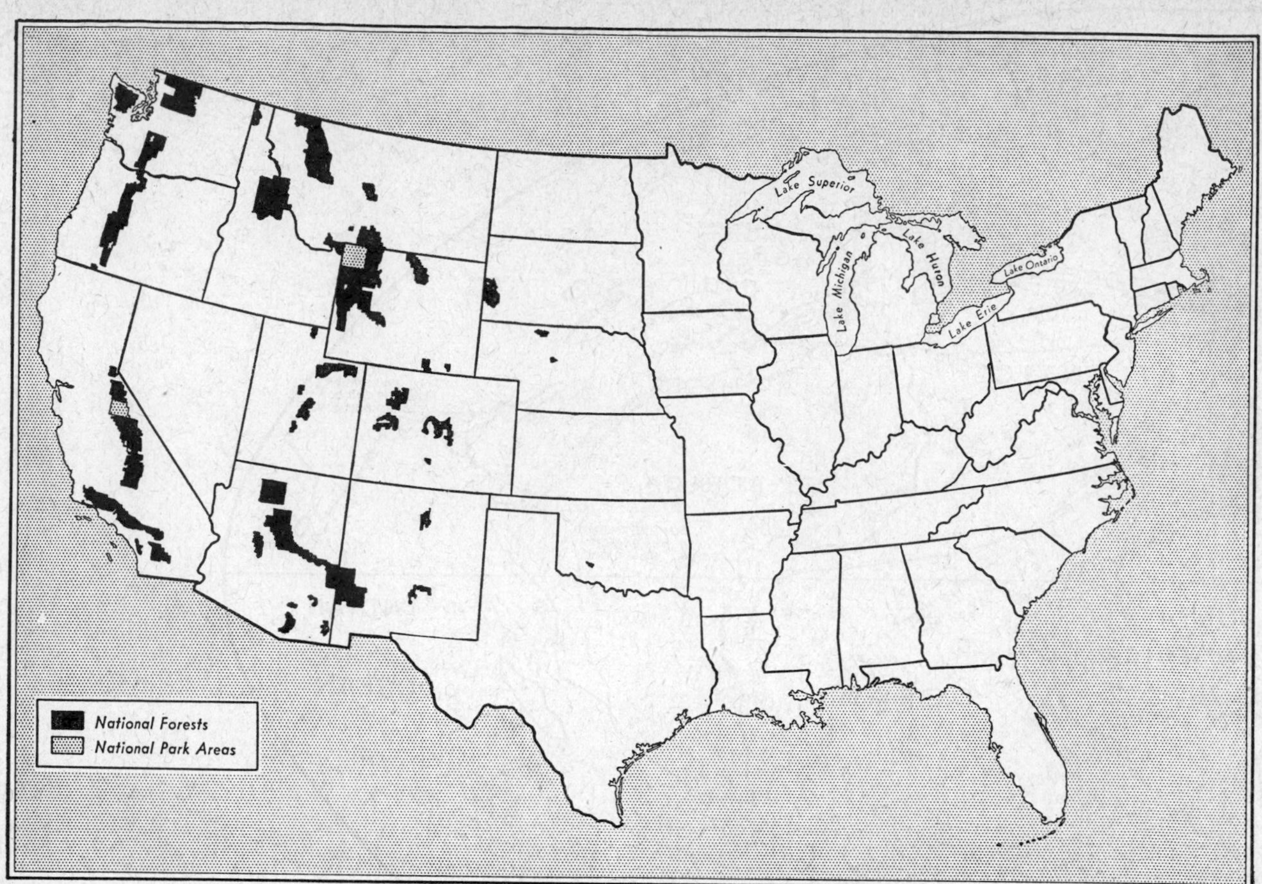

259 National Forests, 1900
Arizona, New Mexico and Oklahoma were still territories at this time

Lake Superior
Lake Michigan
Lake Huron
Lake Ontario
Lake Erie
National Forests
National Park Areas

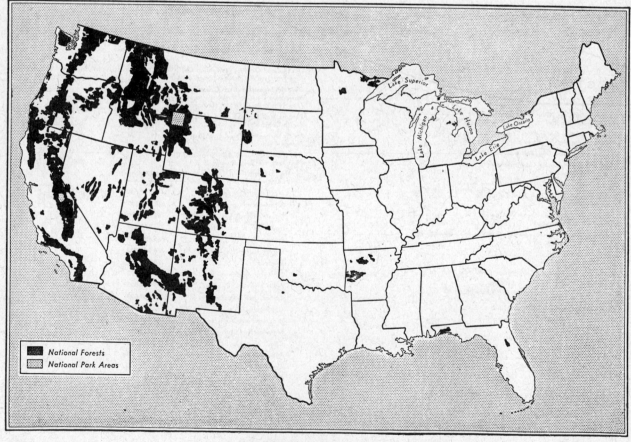

260 National Forests, 1910
Arizona and New Mexico were still territories at this time

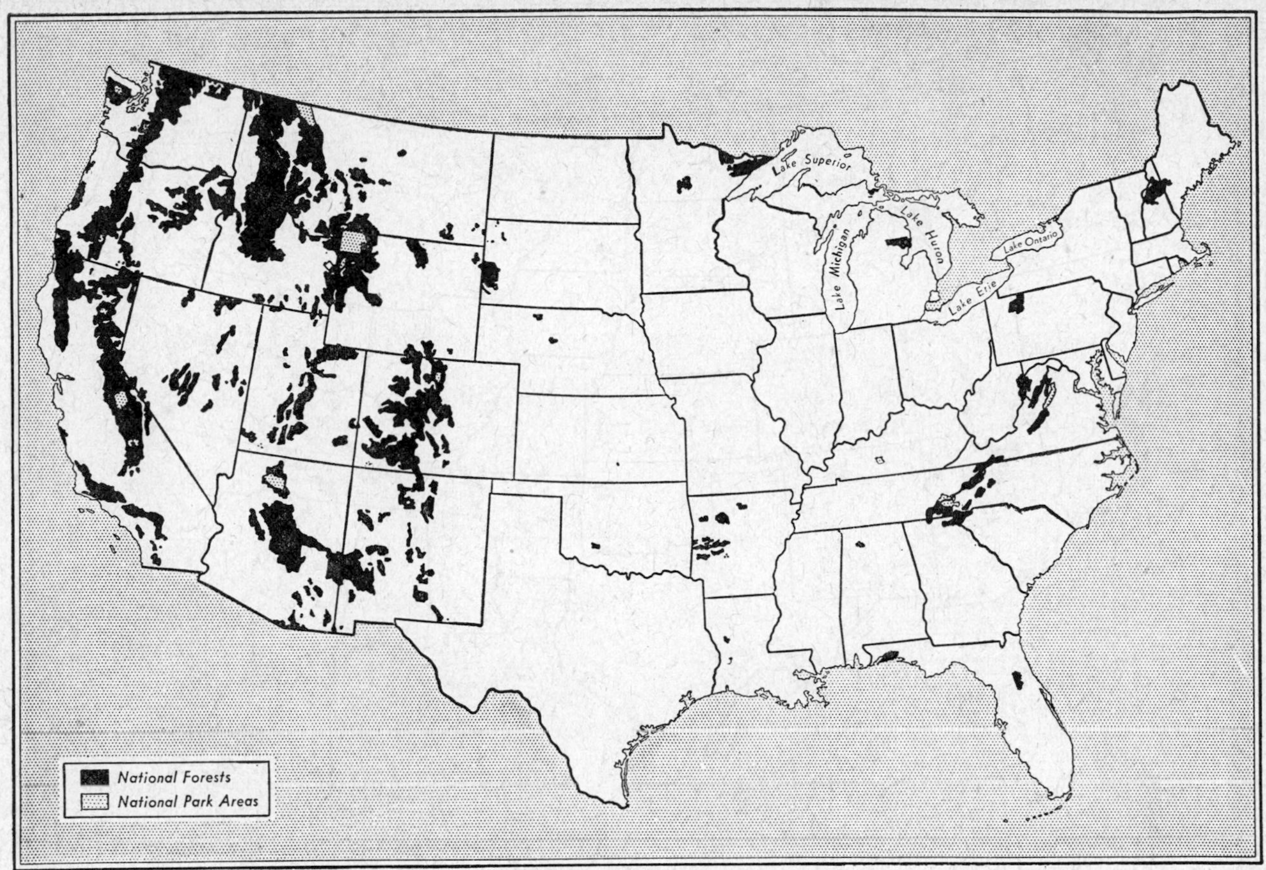

261 National Forests, 1930

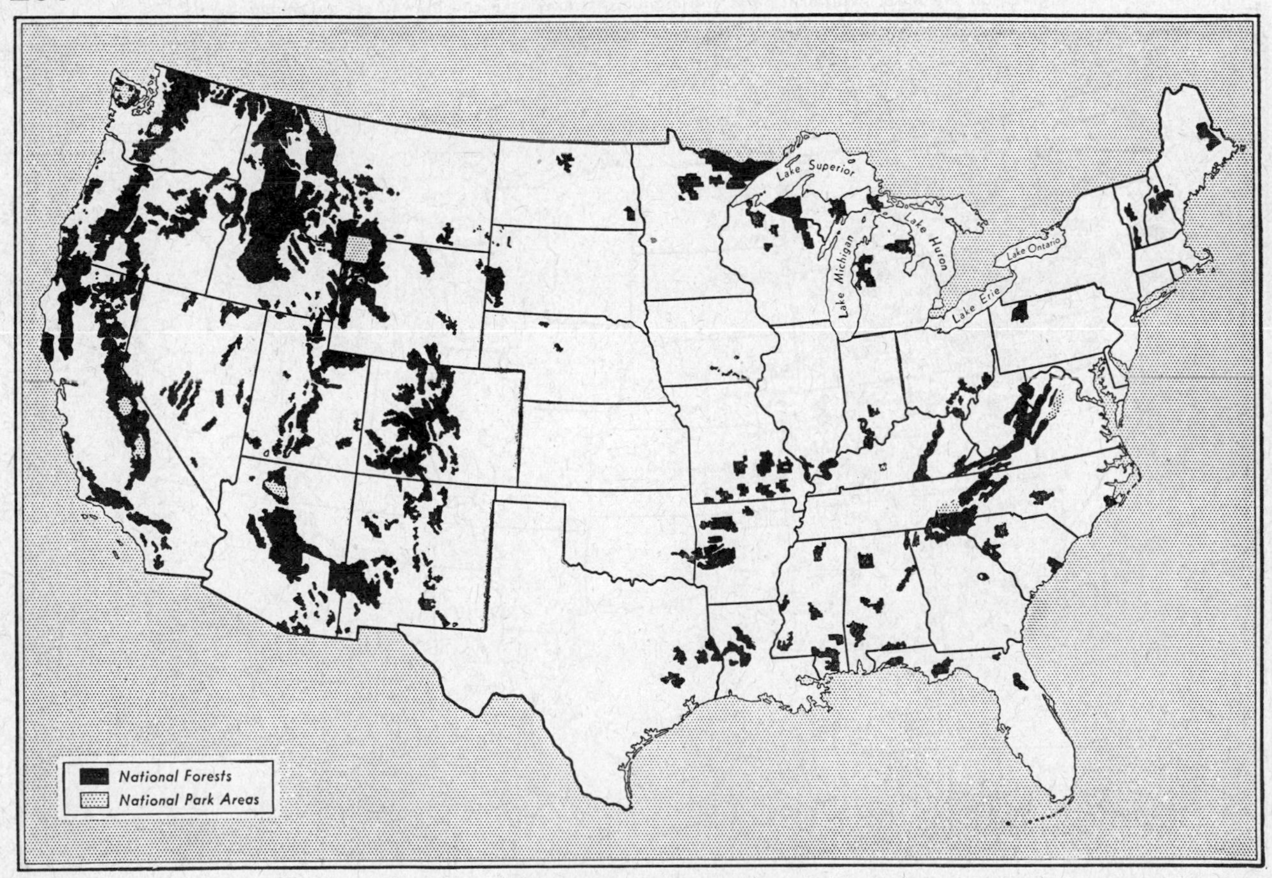

262 National Forests, 1940

NATIONAL MONUMENTS

1. Ackia Battleground — Miss., 1938
2. Andrew Johnson Homestead Project — Tenn., (1935)
3. Arches — Utah, 1929
4. Aztec Ruins — N. Mex., 1923
5. Badlands — S. Dak., 1939
6. Bandelier — N. Mex., 1916
7. Big Hole Battlefield — Mont., 1910
8. Black Canyon of the Gunnison — Colo., 1933
9. Cabrillo — Calif., 1913
10. Canyon De Chelly — Ariz., 1931
11. Capitol Reef — Utah, 1937
12. Capulin Mountain — N. Mex., 1916
13. Casa Grande Ruins — Ariz., 1889
14. Castle Pinckney — S. C., 1924
15. Cedar Breaks — Utah, 1933
16. Chaco Canyon — N. Mex., 1907
17. Channel Islands — Calif., 1938
18. Chiricahua — Ariz., 1907
19. Colorado — Colo., 1911
20. Craters of the Moon — Idaho, 1924
21. Death Valley — Calif., Nev., 1933
22. Devil Postpile — Calif., 1911
23. Devil's Tower — Wyo., 1906
24. Dinosaur — Utah, Wyo., 1915
25. El Morro — N. Mex., 1906
26. Father Millet Cross — N. Y., 1925
27. Fort Frederica Project — Ga. (1936)
28. Fort Jefferson — Fla., 1935
29. Fort Laramie — Wyo., 1938
30. Fort Marion — Fla., 1924
31. Fort Matanzas — Fla., 1924
32. Fort Pulaski — Ga., 1924
33. Fort Stanwix Project — N. Y. (1935)
34. Fossil Cycad — S. Dak., 1922
35. George Washington Birthplace — Va., 1930
36. Gila Cliff Dwellings — N. Mex., 1907
37. Gran Quivira — N. Mex., 1909
38. Grand Canyon — Ariz., 1932
39. Great Sand Dunes — Colo., 1932
40. Holy Cross — Colo., 1929
41. Homestead — Nebr., 1939
42. Hovenweep — Utah-Colo., 1923
43. Jewel Cave — S. Dak., 1908
44. Joshua Tree — Calif., 1936
45. Lava Beds — Calif., 1925
46. Lehman Caves — Nev., 1922
47. Meriwether Lewis — Tenn., 1925
48. Montezuma Castle — Ariz., 1906
49. Mound City Group — Ohio, 1923
50. Muir Woods — Calif., 1908
51. Natural Bridges — Utah, 1908
52. Navajo — Ariz., 1909
53. Ocmulgee — Ga., 1936
54. Oregon Caves — Ore., 1909
55. Organ Pipe Cactus — Ariz., 1937
56. Palm Canyon Project — Calif. (1922)
57. Patrick Henry Project — Va. (1935)
58. Perry's Victory and International Peace Memorial — Ohio, 1936
59. Petrified Forest — Ariz., 1906
60. Pinnacles — Calif., 1908
61. Pioneer Project — Ky. (1934)
62. Pipe Spring — Ariz., 1923
63. Pipestone — Minn., 1937
64. Rainbow Bridge — Utah, 1910
65. Saguaro — Ariz., 1933
66. Scotts Bluff — Nebr., 1919
67. Shoshone Cavern — Wyo., 1909
68. Statue of Liberty — N. Y., 1924
69. Sunset Crater — Ariz., 1930
70. Timpanogos Caves — Utah, 1922
71. Tonto — Ariz., 1907
72. Tumacacori — Ariz., 1908
73. Verendrye — N. Dak., 1917
74. Walnut Canyon — Ariz., 1915
75. Wheeler — Colo., 1908
76. White Sands — N. Mex., 1933
77. Whitman Project — Wash. (1936)
78. Wupatki — Ariz., 1924
79. Yucca House — Colo., 1919
80. Zion — Utah, 1937

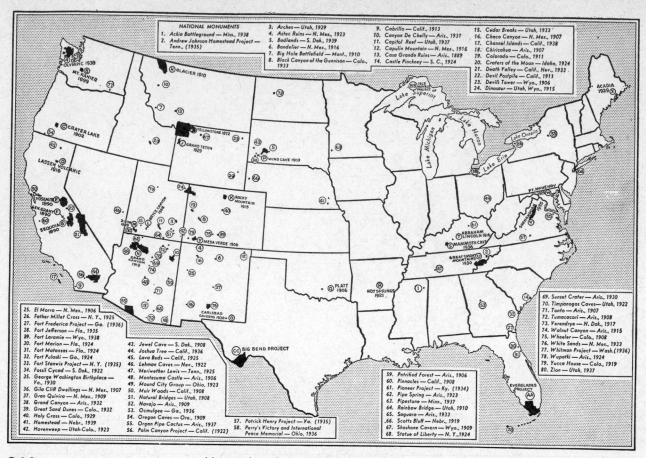

263 National Parks and National Monuments

Numbers = national monuments; Letters = national parks. Names and dates of establishment of the national parks are given on the map. National parks and monuments in Alaska and Hawaii are not included.

Black areas are irrigated

Outlined areas are susceptible of irrigation (in western states only)

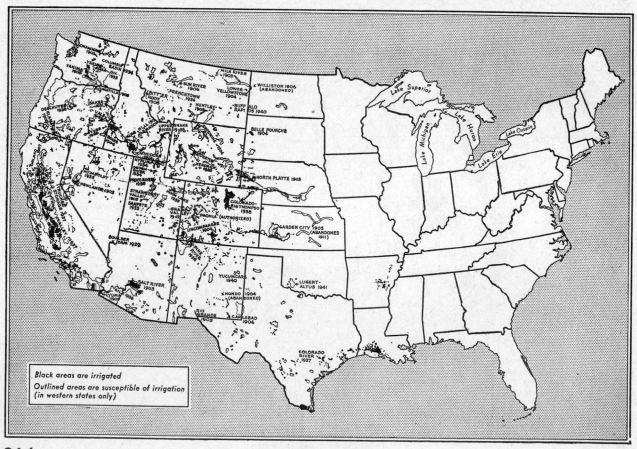

264 Irrigated Lands, 1940

Federal irrigation projects are labelled. Dates are those of the initiation of the project

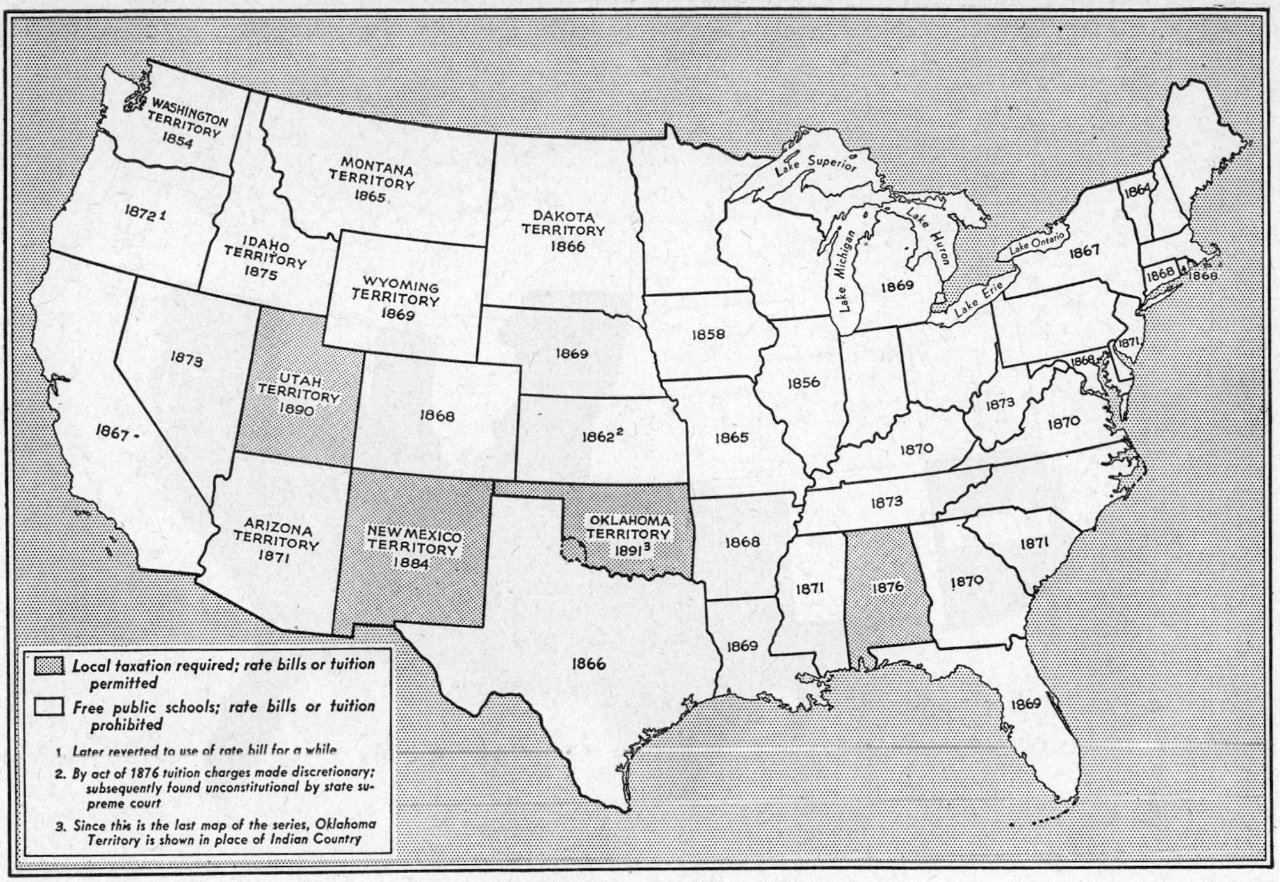

Local taxation required; rate bills or tuition permitted

Free public schools; rate bills or tuition prohibited

1. *Later reverted to use of rate bill for a while*
2. *By act of 1876 tuition charges made discretionary; subsequently found unconstitutional by state supreme court*
3. *Since this is the last map of the series, Oklahoma Territory is shown in place of Indian Country*

265 State Public School Legislation, 1875

Dates are those for establishment of free schools including those after 1875

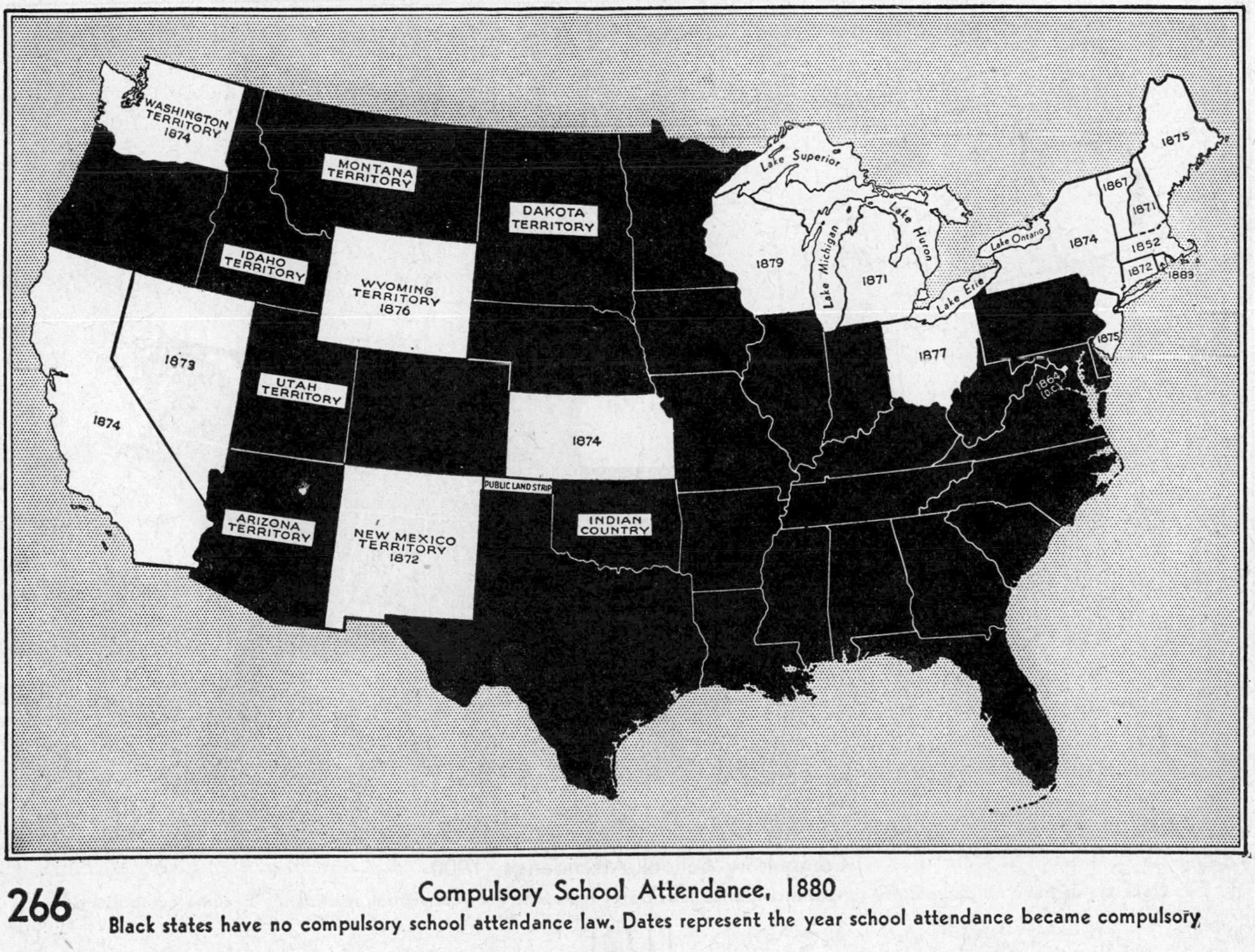

266 Compulsory School Attendance, 1880

Black states have no compulsory school attendance law. Dates represent the year school attendance became compulsory

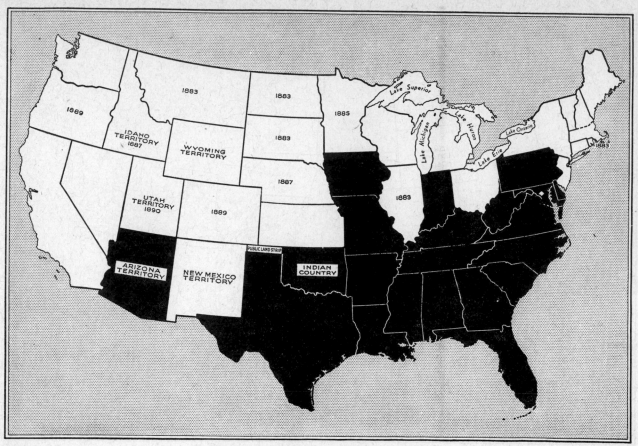

267 Compulsory School Attendance, 1890

Black states have no compulsory school attendance law. Dates represent the year school attendance became compulsory

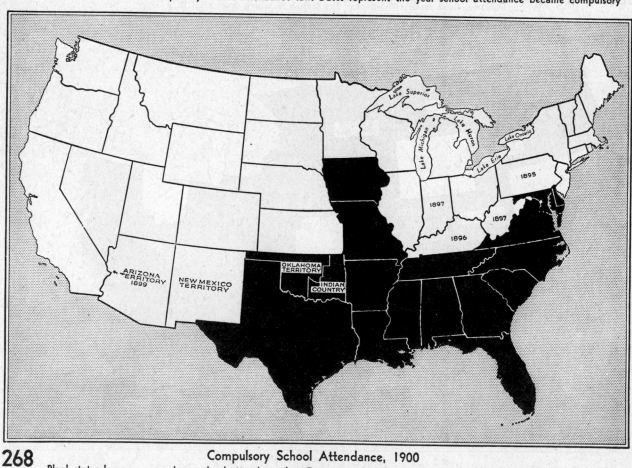

268 Compulsory School Attendance, 1900

Black states have no compulsory school attendance law. Dates represent the year school attendance became compulsory

Lake Superior
Lake Michigan
Lake Huron
Lake Ontario
Lake Erie
1902
1905
1907
1909
1915
1910
1918
1915
1916
1905
1907
1915
1908
1902
1907
1915

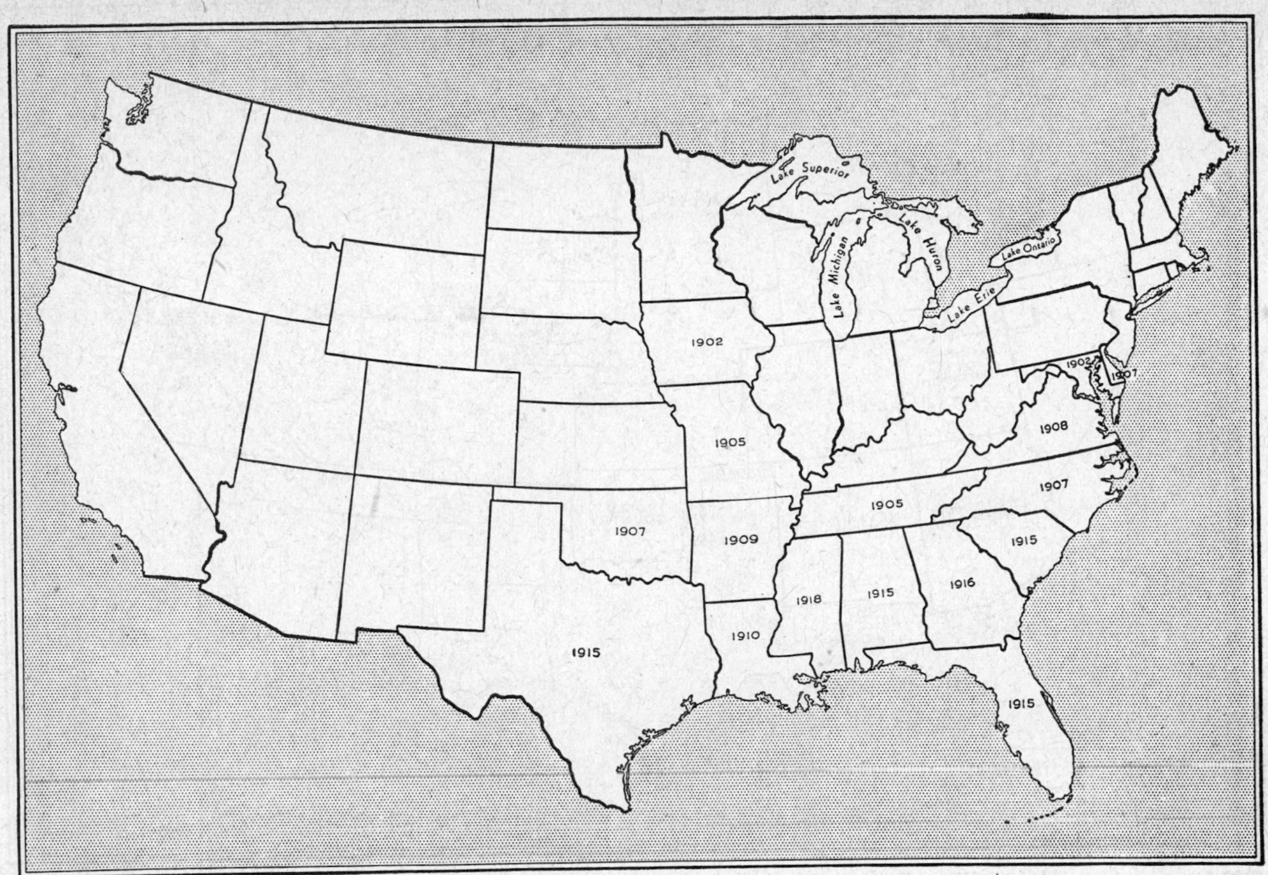

269 Compulsory School Attendance, 1920

Dates represent the year school attendance became compulsory

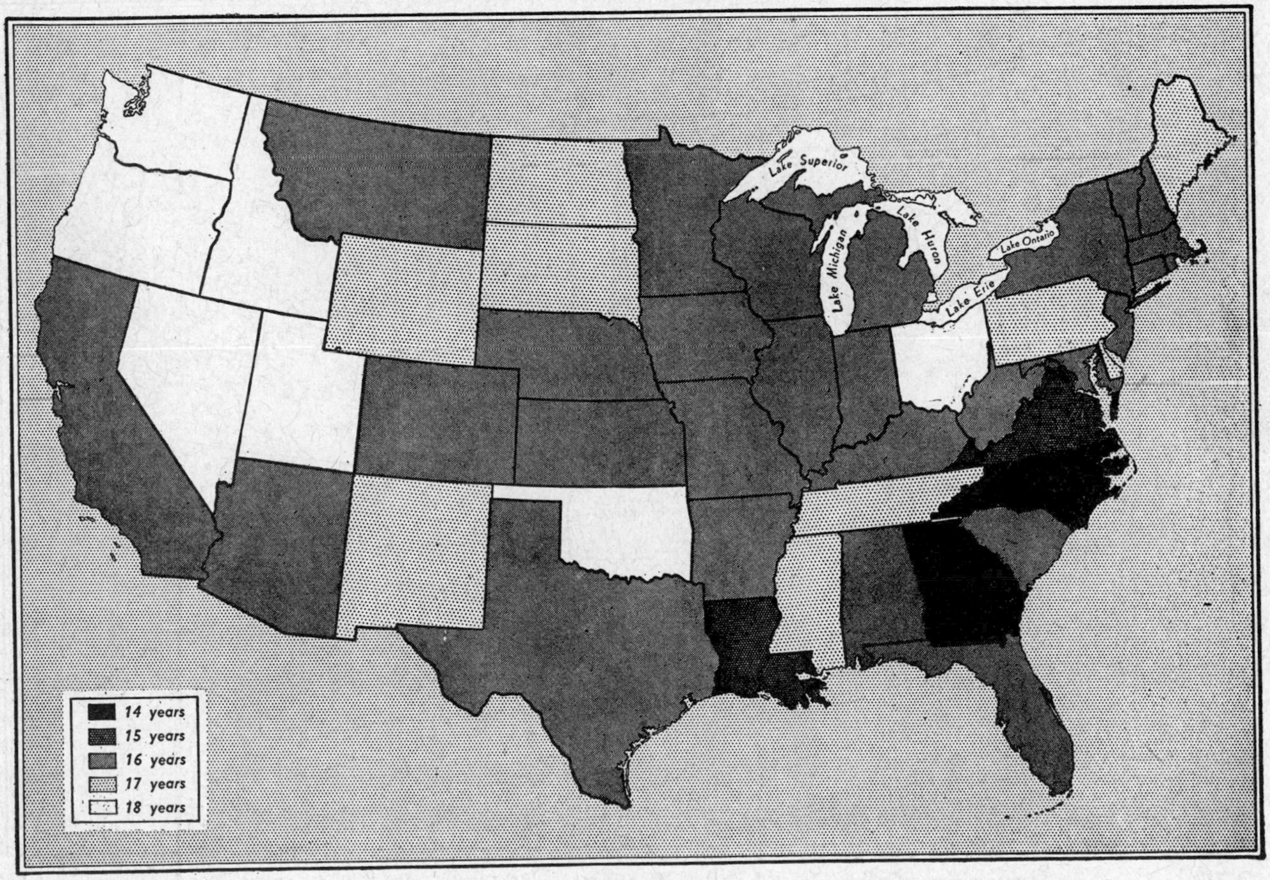

Lake Superior
Lake Michigan
Lake Huron
Lake Ontario
Lake Erie
14 years
15 years
16 years
17 years
18 years

270 Compulsory School Attendance: Age Limits, 1940

WASHINGTON TERRITORY
MONTANA TERRITORY
DAKOTA TERRITORY
IDAHO TERRITORY
WYOMING TERRITORY
UTAH TERRITORY
COLORADO TERRITORY
ARIZONA TERRITORY
NEW MEXICO TERRITORY
NO MAN'S LAND
INDIAN COUNTRY
Lake Superior
Lake Michigan
Lake Huron
Lake Ontario
Lake Erie

• Men's + Coeducational
– Women's ∘ Public institutions

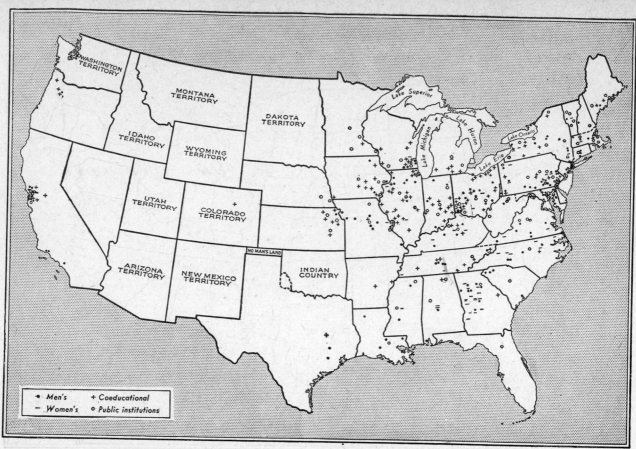

271 Universities, Colleges, and Other Institutions of Higher Learning, 1870

Location of symbols is only approximate, especially in urban centers

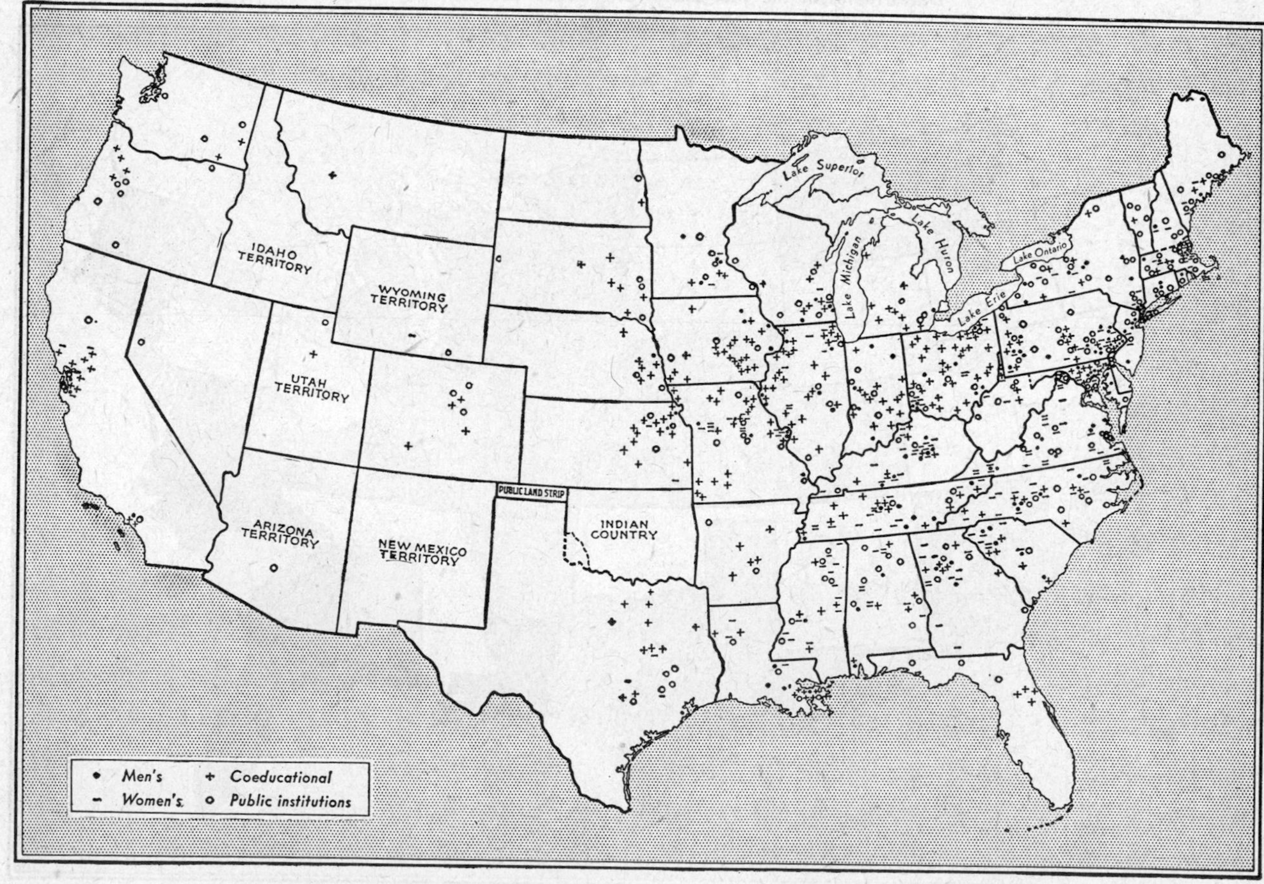

272 Universities, Colleges, and Other Institutions of Higher Learning, 1890

Location of symbols is only approximate, especially in urban centers

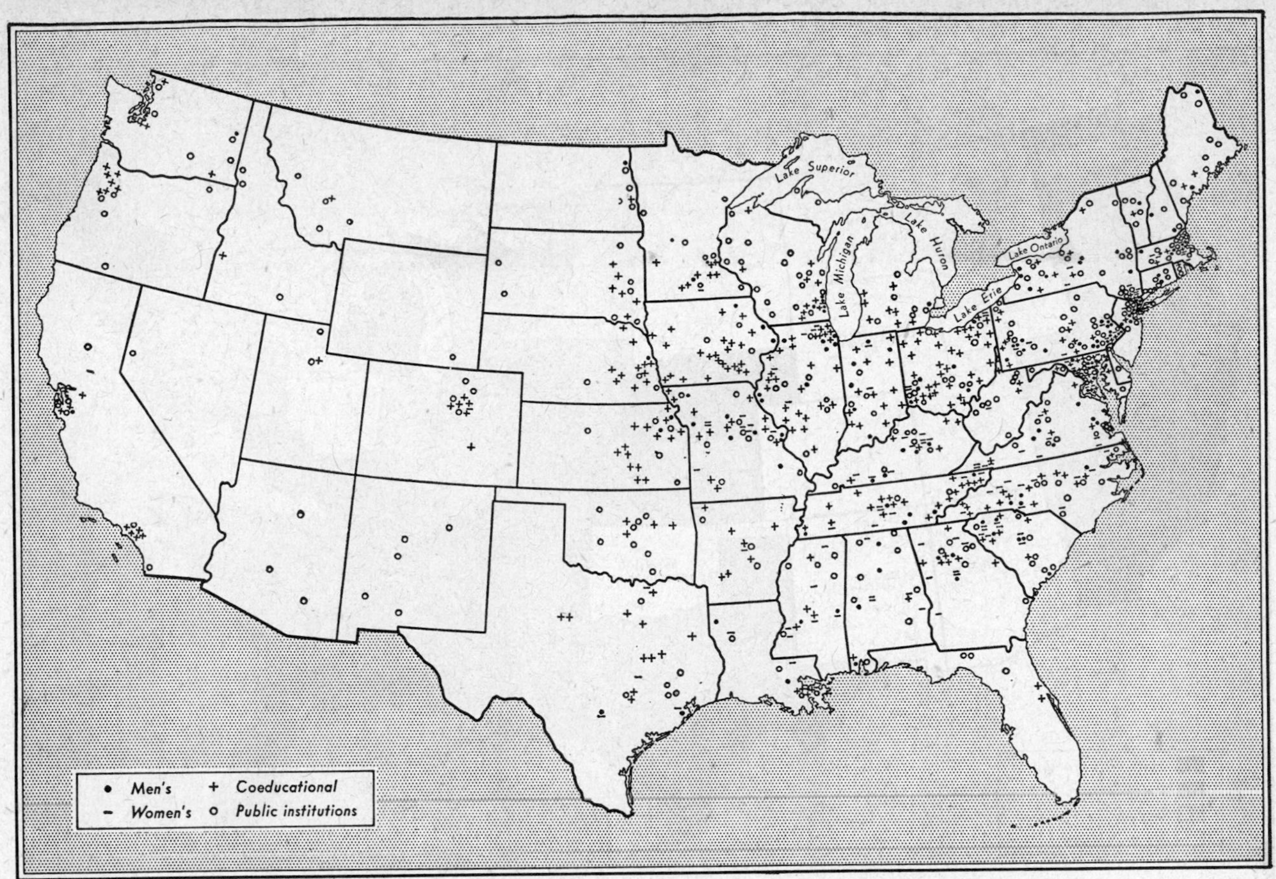

273 Universities, Colleges, and Other Institutions of Higher Learning, 1910

Arizona and New Mexico were still territories at this time

Location of symbols is only approximate, especially in urban centers

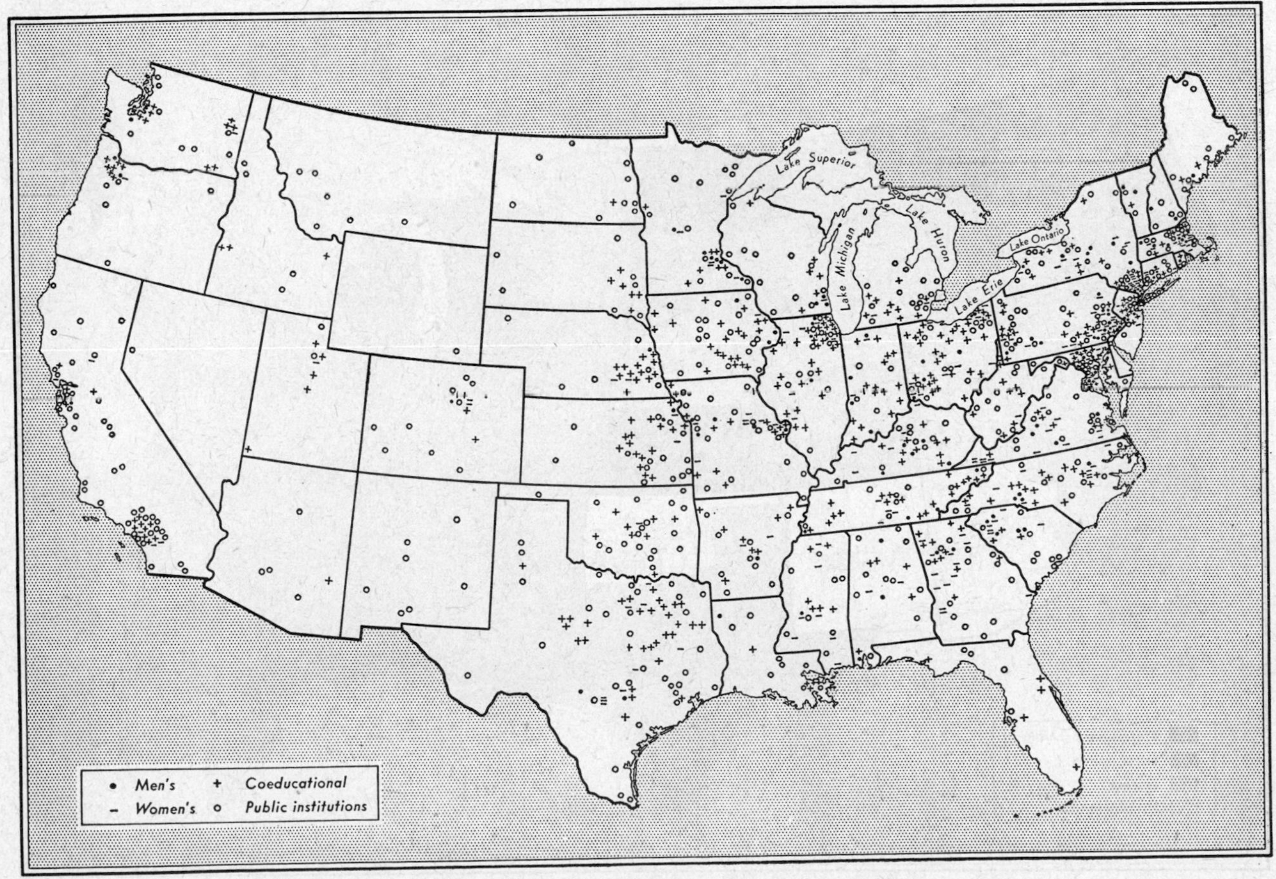

274 Universities, Colleges, and Other Institutions of Higher Learning, 1930

Location of symbols is only approximate, especially in urban centers

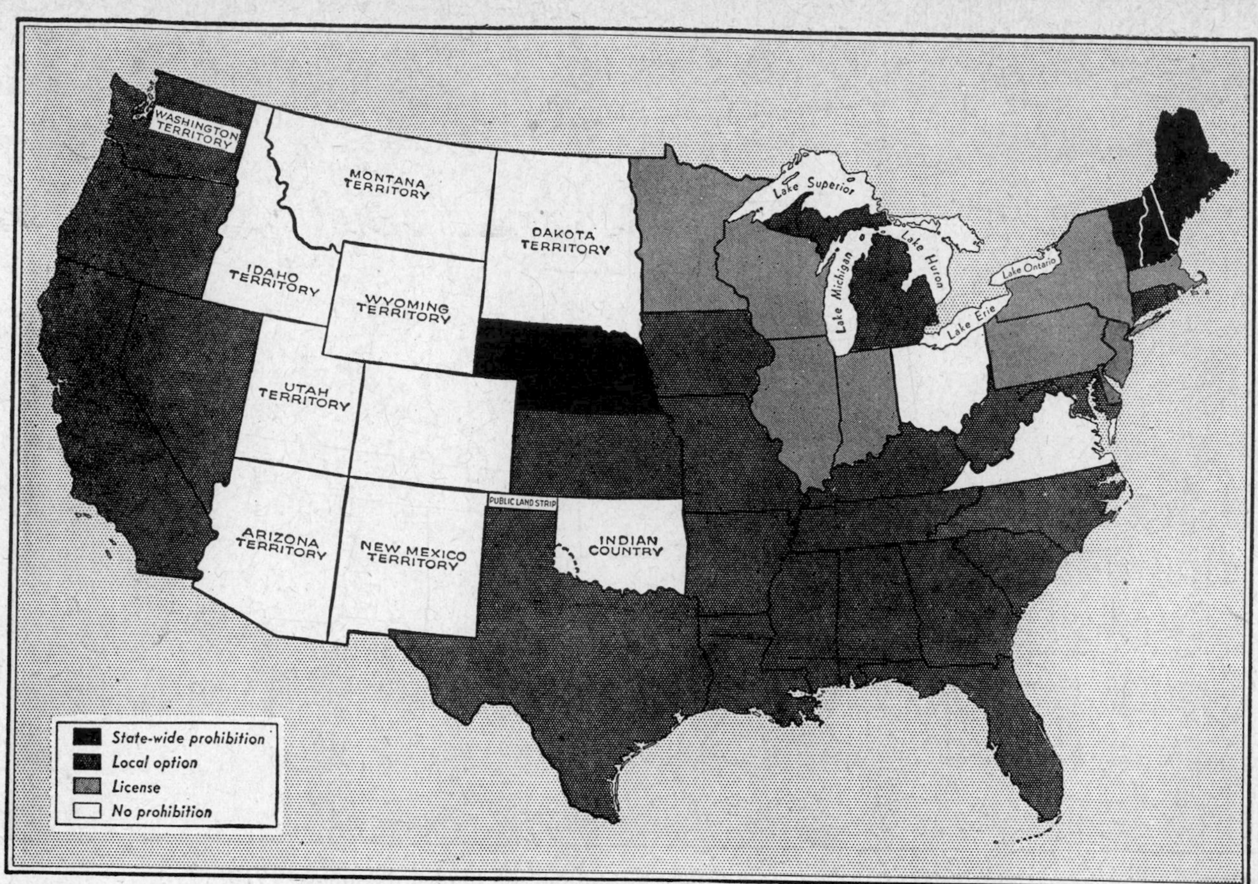

275 Prohibition, 1880
Prohibition on Indian Reservations not shown

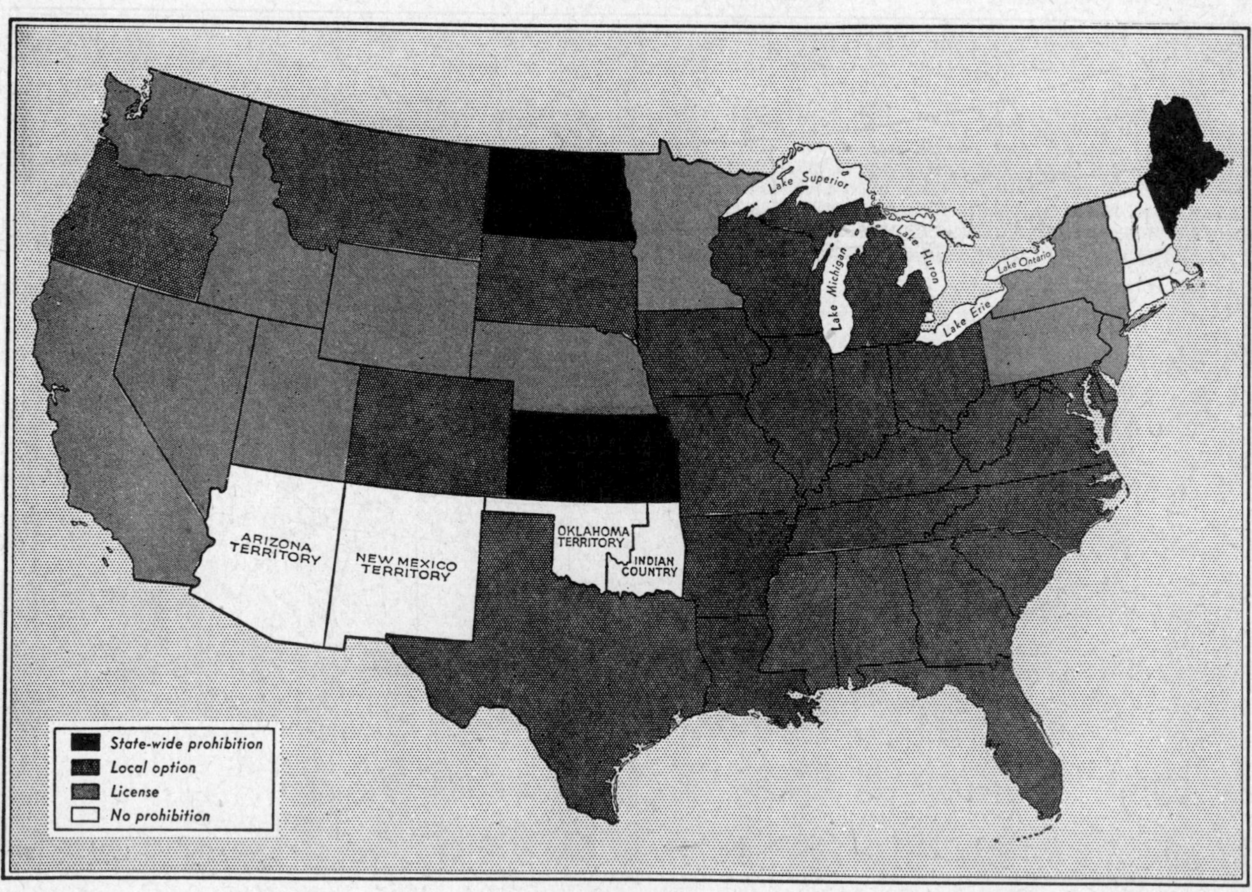

276 Prohibition, 1906
Prohibition on Indian Reservations not shown

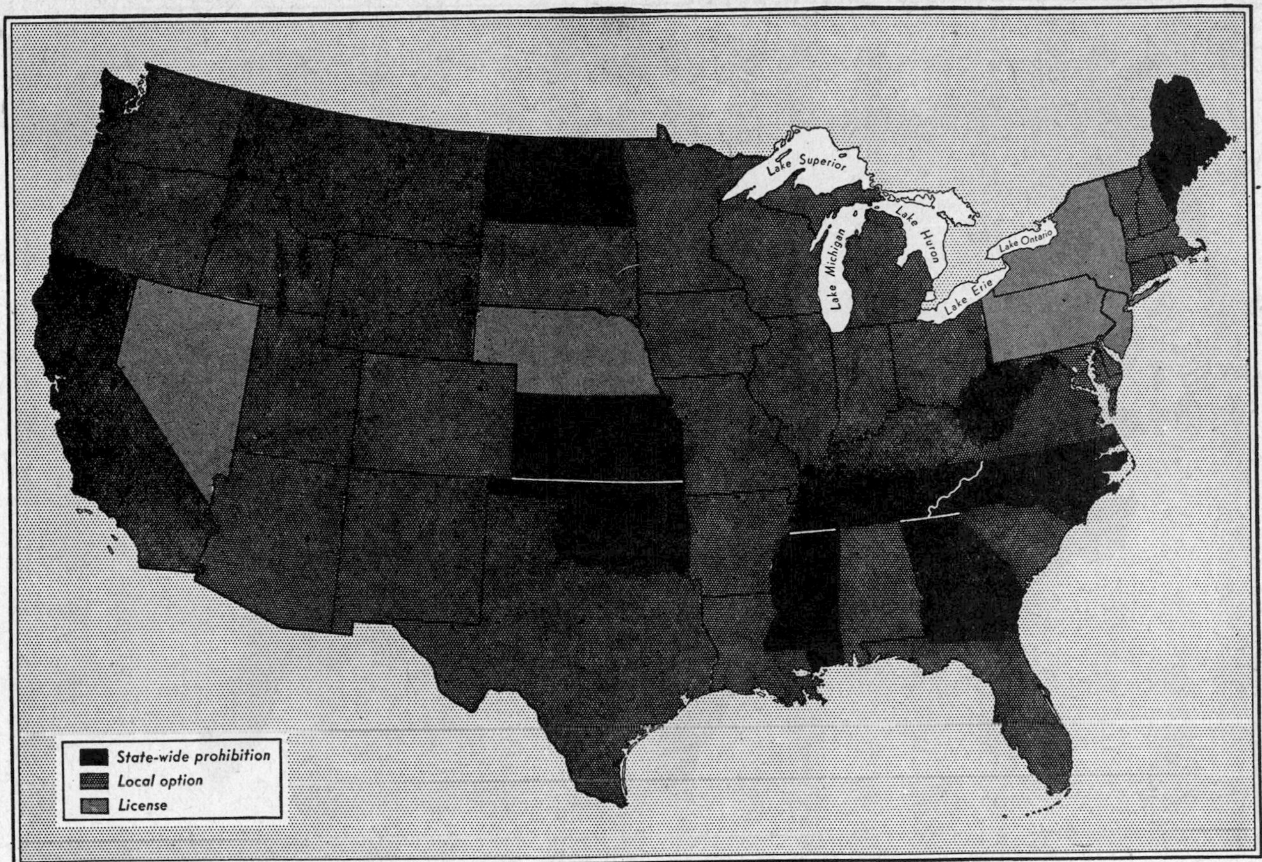

277 Prohibition, 1915

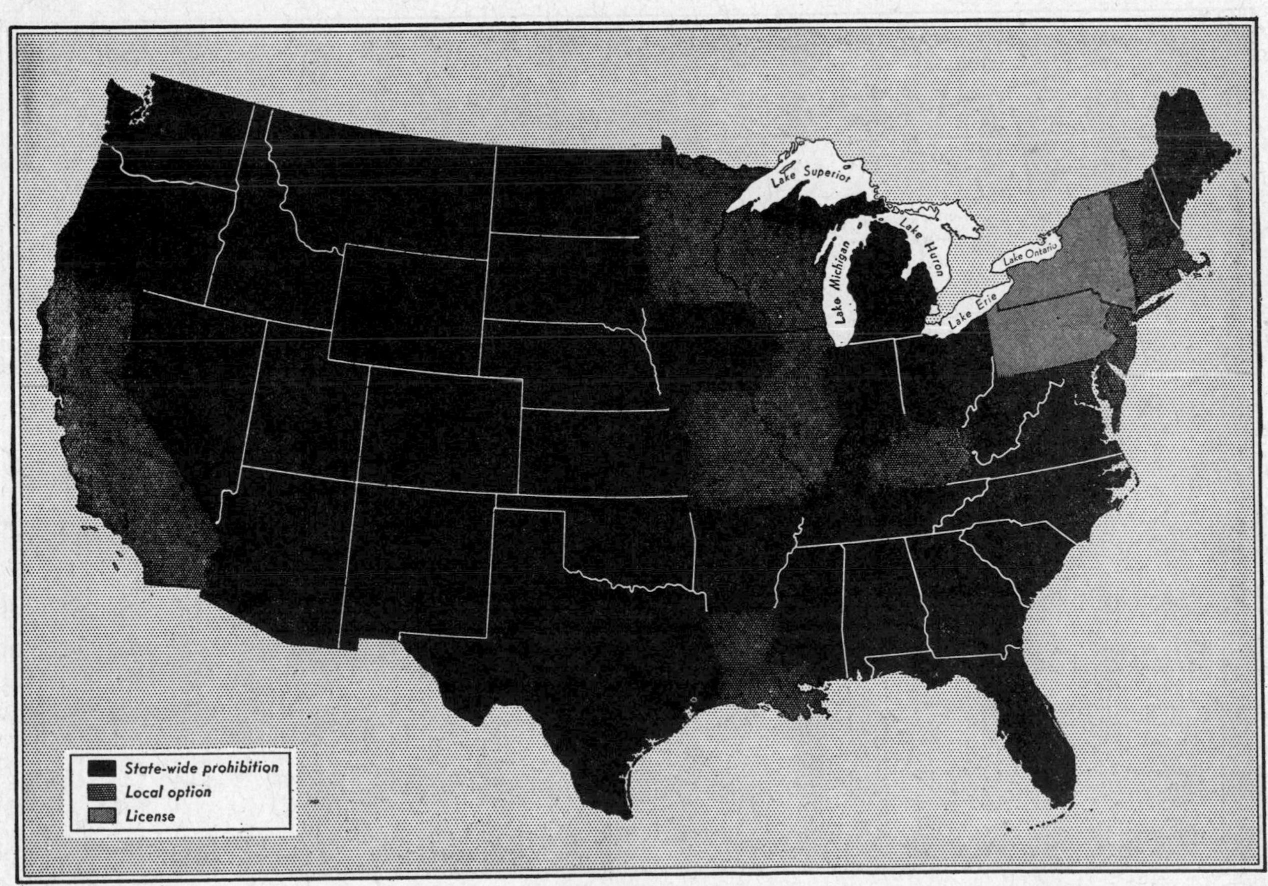

278 Prohibition, 1919

Lake Superior
Lake Michigan
Lake Huron
Lake Ontario
Lake Erie
Dry counties
Wet counties

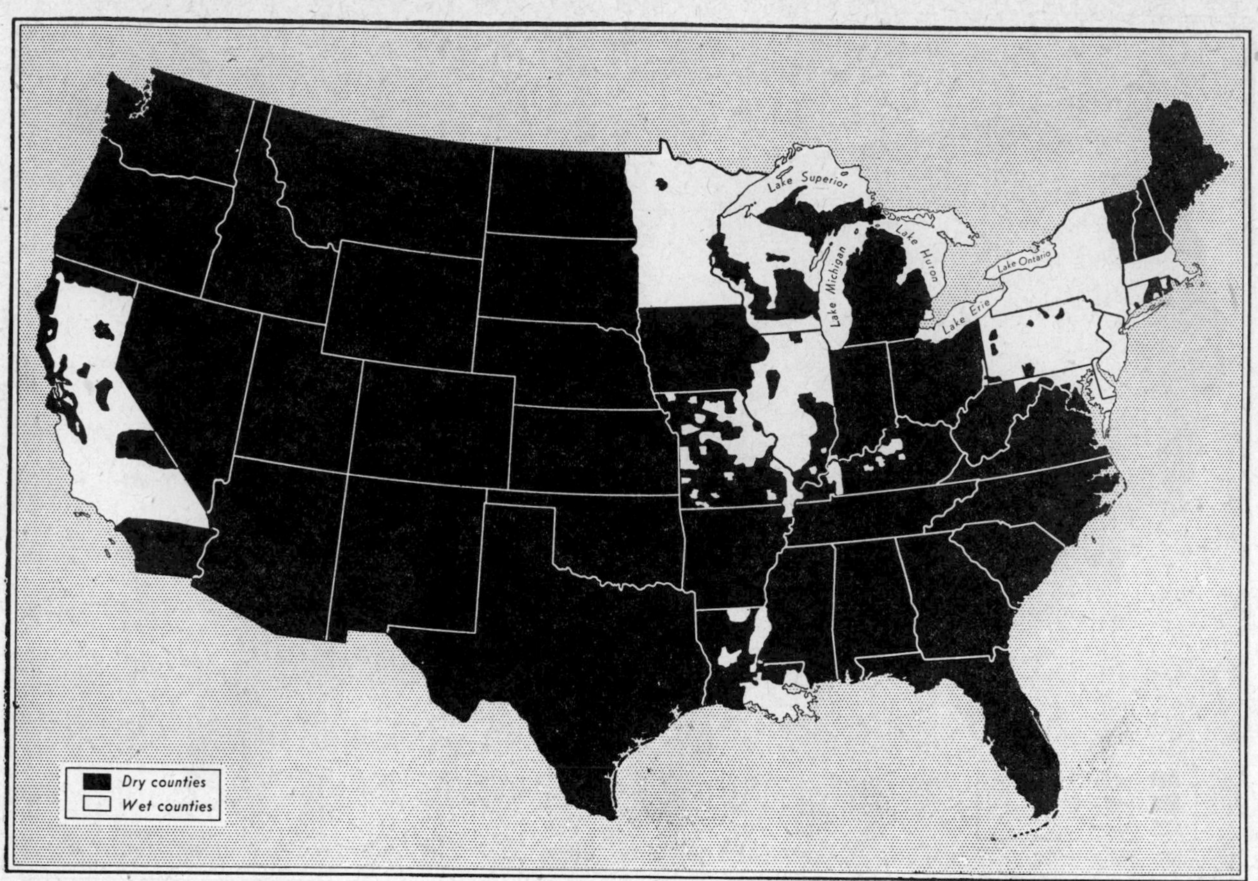

279 Dry Counties, 1919

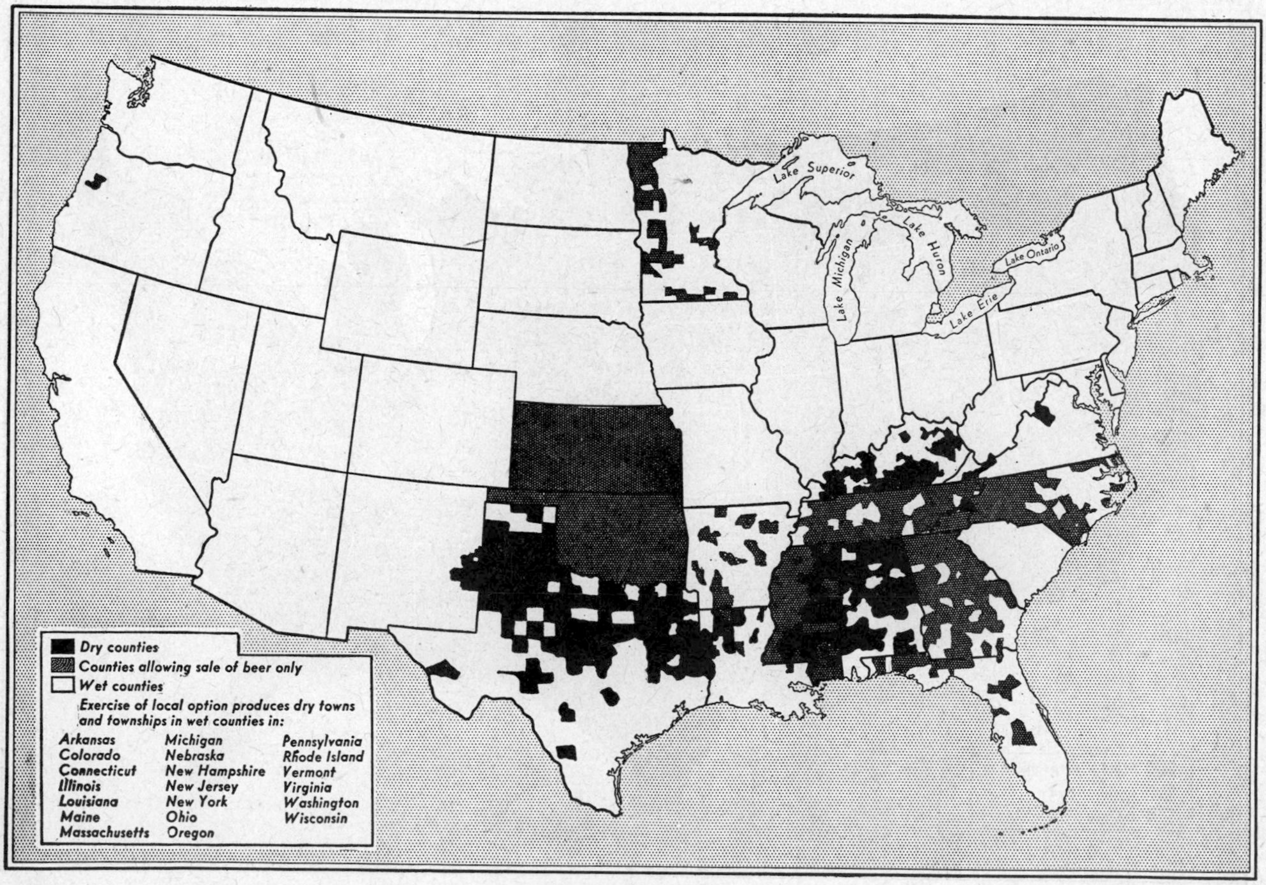

Lake Superior
Lake Michigan
Lake Huron
Lake Ontario
Lake Erie
Dry counties
Counties allowing sale of beer only
Wet counties
Exercise of local option produces dry towns and townships in wet counties in:
Arkansas
Colorado
Connecticut
Illinois
Louisiana
Maine
Massachusetts
Michigan
Nebraska
New Hampshire
New Jersey
New York
Ohio
Oregon
Pennsylvania
Rhode Island
Vermont
Virginia
Washington
Wisconsin

280 Dry Counties, 1942

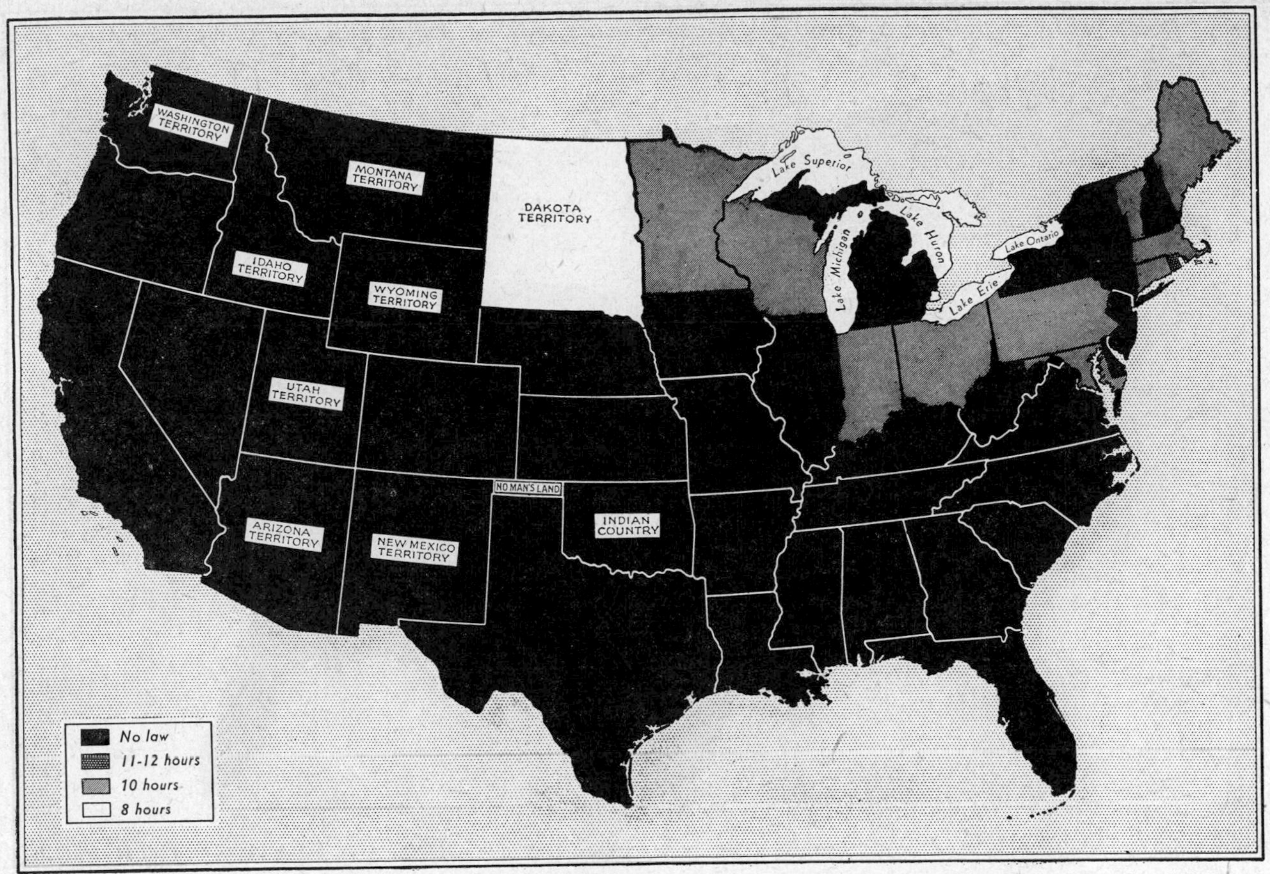

281 Child Labor: Manufacturing and/or Mercantile Employment, 1880

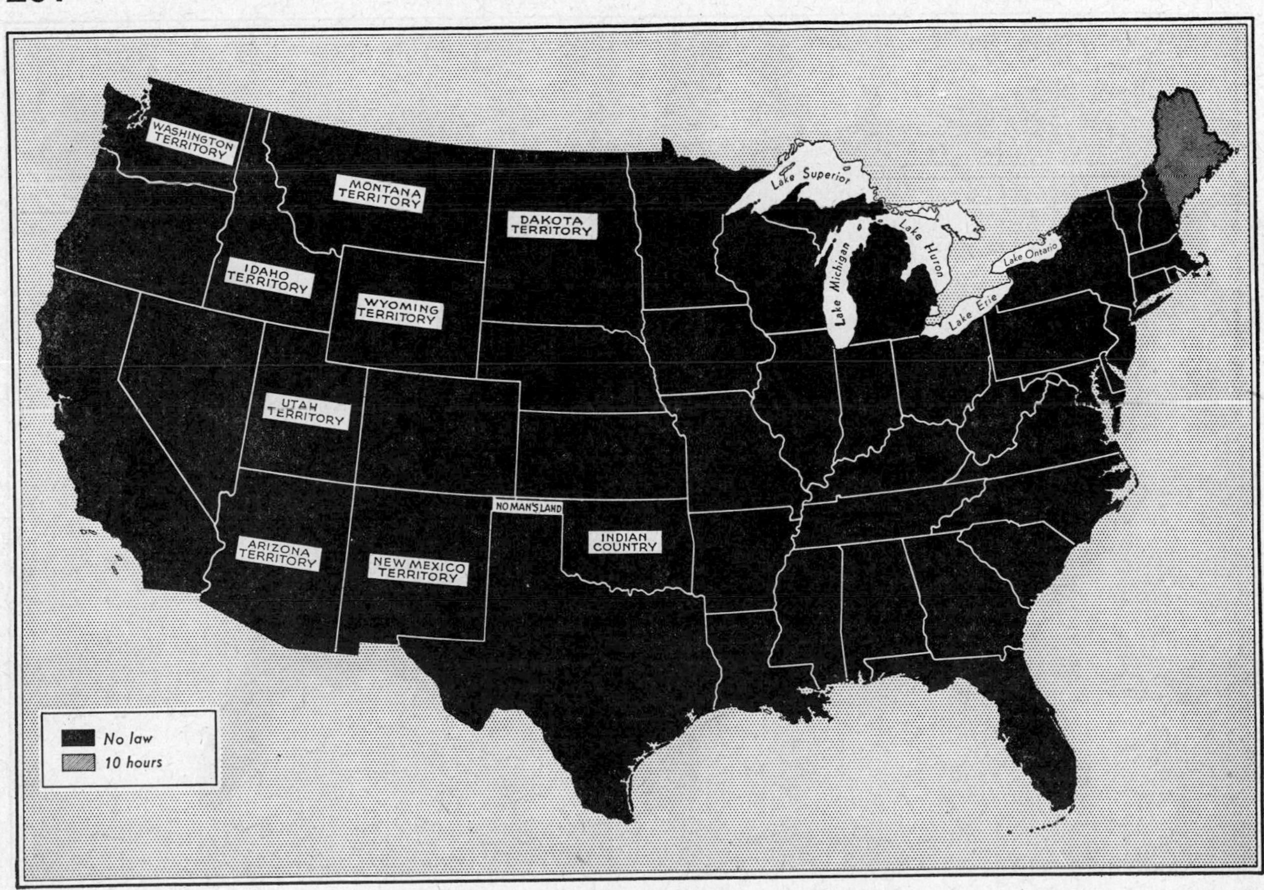

282 Child Labor: Any Gainful Occupation, 1880

Maps on this page show only laws of general applicability, without indicating occasional limitations in specified industries

Lake Superior
Lake Michigan
Lake Huron
Lake Ontario
Lake Erie
IDAHO TERRITORY
WYOMING TERRITORY
ARIZONA TERRITORY
NEW MEXICO TERRITORY
PUBLIC LAND STRIP
INDIAN COUNTRY
No law
10 hours
8 hours

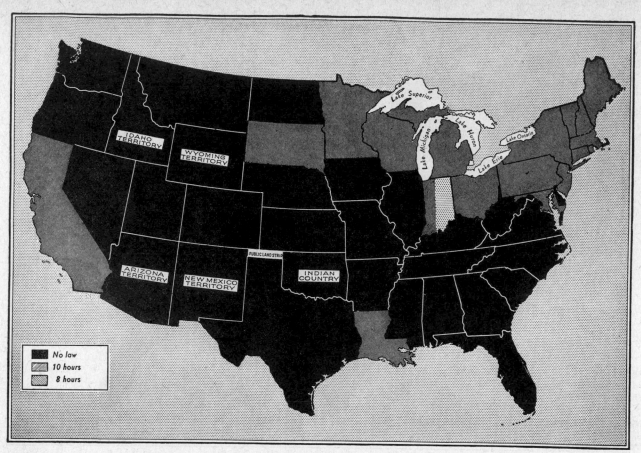

283 Child Labor: Manufacturing and/or Mercantile Employment, 1890

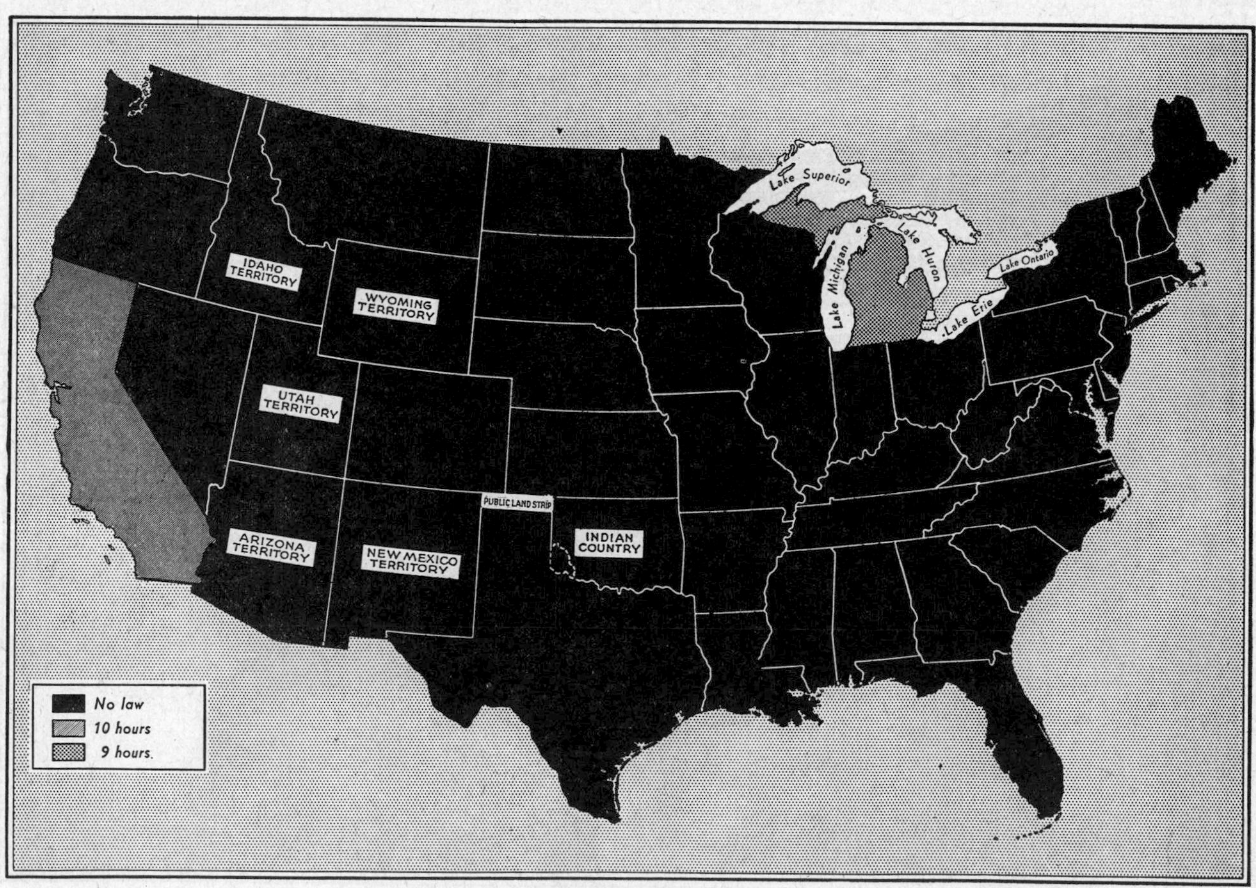

284 Child Labor: Any Gainful Occupation, 1890

Maps on this page show only laws of general applicability, without indicating occasional limitations in specified industries

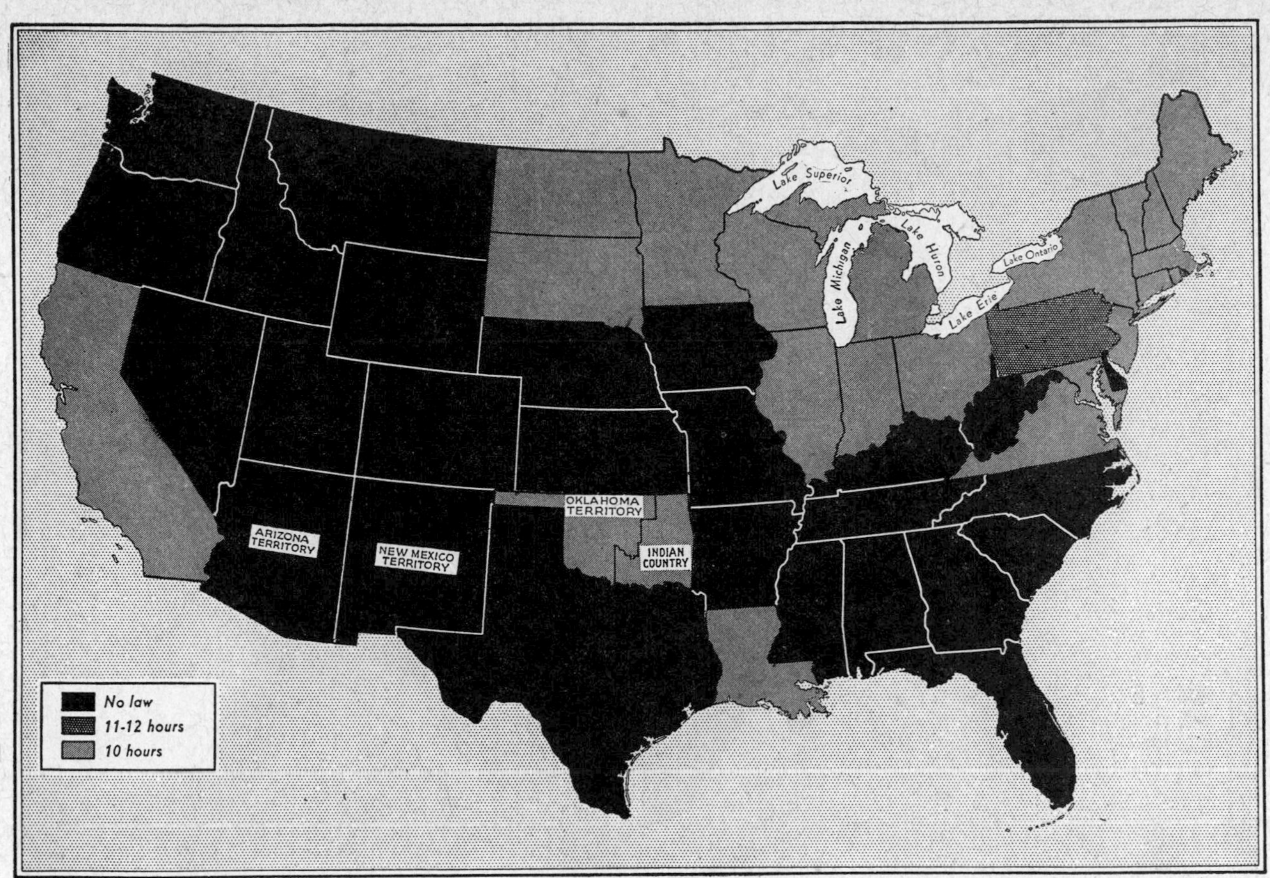

285 Child Labor: Manufacturing and/or Mercantile Employment, 1900

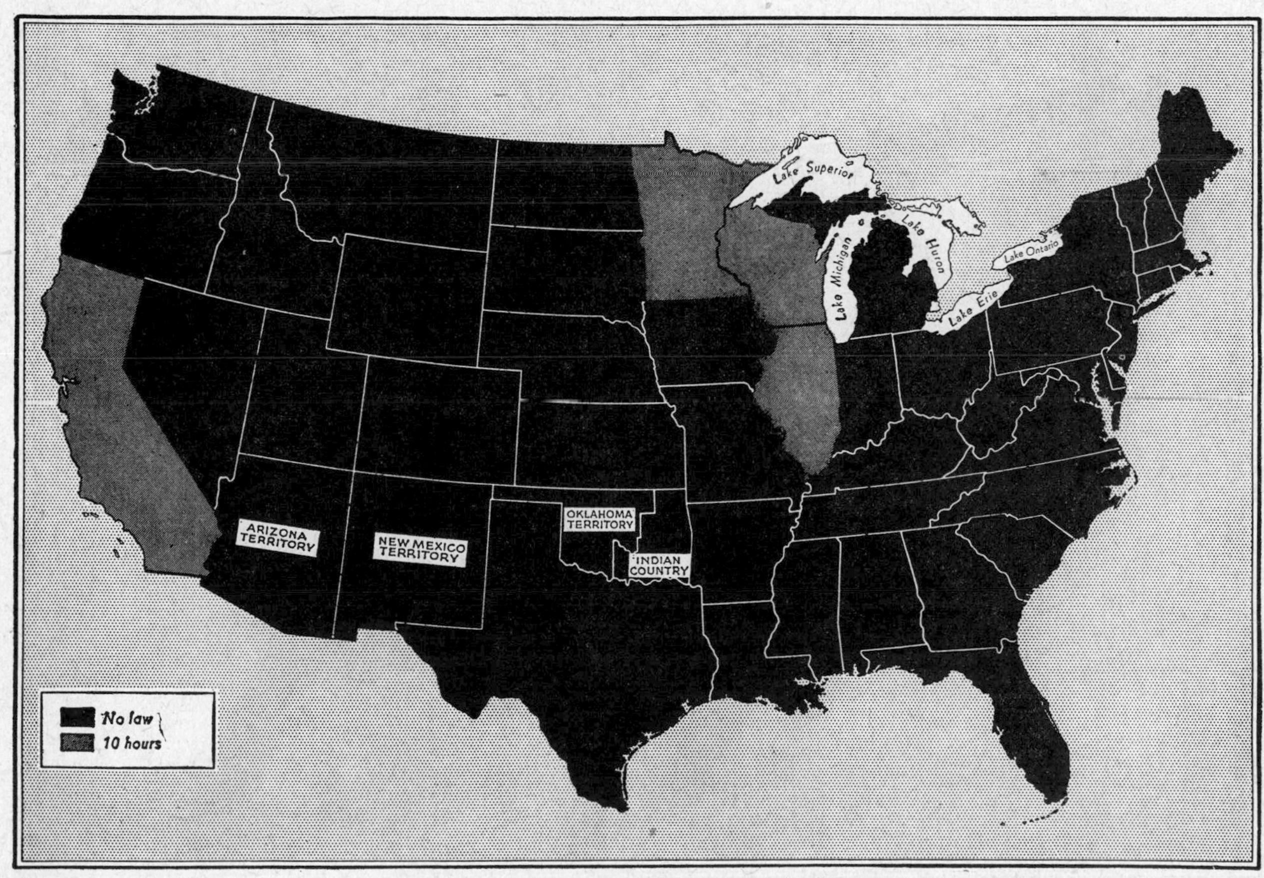

286 Child Labor: Any Gainful Occupation, 1900

Maps on this page show only laws of general applicability, without indicating occasional limitations in specified industries

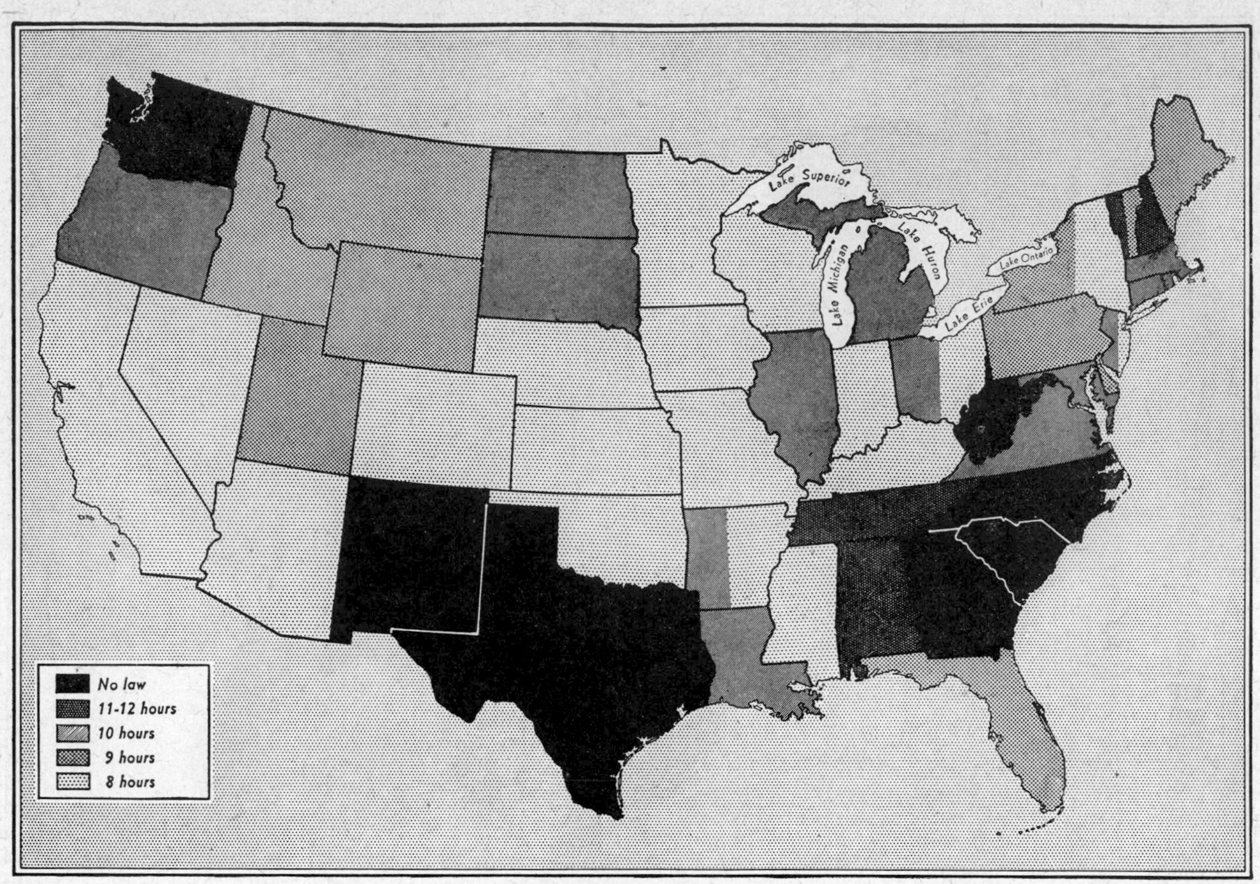

287 Child Labor: Manufacturing and/or Mercantile Employment, 1915

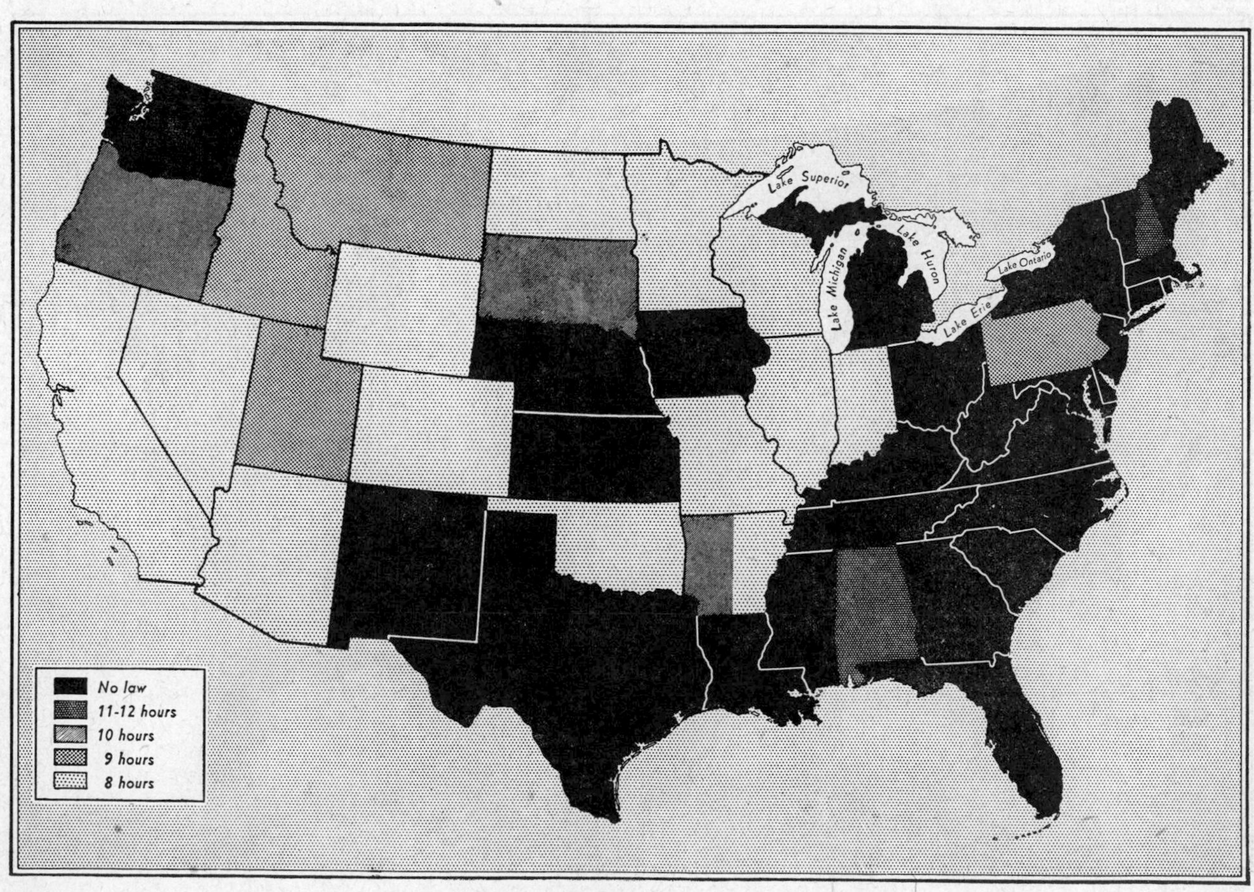

288 Child Labor: Any Gainful Occupation, 1915

Maps on this page show only laws of general applicability, without indicating occasional limitations in specified industries

Lake Superior
Lake Michigan
Lake Huron
Lake Ontario
Lake Erie
No law
11-12 hours
10 hours
9 hours
8 hours

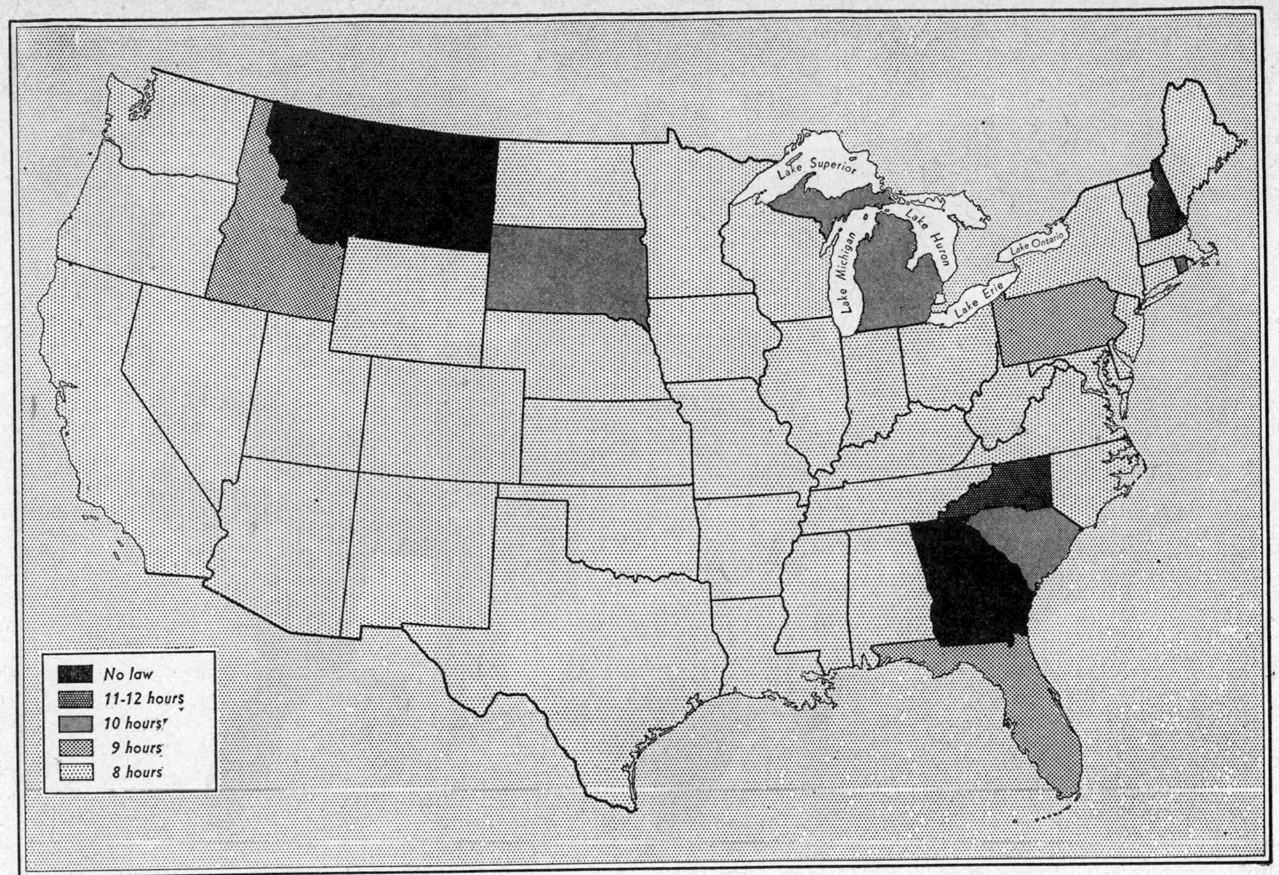

289

Child Labor: Manufacturing and/or Mercantile Employment, 1930

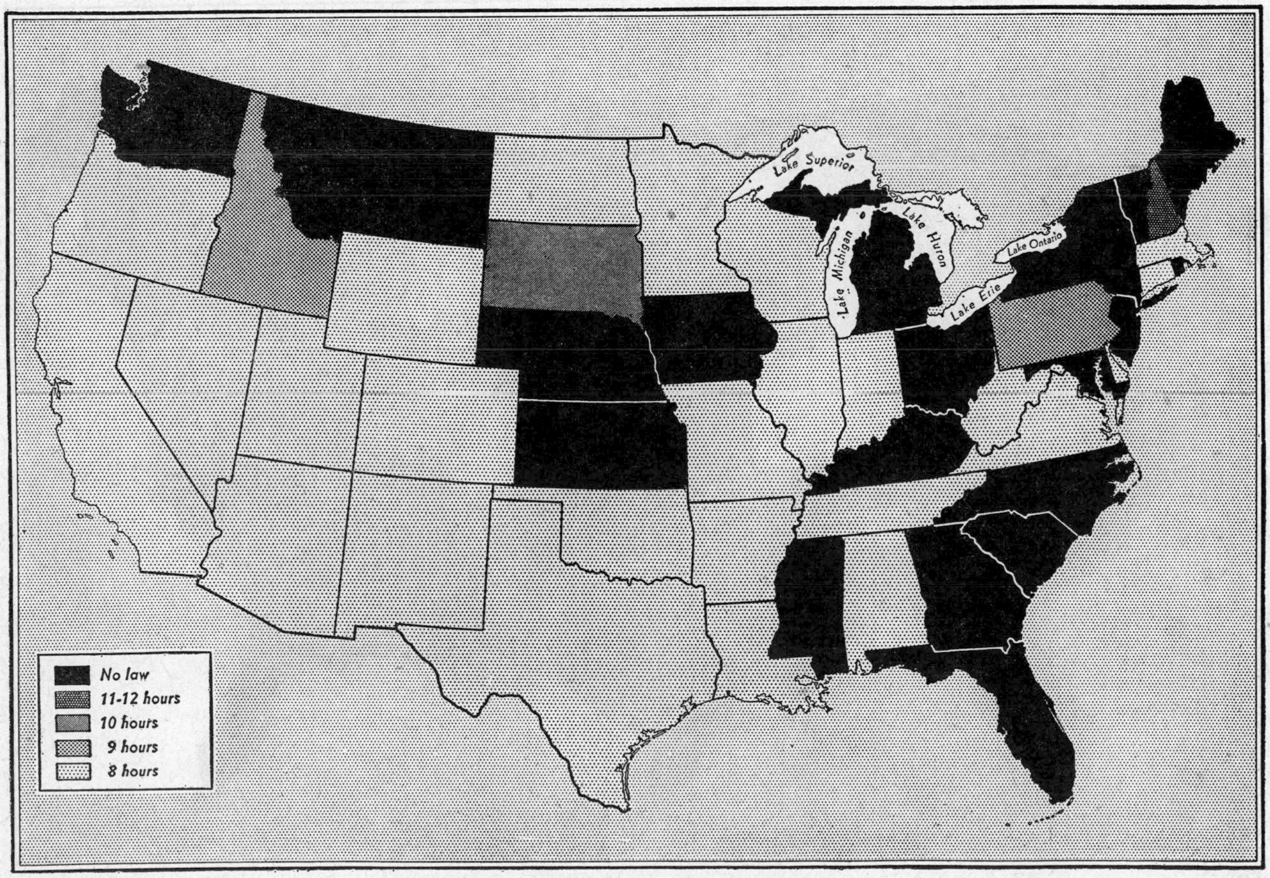

Lake Superior
Lake Michigan
Lake Huron
Lake Ontario
Lake Erie
No law
11-12 hours
10 hours
9 hours
8 hours

290

Child Labor: Any Gainful Occupation, 1930

Maps on this page show only laws of general applicability, without indicating occasional limitations in specific industries

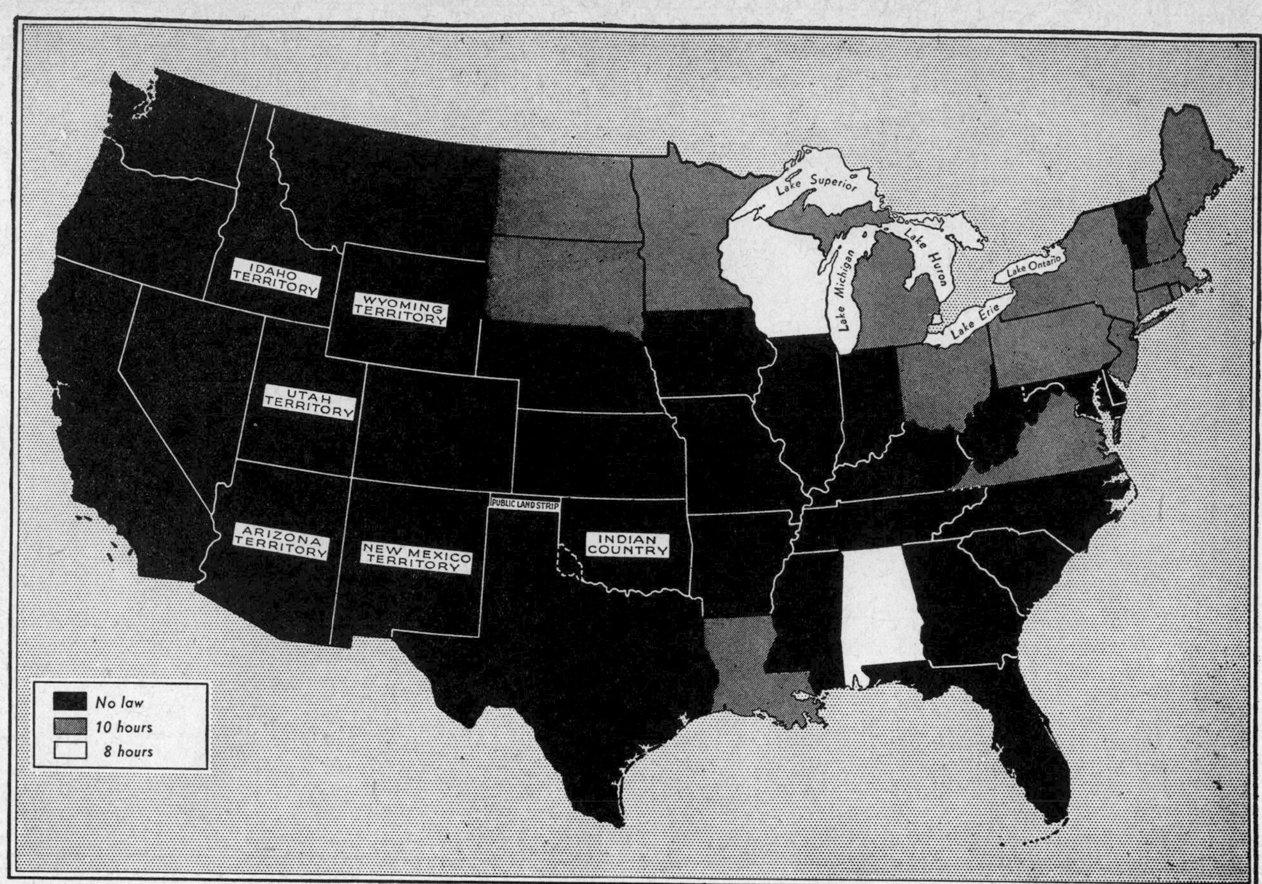

291 Women's Hours of Work, 1890

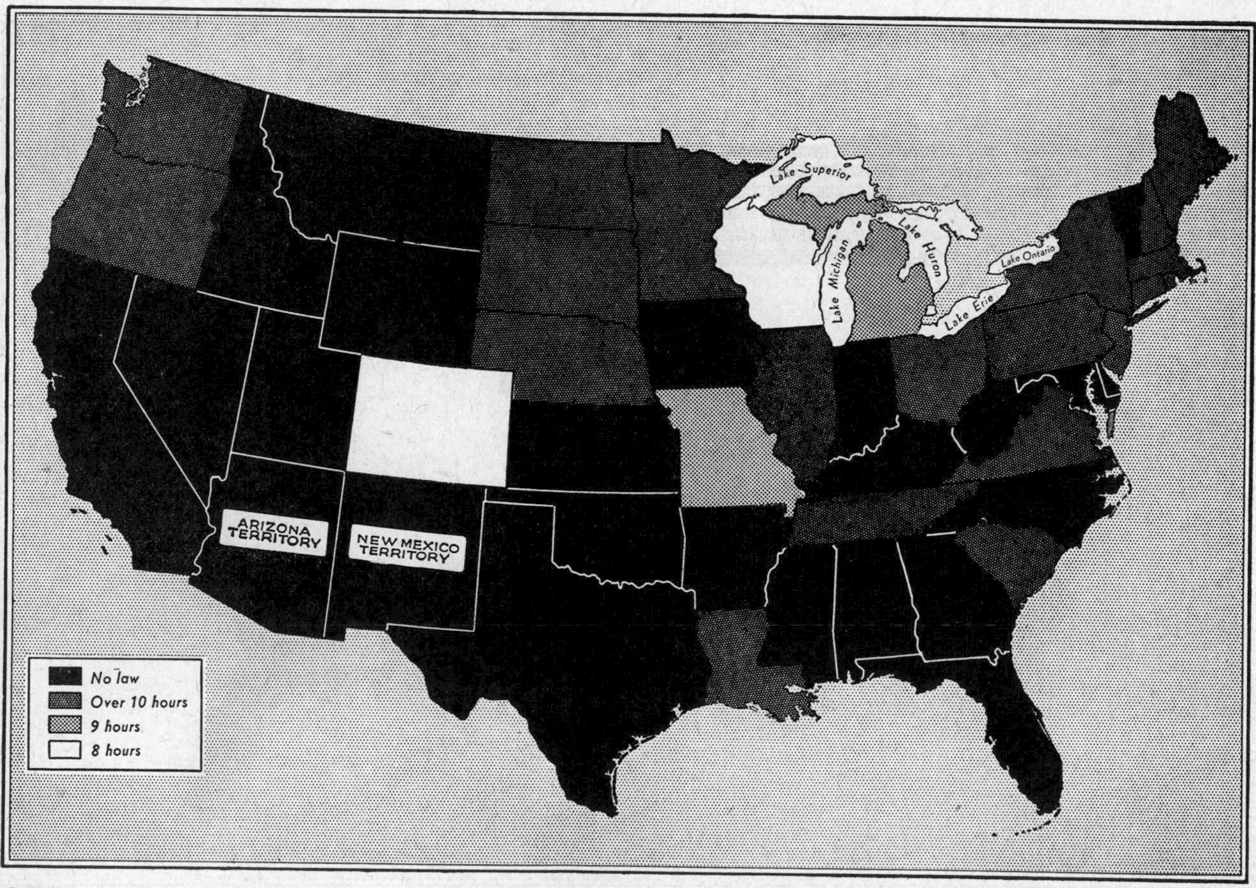

292 Women's Hours of Work, 1910

Maps on this page show only laws of general applicability, without indicating occasional limitations in specified industries

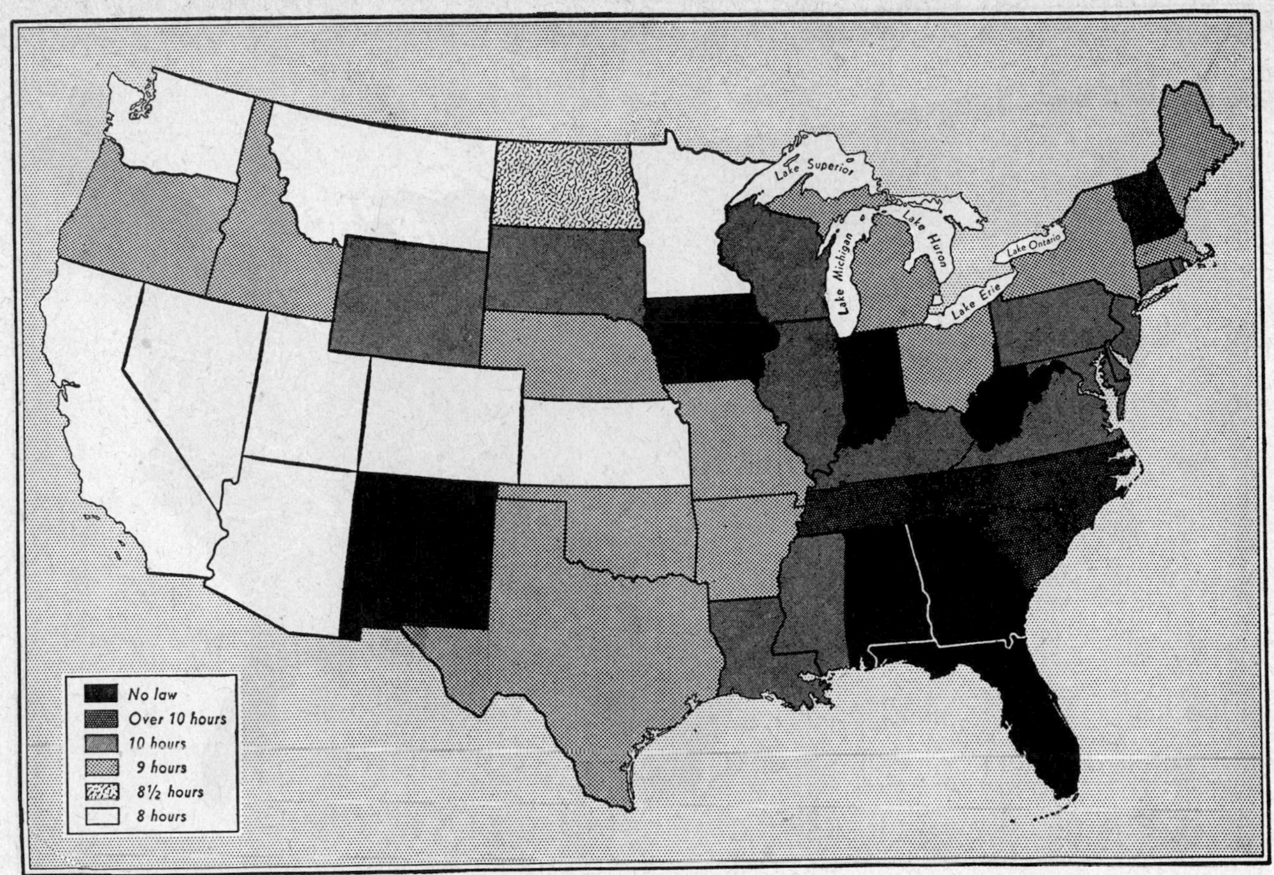

293

Women's Hours of Work, 1920

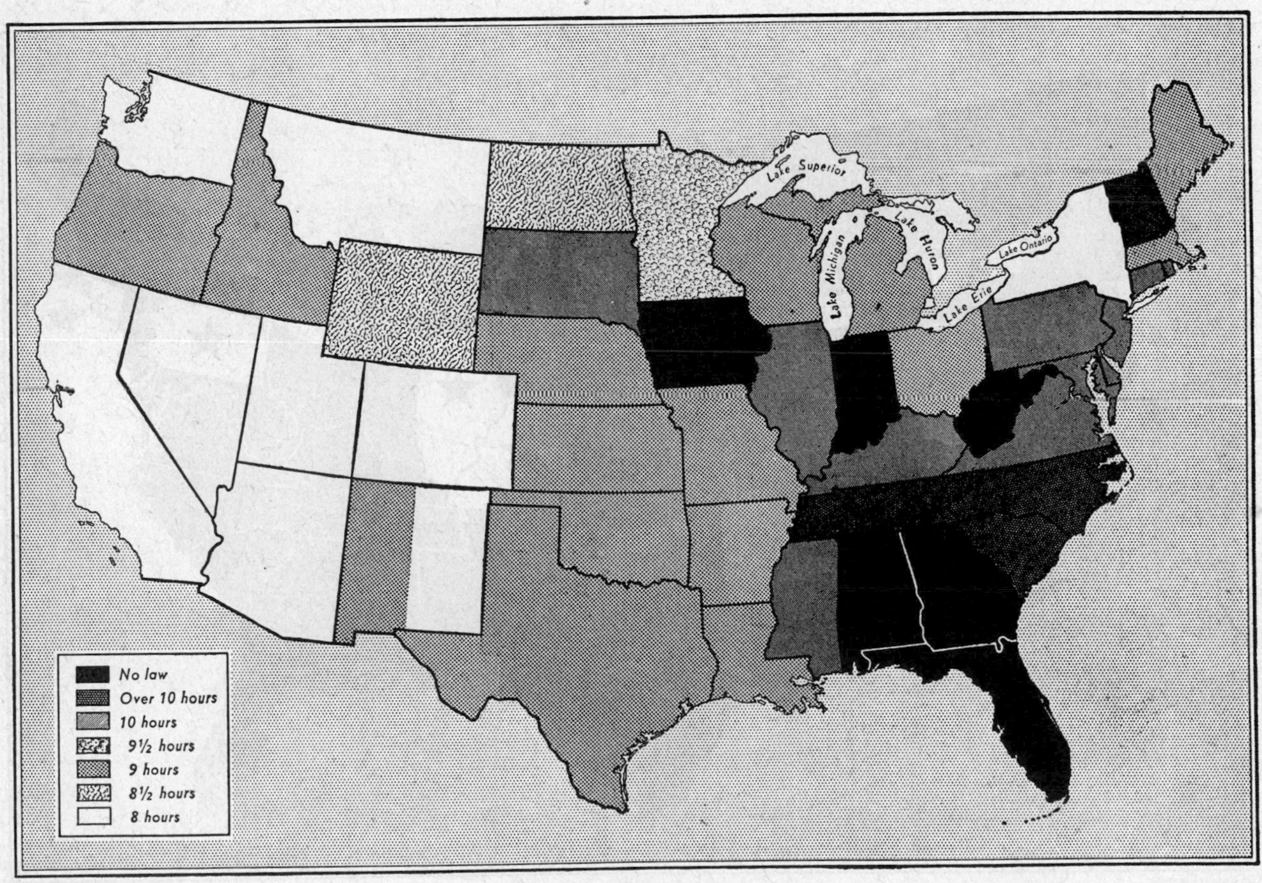

294

Women's Hours of Work, 1930

Maps on this page show only laws of general applicability, without indicating occasional limitations in specified industries

No law
8 hours in dangerous occupations
8 hours on public works

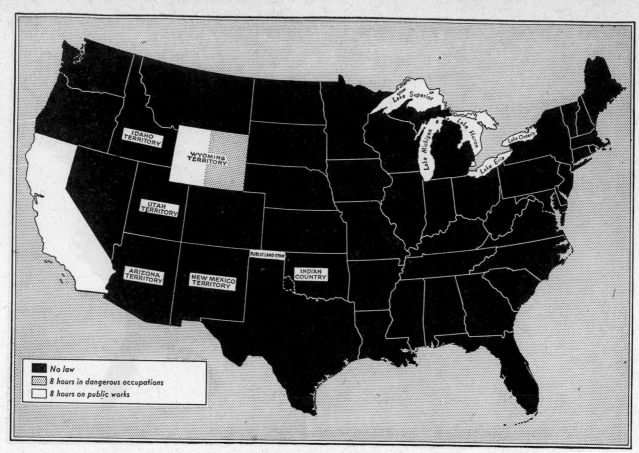

295 Men's Hours of Work: Public Works and Dangerous Occupations, 1890

No law
10 hours
8 hours
★ Limitations effective unless otherwise specified in worker's contract

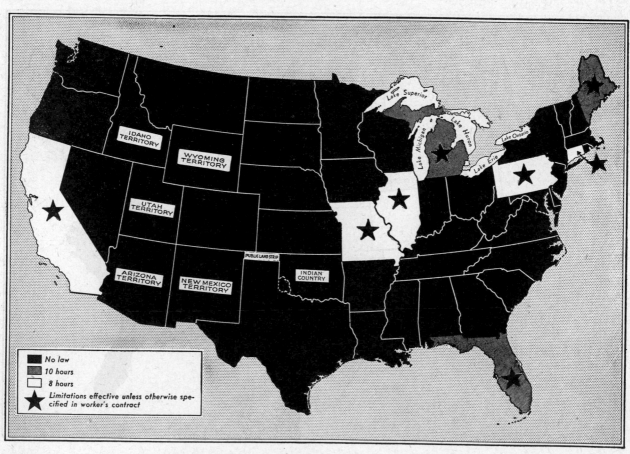

296 Men's Hours of Work: General Occupations, 1890
No indication is made of occasional limitations in specified industries

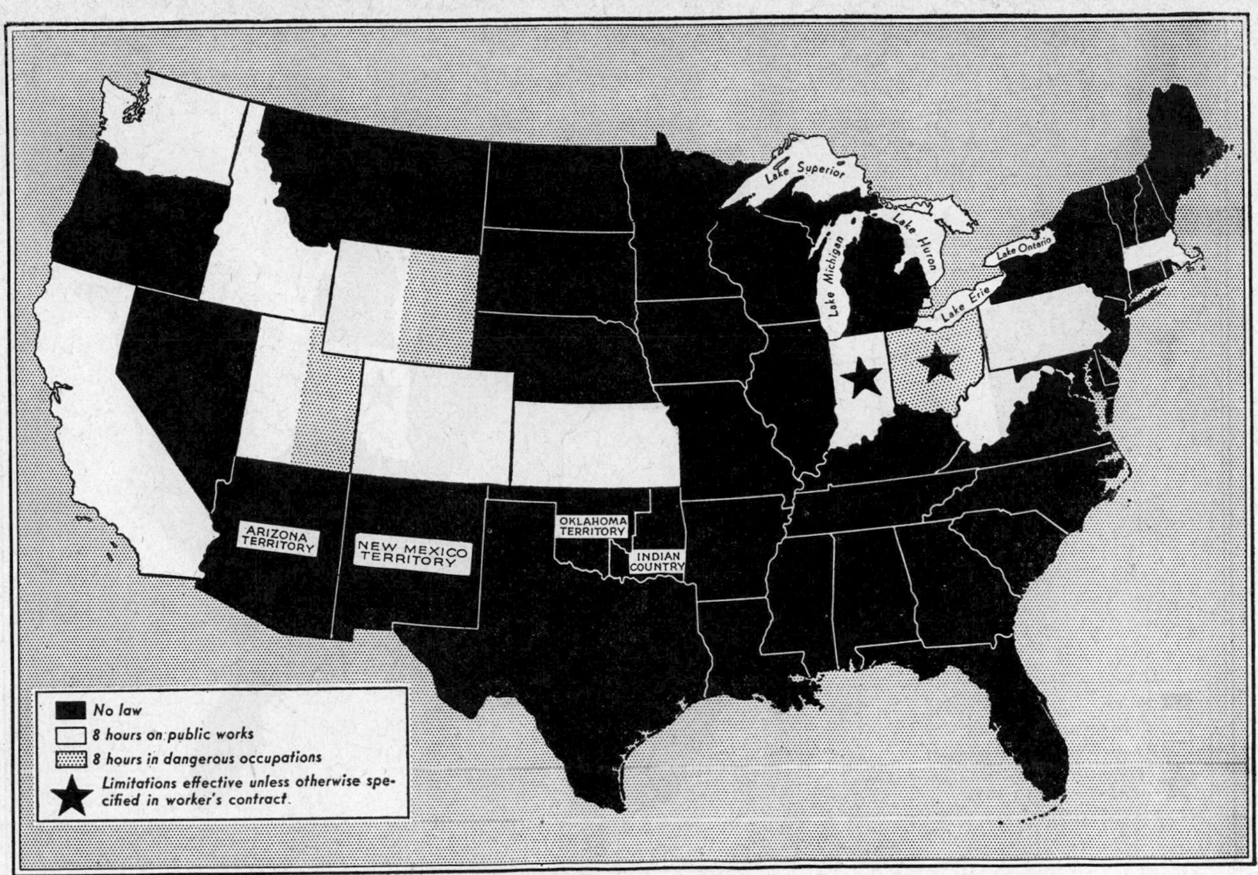

297 Men's Hours of Work: Public Works and Dangerous Occupations, 1900

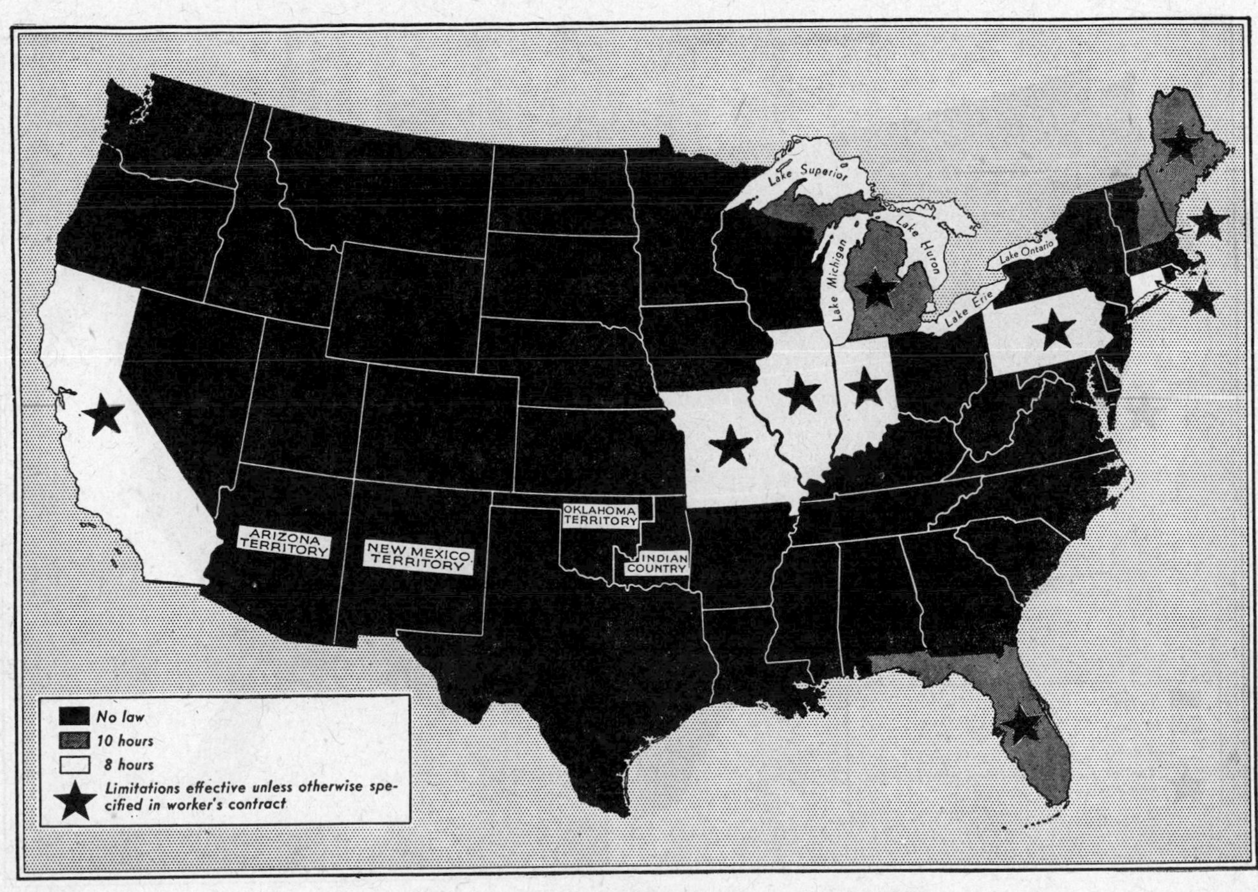

298 Men's Hours of Work: General Occupations, 1900

No indication is made of occasional limitations in specified industries

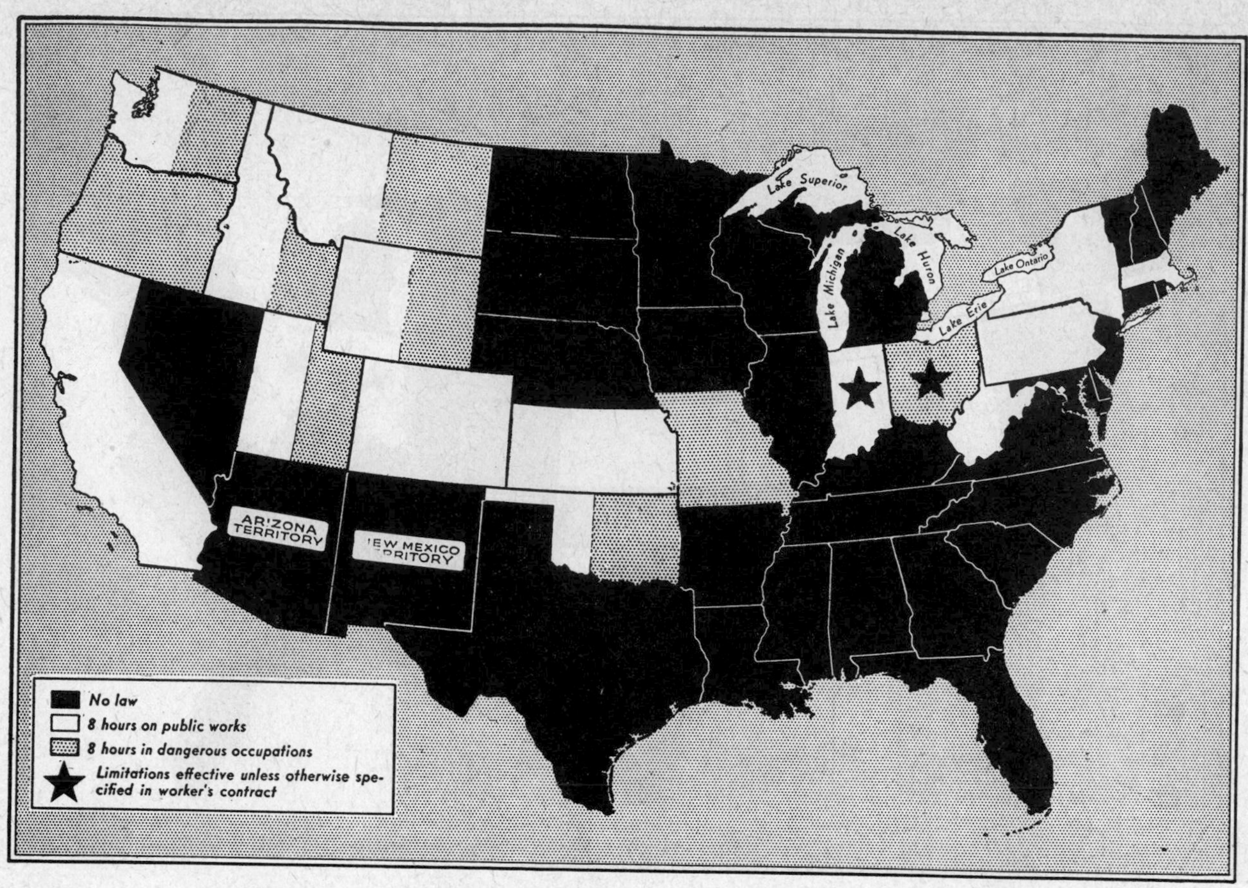

299 Men's Hours of Work: Public Works and Dangerous Occupations, 1910

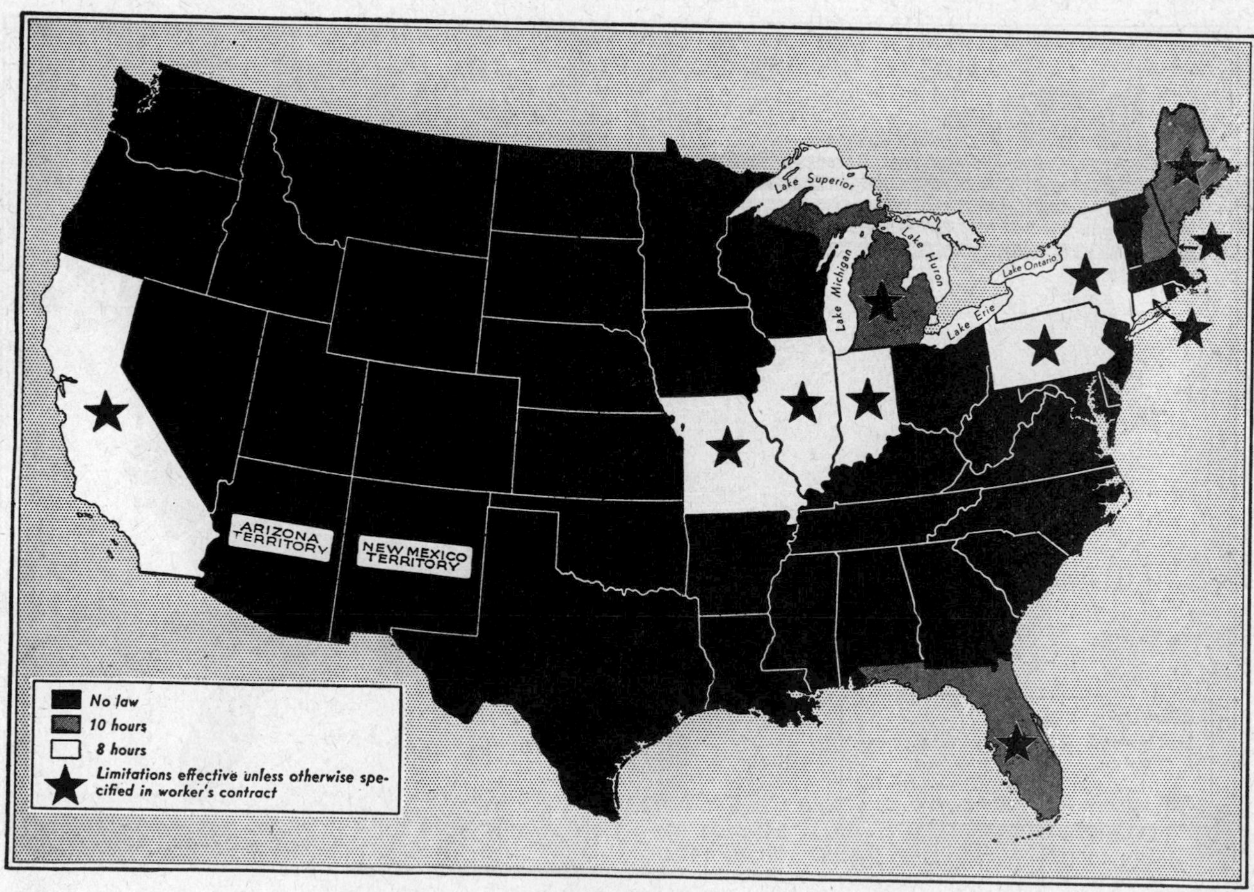

300 Men's Hours of Work: General Occupations, 1910

No indication is made of occasional limitations in specified industries

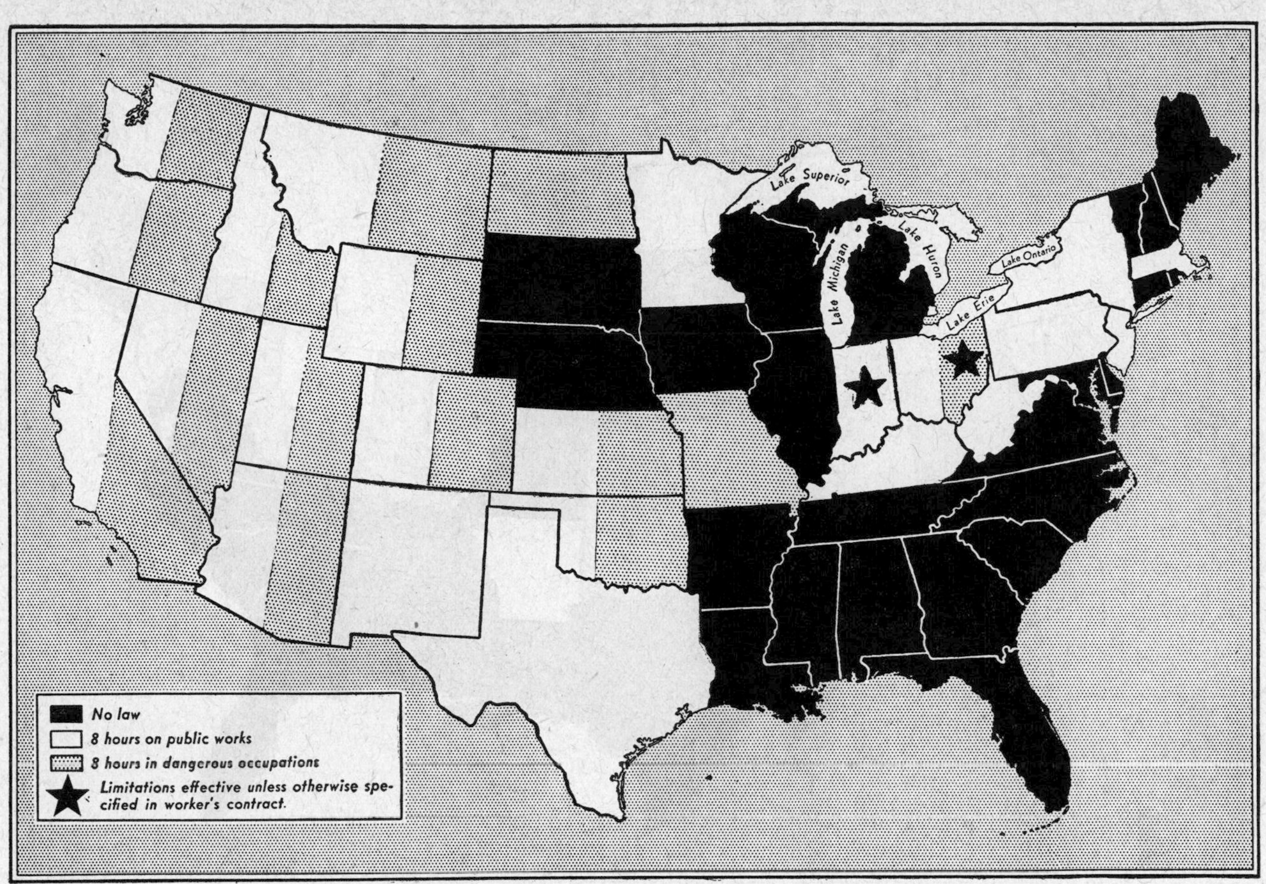

301 Men's Hours of Work: Public Works and Dangerous Occupations, 1920

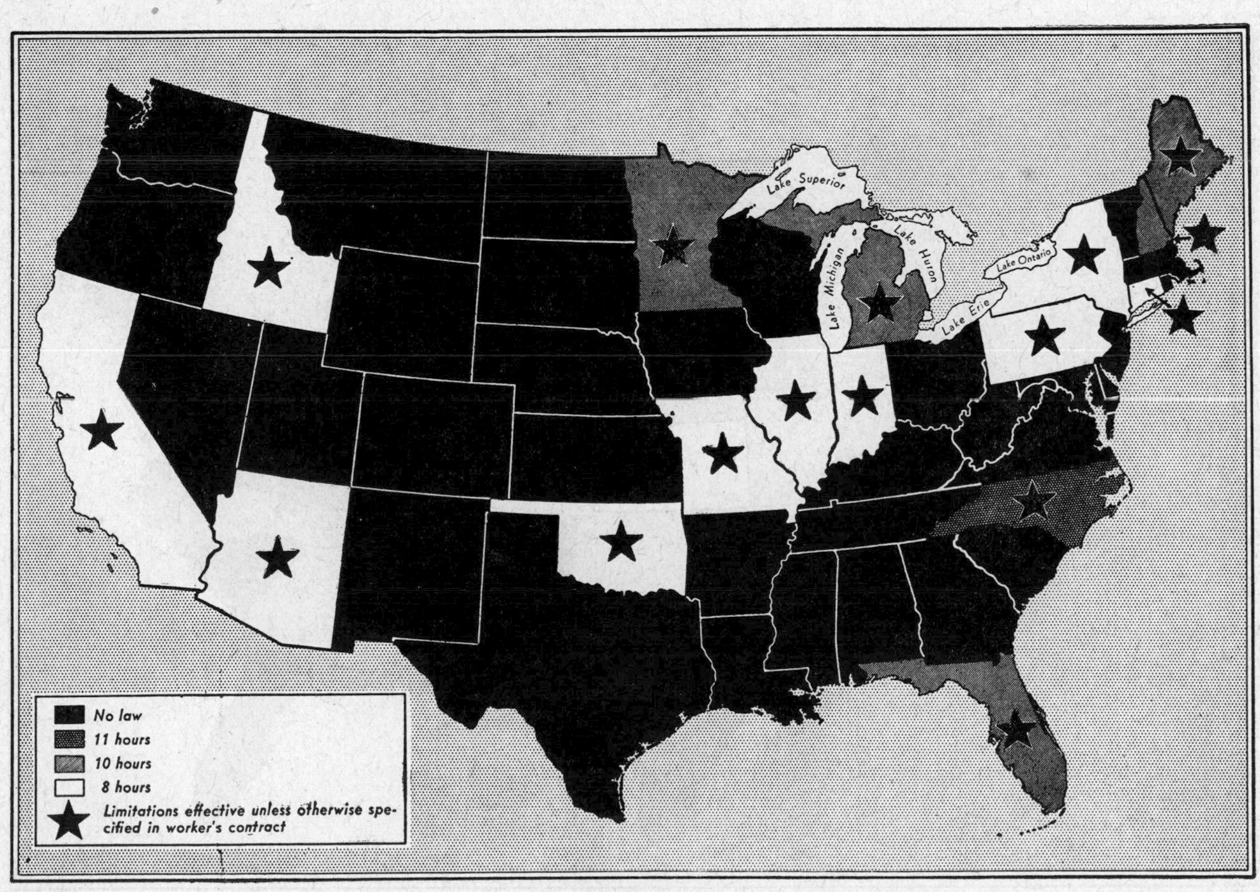

302 Men's Hours of Work: General Occupations, 1920

No indication is made of occasional limitations in specified industries

Lake Superior
Lake Michigan
Lake Huron
Lake Ontario
Lake Erie
States which have rejected the amendment
States which have not yet ratified the amendment
States which have ratified the amendment after having rejected it by vote of both houses
States which have ratified

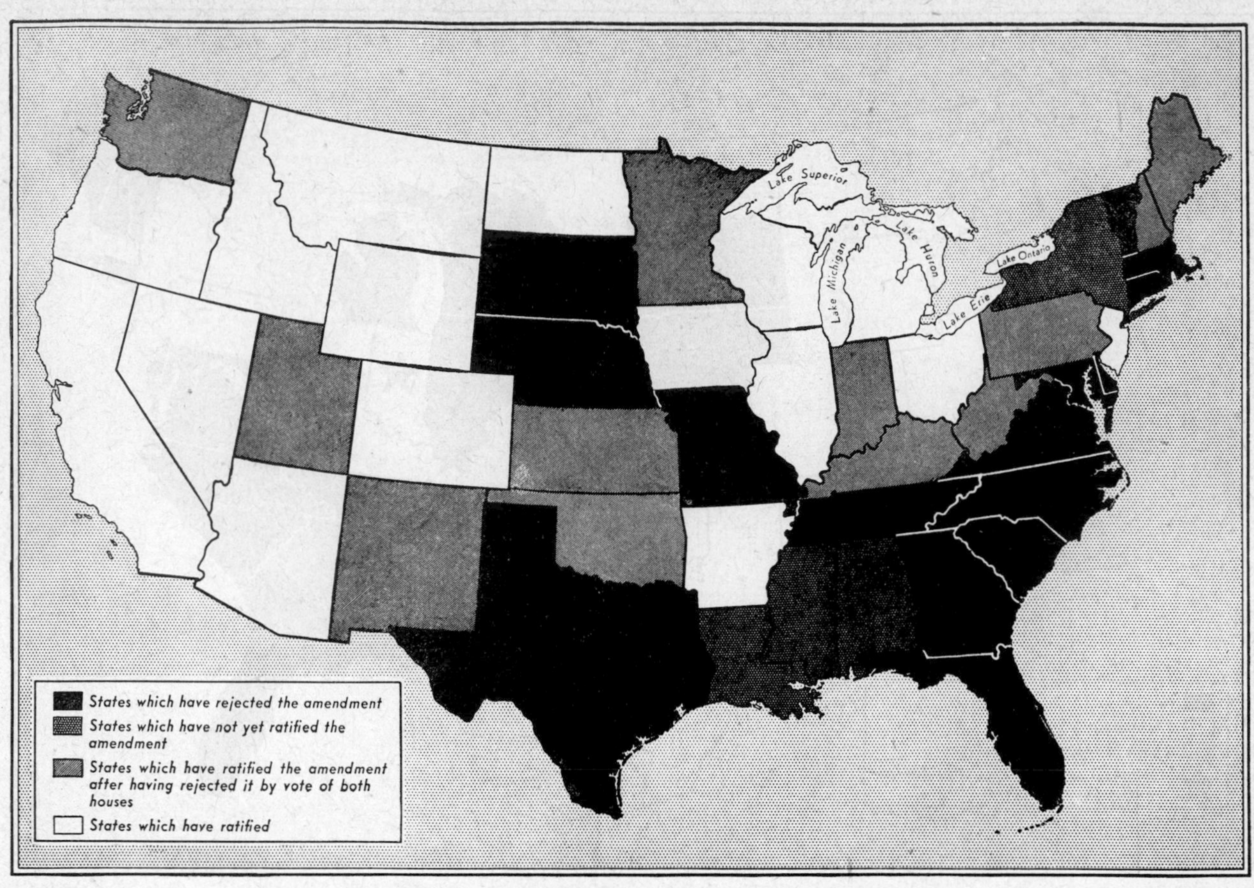

303 State Action on Proposed Federal Child Labor Amendment

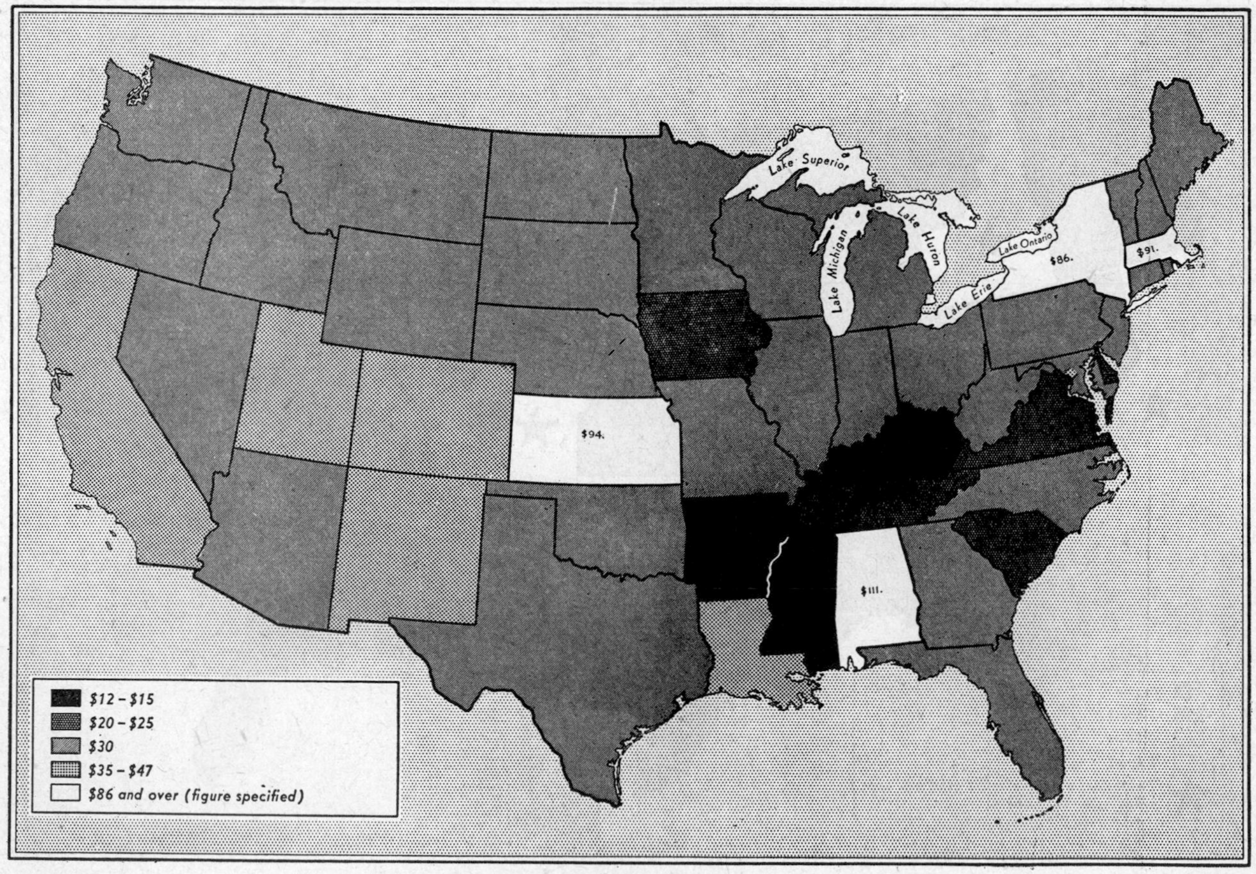

Lake Superior
Lake Michigan
Lake Huron
Lake Ontario
Lake Erie
$86.
$91.
$94.
$111.
$12 – $15
$20 – $25
$30
$35 – $47
$86 and over (figure specified)

304 Old Age Assistance: Maximum Benefit Payments, 1940

Section V

WORLD MAPS

The problems of modern America as a world power can be assessed only in relation to the resources and potentialities of our neighbors all over the world among whom we will always find some friends, some enemies. Those problems, whether their solutions be undertaken in cooperation or in competition with the other nations, can be sensibly approached only through the study of the consumption and distribution of world resources.

We face these problems—as represented very incompletely in the maps of the American Empire of 1941 and those showing the distribution of the major known world natural resources and crops—in a spirit very different from that of 1920, or even of 1937. At that time national interest and national study centered on the domestic scene and domestic problems with only slight general appreciation of the forces outside our borders which have played and will play a vital and decisive role in determining the future of this nation. Only careful, sober, intelligent study can light the way to the better future which we still see but as "through a glass, darkly." In the hope that these maps may in some small measure contribute to a fuller, better-rounded appreciation of America, its past and its potential future, the authors offer this book to its public.

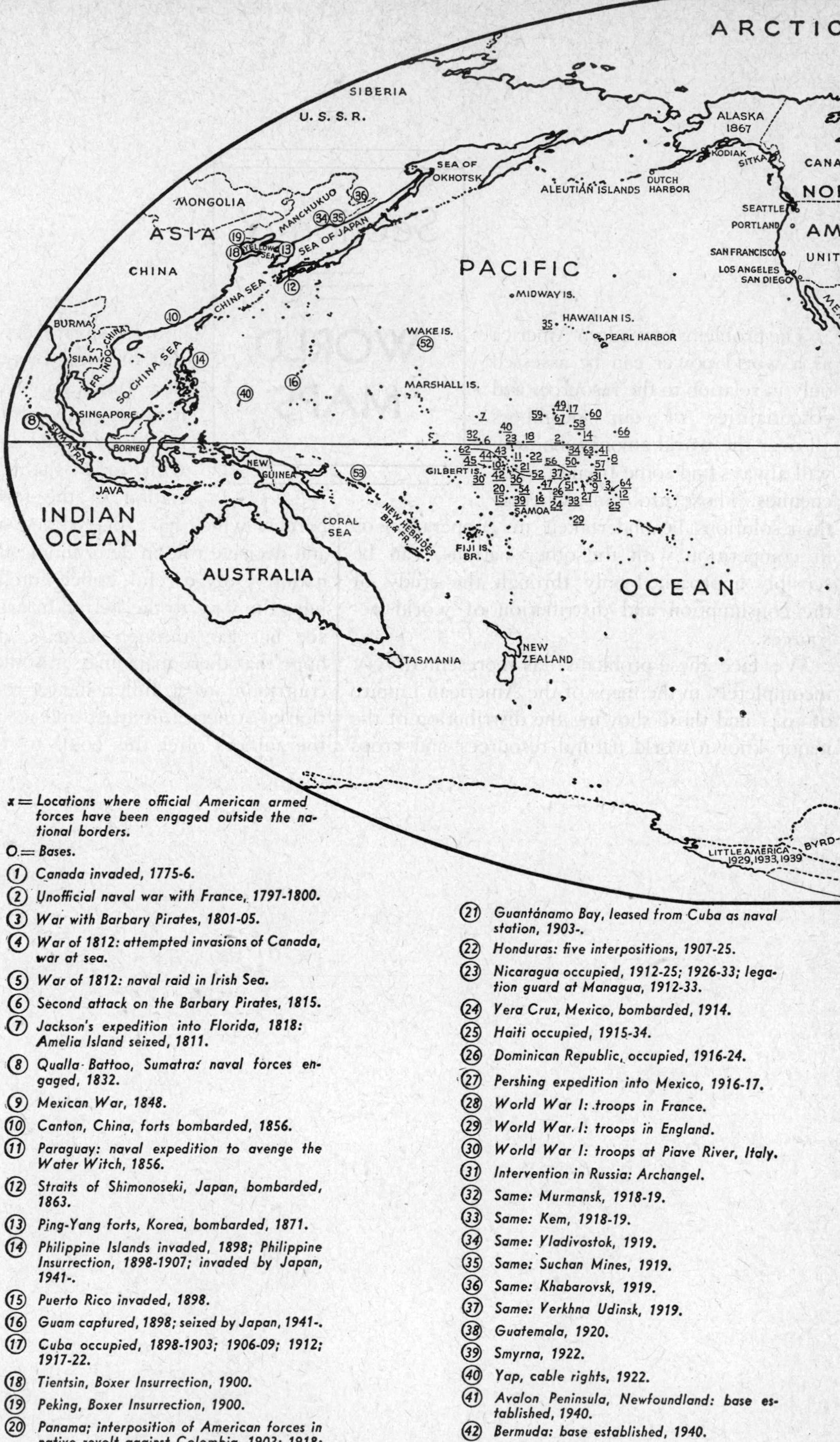

x = Locations where official American armed forces have been engaged outside the national borders.

O = Bases.

(1) Canada invaded, 1775-6.
(2) Unofficial naval war with France, 1797-1800.
(3) War with Barbary Pirates, 1801-05.
(4) War of 1812: attempted invasions of Canada, war at sea.
(5) War of 1812: naval raid in Irish Sea.
(6) Second attack on the Barbary Pirates, 1815.
(7) Jackson's expedition into Florida, 1818: Amelia Island seized, 1811.
(8) Qualla-Battoo, Sumatra: naval forces engaged, 1832.
(9) Mexican War, 1848.
(10) Canton, China, forts bombarded, 1856.
(11) Paraguay: naval expedition to avenge the Water Witch, 1856.
(12) Straits of Shimonoseki, Japan, bombarded, 1863.
(13) Ping-Yang forts, Korea, bombarded, 1871.
(14) Philippine Islands invaded, 1898; Philippine Insurrection, 1898-1907; invaded by Japan, 1941-.
(15) Puerto Rico invaded, 1898.
(16) Guam captured, 1898; seized by Japan, 1941-.
(17) Cuba occupied, 1898-1903; 1906-09; 1912; 1917-22.
(18) Tientsin, Boxer Insurrection, 1900.
(19) Peking, Boxer Insurrection, 1900.
(20) Panama; interposition of American forces in native revolt against Colombia, 1903; 1918; 1925.
(21) Guantánamo Bay, leased from Cuba as naval station, 1903-.
(22) Honduras: five interpositions, 1907-25.
(23) Nicaragua occupied, 1912-25; 1926-33; legation guard at Managua, 1912-33.
(24) Vera Cruz, Mexico, bombarded, 1914.
(25) Haiti occupied, 1915-34.
(26) Dominican Republic, occupied, 1916-24.
(27) Pershing expedition into Mexico, 1916-17.
(28) World War I: troops in France.
(29) World War I: troops in England.
(30) World War I: troops at Piave River, Italy.
(31) Intervention in Russia: Archangel.
(32) Same: Murmansk, 1918-19.
(33) Same: Kem, 1918-19.
(34) Same: Vladivostok, 1919.
(35) Same: Suchan Mines, 1919.
(36) Same: Khabarovsk, 1919.
(37) Same: Verkhna Udinsk, 1919.
(38) Guatemala, 1920.
(39) Smyrna, 1922.
(40) Yap, cable rights, 1922.
(41) Avalon Peninsula, Newfoundland: base established, 1940.
(42) Bermuda: base established, 1940.
(43) Exuma Island: base established, 1940.

Amer

Names of the countries on this map will be useful in connection with the maps of world resources

(44) *Jamaica: base established, 1940.*
(45) *Antigua: base established, 1940.*
(46) *Aruba, Bonair, Curaçao: occupied, 1940.*
(47) *St. Lucia: base established, 1940.*
(48) *Trinidad: base established, 1940.*
(49) *Georgetown, British Guiana: base established, 1940.*
(50) *Greenland: protectorate, 1941.*
(51) *Iceland: protectorate, 1941.*
(52) *Wake Island, seized by Japan, 1941.*
(53) *Solomon Islands, seized by Japan, 1942; part retaken by U. S. in early August, 1942; battle joined in October, 1942.*

1 Alacrans Is., b. 1884
2 America Islands, b. 1860
3 Anne's, b. 1860
4 Arenas Key, b. 1879
5 Arenas Is., b. 1880
6 Baker, b. 1856; 1930
7 Barber's, b. 1860
8 Barren Is., b. 1859
9 Bauman's, b. 1860
10 Birnie Is., b. 1860
11 Canton, b. 1859; 1939
12 Caroline Atoll, b. 1860
13 Chincha Is., b. 1850
14 Christmas Is., b. 1859
15 Clarence Is., b. 1860
16 Dangerous Is., b. 1860
17 Dangers Rock I., b. 1860
18 Davids Is., b. 1860
19 De Anes Is., b. 1880
20 Duke of York Is., b. 1860
21 Enderbury Is., b. 1859, 1860
22 Farmers Is., b. 1860
23 Favorite Is., b. 1860
24 Flint I., b. 1860
25 Flint's Is., b. 1860
26 Frances Is., b. 1860
27 Frienhaven Is., b. 1860
28 Gallego Is., b. 1860
29 Ganges Is., b. 1860
30 Gardner Is., b. 1860
31 Groninque Is., b. 1860
32 Howland Is., 1858
33 Humphrey's Is., b. 1860
34 Jarvis, b. 1856
35 Johnston Is., b. 1859; 1898
36 Kemn's Is., b. 1860
37 Liderons Is., b. 1860
38 Lobos Is., b. 1852
39 Low Is., b. 1860
40 Mackin or Makin Is., b. 1860
41 Malden's Is., b. 1859
42 Mary Letitia I., b. 1860
43 Mary's Is., b. 1860
44 Mathews Is., b. 1860
45 McKean I., b. 1859
46 Morant Keys, b. 1879
47 Nassau, b. 1860
48 Navassa, b. 1858; 1916
49 Palmyra Is., b. 1860; 1898
50 Penhuyns Is., b. 1860
51 Pescador Is., b. 1860
52 Phoenix Is., b. 1859, 1860
53 Prospect Is., b. 1860
54 Quiros Is., b. 1860
*55 Quito Sueño, b. 1869; 1919**
56 Rierson's Is., b. 1860
57 Rogewein's Is., b. 1860
58 Rondacor, b. 1869; 1919
59 Samarang Is., b. 1860
60 Sarah Anne Is., b. 1860
61 Serranilla Keys, b. 1879, 1880; 1919
62 Sidney's Is., b. 1860
63 Starbuck Is., b. 1860
64 Staver's Is., b. 1860
65 Swan Is., 1919
66 Walkers Is., b. 1860
67 Washington Is., b. 1860
68 Western Triangles, b. 1880
** Title cleared with Colombia, 1929.*

Base Map by Permission of Denoyer-Geppert Company, Chicago

pire, 1942

os that follow. The islands bonded under the Guano Act of 1856 are indicated by "b." before the date.

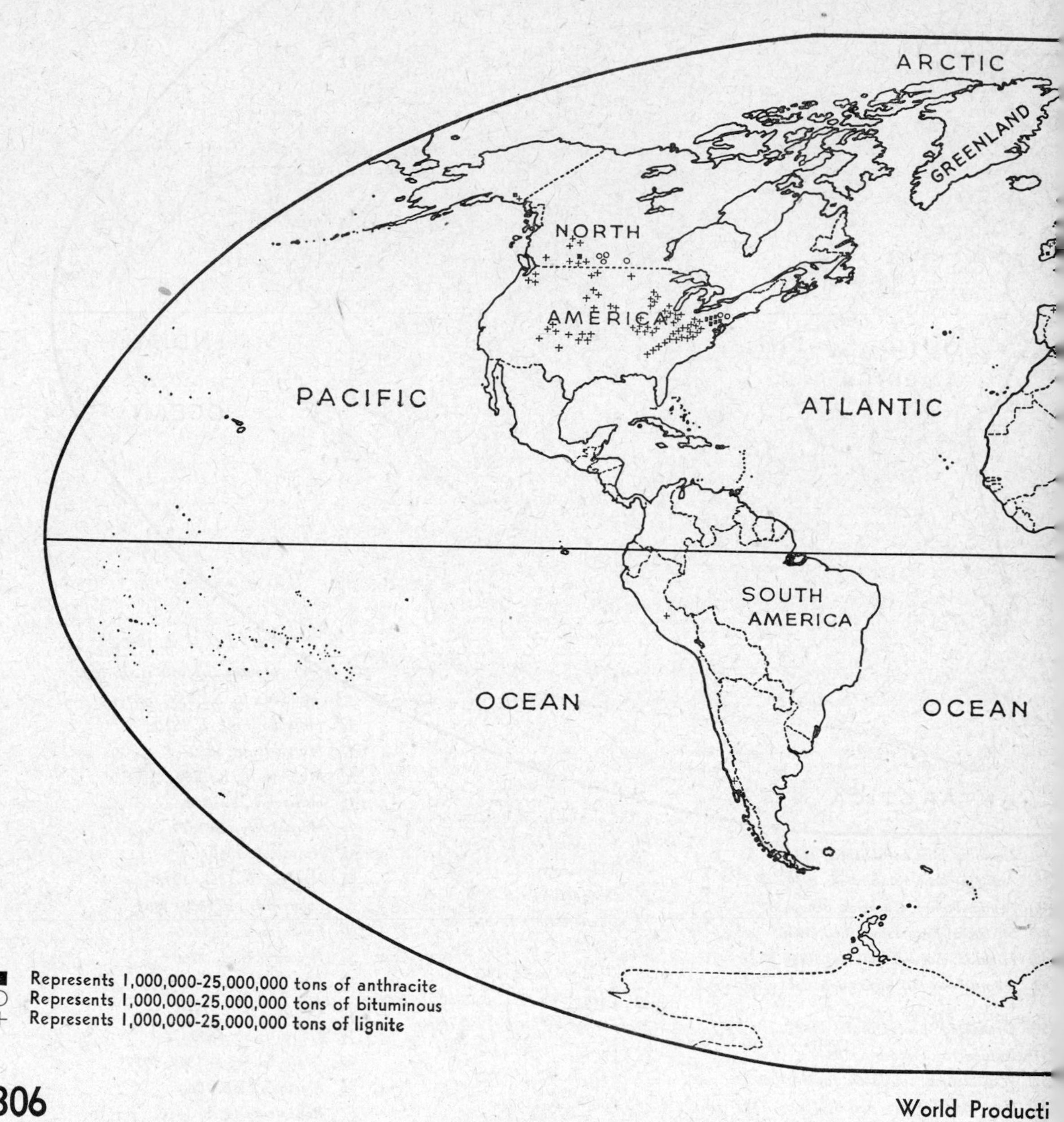

■ Represents 1,000,000-25,000,000 tons of anthracite
○ Represents 1,000,000-25,000,000 tons of bituminous
+ Represents 1,000,000-25,000,000 tons of lignite

306

World Producti

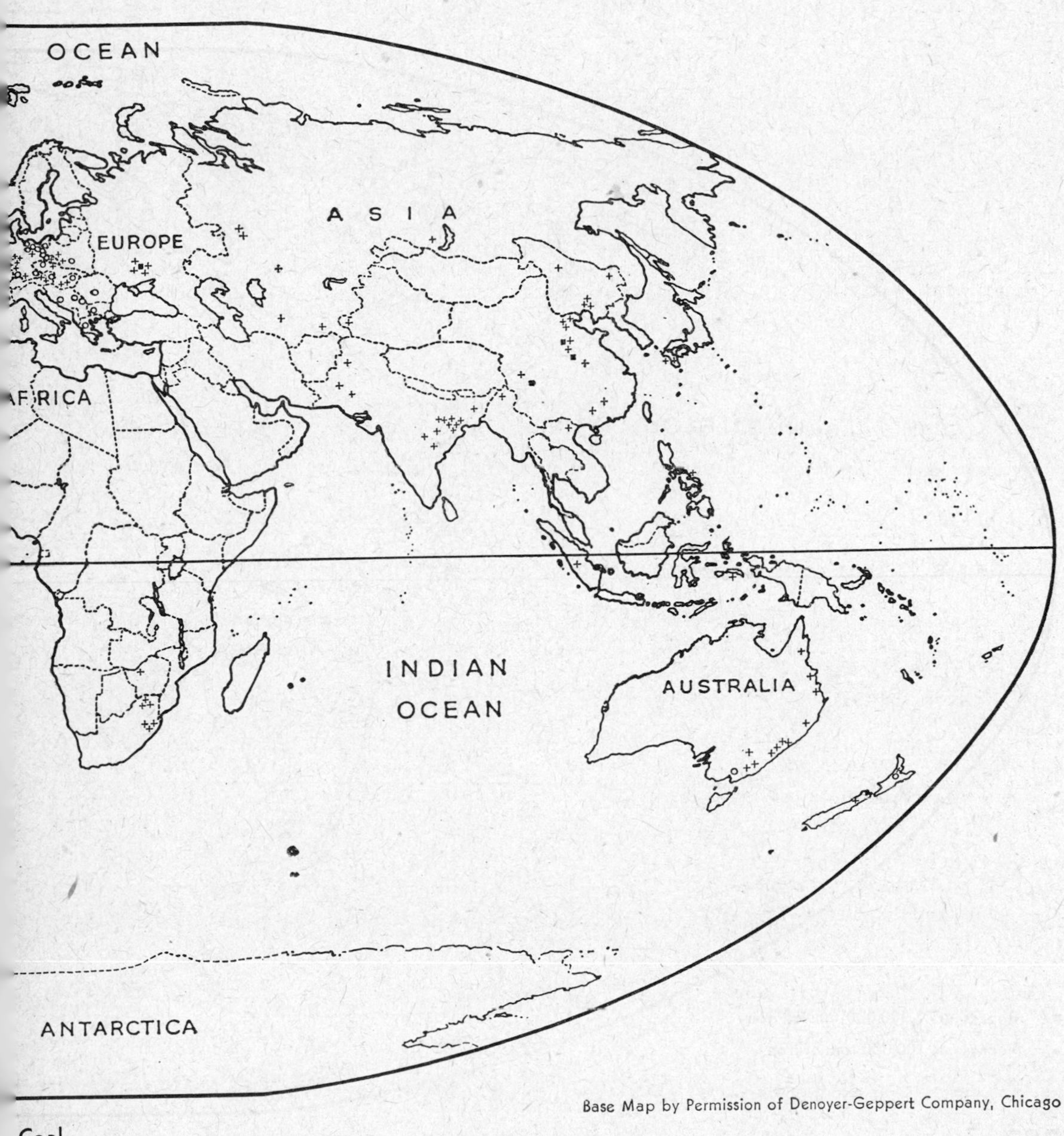

Base Map by Permission of Denoyer-Geppert Company, Chicago

Coal

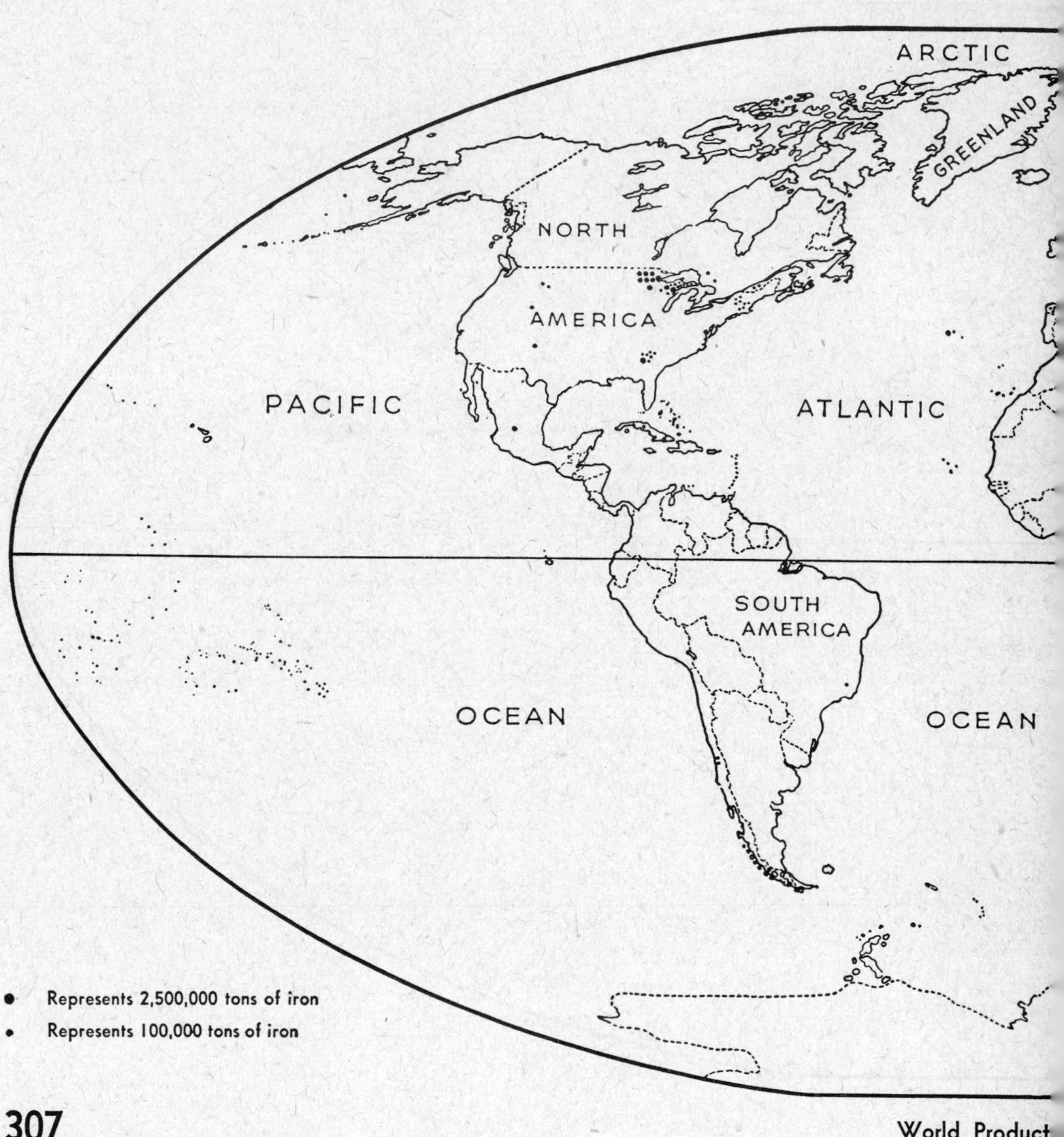

307

World Product

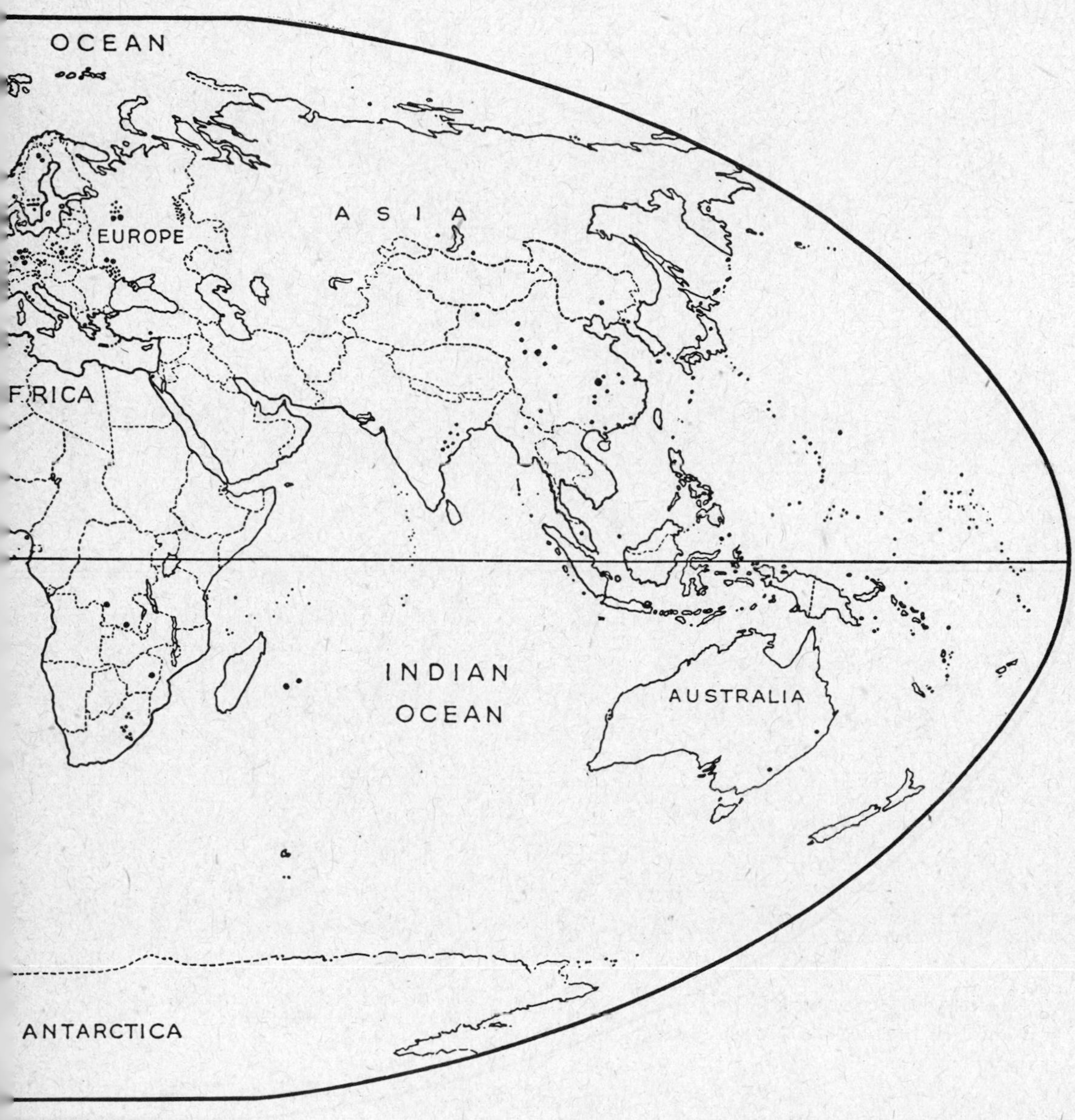

on

Base Map by Permission of Denoyer-Geppert Company, Chicago

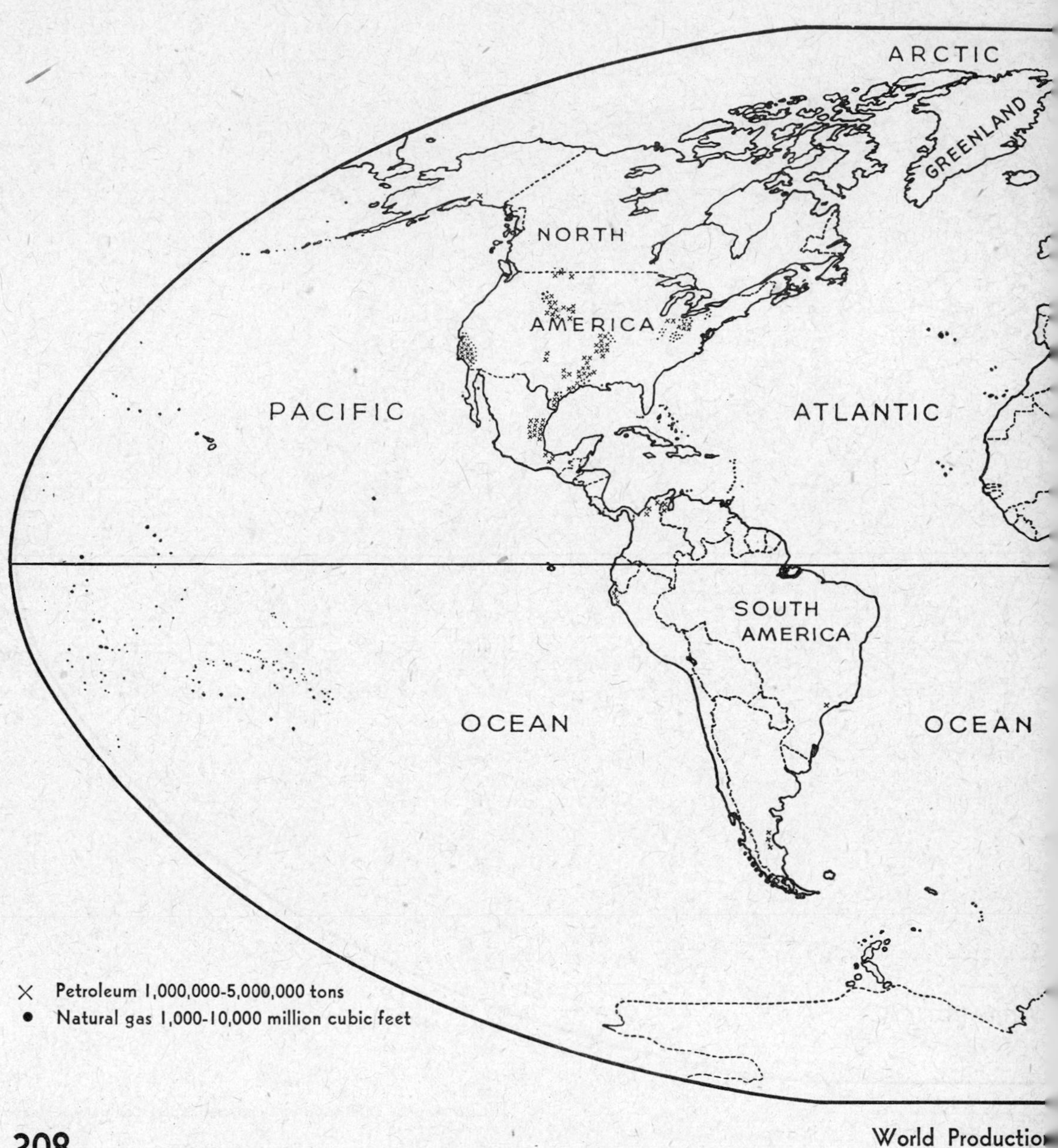

308

World Productio

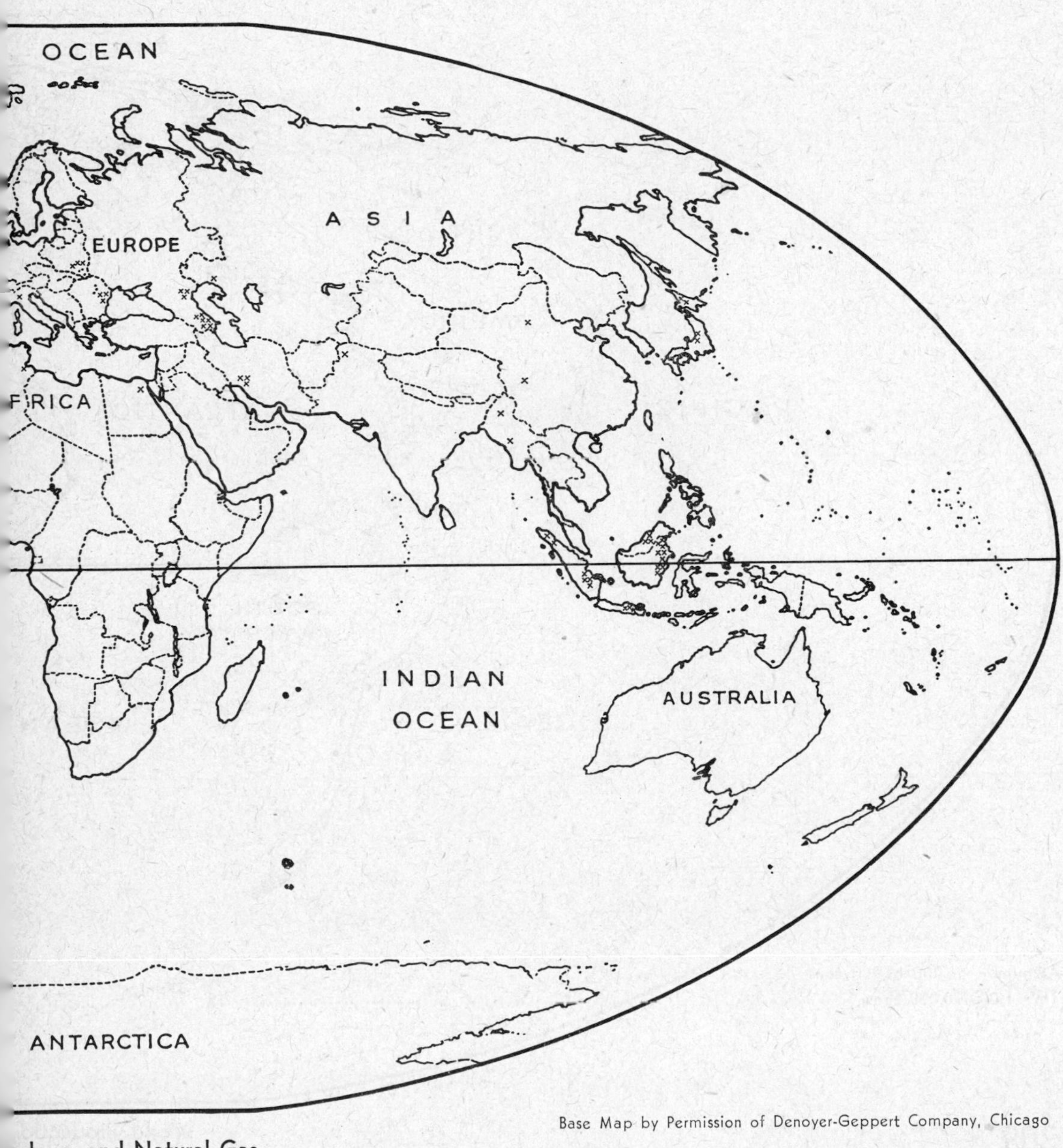

Base Map by Permission of Denoyer-Geppert Company, Chicago

oleum and Natural Gas

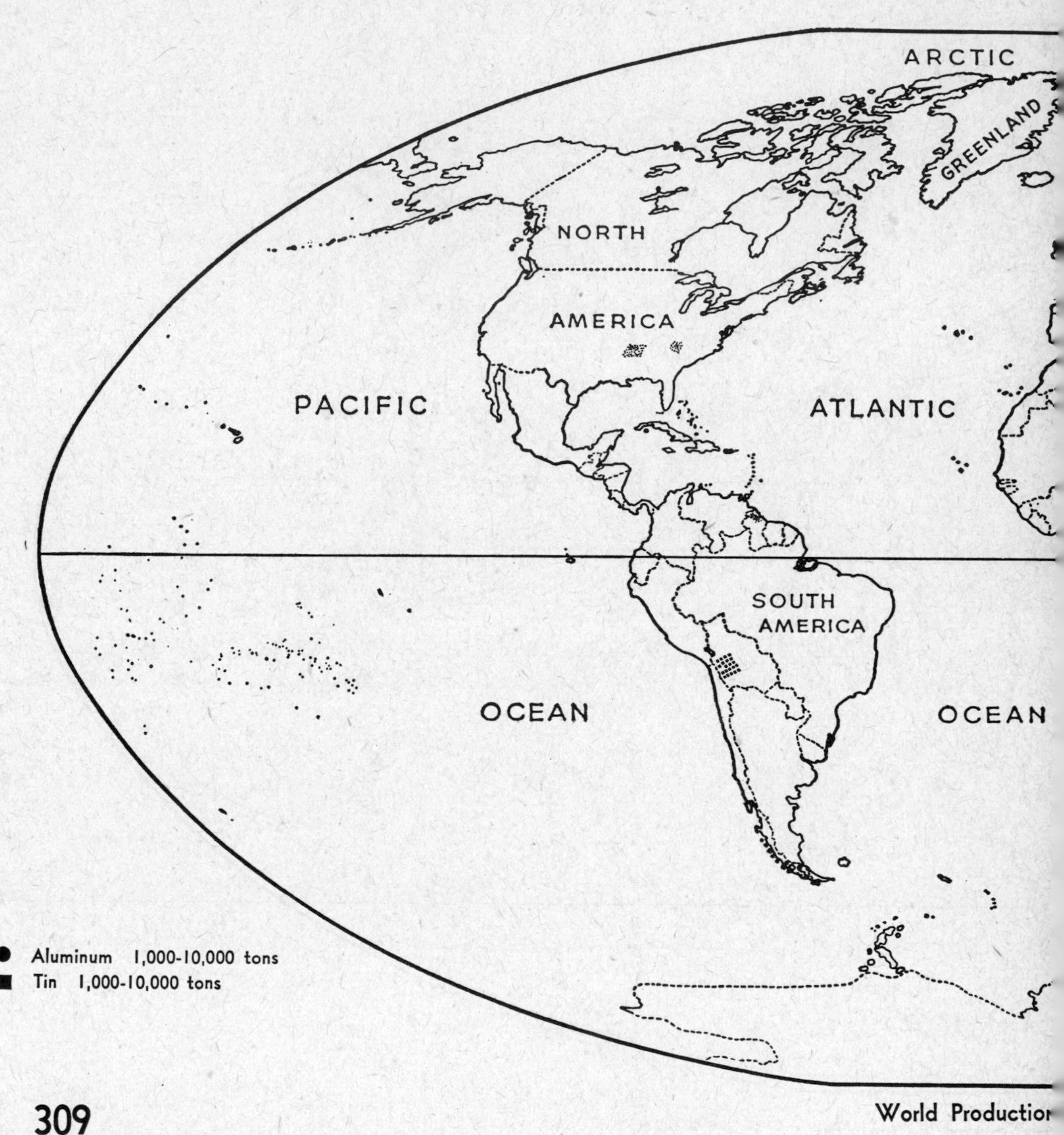

309 World Productio

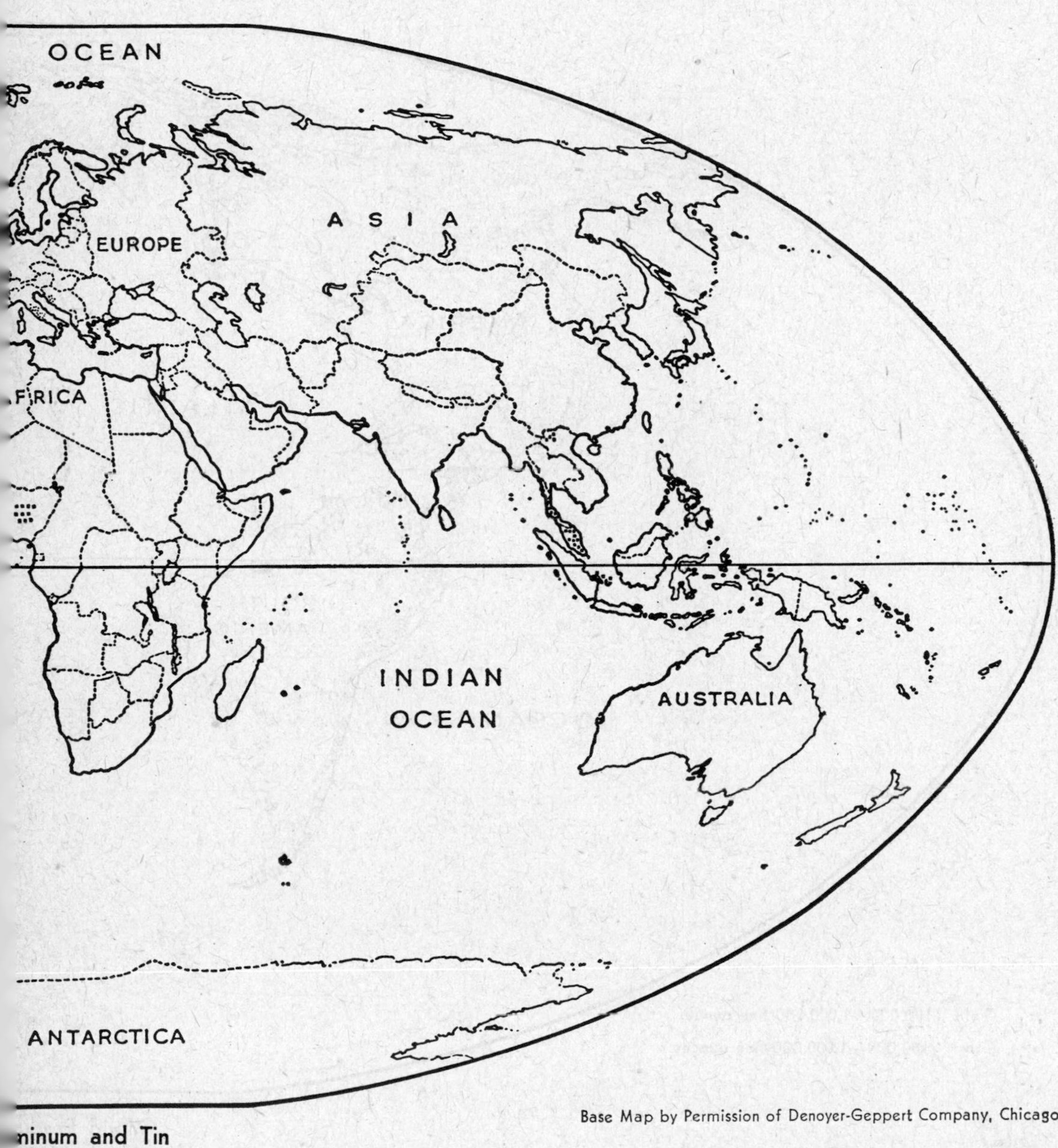

minum and Tin

Base Map by Permission of Denoyer-Geppert Company, Chicago

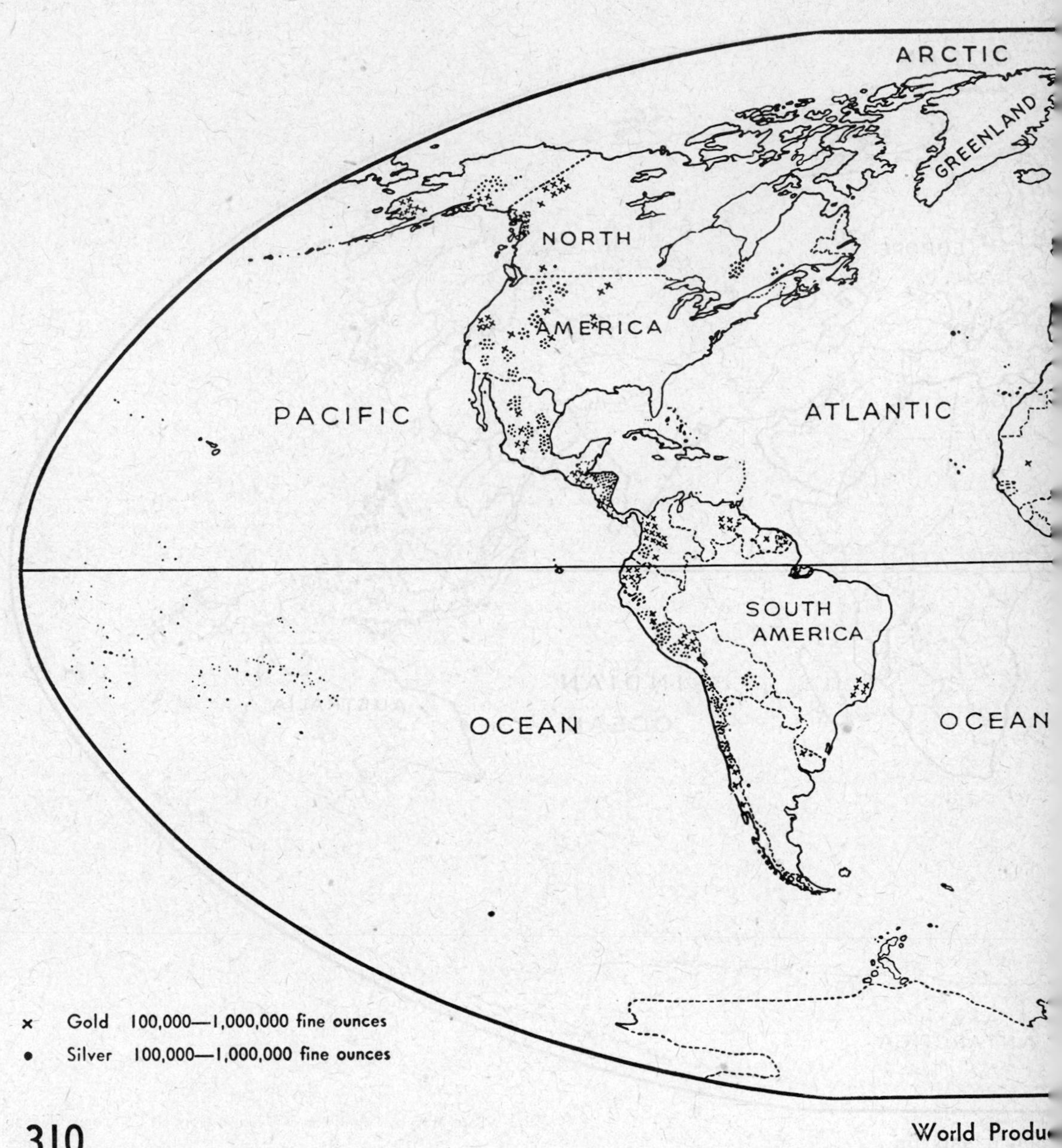
ARCTIC
GREENLAND
NORTH
AMERICA
PACIFIC
ATLANTIC
SOUTH
AMERICA
OCEAN
OCEAN
× Gold 100,000—1,000,000 fine ounces
• Silver 100,000—1,000,000 fine ounces

310

World Produ

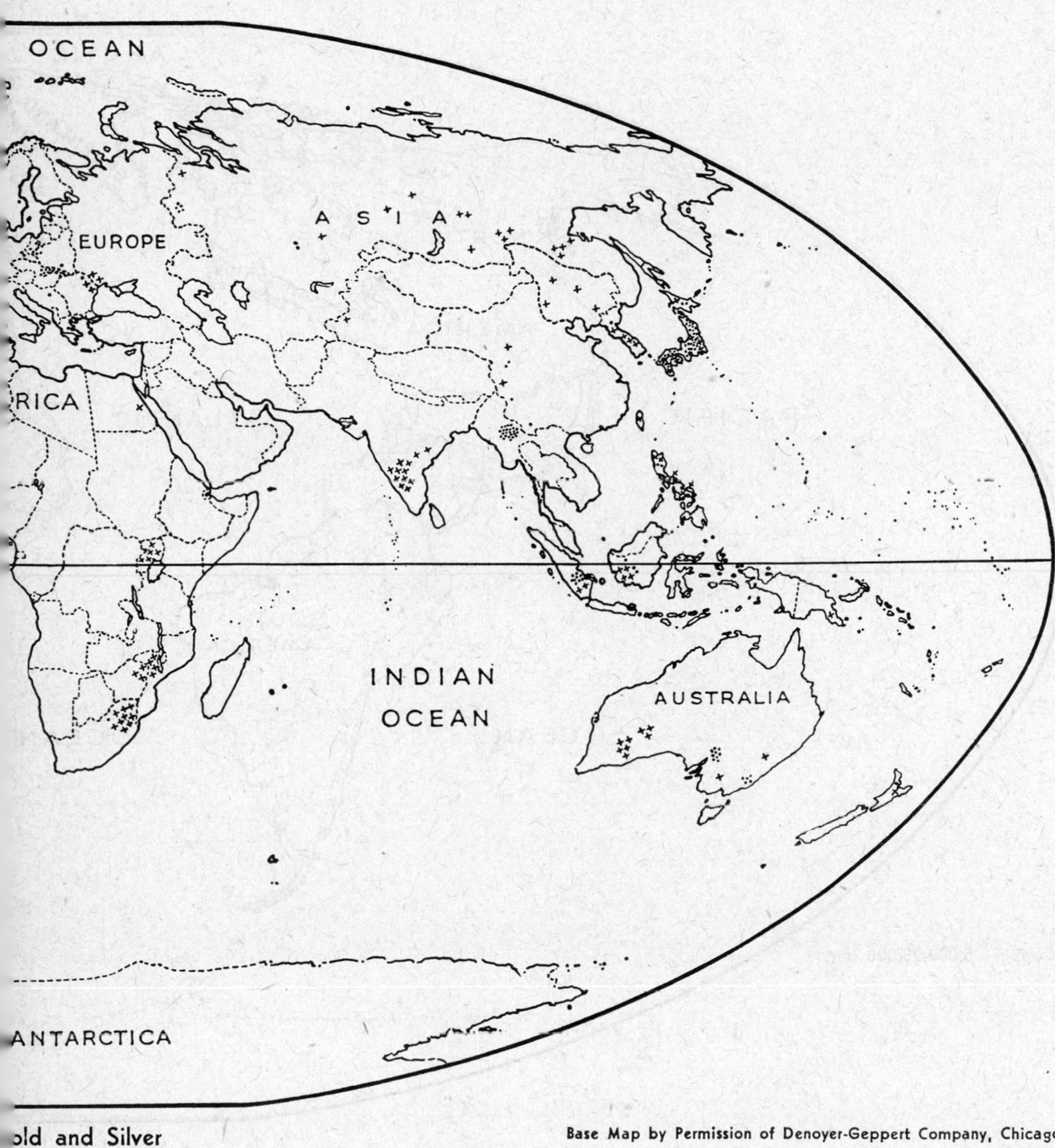

old and Silver

Base Map by Permission of Denoyer-Geppert Company, Chicago

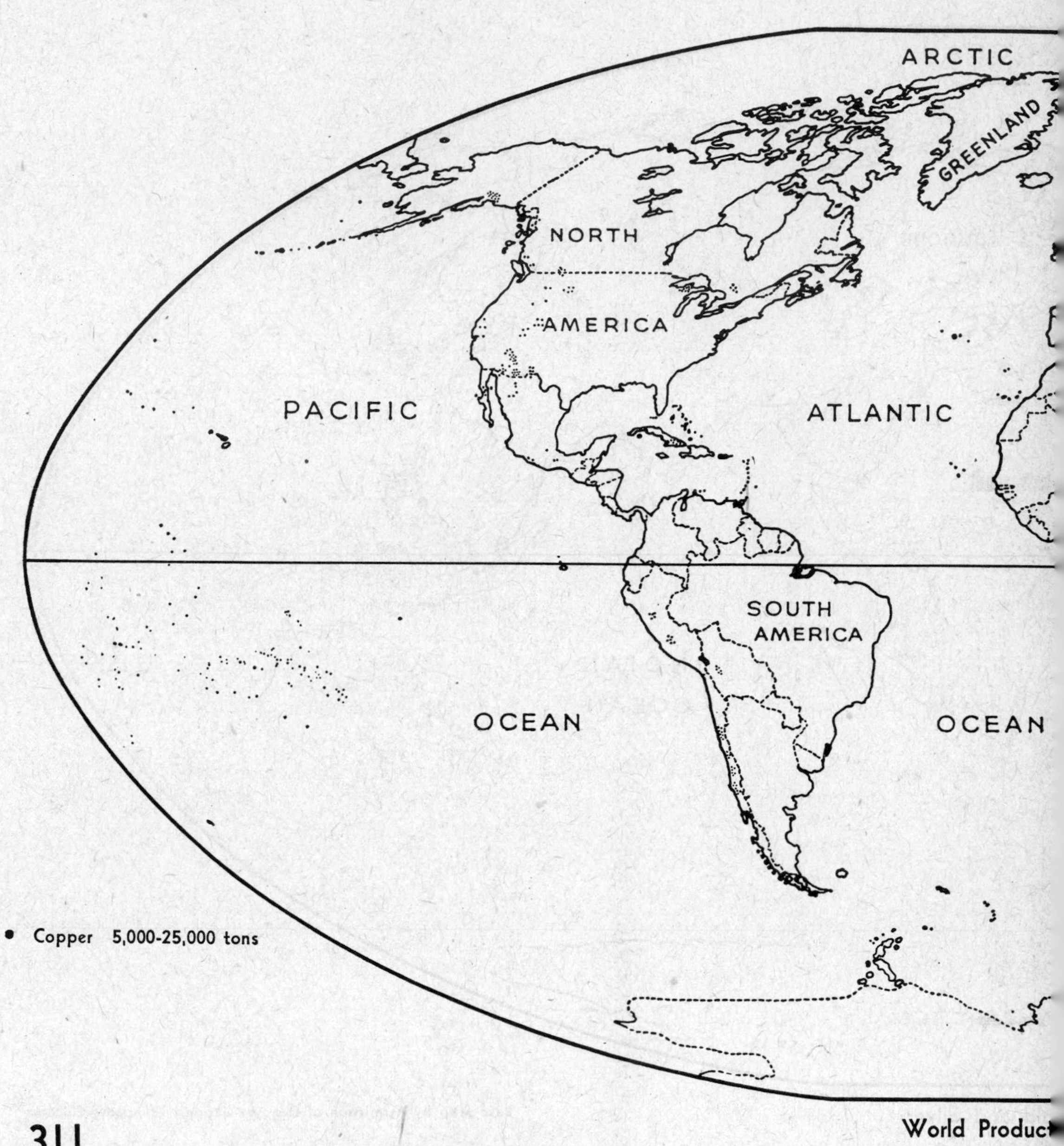

311

World Product

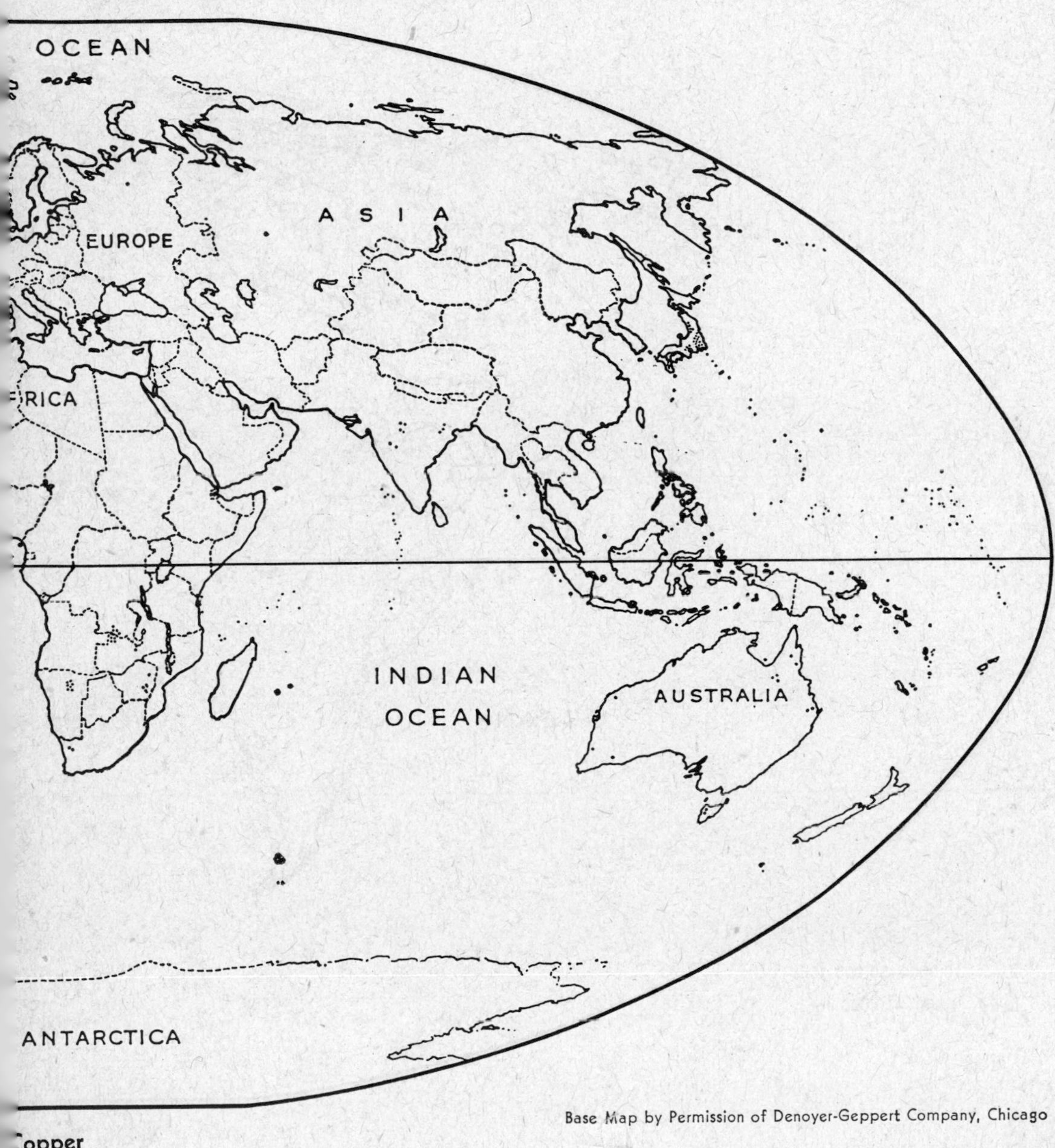

Base Map by Permission of Denoyer-Geppert Company, Chicago

Copper

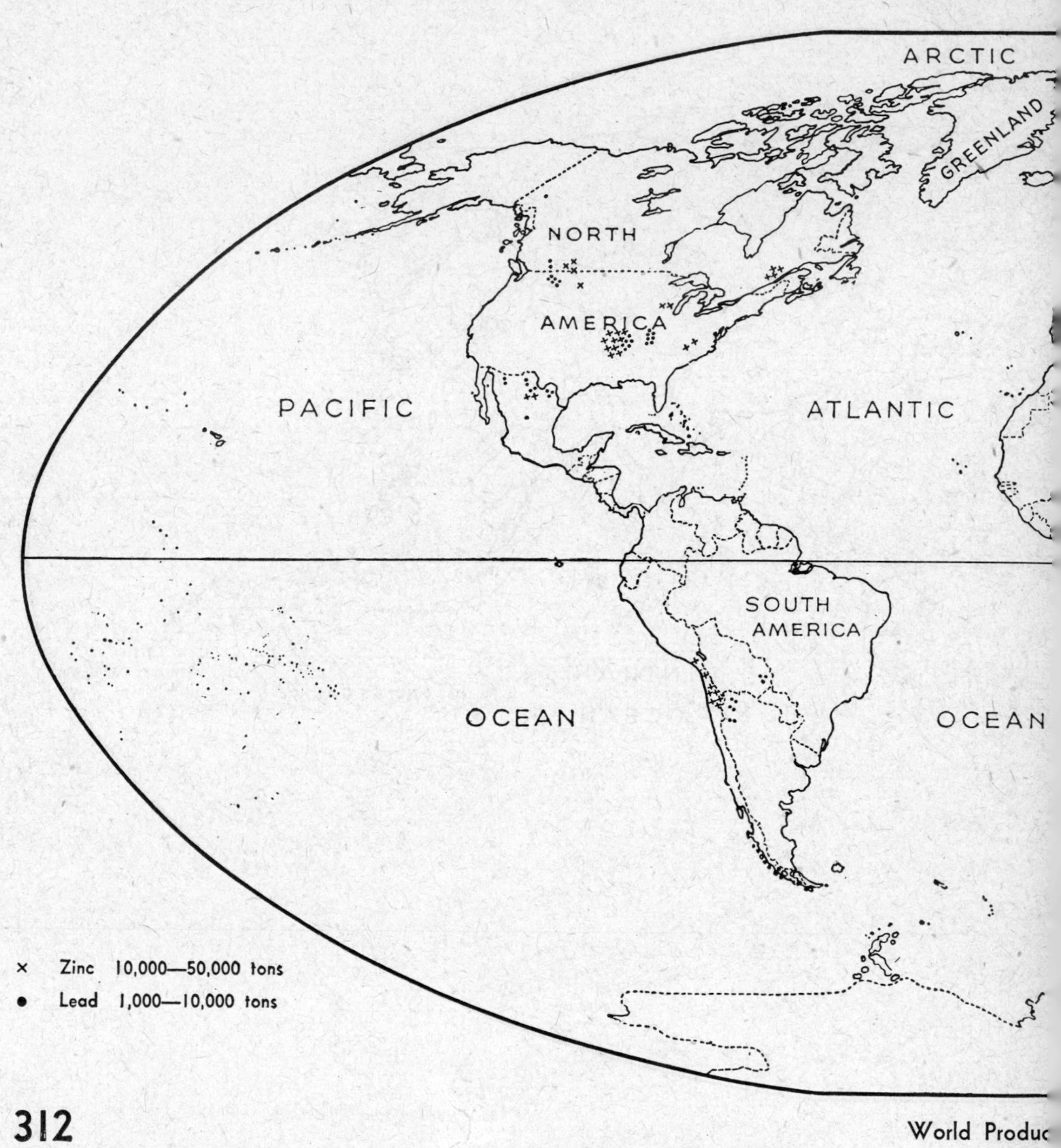

312

World Produc

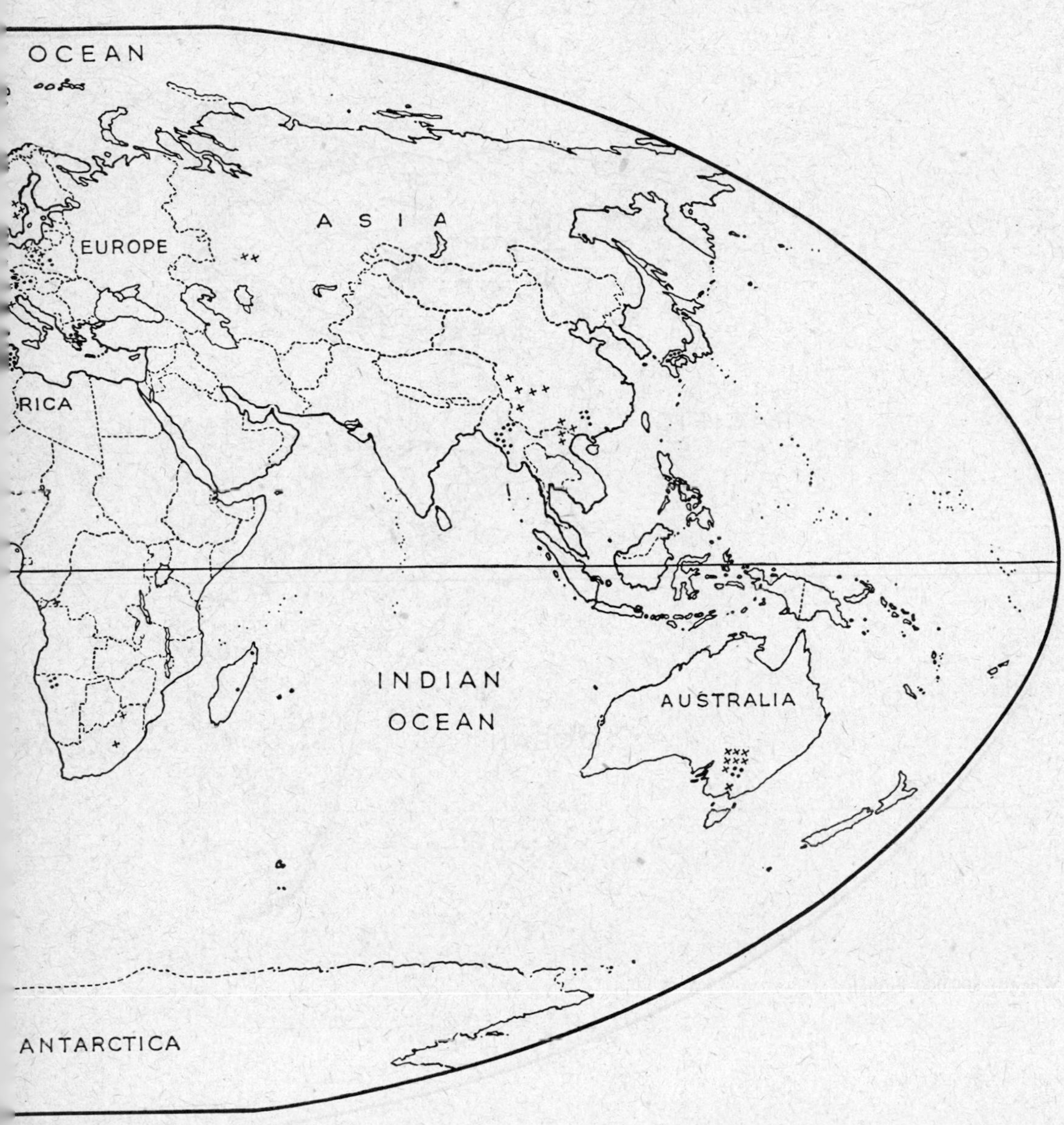

ːinc and Lead

Base Map by Permission of Denoyer-Geppert Company, Chicago

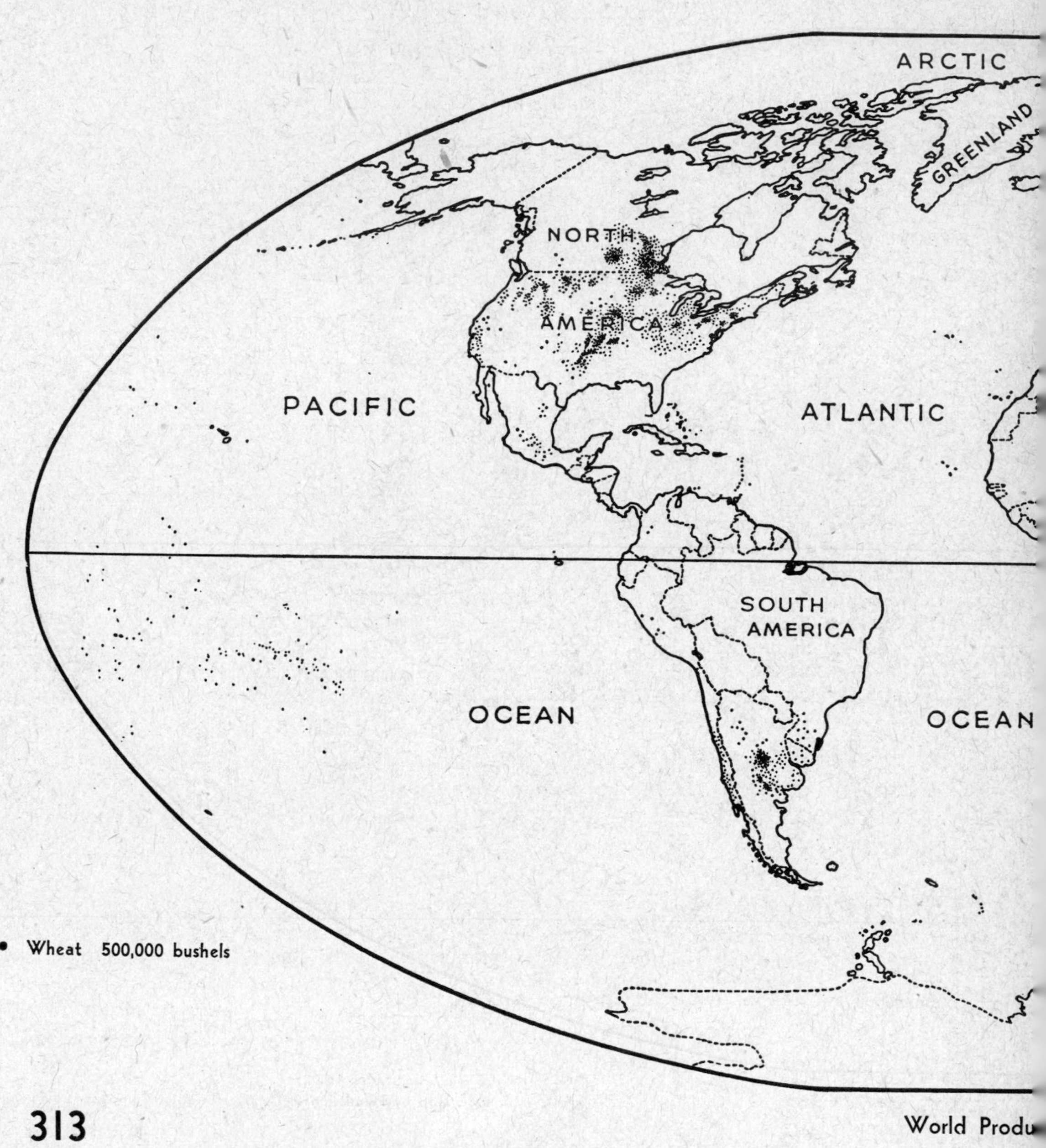

313

World Produ

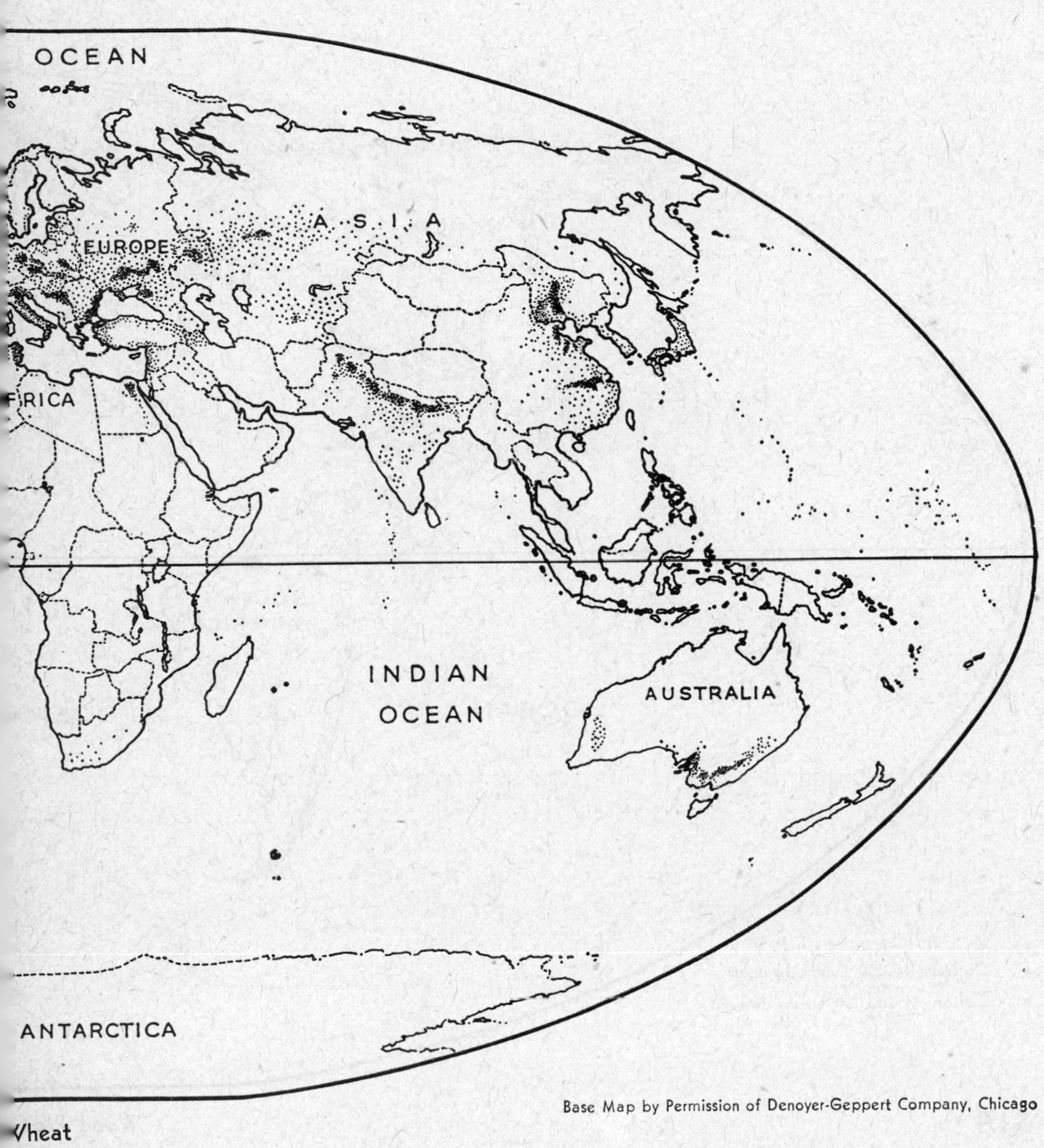

Base Map by Permission of Denoyer-Geppert Company, Chicago

Vheat

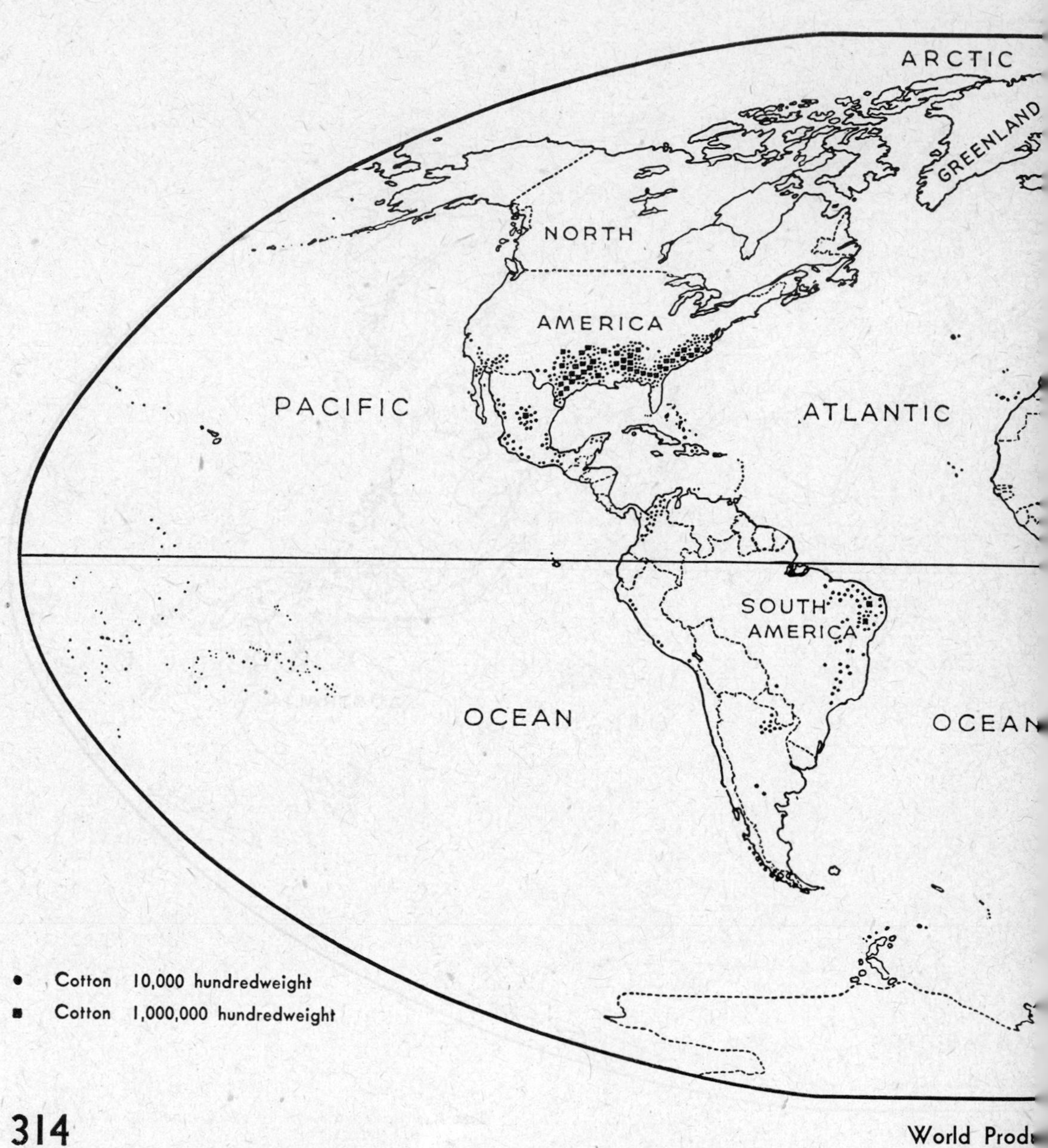

• Cotton 10,000 hundredweight
■ Cotton 1,000,000 hundredweight

314

World Prod

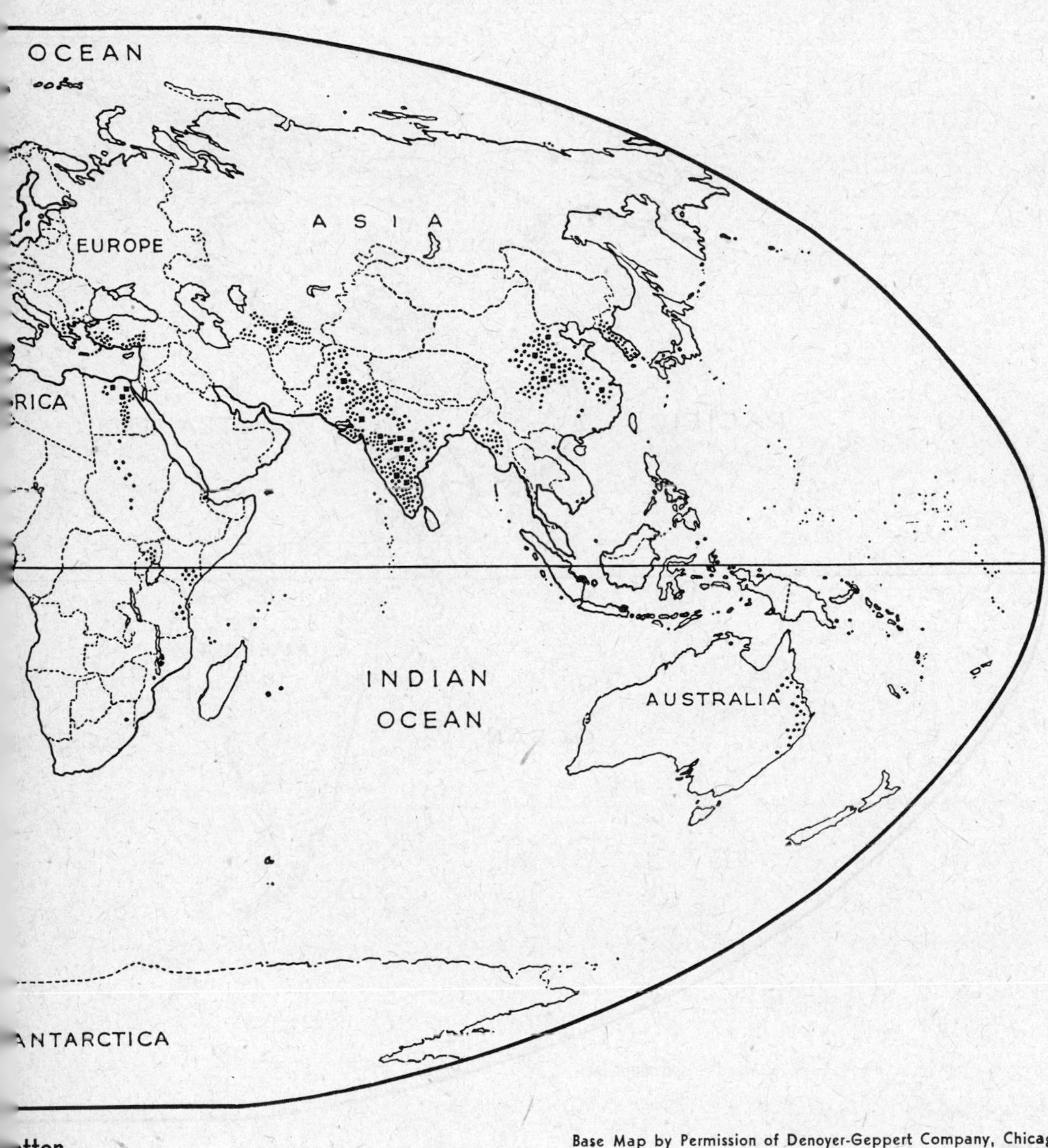

tton

Base Map by Permission of Denoyer-Geppert Company, Chicago

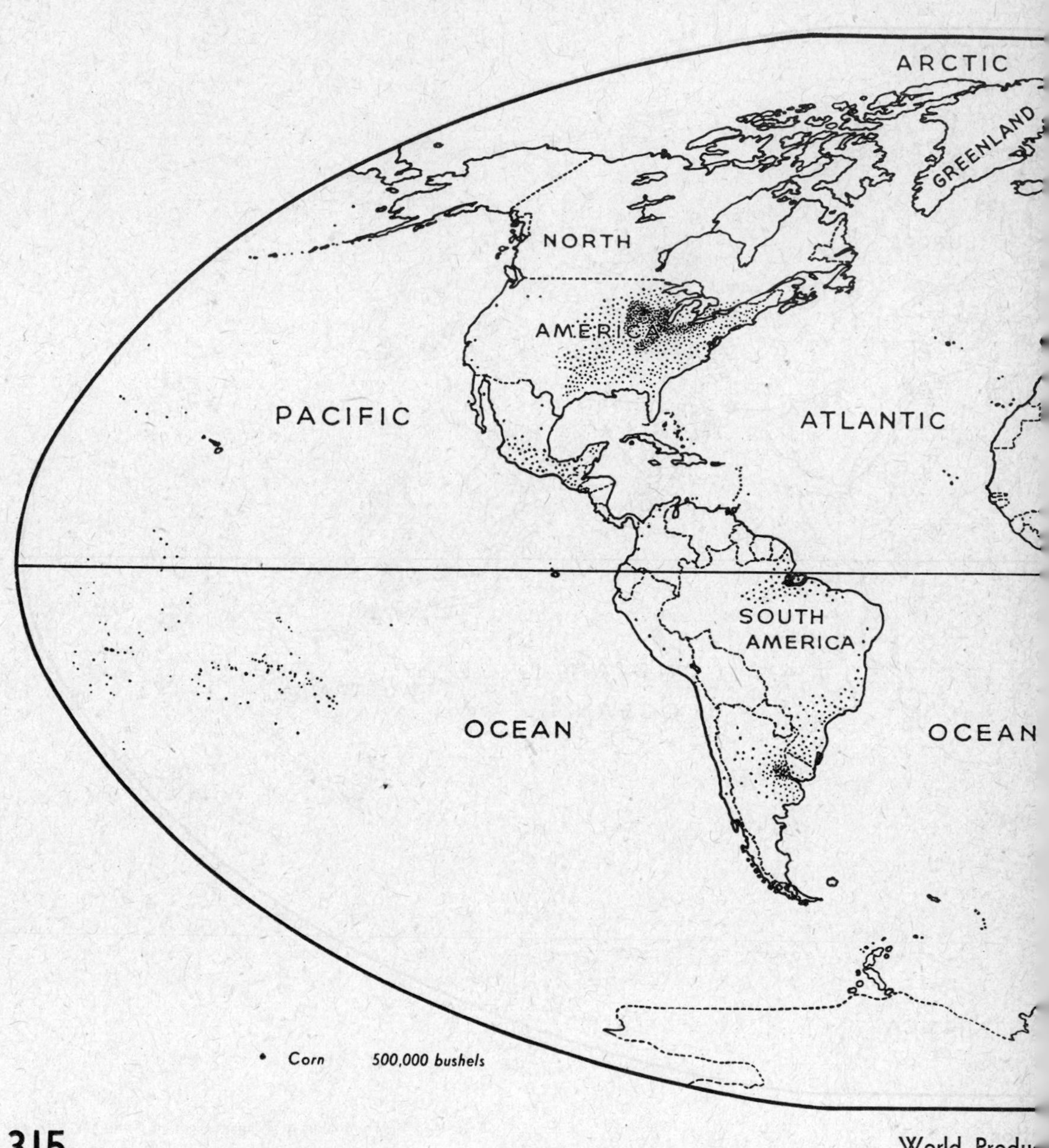

315

World Produ

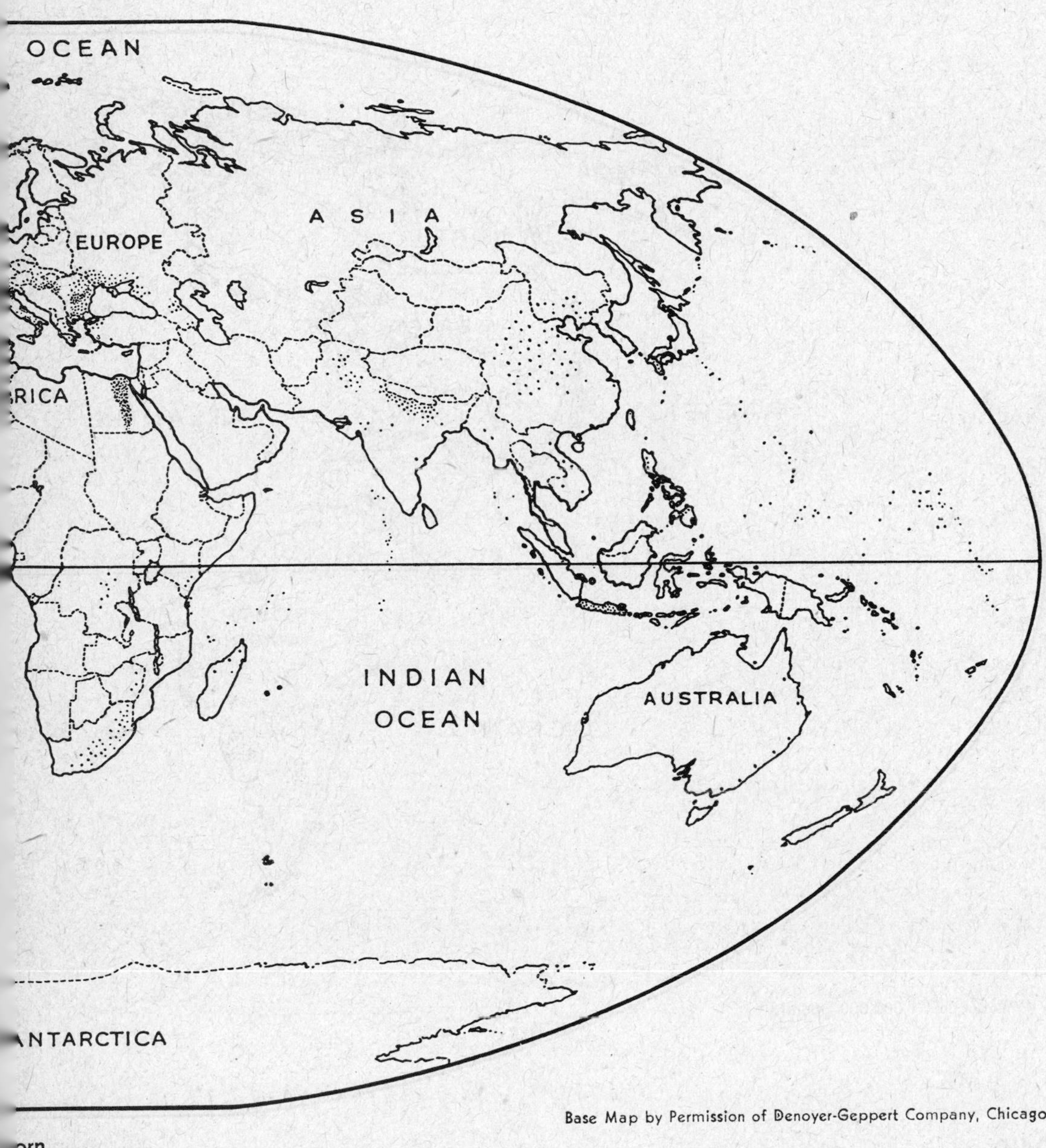

Base Map by Permission of Denoyer-Geppert Company, Chicago

orn

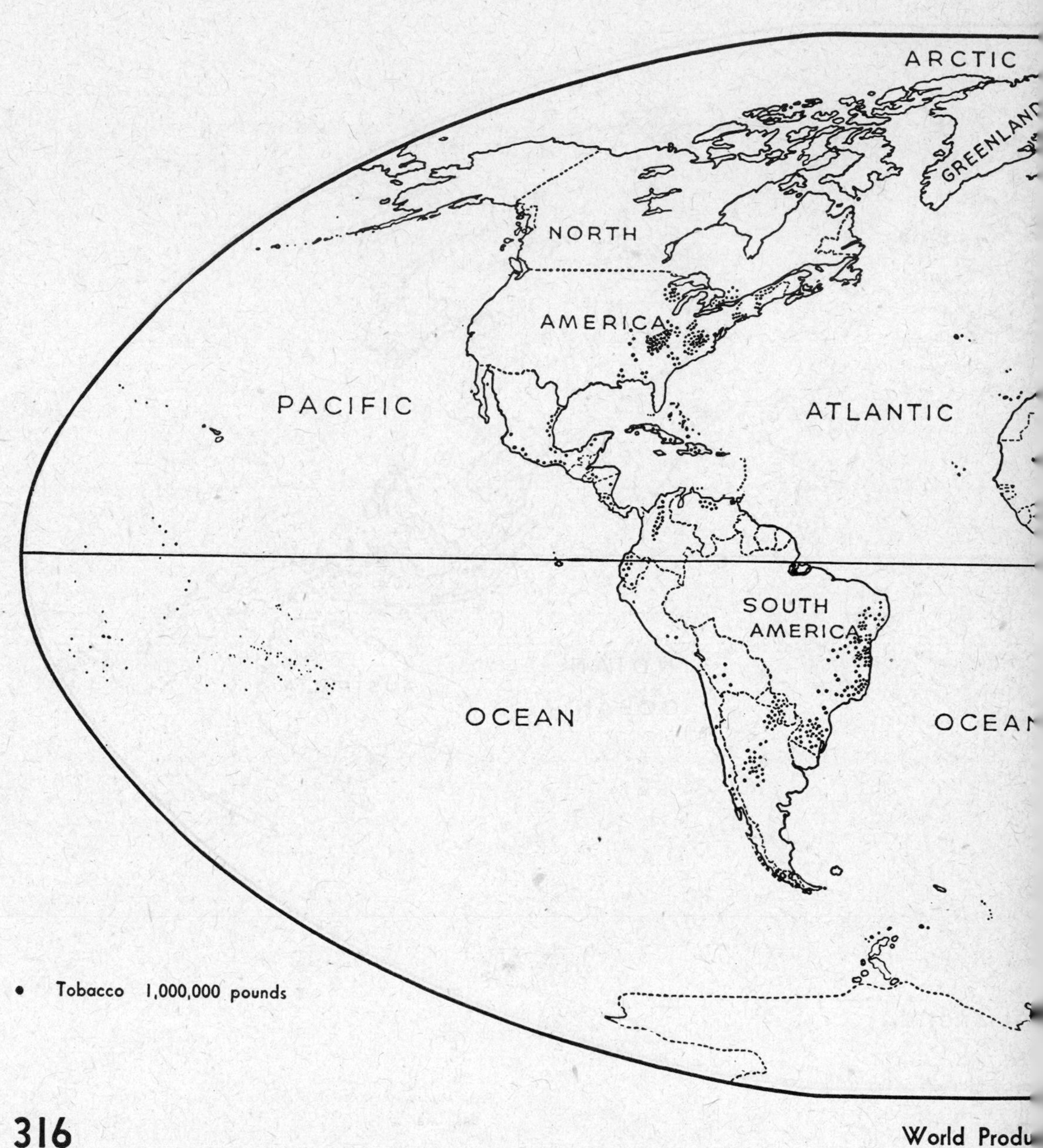
ARCTIC
GREENLAND
NORTH
AMERICA
PACIFIC
ATLANTIC
SOUTH
AMERICA
OCEAN
• Tobacco 1,000,000 pounds

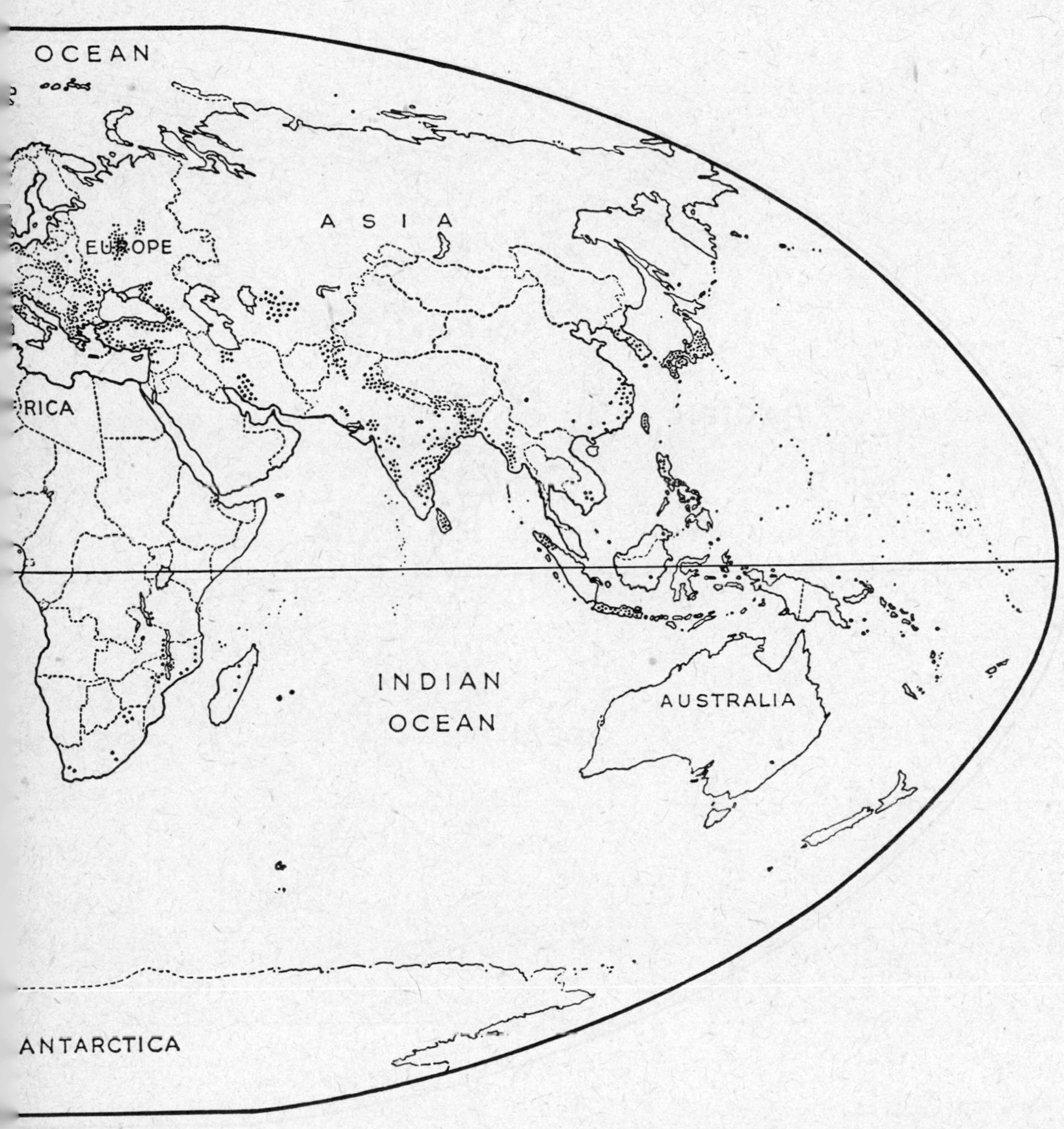

bacco

Base Map by Permission of Denoyer-Geppert Company, Chicago

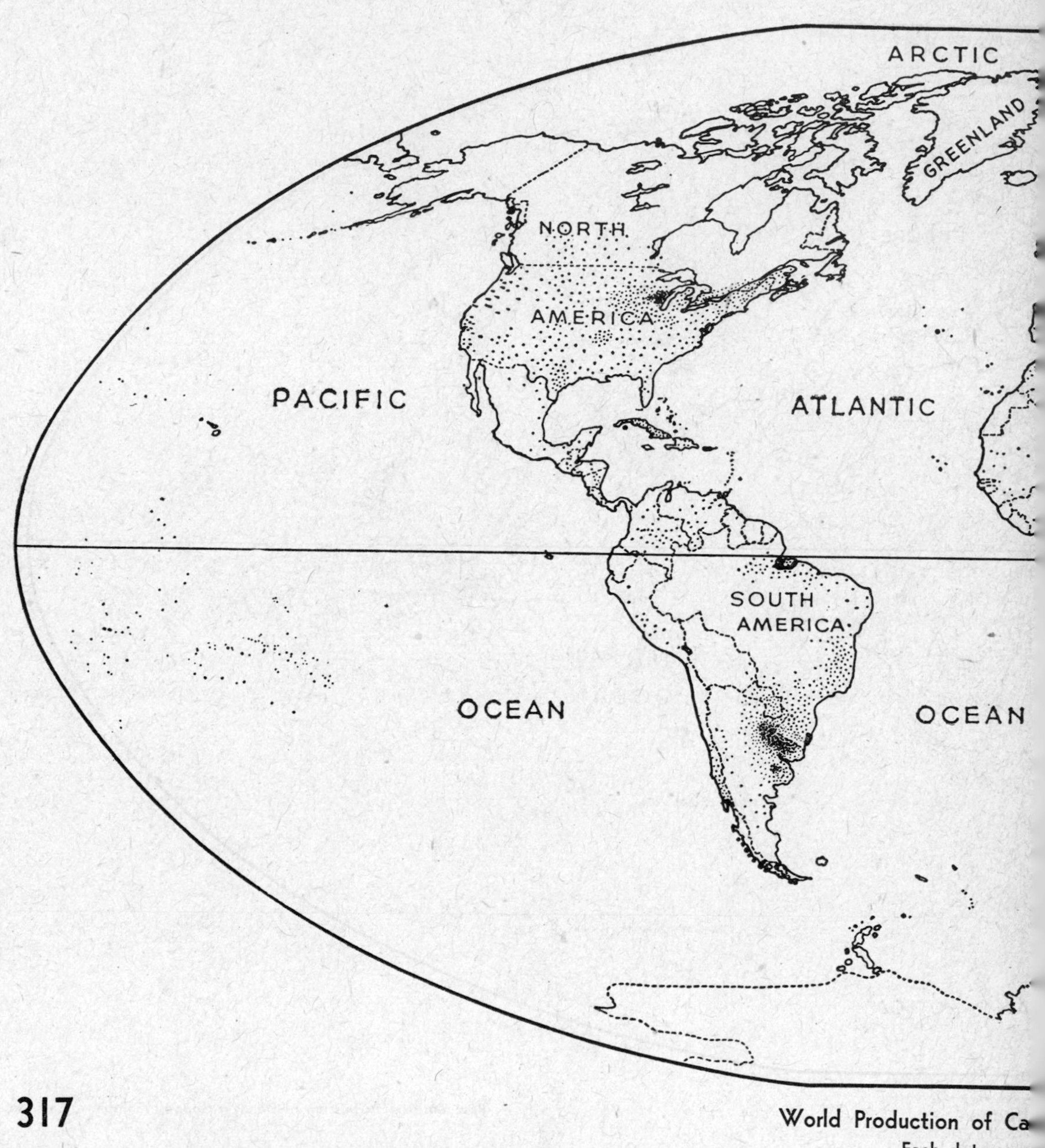

317 World Production of Ca

Each dot repre

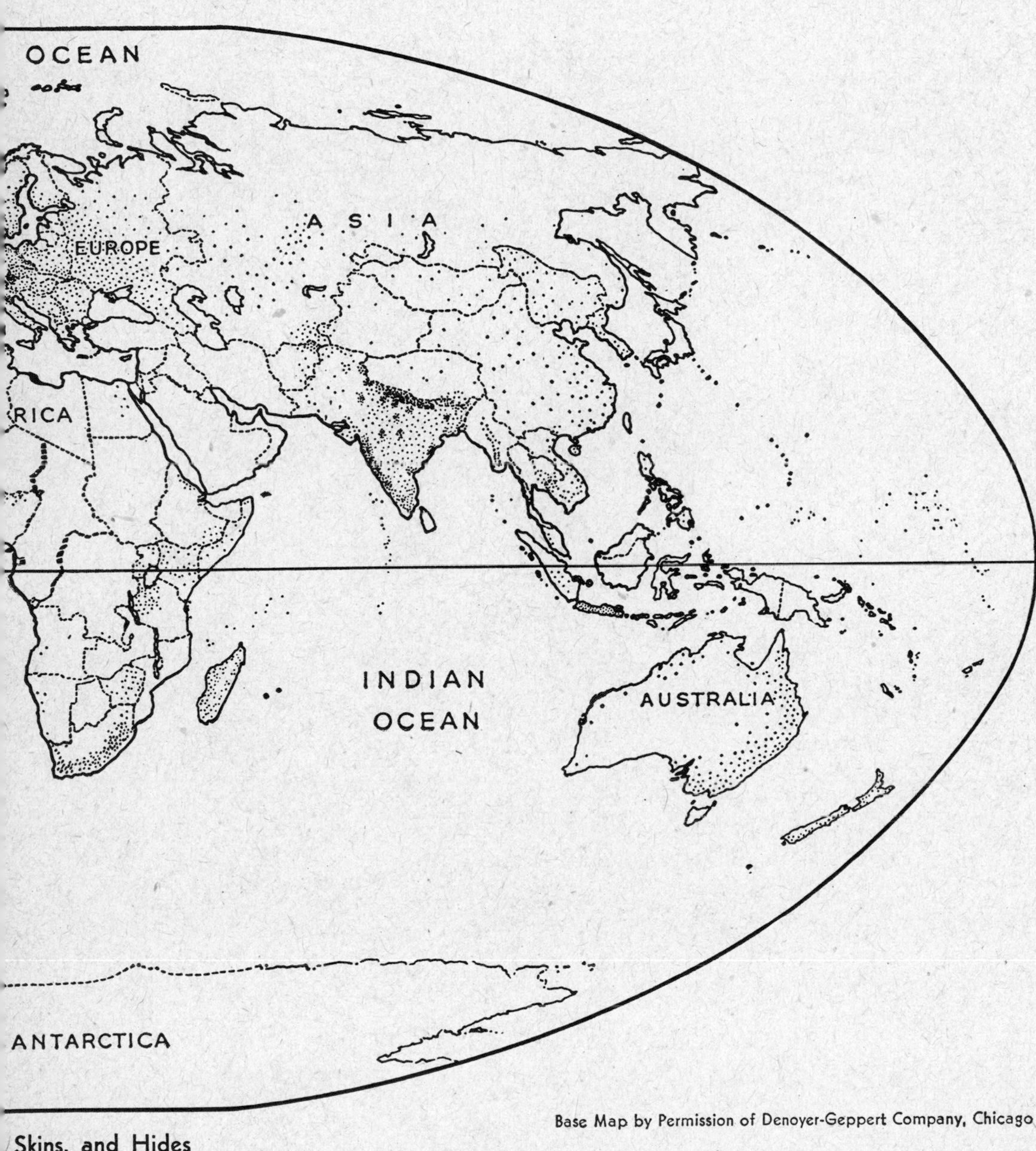

Base Map by Permission of Denoyer-Geppert Company, Chicago

Skins, and Hides
0 head

APPENDICES

	Date of Admission	1770	1780	1790	1800	1810	1820	1830	1840
New Hampshire		60,000	84,500	141,885	183,858	214,460	244,161	269,328	284,574
Massachusetts		265,000	307,000	378,787	422,845	472,040	523,287	610,408	737,699
Connecticut		175,000	203,000	237,946	251,002	261,942	275,248	297,675	309,978
Rhode Island		55,000	52,000	68,825	69,122	76,931	83,059	97,199	108,830
New York		160,000	200,000	340,120	589,051	959,049	1,372,812	1,918,608	2,428,921
New Jersey		110,000	137,000	184,139	211,149	245,562	277,575	320,823	373,306
Pennsylvania		250,000	335,000	434,373	602,365	810,091	1,049,485	1,348,233	1,724,033
Delaware		25,000	37,000	59,096	64,273	72,674	72,749	76,748	78,085
Maryland		200,000	250,000	319,728	341,548	380,546	407,350	447,040	470,019
Virginia		450,000	520,000	747,610	880,200	974,600	1,065,366	1,211,405	1,239,797
North Carolina		230,000	300,000	393,751	478,103	555,500	638,829	737,987	753,419
South Carolina		140,000	160,000	249,073	345,591	415,115	502,741	581,185	594,398
Georgia		26,000	55,000	82,548	162,686	252,433	340,989	516,823	691,392
Vermont	1791	—	—	—	154,465	217,895	235,981	280,652	291,948
Kentucky	1792	—	—	—	220,955	406,511	564,317	687,917	779,828
Tennessee	1796	—	—	—	105,602	261,727	422,823	681,904	829,210
District of Columbia	(1800)	—	—	—	14,093	24,023	33,039	39,834	43,712
Ohio	1803	—	—	—	—	230,760	581,434	937,903	1,519,467
Louisiana	1812	—	—	—	—	—	153,407	215,739	352,411
Indiana	1816	—	—	—	—	—	147,178	343,031	685,866
Mississippi	1817	—	—	—	—	—	75,448	136,621	375,651
Illinois	1818	—	—	—	—	—	55,211	157,445	476,183
Alabama	1819	—	—	—	—	—	127,901	309,527	590,756
Maine	1820	—	—	—	—	—	298,335	399,455	501,793
Missouri	1821	—	—	—	—	—	—	140,455	383,702
Arkansas	1836	—	—	—	—	—	—	—	97,574
Michigan	1837	—	—	—	—	—	—	—	212,267
Florida	1845	—	—	—	—	—	—	—	—
Texas	1845	—	—	—	—	—	—	—	—
Iowa	1846	—	—	—	—	—	—	—	—
Wisconsin	1848	—	—	—	—	—	—	—	—
California	1850	—	—	—	—	—	—	—	—
Minnesota	1858	—	—	—	—	—	—	—	—
Oregon	1859	—	—	—	—	—	—	—	—
Kansas	1861	—	—	—	—	—	—	—	—
West Virginia	1863	—	—	—	—	—	—	—	—
Nevada	1864	—	—	—	—	—	—	—	—
Nebraska	1867	—	—	—	—	—	—	—	—
Colorado	1876	—	—	—	—	—	—	—	—
North Dakota	1889	—	—	—	—	—	—	—	—
South Dakota	1889	—	—	—	—	—	—	—	—
Montana	1889	—	—	—	—	—	—	—	—
Washington	1889	—	—	—	—	—	—	—	—
Idaho	1890	—	—	—	—	—	—	—	—
Wyoming	1890	—	—	—	—	—	—	—	—
Utah	1896	—	—	—	—	—	—	—	—
Oklahoma	1907	—	—	—	—	—	—	—	—
New Mexico	1912	—	—	—	—	—	—	—	—
Arizona	1912	—	—	—	—	—	—	—	—
Totals		2,205,000	2,781,000	3,929,214	5,308,483	7,239,881	9,638,453	12,866,020	17,069,453

POPULATION, 1770-1940

1850	1860	1870	1880	1890	1900	1910	1920	1930	1940
317,976	326,073	318,300	346,991	376,530	411,588	430,572	443,083	465,293	491,524
994,514	1,231,066	1,457,351	1,783,085	2,238,947	2,085,346	3,336,416	3,852,356	4,249,614	4,316,721
370,792	460,467	537,454	622,700	746,258	908,420	1,114,756	1,380,631	1,606,903	1,709,242
147,545	174,620	217,353	276,531	345,506	428,556	542,610	604,397	687,497	713,346
3,097,394	3,880,735	4,382,759	5,082,871	6,003,174	7,268,894	9,113,614	10,385,227	12,588,066	13,479,142
489,555	672,035	906,096	1,131,116	1,444,933	1,883,669	2,537,167	3,155,900	4,041,334	4,160,165
2,311,786	2,906,215	3,521,951	4,282,891	5,258,113	6,302,115	7,665,111	8,720,017	9,631,350	9,900,180
91,532	112,216	125,015	146,608	168,493	184,735	202,322	223,003	238,386	266,505
583,034	687,049	780,894	934,943	1,042,390	1,188,044	1,295,346	1,449,661	1,631,526	1,821,244
1,421,611	1,596,318	1,225,163*	1,512,565	1,655,980	1,854,184	2,061,612	2,309,187	2,421,851	2,677,773
869,039	992,622	1,071,361	1,399,750	1,617,949	1,893,810	2,206,287	2,559,123	3,170,276	3,571,623
668,507	703,708	705,606	995,577	1,151,149	1,340,316	1,515,400	1,683,724	1,738,765	1,899,804
906,185	1,057,286	1,184,109	1,542,180	1,837,353	2,216,331	2,609,121	2,895,832	2,908,506	3,123,723
314,120	315,098	330,551	332,286	332,422	343,641	355,956	352,428	359,611	359,231
982,405	1,155,684	1,321,011	1,648,690	1,858,635	2,147,174	2,289,905	2,416,630	2,614,589	2,845,627
1,002,717	1,109,801	1,258,520	1,542,359	1,767,518	2,020,616	2,184,789	2,337,885	2,616,556	2,915,841
51,687	75,080	131,700	177,624	230,392	278,718	331,069	437,571	486,869	663,091
1,980,329	2,339,511	2,665,260	3,198,062	3,672,329	4,157,545	4,767,121	5,759,394	6,646,697	6,907,612
517,762	708,002	726,915	939,946	1,118,588	1,381,625	1,656,388	1,798,509	2,101,593	2,363,880
988,416	1,350,428	1,680,637	1,978,301	2,192,404	2,516,462	2,700,876	2,930,390	3,238,503	3,427,796
606,526	791,305	827,922	1,131,597	1,289,600	1,551,270	1,797,114	1,790,618	2,009,821	2,183,796
851,470	1,711,951	2,539,891	3,077,871	3,826,352	4,821,550	5,638,591	6,485,280	7,630,654	7,897,241
771,623	964,201	996,992	1,262,505	1,513,401	1,828,697	2,138,093	2,348,174	2,646,248	2,832,961
538,169	628,279	626,295	648,936	661,086	694,466	742,371	768,014	797,423	847,226
682,044	1,182,012	1,721,295	2,168,380	2,679,185	3,106,665	3,293,335	3,404,055	3,629,367	3,784,664
209,897	435,450	488,471	802,525	1,128,211	1,311,564	1,574,449	1,752,204	1,854,482	1,949,387
397,654	749,113	1,184,059	1,636,937	2,093,890	2,420,982	2,810,173	3,668,412	4,842,325	5,256,106
87,445	140,424	187,748	269,493	391,422	528,542	752,619	968,470	1,468,211	1,897,414
212,592	604,215	818,579	1,591,749	2,235,527	3,048,710	3,896,542	4,663,228	5,824,715	6,414,824
192,214	674,913	1,194,020	1,624,615	1,912,297	2,231,853	2,224,775	2,404,021	2,470,939	2,538,268
305,391	775,881	1,054,670	1,315,497	1,693,330	2,069,042	2,333,860	2,632,067	2,939,006	3,137,587
92,597	379,994	560,247	864,694	1,213,398	1,485,053	2,377,549	3,426,861	5,677,251	6,907,387
—	172,023	439,706	780,773	1,310,283	1,751,394	2,075,708	2,387,125	2,563,953	2,792,300
—	52,465	90,923	174,768	317,704	413,536	672,765	783,389	953,786	1,089,684
—	—	364,399	996,096	1,428,108	1,470,495	1,690,949	1,769,257	1,880,999	1,801,028
—	—	442,014	618,457	762,794	958,800	1,211,119	1,463,701	1,729,205	1,901,974
—	—	42,491	62,266	47,355	42,335	81,875	77,470	91,058	110,247
—	—	122,993	452,402	1,062,656	1,066,300	1,192,214	1,296,372	1,377,963	1,315,834
—	—	—	194,327	413,249	539,700	799,024	939,629	1,035,791	1,123,296
—	—	—	—	190,983	391,146	577,056	646,872	680,845	641,935
—	—	—	—	348,600	401,570	583,888	636,547	692,849	642,961
—	—	—	—	142,924	243,329	376,053	548,889	837,606	559,456
—	—	—	—	357,232	518,103	1,141,990	1,356,621	1,563,396	1,736,191
—	—	—	—	88,548	161,772	325,594	431,866	445,032	524,873
—	—	—	—	62,555	92,531	145,965	194,402	225,565	250,742
—	—	—	—	—	276,749	373,351	449,396	507,847	550,310
—	—	—	—	—	—	1,657,155	2,028,283	2,396,040	2,336,434
—	—	—	—	—	—	—	360,350	423,317	531,818
—	—	—	—	—	—	—	334,162	435,573	499,261
23,191,876	31,443,321	38,558,371	50,155,783	62,947,714	75,994,575	91,972,266	105,710,620	122,775,046	131,669,275

* West Virginia was separated from Virginia in 1863.

APPENDIX II

PRESIDENTIAL ELECTIONS

These tables are arranged so as to show the votes of one party in the same relative position throughout. Thus, after 1800, the first column shows, not necessarily the winning candidate, but the candidate of the Democratic party, while the second column shows the vote of the Whig and later of the Republican candidate. This gives the best possible chance to compare the shifts of voting strength between the parties from one election to the next. States are arranged in the order of their admission. Capitals mark the name of the successful candidate. Bold-face figures show the majority or plurality candidate in each state.

Only the electoral votes are given through 1824. Popular votes were taken in but a few of the states prior to that time, and where taken, the statistics are both hard to get and unreliable. Since prior to the passage of the Twelfth Amendment, members of the Electoral College put the names of two men on their ballots, the man receiving the highest number to become President, and the next highest, Vice-President, the names of both appear on the tally of the ballot through 1800. Up to that date, the name of the successful presidential candidate appears in capitals, that of the vice-presidential candidate in italicized capitals.

Correlation of these tables to the suffrage maps will be rewarding. The astounding increase of vote totals in many states between 1820 and 1828 is not to be accounted for by population increase alone. And there are many instances where small popular votes in states maintaining tax-paying qualifications yet having their electoral vote based on the total of the white population plus three-fifths of the slaves, had equal weight in the Electoral College with more democratic states casting much larger popular votes.

"LEGIS." indicates that the electors were chosen by the Legislature, not by popular vote. "UNAN." indicates that the successful candidate in that state had no formal opposition. "Maj." is used in the one case where the full vote totals appear to be unobtainable, but where the figure of the majority of the successful candidate over his opposition is available.

Owing to incomplete reporting by many states, the figures on minor party votes are inconclusive and incomplete. The official national totals of minor candidates are given below the totals of the major parties. The later figures are based on the official returns compiled by the Clerk of the House of Representatives. Returns in the early elections were taken from the *American* and the *Tribune Almanacs*. Electoral votes are published in the *Annals of Congress*, and for 1824 in the *Register of Debates*.

PRESIDENTIAL ELECTORAL VOTES TO 1824

	1788												1792					1796												
	WASHINGTON	*ADAMS*	Huntingdon	Jay	Hancock	Harrison	G. Clinton	Rutledge	Milton	Amesbury	Telfair	Lincoln	WASHINGTON	*ADAMS*	G. Clinton	Jefferson	Burr	ADAMS	*JEFFERSON*	Washington	T. Pinckney	Burr	S. Adams	Ellsworth	S. Johnston	Iredell	Jay	G. Clinton	C. C. Pinckney	J. Henry
New Hampshire	5	5											6	6				6						6						
Massachusetts	10	10											16	16				16			13			1	2					
Connecticut	7	5	2										9	9				9			4						5			
New Jersey	6	1		5									7	7				7			7									
Pennsylvania	10	8			2								15	14	1			1	14		2	13								
Delaware	3			3									3	3				3			3									
Maryland	6					6							8	8				7	4		4	3								2
Virginia	10	5		1	1		3						21		21			1	20	1	1	1	15					3		
South Carolina	7				1			6					8	7			1		8		8									
Georgia	5								2	1	1	1	4		4				4									4		
New York													12		12			12			12									
North Carolina													12		12			1	11	1	1	6				3			1	
Rhode Island													4			4		4						4						
Vermont													3	3				4			4									
Kentucky													4	4					4			4								
Tennessee																			3			3								
TOTALS	69	34	2	9	4	6	3	6	2	1	1	1	132	77	50	4	1	71	68	2	59	30	15	11	2	3	5	7	1	2

PRESIDENTIAL ELECTORAL VOTES TO 1824

	1800					1804		1808			1812		1816		1820		1824			
	JEFFERSON (D)	*BURR* (D)	Adams (F)	Pinckney (F)	Jay (F)	JEFFERSON (D)	Pinckney (F)	MADISON (D)	G. Clinton	Pinckney (F)	MADISON (D)	D. Clinton (F)	MONROE (D)	King (F)	MONROE (D)	J. Q. Adams	Jackson (D)	J. Q. ADAMS (NR)‡	Crawford (D)	Clay (NR)
New Hampshire			6	6		7				7		8	8		7	1		8		
Massachusetts			16	16		19				19		22		22	15			15		
Connecticut			9	9			9			9		9		9	9			8		
Rhode Island			4	3	1	4				4			4		4			4		
New York	12	12				19		13	6			29	29		29		1	26	5	4
New Jersey			7	7		8		8				8	8		8		8			
Pennsylvania	8	8	7	7		20		20			25		25		24		28			
Delaware			3	3			3			3		4		3	4			1	2	
Maryland	5	5	5	5		9	2	9		2	6	5	8		11		7	3	1	
Virginia	21	21				24		24			25		25		25				24	
North Carolina	8	8	4	4		14		11		3	15		15		15		15			
South Carolina	8	8				10		10			11		11		11		11			
Georgia	4	4				6		6			8		8		8				9	
Vermont			4	4		6		6			8		8		8			7		
Kentucky	4	4				8		7			12		12		12					14
Tennessee	3	3				5		5			8		8		7		11			
Ohio						3		3			7		8		8					16
Louisiana											3		3		3		3	2		
Indiana													3		3		5			
Mississippi															2		3			
Illinois															3		2	1		
Alabama															3		5			
Maine															9			9		
Missouri															3†					3
TOTALS	73*	73*	65	64	1	162	14	122	6	47	128	89	183	34	208	[1	99	84	41	37

* Elected by the House of Representatives.
† Vote not allowed.
‡ Elected by the House of Representatives.

PRESIDENTIAL ELECTIONS, 1824–1940

	1824				1828		1832		1836	
	Jackson (D)	J. Q. ADAMS (NR)	Crawford (D)	Clay (NR)	JACKSON (D)	J. Q. Adams (NR)	JACKSON (D)	Clay (W)	VAN BUREN (D)	Others W, (etc.)
New Hampshire	643	**4,170**			20,692	**24,076**	**25,486**	19,010	**18,722**	6,228
Massachusetts		**30,687**	6,616		6,019	**29,836**	14,545	**33,003**	33,501	**41,093†**
Connecticut		**7,587**	1,978		4,448	**13,829**	11,269	**17,755**	**19,234**	18,466
Rhode Island		**2,145**	200		821	**2,754**	2,126	**2,810**	**2,964**	2,710
New York		LEGIS. SPLIT TICKET			**140,763**	135,413	**168,497**	154,896	**166,815**	138,543
New Jersey	**10,985**	9,110	1,196		21,950	**23,758**	**23,856**	23,393	26,347	**26,892‡**
Pennsylvania	**36,100**	5,440	4,206	1,609	**101,652**	50,848	**90,983**	66,716	**91,475**	87,111
Delaware		LEGIS. SPLIT TICKET			4,349	**4,769**	4,110	**4,276**	4,155	**4,738‡**
Maryland	14,523	**14,632**	3,646	695	24,578	**25,759**	19,156	**19,160**	22,167	**25,852‡**
Virginia	2,861	3,189	**8,849**	416	**26,752**	12,101	**33,609**	11,451	**30,261**	23,368
North Carolina	**20,415**	15,621			**37,857**	13,918	**24,862**	4,563	**26,910**	23,626
South Carolina	LEGIS.				LEGIS.		**			LEGIS.§
Georgia			LEGIS.		**18,709**		**20,750**		22,126	**24,930‖**
Vermont		LEGIS.			8,205	**24,784**	7,870	**11,152***	14,037	**20,991‡**
Kentucky	6,453			**16,782**	**39,084**	31,172	36,247	**43,396**	33,435	**36,955‡**
Tennessee	**20,197**	216	312		**44,090**	2,240	**28,740**	1,436	26,120	**35,962‖**
Ohio	18,457	12,280		**19,255**	**67,597**	63,396	**81,246**	76,349	96,948	**105,405‡**
Louisiana	LEGIS. SPLIT				**4,605**	4,097	**4,049**	2,528	**3,653**	3,383
Indiana	**7,343**	3,095		5,315	**22,237**	17,052	**31,552**	15,472	32,480	**41,381‡**
Mississippi	**3,234**	1,694	119		**6,763**	1,581	**5,919**		**9,979**	9,688
Illinois	**1,901**	1,542	219	1,047	**6,763**	1,581	**14,147**	5,429	**18,097**	14,983
Alabama	**9,443**	2,416	1,680	67	**17,138**	1,938	UNAN.		10,068¶	**15,637**
Maine	2,330	**6,870**			13,927	**20,773**	**33,291**	27,204	**22,300**	15,239
Missouri	987	311		**1,401**	**8,232**	3,422	**5,192 maj.**		**10,995**	8,337
Arkansas									**2,400**	1,238
Michigan									**7,360**	4,000
TOTALS	**152,899**	105,321	47,265	47,087	**650,028**	512,158	**687,502**	550,189	**762,149**	736,736

Wirt 33,108.

* Electoral vote cast for Wm. Wirt, Anti-Masonic.
** Legislature cast vote for Floyd.
† Electoral vote cast for Webster (W).
‡ Electoral vote cast for Harrison (W).
§ Electoral vote cast for Mangum.
‖ Electoral vote cast for H. White.
¶ Electoral vote cast for Van Buren (D).

	1840			1844			1848			1852		
	Van Buren (D)	HARRISON (W)	Birney (L)	POLK (D)	Clay (W)	Birney (L)	Cass (D)	TAYLOR (W)	Van Buren (FS)	PIERCE (D)	Scott (W)	Hale (FS)
New Hampshire	**32,670**	26,434	126	**27,150**	17,866	4,161	**27,763**	14,781	7,560	**28,997**	16,147	6,695
Massachusetts	51,948	**72,874**	1,621	52,985	**66,872**	10,830	35,284	**61,072**	38,133	46,880	**56,063**	29,993
Connecticut	**35,296**	31,601	174	29,841	**32,842**	1,943	7,046	**30,314**	5,005	**33,249**	30,359	3,160
Rhode Island	3,301	**5,278**	42	4,848	**7,323**	107	3,600	**6,689**	705	**8,735**	7,626	644
New York	212,519	**225,812**	2,798	**237,588**	232,473	15,812	114,592	**218,551**	120,519	**262,083**	234,882	25,329
New Jersey	31,034	**33,362**	69	37,495	**38,318**	131	36,830	**40,009**	849	**44,305**	38,556	350
Pennsylvania	143,676	**144,019**	343	**167,535**	161,203	3,126	172,661	**186,113**	11,263	**198,568**	179,122	8,524
Delaware	4,884	**5,967**		5,969	**6,257**		5,910	**6,440**	80	**6,318**	6,293	62
Maryland	28,752	**33,528**		33,676	**35,984**		34,528	**37,702**	125	**40,022**	35,077	54
Virginia	**43,893**	42,501		**49,417**	43,677		**46,586**	45,124	9	**72,413**	57,132	
North Carolina	34,218	**46,676**		39,287	**43,232**		38,869	**43,519**	85	**39,744**	39,058	59
South Carolina	LEGIS.			LEGIS.			LEGIS.			LEGIS.		
Georgia	31,933	**40,264**		**44,155**	42,106		44,736	**47,603**		**34,705**	16,660	
Vermont	18,009	**32,445**	319	18,041	**26,700**	3,957	10,948	**23,122**	13,857	13,044	**22,173**	8,621
Kentucky	32,616	**58,489**		51,980	**61,262**		49,720	**67,141**		53,806	**57,068**	265
Tennessee	48,289	**60,391**		59,915	**60,039**		58,419	**64,705**		57,018	**58,898**	
Ohio	124,782	**148,157**	903	149,061	**155,113**	8,050	**154,783**	138,356	35,494	**169,220**	152,526	31,682
Louisiana	7,617	**11,297**		**13,417**	12,818		15,380	**18,273**		**18,647**	17,255	
Indiana	51,695	**65,308**		**70,181**	67,867	2,106	**74,745**	69,907	8,100	**95,299**	80,901	6,934
Mississippi	16,995	**19,518**		**25,188**	19,193		**26,555**	25,821		**26,876**	17,548	
Illinois	**47,476**	45,537	149	**55,515**	45,612	3,579	**56,629**	53,215	15,804	**80,597**	64,934	9,966
Alabama	**33,991**	28,471		**36,223**	24,850		**31,363**	30,482		**26,881**	15,038	
Maine	46,201	**46,612**	194	**45,719**	34,378	4,836	**40,195**	35,273	12,157	**41,609**	32,534	8,030
Missouri	**29,760**	22,972		**41,369**	31,251		32,671	**40,077**		**36,642**	28,944	
Arkansas	**6,049**	4,363		**9,546**	5,504		**9,300**	7,588		**12,173**	7,401	
Michigan	21,098	**22,907**	321	**27,703**	24,223	3,632	**30,687**	23,940	10,389	**41,842**	33,860	7,237
Florida							3,238	**4,539**		**4,318**	2,875	
Texas							**8,801**	3,777		**13,552**	4,995	
Iowa							**12,051**	10,557	1,126	**8,624**	7,444	777
Wisconsin							**15,001**	13,747	10,417	**33,658**	22,240	8,814
California										**39,665**	34,971	100
TOTALS	1,128,702	**1,274,783**	7,609	**1,335,834**	1,297,033	62,270	1,222,455	**1,362,031**	291,678	**1,590,490**	1,378,589	157,296

	1856			1860				1864		1868	
	BUCHANAN (D)	Fremont (R)	Fillmore (A)	Douglas (D)	Breckenridge (SRD)	LINCOLN (R)	Bell (CU)	McClellan (D)	LINCOLN (U)	Seymour (D)	GRANT (R)
New Hampshire	32,567	**38,158**	414	25,811	2,112	**37,519**	441	32,871	**36,400**	31,224	**38,191**
Massachusetts	39,240	**108,190**	19,626	34,372	5,939	**106,533**	22,331*	48,745	**126,742**	59,408	**136,477**
Connecticut	34,995	**42,715**	2,615	38,516	34,334	**39,173**	6,817	42,285	**44,691**	47,600	**50,641**
Rhode Island	**6,680**	1,467	1,675	7,707*		**12,244**		8,718	**14,349**	6,548	**12,993**
New York	195,878	**274,705**	124,604	303,329*		**353,804**		361,986	**368,735**	**429,883**	419,883
New Jersey	**46,943**	28,531	24,115	**62,801***		58,324		**68,124**	60,723	**83,001**	80,121
Pennsylvania	**230,154**	147,350	82,178	16,765	178,871*	**268,030**	12,776	276,316	**296,391**	313,382	**342,281**
Delaware	**8,003**	306	6,175	1,023	**7,337**	3,815	3,863	**8,767**	8,155	**10,980**	7,623
Maryland	**39,115**	281	47,462	5,966	**42,482**	2,294	41,760	32,739	**40,153**	**62,357**	30,438
Virginia	**89,975**	291	60,039	16,290	74,323	1,929	**74,681**				
North Carolina	**48,246**		36,886	2,701	**48,539**		44,990			84,090	**96,226**
South Carolina	LEGIS.				LEGIS.					45,237	**62,301**
Georgia	**56,617**		42,372	11,590	**51,889**		42,886			**102,822**	57,134
Vermont	10,577	**39,561**	511	6,849	218	**33,808**	1,969	13,321	**42,419**	12,045	**44,167**
Kentucky	**72,917**	369	65,822	25,651	66,058	1,364	**66,058**	**64,301**	27,786	**115,889**	39,566
Tennessee	**73,638**		66,178	11,350	64,709		**69,274**			26,311	**56,757**
Ohio	170,874	**187,497**	28,125	187,232	11,405	**231,610**	12,194	205,568	**265,154**	84,090	**96,226**
Louisiana	**22,169**		20,709	7,625	**22,681**		20,204			**80,225**	33,263
Indiana	**118,672**	94,816	23,386	115,509	12,295	**139,033**	5,306	130,233	**150,422**	166,980	**176,552**
Mississippi	**35,665**		24,490	3,283	**40,797**		25,040				
Illinois	**104,279**	96,280	37,451	160,215	2,404	**172,161**	4,913	158,730	**189,496**	199,143	**250,293**
Alabama	**46,817**		28,557	12,651	**48,831**		27,875			72,086	**76,366**
Maine	38,035	**65,514**	3,233	26,693	6,368	**62,811**	2,046	46,992	**68,114**	42,396	**70,426**
Missouri	**58,164**		48,524	**58,801**	31,317	17,028	58,372	31,678	**72,750**	59,788	**85,651**
Arkansas	**21,908**		10,816	5,227	**28,732**		20,094			19,078	**22,152**
Michigan	52,139	**71,762**	1,560	65,057	805	**88,480**	405	74,604	**91,521**	97,069	**138,550**
Florida	**6,368**		4,843	367	**8,543**		5,437				LEGIS.
Texas	**28,575**		15,244		**47,548**		15,438*				
Iowa	36,241	**44,127**	9,944	55,111	1,048	**70,409**	1,763	49,596	**89,075**	74,040	**120,399**
Wisconsin	52,867	**66,092**	579	65,021	888	**86,110**	161	65,884	**83,458**	84,710	**108,857**
California	**42,460**	16,721	28,327	38,516	34,334	**39,173**	6,817	43,841	**62,134**	54,078	**54,592**
Minnesota				11,920	748	**22,069**	62	17,375	**25,000**	28,072	**43,542**
Oregon				3,951	5,006	**5,270**	183	8,457	**9,888**	**11,125**	10,961
Kansas								3,691	**16,441**	14,019	**31,049**
West Virginia								10,438	**23,152**	20,306	**29,025**
Nevada								6,594	**9,826**	5,218	**6,480**
Nebraska										5,439	**9,729**
TOTALS	**1,850,960**	1,334,553	885,960	1,365,976	847,953	**1,857,610**	590,631	1,811,754	**2,223,035**	2,703,249	**3,012,833**

* Fusion

	1872		1876			1880			1884	
	Greeley (D & LR)	GRANT (R)	Tilden (D)	HAYES (R)	Cooper (G)	Hancock (D)	GARFIELD (R)	Weaver (G)	CLEVELAND (D)	Blaine (R)
New Hampshire	31,425	37,168	38,510	41,540		40,797	44,856	528	39,198	43,254
Massachusetts	59,269	133,472	108,777	150,063		111,960	165,205	4,548	122,481	146,724
Connecticut	45,880	50,626	61,934	59,084	774	61,415	67,071	868	67,182	65,898
Rhode Island	5,329	13,665	10,712	15,787	60	10,779	18,195	236	12,391	19,030
New York	387,281	440,736	521,949	489,207	1,987	534,511	555,544	12,373	563,154	562,005
New Jersey	76,456	91,656	115,962	103,517		122,565	120,555	2,617	127,784	123,433
Pennsylvania	212,041	349,589	366,158	384,142	7,187	407,502	444,713	20,648	392,785	473,804
Delaware	10,208	11,115	13,381	10,572		15,181	14,138	121	16,976	13,053
Maryland	67,687	66,760	91,780	71,981		93,706	78,515	818	96,932	85,699
Virginia	91,654	93,468	139,670	95,558		128,568	84,020		145,497	139,356
North Carolina	70,094	94,769	125,427	108,417		124,208	115,874	1,126	142,592	125,068
South Carolina	22,703	72,290	90,906	91,870		112,312	58,071	566	69,890	21,733
Georgia	76,356	62,550	130,088	50,446		102,470	54,086	969	94,667	48,603
Vermont	10,927	41,481	20,350	44,428		19,316	45,567	1,215	17,331	39,514
Kentucky	99,995	88,766	159,690	97,156	1,994	149,068	106,306	11,499	152,961	118,122
Tennessee	94,218	84,930	133,166	89,596		130,381	98,760	5,465	133,324	124,093
Ohio	244,321	281,852	323,182	330,698	3,057	340,821	373,048	6,456	368,280	400,082
Louisiana	57,029	71,663	70,508	75,135		65,067	38,637	439	62,540	46,347
Indiana	163,632	186,147	213,526	208,011		225,552	232,164	12,986	244,900	238,463
Mississippi	42,288	82,175	112,173	52,605		75,750	34,854	5,797	76,510	43,509
Illinois	189,438	241,944	258,601	278,232	17,233	277,321	318,037	26,358	312,351	337,469
Alabama	79,444	90,272	102,002	68,230		91,185	56,221	4,642	93,951	59,591
Maine	29,087	61,422	49,823	66,300		65,171	74,039	4,408	52,140	72,209
Missouri	151,434	119,116	203,077	145,029	3,498	208,609	153,567	35,135	235,988	202,929
Arkansas	37,927	41,373	58,071	38,669		60,775	42,436	4,079	72,927	50,895
Michigan	77,020	136,199	141,095	166,534	9,060	131,301	185,190	34,895	149,835	192,669
Florida	15,427	17,763	22,923	23,849		27,964	23,654		31,766	28,031
Texas	66,500	47,406	104,755	44,800		156,428	57,893	27,405	225,309	93,141
Iowa	71,179	131,566	112,121	171,326	9,431	105,845	183,904	32,327	177,316	197,088
Wisconsin	86,477	104,992	123,927	130,068	1,509	114,634	144,897	7,980	146,453	161,135
California	40,718	54,020	75,845	78,614	44	80,426	80,348	3,392	89,288	102,416
Minnesota	35,211	55,708	48,587	72,955	2,389	53,315	93,902	3,267	70,065	111,685
Oregon	7,742	11,818	14,157	15,214		19,955	20,619	245	24,604	26,860
Kansas	32,390	67,048	37,902	78,354	7,770	59,801	121,549	19,851	90,132	154,406
West Virginia	29,533	32,323	55,584	41,392		57,391	46,243	9,079	67,331	63,913
Nevada	6,236	8,413	9,308	10,383		8,619	7,878		5,578	7,193
Nebraska	7,812	18,329	17,554	31,917	2,320	28,523	54,979	3,950	54,391	76,912
Colorado						24,647	27,450	1,435	27,723	36,290
TOTALS	2,834,079	3,597,070	4,284,885	4,033,950	81,740	4,442,035	4,449,053	307,306	4,911,017	4,848,331

O'Conner (NLR) 29,408
Black (Pro) 5,608

Smith (Pro) 9,552

Dow (Pro) 10,487

St. John (Pro) 151,809
Butler (G) 133,825

	1888		1892			1896	
	Cleveland (D)	HARRISON (R)	CLEVELAND (D)	Harrison (R)	Weaver (P)	Bryan (D & P)	McKINLEY (R)
New Hampshire	43,456	45,728	43,081	45,658	293	21,651	57,444
Massachusetts	151,905	183,892	176,858	202,927	3,348	121,385	278,976
Connecticut	74,922	74,586	82,395	77,032	809	56,740	110,285
Rhode Island	17,520	21,969	24,336	26,975	228	14,459	37,437
New York	635,965	650,338	654,900	609,459	16,436	551,513	819,838
New Jersey	151,508	144,360	171,066	156,101		133,695	221,371
Pennsylvania	446,633	526,091	452,264	516,011	8,714	433,228	728,300
Delaware	16,414	12,973	18,581	18,077		13,425	16,883
Maryland	106,168	99,986	113,866	92,736	796	104,746	136,978
Virginia	151,979	150,449	193,977	113,256	12,275	154,985	135,388
North Carolina	148,336	134,784	133,098	100,565	44,732	174,488	155,243
South Carolina	65,825	13,740	54,698	13,384	2,410	58,801	9,313
Georgia	100,472	40,453	129,386	48,305	42,937	94,733	60,107
Vermont	16,785	45,192	16,325	37,992	44	10,607	50,991
Kentucky	183,800	155,134	175,461	135,441	23,500	217,890	218,171
Tennessee	158,779	138,988	136,594	99,851	23,730	168,847	149,703
Ohio	396,455	416,054	404,115	405,187	14,852	477,497	525,991
Louisiana	85,032	30,701	87,662	27,903		77,175	22,037
Indiana	261,013	263,361	262,740	255,615	22,208	305,573	323,754
Mississippi	85,467	31,120	40,288	1,342	10,102	63,793	5,123
Illinois	348,371	370,475	426,281	399,288	22,207	464,523	607,130
Alabama	117,320	56,197	138,138	9,197	85,181	131,226	54,737
Maine	50,437	72,656	48,024	62,878	2,045	34,587	80,461
Missouri	261,943	236,252	268,188	226,918	41,213	313,576	239,333
Arkansas	86,717	60,245	87,834	46,974	11,831	110,103	37,512
Michigan	213,469	236,387	202,296	222,708	19,931	237,268	293,582
Florida	39,656	26,659	30,143		4,843	32,736	11,288
Texas	234,883	88,280	239,148	81,444	99,418	361,224	158,894
Iowa	179,877	211,598	196,367	219,795	20,595	289,293	223,741
Wisconsin	155,243	176,555	177,335	170,846	9,909	165,349	268,051
California	117,729	124,816	118,174	117,962	25,311	144,618	146,688
Minnesota	104,385	142,492	100,920	122,823	29,313	139,735	193,503
Oregon	26,522	33,291	14,243	35,002	26,965	46,739	48,779
Kansas	102,745	182,904		157,241	163,111	172,915	159,345
West Virginia	78,677	78,171	84,467	80,293	4,166	94,488	105,379
Nevada	5,149	7,088	714	2,711	7,264	8,376	1,938
Nebraska	80,542	108,425	24,943	87,227	83,134	115,999	103,064
Colorado	37,567	50,774		38,620	53,584	161,269	26,279
North Dakota				17,506	17,700	20,686	26,335
South Dakota			9,081	34,888	26,544	41,225	41,042
Montana			17,581	18,851	7,334	42,537	10,494
Washington			29,844	36,460	19,105	51,646	39,153
Idaho			2	8,799	10,520	23,135	6,314
Wyoming				8,454	7,722	10,375	10,072
Utah						64,607	13,491
Oklahoma							
New Mexico							
Arizona							
TOTALS	5,540,050	5,444,337	5,554,414	5,190,802	1,027,329	6,467,946	7,035,638

Fisk (Pro) 259,125
Streeter (UL) 146,897
Cowdrey (UL) 2,418

Bidwell (Pro) 271,058

Palmer (ND) 131,529
Levering (Pro) 141,676

	1900		1904		1908	
	Bryan (D)	McKINLEY (R)	Parker (D)	ROOSEVELT (R)	Bryan (D)	TAFT (R)
New Hampshire	35,489	**54,798**	33,905	**54,180**	33,655	**53,149**
Massachusetts	157,016	**239,147**	165,722	**257,822**	155,543	**265,966**
Connecticut	74,014	**102,572**	72,909	**111,089**	68,255	**112,915**
Rhode Island	19,812	**33,784**	24,839	**41,605**	24,706	**43,942**
New York	678,425	**822,013**	683,981	**859,533**	667,468	**870,070**
New Jersey	164,879	**221,754**	164,367	**245,164**	182,567	**265,326**
Pennsylvania	424,232	**712,665**	335,430	**840,949**	448,782	**745,779**
Delaware	18,386	**22,535**	19,359	**23,712**	22,071	**25,114**
Maryland	122,237	**136,185**	109,446	**109,497**	115,908	**116,513**
Virginia	**146,080**	115,865	**86,548**	47,880	**82,946**	52,573
North Carolina	**157,752**	133,081	**124,121**	82,625	**136,995**	114,937
South Carolina	**47,283**	3,579	**52,563**	2,554	**62,200**	3,965
Georgia	**81,700**	35,056	**83,472**	24,003	**72,413**	41,692
Vermont	12,849	**42,596**	9,777	**40,459**	11,496	**39,552**
Kentucky	**234,899**	226,801	**217,170**	205,277	**244,092**	235,711
Tennessee	**145,356**	123,180	**131,653**	105,369	**135,608**	118,324
Ohio	474,882	**543,918**	344,940	**600,095**	502,721	**572,311**
Louisiana	**53,671**	14,233	**48,708**	5,205	**63,568**	8,958
Indiana	309,584	**336,063**	274,345	**368,289**	338,262	**348,993**
Mississippi	**51,706**	5,753	**53,374**	3,187	**60,287**	4,363
Illinois	503,061	**597,985**	327,606	**632,645**	450,810	**629,932**
Alabama	**96,368**	55,634	**79,857**	22,472	**74,374**	25,308
Maine	36,823	**65,435**	27,648	**64,438**	35,403	**66,987**
Missouri	**351,992**	314,092	296,312	**321,449**	346,574	**347,203**
Arkansas	**81,091**	44,770	**64,434**	46,860	**87,015**	56,760
Michigan	211,685	**316,269**	135,392	**364,957**	175,771	**335,580**
Florida	**28,007**	7,314	**27,046**	8,314	**31,104**	10,654
Texas	**267,432**	130,641	**167,200**	51,242	**217,302**	65,666
Iowa	209,265	**307,808**	149,141	**307,907**	200,771	**275,210**
Wisconsin	159,279	**265,756**	124,107	**280,164**	166,632	**247,747**
California	124,985	**164,755**	89,404	**205,226**	127,492	**214,398**
Minnesota	112,901	**190,461**	55,187	**216,651**	109,401	**195,843**
Oregon	33,385	**46,526**	17,521	**60,455**	38,049	**62,530**
Kansas	162,601	**185,955**	86,174	**212,955**	161,209	**197,216**
West Virginia	98,807	**119,829**	100,881	**132,628**	114,418	**137,869**
Nevada	**6,347**	3,849	3,982	**6,864**	**11,212**	10,775
Nebraska	114,013	**121,835**	52,921	**138,558**	**131,099**	126,997
Colorado	**122,733**	93,039	100,105	**134,687**	**126,644**	123,700
North Dakota	20,531	**35,898**	14,273	**52,595**	32,885	**57,680**
South Dakota	39,544	**54,530**	21,969	**72,083**	40,266	**67,536**
Montana	**37,145**	25,373	21,773	**34,932**	29,326	**32,333**
Washington	44,833	**57,456**	28,098	**101,540**	58,691	**106,062**
Idaho	**29,414**	27,198	18,480	**47,783**	36,162	**52,621**
Wyoming	10,164	**14,482**	8,930	**20,489**	14,918	**20,846**
Utah	45,006	**47,089**	33,413	**62,466**	42,601	**61,028**
Oklahoma					**122,363**	110,474
New Mexico						
Arizona						
TOTALS	6,358,071	**7,219,530**	5,084,491	**7,628,834**	6,409,106	**7,679,006**

Woolley (Pro) 209,166, Debs (Soc) 44,768, Swallow (Pro) 259,257, Debs (Soc) 402,400, Chafin (Pro) 252,683, Debs (Soc) 420,820

	1912			1916		1920	
	WILSON (D)	Taft (R)	Roosevelt (P)	WILSON (D)	Hughes (R)	Cox (D)	HARDING (R)
New Hampshire	**34,724**	32,927	17,794	**43,781**	43,725	62,662	**95,196**
Massachusetts	**173,408**	155,948	142,228	247,885	**268,784**	276,691	**681,153**
Connecticut	**74,561**	68,324	34,129	99,786	**106,514**	120,721	**229,238**
Rhode Island	**30,412**	27,703	16,878	40,394	**44,858**	55,062	**107,463**
New York	**655,475**	455,428	390,021	759,426	**869,115**	731,238	**1,871,167**
New Jersey	**170,282**	88,834	145,409	211,645	**269,352**	258,229	**611,670**
Pennsylvania	395,637	273,360	**444,894**	521,784	**703,823**	503,202	**1,218,215**
Delaware	**22,631**	15,997	8,886	24,753	**26,001**	39,911	**52,858**
Maryland	**112,674**	54,956	57,789	**138,359**	117,347	180,626	**236,117**
Virginia	**90,332**	23,288	21,777	**102,824**	49,356	**141,670**	87,456
North Carolina	**144,507**	29,139	69,130	**168,383**	120,890	**305,447**	232,848
South Carolina	**48,357**	536	1,293	**61,846**	1,550	**64,170**	2,244
Georgia	**93,076**	5,191	21,980	**125,845**	11,225	**107,162**	43,720
Vermont	15,334	**23,332**	22,132	22,739	**40,295**	20,919	**68,212**
Kentucky	**219,584**	115,512	102,766	**269,990**	241,854	**456,497**	452,480
Tennessee	**130,335**	59,444	53,725	**153,282**	116,223	206,558	**219,829**
Ohio	**424,834**	278,168	229,807	**604,161**	514,753	780,037	**1,182,022**
Louisiana	**60,971**	3,834	9,323	**79,875**	6,466	**87,519**	38,538
Indiana	**281,890**	151,267	162,007	334,063	**341,005**	511,364	**696,370**
Mississippi	**57,227**	1,595	3,645	**80,422**	4,253	**69,277**	11,576
Illinois	**405,048**	253,593	386,478	950,229	**1,152,549**	534,395	**1,420,480**
Alabama	**82,438**	9,732	22,680	**99,409**	22,809	**163,254**	74,690
Maine	**51,113**	26,545	48,495	64,127	**69,506**	58,961	**136,355**
Missouri	**57,227**	1,595	3,645	**398,025**	369,339	574,799	**727,162**
Arkansas	**68,838**	24,467	21,673	**112,148**	47,148	**107,408**	71,117
Michigan	150,751	152,244	**214,584**	285,151	**339,097**	233,450	**762,865**
Florida	**36,417**	4,279	4,535	**55,984**	14,611	**90,515**	44,853
Texas	**219,489**	26,745	28,530	**286,514**	64,999	**288,767**	114,269
Iowa	**185,325**	119,805	161,819	221,699	**280,449**	227,921	**634,674**
Wisconsin	**164,228**	130,695	62,460	193,042	**221,323**	113,422	**498,576**
California	283,436	3,914	**283,610**	**466,200**	462,394	229,191	**624,992**
Minnesota	106,426	64,334	**125,856**	179,152	**179,544**	142,994	**519,421**
Oregon	**47,064**	34,673	37,600	120,187	**126,813**	80,019	**143,592**
Kansas	**143,663**	74,845	120,210	**314,588**	277,658	185,464	**369,268**
West Virginia	**113,046**	56,667	78,977	140,403	**143,124**	220,789	**282,007**
Nevada	**7,986**	3,196	5,620	**17,776**	12,127	9,851	**15,479**
Nebraska	**109,008**	54,029	72,614	**158,827**	117,257	119,608	**247,498**
Colorado	**114,232**	58,386	72,306	**178,816**	102,308	104,936	**173,248**
North Dakota	**29,555**	23,090	25,726	**55,206**	53,471	37,422	**160,072**
South Dakota	48,942		**58,811**	59,191	**64,217**	35,938	**110,692**
Montana	**27,941**	18,512	22,456	**101,063**	66,750	57,372	**109,430**
Washington	86,840	70,445	**113,698**	**183,388**	167,244	84,298	**223,137**
Idaho	**33,921**	32,810	25,527	**70,054**	55,368	46,579	**88,975**
Wyoming	**15,310**	14,560	9,232	**28,316**	21,698	17,429	**35,091**
Utah	36,579	**42,100**	24,174	**84,025**	54,137	56,639	**81,555**
Oklahoma	**119,156**	90,786		**148,113**	97,233	215,808	**243,464**
New Mexico	**22,139**	17,900	8,347	**33,693**	31,163	46,668	**57,634**
Arizona	**10,324**	3,021	6,949	**112,148**	47,148	29,546	**37,016**
TOTALS	**6,286,214**	3,483,922	4,126,020	**9,129,606**	8,538,221	9,147,353	**16,152,200**

Chafin (Pro) 208,923, Debs (Soc) 897,011, Reimer (Soc Lab) 29,079, Hanley (Pro) 220,506, Benson (Soc) 585,113, Reimer (Soc Lab) 13,403
Watkins (Pro) 189,408, Debs (Soc) 919,799, Christensen (FL) 265,411

	1924			1928		1932	
	Davis (D)	COOLIDGE (R)	La Follette (P) * (and Soc.)	Smith (D)	HOOVER (R) *(and Anti-Smith Democrat)	ROOSEVELT (D)	Hoover (R)
New Hampshire	57,201	**98,575**	8,993	80,715	**115,404**	100,680	**103,629**
Massachusetts	280,884	**703,489**	141,225	**792,758**	775,566	**800,148**	736,959
Connecticut	110,184	**246,322**	42,416	252,040	**296,614**	281,632	**288,420**
Rhode Island	76,606	**125,286**	7,628	**118,973**	117,522	**146,604**	115,266
New York	950,796	**1,820,058**	467,293*	2,089,863	**2,193,344**	**2,534,959**	1,937,963
New Jersey	298,043	**676,277**	109,028	616,517	**926,050**	**806,630**	775,684
Pennsylvania	409,192	**1,401,481**	307,567	1,067,586	**2,055,382**	1,295,948	**1,453,540**
Delaware	33,445	**52,441**	4,979*	36,643	**68,860**	54,319	**57,074**
Maryland	148,072	**162,414**	47,157	223,626	**301,479**	**314,314**	184,184
Virginia	**139,797**	73,359	10,379	140,146	**164,609**	**203,979**	89,637
North Carolina	**284,270**	191,753	6,651	287,078	**348,992**	**497,566**	208,344
South Carolina	**49,008**	1,123	620	**62,700**	3,188	**102,347**	1,978
Georgia	**123,200**	30,300	12,691	**129,602**	99,369*	**234,118**	19,863
Vermont	16,124	**80,498**	5,964	44,440	**90,404**	56,266	**78,984**
Kentucky	374,855	**398,966**	38,465	381,070	**558,064**	**580,574**	394,716
Tennessee	**158,404**	130,882	10,656	167,343	**195,388**	**259,817**	126,806
Ohio	477,888	**1,176,130**	357,948	864,210	**1,627,546**	**1,301,695**	1,227,697
Louisiana	**93,218**	24,670	4,063	**164,655**	51,160	**249,418**	18,853
Indiana	492,245	703,042	71,700	562,691	**848,290**	**862,054**	677,184
Mississippi	**100,475**	8,546	3,494	**124,539**	27,153	**140,168**	5,180
Illinois	576,975	**1,453,321**	432,027	1,313,817	**1,768,141**	**1,882,304**	1,432,756
Alabama	**112,966**	45,005	8,084	**127,797**	120,725	**207,910**	34,675
Maine	41,964	**138,440**	11,382	81,179	**179,923**	128,907	**166,631**
Missouri	572,753	**648,486**	84,160	662,562	**834,080**	**1,025,406**	564,713
Arkansas	**84,795**	40,564	13,173	**119,196**	77,751	**189,602**	28,467
Michigan	152,238	**874,631**	122,014	396,762	**965,396**	**871,700**	739,894
Florida	**62,083**	30,633	8,625	101,764	**144,168**	**206,307**	69,170
Texas	**484,605**	130,023	42,881	341,032	**367,036**	**760,348**	97,959
Iowa	162,600	**537,635**	272,243	378,936	**623,818**	**598,019**	414,433
Wisconsin	68,115	311,614	**453,678**	450,259	**544,205**	**707,410**	347,741
California	105,514	**733,250**	424,649*	614,365	**1,147,929**	**1,324,157**	847,902
Minnesota	55,913	**420,759**	339,192	396,451	**560,977**	**600,806**	363,959
Oregon	67,589	**142,579**	68,403	109,223	**205,341**	**213,871**	136,019
Kansas	156,319	**407,671**	98,461	193,003	**513,672**	**424,204**	349,498
West Virginia	257,232	**288,635**	36,723	263,784	**375,551**	**405,124**	330,731
Nevada	5,909	**11,243**	9,769	14,090	**18,327**	**28,756**	12,674
Nebraska	137,289	**218,585**	106,701	197,959	**345,745**	**359,082**	201,177
Colorado	75,238	**195,171**	69,945	133,131	**253,872**	**250,877**	189,617
North Dakota	13,858	**94,931**	89,922	106,648	**131,441**	**178,350**	71,772
South Dakota	27,214	**101,299**	75,355	102,660	**157,603**	**183,515**	99,212
Montana	33,805	**74,138**	65,876	78,578	**113,300**	**127,286**	78,078
Washington	42,842	**220,224**	150,727	156,772	**335,844**	**353,260**	208,645
Idaho	24,256	**69,879**	54,160	53,074	**99,848**	**109,479**	71,312
Wyoming	12,868	**41,858**	25,174	29,299	**52,748**	**54,370**	39,583
Utah	47,001	**77,327**	32,662	80,985	**94,618**	**116,750**	84,795
Oklahoma	**255,798**	226,242	41,141	219,174	**394,046**	**516,468**	188,165
New Mexico	48,542	**54,745**	9,543	48,211	**69,645**	**95,089**	54,217
Arizona	26,235	**30,516**	17,210	38,537	**52,533**	**79,264**	36,104
Totals	8,385,586	**15,725,016**	4,822,856	15,016,443	**21,392,190**	**22,821,857**	15,761,841

Foster (W) 33,361, Faris (Pro) 57,551, Johns (Soc Lab) 38,958, Nations (A) 23,867, Wallace (CL) 2,778, Thomas (Soc) 267,420, Foster (C) 48,770,
Varney (Pro) 20,106, Reynods (Soc Lab) 21,603, Webb (FL) 6,390, Foster (C) 102,991, Upshaw (Pro) 81,869,
Reynolds (Soc Lab) 33,275, Coxey (FL) 7,309, Harvey (Lib) 53,425

	1936			1940	
	ROOSEVELT (D & AL)	Landon (R)	Lemke (U)	ROOSEVELT (D & AL)	Willkie (R) * (and Ind. Dem.)
New Hampshire	**108,460**	104,642	4,819	**125,292**	110,127
Massachusetts	**942,716**	768,613	118,369	**1,076,522**	939,700
Connecticut	**382,129**	278,685		**417,621**	361,819
Rhode Island	**165,238**	125,031	19,569	**181,746**	138,432
New York	**3,293,222**	2,180,670		**3,251,918**	3,027,478
New Jersey	**1,083,549**	719,421	9,045	**1,016,404**	944,876
Pennsylvania	**2,353,788**	1,690,300	67,467	**2,171,035**	1,889,848
Delaware	**69,702**	54,014	442	**74,599**	61,440
Maryland	**389,612**	231,435		**384,546**	269,534
Virginia	**161,083**	76,366	233	**160,198**	82,895
North Carolina	**616,141**	223,283	2	**609,015**	213,633
South Carolina	**113,791**	1,646		**95,470**	1,727
Georgia	**255,364**	36,942		**265,194**	46,362*
Vermont	62,124	**81,023**		64,269	**78,371**
Kentucky	**541,944**	369,702	12,501	**557,222**	410,384
Tennessee	**327,083**	146,516	696	**351,601**	169,153
Ohio	**1,747,122**	1,127,709	132,212	**1,733,139**	1,568,773
Louisiana	**292,894**	36,791		**319,751**	52,446
Indiana	**934,974**	691,570	19,407	874,063	**899,466**
Mississippi	**157,318**	4,418		**168,252**	7,364
Illinois	**2,282,999**	1 570,393	86,439	**2,142,934**	2,047,240
Alabama	**238,195**	35,358	549	**250,726**	42,174
Maine	126,333	**168,823**	7,581	156,478	**163,951**
Missouri	**1,111,043**	697,891	14,630	**958,746**	871,009
Arkansas	**146,765**	32,039	4	**158,622**	42,121
Michigan	**1,016,794**	699,733	75,795	1,032,991	**1,039,917**
Florida	**249,117**	78,248		**359,334**	126,158
Texas	**734,485**	103,874	3,281	**840,151**	199,152
Iowa	**621,756**	487,977	29,687	578,800	**632,370**
Wisconsin	**802,984**	380,828	60,297	**704,821**	679,206
California	**1,766,836**	836,481		**1,877,618**	1,351,419
Minnesota	**698,811**	350,461		644,196	596,274
Oregon	**266,733**	122,706	21,831	**258,415**	219,555
Kansas	**464,520**	397,727	494	364,725	**489,169**
West Virginia	**502,582**	325,258		**495,662**	372,414
Nevada	**31,925**	11,923		**31,945**	21,229
Nebraska	**347,454**	248,731	12,847	263,677	**352,201**
Colorado	**295,021**	181,267	9,962	265,554	**279,576**
North Dakota	**163,148**	72,751	36,708	124,036	**154,590**
South Dakota	**160,137**	125,977		131,362	**177,065**
Montana	**159,690**	63,598	5,549	**145,698**	99,579
Washington	**459,579**	206,892	17,463	**462,145**	322,123
Idaho	**125,683**	66,256	7,684	**127,842**	106,553
Wyoming	**62,624**	38,739	1,653	**59,287**	52,633
Utah	**150,246**	64,550		**154,277**	93,151
Oklahoma	**501,069**	245,122		**474,313**	348,872
New Mexico	**105,838**	61,710	924	**103,699**	79,315
Arizona	**86,722**	33,433		**95,267**	54,030
Totals	**27,476,673**	16,679,583	882,479	**27,243,466**	22,304,755

Browder (C) 80,150, Colvin (Pro) 37,847, Aiken (Soc Lab) 12,777, Thomas (Soc) 99,557, Browder (C) 46,251, Babson (Pro) 57,812, Aiken (Soc Lab) 14,861

APPENDIX III

IMMIGRATION BY COUNTRY OF ORIGIN, 1831-1940

	1831–40	1841–50	1851–60	1861–70	1871–80	1881–90	1891–1900	1901–10	1911–20	1921–30	1931–40
Austra-Hungary				7,800	72,969	353,722	592,707	2,145,266	896,342	63,548	7,861*
Belgium	22	5,094	4,738	6,734	7,221	20,174	18,167	41,635	33,746	15,846	4,817
Bulgaria							160	39,280	22,533	2,945	938
Czechoslovakia									3,426	102,194	14,393
Denmark	1,063	539	3,749	17,094	31,771	88,132	50,231	65,285	41,983	32,430	2,559
France	45,575	77,262	76,358	35,984	72,201	50,463	30,770	73,739	61,897	49,610	12,623
Germany	152,454	434,626	951,667	787,468	717,182	452,970	505,152	341,498	143,945	412,202	117,621§
Greece						2,053	15,979	167,519	184,201	51,084	9,119
Italy	2,253	1,870	9,231	11,728	55,762	307,310	651,893	2,045,877	1,109,524	455,315	68,028
Netherlands	1,412	8,251	10,789	9,102	16,541	53,701	26,758	48,262	43,718	26,946	7,150
Norway } Sweden }	1,201	13,903	20,931	109,298							
Norway					95,323	176,586	95,014	190,505	66,393	68,531	4,740
Sweden					115,922	391,776	226,266	249,534	95,074	97,249	3,960
Poland†	—	—	1,164	2,027	12,970	51,806	96,720	—	4,813	227,734	17,026
Roumania						5,938	12,750	53,008	13,311	67,646	3,871
Russia‡	646	656	1,621	4,536	52,254	265,089	602,011	1,597,306	921,957	78,433	1,356
Spain } Portugal }	2,954	2,759	10,353	8,493							
Spain					5,266	4,418	8,731	27,935	68,611	28,958	3,258
Portugal					4,627	11,917	27,323	69,149	89,732	29,994	3,329
Switzerland	4,821	4,644	25,011	23,286	28,293	81,988	31,179	34,922	23,091	29,676	5,512
Turkey in Europe						1,185	3,786	119,256	77,210	14,659	737
United Kingdom											
England	7,611	32,092	247,125	222,277	437,706	644,680	216,726	388,017	249,944	157,420	21,756
Ireland	207,381	780,719	914,119	435,778	436,871	655,482	388,416	339,065	146,181	220,591	13,167
Scotland	2,667	3,712	38,331	38,768	87,564	149,869	44,188	120,469	78,357	159,781	6,887
Wales	185	1,261	6,319	4,313	6,631	12,640	10,557	17,464	13,107	13,012	735
Not Specified	65,347	229,979	132,199	349,538	16,142	168	67				
Other Europe	96	155	116	210	658	1,346	122	665	18,238	22,983	8,865
Total Europe	495,688	1,597,522	2,453,821	2,074,434	2,274,874	4,783,413	3,655,673	8,175,296	4,407,336	2,427,787	340,308
Canada and Newfoundland¶			59,304	153,878	383,640	393,304	3,311	179,226	742,185	924,515	108,527
Mexico¶			3,078	2,191	5,162	1,913	971	49,642	219,004	459,287	22,319
Central America			449	95	157	404	549	8,192	17,159	15,769	5,861
South America			1,224	1,397	1,128	2,304	1,075	17,280	41,899	42,215	7,803
West Indies			10,660	9,046	13,957	29,042	33,066	107,548	123,424	74,899	15,502
Total America			74,715	166,607	404,044	426,967	38,972	361,888	1,143,671	1,516,685	160,012
China	8	35	41,397	64,301	123,200	61,711	14,799	20,005	21,270	29,907	4,928
Japan							25,942	129,797	83,837	33,462	1,948
Turkey in Asia							26,799	77,393	79,389	19,165	328
Other Asia	40	47	61	308	603	6,669	3,696	15,772	8,055	14,866	8,140
Total Asia	48	82	41,458	64,609	123,803	68,380	71,236	243,567	192,559	97,400	15,344
Africa			210	312	358	857	350	7,368	8,443	6,286	1,750
Australia, Tasmania, New Zealand				36	9,886	7,017	2,740	11,975	12,348	8,299	2,231
Pacific Islands					1,028	5,557	1,225	1,049	1,079	427	780
All other countries			29,169	17,969	790	789	14,063	33,523#	1,147	228	—
TOTAL IMMIGRATION	495,736	1,597,604	2,599,373	2,323,967	2,814,783	5,292,980	3,784,259	8,834,666	5,766,583	4,057,112	535,569

* Hungary only.
† From 1899–1919 Poland is included with Austria-Hungary, Germany and Russia.
‡ Including Finland 1831–1920.
§ Includes Austria.
¶ No reports from 1886–1893.
# Includes 32,897 persons returning to their homes in U.S. After 1906 such aliens have been considered non-immigrants.

APPENDIX IV

IMPORTS AND EXPORTS, 1799-1938

DOMESTIC EXPORTS BY CLASSIFICATION, 1800*

Products of the Sea	
Dried Salt Fish	$ 1,620,000
Pickled Fish	560,000
Whale Oil and Bone	280,000
Spermaceti Oil and Candles	175,000
	2,635,000
Produce of the Forest	
Ginseng, Peltry, etc.	630,000
Naval Stores	460,000
Pearl and Pot Ashes	735,000
Lumber, Masts, etc.	2,800,000
	4,850,000
Agriculture	
Animal Food and Animals	4,135,000
Vegetable Food	14,080,000
Tobacco	6,230,000
Cotton	7,920,000
	32,995,000
Manufactures	
From Domestic Material	790,000
From Foreign Material	565,000
	1,355,000
Total Domestic Exports	42,235,000

IMPORTS BY CLASSIFICATION, 1800

Merchandise Paying ad Valorem Duties	$39,489,000
Salt, Nails, Lead, Steel, Beer, Cheese, Shoes and Coals	1,917,000
Rum	3,881,000
Coffee	8,373,000
Sugar	7,794,000
Molasses	1,930,000
Cotton, Cocoa, Indigo, Pepper and Pimento	2,257,000
Hemp, Soap, Candles, etc.	1,600,000
Brandy and Geneva	2,253,000
Wines	2,962,000
Teas	2,360,000
Total Imports	75,316,000
From Great Britain	35,970,000
From Rest of World	39,346,000
	75,316,000

IMPORTS BY COUNTRY OF ORIGIN, 1799

(Goods Imported in Amounts totalling at least 100,000 Units)

BOURBON AND MAURITIUS	
Coffee	692,284 lbs.
Brown Sugar	299,465 lbs.
Cotton	264,667 lbs.
BRITISH AMERICAN COLONIES	
Salt	114,296 lbs.
BRITISH EAST INDIES	
Coffee	729,475 lbs.
Brown Sugar	1,689,113 lbs.
Cotton	673,149 lbs.
BRITISH WEST INDIES	
Foreign Distilled Spirits from Materials Other than Grain	3,470,468 gals.
Molasses	1,456,433 gals.
Coffee	778,571 lbs.
Cocoa	368,821 lbs.
Brown Sugar	10,703,771 lbs.
CAPE VERDE ISLANDS	
Salt	2,388,876 lbs.
CHINA AND EAST INDIES GENERALLY	
Tea	
Bohea	3,885,280 lbs.
Souchong	260,531 lbs.
Hyson	284,328 lbs.
Other Green	541,921 lbs.
DANISH WEST INDIES	
Foreign Distilled Spirits from Materials Other than Grain	1,006,100 gals.
Coffee	2,023,108 lbs.
Cocoa	106,185 lbs.
Brown Sugar	5,928,887 lbs.
Loaf Sugar	108,036 lbs.
Salt	386,276 lbs.
ENGLAND, MAN, AND BERWICK	
Beer, Ale, and Porter	331,391 gals.
Cheese	222,647 lbs.
Nails and Spikes	3,699,159 lbs.
Lead	2,844,522 lbs.
Salt	7,671,546 lbs.
Coal	155,678 bu.
FLORIDAS AND LOUISIANA	
Brown Sugar	751,512 lbs.
Cotton	842,200 lbs.
FRANCE	
Foreign Distilled Spirits from Materials Other than Grain	446,416 gals.
FRENCH WEST INDIES	
Foreign Distilled Spirits from Materials Other than Grain	500,009 gals.
Molasses	101,459 gals.
Coffee	4,918,422 lbs.
Brown Sugar	4,311,837 lbs.
Salt	332,115 lbs.
GUERNSEY, JERSEY, SARK, etc.	
Salt	362,600 lbs.
HAMBURG, BREMEN	
Foreign Distilled Spirits	
From Grain	136,969 gals.
From Other Materials	198,429 gals.
ITALY	
Foreign Distilled Spirits from Materials Other than Grain	276,980 gals.
Soap	535,818 lbs.
MANILA AND OTHER PHILIPPINE ISLANDS	
Brown Sugar	121,523 lbs.
OTHER SPANISH AMERICAN COLONIES	
Cocoa	117,586 lbs.
Brown Sugar	279,870 lbs.
Loaf Sugar	301,340 lbs.
PORTUGAL	
Wines Other than Sherry	420,856 gals.
Salt	13,919,452 lbs.
SCOTLAND	
Nails and Spikes	133,721 lbs.
SPAIN	
Sherry	568,077 gals.
Other Wines	348,297 gals.
Foreign Distilled Spirits from Materials Other than Grain	1,203,170 gals.
Salt	371,682 lbs.
SPANISH WEST INDIES	
Molasses	2,046,241 gals.
Coffee	3,919,287 lbs.

* For amount of exports by countries, see Map 126.

Cocoa	3,575,489 lbs.
Brown Sugar	32,095,424 lbs.
Loaf Sugar	33,316,291 lbs.
Salt	291,653 lbs.
SWEDISH WEST INDIES	
Coffee	175,213 lbs.
Brown Sugar	2,784,697 lbs.
TENERIFFE AND OTHER CANARIES	
Wines Other than Sherry	187,880 gals.
UNITED NETHERLANDS	
DUTCH EAST INDIES	
Coffee	6,238,457 lbs.
Brown Sugar	1,718,199 lbs.
DUTCH WEST INDIES	
Foreign Distilled Spirits from Grain	300,768 gals.
Coffee	10,346,612 lbs.
Cocoa	1,796,611 lbs.
Brown Sugar	8,454,210 lbs.
Molasses	367,824 gals.
Cotton	1,143,681 lbs.
Salt	104,632 lbs.
WEST INDIES GENERALLY	
Brown Sugar	782,370 lbs.

DOMESTIC EXPORTS BY CLASSIFICATION, 1851*

Products of the Sea	
Whale and Fish Oil	$ 882,485
Spermaceti Oil	1,044,967
Whalebone	689,662
Spermaceti Candles	195,916
Dried Fish or Cod Fisheries	367,729
Pickled Fish	113,932
	3,294,692
Products of the Forest	
Staves, Shingles, Boards	2,348,621
Other Lumber	205,190
Masts and Spars	70,095
Oak Bars and Other Dye	355,477
Wood Manufactures	2,076,395
Naval Stores, Tar, Pitch, Rosin, Turpentine	1,063,842
Ashes, Pot and Pearl	649,091
Ginseng	100,549
Skins and Furs	977,762
	7,847,021
Agriculture	
Products of Animals	
Beef, Tallow, Hides, Horned Cattle	1,689,958
Butter and Cheese	1,124,652
Pork, Bacon, Lard, Live Hogs	4,368,015
Horses and Mules	198,155
Sheep	18,875
	7,399,655
Vegetable Food	
Wheat	1,025,732
Flour	10,524,331
Indian Corn	1,762,549
Indian Meal	622,866
Rye Meal	145,802
Rye, Oats, Small Grain	120,630
Biscuit or Ship Bread	354,286
Potatoes	79,314
Apples	71,367
Rice	2,170,927
Indigo	2,803
Cotton	112,315,327
Tobacco	9,219,251
Hemp	29,114
Flaxseed	18,988
Brown Sugar	29,170
Hops	11,636
	145,903,778

* For amounts of exports by countries and commodities exported in amounts over $1,000,000, see Map 127.

Manufactures	
Wax	122,835
Refined Sugar	219,588
Chocolate	3,255
Spirits From Grain	36,084
Spirits From Molasses	239,622
Molasses	16,830
Vinegar	16,951
Beer, Ale, Porter, Cider	57,975
Linseed Oil and Turpentine	145,410
Household Furniture	362,830
Coaches and Carriages	199,421
Hats	103,768
Saddlery	30,100
Tallow Candles and Soap	609,732
Snuff and Tobacco	143,547
Leather, Boots and Shoes	458,838
Cordage	52,054
Gunpowder	154,257
Salt	61,424
Lead	11,774
Iron	
Pig, Bar, Nails	215,652
Castings	164,425
Manufactures	1,875,621
Copper and Brass	91,871
Medicinal Drugs	351,585
Cotton Piece Goods	7,241,205
Hemp and Flax	
Cloth and Thread	1,647
Bags and Manufactures	6,376
Wearing Apparel	1,211,894
Earthen and Stoneware	23,096
Combs and Buttons	27,334
Brushes	8,257
Billiard Tables and Apparatus	1,798
Umbrellas, Parasols	22,260
Leather and Morocco Skins	13,309
Fire Engines and Apparatus	9,488
Printing Presses and Type	71,401
Musical Instruments	55,700
Books and Maps	153,912
Paper and Stationery	155,664
Paints and Varnish	109,834
Manufactures of Glass	185,436
Manufactures of Tin	27,823
Manufactures of Pewter and Lead	16,426
Manufactures of Marble and Stone	41,449
Manufactures of Gold and Silver	68,639
Gold and Silver Coin	18,069,580
Artificial Flowers and Jewelry	121,013
Trunks	12,207
Brick and Lime	22,045
Coal	163,977
Ice	106,805
Articles Not Mentioned	
Manufactured	3,793,341
Raw	1,166,898
TOTAL EXPORTS	196,689,718

IMPORTS BY CLASSIFICATION—JULY 1, 1849-JUNE 30, 1850

(Goods Imported in Amounts totalling at least $250,000)

FREE OF DUTY

Specie	
Gold	$1,600,722
Silver	2,825,770
Teas	4,588,373
Coffee	11,215,076
Copper, in plates for sheathing ships	715,614
Sheathing metal	484,168

PAYING DUTY

Manufactures of wool	
Cloths and cassimeres	$6,184,190
Merino shawls of wool	935,348
Blankets	1,244,335

Hosiery and articles on frames	$ 718,135
Worsted stuff goods	5,004,250
Other manufactures	1,880,526
Carpeting	
Brussels, Turkey, and treble ingrained	573,723
Manufactures of cotton	
Printed, stained, or colored	13,640,291
White or uncolored	1,773,302
Tamboured or embroidered	1,267,286
Hosiery and articles made on frames	1,588,173
Twist, yarn, and thread	799,156
Other manufactures	858,422
Manufactures of silk	
Piece goods	14,459,560
Hosiery and articles made on frames	616,217
Sewing silk	489,487
Tamboured or embroidered	1,131,462
Other manufactures	925,567
Raw silk	386,281
Silk and worsted goods	1,653,809
Manufactures of flax	
Linens, bleached or unbleached	7,063,194
Other manufactures	1,071,490
Cotton bagging	251,905
Clothing	
Articles of wear	734,268
Cotton insertings, trimmings, etc.	672,627
Gunny cloth	331,035
Hats, caps, bonnets, etc.	
Leghorn, straw, grass, chip, etc.	1,163,485
Manufactures of iron and steel	
Firearms not specified	354,877
Cutlery not specified	1,274,838
Manufactures of, not specified	3,427,180
Chain cables	299,811
Sheet iron	659,058
Pig iron	950,660
Bar, unmanufactured by rolling	7,397,166
Bar, unmanufactured otherwise	744,735
Steel Cast, shear, and German	1,106,891
Copper and manufactures of	
In pigs, bars and old	1,167,411
Manufactures of, not specified	320,297
Tin and manufactures of	
In pigs and bars	654,410
In plates and sheets	2,457,753
Lead and manufactures of	
Pig, bar, sheet and old	1,182,597
Manufactures of gold and silver	
Jewelry, real or imitations of	352,287
Watches, and parts of	1,633,921
Buttons and button-moulds	$ 424,518
Glass, polished plate	263,197
Books, printed in English	341,755
Leather	
Skins, tanned and dressed	863,201
Gloves	788,067
Manufactures of, not specified	258,732
Wares	
China, porcelain, earthen and stone	2,601,393
Furs	
Hatter's furs, dressed or undressed, not on the skin	807,506
Wood, manufactures of	353,981
Wood, unmanufactured	
Dye wood in sticks	478,112
Raw hides and skins	4,799,031
Gunny bags	286,426
Flaxseed or linseed	324,811
Wool, unmanufactured	1,681,691
Wines, in casks	
Port	305,454
Claret	267,445
Wines, in bottles	
Champagne	432,410
Foreign Distilled Spirits	
Brandy	2,659,537
From grain	361,078
Molasses	2,890,185
Linseed oil	848,672
Sugar	
Brown	6,659,543
White, clayed, or powdered	846,939
Raisins	700,977
Saltpetre, crude	712,915
Indigo	903,031
Opium	362,605
Soda ash	714,718
Tobacco	
Unmanufactured	272,438
Cigars	1,469,097
Hemp, unmanufactured	579,814
Manila, sun, and other hemp of India	659,362
Rags of all kinds	748,707
Salt	1,237,186
Coal	378,817
Breadstuffs	
Wheat	907,922
Wheat-flour	1,194,469
Fish	
Mackerel	335,736
Total Imports	178,138,318

IMPORTS BY COUNTRY OF ORIGIN, 1850

(Goods Imported in Amounts totalling at least $250,000)

ARGENTINE REPUBLIC		
Raw Hides and Skins	$ 1,587,958	
Wool—Unmanufactured	877,900	10,176,966 lbs.
BELGIUM		
Wool Cloths and Cassimeres	769,799	
BRAZIL		
Raw Hides and Skins	463,848	
Brown Sugar	292,664	7,033,366 lbs.
BRITISH EAST INDIES		
Gunny Cloth	316,402	
Raw Hides and Skins	438,560	
Gunny Bags	264,761	
Flaxseed or Linseed	256,667	592,060 bu.
Saltpetre—Crude	698,714	15,163,351 lbs.
CANADA		
Wheat	907,615	1,237,336 bu.
Wheat Flour	1,194,094	286,244 cwt.
CHILE		
Copper—in Pigs, Bars, and Old	1,008,044	

CHINA		
Silk Piece Goods	$ 912,428	
Silk Articles Tamboured or Embroidered	322,099	
CUBA		
Molasses	2,434,856	21,395,107 gals.
Brown Sugar	4,399,213	127,767,543 lbs.
Cigars	1,416,694	112,069 M.
DUTCH WEST INDIES		
Raw Hides and Skins	346,792	
ENGLAND		
Hats		
Leghorn, Straw, etc.	593,263	
Chain Cables	295,948	10,837,056 lbs.
Pig Iron	534,102	825,195 cwt.
Iron, Bar—Manufactured by Rolling	6,737,571	4,623,379 cwt.
Steel, Cast, Shear and German	1,050,842	93,499 cwt.
Tin in Plates and Sheets	2,426,059	
Lead—Pig, Bar, Sheet and Old	514,878	14,908,101 lbs.
Watches and Parts Thereof	563,766	
Printed Books and Magazines in English	337,417	
China, Porcelain, Earthen and Stone Ware	2,250,643	
Raw Hides and Skins	303,074	
Wool, Unmanufactured	267,459	1,927,403 lbs.
Linseed Oil	766,879	
Indigo	407,336	585,359 lbs.
Soda Ash or Barilla	656,239	28,847,219 lbs.
Salt	825,208	6,266,888 bu.
Silk		
Silk Piece Goods	2,635,028	
Hosiery and Articles Made on Frames	487,011	
Articles Tamboured or Embroidered	282,452	
Other Manufactures	715,821	
Silk and Worsted Goods	714,284	
Linens	6,263,367	
Other Flax Manufactures	861,317	
Articles of Wear	358,140	
Cotton Laces	628,450	
Wool Cloths and Cassimeres	2,749,578	
Merino Shawls of Wool	398,170	
Wool Blankets	1,159,575	
Hosiery and Articles on Frames (wool)	659,676	
Worsted Stuff Goods	3,505,403	
Wool Manufactures not Specified	1,255,328	
Wool Carpeting—Brussels, Turkey, and Treble Ingrained	542,554	593,399 yds.
Cotton—Printed, Stained or Colored	10,674,689	
White or Uncolored	1,571,820	
Tamboured or Embroidered	741,037	
Hosiery and Articles Made on Frames	314,763	
Twist, Yarn and Threads	695,475	
Other Manufactures	763,228	
FRANCE ON THE ATLANTIC		
Worsted Stuff Goods	1,176,458	
Cotton, Tamboured or Embroidered	352,773	
Silk Piece Goods	8,246,163	
Tamboured or Embroidered	418,823	
Silk and Worsted Goods	793,398	
Articles of Wear	332,004	
Watches and Parts	1,040,355	
Skins, Tanned and Dressed	609,744	
Leather Gloves	492,720	
China, Porcelain, Earthen and Stone Ware	272,489	
Hatter's Furs	378,020	
Champagne	425,829	84,319 doz. bottles
Brandy	2,512,041	3,963,107 gals.
HANSE TOWNS		
Wool Cloths and Cassimeres	933,998	
Cotton—Printed, Stained or Colored	348,998	
Hosiery and Articles Made on Frames (Cotton)	1,095,944	
Silk Piece Goods	2,530,726	
ITALY		
Hats—Leghorn, Straw, etc.	292,911	
Rags of all Kinds	419,524	10,277,337 lbs.
MANILA AND OTHER PHILIPPINE ISLANDS		
Brown Sugar	333,830	11,087,349 lbs.
Manila, Sun, and other Hemp of India, etc.	477,766	79,702 cwt.

OTHER SPANISH WEST INDIES

Brown Sugar	$1,410,052	44,937,652 lbs.

PORTUGAL

Port	264,188	527,161 gals.

RUSSIA

Hemp	259,230	34,405 cwt.

SCOTLAND

Cotton—Printed, Stained or Colored	988,587	
Linens	343,859	
Pig Iron	290,553	

SPAIN ON THE MEDITERRANEAN

Lead—Pig, Bar, Sheet and Old	312,117	9,887,847 lbs.
Raisins	685,107	20,081,753 lbs.

SWEDEN AND NORWAY

Iron, Bar—Manufactured Otherwise than by Rolling	696,202	270,210 cwt.

VENEZUELA

Raw Hides and Skins	959,048	

IMPORTS AND EXPORTS BY CLASSIFICATION, 1900-1938

	1900		1938 (To nearest thousand dollars)	
	Imports	Exports*	Imports	Exports*
Agricultural Implements and Machinery		$ 16,099,149	$ 3,920,000	
Animals	$ 4,530,950	43,585,031	9,388,000	$ 412,000
Antimony			1,095,000	
Art Works	2,608,891		16,774,000	1,022,000
Aluminum			6,900,000	6,944,000
Beads	1,777,670		1,357,000	
Books, Maps	3,671,626	2,943,435	9,038,000	23,000,000
Brass and Bronze		1,866,727		7,945,000
Breadstuffs	1,803,729	262,744,078	11,785,000	235,452,000
Bristles	2,652,867			
Carriages, Cars, etc.		9,905,610	2,373,000	
Cement	3,270,916		1,450,000	
Chemicals	53,705,152	13,203,610	37,749,000	82,747,000
Clocks and Watches	1,750,551	1,977,694	8,927,000	2,506,000
Coal	4,476,736	19,502,000	3,354,000	52,740,000
Cocoa (crude)	5,657,283		20,139,000	
Coffee	52,467,943		137,824,000	1,911,000
Coke		1,233,921	1,094,000	5,158,000
Copper and Manufactures of	12,457,470	97,852,960	37,872,000	86,809,000
Cork	1,909,483		3,711,000	
Cotton—Manufactures	41,296,239	24,003,087	56,100,000	52,833,000
Unmanufactured	7,960,945	241,832,737	9,615,000	228,647,000
Diamonds			28,777,000	
Other Precious Stones			1,816,000	
Drugs and Herbs			8,979,000	1,871,000
Earthen, Stone and China Ware	8,645,265		8,094,000	7,835,000
Electrical Machinery			2,019,000	102,136,000
Feathers	4,078,925			
Fertilizers	1,697,986	7,218,224	36,496,000	16,486,000
Fibers (Vegetable) and Grasses—Manufactures of	57,933,176	4,441,835		1,027,000
Fish	7,472,057	5,427,469	28,349,000	13,798,000
Fruits and Nuts	19,263,592	11,642,662	55,117,000	99,061,000
Furs and Skins and Manufactures of	12,160,154	4,503,968	45,873,000	14,130,000
Glass and Glassware	5,037,931	1,936,119	6,528,000	8,332,000
Glucose and Grape Sugar		3,600,139		
Glue		2,349,014		
Grease		2,944,322		
Gums, rosins			8,563,000	
Gunpowder and Firearms		1,891,604		8,006,000
Hair and Manufactures of	2,694,190		2,947,000	2,223,000
Hats and Bonnets	2,092,801			

* For amounts of exports by countries see Maps 257 and 258.

	1900		1938	
	Imports	Exports*	Imports	Exports*
Hay	$ 1,019,743			
Hides and Skins (not Furred)	57,935,698		$ 29,883,000	$ 4,751,000
Hide Cuttings	1,223,521			
Hops		$ 1,707,660		
Household and Personal Effects	2,007,805	2,506,669	5,405,000	7,283,000
India Rubber, Manufactures of	31,376,867	2,631,641	(see Rubber)	
Industrial Machinery			9,586,000	269,908,000
Iron Ore			5,288,000	1,954,000
Iron and Steel Manufactures	20,478,728	121,913,548	34,577,000	252,792,000
Jewelry	17,783,076			2,601,000
Jute, Manufactures of			33,478,000	1,164,000
Lead and Manufactures of	3,156,250		2,113,000	3,936,000
Leather and Manufactures of	13,292,196	27,293,010	15,488,000	20,711,000
Manganese	2,693,003			
Malt Liquors	1,727,256	2,139,216		466,000
Marble and Stone and Manufactures of	1,028,550	1,677,169		
Matting for Floors	2,674,911			
Meat and Dairy Products	2,285,383	184,453,055	41,821,000	34,554,000
Metals	5,570,127			
Miscellaneous Office Supplies				6,088,000
Miscellaneous Textiles			9,458,000	12,295,000
Musical Instruments	1,090,541	1,958,779	3,831,000	2,815,000
Naval Stores		12,474,194		12,329,000
Nickel	1,070,980	1,219,812	13,089,000	2,504,000
Nursery Stock			3,633,000	
Oils				
Mineral		76,611,750		
Vegetable	3,811,721	16,349,056	47,090,000	3,349,000
Animal (Edible)				19,099,000
(Inedible)			5,524,000	
Oilseeds			34,663,000	2,144,000
Oil Cake (Meal)				
Cotton Seed		11,229,188		
Flaxseed or Linseed		5,528,331		
Other Non-Metallic Minerals			14,893,000	28,187,000
Other Vegetable Fibers			20,332,000	
Paints	1,535,461	1,902,367	1,368,000	18,655,000
Paper and Manufactures of	7,057,423	6,215,833	199,341,000	37,355,000
Paraffin		8,602,723		
Petroleum and Products			39,461,000	388,606,000
Photographic Materials		1,386,122	8,712,000	19,867,000
Platinum	1,193,475		3,627,000	1,157,000
Plumbago	2,345,294			
Quicksilver		1,071,585		
Rayon Material			6,966,000	
Rice	2,279,036			
Rubber and Manufactures of	(see India Rubber)		134,541,000	27,181,000
Seeds (Except Oilseeds)	1,795,048	7,036,982	5,917,000	1,972,000
Shells	2,107,665			
Silk—Unmanufactured	45,329,760		89,252,000	
Manufactured	30,894,373		8,272,000	6,064,000
Soap and Toilet Preparations		1,774,024	2,409,000	8,964,000
Spices	3,401,265		11,089,000	
Spirits, Distilled	3,609,831	2,278,111	62,207,000	
Starch		2,604,362		4,284,000
Sugar, Molasses and Confectionery	100,279,074	3,697,671	141,751,000	7,364,000
Sulpher Ore	1,224,711			
Tea	10,558,110		18,313,000	
Tin—Bars and Blocks	19,104,301		44,860,000	
Tobacco	15,661,360	35,432,512	39,211,000	170,028,000
Toys	2,923,984		2,557,000	5,098,000

	1900		1938	
	Imports	Exports*	Imports	Exports*
Vegetables	$ 2,935,077	$ 2,853,278	$ 16,131,000	$ 13,312,000
Vegetable Dyeing Extracts		5,040,000		1,239,000
Woods and Manufactures of	20,591,908	50,598,416	31,637,000	55,886,000
Wool and Manufactures of	36,425,382	1,300,362	40,358,000	3,040,000
Wines	7,421,495		8,511,000	
Zinc		1,669,215		1,521,000
Totals	849,941,184	1,394,483,082	1,960,428,000	3,094,440,000

IMPORTS BY COUNTRY OF ORIGIN, 1900

(Goods Imported in Amounts totalling at least $2,500,000)

ARGENTINA	$ 3,266,952	20,524,395 lbs.
Hides of Cattle	3,266,952	20,524,395 lbs.
BRAZIL		
Coffee	33,905,059	596,231,207 lbs.
India Rubber	17,876,121	28,026,714 lbs.
BRITISH AUSTRALASIA		
Wool—Unmanufactured	2,933,751	11,007,947 lbs.
BRITISH COLUMBIA		
Coal (Bituminous)	2,864,237	750,205 tons
BRITISH EAST INDIES		
Jute and Jute Butts	3,440,252	6,682 lbs.
Goat Skins	5,598,937	22,277,999 lbs.
Hides of Cattle	4,267,892	35,312,183 lbs.
Tin—Bars, Blocks	10,220,490	
BRITISH GUIANA		
Sugar Cane	3,779,398	
BRITISH WEST INDIES		
Sugar cane	4,603,409	
CANADA		
Wood—Unmanufactured	7,464,208	
CHINESE EMPIRE		
Silk—Raw	12,171,309	3,854,657 lbs.
CUBA		
Sugar cane	18,243,635	
Tobacco—Leaf	7,382,423	11,272,334 lbs.
DUTCH EAST INDIES		
Sugar cane	24,170,081	
Coffee	2,935,661	17,313,728 lbs.
FRANCE		
Cotton, Laces and Edgings	3,666,213	
Goat Skins	2,809,291	9,568,071 lbs.
Silk		
Dress and Piece Goods	7,104,208	
Laces and Embroideries	2,357,413	
Wines	3,853,547	
GERMANY		
Chemicals, Drugs, Dyes	3,145,254	
Cotton, Knit Goods	4,185,229	
Earthen, Stone and China Ware	2,619,737	
Hides other than Cattle	2,774,117	14,743,426 lbs.
Leather, Gloves	2,785,103	
Toys	2,674,035	
ITALY		
Lemons	3,581,374	
Raw Silk	10,816,084	2,217,879 lbs.
JAPAN		
Silk—Raw	19,686,132	4,765,091 lbs.
MEXICO		
Copper and Manufactures of	2,837,775	21,521,755 lbs.
Coffee	3,312,608	35,327,921 lbs.
Lead and Manufactures of	2,540,101	173,290,198 lbs.
Sisal Grass	11,533,772	75,241 tons

	Value	Quantity
NETHERLANDS		
Tobacco Leaf	$ 4,558,143	
Diamonds	3,424,219	
SWITZERLAND		
Cotton Laces, Edgings	8,070,107	
Silk Dress Goods	2,797,876	
UNITED KINGDOM		
Copper and Manufactures of	7,856,350	50,469,062 lbs.
Cotton		
Laces, Edgings, etc.	4,762,339	
Other Manufactures	3,530,701	
Furs	2,403,562	
Hides other than Cattle	4,986,378	30,132,807 lbs.
India Rubber	5,562,680	8,611,061 lbs.
Iron and Steel		
Tin Plates, Terne Plates, and Taggers Tin	4,770,846	147,260,787 lbs.
Machinery	2,540,580	
Jewelry	2,961,553	
Diamonds	2,560,106	
Tin, Bars, Blocks	7,177,134	
Wool		
Unmanufactured	2,618,164	
Cloth	3,660,501	
Dress Goods	2,526,171	
Vegetable Fibers		
Fabrics	4,674,524	
Others	11,350,168	
VENEZUELA		
Coffee	3,532,511	42,444,443 lbs.

IMPORTS BY COUNTRY OF ORIGIN, 1938

(Goods Imported in Amounts totalling at least $5,000,000)

	Value	Quantity
ARGENTINA		
Flaxseed	$18,559,181	14,342,302 bu.
BELGIUM		
Diamonds, Cut but Unset	13,869,072	287,144 carats
BRAZIL		
Cocoa	8,258,343	185,404,734 lbs.
Coffee	67,425,594	1,200,252,783 lbs.
BRITISH INDIA		
Jute Manufactures, Burlaps	24,766,432	460,385,530 lbs.
BRITISH MALAYA		
Rubber, Crude and Milk of	75,502,548	547,933,508 lbs.
Tin Bars, Blocks, Pigs, etc.	32,952,813	82,146,688 lbs.
CANADA		
Whiskey	10,597,200	3,559,988 pf. gal.
Sawed Boards and Lumber	11,387,593	469,032 M. ft.
Shingles	5,029,847	1,846,931 sq. ft.
Pulp Woods	11,038,380	1,293,930 cords
Nickel Pigs, Ingots, etc.	10,733,051	43,003,757 lbs.
Woodpulp	22,125,235	467,443 tons
Asbestos, Unmanufactured	5,066,762	148,277 tons
Standard Newsprint Paper	89,236,227	3,926,872,788 lbs.
Copper for Smelting, Refining and Export	5,709,315	57,223,466 lbs.
CEYLON		
Tea	6,707,337	22,144,688 lbs.
Rubber Other than Latex (Crude)	8,493,595	55,492,395 lbs.
CHILE		
Copper for Smelting, Refining and Export	10,997,933	121,873,886 lbs.
Sodium Nitrate	10,689,289	575,841 tons
CHINA		
Tung Oil	11,133,149	100,054,026 lbs.
COLOMBIA		
Coffee	45,829,541	452,889,916 lbs.
CUBA		
Cane Sugar	76,828,540	3,757,885,930 lbs.
FINLAND		
Sulphite Wood Pulp	7,160,166	170,368 tons
Standard Newsprint Paper	5,414,353	302,267,256 lbs.

	Value	Quantity
FRENCH INDO-CHINA		
Rubber, Crude	$ 6,746,806	45,253,662 lbs.
GREECE		
Cigarette Leaf Tobacco	11,161,501	19,547,404 lbs.
HONDURAS		
Bananas	5,126,425	9,888,812 bunches
ITALY		
Olive Oil, Edible	5,721,845	40,489,657 lbs.
JAPAN		
Raw Silk	83,651,240	51,323,148 lbs.
MEXICO		
Bananas	6,786,229	15,497,429 bunches
Copper for Smelting, Refining and Export	5,603,972	64,918,580 lbs.
NETHERLANDS INDIES		
Rubber Other than Latex (Crude)	33,821,016	233,699,208 lbs.
Palm Oil	7,922,569	228,309,060 lbs.
NETHERLANDS WEST INDIES		
Fuel Oil Including Top, Crude	5,853,181	7,047,695 bbl.
Fuel Oil Free for Supplies to Vessels	9,637,345	17,873,167 bbl.
PERU		
Copper for Smelting, Refining and Export	6,952,443	74,122,323 lbs.
PHILIPPINE ISLANDS		
Cane Sugar	50,588,110	303,298,647 lbs.
Copra Seed	8,847,867	490,647,785 lbs.
Coconut Oil	11,399,826	363,919,285 lbs.
Cotton Wearing Apparel	5,651,318	
POLAND AND DANZIG		
Hams, Shoulders, Bacon	8,772,194	32,592,905 lbs.
RUSSIA		
Lamb, Kid, Sheep and Goatskin Furs	6,705,408	975,636 furs
SALVADOR		
Coffee	5,549,583	71,265,767 lbs.
SWEDEN		
Sulphite Wood Pulp	18,095,191	438,483 tons
Sulphate Wood Pulp	13,955,623	349,383 tons
SWITZERLAND		
Watches and Watch Movements	6,549,488	2,393,830 units
TURKEY		
Cigarette Leaf, Unstemmed	11,125,419	24,421,851 lbs.
UNITED KINGDOM		
Whiskey	31,831,026	6,672,863 pf. gal.
VENEZUELA		
Crude Petroleum	14,965,293	20,846,477 bbl.

EXPORTS BY COUNTRY, 1938

(In Amounts of $10,000,000 and more)

United Kingdom	$520,878,000
Canada	467,767,000
Japan	239,662,000
British Africa	158,023,000
France	133,872,000
Germany	107,130,000
Netherlands	96,732,000
Argentina	86,793,000
Philippine Islands	86,464,000
Sweden-Norway	84,794,000
Belgium	76,942,000
Cuba	76,331,000
China (including Hong Kong and Kwantung)	73,012,000
Russia	69,691,000
Australia	68,992,000
Mexico	62,016,000
Brazil	61,957,000
Italy	58,292,000
Venezuela	52,278,000
Dutch West Indies	42,767,000
Colombia	$40,862,000
British India	33,441,000
Dutch East Indies	27,518,000
Ireland	27,259,000
Czechoslovakia	26,526,000
Denmark	24,814,000
Poland, Danzig	24,695,000
Chile	24,603,000
New Zealand	23,461,000
British West Indies	21,564,000
Peru	16,892,000
Canal Zone	14,242,000
Egypt	13,317,000
Turkey	13,218,000
Spain	12,266,000
Finland	11,991,000
Portugal	10,950,000
Switzerland	10,596,000
Panama	10,165,000

APPENDIX V

RAILROAD MILEAGE, 1840-1940

Year	Mileage	Year	Mileage	Year	Mileage
1840	2,818	1880	93,267	1920	252,845
1850	9,021	1890	167,191	1930	249,052
1860	30,626	1900	198,964	1940	233,670
1870	52,922	1910	249,992		

APPENDIX VI

INITIATIVE, REFERENDUM, AND RECALL

	Initiative	Referendum	Recall		
			State-wide	Local	Judicial
Alabama	1907	1907			
Arkansas	1910	1911			
Arizona	1911	1910	1912		
California	1911–12	1911–12	1911		
Colorado	1910	1910	1912		
Idaho	1911–12	1911–12	1912§		
Indiana		1901 †			
Kansas			1914		
Louisiana			1914§		
Maryland		1915			
Massachusetts	1918	1918			
Michigan	1908¶	1908¶			
	1913	1913	1913§		
Mississippi	1908	1908			
Missouri	1908	1908			
Montana	1906‡	1906‡			
Nebraska	1911–12	1911–12			
Nevada	1911–12	1904	1912		
New Mexico		1911			
North Dakota	1911–12	1911–12	1914		
Ohio	1911	1911	1913	1911	
Oregon	1902	1902	1908		1908
South Carolina					1910
South Dakota	1898	1898		1907	
Utah	1900*	1900†			
Washington	1911–12	1911–12	1912§	1907	
Wisconsin			1926	1911	

* Ineffective: legislation has failed to render available the provision in the constitution.
† Impractical and ineffective.
‡ Modified.
¶ Conditional.
§ Except Judges.

Index

Since the primary purpose of the index is to help the user locate the place or places in which he is interested, the territorial abbreviations appearing after most place names are designed to help that search, even if strict accuracy of terminology is thereby sacrificed. This is particularly true in Colonial Spanish America, where non-Spanish terms such as "Spanish Central America" and "Spanish South America" are used in place of the more euphonious but less well known "Nueva España," "Nueva Leon," "Nueva Estremadura," or "Castillo del Oro." Similarly in Canada "Ont." (Ontario) refers to the territory embraced within the borders of Ontario today, but is used also instead of upper and lower Canada throughout the period of British control of that area.

Since the secondary purpose of the index is to increase the instruction the *Atlas* is intended to offer, old-time geographical terminology is used in colonial America except in the Spanish areas. Thus one may find "Vincennes" listed as "Fr. Ill." in one place, referring to the French term for that region, the "Illinois Country"; in another as "P.Q." for the period when the town was governed by the British who, by the act of 1774, assigned that territory to the Province of Quebec; still later, of course, as "Ind." for Indiana. This device, though it produces some startling juxtapositions in the index, should prove helpful to the teacher who works with his or her class through the index.

The following abbreviations are used in the index:

Ala. Alabama
Alb. Province of Alberta, Canada
Arg. Argentina
Ark. Arkansas
Ariz. Arizona
B.C. Province of British Columbia, Canada
Belg. Belgium
Bol. Bolivia
Br. British
B.W.I. British West Indies
C.A. Central America
Cal. California
Can. Canada
Col. Colombia
Colo. Colorado
Conn. Connecticut
D.C. District of Columbia
D.E.I. Dutch East Indies
Del. Delaware
Dist. District
D.W.I. Dutch West Indies
Ec. Ecuador
Eng. England
Fla. Florida
Fr. France, French
Fr. Ill. French Illinois (loose term covering the Ohio Valley, etc.)
Ga. Georgia
G.B. Great Britain
Ger. Germany
Ida. Idaho
Ill. Illinois
Ind. Indiana
Ind. Co. Indian Country (in all cases where used, applies to territory later included in Oklahoma)
Is. Island
Kan. Kansas
Ky. Kentucky
La. Louisiana (to America a territory and later a state; to France, the Mississippi Valley, except the loosely defined "Illinois Country"—see *Fr. Ill.*; to Spain, the Mississippi Valley; West Florida was included by France, excluded by Spain).
Lab. Labrador
L.I. Long Island, N.Y. (used only in sense of colonial period to distinguish British colonial settlements from those of New Netherlands in the western end of the island)
Mass. Massachusetts, and Massachusetts Bay
Md. Maryland
Me. Maine
Mex. Mexico
Mich. Michigan
Minn. Minnesota
Miss. Mississippi
Mo. Missouri
Mont. Montana
Mts. Mountains
N.B. New Brunswick, Canada
N.C. North Carolina
N. Dak. North Dakota
Neb. Nebraska
Neth. Netherlands
Nev. Nevada
Nfld. Newfoundland
Nic. Nicaragua
N.H. New Hampshire
N.J. New Jersey
N. Mex. New Mexico
N. Neth. New Netherland
N. Sco. Nova Scotia, Canada
N. Swe. New Sweden
N.W. Terr. Northwest Territory, or Territory Northwest of the River Ohio (used, beginning in 1783 for convenience, for territory included in the Northwest Territory in 1787)
N.Y. New York
Okla. Oklahoma
Ont. Province of Ontario, Canada; used in earlier days in place of Upper and Lower Canada
Ore. Oregon
Pa. Pennsylvania
Pan. Panama
Para. Paraguay
P.E.I. Prince Edwards Island, Canada
Penin. Peninsula
P.Q. Province of Quebec, Canada (used for the period of British rule and the Dominion, including territory under the Quebec Act of 1774 to 1783. *See also Que.*)
P.R. Puerto Rico
Que. French Quebec (used loosely to cover Great Lakes basin.—*See also P.Q.*)

R. River
R.I. Rhode Island
R.I. and P. P. Rhode Island and Providence Plantation (used for colonial Rhode Island)
S.A. South America
Sask. Province of Saskatchewan, Canada
S.C. South Carolina
Sd. Sound
S. Dak. South Dakota
S. Dom. Santo Domingo
Sp. Spain, Spanish
Sp. C.A. Spanish Central America (a loose term applied to modern Central America in place of the Spanish colonial terms which are unfamiliar in the United States, such as Castillo del Oro, Nueva Estremadura, etc.)
Sp. Cal. Spanish California (including Upper and Lower California)
Sp. Cuba Spanish or colonial Cuba
Sp. Fla. Spanish Florida
Sp. Mex. Spanish or colonial Mexico
Sp. N. Mex. Spanish New Mexico (the Spanish colony centering about Santa Fé)
Sp. S.A. Spanish South America (a loose term applied in these maps only to the Spanish Main and Nueva Andalusia)
Sp. Tex. Spanish Texas (applied loosely to Texas before the Revolution of 1835)
Str. Strait
Sts. Straits
Tenn. Tennessee
Tex. Texas
T.H. Territory of Hawaii
Urug. Uruguay
USSR Union of Socialist Soviet Republics
Ven. Venezuela
Vt. Vermont
Wash. Washington (State)
W.I. West Indies
Wisc. Wisconsin
W. Can. West Canada (used for colonial period for the territory lying west of the Great Lakes and Mississippi River watersheds)
W. Va. West Virginia (after 1863: *Va.* to that time)
Wyo. Wyoming

Aberdeen, S. Dak., 1
Abilene, Kan., and Chisholm Trail, 226
Abingdon, Va., 58
Abolition, 1800, 149; 1821, 150; 1840, 151; 1850, 152; 1854, 153; 1860, 154; 1863–4, 155; 1865–8, 156
Abnaki Indians, Me., 19
Abraham Lincoln National Park, Ky., 263
Acadia National Park, Me., 263
Acapulco, Mex., in the Mexican War, 97; Sp. Mex., 21
Accau, route of, 28
Ackia Battleground National Monument, Miss., 263
Acoma, Sp. N. Mex., 35
Acre, S.A., 4
Aden, 305
AEF in Europe, World War I, 213
Afghanistan, 305
Agawam, Mass., 27
Age of discovery, 20
Agriculture, *see* Cattle, Corn, Cotton, Crop Areas, Drought Frequency, Farm Tenancy, Farming, Regionalized Types of, Improved Acreage, Soil Regions, Tobacco, Wheat
Airlines, 1922, 253; 1930, 254; 1940, 255
Akari Mts., S.A., 4
Akron, Ohio, 1
Alabama R., Ala., 2
Alacrans Is., claimed by U. S., 305*n*
Alamo, Tex., 97
Alaska, 3, 305; physical features of, 2, 3; border dispute, 209; airline connections from continental U. S. to, 255; annexed, 257*n*
Alaska, Gulf of, 3
Alaska Mts., 2, 3
Alaska Penin., 2, 3
Alaska R., 3
Albany, N. Y., 1; in Seven Years' War, 34; and Underground Railway, 146
Albany R., Ont., 3
Albemarle-Chesapeake Canal, Va.-N.C., 250
Albemarle Sd., N.C., 2
Alberta, prov. of, 3
Albuquerque, routes of, 20
Albuquerque, N. Mex., 1; Sp. N. Mex., 35; in the Mexican War, 97; and mail routes, *circa* 1850, 116; in the Civil War, 160
Aleutian Is., Alaska, 2, 305
Alexander, Sir Wm., charter grants to, 22
Alexandria-Georgetown Canal, Va.-D.C., 117
Alexandria, La., in the Civil War, 159, 160
Alexandria, Va., 1; in War of 1812, 95; and domestic routes of slave trade, 146
Algeria, 305
Aliens, enfranchisement of, 197
Allegheny Plateau, 2
Allegheny R., Pa., 2
Allentown, Pa., 1
Allouez, route of, 28
All Saints Bay, Brazil, 4
Almaden, Sp. Mex., 21
Aluminum, world production of, 309
Alsace, prov. of, 213
Alta California, 35
Altamaha R., Ga., 2
Altar, Sp. Mex., 35
Amazon R., S.A., 4; American exploration of, 127*n*
Amchitka Is., Alaska, 2
Amelia Is., Fla., 126
Amendments to the Constitution, *see* Constitution
America Is., claimed by U. S., 305*n*
American Empire, 305
American Expeditionary Force, *see* AEF
American explorations in West, 59
American Line Steamship Corp., subsidized routes of, 258
American Mail Line, subsidized routes of, 258
American occupation zone, Ger., World War I, 213
American Scantic Lines, subsidized routes of, 258
American South African Line, subsidized routes of, 258
American West African Line, subsidized routes of, 258
Amersfoert, N. Neth., 24
Amherst, routes of in the Seven Years' War, 34
Amherstburg, Ont., 94
Amsterdam, Neth., 213
Amur R., Siberia, 127*n*
Anaconda, Mont., 1, 6
Andes Mts., S.A., 4
Andorra, Republic of, 213
Andreanof Is., Alaska, 2
Andrew Johnson Homestead Project, Tenn., 263
Anglo-Egyptian Sudan, 305

Angmagssalik, Greenland, 3
Angola, 305
Annapolis, Md., 1, 26, 29
Anne's Is., claimed by U.S., 305*n*
Antarctica, discovery of by Wilkes, 126*n;* Little America, etc., 305
Anthracite coal deposits, U.S., 8
Anticosti Is., Can., 2, 3
Antietam, Md., in the Civil War, 158
Antigua, B.W.I., 2; U.S. base at, 258*n*, 305*n*
Antilla, W. I., U.S. airline connections to, 254, 255
Antofagasta, Chile, 4
Anza, route of, 35
Apache Indians, 19
Apalachicola arsenal, Ga., 157
Apalachicola R., Fla., 2, 60, 62
Appalachian Mts., 2
Appalachian oil field, 9
Appomattox Court House, Va., in the Civil War, 161
Arabia, 305
Arabian Sea, 305
Araguaya R., Brazil, 4
Arapahoe Indians, Wyo.-Mont., 19
Archangel, USSR, U.S. intervention at, 258*n*, 305*n*
Arches National Monument, Utah, 263
Arctic Circle, 3
Arctic Ocean, 2, 3
Arenas Is., claimed by U.S., 305*n*
Arenas Key, claimed by U.S., 305*n*
Arequipa, Peru, 4
Argentina, 4, 305
Arica, Chile, 4
Arizona Territory, 165
Arizpe, Sp. Mex., 35
Arkansas Indians, Ark.-Okla., 19
Arkansas Post, Ark., 59; in the Civil War, 159
Arkansas R., 2, 58, 97
Arkansas Territory, 66, 67
Army camps, World War I, 212
Army construction projects, U.S., 212
Army embarkation ports, World War I, 212
Arnold, routes of, in the Revolution, 46, 47; route as British general in the Revolution, 50
Aroostook War, 127*n*
Arrow Lake, Ont., 73
Aruba, D.W.I., 4; intervention in, 258*n*, 305*n*
Ashburton Line, proposed for Oregon, 72
Ashe, route of, in the Revolution, 49
Ashcville, N.C., 1
Ashley, route of, 59
Ashley's Post, Utah, 58
Aspinwall, William F., at Panama, 127*n*
Astoria, Ore., 1; *see also* Ft. Clatsop
Astorians, route of, 58
Assiniboin Indians, Minn., 19
Asuncion, Para., 4
Atchinson, Kan., 1
Athabaska R., Can., 2, 3
Athens Canal, Ohio, 117
Atitlan, Sp. Mex., 21
Atlanta, Ga., 1; in the Civil War, 160; Federal Reserve Bank, 246
Atlantic and Caribbean Steam Navigation Co., subsidized routes of, 258
Atlantic City, N.J., 1
Atlantic Ocean, 2
Atrato R., Col., 4
Attawapiskat R., Ont., 3
Attu Is., Alaska, 2
Augusta, Ga., 1, 58; in the Revolution, 49; branch of Second Bank of the U.S. at, 112
Augusta arsenal, Ga., 157
Augusta Canal, Ga., 118
Augusta, Me., 1
Austin, Tex., 1, 97
Australia, 305; U.S. troops in, 258*n*
Austria, 305
Avalon Penin., Nfld., 3; U.S. base at, 258*n*, 305*n*
Averasboro, N.C., in the Civil War, 161
Ayllon, route of, 21
Azores Is., 41
Aztec Ruins National Monument, N. Mex., 263

Badlands National Monument, S. Dak., 263
Baffin Bay, 2, 3, 305
Baffin Land, Can., 2, 3
Bahama Is., 2, 21
Bahia, Brazil, 4
Bahia Blanca, Arg., 4
Bahia Hondo, Cuba, U.S. base rights at, 258*n*, 305
Baker Is., claimed by U.S., 305*n*
Baker Reclamation Project, Ore., 264
Balboa, route of, 21
Balearic Is., Sp., 213
Balfour, route of, in the Revolution, 50
Baltic Sea, 305
Baltimore, Lord, charter grant to, 22
Baltimore, Md., 1, 7, 9, 26, 31, 58; in the War of 1812, 95; branch of First Bank of the U.S. at, 111; Second Bank, 112; and domestic routes of slave trade, 146; and Underground Railway, 146; embarkation port, World War I, 212
Bandelier National Monument, N. Mex., 263
Bandera, Tex., and Western Trail, 226
Banff, Alb., 3
Bangor, Me., 1; in the War of 1812, 95
Bank of the United States, First, branches, 111; Second, branches, 112
Banks, 1800, 111; 1830, 112; 1850, 113; 1880, 245; Federal Reserve districts and branches, 246
Banks, routes of, in the Civil War, 159, 160
Banks Is., Can., 3
Banks of Newfoundland, 41
Bannock Indians, Ida.-Mont., 19
Baranquilla, Col., 4
Barbados, W. I., 4
Baranof Is., Alaska, 3
Barber's Is., claimed by U.S., 305*n*
Barcelona, Sp., 213
Barents Sea, 305
Barren Is., claimed by U.S., 305*n*
Baton Rouge, La., 1, 9; in the Revolution, 49; in the Civil War, 158, 159
Baton Rouge arsenal, La., 157
Bastidas, route of, 21
Bauman's Is., claimed by U.S., 305*n*
Baxter Springs, Kan., and the Shawnee Trail, 226
Bay City, Mich., 1
Bay of Fundy, Can., 3
Bayonne, Fr., and U.S. in World War I, 213
Beaufort, S.C., 29
Beaufort Sea, 3
Beausejour, Can., in the Seven Years' War, 34
Bedford, Va., in the Revolution, 51
Beef, U. S. production of, 1940, 230; world production of, 317
Beeverwyak, N. Neth. (N.Y.), 24
Belcher Is., Can., 3

All numbers refer to maps, not pages

Belen, Sp. Mex., 35
Belfast, Me., in the War of 1812, 95
Belgian Congo, 305
Belgium, 305
Bellefonte, Pa., and nearby canal, 117; on commercial airline, 1922, 253
Belle Fourche Reclamation Project, S. Dak., 264
Bell, route of, 59
Bengal, Bay of, 305
Bennett Is., Siberia, claimed by U.S., 257*n*
Bennington, Vt., in the Revolution, 47
Benton, Mont., *see* Ft. Benton
Bentonville, N.C., in the Civil War, 161
Bent's Fort, Colo., 58, 59; in the Mexican War, 97
Bergen, N. Neth. (N.J.), 24
Bering Sea, 2, 3
Bermejo R., S.A., 4
Berkeley, charter grant to, 25
Berlin, Ohio, in the Civil War, 159
Bermuda, 2; U.S. airline connections to, 255; U.S. base at, 258*n*, 305, 305*n*
Bienville, route of, 30
Big Bend National Park Project, Tex., 263
Big Hole Battlefield National Monument, Mont., 263
Big Horn Mts., 2
Bilbao, Sp., 213
Bill of Rights, *see* Constitution (First ten amendments)
Billings, Mont., 1
Binghamton, N.Y., 1
Birmingham, Ala., 1, 7
Birnie Is., claimed by U.S., 305*n*
Bisbee, Ariz., 1, 6
Bismarck, N. Dak., 1
Bitterroot Range, Mont., etc., 2
Bitterroot Reclamation Project, Mont., 264
Bituminous coal deposits, U.S., 8
Black Canyon of the Gunnison National Monument, Colo., 263
Blackfeet Indians, Mont., 19
Black Hills, S. Dak., 2, 6
Black River Canal, N.Y., 118
Black Rock Desert, Nev., 2
Black Rock, N.Y., in the War of 1812, 94
Black Sea, 305
Blackstock, S.C., in the Revolution, 50
Blackstone Canal, Mass.-R.I., 117
Black Warrior incident, 127*n*
Blanca Bay, Arg., 4
Bloody Marsh, Ga., in the War of the Austrian Succession, 32
Blue Mts., 2
Blue Ridge Mts., N.C.-Va., 2
Blunt, route of, in the Civil War, 158
Bogotá, Col., 4
Boise, Ida., 1; *see also* Ft. Boise
Boise Reclamation Project, Ida., 264
Bolivia, 4, 305
Bonaire, D.W.I., 4; intervention in, 258*n*, 305*n*
Bonin Is., claimed by U.S., 127*n*
Boonesboro, Ky., 58
Boone's Wilderness Trail, Ky., 58
Boothia Penin., 3
Bosque, route of, 35
Bordeaux, Fr., disembarkation port, World War I, 213
Borneo, 305
Boston, Mass., 1, 22, 27; in the War of the League of Augsburg, 28; in the War of the Spanish Succession, 30; in the Revolution, 46, 48; in the War of 1812, 95; branch of First Bank of the U.S. at, 111; Second Bank, 112; and Underground Railway, 146; embarkation port, World War I, 212; Federal Reserve Bank, 246; base at, 305
Boston Mts., 2
Botwood, Nfld., 3
Boulder, Colo., 1
Boulder Dam, 264
Bounty lands, for Revolutionary soldiers, 53; for veterans of the War of 1812, 95
Bourgemont, route of, 32
Boxer Rebellion, China, sites of U.S. intervention in, 257*n*
Boyd, route of, in the Revolution, 49
Braddock, route of, in the Seven Years' War, 34
Braddock's Road, Pa.-Md., 58
Bradstreet, route of, in Seven Years' War, 34
Bragg, routes of, in the Civil War, 158
Branco R., Brazil, 4
Brandenburg, Ky., in the Civil War, 159
Brandywine, Pa., in the Revolution, 47
Brant, route of, in the Revolution, 48
Brazil, 4, 305
Brazito, N. Mex., in the Mexican War, 97
Brazos R., Tex., 2, 97
Brest, Fr., disembarkation port, World War I, 213
Breuckelen (Brooklyn), N. Neth. (N.Y.), 22, 24
Brewster, Mass., in the War of 1812, 95
Briar Creek, Ga., in the Revolution, 49
Bridgeport, Conn., 1
Bristol Bay, Alaska, 2, 3
Bristol, Eng., disembarkation port, World War I, 213
British colonies and charter grants, 1660, 22; 1700, 25; 1750, 26; colonies, 1763–1775, 36
British Columbia, prov. of, 3
British Guiana, 4, 305; U.S. base at Georgetown, 305*n*
British Isles, 305
Brock, route of, in the War of 1812, 93
Brooklyn (Breuckelen), N. Neth. (N.Y.), 22, 24
Brown, Jacob, route of, in the War of 1812, 95
Brownsville, Tex., 1
Brunswick, Ga., 1; in the War of the Austrian Succession, 32; and Brunswick Canal, 118
Brunswick, Me., 26
Brunswick Canal, Ga., 118
Bruselas, Sp. C.A., 21
Bryan, Ohio, on commercial airline, 1922, 253
Bryce Canyon National Park, Utah, 263
Buchanan, Va., terminus of James River and Kanawha Canal, 118
Buell, route of, in the Civil War, 158
Buena Vista, Cal., Naval Oil Reserve, 9
Buena Vista, Mex., in the Mexican War, 97
Buenos Aires, Arg., 4
Buffalo, N.Y., 1, 58; in the War of 1812, 95; branch of Second Bank of the U.S. at, 112; and nearby canals, 117; and Underground Railway, 146
Buffalo Rapids Reclamation Project, Mont., 264
Bulgaria, 305
Bull Run, Va., in the Civil War, 157
Burgoyne, routes of, in the Revolution, 46, 47
Burlington, Vt., 1
Burma, 305
Burnside, routes of, in the Civil War, 159
Butler, route of, in the Revolution, 48
Butterfield Overland Mail, 116
Butte, Mont., 1, 6
Byrd-Ellsworth Sector, Antarctica, 305

Cabot, routes of, 20

All numbers refer to maps, not pages

Cabot Str., Nfld.-N. Sco., 3
Cabral, route of, 20
Cabrillo, route of, 21
Cabrillo National Monument, Cal., 263
Caddo Indians, Tex.-La., 19
Cagayan Sulú and Sibitú, purchased from Spain, 257*n*
Cahokia, Fr. Ill., 30; P.Q., in the Revolution, 48
Cairo, Ill., and Underground Railway, 146; in the Civil War, 158
Caldwell, Kan., and Chisholm Trail, 226
Calgary, Alb., 3
California, Alta, 35
California Cut-off, N. Mex., etc., 58
California, Lower, 98
California, Oregon, and Mexico Steamship Co., routes of, 257
California Trail, 58
Callao, Peru, 4
Calumet, Mich., 6
Calvert (Lord Baltimore), charter grant to, 22
Camarga, Mex., in the Mexican War, 97
Cambridge City, Ohio, and White Water Canal, 118
Cambridge, Mass., in the Revolution, 46
Camden, Ark., in the Civil War, 160
Camden, N.J., 1
Camden, S.C., in the Revolution, 50
Camp Beauregard, La., 212
Camp Bowie, Tex., 212
Camp Cody, N. Mex., 212
Camp Cooper, Tex., 58
Camp Custer, Mich., 212
Camp Devens, Mass., 212
Camp Dix, N.J., 212
Camp Dodge, Iowa, 212
Camp Doniphan, Okla., 212
Camp Fremont, Cal., 212
Camp Funston, Kan., 212
Camp Gordon, Ga., 212
Camp Grant, Ill., 212
Camp Greene, N.C., 212
Camp Hancock, Ga., 212
Camp Jackson, S.C., 212
Camp Kearney, Cal., 212
Camp Lee, Va., 212
Camp Logan, Tex., 212
Camp MacArthur, Tex., 212
Camp McClellan, Ala., 212
Camp Meade, Md., 212
Camp Pike, Ark., 212
Camp Sevier, S.C., 212
Camp Shelby, Miss., 212
Camp Sheridan, Ala., 212
Camp Sherman, Ohio, 212
Camp Taylor, Ky., 212
Camp Travis, Tex., 212
Camp Upton, N.Y., 212
Camp Wadsworth, S.C., 212
Camp Wheeler, Ga., 212
Campbell, routes of, in the Revolution, 48, 49
Campeche Bay, Mex., 2
Campos, Brazil, 4
Canada, 3, 305; physical features of, 2, 3; invasion of, 1775–6, 126; 1812–13, 126; first reciprocity treaty with, 127*n;* revolts of Papineau and Mackenzie, 127*n;* Alaska border dispute, 209; Fenian raids against, 257; Riel rebellion, 257*n*
Canadian R., Okla., etc., 2
Canals, to 1837, 117; 1837–60, 118; after 1860, 250; *see also* by specific name
Canal Zone, 305; leased by U.S., 257*n*
Canton, China, 126; forts bombarded, 305*n*
Canton Is., claimed by U.S., 305*n*
Canton, Miss., in the Civil War, 160
Canyon De Chelly National Monument, Ariz., 263
Cape Anne, Mass., 2
Cape Blanco, Arg., 4
Cape Blanco, Ore., 2
Cape Breton Island, N. Sco., 3
Cape Charles, Va., 2
Cape Chidley, Lab., 3
Cape Cod, Mass., 2
Cape Corrientes, Col., 4
Cape Farewell, Greenland, 2, 3
Cape Fear, N.C., 2
Cape Fear R., N.C., 2
Cape Flattery, Wash., 2
Cape Frio, Brazil, 4
Cape Hatteras, N.C., 2
Cape Henry, Va., 2
Cape Horn, S.A., 4
Cape Huacas, Peru, 4
Cape Mendocino, Cal., 2
Cape Race, Nfld., 2, 3
Cape Sable, Fla., 2
Cape Sable, N. Sco., 3
Cape San Blas, Fla., 2
Cape Tennyson, Can., 3
Capital export, *see* Investments abroad
Capitol Reef National Monument, Utah, 263
Capo de São Roque, Brazil, 4
Capulin Mountain National Monument, N. Mex., 263
Caracas, Ven., 4
Caranchua Indians, Tex., 19
Caribbean Sea, 2, 305; Spanish explorations and settlements in, 21
Carlsbad Caverns National Park, N. Mex., 263
Carlsbad Reclamation Project, N. Mex., 264
Carmen, Mex., in the Mexican War, 97
Carolina proprietors, charter grants to, 25
Carolinas, 22
Caroline Atoll, claimed by U.S., 305*n*
Caroline incident, 127*n*
Carson City, Nev., 1
Cartagena, Col., 4
Carteret, charter grant to, 25
Cartier, routes of, 20
Cartwright, Lab., 3
Casa Grande Ruins National Monument, Ariz., 263
Casas Grandes, Sp. Mex., 35
Cascade Mts., Wash.-Ore., 2
Casco, Me., in the War of the League of Augsburg, 28; in the War of the Spanish Succession, 30
Casper, Wyo., 1
Caspian Sea, 305
Castillo del Oro (C.A.), 21
Castillo, route of, 35
Castle Pinckney National Monument, S.C., 263
Catawba Indians, Ga.-S.C., 19
Cattle areas, 1700, 39; 1775, 40; 1860, 105; 1890, 227; 1920, 228; 1940, 229, 230; world production of, 317
Cattle trails, 226
Cauca R., Col., 4
Cayenne, Fr. Guiana, 4
Cayuga Indians, N.Y., 19
Cayuga-Seneca Canal, N.Y., 118

All numbers refer to maps, not pages

Cedar Bluff, Ala., in the Civil War, 159
Cedar Breaks National Monument, Utah, 263
Cedar Rapids, Iowa, 1
Cenis Indians, Tex., 19
Central Cordillera, S.A., 4
Central Valley Reclamation Project, Cal., 264
Cervera, route of, in the Spanish-American War, 207
Cessions of Western lands, *see* Land Cessions
Ceylon, 305
Chaco Canyon National Monument, N. Mex., 263
Chaco, S.A., 4
Chaleur Bay, Can., 3
Chambersburg, Pa., 160
Champagne-Marne sector, World War I, 213
Champlain, routes of, 28
Champlain-Hudson Canal, N.Y., 117
Chancellor and Willoughby, route of, 20
Chancellorsville, Va., in the Civil War, 159
Channel Islands National Monument, Cal., 263
Charcas, Sp. Mex., 21
Charity schools, *see* Schools, Public, State Legislation
Charlesfort, Carolina, 28
Charleston, S.C., 1, 25, 27, 30; in the Revolution, 46, 49, 50, 51; branch of First Bank of the U.S. at, 111; Second Bank, 112; and domestic routes of slave trade, 146; in the Civil War, 161; base at, 305
Charleston, W. Va., 1
Charleston arsenal, S.C., 157
Charleston-Santee Canal, S.C., 117
Charlestown, S.C., *see* Charleston
Charlotiana, 53
Charlotte, N.C., 1, 33; in the Revolution, 50
Charlottesville, Va., 1, 31; in the Revolution, 51
Charlottetown, P.E.I., 3
Charter grants, 1660, 22; 1700, 25; 1750, 26; to Berkeley and Carteret, 25; Conn. Co., 25; Council for New England, 22; De Mont's Government, 22; Gen. Oglethorpe, 26; Lord Baltimore, 22; Lord Hopton, 22; Mason and Gorges, 22; Mass. Bay Co., 22; Sir Robert Heath, 22; Sir (Lord) William Alexander, 22, 22n; the Carolina Proprietors, 25; Virginia (London) Co., 22; Virginia (Plymouth) Co., 22; William Penn, 25
Chateau Thierry, Fr., and U.S. in World War I, 213
Chateauguay, N.Y., in the War of 1812, 94
Chattahoochee R., Ga.-Fla., 2, 60, 62
Chattanooga, Tenn., 1; in the Civil War, 158, 159, 160
Chaudiere R., P.Q., 3
Chaumont, Fr., and U.S. in World War I, 213
Chehalis Indians, Wash., 19
Chemung Canal, N.Y., 117
Chenango Canal, N.Y., 117
Cheraw, S.C., in the Revolution, 50
Cherbourg, Fr., and U.S. in World War I, 213
Cherry Valley, N.Y., in the Revolution, 48
Cherokee Indians, Tenn.-N.C., 19
Chesapeake and Ohio Canal, 118
Chesapeake Bay, Md. 2
Chester, Ill., and Underground Railway, 146
Chester, Pa., 1
Chesterfield Inlet, Keewatin, 2, 3
Cheyenne, Wyo., 1, 226; and mail routes, 116; on commercial airline, 1922, 253
Cheyenne Indians, Wyo., 19
Chicago, Ill., 1; and Underground Railway, 146; on commercial airline, 1922, 253
Chickamauga, Ga., in the Civil War, 159
Chickasaw Bayou, Miss., in the Civil War, 158
Chickasaw Indians, Ala.-Miss.-Tenn., 19
Chickasaw Landing, Ala., in the Civil War, 161
Chicora, Sp. Fla., 35
Chicoutimi, P.Q., 3
Chihuahua, Mex., 1, 59; in the Mexican War, 97
Child labor, in any gainful occupation, 1880, 282; 1890, 284; 1900, 286; 1915, 288; 1930, 290; in mercantile and manufacturing establishments, 1880, 281; 1890, 283; 1900, 285; 1915, 287; 1930, 289; amendment, votes of the states on, 303
Chile, 4, 305; crisis with, 1891, 257*n*
Chillicothe, Ohio, branch of Second Bank at, 112
China, 305; U.S. interventions in, 127, 257; in Boxer Rebellion, 305*n*; Canton forts bombarded, 305*n*
China Sea, 305
Chincha Is., Peru, 127*n*; claimed by U.S., 305*n*
Chinook Indians, Wash., 19
Chippewa Indians, Minn.-Wisc., 19
Chippewa, Ont., in the War of 1812, 95
Chiricahua National Monument, Ariz., 263
Chisholm Trail, 226
Choctaw Indians, Miss., 19
Chouteau's Landing, Mo., 58
Christianhaab, Greenland, 3
Christmas Is., claimed by U.S., 305*n*
Chrysler's Farm, Ont., in the War of 1812, 94
Chugach Mts., Alaska, 3
Church, route of, in the War of the Spanish Succession, 30
Churchill R., Can., 2, 3
Cienfuegos, Cuba, U.S. airline connections to, 255
Cincinnati, Ohio, 1, 58; in the War of 1812, 94; branch of Second Bank at, 112; and Underground Railway, 146; in the Civil War, 159
Circuit Court boundaries, *see* Courts
Civil War, campaigns of 1861, 157; 1862, 158; 1863, 159; 1864, 160; 1865, 161; line of Northern occupation, 1861, 157; 1862, 158; 1863, 159; 1864, 160; Southern opposition to secession, 148
Clarence Is., claimed by U.S., 305*n*
Clark, and Lewis, route of, 59
Clark, George Rogers, routes of, in the Revolution, 48, 49; land grant to, 53
Clark's Ferry, Pa., and nearby canals, 117
Clatsop Indians, Ore., 19
Cleveland, Ohio, 1, 7, 58; and Underground Railway, 146; Federal Reserve Bank, 246; on commercial airline, 1922, 253
Clinton, Sir Henry, routes of, in the Revolution, 46, 47, 49, 50, 51
Clinton, James, route of, in the Revolution, 48
Coahuilteco Indians, Tex., 19
Coal deposits, U.S., 8; World production of, 306
Coalport Canal, Pa., 117
Coast Mts., Can., 2, 3
Coast Range, Cal., 2
Cockburn, route of, in War of 1812, 95
Coeur d'Alène, Mont., 6
Cold Harbor, Va., in the Civil War, 160
Colleges, 1775, 43; 1800, 134; 1830, 136; 1850, 137; 1870, 271; 1890, 272; 1910, 273; 1930, 274
Collingwood, Ont., and the Underground Railway, 146
Collins Line, route of, 127
Colendonck, N. Neth. (N.Y.), 24
Colima, Sp. Mex., 21
Colombia, 4, 305; (New Granada), Panama transit treaty with, 1846, 127*n*; coaling station contract, 127*n*
Colombian Steamship Co., subsidized routes of, 258
Colonies, British, 1660, 22; 1700, 25; 1750, 26; 1763–75, 36
Colorado-Big Thompson Reclamation Project, Colo., 264

Colorado National Monument, Colo., 263
Colorado Negro R., Arg., 4
Colorado Plateau, 2
Colorado R., Ariz., etc., 2
Colorado R. Reclamation Project, Tex., 264
Colorado R., Tex., 2
Colorado Springs, Colo., 1
Colorado Territory, 90, 165
Columbia Basin irrigation project, Wash., 264
Columbia, Ga., in the Civil War, 161
Columbia, Pa., and nearby canals, 117, 118
Columbia, S.C., 1, 29
Columbia R., Wash., 72
Columbus, routes of, 20, 21
Columbus, Ga., 1
Columbus, Ohio, 1, 58
Colville Indians, Wash., 19
Colville R., Alaska, 2
Comanche Indians, 19
Compañía Exploradora, route of Col. Morgan's, 35
Company's Canal, La., 118
Compulsory school attendance, *see under* Schools
Comstock Lode, Nev., 6
Concepcion, Chile, 4
Concord, N.H., 1
Confederate arsenals, 1861, 157
Confederate States of America, 155
Congo, Belgian, 305
Congress, *see* Senate, or House
Congress Lands, 53
Connecticut, cession of western lands, 56
Connecticut Co., charter grant, 25
Connecticut R., Conn., Mass., etc., 2
Connecticut, Western Reserve of (Ohio), 53
Constitution, distribution of vote on ratification of, 57; ratification of first ten amendments, 82; 11th amend., 83; 13th amend., 162; 14th amend., 163; 15th amend., 164; 16th amend., 198; 17th amend., 199; 18th amend., 200; 19th amend., 201; 20th amend., 202; 21st amend., 203; child labor amend., vote of the states on, 303
Continental divide, 72, 209
Cook Inlet, Alaska, 3
Coos Indians, Ore., 19
Copper, U.S. deposits, 6; world production of, 311
Copper R., Alaska, 3
Coral Sea, 305; battle of, 258*n*
Cordoba, Arg., 4
Cordova, route of, 21
Corinth, Miss., in the Civil War, 158
Corn, 1840, 101; 1860, 102; 1890, 217; 1920, 218; 1940, 219; world production of, 315
Corn Is., Nic., leased, 258*n*
Cornwallis, routes of, in the Revolution, 46, 50, 51
Coro, Ven., 4
Coronado, route of, 21
Coronel, Chile, 4
Corpus Christi, Tex., 1; in the Mexican War, 97; base at, 305
Corrientes, Arg., 4
Corsica Is., Fr., 213
Cortereal, route of, 20
Cortes, routes of, 21
Cotton, 1840, 103; 1860, 104; 1890, 220; 1920, 221; 1940, 222; world production of, 314
Council Bluffs, Iowa, 1, 59
Courts, Federal Circuit and District, 1789, 84; 1801, 85; 1802, 86; 1802, 87; 1807, 88; 1837, 89; 1861, 90; 1873, 204; 1911, 205
Cowpens, S.C., in the Revolution, 51
Crater Lake National Park, Ore., 263
Craters of the Moon National Monument, Ida., 263
Creek Indians, Ala.-Ga., 19
Cripple Creek, Colo., 6
Crooked Lake Canal, N.Y., 117
Crop areas, 1700, 39; 1775, 40; regionalized types of farming, 12; *see also* Cattle, Corn, Cotton, Rice, Tobacco, Wheat
Crow Indians, Mont.-Dak., 19
Crown Point, N.Y., in the Revolution, 46, 47
Croxton, route of, in the Civil War, 161
Cuba, 2; colonial period of, 21; negotiations re, 127*n*, 257*n*; intervention in, 258*n*; occupation of and interventions in, 305*n*
Culebra Is. and Culebrita Is., P.R., purchase of, discussed, 257*n*
Culiacan, Sp. Mex., 21
Culpeper, Va., in the Civil War, 160
Cultivated Land, *see* Improved Acreage
Cumana, Ven., 4
Cumberland, Md., 1, 58; and Underground Railway, 146
Cumberland and Oxford Canal, Me., 117
Cumberland District, Ky-Tenn., 53
Cumberland Gap, Va.-Ky.-Tenn., 53, 58; in the Civil War, 159
Cumberland Mts., 2
Cumberland Pike, 58
Cumberland R., Tenn., 2
Cumberland Sd., Can., 3
Curaçao, D.W.I., 4; intervention in, 258*n*, 305*n*
Curtis, route of, in the Civil War, 158
Curitiba, Brazil, 4
Currituck, N.C., and Albemarle-Chesapeake Canal, 250
Curupira Mts., S.A., 4
Cuzco, Peru, 4
Czecho-Slovakia, 305

Da Gama, routes of, 20
Dahlonega, Ga., 6
Daiquiri, Cuba, in the Spanish-American War, 207
Dakota Indians, Dak.-Minn., 19
Dakota Territory, 90, 165
Dallas, Tex., 1; Federal Reserve Bank, 246
Danbury, Conn., in the Revolution, 47
Dangerous Is., claimed by U.S., 305*n*
Dangers Rock Is., claimed by U.S., 305*n*
Danish West Indies, early negotiations for, 257*n*; annexation, 257*n*
Danville, Va., 1
Darien, Gulf of, 4
Dauphin Is., La., 30
Davenport, Iowa, 1; and Underground Railway, 146
Davids Is., claimed by U.S., 305*n*
Davis, routes of, 20
Davis, route of, in the Civil War, 158
Davis St., Can., 2
Dawson, Yukon Dist., 3
Dayton, Ohio, 1, 58; in War of 1812, 93, 94
Deadwood, S. Dak., 6
De Anes Is., claimed by U.S., 305*n*
Dearborn, route in the War of 1812, 94
Death Valley, Cal., 2
Death Valley National Monument, Cal., 263
De Barras, route of, in the Revolution, 51
Deerfield, Mass., in the War of the Spanish Succession, 30
De Grasse, routes of, in the Revolution, 51

Delaware and Hudson Canal, N.Y., 117
Delaware and Raritan Canal, N.J., 118
Delaware Bay, 2; in the Revolution, 48
Delaware Division Canal, N.J.-Pa., 117
Delaware Indians, Del., 19
Delaware R., N.J.-Pa., etc., 2
De Leon, routes of, 21, 35
De Mont, charter grant to, 22
Denmark, 305
Denonville, route of, 28
Denver, Colo., 1, 6; and mail routes, *circa* 1859, 116
Denver Service (mail), 116
De Rouville, route of, in the War of the Spanish Secession, 30
Deschutes R., Ore., 72
Deschutes Reclamation Project, Ore., 264
Desert vegetation, 10
Des Moines, Iowa, 1; and Underground Railway, 146
De Soto, route of, 21
D'Estaing, routes of, in the Revolution, 48, 49
Detroit, Mich., 1, 7; Que., 30; N.W. Terr., 52; in War of 1812, 93, 94; and Underground Railway, 146
De Vaca, routes of, 21, 35
Devil Postpile National Monument, Cal., 263
Devil's Is., S.A., 4
Devil's Tower National Monument, Wyo., 263
Diaz, route of, 20, 21
Dinosaur National Monument, Utah-Wyo., 263
Diomede Is., Alaska, 3
Discovery, routes of, 20, 21
Disko Bay, Greenland, 3
District Courts, *see* Courts
Dixon Entrance, Alaska, 3
Doan's Store, Tex., 226
Dobbs Ferry, N.Y., in the Revolution, 51
Doce R., Brazil, 4
Dodge City, Kan., and Western Trail, 226
Dog Lake, Ont., 73
Dog R., Ont., 73
Dollier, route of, 28
Dollar Steamship Co., subsidized routes of, 258
Dolores, Sp. Mex., 35
Dolores, Sp. Tex., 35
Dominguez and Escalante, route of, 35
Dominica, W.I. 21
Dominican Republic, intervention in, 258*n;* occupation of, 305
Dominion of New England, 25*n*
Doniphan, route of, in the Mexican War, 97
Dover, Del., 1; and Underground Railway, 146; base at, 305
Dover, N.H., 22
Downie, route in the War of 1812, 95
Drainage basins, U.S., 5
Drake, Sir Francis, routes of, 20
Drought frequency, U.S., 16
Dubawnt R., Can., 3
Dubuque, Iowa, 1
Duluth, Minn., 1, 7
Duluth, route of, 28
Dunbar, route of, 59
Dunmore, attack on Newport by, 46
Durango, Sp. Mex., 21
Durham, N.C., 1
Durham Station, N.C., in the Civil War, 161
Duke of York Is., claimed by U.S., 305*n*
Dutch Guiana (Surinam), 4, 305
Dutch Harbor, Alaska, 2, naval base at, 305
Du Tisné, route of, 32
Early, routes of in the Civil War, 160
Early settlements, Dutch, 23, 24; English, 23, 24, 25, 27, 29, 31, 33; French, 28, 30, 32, 34; Spanish, 21, 35; Swedish, 23
East Cape, Alaska, 3
East Florida, British, 36
East New Jersey, 25
Easter Is., 305
Eastern Cordillera, S.A., 4
Eastern Division Canal, Pa., 117
Eastern Steamship Lines, subsidized routes of, 258
Easton, Pa., and nearby canals, 117
Ebenezer, Ga., 26
Ecuador, 4, 305
Edenton (Queen Anne's Creek), N.C., 29
Edmonton, Alb., 3
Egg Island, Gulf of St. Lawrence, 30
Egypt, 305
El Caney, Cuba, battle of, 207
Elcano, route of, 20
Electric power transmission lines, 1922, 214; 1935, 242
Elgin, Ill., 1
Elizabethtown, N.J., 25
Elkhart, Ind., 1
Elko, Nev., on commercial airline, 1922, 253
Ellesmere Is., Can., 3
El Morro National Monument, N. Mex., 263
El Paso, Tex., 1, 9; Sp. Tex., 35; in the Mexican War, 97; and mail routes, *circa* 1858, 116
Embargo, House vote on, 91
Embarkation ports, World War I, 212
Embarrass R., Minn., 73
Enderbury Is., claimed by U.S., 305*n*
Endicott Mts., Alaska, 2, 3
England, U.S. forces in, 258*n*, 305
English expansion, to 1697, 27; to 1713, 29; to 1744, 31; to 1763, 33
English R., Ont., 3
Enumerated goods, 41
Equator, in S.A., 4
Erie, Pa., 1, 58; *see also* Presqu'Isle
Erie Canal, N.Y., 58, 117
Erie (Pa.) Canal, Pa., 118
Erie Indians, Ohio-Pa., 19
Erie Triangle, ceded by New York to U.S., 56
Eritrea, 305; U.S. base at, 258*n*
Erosion areas, U.S., 13
Escalante, route of, 35
Esopus, N. Neth. (N.Y.), 24
Española (Haiti), 21
Espejo, route of, 21
Espinoza, route of, 21
Espiritu Santo, Sp. Mex., 21
Essequibo R., S.A., 4
Esthonia, 305
Ethiopia, 305
Europe, U.S. airline connections to, 255; *see also* names of specific countries
Evansville, Ind., 1; and Underground Railway, 146
Everglades, Fla., 2
Everglades National Park Project, Fla., 263
Everett, Wash., 1
Exeter, N.H., 22, 27
Expansion, U.S., 1775–1830, 126; 1830–1860, 127; 1904–1942, 258; English, to 1697, 27; to 1713, 29; to 1744, 31; to 1763, 33; French, to 1697, 28; to 1713, 30; to 1744, 32; to 1763, 34
Explorations, in Caribbean and Mexico, 19, 21; English

20; French, 20; Portuguese, 20; routes of, 1492–1587, 20; Spanish, 20; French in Gt. Lakes and Miss. Valley, 28; in New Mexico, etc., 35; U.S. in West, 59
Exports and imports, colonial, 41; 1800, 126; 1850, 127; 1900, 257; 1938, 258
Export Steamship Corp., subsidized routes of, 258
Exuma Is., B.W.I., U.S. base at, 258*n*, 305*n*

Fagundes, route of, 20
Fairfield Canal, N.C., 250
Fairfield, Conn., in the Revolution, 49
Falkland Is., S.A., 4, 305
Fall River, Mass., 1
Falls of the Ohio, 2
Fallen Timbers, Ohio, battle site, 53
Falmouth, Eng., disembarkation point, World War I, 213
Falmouth, Va., in the Civil War, 159
Fargo, N.D., 1
Farmers Is., claimed by U.S., 305*n*
Farming, regionalized types of, 12; *see also* Cattle, Corn, Crop Areas, Drought Frequency, Farm Tenancy, Improved Acreage, Rice, Soil Regions, Tobacco, Wheat
Farmington Canal, Conn., 117
Farm Tenancy, 1880, 237; 1910, 238; 1920, 239; 1930, 240
Farnham, route of, 59
Farragut, routes of, in Civil War, 157, 159, 160, 161
Father Millet Cross National Monument, N.Y., 263
Favorite Is., claimed by U.S., 305*n*
Fayetteville, N. C., branch of Second Bank at, 112
Fayetteville arsenal, N. C., 157
Federal highways, *see under* Roads and Highways, Post Roads
Federal Reserve bank, districts and branches, 246
Fenian raids, 257*n*
Ferguson, route of, in the Revolution, 50
Fernandina, Ga., in the War of the Austrian Succession, 32; in the Civil War, 158, 159
"Fifty-four, forty," 209
Fiji Is., 305
Finland, 305
Five Nations, N.Y., 19
Flagstaff, Ariz., 1
Flatbush (Midwout), N. Neth. (N.Y.), 24
Flathead Indians, Mont., 19
Flint, Mich., 1
Flint Is., claimed by U.S., 305*n*
Flint R., Fla. Ga., 2, 60, 61, 62
Flint's Is., claimed by U.S., 305*n*
Florida, Jackson's invasion of, 1818, 95
Florida Territory, 67
Flushing (Otissingen), N. Neth. (N.Y.), 24
Fonseca, Gulf of, *see* Gulf of Fonseca
Forbes, route of in Seven Years' War, 34
Forbes Road, Pa., 34, 58
Foreign investments, *see* Investments abroad
Forestation and vegetation belts, U.S., 10
Forest, route of, in the Civil War, 160
Formosa, seizure of, recommended, 127*n*
Ft. Anne, N.Y., 29
Ft. Argyle, Ga., 31
Ft. Arkansas, La., 28
Ft. Assumption, La., 32
Ft. Augusta, Ga., 26, 31
Ft. Augusta, Pa., 33
Ft. Beauharnais, Fr. Ill., 32
Ft. Bedford, Pa., 33
Ft. Benton, Mont., 58
Ft. Beversrede, N. Neth., 23
Ft. Bliss, N. Mex., in the Civil War, 160
Ft. Boise, Ida., 58
Ft. Bonneville, Wyo., 58
Ft. Bourbon, W. Can., 32
Ft. Bridger, Wyo., 58; and mail routes, *circa* 1851, 116
Ft. Brown, Tex., in the Mexican War, 97
Ft. Budd, N.Y., in the Seven Years' War, 34
Ft. Bull, N.Y., 33
Ft. Caroline, Carolina, 28
Ft. Caroline, Fla., 35
Ft. Carillon, Que. (N.Y.) 34.
Ft. Casimir, N. Swe., 23
Ft. Chambly, Que., 28; in the Revolution, 46
Ft. Charles, Va., 27
Ft. Charlotte, Savannah R., in the Revolution, 49
Ft. Chartres, Fr. Ill., 32
Ft. Chequamegon, Que., 32
Ft. Chiswell, Va., 33
Ft. Christina, N. Swe., 23
Ft. Clark, N. Dak., 58
Ft. Clatsop, Ore., 58
Ft. Clinton, N.Y., 33
Ft. Colville, Wash., 58
Ft. Condé, La., 30
Ft. Craig, N. Mex., 58; in the Civil War, 157
Ft. Craven, N.Y., 33
Ft. Crawford, Wisc., 58
Ft. Crevecoeur, Fr. Ill., 28
Ft. Cumberland. Pa., 33, 34
Ft. Dauphin, W. Can., 32
Ft. Dearborn, Ill., 58
Ft. Defiance, Ohio, in War of 1812, 94
Ft. de la Presentation, Que., 34
Ft. de la Reine, W. Can., 32
Ft. D'Huillier, Fr. Ill., 30
Ft. Denonville, Que., 28
Ft. des Abitibis, Que., 28
Ft. Dodge, Kan., 58
Ft. Donelson, Tenn., in the Civil War, 158
Ft. Dummer, Mass., 31
Ft. Duquesne, Que., 34
Ft. Edward, N.Y., 33
Ft. Erie, Ont., in the War of 1812, 95
Ft. Fisher, N.C., in the Civil War, 161
Ft. Frederic, N.Y., 32
Ft. Frederica National Monument Project, Ga., 263
Ft. Frederick, Md., 33
Ft. Frontenac, Que., 28; in the Seven Years' War, 34
Ft. Gadsden, Fla., in the First Seminole War, 95
Ft. George, N.Y., 33
Ft. George, Ont., in the War of 1812, 94
Ft. George, P.Q., 3
Ft. Gibson, Ind. Co., 58; and the Shawnee Trail, 226
Ft. Good Hope, N. Neth. (Conn.), 24
Ft. Granville, Pa., 33
Ft. Griffin, Tex., and Western Trail, 226
Ft. Hall, Ida., 58
Ft. Halifax, Me., 33
Ft. Harris, Pa., 33
Ft. Henry, Ida., 58
Ft. Henry, P.Q., in the Revolution, 48
Ft. Henry, Tenn., in the Civil War, 158
Ft. Herkimer, N.Y., 31
Ft. Jackson, Ala., in the War of 1812, 95
Ft. Jackson, La., in the Civil War, 158
Ft. Jefferson National Monument, Fla., 263
Ft. Kaministiquia, Que., 28

Ft. Kearney, Neb., 58; and the Overland Mail, 116
Ft. King George, Ga., 31
Ft. Laramie, Wyo., 58
Ft. Laramie National Monument, Wyo., 263
Ft. La Baye, Que., 32
Ft. La Jonquiere, W. Can., 34
Ft. La Motte, Que., 28
Ft. Latourette, Que., 28
Ft. Leavenworth, Kan., 58; in the Mexican War, 97
Ft. Le Boeuf, Que., 34
Ft. Levis, Que., in the Seven Years' War, 34
Ft. Ligonier, Pa., 34
Ft. Lookout, S. Dak., 58
Ft. Loudoun, Pa., 33, 34
Ft. Loyal, Me., 27; in the War of the League of Augsburg, 28
Ft. Mackinac, Mich., in War of 1812, 93
Ft. Mackinac, Que., 30
Ft. Macon, N.C., in the Civil War, 158
Ft. Malden, P.Q., in the Revolution, 48; Ont., in War of 1812, 93, 94
Ft. Mandan, N. Dak., 58
Ft. Manchac, La., in the Revolution, 49
Ft. Marion National Monument, Fla., 263
Ft. Massac, La., 34
Ft. Massachusetts, Mass., in the War of the Austrian Succession, 32
Ft. Matanzas National Monument, Fla., 263
Ft. Maurepas, La., 30
Ft. Maurepas, W. Can., 32
Ft. McHenry, Md., in the War of 1812, 95
Ft. McHenry National Park, Md., 263
Ft. Meigs, Ohio, in the War of 1812, 94
Ft. Miami, Fr. Ill., 30; N. W. Terr., 52
Ft. Michipicton, Que., 32
Ft. Mims massacre, 94
Ft. Montgomery, N.Y., in the Revolution, 47
Ft. Moore, Ga., 31
Ft. Nassau, N. Neth., 23, 24
Ft. Necessity, Pa., 34
Ft. New Elfsborg, N. Swe., 23
Ft. New Gothenburg, N. Swe., 23
Ft. New Korsholm, N. Swe., 23
Ft. Niagara, N.Y., Que., 28, 34; in the Revolution, 48, 52; in the War of 1812, 94
Ft. Nicholson, N.Y., 29
Ft. Nisqually, Wash., 58
Ft. Orange, N. Neth., 24
Ft. Orleans, Fr. Ill., 32
Ft. Osage, Mo., 58
Ft. Oswego, N.Y., 31
Ft. Ouiatanon, Fr. Ill., 32
Ft. Panmure (Natchez), La., in the Revolution, 49
Ft. Pentagoet, Me., 27
Ft. Pickens, Fla., in the Civil War, 157
Ft. Pierre, S. Dak., 58, 59
Ft. Pillow, Tenn., in the Civil War, 160
Ft. Pitt, Pa., 33, 53; in the Revolution, 48
Ft. Presqu'Isle, Que., 34
Ft. Prince George, S.C., 33
Ft. Prudhomme, La., 28
Ft. Pulaski, Ga., in the Civil War, 158, 159
Ft. Pulaski National Monument, Ga., 263
Ft. Radisson, Que., 28
Ft. Randall, Neb., 58
Ft. Redstone, Pa., in the Revolution, 48
Ft. Reliance, Mackenzie Dist., 3
Ft. Richelieu, Que., 28
Ft. Riley, Kan., 58
Ft. Ripley, Minn., 58
Ft. Rosalie, La., 32
Ft. Rouge, W. Can., 32
Ft. Rouillé, Que., 32, 34
Ft. Royal, Me., in the War of the League of Augsburg, 28
Ft. St. Antoine, Fr. Ill., 28
Ft. St. Charles, W. Can., 32
Ft. St. Croix, Fr. Ill., 28
Ft. Ste. Genevieve, La., 32
Ft. St. Jean, Que., 28
Ft. St. John, Que., 34
Ft. St. Joseph, Fr. Ill., 28
Ft. St. Joseph, Que., 28; in the Revolution, 51
Ft. St. Louis, Fr. Ill., 28
Ft. St. Louis, La., 28, 30
Ft. St. Nicholas, Fr. Ill., 28
Ft. St. Pierre, W. Can., 32
Ft. St. Phillip, La., in the War of 1812, 95
Ft. St. Vrain, Colo., 58
Ft. Saratoga, N.Y., 29
Ft. Scott, Ga., in First Seminole War, 95
Ft. Shirley, Pa., 33
Ft. Smith, Ark., 1, 58, 59; and mail routes, *circa* 1858, 116
Ft. Snelling, Minn., 58, 59
Ft. Stanwix National Monument Project, N.Y., 263
Ft. Stanwix, N.Y., 33; in the Revolution, 47
Ft. Stephenson, Ohio, in the War of 1812, 94
Ft. Sumter, S.C., in the Civil War, 157
Ft. Sunbury, Ga., in the Revolution, 49
Ft. Tadoussac, Que., 28
Ft. Tecumseh, S. Dak., 58
Ft. Ticonderoga, N.Y., 34; in the Revolution, 46, 47
Ft. Tombecbé, La., 32
Ft. Toulouse, La., 32
Ft. Trinity, N. Neth., 23
Ft. Uintah, Utah, 58
Ft. Union, N. Mex., 58; in the Civil War, 157, 160
Ft. Vancouver, Wash., 58, 59
Ft. Venango, Que., 34
Ft. Vincennes, Fr. Ill., 32
Ft. Wagner, S.C., in the Civil War, 159
Ft. Walla Walla, Wash., 58, 59
Ft. Washita, Ind. Co., 58
Ft. Wayne, Ind., 1, 58; P.Q., in the Revolution, 48
Ft. Western, Me., 33
Ft. William, Ont., 3
Ft. William, Ore., 58
Ft. William Henry, N.Y., 33; in the Seven Years' War, 34
Ft. Williams, N.Y., 33
Ft. Worth, Tex., 1; and the Shawnee Trail, 226
Ft. Yuma, Ariz., 58
Fortress Monroe, Va., in the Civil War, 157
Fossil Cyacid National Monument, S. Dak., 263
Fowler, route of, 59
Foxe Channel, Can., 3
France, 305; U.S. boundary proposals by, after the Revolution, 52; U.S. forces in, 213, 258*n*, 305*n*
Frances Is., claimed by U.S., 305*n*
Franchise qualifications, 1775, 42; 1780, 74; 1790, 75; 1800, 76; 1820, 77; 1830, 78; 1840, 79; 1850, 80; 1860, 81; 1870, 186; 1880, 187; 1900, 188; 1910, 189; 1940, 190; literacy requirement, 196; alien enfranchisement, 197; *see also* Womens Suffrage
Frankfort, Ky., 1, 58; and domestic routes of slave trade 146; in the Civil War, 158
Franklin, Dist. of, Can., 3
Franklin, "state" of, Tenn., 53

Franklin, Tenn., in the Civil War, 160
Fraser R., Can., 2, 3
Fredericksburg, Va., in the Civil War, 158, 159
Frederickshaab, Greenland, 3
Frederickton, Md., in the War of 1812, 95
Fredericton, N.B., 3
Freeman, route of, 59
Free Schools, *see* Schools, Public, State Legislation
Fremont, routes of explorations, 59; route of in the Mexican War, 97
French and Indian War (Seven Years' War), 34
French and Indian Wars, 28, 30, 32, 34
French Equatorial Africa, 305
French expansion, to 1697, 28; to 1713, 30; to 1744, 32; to 1763, 34
French Guiana, 4, 305
French Indo-China, 305
French invasion of Mexico, 257*n*
French Louisiana, W. Fla. border of, 60
French Somaliland, 305
French West Africa, 305
Frenchtown Reclamation Project, Mont., 264
Fresno, Cal., 1
Frienhaven Is., claimed by U.S., 305*n*
Frobisher, route of, 20
Frobisher Bay, Can., 3
Fronteras, Sp. Mex., 35
Frontier of settlement, 1660, 22; 1700, 25; 1750, 26; 1775, 37; after 1790 *see* Population, density of
Fundy, Bay of, 3
Fur trade routes, Indian, *circa* 1750, 33

Gadsden Purchase, 127*n*
Galapagos Is., 4
Gallego Is., claimed by U.S., 305*n*
Galleons, Spanish, routes of, 20
Galveston, Tex., 1, 9; in the Mexican War, 97; and domestic routes of slave trade, 146; base at, 305
Galveston and Brazos Canal, Tex., 118
Galvez, routes of, in the Revolution, 49, 50, 51
Ganges Is., claimed by U.S., 305*n*
Garces, route of, 35
Garden City Reclamation Project, Kan., 264
Gardner Is., claimed by U.S., 305*n*
Gardoqui's proposed lines of W. Florida, 61
Garfield, route of, in Civil War, 158
Gary, Ind., 1, 7
Gas, Natural, *see* Natural Gas
Gaspé Penin, P.Q., 3
Gates, routes of, in the Revolution, 47, 50
General Grant National Park, Cal., 263
Genesee Turnpike, N.Y., 58
Genesee Valley Canal, N.Y., 118
Genoa, Italy, 213
Georgetown, Br. Guiana, 4; U.S. base at, 258*n*, 305*n*
Georgetown, S.C., in the Civil War, 161
George Washington Birthplace National Monument, Va., 263
Georgia, military lands, 53; cession of western lands, 55
Georgia, Sts. of, B.C., 3
Georgia Co. lands, 53
Georgia Mississippi Co. lands, 53
Georgian Bay, Lake Huron, 2, 3
German-born population, *see under* Population
Germantown, Pa., in the Revolution, 47
Germany, 305; European battlefront, 213; Rhineland occupation, 258*n*
Gettysburg, Pa., in the Civil War, 159
Ghent, Belg., 213
Gila Cliff Dwellings National Monument, N. Mex., 263
Gila R., Ariz., 2, 97
Gila Reclamation Project, Ariz., 264
Gilbert Is., 305; raided by U.S., 258*n*
Glacier National Park, Mont., 263
Glasgow, Scot., disembarkation port, World War I, 213
Gloucester, Mass., 22, 27; in the War of 1812, 95
Godhavn, Greenland, 3
Godthaab, Greenland, 3
Gold Coast, 305
Gold, U.S. deposits, 6; world production of, 310
Goldfield, Nev., 6
Goldsboro, N.C., in the Civil War, 161
Good Hope, Mackenzie Dist., 3
Gordillo, route of, 21
Gorges, charter grant to, 22
Grain areas, 1700, 39; 1775, 40; *see also* Wheat
Grace Steamship Co., subsidized routes of, 258
Granada, Sp. C.A. (Nic.), 21
Gran Chaco, Para.-Bol., 4
Gran Quivira National Monument, N. Mex., 263
Grand Canyon National Monument, Ariz., 263
Grand Canyon National Park, Ariz., 263
Grand Forks, N. Dak., 1
Grand Rapids, Mich., 1
Grand Teton National Park, Wyo., 263
Grand Valley Reclamation Project, Colo., 264
Grande R., Brazil, 4
Grande R., Bol., 4
Grant, routes of in the Civil War, 158, 159, 160, 161
Graves, route of in the Revolution, 51
Grays Harbor, Wash., 2
Great Bear Lake, Can., 2, 3
Great Britain, *see also* British Colonies; English expansion; Revolution; Trade; U.S. forces in, 258*n*, 305
Great Corn Is., Nic., leased, 258*n*
Great Falls, Mont., 1
Great Harbor, Conn., 27
Great Lakes, 2
Great National Road, 58
Great Salt Lake, Utah, 2
Great Salt Lake Desert, Utah, 2
Great Sand Dunes National Monument, Colo., 263
Great Slave Lake, Can., 2,3
Great Smoky Mountains National Park, N.C.-Tenn., 263
Great Warrior Path, Tenn. to Ohio, 33
Greece, 305
Green Mts., Vt., 2
Green R., Ky., 53
Greenbriar R., W. Va., 53
Greene, routes of, in the Revolution, 50, 51
Greenland, 3, 305; occupied by U.S., 258*n*; U.S. protectorate, 305*n*
Greensboro, N.C., 1
Greenwich, Conn., 22
Greenville, S.C., 1
Grenada, 4
Greytown, Nic., bombarded, 127*n*; and Polk Corollary, 217*n*; British seize customs at, 257*n*
Grierson, route of, in the Civil War, 159
Grijalva, route of, 21
Groninque Is., claimed by U.S., 305*n*
Guadalajara, route of, 35
Guadalupe Hidalgo, Mex., in the Mexican War, 97
Guadalupe (El Paso), Sp. Tex., 35
Guadalupe (Guadeloupe), Sp. Mex., 21
Guadeloupe (Guadelupe), Sp. Mex., 21

All numbers refer to maps, not pages

Guale, Sp. Fla., 21, 35
Guam, annexed, 257*n*; captured, 305; invaded by Japan, 258*n*, 305*n*
Guano Is., 257*n*; claimed by U.S., 305*n*
Guantanamo, Cuba, U.S. naval base, 258*n*, 305*n*
Guapore R., S.A., 4
Guatemala, Sp. C.A., 21; intervention in, 258*n*, 305*n*
Guevara, route of, 20
Guayaquil, Ec., 4
Guayaquil, Gulf of, 4
Guayamas, Sp. Mex., 35; Mex., in the Mexican War, 97
Guevavi, Sp. Mex., 35
Guiana, Br., Fr., Dutch, 305
Guilford, N.C., in the Revolution, 51
Gulf Mail Steamship Co., subsidized routes of, 258
Gulf of Alaska, 3
Gulf of California, Mex., 2
Gulf of Darien, Col., 2, 4
Gulf of Fonseca, C.A., 127*n;* naval lease in, 258*n*
Gulf of Guayaquil, Ec., 4
Gulf of Honduras, C.A., 2
Gulf of Mexico, 2, 305
Gulf of Panama, 4
Gulf of St. Lawrence, Can., 2
Gulf of San Jorge, Arg., 4
Gulf of San Matias, Arg., 4
Gulf of Trieste, Ven., 4
Gulf of Venezuela, 4
Gulf oil field, 9
Gulfport, Miss., 1
Gunnison National Monument, Black Canyon of the, Colo., 263

Hackensack, N. Neth. (N.J.), 24
Hackensack R., N. Neth. (N.J.),24
Hadley, Mass., 27
Hague, Neth., 213
Haiti, 2, 21; Mole of St. Nicholas offered to U.S. by, 257*n;* protectorate question, 257*n;* intervention in, 258*n;* occupation of, 305*n*
Halifax, N. Sco., 3; embarkation port, World War I, 212
Hamilton, route of, in the Revolution, 48
Hamilton, Ont., 1, 3; in the War of 1812, 94
Hamilton R., Lab., 3
Hampden, raids in the War of 1812, 95
Hampshire and Hampden Canal, Mass., 117
Hampton, route in the War of 1812, 94
Harbor Grace, Nfld., 3
Harper's Ferry,W. Va., in the Civil War, 158
Harrisburg, Pa., 1
Hartford, Conn., 1, 24, 27; in the Revolution, 46; branch of Second Bank of the U.S. at, 112; and Underground Railway, 146
Hartford, Treaty of, shown, 56
Hatteras Inlet, N.C., in the Civil War, 158
Havana, Cuba, 21; in the Spanish-American War, 207; U.S. airline connections to, 254
Haverhill, Mass., in the War of the Spanish Succession, 30
Havre de Grace, Md., in the War of 1812, 95; and Susquehanna and Tidewater Canal, 118
Hawaii, 305; early protectorate and base, 127*n;* U.S. airline connections to, 255; relations with, 1867–1898, 257*n*
Hawkesbury, N. Sco., 3
Hay River, Can., 3
Heath, Sir Robert, charter grant to, 22
Heemstede (Hempstead), N. Neth. (N.Y.), 24
Helena, Ark., 1; in the Civil War, 160
Helena, Mont., 1, 6
Helgoland, Ger., 213
Hemisphere neutrality zone, World War II, 258
Hempstead (Heemstede), N. Neth. (N.Y.), 22, 24
Henrietta Is., Siberia, claimed by U.S., 257*n*
Hennepin, routes of, 28
Herkimer, route of, in the Revolution, 47
Hermosillo, Mex., 1
Herron, route of, in the Civil War, 158
Hides and skins, world production of, 317
Highways, *see* Roads and Highways
Hillsboro, N.C., in the Revolution, 51
Hindman, route of, in the Civil War, 158
Hoboken, N. Neth. (N.J.), 24
Hocking Canal, Ohio, 118
Holland, 305
Holly Springs, Miss., in the Civil War, 158
Holy Cross National Monument, Colo., 263
Holyoke, Mass., 1
Homestead National Monument, Neb., 263
Hondo Reclamation Project, N. Mex., 264
Honduras, interventions in, 257*n*, 305*n*
Honolulu, T.H., U.S. airline connections to, 255
Hood, route of, in the Civil War, 160
Hooker, routes of, in the Civil War, 159
Hopedale, Lab., 3
Hopi Indians, Ariz., 19
Hopton, Lord, charter grant to, 22
Horseshoe Bend, Ala., in the War of 1812, 95
Hot Springs, Ark., 1
Hot Springs National Park, Ark., 263
Hours of work, men, in general occupations, 1890, 296; 1900, 298; 1910, 300; 1920, 302; in public works and dangerous occupations, 1890, 295; 1900, 297; 1910, 299; 1920, 301
Hours of work, women, limitations on, 1850, 139; 1890, 291; 1910; 292; 1920, 293; 1930, 294
House vote, on passage of the Embargo, 91; on war resolution, 1812, 92; on the Mexican War, 96; on resolution declaring war with Spain, taken prior to submission of Senate amendments, Apr. 13, 1898, 206; on entry into World War I, 210
Houston, Tex., 1, 9
Hovenweep National Monument, Utah-Colo., 263
Howe brothers, routes of, in the Revolution, 46, 47, 48, 49
Howland Is., claimed by U.S., 305*n*
Hudson Bay, Can., 2, 3
Hudson R., N.Y., 2
Hudson Str., Can., 2, 3
Hull, route of, in the War of 1812, 93
Humboldt irrigation project, Nev., 264
Humboldt R., Nev., 2
Humphrey's Is., claimed by U.S., 305*n*
Hungary, 305
Huntington, N.Y., 22; in the Revolution, 49
Huntington, Pa., and nearby canals, 117
Huntley Reclamation Project, Mont., 264
Huntsville, Ala., in the War of 1812, 95
Hyrum Reclamation Project, Utah, 264

Iceland, 2; occupied by U.S., 258*n;* U.S. protectorate, 305*n*
Ichuse, Sp. Fla., 21, 35
Idaho City, Ida., 6
Idaho Territory, 165
Iguassu Falls, Brazil, 4
Illinois Indians, Ill., 19
Illinois-Indiana oil field, 9
Illinois-Michigan Canal, 118
Illinois R., Ill., 2
Illinois-Rock Island Canal, Ill., 205

All numbers refer to maps, not pages

Illinois Territory, 92
Imports and exports, colonial, 41; 1800, 126; 1850, 127; 1900, 257; 1938, 258
Improved Acreage, 1850, 107; 1870, 231; 1880, 232; 1900, 233; 1910, 234; land in harvested crops, 1920, 235; acreage in harvested crops, 1930, 236
Income tax, ratification of 16th amend. to the Constitution, 198
Independence, Mo., 59; and mail routes, *circa* 1850, 116
India, 305
Indian cession, line of, 1790, 63; 1810, 65; 1830, 67; 1850, 69
Indian fur trade routes, *circa* 1750, 33
Indian Ocean, 305
Indian tribes, U.S., 19
Indiana Territory, 85, 92
Indianapolis, Ind., 1, 58
Indigo areas, 40
Indo-China, Fr., 305
Industrial areas, *see* Manufacturing areas
Inter-coastal Waterways, 250
Interpositions of force, *see* Expansion, U.S.
Interventions, *see* Expansion, U.S.
Investments abroad, 1900, 257; 1938, 258
Iowa City, Iowa, on commercial airline, 1922, 253
Iowa Indians, Iowa, 19
Iowa Territory, 68
Iquitos, Peru, 4
Iran, 305
Iraq, 305
Ireland, Northern, U.S. troops in, 258*n*
Irish-born population, *see under* Population
Iron, U.S. deposits, 7; world production of, 307
Iron works, 1775, 38
Irondequoit Bay, N.Y., 28
Ironton, Ohio, and Underground Railway, 146
Iroquois Indians, N.Y.-Pa., 19
Irrigation, areas now irrigated or subject to irrigation, 264
Island No. 10, Miss. R., in the Civil War, 158
Isle de Lobos, Mex., in the Mexican War, 97
Isle of Orleans, La., 60, 62
Isle of Pines, Cuba, 2; claimed by U.S., 257*n*
Isle Royale, Mich., 73
Isle Royale National Park Project, Mich., 263
Isthmus of Tehuantepec, Mex., 2
Italian East Africa, 305
Italy, 305; U.S. forces in, 258*n*, 305*n*

Jackson, Miss., 1; and domestic routes of slave trade, 146; in the Civil War, 159, 160
Jackson, Tenn., in the Civil War, 160
Jackson's Florida campaign, 1818, 95
Jacksonville, Fla., 1; in the Civil War, 158, 159, 160; base at, 305
Jamaica, B.W.I., 2; U.S. base at, 258*n*, 305*n*
Jamaica (Rustdorf), N. Neth. (N.Y.), 24
James Bay, Can., 2, 3
James R., Va., 2
James River and Kanawha Canal, Va., 118
James River Canal, Va., 117
Jamestown, Va., 22, 27
Japan, Sea of, 305
Japan, Sts. of Shimonoseki bombarded, 305*n*
Jarvis Is., claimed by U.S., 305*n*
Java, D.E.I., 305; U.S. troops in, 258*n*
Jeanette Is., Siberia, claimed by U.S., 257*n*
Jefferson City, Mo., 1
Jenkins Ferry, Ark., in the Civil War, 160
Jenkinson, route of, 20
Jequitinhonha R., Brazil, 4
Jersey City, N.J., 1
Jewel Cave National Monument, S. Dak., 263
John Day R., Ore., 72
Johnson, route of, in the Seven Years' War, 34
Johnston Is., claimed by U.S., 305*n*
Johnstown, Pa., 1
Joliet, route of, 28
Joliet, Ill., 1
Jonesboro, Tenn., in the Civil War, 161
Joplin, Mo., 1, 6
Joshua Tree National Monument, Cal., 263
Joutel, route of, 28
Juana (Cuba), 21
Juan de Fuca, Sts. of, 2, 3; island in, seized by U.S., 127*n*
Julianehaab, Greenland, 3
Juman, Sp. Tex., 35
Junction Canal, Pa., 118
Junction City, Kan., and the Western Shawnee Trail, 226
Juneau, Alaska, 3, 209
Juniata Division Canal, Pa., 117
Jurua R., Brazil, 4

Kanagawa, Treaty of, 127*n*
Kansas City, Kan., 1
Kansas City, Mo., 1; and the Overland Mail, 116; and cattle country, 226; Federal Reserve Bank, 246
Kansas R., Kan., 2
Kansas Territory, 70
Kaskaskia, Fr. Ill., 30; P.Q., in the Revolution, 48, 49
Kearny, route of, in the Mexican War, 97
Keewatin, Dist. of, 3
Kem, USSR, U.S. forces at, 258*n*, 305*n*
Kemn's Is., claimed by U.S., 305*n*
Kendrick irrigation project, Wyo., 264
Kennebec R., Me., 2
Kent Island, Md., 27
Kentucky, lands relinquished to, 55
Kentucky R., Ky., 53
Kenya, 305
Kettle Creek, Ga., in the Revolution, 49
Kettleman Hills oil fields, Cal., 9
Key West, Fla., 1; in the Spanish-American War, 207; base at, 305
Khabarovsk, USSR, U.S. forces at, 258*n*, 305*n*
Kickapoo Indians, Wisc.-Ill., 19
Kievits Hoeck, N. Neth. (Conn.), 24
King George's War (War of the Austrian Succession), 32
King Hill Reclamation Project, Ida., 264
King William's War (War of the League of Augsburg), 28
Kings Mountain, S.C., in the Revolution, 50
Kingston, N.Y., and Delaware and Hudson Canal, 117
Kingston, Ont., 3; and Underground Railway, 146
Kino, Fr., route of, 35
Kiowa Indians, Colo., etc., 19
Kiska Is., Alaska, 2
Kittaning Path, 33
Klamath Indians, Ore., 19
Klamath Reclamation Project, Ore., 264
Klikitat Indians, Wash., 19
Klondike region, 3, 209
Knoxville, Tenn., 1, 58; and domestic routes of slave trade, 146; in the Civil War, 158, 159, 161
Knyphausen, route of, in the Revolution, 50
Kodiak, Alaska, base at, 305
Kodiak Is., Alaska, 2, 3
Korea, Ping-Yang forts bombarded, 257*n*, 305*n*
Kuskokwim R., Alaska, 2, 3

All numbers refer to maps, not pages

La Bahia, Sp. Tex., 35
La Bahia del Espiritu Santo, Sp. Tex., 35
Labor, *see* Hours of Work, Child Labor
Labrador, 3, 305
La Cosa, routes of, 21
La Croix Lake, Ont., 73
LaFayette, route of, in the Revolution, 51
La Florida, 35
La Grange, Tenn., in the Civil War, 159
La Harpe, route of, 32
La Havre, Fr., disembarkation port in World War I, 213
Lake Athabaska, Can., 2, 3
Lake Borgne, La., in the War of 1812, 95
Lake Dos Patos, Brazil, 4
Lake Erie, U.S.-Can., 2
Lake Huron, U.S.-Can., 2
Lake Manitoba, Man., 2, 3
Lake Maracaibo, Ven., 2, 4
Lake Melville, Lab., 3
Lake Michigan, U.S., 2
Lake Nipigon, Ont., 2, 3
Lake Nipissing, Ont., 3, 52
Lake of the Woods, 2, 3
Lake Okeechobee, Fla., 2
Lake Ontario, Can.-U.S., 2
Lake St. Clair, Mich.-Ont., 2
Lake Saranaga, Ont., 73
Lake Superior, Can.-U.S., 2
Lake Superior-Rainy Lake border dispute, 1826–42, 73
Lake Titicaca, S.A., 4
Lake Winnedago, Ont., 73
Lake Winnipeg, Man., 2, 3
Lake Winnipegosis, Man., 2, 3
Lake Wollaston, Can., 2
La Junta, Sp. Mex., 35
Lampazos, Sp. Mex., 35
Land cessions, New York, 54; Georgia, 55; Virginia, 55; Connecticut, 56; Massachusetts, 56; New Hampshire, 56; North Carolina, 56; South Carolina,
Land in Cultivation, *see* Improved Acreage
Land retirement areas, U.S., 14
Lands End, Eng., 213
Lansing, Mich., 1
La Pallice, Fr., and U.S. in World War I, 213
La Paz, Bol., 4
La Paz, Sp. Mex., settlements at, 21; in the Mexican War, 97
La Plata, Arg., 4
La Pointe, Que., 28
La Purissima Concepcion, Sp. Cal., 35
Laramie, Wyo., 1
Laredo, Sp. Tex., 35
La Salle, Ill., 250
La Salle, routes of, 28
La Soledad, Sp. Cal., 35
Las Palmas, claimed by U.S., 257*n*
Lassen Pass, Cal., 58
Lassen Volcanic National Park, Cal., 263
Latvia, 305
Laurentian Mts., Can., 2
Lava Beds National Monument, Cal., 263
La Verendrye bros., routes of, 32
Lawrence, Kan., 1; and Underground Railway, 146
Lawrence, Mass., 1
Lead, S. Dak., 6
Lead, U.S. deposits, 6; world production of, 312
Leadville, Colo., 6
Leavenworth, Kan., 1; and the Overland Mail, 116
Lebanon, Ky., in the Civil War, 159
Lee, routes of, in the Civil War, 158, 159
Lehman Caves National Monument, Nev., 263
Léon, Sp. C.A., 21
Léon, Sp. Mex., 21
Les Sables d'Olenne, Fr., and U.S. in World War I, 213
Lesser Antilles, 4
Le Sueur, route of, 30
Lethbridge, Alb., 3
Levis, P.Q., 3
Lewis and Clark, route of, 59
Lewiston, Me., 1
Lexington, Ky., 1; branch of Second Bank at, 112; in the Civil War, 158
Liard R., Can., 2, 3
Liberia, 305; financial protectorate, 258*n*
Libya, 305
Liderons Is., claimed by U.S., 305*n*
Lignite deposits, U.S., 8
Lima-Indiana oil field, 9
Lima, Peru, 4
Lincoln, route of, in the Revolution, 49
Lincoln, Neb., 1
Liquor license, *see* Prohibition
Literacy qualification for the suffrage, 196
Lithuania, 305
Little America, Antarctica, 305
Little Colorado R., 2
Little Corn Is., Nic., leased, 258*n*
Little Rock, Ark., 1; in the Civil War, 160
Little Rock arsenal, Ark., 157
Little Slave Lake, Alb., 2, 3
Liverpool, Eng., disembarkation port, World War I, 213
Lobos Is., Peru, 127*n*; claimed by U.S., 305*n*
Local option, *see* Prohibition
London, Eng., disembarkation port, World War I, 213
London, Ont., 3
Long, routes of, 59
Long Beach, Cal., 1
Long Island, N.Y., 2
Long Island Bay, N.Y., 46
Lopez expedition, Cuba, 127*n*
Loreto, Sp. Mex., 35
Lorraine, prov. of, 213
Los Adaes, Sp. Tex., 35
Los Ais, Sp. Tex., 35
Los Angeles, Cal., 1, 9; Sp. Cal., 35; Cal., 58, 59; in the Mexican War, 97; and mail routes, *circa* 1854, 116; base at, 305
Los Cayos (Bahamas), 21
Louisbourg, Can., 3; in War of the Austrian Succession, 32
Louisiana, Fr., border with W. Fla., 60; Sp., 35; border with W. Fla., 61; Territory of, 88
Louisville, Ky., 1; branch of Second Bank at, 112; and Underground Railway, 146
Louisville-Portland Canal, Ky.-Ohio, 117
Low Is., claimed by U.S., 305*n*
Lowell, Mass., 1
Lower California, Sp., 98
Lower California Penin., Mex., 2
Lower Shawnee Town, 33
Lower Yellowstone Reclamation Project, Mont.-N. Dak., 264
Lugert-Altus Reclamation Project, Okla., 264
Lundy's Lane, Ont., in the War of 1812, 95
Luxemburg, duchy of, 213
Lynchburg, Va., 1; in the Civil War, 161
Lynn, Mass., 1

All numbers refer to maps, not pages

Lyon, Fr., and U.S. in World War I, 213
Lyon, route of, in the Civil War, 157

Macassar Sts., battle of, 258*n*
McClellan, routes of, in the Civil War, 158
McCulloch, route of, in the Civil War, 157
McDowell, route of, in the Civil War, 157
McKean Is., claimed by U.S., 305*n*
Mackenzie, Dist. of, 3
Mackenzie, revolt of, Can., 127*n*
Mackenzie R., Can., 2, 3
McLernand, route of, in the Civil War, 159
Macon, Ga., 1, in the Civil War, 160, 161
McPherson, Mackenzie Dist., 3
Madagascar, 305
Madeira Is., 41
Madeira R., Brazil, 4
Madison, Wisc., 1
Magdalena R., Col., 4
Magellan, route of, 20
Magnetic Pole, North, 3
Maine, British occupation of, in War of 1812, 95
Maine, border proposals, 1782–3, 52; border dispute, 1821–42, 71; award by King of the Netherlands, 1831, 71
Makin Is., claimed by U.S., 305*n*
Malden's Is., claimed by U.S., 305*n*
Malinger R., Ont., 73
Mallets, routes of, 32
Mamor R., Bol., 4
Mammoth Cave National Park, Ky., 263
Manaos, Brazil, 4
Manchester, Eng., disembarkation port, World War I, 213
Manchester, N.H., 1
Manchukuo, 305
"Manifest Destiny," 127
Manila, P.I., U.S. airline connections to, 255
Manila Bay, P.I., battle of, 207*n*
Manitoba, prov. of, 3
Manitoulin Is., Ont., 3
Manufacturing areas, 1775, 38; 1810, 108; 1840, 109; 1860, 110; 1900, 243; 1940, 244
Manzanillo, Mex., in the Mexican War, 97
Maranhao, Brazil, 4
Marañon R., S.A., 4
March, route of, in the War of the Spanish Succession, 30
Marcus Is., raided by U.S., 258*n*
Marietta, N.W. Terr., 53
Marion, routes of, in the Revolution, 50, 51
Maroni R., S.A., 4
Marquette, route of, 28
Marseilles, Fr., disembarkation port, World War I, 213
Marshall Is., 305; raided by U.S., 258*n*
Martinio (Martinique), 21
Martinique (Martinio), 21
Maryland, colony, 22; military lands, 53
Mary Letitia Is., claimed by U.S., 305*n*
Mary's Is., claimed by U.S., 305*n*
Mason, charter grant to, 22
Massachusetts Bay, Mass., 2
Massachusetts Bay Colony, 22
Massachusetts Bay Co., charter grant to, 22
Massachusetts, cession of western lands, 56
Massachusetts Indians, Mass., 19
Matamoras, Mex., in the Mexican War, 97
Matanuska, Alaska, 3
Matanzas, Cuba, in the Spanish-American War, 207
Matehuala, Sp. Mex., 21
Mathews Is., claimed by U.S., 305*n*
Matto Grosso plateau, Brazil, 4
Maumee R., Ohio, 53
Maury, exploration of Amazon, 127*n*
Mazatlan, Mex., in the Mexican War, 97
Meade, routes of, in the Civil War, 159
Medellin, Sp. Mex., 21
Mediterranean Sea, 213, 305
Meewoc Indians, Cal., 19
Melville Is., Can., 3
Memphis, Tenn., 1, 58; and domestic routes of slave trade, 146; in the Civil War, 158, 159, 160
Mendoza, route of, 35
Menominee Indians, Wisc.-Minn., 19
Meridian, Miss., in the Civil War, 160
Meriwether Lewis National Monument, Tenn., 263
Merrimack R., N.H., and Mass., 2
Mesa Verde National Park, Colo., 263
Meuse-Argonne sector, Fr., World War I, 213
Mexicali, Mex., 1
Mexican War, House vote on, 96; campaigns of, 97; peace proposals, 98
Mexico, 305; physical features of, 2; Spanish explorations and settlements in, 21; Tehuantepec R.R., mentioned, 58; war with, 97; border problems with, 1821–57, 98; annexations and proposed annexations from, 127*n;* French invasion of, 257*n;* intervention in, 258*n;* Pershing expedition into, 305*n*
Mexico City, Mex., in the Mexican War, 97; U.S. airline connections to, 254, 255
Miami, Fla., 1
Miami Canal, Ohio, 117
Miami R., Ohio, 2
Michigan Territory, 66
Michillimackinac, Que., 28; N.W. Terr., 52
Mid-Continent oil field, 9
Middle Plantations (Williamsburg), Va., 27
Middlesex Canal, Mass., 117
Middletown, Conn., branch of Second Bank at, 112
Midway Is., 305; discovered, 127*n*
Midwout (Flatbush), N. Neth. (N.Y.), 24
Migration, routes of westward, 58
Mile Run, Va., in the Civil War, 159
Milk River Reclamation Project, Mont., 264
Military bounty lands, for Revolutionary soldiers, 53; for veterans of the War of 1812, 95
Mille Lacs, Ont., 73
Milwaukee, Wisc., 1, 7
Minas Novas, Brazil, 4
Minidoka Reclamation Project, Ida., 264
Minneapolis, Minn., 1; Federal Reserve Bank at, 246
Minnesota Territory, 69
Miquelon, off Nfld., 3
Mission Indians, Cal., 19
Mississippi R., 2
Mississippi Shipping Co., subsidized routes of, 258
Mississippi Territory, 62, 88
Missouri Indians, Mo.-Kan., 19
Missouri R., 2, 58
Missouri Territory, 66
Missoula, Mont., 1
Mobile Act, 1804, 126*n*
Mobile, Ala., 1, 58; Fla., 60; in the Revolution, 50; Ala., in the War of 1812, 95; branch of Second Bank at, 112; domestic routes of slave trade, 146; in the Civil War, 160, 161
Mobile Forts, Ala., in the Civil War, 160
Modoc Indians, Ore., 19

Mohawk Indians, N.Y., 19
Mohawk Path, 33
Mohawk R., N.Y., 24
Mohican Indians, N.Y., 19
Mojave Desert, Ariz., 2
Mojave Indians, Ariz., 19
Mole of St. Nicholas, Haiti, offered U.S., 257*n*
Monacan Indians, Va., 19
Moncks Corners, S.C., in the Revolution, 50
Monckton, route of, in the Seven Years' War, 34
Monclova, Sp. Mex., 35
Moncton, N.B., U.S. airline connections to, 255
Mondidier sector, Fr., World War I, 213
Moneton Indians, W. Va., 19
Mongolia, China, 305
Monmouth, N.J., in the Revolution, 48
Monocacy, Va., 160
Monongahela Canal, Pa., 118
Monongahela R., Pa., 2
Montana Territory, 165
Montcalm, routes of, in the Seven Years' War, 34
Monterey Bay, Cal., 2
Monterey, Cal., 1, 9, 59; Sp. Cal., 35; in the Mexican War, 97
Monterrey, Mex., 1, 21, 35; in the Mexican War, 97
Montes Claros, Sp. Mex., 35
Montevideo, Urug., 4
Montezuma Castle National Monument, Ariz., 263
Montgomery, route of in Mexican War, 97
Montgomery, Ala., 1, 58, 61; and domestic routes of slave trade, 146; in the Civil War, 161
Montiano, route of, 1742, 32
Montpelier, Vt., 1
Montreal, P.Q., 1, 3, 9; Que., in the War of the League of Augsburg, 28; in the War of the Spanish Succession, 30; in the Seven Years' War, 34; P.Q., in the Revolution, 46, 47; in the War of 1812, 95; telegraph line to, 122; and Underground Railway, 146; embarkation port, World War I, 212
Moon Lake Reclamation Project, Utah, 264
Moore, campaign against St. Augustine, 1702, 30
Moosejaw, Sask., 3
Moosonee, Ont., 3
Morant Keys, claimed by U.S., 305*n*
Morgan, Compañía Exploradora route of, 35
Morgan, route of, 59
Morgan, route of in the Civil War, 159
Mormon migration, route of, 58
Morocco, 305
Morris Canal, N.J., 117
Morristown, N.J., in the Revolution, 47, 50
Moscoso, route of, 21
Moultrie, route of, in the Revolution, 49
Mound City Group National Monument, Ohio, 263
Mt. Aconcagua, S.A., 4
Mt. Chimborazo, Ec., 4
Mt. Cotopaxi, Ec., 4
Mt. Hubbard, Alaska, 3
Mt. Illampu, Bol., 4
Mt. Illimani, Bol., 4
Mt. McKinley, Alaska, 3
Mt. Rainier National Park, Wash., 263
Mt. St. Elias, Alaska, 3, 209
Mt. Vernon arsenal, Miss., 157
Mt. Whipple, Alaska, 209
Mozambique, 305
Muir Woods National Monument, Cal., 263
Mulcaster, route of in War of 1812, 94
Munson Steamship Line, subsidized routes of, 258
Murfreesboro, Tenn., in the Civil War, 159
Murmansk, USSR, U.S. forces at, 258*n*, 305*n*
Murray, route of in the Seven Years' War, 34
Muskingum Canal, Ohio, 118

Nantes, Fr., and U.S. in World War I, 213
Narantsouck Mission, Me., 32
Narragansett Bay, R.I., 2
Narragansett Indians, R.I.-Mass., 19
Nashua, N.H., 1
Nashville, Tenn., 1, 58; and domestic routes of slave trade, 146; in the Civil War, 158, 159, 160
Nassau, Bahamas, U.S. airline connections to, 254, 255
Nassau Is., claimed by U.S., 305*n*
Natal, Brazil, 4
Natchez, Miss., 1, 58; and domestic routes of slave trade, 146
Natchitoches, La., 32, 59
National Army camps, World War I, 212
National Cattle Trail, proposed, 226
National Forests, 1900, 259; 1910, 260; 1930, 261; 1940, 262
National Guard Camps, World War I, 212
National Monuments, 263
National Parks, 1900, 259; 1910, 260; 1930, 261; 1940, 262; named, 263
National Road, Old (or Great), 58
Natural Bridges National Monument, Utah, 263
Natural Gas, U.S. fields, 9; world production of, 308
Natural Resources, U.S., gold, silver, zinc, lead, copper, 6; iron, 7; coal, 8; oil and natural gas, 9; world 306–317
Nauvoo, Ill., 58
Navajo Indians, Ariz.-N. Mex., 19
Navajo National Monument, Ariz., 263
Navassa Is., claimed by U.S., 127*n*, 305*n*
Navy, North Sea mine field, World War I, 213; bases, 305
Nebraska Territory, 70
Negro, *see* Abolition, Slavery, Population—Negro
Negro R., Brazil, 4
Nelson R., Can., 2, 3
Nemacolins Path, 33
Neosho, Mo., and mail routes, *circa* 1858, 116
Nepal, 305
Netherlands, The, 305
Neutrality Zone, World War II, 258; extended, 258
Nevada Territory, 90
New Amsterdam, N. Neth. (N.Y.), 24
New Amstel, N. Neth. (Del.), 23
Newark, N.J., 1, 25
New Bedford, Mass., 1; in the War of 1812, 95; and the Underground Railway, 146
New Bern, N.C., 1, 29; and the Underground Railway, 146; in the Civil War, 158, 159
New Bern-Beaufort Canal, N.C., 250
New Brunswick, N.J., and Delaware and Raritan Canal, 118
New Brunswick, prov. of, 3
Newburyport, Mass., 1; in the Revolution, 46
New Castle, N. Neth., 23; Del., 25
New England, Dominion of, 25*n*; United Cols. of, 22*n*
Newfoundland, 2, 3, 305; U.S. base at Avalon Penin., 305*n*
Newfoundland Banks, 41
New Granada, Panama transit rights, 127*n*
New Guinea, 305
New Hampshire, cession of Vermont claims, 56; for "New Hampshire Grants," *see* Vermont
New Haven, Conn., 1; in the Revolution, 49; and the Underground Railway, 146
New Haven colony, 22
New Hebrides, 305

New Inverness, Ga., 26
New Jersey, East, 25; West, 25
Newlands Reclamation Project, Nev., 264
New London, Conn., 1, 22; in the Revolution, 51; in the War of 1812, 94, 95; base at, 305
New Mexico, Sp., 35, 98
New Mexico Territory, 70, 90, 122, 165
New Netherland, 22; northern part, 24, southern part, 23
New Orleans, La., 1, 9, 32, 58, 60; in the Revolution, 49, 50; in the War of 1812, 95; branch of First Bank of the U.S. at, 111; Second Bank, 112; and domestic routes of slave trade, 146; in the Civil War, 158, 159; base at, 305
New Orleans and Orleans Bank Canal, La., 117
New Paltz, N. Neth. (N.Y.), 24
Newport, R.I., 22, 27; in the Revolution, 46, 48, 49, 51
Newport News, Va., 1; embarkation port, World War I, 212
Newspapers, 1725, 44; 1775, 45; 1800, 135; 1860, 138
New Sweden, 23
Newton, Kan., and the Chisholm Trail, 226
Newtown (Wilmington), N.C., 31
New Utrecht, N. Neth., 24
New York, charter borders, 22; cession of western lands, 54; military lands, 53
New York, N.Y., 1; in the Revolution, 48, 49, 50, 51; branch of First Bank of the U.S. at, 111; Second Bank, 112; and Underground Railway, 146; Federal Reserve Bank, 246; embarkation port, World War I, 212; on commercial airline, 1922, 243; base at, 305
New York and Cuba Mail Steamship Co., subsidized routes of, 258
New York and Pennsylvania Canal, 118
New York and Puerto Rico Steamship Co., subsidized routes of, 258
New Zealand, 305
Nez Perce Indians, Ida.-Mont., 19
Nicaragua, interventions in, financial protectorate, 258*n*, 305*n*; Vanderbilt Transfer, mentioned, 58
Nicaraguan Canal, Hise treaties, 127*n*
Nicholls, route of, in the War of 1812, 95
Nicholson, route of, in the War of the Spanish Succession, 30
Nickel deposits, Sudbury, Ont., 6
Nicolet, route of, 28; 1838–9, 59
Nicuesa, route of, 21
Nieu Amsterdam, N. Neth., 24
Nieu Utrecht, N. Neth., 24
Nigeria, 305
Ninety-six, S.C., in the Revolution, 50, 51
Niteroi, Brazil, 4
No Man's Land, Okla., 165
Nombre de Dios (Pan.), 4; Sp. C.A., 21
Nome, Alaska, 3
Norfolk, Va., 1; in the Revolution, 46; in War of 1812, 94, 95; branch of First Bank of the U.S. at, 111; Second Bank, 112; and domestic routes of slave trade, 146; and Underground Railway, 146; in the Civil War, 158; and Albemarle-Chesapeake Canal, 250; base at, 305
Norridgewock, Me., 31
North Carolina, military lands, 53; cession of western lands, 56
North Magnetic Pole, 3
North Platte, Neb., on commercial airline, 1922, 253
North Platte R., Neb., etc., 2
North Saskatchewan R., Can., 2, 3
North Sea, 305; minefield, World War I, 213
Northampton, Mass., and Hampshire and Hampden Canal, 117
Northern Division Canal, Pa., 117
Northern Rhodesia, 305
Northwest posts, 52, 126
Northwest Territories, Can., 3
Norton Sd., Alaska, 2
Norwalk, Conn., in the Revolution, 49
Norway, 305
Norwegian-born population, *see under* Population
Novaya Zemlya, USSR, 305
Nova Scotia, prov. of, 2, 3
Noyon, Fr., in World War I, 213
Nueces R., Tex., 2, 97
Nueva Andalusia, Sp. C.A., 21
Nueva España, 21
Nueva Estremadura, Sp. Mex., 21
Nueva Galicia, Sp. Mex., 21
Nueva Leon, Sp. Mex., 21
Nunivak Is., Alaska, 2, 3

Oakland, Cal., 1, 9; and mail routes, *circa* 1850, 116
Ocampo, route of, 21
Ocean Steam Navigation Co., routes of, 127
Oceanic and Oriental Navigation Co., subsidized routes of, 258
Ocmulgee National Monument, Ga., 263
Ogallala, Neb., and Western Trail, 226
Ogden, Utah, 1
Ogden River reclamation project, Utah, 264
Ogdensburg, N.Y., 1
Ohio and Pennsylvania Canal, 118
Ohio Canal, Ohio, 58, 117
Ohio Co. lands, 53
Ohio R., 2, 58
Ohio Territory, 85
Oil fields, U.S., 9; world production, 307
Ojeda, routes of, 20, 21.
Okanogan Reclamation Project, Wash., 264
Okkak, Lab., 3
Oklahoma City, Okla., 1
Oklahoma Territory, 168
Old-age assistance, maximum benefit payments by the states, 304
Old National Road, 58
Olean, N.Y., and Genesee Valley Canal, 118
Olympia, Wash., 1
Olympic National Park, Wash., 263
Omaha, Neb., 1, 58; and the Overland Mail, 116; on commercial airline, 1922, 253
Omaha Indians, Neb., 19
Oman, 305
Oñate, routes of, 21, 35
Oneida Indians, N.Y., 19
Onondaga Indians, N.Y., 19
Ontario, prov. of, 3
Oregon border dispute, 1826–72, 72
Oregon Caves National Monument, Ore., 263
Oregon Country, 66; border problem, 127*n*; northern limits, 209
Oregon Territory, 69, 122
Oregon Trail, 58
Organ Pipe Cactus National Monument, Ariz., 263
Orinoco R., S.A., 4
Oriskany, N.Y., in the Revolution, 47
Orkney Is., G.B., 213
Orland Reclamation Project, Cal., 264
Orleans, Territory of, 88
Osage Indians, Kan.-Mo., 19
Osawatomie, Kan., and Underground Railway, 146
Ostend Manifesto, 127*n*
Oswego, N.Y., 1, 52; in the Seven Years' War, 34; in the

Revolution, 47; and Oswego Canal, 117; and Underground Railway, 146
Oswego Canal, N.Y., 117
Ottawa, Ont., 1, 3
Ottawa Indians, Mich., 19
Ottawa R., Can., 2, 3
Otissingen (Flushing), N. Neth. (NY.), 24
Ouachita Mts., 2
Overland Mail, 116
Owyhee Reclamation Project, Ore.-Ida., 264
Oxford, Miss., in the Civil War, 158
Ozark Mts., Ark., 2

Paanpack (Troy), N. Neth. (N.Y.), 24
Pacific Argentine Brazil Line, subsidized routes of, 258
Pacific Mail Steamship Co., routes of, 127
Pacific Ocean, 2
Packenham, route in the War of 1812, 95
Paducah, Ky., in the Civil War, 158, 160
Pago Pago, Samoa, base at, 257*n*
Painted Desert, Ariz., 2
Paiute Indians, Nev.-Utah, 19
Palm Beach, West, Fla., 1
Palm Canyon National Monument Project, Cal., 263
Palmyra Is., claimed by U.S., 305*n*
Pamlico Sd., N.C., 305*n*
Panama, early American transit facilities at, 127*n;* interventions in, 258*n*, 305*n*
Panama Canal, 2; transit rights in treaty of 1846, 127*n*
Panama City, Pan., 4, 305; Sp. C.A., 21
Panama Conference neutrality zone, World War II, 258
Panama, Gulf of, 4
Panama Mail Steamship Co., subsidized routes of, 258
Panama Railroad, 127*n;* mentioned, 58
Panuco R., Mex., 97
Panzacola (Pensacola), Sp. Fla., 35
Paonia Reclamation Project, Colo., 264
Papineau, revolt of, Can., 127*n*
Para, Brazil, 4
Para R., Brazil, 4
Paracima Mts., S.A., 4
Paraguay, 4, 305; punitive expedition against, 127*n*, 305*n*
Paraguay R., S.A., 4
Paramaribo, Surinam, 4
Paraná R., S.A., 4
Paranahyba R., Brazil, 4
Parecis Mts., S.A., 4
Paria Bay, Ven., 4
Parima Mts., S.A., 3
Paris, Fr., and U.S. in World War I, 213
Paris, Peace of, 52
Parnahyba R., Brazil, 4
Parral, Sp. Mex., 35
Parras, Mex., in the Mexican War, 97
Parras, Sante Marie de, Sp. Mex., 21
Passaic R., N. Neth. (N.J.), 24
Patagonia, Arg., 4
Paterson, N.J., 1
Patrick Henry National Monument Project, Va., 263
Patterson, route of, in the Mexican War, 97
Pattie, route of, 59
Patzcuaro, Sp. Mex., 21
Paulus Hoeck (Hook), N. Neth. (N.J.), 24
Pauper Schools, *see* Schools, Public, State Legislation
Pawnee Indians, Kan.-Neb., 19
Pawtucket and Lowell Canal, R.I.-Mass., 117
Pea Ridge, Ark., in the Civil War, 158
Peace of Paris, 52
Peace R., Can., 2, 3
Pearl Harbor, T.H., acquired, 257*n;* base at, 305
Pearl R., Miss., 2, 60, 62
Pecos, Sp. N. Mex., 35
Pecos R., N. Mex.-Tex., 2
Pedee R., S.C., 2
Peekskill, N.Y., in the Revolution, 47, 51
Peking, China, and Boxer Rebellion, 305*n*
Pemaquid, Me., 27; in the War of the League of Augsburg, 28
Penhuyns Is., claimed by U.S., 305*n*
Peninsula Campaign, Civil War, 158
Penn, William, charter grant to, 25
Penn's Neck Canal, 250
Pennsylvania, charter borders, 25; donation and depreciation lands, 53; lands relinquished to by Conn., 56
Penobscot, Me., 27
Penobscot Indians, Me., 19
Penobscot R., Me., 2
Pensacola, Fla., 1, 30; Sp. Fla., 35, 60; in the Revolution, 51; in the War of 1812, 95; in the Seminole War, 95; in the Civil War, 158, 159; base at, 305
Peoria, Ill., 1
Pepperell, route of, in the War of the Austrian Succession, 32
Pequot Indians, Mass.-Conn., 19
Perdido R., Fla., 2, 60, 62
Pernambuco, Brazil, 4
Perry, route of, on Lake Erie, War of 1812, 94
Perry's Victory and International Peace Memorial National Monument, Ohio, 263
Perryville, Ky., in the Civil War, 158
Pershing's pursuit of Villa, 258*n*
Persian Gulf, 305
Peru, 4, 305
Pescador Is., claimed by U.S., 305*n*
Peterboro, Ont., 3
Petersburg, Va., 1; in the Revolution, 51; and domestic routes of slave trade, 146; in the Civil War, 161
Petrified Forest National Monument, Ariz., 263
Petroleum, U.S. fields, 9; world production of, 308
Philadelphia, Pa., 1, 7, 25, 27; in the Revolution, 47, 48; and Delaware Division Canal, 117; and Underground Railway, 146; embarkation port, World War I, 212; Federal Reserve Bank, 236; base at, 305
Philippine Is., annexed, 257*n;* insurrection, 258*n;* invaded by Japan, 258*n*, 305*n*
Phips, route of in the War of the League of Augsburg, 28
Phoenix, Ariz., 1
Phoenix Is., claimed by U.S., 305*n*
Pickawillany, Ohio, 33
Pickawillany Trail, Ohio, 33
Pickens, route of in the Revolution, 49
Piedmont region, U.S., 2
Pierre, S. Dak., 1; *see also* Ft. Pierre
Pigeon R., Ont., 73
Pike, routes of, 59
Pike's Peak, Colo., 59
Pilcomayo R., S.A., 4
Pima Indians, Ariz., 19
Pine River Reclamation Project, N. Mex., 264
Pineda, routes of, 20, 21
Ping-Yang forts, Korea, bombarded, 257*n*, 305*n*
Pinnacles National Monument, Cal., 263
Pinzon, routes of, 20, 21
Pioneer National Monument Project, Ky., 263
Pipelines, U.S., 9
Pipe Spring National Monument, Ariz., 263

Pipestone National Monument, Minn., 263
Piscatauqua, Me., 27
Pitiqui, Sp. Mex., 35
Pittsburgh, Pa., 1, 7, 9, 58; branch of Second Bank at, 112; *see also* Ft. Pitt
Pizzaro, beginning of route of, 21
Placerville, Ida., 6
Platt National Park, Okla., 263
Plata R., S.A., 4
Platte R., U.S., 2
Plattsburg, N.Y., in the War of 1812, 94, 95
Pleasant Hill, La., in the Civil War, 160
Plymouth Colony, 22
Plymouth, Eng., disembarkation port, World War I, 213
Plymouth, Mass. Bay, 27; in the War of 1812, 95
Pocatello, Ida., 1
Pocomtuck Indians, Mass., 19
Point au Fer, N.Y., 52
Point Barrow, Alaska, 2, 3
Point Conception, Cal., 2
Point de Aguja, Peru, 4
Poland, 305
Poll Tax, 1940, 190
Ponca Indians, Neb.-Dak., 19
Pony Express, 116
Population, density of, 1790, 63; 1800, 64; 1810, 65; 1820, 66; 1830, 67; 1840, 68; 1850, 69; 1860, 70; 1870, 165; 1880, 166; 1890, 167; 1900, 168; 1910, 169; 1920, 170; 1930, 171; Dutch origin, 1775, 37; English origin, 1775, 37; foreign-born, proportion to total population, 1860, 174; 1880, 175; 1900, 176; German origin, 1775, 37; German-born, proportion to total population, 1880, 183; 1900, 184; 1930, 185; Irish-born, proportion to total population, 1880, 180; 1900, 181; 1930, 182; Negro (Free Negro), 1860, 145; proportion to population, 1900, 172; 1930, 173; Scots-Highland origin, 1775, 37; Scots-Irish origin, 1775, 37; Swedish and Norwegian-born, proportion to total population, 1880, 177; 1900, 178; 1930, 179
Porcupine R., Alaska, 3
Port Arthur, Ont., 3
Port Gibson, Miss., in the Civil War, 159
Port Hudson, La., in the Civil War, 159
Port Nelson, Man., 3
Port Royal, N. Sco., in the War of the Spanish Succession, 30
Port Royal, S.C., 25, in the War of the Spanish Succession, 30; in the Civil War, 157, 158, 159
Porter, route of, in the Civil War, 160
Portland, Me., 1, 9; branch of Second Bank at, 112; and the Underground Railway, 146; embarkation port in World War I, 212; base at, 305
Portland, Ore., 1; and mail routes, *circa* 1861, base at, 305; *see also* Ft. William
Porto Alegre, Brazil, 4
Porto Bello, Pan., 4
Portola, route of, 35
Portsmouth, Eng., 213
Portsmouth, N.H., 1; branch of Second Bank at, 112; base at, 305
Portsmouth, Ohio, and the Underground Railway, 146
Portugal, 305
Post Roads, 1804, 114; 1834, 115; Overland Mail and Pony Express, 116
Potomac, circumnavigation of globe by, 127*n*
Potomac R., Md.-Va., 2
Potosí, Bol., 4
Pottawatomie Indians, Mich., 19
Poughkeepsie, N.Y., 1
Pourée, route of, in the Revolution, 51
Power transmission lines, 1922, 241; 1935, 242
Powhattan Indians, Va., 19
Prairie du Chien, Wisc., 58, 59
Prairie Grove, Ark., in the Civil War, 158
Precipitation, U.S., 15; drought frequency, 16
Presqu'Isle (Erie), Que., 34; Pa., in War of 1812, 94
Prestonburg, Ky., in the Civil War, 158
Prevost, route of in the Revolution, 49; in the War of 1812, 95
Price, routes of, in the Civil War, 158, 160
Primeria Alta, Sp. Cal., 35
Prince Edward Island, prov. of, 3
Prince George, B.C., 3
Prince of Wales Is., Alaska, 209
Prince Rupert, B.C., 3
Princeton, N.J., in the Revolution, 47
Prince William Sd., Alaska, 3
Proclamation Line of 1763, 36
Proctor, route of in the War of 1812, 94
Prohibition, 1846, 132; 1856, 133; 1880, 275; 1906, 276; 1915, 277; 1919, 278; dry counties, 1919, 279; 1940, 280; ratification of the 18th amend., 200; repeal (21st amend.), 203
Prospect Is., claimed by U.S., 305*n*
Providence, Md., 22
Providence, R.I., 1, 22; branch of Second Bank at, 112
Providence Plantations colony, 22
Provo River Irrigation Project, Utah, 264
Provo, Utah, 1
Public Domain, *see* Land cessions
Public Land Strip, (Okla.), 166
Public School Legislation, *see* Schools, State Public Legislation
Puebla, Mex., in the Mexican War, 97
Pueblo, Colo., 1
Pueblo Indians, N. Mex., 19
Puerto, Santiago (Jamaica), 21
Puerto Rico, 2, 21; in the Spanish-American War, 207*n*, 305*n*; annexed, 257*n*
Puget Sd., Wash., 2, 72
Purus R., Brazil, 4
Put-in-Bay, Ohio, 94
Putumayo R., S.A., 4

Qualla Battoo, Sumatra, 127*n*, 305*n*
Qu'Appelle R., Can., 3
Quebec, P.Q., 1, 3; Que., in the War of the League of Augsburg, 28; in the Seven Years' War, 34; P.Q., in the Revolution, 46; embarkation port, World War I, 212
Quebec, prov. of, 3, 53
Quebec Act of 1774, 36
Queen Anne's Creek (Edenton), N.C., 29
Queen Anne's War (War of the Spanish Succession), 30
Queen Charlotte Is., B.C., 3
Queenstown Heights, Ont., in War of 1812, 93
Queretaro, Sp. Mex., 21
Quexaltenango, Sp. Mex., 21
Quiros Is., claimed by U.S., 305*n*
Quitman expedition, 127*n*
Quito, Ec., 4
Quito Sueño Is., claimed by U.S., title established, 305*n*
Quivira, 35

Racine, Wisc., 1
Railroads, 1840, 119; 1850, 120; 1860, 121; 1870, 247; 1880, 248; land grants to, 249
Rainbow Bridge National Monument, Utah, 263

All numbers refer to maps, not pages

Rainfall, U.S., 15; drought frequency, 16
Rainy Lake, Minn.-Ont., 3, 73
Rainy R., Can.-U.S., 73
Raisin R., Mich., 94
Raleigh, N.C., 1
Ramsey's Mill, N.C., in the Revolution, 51
Rapid City, S. Dak., 6
Rates of travel, 1800, 123; 1830, 124; 1860, 125; 1930, 256
Rawdon, route of in the Revolution, 51
Rawlins, Wyo., on commercial airline, 1922, 253
Rayneval boundary proposals after the Revolution, 52
Reading, Pa., 1; and nearby canals, 117
Recife, Brazil, 4
Reclamation, areas now irrigated or susceptible of irrigation, projects, 264
Red R., La.-Ark.-Tex.-Okla., 2, 97
Red R., U.S.,-Can., 2, 3
Red Sea, 305
Regina, Sask., 3
Reims, Fr., in World War I, 213
Reindeer Lake, Sask., 3
Reno, Nev., 1; on commercial airline, 1922, 253
Rensselaerswyck, N. Neth. (N.Y.), 24
Republican R., Kan.-Neb., 2
Revolt of Mackenzie, Upper Canada, 127*n;* of Papineau, Lower Canada, 127*n;* of Riel, Can., 257*n*
Revolutionary War Campaigns 46, 47, 48, 49, 50, 51; Peace of Paris, 52
Reykjavik, Iceland, 3
Rhineland, occupation of, 258*n*
Rhode Island and Providence Plantations, 25
Rhodesia, 305
Rice areas, 1775, 40
Richelieu R., P.Q., 3
Richmond, Va., 1, 31, 58; in the Revolution, 50; branch of Second Bank of the U.S. at, 112; and domestic routes of slave trade, 146; in the Civil War, 158, 160, 161; Federal Reserve Bank at, 246
Richmond Canal, Va., 117
Rich Mountain, W. Va., in the Civil War, 157
Ridgefield, Conn., in the Revolution, 47
Ridley expedition, 127*n*
Riel rebellion, Can., 257*n*
Rierson's Is., claimed by U.S., 305*n*
Rigaud, route of, in the War of the Austrian Succession, 32
Rio de Janeiro, Brazil, 4
Rio de Oro, 305
Rio Grande, U.S.-Mex., 97
Rio Grande do Sul, Brazil, 4
Rio Grande Reclamation Project, N. Mex.-Tex., 264
Ripley, Ohio, and Underground Railway, 146
Riverton Reclamation Project, Wyo., 264
Roads and highways, land grants to wagon roads, 249; U.S. highways, 1925, 251; 1935, 252; *see also* Post Roads; *see also* by specific name
Roanoke, Va., 1
Roanoke Is., Carolina, 2, 22, 27; in the Civil War, 158
Roanoke R., N.C., 2
Robertson Trail, 58
Rochambeau, routes of in the Revolution, 51
Rochester, N.Y., 1, 58; and nearby canals, 117
Rochefort, Fr., and U.S. in World War I, 213
Rock Island, Ill., 1, 250
Rock Springs, Wyo., on commercial airline, 1922, 253
Rocky Mts., 2; Can., 3
Rocky Mountain National Park, Colo., 263
Rogewein's Is., claimed by U.S., 305*n*
Romaine R., P.Q., 3
Roncador Key, claimed by U.S., 305*n*
Roncador Mts., Brazil, 4
Roosevelt Steamship Co., subsidized routes of, 258
Rosario, Arg., 4
Rosario, Sp. Tex., 35
Rosecrans, routes of in the Civil War, 157, 159
Ross, route of in the War of 1812, 95
Roswell, N. Mex., 1
Rotterdam, Neth., 213
Rouen, Fr., and U.S. in World War I, 213
Rouse's Point, N.Y., 1
Rui, route of, 35
Rumania, 305
Rush-Bagot agreement, 126*n*
Russia, Ukase of 1821, 126*n;* Archangel expedition, 258*n;* U.S. forces in, after World War I, 258*n*, 305
Rustdorf (Jamaica), N. Neth. (N.Y.), 24
Rutland, Vt., 1

Saar basin, Ger., 213
Saavedra, route of, 20
Sabine Cross Roads, La., in the Civil War, 160
Sabine R., Tex.-La., 2, 97
Sac and Fox Indians, Wisc., 19
Sackett Harbor, N.Y., in the War of 1812, 94
Saco, Me., 22, 27
Sacramento, Cal., 1; in the Mexican War, 97; and mail routes, *circa* 1858, 116
Sacramento Mts., Mex., 2
Sagadahoc, Me., 27
Saguaro National Monument, Ariz., 263
Saguenay R., P.Q., 3
St. Augustine, Fla., 1; Sp. Fla., 21, 35; attacked 1702, 30; in the War of the Austrian Succession, 32; in the Civil War, 158, 159
St. Bartholomew Is., W.I., purchase contemplated, 257*n*
St. Catherines, Ont., and the Underground Railway, 146
St. Denis, route of, 32
St. Denis, La., 30
St. Eustatius Is., W.I., 2
St. Francis de Sales, Que., 28
St. Francis Xavier, Fr. Ill., 28
St. Ignace, Que., 28
St. John, N.B., 47
St. John R., Me., 2
St. Johns, Nfld., 3; embarkation port, World War I, 212
St. Johns, P.Q., in the Revolution, 46
St. Joseph, Mo., 1; and the Overland Mail, 116
St. Lawrence Is., Alaska, 2, 3
St. Lawrence R., 2, 3; free navigation of secured, 257*n*
St. Leger, route of, in the Revolution, 47
St. Louis, Mo., 1, 9, 58, 59; in the Revolution, 5; branch of Second Bank of the U.S. at, 112; and mail routes, *circa* 1858, 116; Federal Reserve Bank, 246
St. Louis R., Minn., 73
St. Lucia, B.W.I., 2; U.S. base at, 258*n*, 305*n*
St. Marks, Fla., in the First Seminole War, 95
St. Mary's, Md., 22, 27
St. Mary's R., Fla.-Ga., 2
St. Mary's R., Ont.-Mich. 2
St. Matthew Is., Alaska, 2
St. Maurice R., P.Q., 3
St. Mihiel sector, Fr., World War I, 213
St. Nazaire, Fr., disembarkation port, World War I, 213
St. Paul, Minn., 1
St. Petersburg, Fla., 1
St. Pierre Is., off Nfld., 3
St. Xavier del Bac, Sp. Mex., 35

All numbers refer to maps, not pages

Salado R., Arg., 4
Salem, Mass., 27
Salem, N.J., 25
Salem, Ore., 1
Salinan Indians, Cal., 19
Salisbury, N.C., 58; and domestic routes of slave trade, 146; in the Civil War, 161
Salmon Falls, N.H., in the War of the League of Augsburg, 28
Saltillo, Sp. Mex., 21; in the Mexican War, 97
Salt Lake City, Utah, 1, 6, 58, 59; and mail routes, *circa* 1851, 116; on commercial airline, 1922, 253
Salton Sea, Cal., 2
Salt River Reclamation Project, Ariz., 264
Saludo R., Arg., 4
Samana Bay, S. Dom., 2; negotiations re, 257*n*
Samoa, 305; negotiations re, 257*n*
Sampson, route of, in the Spanish-American War, 207
San Antonio de Bejar, Sp. Tex., 35
San Antonio, Sp. Fla., 21, 35
San Antonio, Tex., 1; and mail routes, 1854, 116; and cattle trails, 226
San Augustin, Sp. Tex., 35
San Blas, Mex., in the Mexican War, 97
San Buenaventura, Sp. Cal., 35
San Carlos Borromeo, Sp. Cal., 35
San Diego, Cal., 1, 59; in the Mexican War, 97; and mail routes, *circa* 1857, 116; base at, 305
San Diego de Alcala, Sp. Cal., 35
San Dionysio, Sp. Cal., 35
San Esteban, Sp. Mex., 21
San Felipé, Sp. Mex., 21
San Felipe Orista, Sp. Fla., 35
San Fernando Re de España, Sp. Cal., 35
San Francisco, Cal., 1, 6, 97; (de Assisi), 35, 59; and mail routes, *circa* 1858, 116; Federal Reserve Bank, 246; on commercial airline, 1922, 253; base at, 305
San Francisco Bay, Cal., 2
San Francisco de la Espada, Sp. Tex., 35
San Francisco de los Nechas, Sp. Tex., 35
San Francisco de los Tejas, Sp. Tex., 35
San Francisco de Solano, Sp. Cal., 35
San Francisco de Borja, Sp. Mex., 35
San Geronimo, Sp. Mex., 21
San Jacinto, Tex., battle site, 97
San José, Mex., in the Mexican War, 97
San José, Sp. Cal., 35
San Juan, Sp. Mex., 21
San Juan Bautista, P.R., 21
San Juan Bautista, Sp. Cal., 35
San Juan Capistrano, Sp. Cal., 35
San Juan de los Caballeros, Sp. N. Mex., 35
San Juan Hill, Cuba, battle of, 207
San Luis, Sp. Fla., 35
San Luis, Sp. Mex., 21
San Luis, Sp. Tex., 35
San Luis Bautista, Sp. Tex., 35
San Luis Obispo, Sp. Cal., 35
San Luis Obispo Bay, Cal., 2
San Luis Potosi, Sp. Mex., 21; Mex., in border proposals, 98
San Luis Rey de Francia, Sp. Cal., 35
San Mateo, Sp. Fla., 21, 35
San Matias, Gulf of, 4
San Miguel, Sp. Fla., 35
San Miguel Archangel, Sp. Cal., 35
San Miguel de Cuellar, Sp. Tex., 35
San Miguel de Gualdape, Sp. Tex., 35
San Rafael Archangel, Sp. Cal., 35
San Salvador, Sp. C.A., 21
San Sebastian, Sp. S.A., 21
San Xavier, Sp. Tex., 35
Sandusky, Ohio, and Underground Railway, 146
Sandy Hook, N.J., in the Revolution, 48
Sangre de Cristo Mts., 2
Sanpete Reclamation Project, Utah, 264
Santa Barbara, Brazil, 4
Santa Barbara, Cal., 1; Sp. Cal., 35
Santa Barbara, Sp. Mex., 21
Santa Cruz de Nanipacna, Sp. Fla., 21, 35
Santa Cruz, Sp. Cal., 35
Santa Elena, Sp. Fla., 35
Santa Fé, Arg., 4
Santa Fé, N. Mex., 1, Sp. Mex., 32, 35; N. Mex., 58, 59; in the Mexican War, 97; and mail routes, *circa* 1850, 116; in the Civil War, 160
Santa Fé de Guanajuato, Sp. Mex., 21
Santa Fé Trail, 58
Santa Maria, Sp. Cal., 35
Santa Marie de Parras, Sp. Mex., 21
Santa Marie la Antigua del Darien, Sp. S.A., 21
Santa Rosa Mts., 2
Santa Ynez, Sp. Cal., 35
Santee Indians, N.-S.C., 19
Santee R., S.C., 2
Santiago, Arg., 4
Santiago, Chile, 4
Santiago, Cuba, 21; in the Spanish-American War, 207
Santiago (Jamaica), 21
Santiago Mts., Mex., 2
Santo Domingo (city), 21
Santo Domingo, protectorate offer, 127*n*
Santos, Brazil, 4
São Domingos Mts., Brazil, 4
São Francisco R., Brazil, 4
São Paulo, Brazil, 4
Sarah Anne Is., claimed by U.S., 305*n*
Sarah Lake, Ont., 73
Saramang Is., claimed by U.S., 305*n*
Saratoga, N.Y., in the Revolution, 47
Saratoga Springs, N.Y., 1
Sardinia, Is. of, 213
Saskatchewan, prov. of, 3
Saskatoon, Sask., 3
Saudi Arabia, 305
Sault Ste. Marie, Ont., 3; Que., 28
Saunders, route of in the Seven Years' War, 34
Savannah, Ga., 1, 26, 31; in the Revolution, 48, 49; branch of First Bank of the U.S. at, 111; Second Bank, 112; and domestic routes of slave trade, 146; in the Civil War, 160, 161
Savannah Canal, Ga., 117
Savannah-Ogeechee Canal, Ga., 118
Savannah R., Ga., 2
Saybrook, Conn., 27
Scapa Flow, Orkney Is., 213
Schenectady, N.Y., 1; N. Neth., 24; in the War of the League of Augsburg, 28
Schley, route of in the Spanish-American War, 507
Schofield, route of in the Civil War, 161
Schoolcraft, route of, 59
Schools, compulsory attendance, 1880, 266; 1890, 267; 1900, 268; 1920, 269; age limits of 1940, 270
Schools, Public, State Legislation, 1790, 128; 1820, 129; 1830, 130; 1855, 131; 1875 ff., 265
Scioto R., Ohio, 2

Scituate, Mass., in the War of 1812, 95
Scott, routes of in the Mexican War, 97
Scotts Bluff National Monument, Neb., 263
Scranton, Pa., 1
Sea of Japan, 305
Sea of Okhotsk, 305
Seattle, Wash., 1; base at, 305
Secession, distribution of opposition to, in South, 148
Sedan, Fr., in World War I, 213
Segura Mission, Sp. Fla., 35
Selma, Ala., 1; in the Civil War, 161
Seminole Indians, Fla., 19
Seminole War, 1818, 95
Senate vote on ratification of the Treaty of Paris, Feb. 6, 1899, 208; of the Versailles Treaty without reservations, Nov. 19, 1919, 211
Senators, direct election of, ratification of 17th amend. to the Constitution, 199
Seneca Indians, N.Y., 19
Sequoia National Park, Cal., 263
Sequeira, route of, 20
Serranilla Keys, claimed by U.S., title established, 305*n*
Service of Supply, U.S. Army in France, World War I, 213
Seven Days, battle of, in Civil War, 158
Seven Ranges, N.W. Terr., 53
Seven Years' War (French and Indian War), 34
Severn, Ont., 3
Severn R., Ont., 3
Sevier Lake, Utah, 58
Seward Penin., Alaska, 3
Shafter, route of in the Spanish-American War, 207
Shawinigan Falls, P.Q., 3
Shawnee Indians, Ohio-Ind., 19
Shawnee Trail, 226
Sheet erosion areas, U.S., 13
Shenandoah National Park, Va., 263
Shenandoah Valley, Va., 58
Sherbrooke, P.Q., 3
Sheridan, route of in the Civil War, 160, 161
Sherman, routes of in the Civil War, 158, 159, 160, 161
Shetland Is., G.B., 213
Shiloh, Tenn., in the Civil War, 158
Shimonoseki, Sts. of, bombarded, 257*n*
Ship Island, Miss., in Civil War, 157, 158
Shipping subsidies, in 1850, 127; under act of 1864, 257; under act of 1891, 257; under act of 1936, 258
Shoshone Cavern National Monument, Wyo., 263
Shoshone Indians, Ida., 19
Shoshone Reclamation Project, Wyo., 264
Shreveport, La., 1, 9
Siam (Thailand), 305; trade treaties with, 127*n*
Siberia, USSR, 3, 305
Sibley, exploration by, 59
Sibley, route of in the Civil War, 160
Siboney, Cuba, in the Spanish-American War, 207
Sidney's Is., claimed by U.S., 305*n*
Sierra Leone, 305
Sierra Madre Occidental, Mex., 2
Sierra Madre Oriental, Mex., 2
Sierra Nevada, Cal., 2
Silao, Sp. Mex., 21
Sillery, Que., 28
Silver, U.S. deposits, 6; world production of, 310
Silver City, Ida., 6
Silver City, N. Mex., 6
Silver Creek, Nev., 6
Silver Peak, Nev., 6
Silver Plume, Colo., 6
Simpson, Mackenzie Dist., 3
Singapore, 305
Sioux City, Iowa, 1
Sioux Falls, S. Dak., 1
Sioux Indians, 19
Sitka, Alaska, 3, 209; base at, 305
Skagway, Alaska, 3, 209
Skenesboro, N.Y., in the Revolution, 47
Skins and hides, world production of, 317
Slave R., Can., 3
Slavery, *see also* Abolition; proportion of slaves to total population, 1790, 141; 1800, 142; 1840, 143; 1860, 144; slaves per slaveholder, 1860, 147
Slave trade, domestic routes of, 146
Sloat, route of in Mexican War, 97
Smith, route of, 59
Smith, route of in the Civil War 158, 160
Smyrna, Turkey, interposition at, 258*n*, 305*n*
Snake Indians, Ida., 19
Snake R., Ida., 72
Social security, maximum benefit payments in old age assistance, 304
Soil regions, U.S., 11
Solimoes R., Brazil, 4
Solis, route of, 21
Solomon Is., in World War II, 305*n*
Somaliland, 305
Sonoma, Cal., in the Mexican War, 97
Sonora, Mex., invaded, 127*n*
S.O.S., *see* Services of Supply
South Africa, Union of, 305
South America, physical features of, 4
South Atlantic Steamship Co., subsidized routes of, 258
South Bend, Ind., 1
South Carolina, military lands, 53; cession of western lands, 56
South Carolina Yazoo Co. lands, 53
South China Sea, 305
South Pass, Wyo., 58, 59
South Platte R., Colo.-Neb., 2
South Saskatchewan R., Alb.-Sask., 2, 3
Southern Indian Lake, Man., 3
Southern Rhodesia, 305
Southampton, Eng., disembarkation port, World War I, 213
Southampton, L.I., 27
South West Africa, 305
Spain, 305; participation in the Revolution, 49, 50, 51; U.S. boundary proposals by, after the Revolution, 52
Spanish-American War, House vote on declaration of, 206; campaigns of, 207; Senate vote on peace treaty, 208
Spanish explorations and settlements in Mexico and the Caribbean, 21
Spanish galleons, routes of, 20
Spanish Lower California, 98
Spanish Main, 21
Spanish New Mexico, 98
Spanish Texas, 21, 98; approximate border of, 97
Spanish Trail, 58
Spanish Upper California, 98
Spartanburg, S.C., 1
Spitsbergen, 305
Springfield, Ill., 1
Springfield, Mass., 1
Springfield, Mo., in the Civil War, 157, 158
Springfield, N.J., in the Revolution, 50
Spokane, Wash., 1
Spokane Indians, Wash., 19
Staked Plain, Tex., 2

Stanley, Falkland Is., 4
Stanley, Sask., 3
Starbuck Is., claimed by U.S., 305*n*
Starkville, Miss., in the Civil War, 159
Staten Is., N. Neth. (N.Y.), 24
States Steamship Co., subsidized routes of, 258
Statue of Liberty National Monument, N.Y., 263
Staunton, Va., 160, 161
Staver's Is., claimed by U.S., 305*n*
Steamship routes subsidized, 1850, 127; under the act of 1864, 257; under act of 1891, 257; under act of 1936, 258
Steele, route of in the Civil War, 160
Stockton, route of in the Mexican War, 97
Stockton, Cal., and mail routes, *circa* 1850, 116
Stoneman, route of in the Civil War, 111
Stonington, Conn., in War of 1812, 94, 95
Stono Ferry, S.C., in the Revolution, 49
Stony Creek, Ont., in the War of 1812, 95
Stony Point, N.Y., in the Revolution, 49
Straits of Belle Isle, Nfld.-Lab., 3
Straits of Georgia, B.C., 3
Straits of Juan de Fuca, Wash.-B.C., 2, 3, 72
Straits of Magellan, S.A., 4
Strawberry Valley Reclamation Project, Utah, 264
Streight, route of in the Civil War, 159
Sublette Cut-off, 58
Sub-marginal land areas, U.S., 14
Submarine zones, World War I, 213; safety zone to Greece, via Mediterranean, 213; World War II, 258
Subsidies, *see* Shipping subsidies
Suchan Mines, USSR, U.S. forces at, 258*n*, 305*n*
Sucre, Bol., 4
Sudan, 305
Sudbury, Ont., 3, 6
Suffrage, *see* Franchise
Sullivan, route of in the Revolution, 48
Sumatra, D.E.I., 305; Qualla Battoo bombarded, 305*n*
Sunbury, Pa., and nearby canal, 117
Sun River Reclamation Project, Mont., 264
Sunset Crater National Monument, Ariz., 263
Superior, Wisc., 1, 7
Surinam, 4; intervention in, 258*n*
Susitna R., Alaska, 3
Susquehanna and Tidewater Canal, 118
Susquehanna Division Canal, Pa., 117
Susquehanna Indians, Pa., 19
Susquehanna R., Pa., 2
Sutter's Mill (Fort), Cal., 6, 58, 97
Suwanee R., Fla., in the 1st Seminole War, 95
Swains Is., 127*n*
Swan Is., claimed by U.S., 305*n*
Sweden, 305
Swedish- and Norwegian-born population, *see under* Population
Switzerland, 213, 305
Sydney, N. Sco., 3
Symmes Purchase, N.W. Terr., 53
Syracuse, N.Y., 1
Syria, 305

Tacna, Peru, 4
Tacoma, Wash., 1
Tacoma Oriental Steamship Co., subsidized routes of, 258
Tadoussac, P.Q., 3
Taliaferro Canal, Ala., 260
Tallahassee, Fla., 1
Tampa, Fla., 1; in the Spanish-American War, 207; base at, 305
Tampa Bay, Fla., 2
Tampa Inter-Ocean Steamship Co., subsidized routes of, 258
Tampico, Mex., in border proposals, 98; in the Mexican War, 97
Tanana R., Alaska, 2, 3
Tanganyika, 305
Taos, Sp. N. Mex., 35, 59
Tapajoz R., Brazil, 4
Tarleton, routes of in the Revolution, 50, 51
Tasmania, 305
Taylor, routes of in the Mexican War, 97
Tehuantepec, negotiations re, 127 *n*
Tehuantepec R.R., mentioned, 58
Tejas Indians, Tex., 19
Telegraph lines, 1854, 122; first transcontinental line, 122*n*
Temperature, averages in January, U.S., 17; July, 18
Tenancy, Farm, *see* Farm Tenancy
Tennessee Co. lands, 53
Tennessee R., Tenn., etc., 2, 58, 61
Teran, route of, 35
Terre Haute, Ind., 1, 58
Territorial expansion, *see* Expansion, U.S.
Territory northwest of the River Ohio, 63
Texas, colonial period, 21; Spanish, approximate borders of, 97, 98; independence, annexation of, 127*n*
Thailand (Siam), 305
Thames R., Ont., 3; in the War of 1812, 94
The Alamo, Tex., 97
Tibet, 305
Tientsin, China, and Boxer Rebellion, 305*n*
Tierra del Fuego, Arg., 4
Tierra Firme (Spanish Main), 21
Tigre Is., Nic., 127*n*
Timpanogos Caves National Monument, Utah, 263
Timucua Indians, Fla., 19
Tin, world production of, 309
Tobacco areas, 1700, 39; 1775, 40; 1860, 106; 1890, 223; 1920, 224; 1940, 225; world production of, 316
Tobago, 4
Tocantins R., Brazil, 4
Tocobaga, Sp. Fla., 35
Toledo, Ohio, 1; and Underground Railway, 146
Tombigbee R., Ala., 2
Tombstone, Ariz., 6
Tonga, U.S. coaling rights at, 257*n*
Tonto National Monument, Ariz., 263
Tonty, route of, 28
Topeka, Kan., 1; and Underground Railway, 146
Toronto, Ont., 1, 3; in the War of 1812, 94; and Underground Railway, 146
Toul, Fr., and World War I, 213
Toulon, Fr., and U.S. in World War I, 213
Tours, Fr., and U.S. in World War I, 213
Trade, colonial, 41; 1800, 126; 1850, 127; 1900, 257; 1938, 258
Trans-Jordan, 305
Transmission Lines, 1922, 241; 1935, 242
Transylvania, 53
Travel, rates of, 1800, 123; 1830, 124; 1860, 125; 1930, 256
Treaty Line, of 1818, 66, 126; of 1819 (1821), 66, 98; of 1842, 69
Trenton, N.J., 1, 7, 25, 27; in the Revolution, 46, 47; and Delaware Division Canal, 117; and nearby canals, 118; and Underground Railway, 146
"Triangular" trade route, 41
Trieste, Gulf of, 4
Trinidad, 2, 4; U.S. base at, 258*n*, 305*n*
Trinidad, Colo., 1

Tripolitan War, 120*n*
Trois Rivières, P.Q., 3; in the Revolution, 46
Troy, N.Y., 1; and nearby canals, 117
Truckee Storage Project, Nev., 264
Truxillo, Sp. C.A., 21
Tryon, routes of, in the Revolution, 47, 49
Tsinan forts, Shanghai, bombarded, 127*n*
Tubac, Sp. Mex., 35
Tucson, Ariz., 1
Tucuman, Arg., 4
Tucumcari Reclamation Project, N. Mex., 264
Tulsa, Okla., 1, 9
Tumacacori, Sp. Mex., 35
Tumacacori National Monument, Ariz., 263
Tupelo, Miss., in the Civil War, 160
Turkey, 305; U.S. forces at Smyrna, 258*n*, 305*n*
Turnpikes, *see* Roads and Highways, or by specific name
Tuscaloosa, Ala., in the Civil War, 161
Tuscarora Indians, N.C.-Va., 19
Tuskegee, Ala., and domestic routes of slave trade, 146
Tuxpan, Mex., in the Mexican War, 97

Ucayali R., S.A., 4
Ukase of 1821, 126*n*
Ulloa, route of, 21
Ulster, Ireland, U.S. troops in, 258*n*
Umatilla, Ore., and mail routes, *circa* 1863, 116
Umatilla Reclamation Project, Ore., 264
Underground Railway, 146
Ungava Bay, 3
Uncompahgre Reclamation Project, Colo., 264
Union Canal, Pa., 117
Union of South Africa, 305
United Colonies of N. Eng., 22*n*
United Fruit Co., subsidized routes of, 258
United States, states and principal cities, 1; regional watersheds, 5; *see also* specific subject
United States and Brazil Steamship Co., route of, 257
United States Bank, *see* Bank of the United States
United States Lines, subsidized routes of, 258
U.S. Army, World War I home camps and embarkation ports, 212; Services of Supply, zones and bases in France, 213
U.S. states, state capitals, principal cities 1; physical features, 2; boundaries, proposed during Revolution, 52; Treaty Line of 1818, 66; Treaty Line of 1819, 66; Treaty Line of 1842, 69; Lake Superior-Rainy Lake border dispute, 1826–42, 73; Maine border dispute, 1821–42, 71; Oregon border dispute, 1826–72, 72; Mexican border, 1821–57, 69, 98; Rush-Bagot agreement, 126; Treaty of 1818, 126
U.S. Congress, *see* Senate, or House
U.S. Constitution, *see* Constitution
U.S. Navy mine field, North Sea, World War I, 213
Upland, N. Swe. (Pa.), 23
Upper California, Sp., 98
Upper Mississippi Co. lands, 53
Upper Snake River Reclamation Project, Ida., 264
Ures, Sp. Mex., 35
Uribarri, route of, 35
Uruguay, 4, 305
Uruguay R., S.A., 4
Utah Lake, Utah, 2, 58
Utah Territory, 70, 90, 165
Ute Indians, Colo.-Utah, 19
Utica, N.Y., 1; and nearby canals, 117; and Underground Railway, 146

Valcours Is., N.Y., in the Revolution, 46
Valdez Penin., Arg., 4
Valdivia, Chile, 4
Vale Reclamation Project, Ore., 264
Valencia, Sp., 213
Valencia, Ven., 4
Valley Forge, Pa., in the Revolution, 47, 48
Valparaiso, Chile, 4; incident, 257*n*
Vancouver, B.C., 1, 3
Vancouver Is., B.C., 3
Vandalia, Fr. Ill., 53; Ill., 58
Vanderbilt Transfer, Nic., mentioned, 58
Van Rensselaer, route of in the War of 1812, 93
Varckenskill, N. Neth., 23
Vegetation and forestation belts, U.S., 10
Venezuela, 4, 305; crisis between U.S. and Great Britain over, 257*n*
Venezuela, Gulf of, 4
Vera Cruz, Sp. Mex., 21; in the Mexican War, 97; bombarded, 258*n*, 305*n*
Verdun, Fr., and World War I, 213
Verendrye National Monument, N. Dak., 263
Vergennes, boundary proposals after the Revolution, 52
Verkhna Udinsk, USSR, U.S. forces at, 258*n*, 305*n*
Vermillion Lake, Minn., 73
Vermillion R., Minn., 73
Vermont, lands ceded to by New York, 54; by New Hampshire, 56
Verrazano, route of, 20
Versailles, Treaty of, Senate vote on ratification of without reservations, Nov. 19, 1919, 211
Vespucci, routes of, 20, 21
Vial, route of, 35
Vicksburg, Miss., 1, 61; and domestic routes of slave trade, 146; in the Civil War, 158, 159, 160
Victoria, B.C., 3
Victoria, Mex., in the Mexican War, 97
Victoria Is., B.C., 3
Villa, Pershing's expedition after, 258*n*
Villazur, route of, 35
Vincennes, P.Q., in the Revolution, 48, 49
Virgin Islands, 21; early negotiations for, 257*n*; annexation of, 257*n*
Virginia, cession of western lands, 55; military lands, 53
Virginia City, Nev., 6; and mail routes, *circa* 1863, 116
Virginia colony, 22
Virginia (London) Co., charter grant to, 22
Virginia (Plymouth) Co., charter grant to, 22
Virginia Yazoo Co. lands, 53
Virginius incident, and Cuba, 257*n*
Vizcaino, route of, 35
Vladivostok, USSR, U.S. forces at, 258*n*, 305*n*
Vreaeland, N. Neth., 24
Vriesendael (Tappans), N. Neth. (N.Y.), 24

Wabash Canal, Ind., 58
Wabash and Erie Canal, Ohio-Ind., 118
Wabash R., Ind., 53
Waco, Tex., 1
Wager Bay, Keewatin, 3
Wagon Roads, land grants to, 249
Wake Is., 305; claimed, 127; annexed, 257*n*; seized by Japan, 258*n*, 305*n*; raided, 258*n*
Walker, route of, 59
Walker, route of in the War of the Spanish Succession, 30
Walker, Wm., activities of, 127*n*
Walkers Is., claimed by U.S., 305*n*
Walapai Indians, Ariz., 19
Walla Walla, Wash., and mail routes, *circa* 1863, 116; *see*

also Ft. Walla Walla
Walnut Canyon National Monument, Ariz., 263
Wampanoag Indians, Mass., 19
Wanghia, Treaty of, 127*n*
War Between the States; Campaigns of 1861, 157; 1862, 158; 1863, 159; 1864, 160; 1865, 161; line of Northern occupation, 1861, 157; 1862, 158; 1863, 159; 1864, 160; Southern opposition to secession, 148
War of 1812, House vote on war resolution, 92; campaigns of, 93, 94, 95
War of the Austrian Succession (King George's War), 32
War of the League of Augsburg (King William's War), 28
War of the Spanish Succession (Queen Anne's War), 30
Wareham, Mass., and Underground Railway, 146
Wasatch Mts., Utah 2
Washington, Ark., in the Civil War, 160
Washington, D.C., 1; in the War of 1812, 95; First Bank of the U.S. at, 111; Second Bank, 112; and nearby canals, 117; in the Civil War, 157, 158, 159
Washington, George, routes of in the Revolution, 47, 48, 49, 50, 51
Washington Is., claimed by U.S., 305*n*
Washington Territory, 70, 122, 165
Watauga Settlements, N.C., 53
Waterbury, Conn., 1
Watersheds, U.S., 5
Wayne, routes of in the Revolution, 51
Weehawken, N. Neth. (N.J.), 24
Weldon Canal, Va., 117
Wellfleet, Mass., in the War of 1812, 95
Wells, N.H., in the War of the League of Augsburg, 28
Wemyss, route of in the Revolution, 50
West Branch Canal, Pa., 117
West Florida, 36; borders of, after the Treaty of Paris, 1763, 60; 1767–87, 61; 1787–1803, 62; steps in U.S. annexation of, 62; occupation of, 126
West Indies, protectorate moves re, 257*n*
West New Jersey, 25
West Palm Beach, Fla., 1
West Point, N.Y., in the Revolution, 50
Western Cordillera, S.A., 4
Western Reserve (Ohio), 53
Western Shawnee Trail, 226
Western Trail, 226
Western Triangles, claimed by U.S., 305*n*
Westward migration, routes of, 58
Whaling grounds, colonial, 41; 1850, 127
Wheat, 1840, 99; 1860, 100; 1890, 214; 1920, 215; 1940, 216; world production of, 313
Wheeler National Monument, Colo., 263
Wheeling, W.Va., 1; Va., 58; and Underground Railway, 146;
Whitehall, N.Y., and Champlain-Hudson Canal, 117; *see also* Skenesboro
White Horse, Yukon, 3
White Mts., N.H., 2
White Plains, N.Y., in the Revolution, 46, 49
White Sands National Monument, N. Mex., 263
White Water Canal, Ohio, 118
Whitman National Monument Project, Wash., 263
Wichita, Kan., 1
Wichitaw Indians, Okla., 19
Wilderness Campaign, Va., in the Civil War, 160
Wilderness Trail, Ky., 58
Wilhelmshaven, Ger., 213
Wilkes, and discovery of Antarctica, 126*n*
Wilkes-Barre, Pa., 1; and nearby canals, 117
Wilkinson, route of, 59
Wilkinson, routes of in the War of 1812, 94, 95
Willamette Canal, Ore., 250
Willamette R., Ore., 2, 72
Williamsburg (Middle Plantations), Va., 27
Williston Reclamation Project, N. Dak., 264
Willoughby and Chancellor, route of, 20
Wilmington, Del., 1
Wilmington, N.C., 1, 31; in the Revolution, 51
Wilson's Creek, Mo., in the Civil War, 157
Wiltwyck (Kingston), N. Neth. (N.Y.), 24
Wind Cave National Park, S. Dak., 263
Wind erosion, U.S., 13
Winnebago Indians, Wisc., 19
Winnipeg, Man., 3
Winnsboro, S.C., in the Revolution, 50, 51
Winston-Salem, N.C., 1
Winthrop, route of in the War of the League of Augsburg, 28
Wisconsin Territory, 68, 89
Wolfe, route of in the Seven Years' War, 34
Women's Hours of Work, *see* Hours of Work, Women
Women's suffrage, 1860, 140; 1870, 191; 1880, 192; 1900, 193; 1915, 194; 1919, 195; ratification of the 19th amend., 201
Worcester, Mass., 1
World War I, House vote on entry into, 210; Senate vote on Versailles Treaty, 211; home front, 212; National Guard camps, 212; embarkation ports, 212; battle lines of Mar. 31, July 18, Nov. 11, 1918, 213; European front, 213; U.S. battlefields, 213
World War II, Axis submarine blockade limits, 258; neutrality zones, 258; U.S. in, 1941–42, 258
Wrangell, Alaska, 3
Wrangell Is., Siberia, claimed by U.S., 257*n*
Wupatki National Monument, Ariz., 263
Wyandotte Indians, Ohio, 19
Wyeth, route of, 59
Wyoming Territory, 164
Wyoming Valley, Pa., in the Revolution, 48

Xingu R., Brazil, 4

Yakima, Wash., 1
Yakima Indians, Ore., 19
Yakima Irrigation Project, Wash., 264
Yakutat Bay, Alaska, 3
Yamasee Indians, Ga.-S.C., 19
Yap Is., 305*n*
Yapura R., Brazil, 4
Yarmouth, N. Sco., 3
Yavari R., S.A., 4
Yazoo R., Miss., 2
Yellow Sea, 305
Yellowstone National Park, Wyo., etc., 263
Yellowstone R., Wyo., etc., 2
Yemen, 305
Yonkers, N. Neth. (N.Y.), 24
York, Ont., in the War of 1812, 94
York, Pa., 58; in the Revolution, 51
York Factory, Man., 3
Yorktown, Va., in the Revolution, 51
Yosemite National Park, Cal., 263
Youngstown, Ohio, 1, 7
Ypres, Belg., in World War I, 213
Yucatan, Mex., asks protection, 127*n*
Yucatan Sts., Mex., 2
Yucca House National Monument, Colo., 263
Yugoslavia, 305
Yukon Dist., 3
Yukon R., Alaska, 3

All numbers refer to maps, not pages

Yuma, Ariz., 1
Yuma Indians, Ariz., 19
Yuma Reclamation Project, Ariz., 264

Zinc, U.S. deposits, 6; world production of, 312
Zion National Monument, Utah, 263
Zion National Park, Utah, 263
Zone of neutrality patrol, western hemisphere, World War II, 258
Zones of Allied occupation, Ger., World War I, 213
Zuni Indians, N. Mex., 19
Zwaanendael, N. Neth., 23